PENGUIN BOOKS

ROBERT BURNS

Ian McIntyre read Modern Languages at Cambridge, where he was President of the Union. He worked for many years for the BBC: he was the first presenter of the programme *Analysis* and is a former Controller of both Radio 3 and Radio 4. He is also the author of *The Expense of Glory: A Life of John Reith* and *Garrick*, winner of the 1999 Theatre Book Prize.

D1325237

But yet—O L—d—confess I must—
At times I'm fash'd wi' fleshly lust;
And sometimes too, in warldly trust
        The Self gets in,
But thou remembers we are dust,
        Defil'd wi' sin—

O L—d—yestreen—thou kens—wi' Meg—
Thy pardon I sincerely beg!
O may't ne'er be a living plague,
        To my dishonor!
And I'll ne'er lift a lawless leg
        Again upon her.—

Besides, I farther maun avow,
Wi' Leezie's lass, three times—I trow—
But L—d, that friday I was fou
        When I cam near her;
Or else, thou kens, thy servant true
        Had never steer her.—

Maybe thou lets this fleshly thorn
Buffet thy servant e'en & morn,
Lest he o'er proud & high should turn,
        That he's sae gifted;
If sae, thy hand maun e'en be borne
        Untill thou lift it.—

'Holy Willie's Prayer' in Burns's own hand.

IAN McINTYRE

Robert Burns

A Life

PENGUIN BOOKS

PENGUIN BOOKS

Published by the Penguin Group
Penguin Books Ltd, 27 Wrights Lane, London w8 5TZ, England
Penguin Putnam Inc., 375 Hudson Street, New York, New York 10014, USA
Penguin Books Australia Ltd, Ringwood, Victoria, Australia
Penguin Books Canada Ltd, 10 Alcorn Avenue, Toronto, Ontario, Canada M4V 3B2
Penguin Books India (P) Ltd, 11, Community Centre, Panchsheel Park, New Delhi – 110 017, India
Penguin Books (NZ) Ltd, Private Bag 102902, NSMC, Auckland, New Zealand
Penguin Books (South Africa) (Pty) Ltd, 5 Watkins Street, Denver Ext 4, Johannesburg 2094, South Africa

Penguin Books Ltd, Registered Offices: Harmondsworth, Middlesex, England

First published by HarperCollins 1995
Published as a Classic Penguin 2001
1

Copyright © Ian McIntyre, 1995
All rights reserved

*In memory of my Mother and Father
and for wee Alistair*

Allen ... has lent me a quantity of Burns's unpublished and never-to-be-published Letters. They are full of
oaths and obscene songs. What an antithetical mind! –
tenderness, roughness – delicacy, coarseness – sentiment,
sensuality – soaring and grovelling, dirt and deity – all
mixed up in that one compound of inspired clay!

LORD BYRON
Journal, 13th December 1813

Mair nonsense has been uttered in his name
Than in ony's barrin' liberty and Christ.

HUGH MACDIARMID
A Drunk Man Looks at the Thistle, 1926

CONTENTS

LIST OF ILLUSTRATIONS

SOURCE OF ILLUSTRATIONS

1, 3, 7, 8, 9, 13, 16, 17, 19, 20, 23, 34, 35: *The Land of Burns, A Series of Landscapes and Portraits by Professor John Wilson and Robert Chambers. The Landscapes from Paintings made expressly for the work by* D. O. Hill, 2 volumes, Blackie & Son, Glasgow, 1840.

2, 10, 11, 18, 21, 38: Scottish National Portrait Gallery.

4, 5, 12, 26, 29: engravings from *The Antiquities of Scotland* by Francis Grose, 2 volumes, London, 1989-91.

6, 14, 15, 24, 25, 27, 30, 31, 32: caricatures from *A Series of Original Portraits and Caricature Etchings* by John Kay, 2 volumes, Hugh Paton, Carver & Gilder, Edinburgh, 1837-8.

22: engravings from *Old and New Edinburgh: Its History, its People, and its Places*, Cassell, Petter, Galpin & Co., London, Paris and New York, 1883.

28: The National Trust. Photograph by The Courtauld Institute of Art, University of London.

33. The MS is privately owned. Reproduced from the facsimile in the *Memorial Catalogue of the Burns Exhibition*, William Hodge & Company and T. & R. Annan & Sons, Glasgow, 1898.

36. Painting by the Victorian artist W. E. Lockhart (1846-1900).

37. *Punch*, 5th February, 1859.

38. Photograph by Drummond Young of Edinburgh from Scottish National Portrait Gallery.

Illustrations in text:
p. 80: a page from the Glenriddell Manuscripts.
p. 119, 209, 388: caricatures by John Kay.
p. 253. *Memorial Catalogue of the Burns Exhibition.*

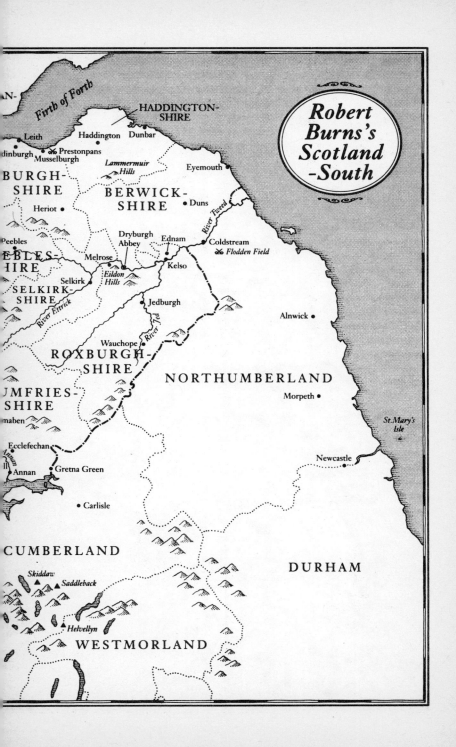

Firth of Forth

HADDINGTON-SHIRE

Leith
dinburgh
Musselburgh
Prestonpans

Haddington
Dunbar

BURGH-SHIRE

Lammermuir Hills

BERWICK-SHIRE

Eyemouth

Heriot

Duns

River Tweed

Peebles

EBLES-HIRE

Dryburgh Abbey

Ednam

Coldstream
Flodden Field

Melrose

Kelso

SELKIRK-SHIRE

Selkirk

Eildon Hills

River Ettrick

Jedburgh

Alnwick

River Ted

Wauchope

ROXBURGH-SHIRE

NORTHUMBERLAND

Morpeth

UMFRIES-SHIRE

St. Mary's Isle

maben

Ecclefechan

Annan
Gretna Green

Newcastle

Carlisle

CUMBERLAND

DURHAM

Skiddaw
Saddleback

Helvellyn

WESTMORLAND

Robert Burns's Scotland -South

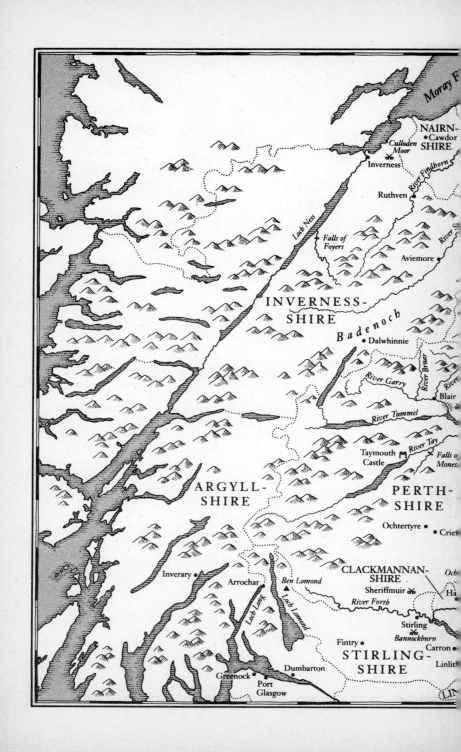

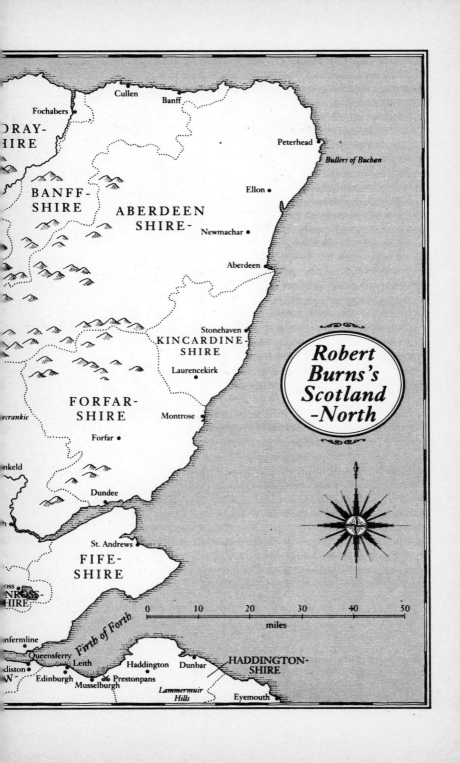

PREFACE

At the end of John Ford's film *The Man Who Shot Liberty Valance*, the newspaper reporter says, 'When the legend conflicts with the facts – print the legend'. That could serve as an epigraph for all too many books about Scotland's national poet. The two-hundredth anniversary of his death seems a good moment to reverse the injunction and look again at the facts. That is the informing principle of this biography.

Burns wrote marvellously vivid letters, and I have used them extensively to let him speak for himself. The first Clarendon Press edition of his correspondence, the work of the American scholar J. De Lancey Ferguson, appeared in 1931 and was a high point of Burns scholarship between the wars. I have generally been guided by the second edition, edited by G. Ross Roy, which appeared in 1985. The idiosyncrasies of Burns's spelling and punctuation have been retained, but his deletions have in most cases been removed.

In quoting from the poems and songs I have followed the 1968 Oxford University Press edition, with its incomparable literary and textual commentary by James Kinsley. My many other debts to earlier writers on Burns are acknowledged in the text and in footnotes.

The roll-call of institutions where I benefited from the knowledge and enthusiasm of the staff is a lengthy one. In Cambridge, the University Library; in Edinburgh, the Scottish Library of the Central Library, the National Library of Scotland and the Scottish National Portrait Gallery; in Glasgow, the Mitchell Library; in London, the London Library, the Map Library and Main Reading Room of the British Library in Bloomsbury and its Newspaper Library at Colindale.

I was greatly helped by a number of firms in the book trade, who were able to trace several rare items for me – Cooper Hay of Glasgow, Deighton, Bell of Cambridge, Peter Eaton of Lilies, David Green of Booksearch (U.K.), Jarndyce of London and McNaughton's Bookshop in Edinburgh.

For advice and help in the course of my research, as for much else over the years, I am grateful to my dear friends Sheila and James Farquhar of Barr; not to have heard Jimmy recite *Tam o' Shanter* on Burns Night is not to have lived. I am also indebted to Cameron Fyfe of the law firm of Ross Harper in Glasgow, Gwyniver Jones of the BBC's Written Archives Centre at Caversham, Colin Kilpatrick, former Honorary Secretary to the Trustees of Burns Monument and Burns Cottage, Maurice Lindsay and James Mackay, themselves both earlier biographers of Burns, and Professor Peter Vanezis, Head of the Department of Forensic Medicine and Science at the University of Glasgow.

For much good advice on matters of style and substance I am again in the debt of my publisher, Stuart Proffitt. I am also grateful to his assistant, Julie Baldwin, for her unfailing readiness to help and for many kindnesses. My editor at HarperCollins was Arabella Quin, and I greatly appreciated her scrupulous attention to what was not the easiest of texts. I am equally grateful to those who worked on the design, production and marketing of the book – Lucy Allen, Vera Brice, Sonia Dobie, Helen Ellis, Margaret Halton, Sarah McLaughlin and Kate Parrish. The index, a model of clarity and coherence, was compiled by Sarah Ereira.

My greatest debt is once more to my wife. She vetted each chapter as it was written, and was ready at all times to discuss points of emphasis or interpretation. She was an unfailing touchstone of taste and of good sense. And she was always there.

One

1759

THE ENTRY IN the Ayr parish register is of the briefest:

Robert Burns, lawful son to William Burns, in Alloway, and Agnes Brown, his spouse, was born January 25, 1759; bapd. 26, by Mr William Dalrymple. Witnesses: John Tennant and Jas. Young.

Scotland's national poet was born in the same year as William Pitt, Schiller and Mary Wollstonecraft, the near contemporary of Robespierre and Mozart, of Nelson and of William Blake. It was the year in which Handel died and in which Haydn composed his first symphony. In London Laurence Sterne was about to achieve celebrity with *Tristram Shandy* and in Geneva Voltaire published *Candide* – it was only two years previously that the unfortunate Admiral Byng had been court-martialled and shot at Portsmouth *pour encourager les autres*. John Wesley – 5000 miles a year, fifteen sermons a week – was at the height of his influence and fame. The outstanding British scientist of the day was Henry Cavendish, although his eccentricity ensured that much of his work, on the nature of oxygen and electricity, remained unknown: 'He rarely spoke,' wrote Sir John Plumb. 'Sometimes he did, and sometimes he did not, communicate his discoveries to the Royal Society.'[1]

Communication was also defective in a physical sense. A project to link the Forth and the Clyde by canal, first proposed in the time of Charles II, had been regularly revived and abandoned, a neglected opportunity deplored in the 1720s by that restless traveller Daniel Defoe: 'It must lie till Posterity, by the rising Greatness of their Commerce, shall not only feel the Want of it, but find themselves inclinable, as well as able, to effect it.'[2] It was only in 1759 that the

1. J.H. Plumb, *England in the Eighteenth Century*, Penguin Books, London, 1950, p. 101. Plumb notes that electricity was not only the subject of scientific research in the eighteenth century but also a fashionable game: 'Louis XV witnessed the administration of an electric shock to a line of monks a mile long and was convulsed with laughter when they all leapt into the air.' (*Ibid.*, pp. 103-4.)
2. Daniel Defoe, *A Tour Through the Whole Island of Great Britain*, 3 volumes, 1724-6. Posterity did not find itself 'inclinable' for some years. The canal was finally opened from sea to sea in 1790. An official party sailed from Port Hamilton to Bowling and a hogshead of water from the

magistrates of Glasgow secured the first Act for improving the harbour and waters of the Clyde.

Tolls had been levied for the maintenance of some Scottish roads before the Union, and the first Turnpike Act – for 'upholding and repairing the Bridges and Highways in the County of Edinburgh' – had been passed in 1714. Many roads in the mid-eighteenth century were still too bad for wheeled traffic, however, and goods were commonly carried in panniers slung on horseback. The first vehicle had begun to ply between Glasgow and Edinburgh only ten years previously, and the 44–mile journey took two days. It would be another thirty years before crowds in Glasgow cheered the arrival of the first mail coach from London.

Much of the greater world still appeared on maps as *terra incognita*. The interiors of Africa, Asia and South America remained unexplored. Australia had not been colonised and no vessel was yet known to have crossed the Antarctic Circle. It would be almost ten years before James Cook sailed out of Plymouth in a converted Whitby collier on his first Pacific voyage; when he did it would take him eight months to reach Tahiti.

Europe was at war. The Austria of Maria Theresa, in coalition with the France of Louis XV, the Russia of Catherine the Great and the Sweden of the ineffectual Adolphus Frederick, were intent on crippling the power of Prussia. When Britain joined her efforts to those of Frederick the Great, she was quickly drawn into renewed maritime and colonial conflict with the French. During 1759 the opposing European armies clashed at Minden; in North America Amherst captured Ticonderoga and Wolfe stormed the Heights of Abraham to take Quebec. The influence of France in India had already been fatally undermined by the victories of Clive; by the end of the Seven Years' War, the British Empire consisted of vastly more than thirteen American colonies.

In little more than a decade the shifts in imperial policy which the war set in motion would carry King George's American subjects to the threshold of independence, but in 1759, in the oldest of those colonies, Thomas Jefferson was still a schoolboy. Elsewhere in Virginia, after six adventurous years in the French and Indian War, a young colonel called George Washington had just resigned his commission, married a rich widow and resumed the agreeable life of a tobacco planter. The fifty-three-year-old Benjamin Franklin – printer, scientist, moralist and sage – was installed in London as agent for the Pennsylvania Assembly, pleading the cause of the colonists against the Proprietors. He travelled north in that year to receive an honorary degree from the University of St Andrews (the town had three thousand inhabitants, forty-two ale houses and twenty students). He was the guest of Lord Kames, judge, philosopher and gentleman farmer, and described his stay as 'six weeks of the densest

Forth was discharged into the Clyde 'as a symbol of the junction of the eastern and western seas.' (Henry Hamilton, *The Industrial Revolution in Scotland*, Clarendon Press, Oxford, 1932, p. 233.)

happiness I have met with in any part of my life.' 'Did not strong connections draw me elsewhere,' he wrote to his hosts, 'I believe Scotland would be the country I should choose to spend the remainder of my days in.'[1]

The Scotland which afforded Franklin such happiness was still in 1759 a fairly recent part of a far from united kingdom. It was only half a century since the Westminster Parliament (to the indignation of some English nationalists) had legislated to create 'one united kingdom by the name of Great Britain,' but it was, as Daniel Defoe had put it, 'a union of policy, not of affection.' For politicians in London it was principally a means of blocking the return of the Roman Catholic Stuarts and of countering the threat posed by their French backers.

Even so, Jacobite armies had twice marched into England in the first half of the century, penetrating as far as Derby and causing a run on the Bank of England. In the late 1750s the slaughter of Culloden had not faded from Scottish minds. The wearing of 'Highland Clothes' was still proscribed and the penalties were severe – six months for a first offence, and for a second offence transportation for seven years 'to any of His Majesty's Plantations beyond the Seas.' One of the more improbable offenders to be apprehended was Oronoce, a black servant of the Laird of Appin.[2] Charles Edward, the ill-tempered Young Chevalier, was not yet 40; there remained to him almost three decades in which to roam drunkenly around Europe, doing impartial violence to his hopeless cause and his unhappy wife.

It was in 1759 that Samuel Johnson published *Rasselas* – his *Dictionary* had established his reputation four years previously, but he still had to struggle for a livelihood. A further four years would pass before he met James Boswell. 'I do indeed come from Scotland,' said the pushy twenty-two-year-old at their first encounter, 'but I cannot help it.' It earned him a celebrated riposte: 'That, Sir, I find, is what a very great many of your countrymen cannot help.'

What Johnson put wittily, others – most notoriously John Wilkes – expressed with virulence. The Act of Union had presented Scots with greatly increased scope to compete for advancement, and this provoked an English backlash. Nobody felt its force more keenly than John Stuart, the third Earl of Bute. Resident in England since the Forty-Five, he became, entirely by chance, a leading figure at the court of the Prince and Princess of Wales and the tutor and close friend of their son.[3] When the latter succeeded as George III Bute was made Groom of the Stole and First Gentleman of the Bedchamber; popular

---

1. *The Papers of Benjamin Franklin*, ed. L.W. Labaree and Whitfield Bell et al. (to vol. 14); W.B. Willcox et al. (vol. 15–), New Haven, Yale University Press, 1959–, ix, 9.
2. The Act of 1746 (19 Geo. II, c. 39) was specific about the items of apparel which were forbidden – 'the Plaid, Philebeg, or little Kilt, Trowse, Shoulder Belts, or any part whatsoever of what peculiarly belongs to the Highland Garb.' Officers and soldiers were excluded. See J. Telfer Dunbar, *History of Highland Dress*, B.T. Batsford Ltd., London, 1979.
3. Bute happened to be at the Egham races one day in 1747. The Prince of Wales was also present. When a sudden downpour prevented the departure of the royal party, Bute found himself summoned to the Prince's tent to make up a whist party.

conjecture had it that he was more frequently in the bedchamber of the king's mother, the Dowager Princess. The Wilkesite mob found it amusing to burn petticoats (representing the princess) and jackboots (a pun of sorts on Bute's name) outside his town residence:

> This was not an attack on immorality in high places. The accusation that one Scottish minister was penetrating the mother of the King of England was symbolic shorthand for the real anxiety: namely, that large numbers of Scots were penetrating England itself, compromising its identity, winning access to its riches and cutting out English men. As the princess was made to say in one splendidly filthy cartoon, her hand located firmly under Lord Bute's kilt: 'A man of great parts is sure greatly to rise.'[1]

One of the fellow-Scots who prospered under Bute's patronage was the painter Allan Ramsay, and it was in 1759 that Horace Walpole paid tribute to the 'delicacy' of his style; as a painter of women, he said, he was superior to Reynolds. Another member of the Scottish diaspora who swam for a time into Bute's orbit was the prickly Tobias Smollett. He was briefly in the Marshalsea in that year for a libellous attack on an admiral, but his controversial *History of England* had sold well and he had had a success at Drury Lane with a naval farce staged by Garrick.

The Union had offered many Scots the opportunity 'greatly to rise' in a commercial sense. Scotland's ships were no longer excluded from England's enormous colonial markets, and the restrictions which had hampered trade with her prosperous southern neighbour were removed. Initially many Scottish industries took a severe mauling from their English competitors (linen was an exception), but after the collapse of the Forty-Five a new spirit of enterprise became apparent, and Scotland entered on a period of sustained economic expansion.

The Industrial Revolution, conventionally reckoned to have been underway in England by the 1760s, came more slowly north of the border, but the year of Robert Burns's birth was also the year in which the celebrated Carron Iron Works was founded – the first concern to use native ironstone and to employ coal for the smelting process. The company's main business was casting, and its chief product cannon. It took some years before they could match the standards of the great English ironworks and their guns were rejected time and again by the Office of Ordnance. 'Irregularity in the weight of our guns is alarming,' wrote one of the partners in 1767. 'Until we have proof of our guns I cannot speak about Portugal, Ireland, or the East India Company.'[2] It

1. Linda Colley, *Britons: Forging the Nation 1707–1837.* Yale University Press, New Haven and London, 1992, p. 122.
2. Quoted in Hamilton, *op. cit.*, p. 158.

was another of the Carron partners who encouraged and financed the early experiments of James Watt.

Four years before the birth of Burns there had been a census. The population of Scotland had been put at 1,255,663 and of Ayrshire at some 59,000. The county had only three towns of any size – Kilmarnock, Irvine and Ayr. The largest of them, Kilmarnock, known for its production of striped woollen bonnets called 'Kilmarnock cowls' had fewer than 4,500 people; the smallest, Ayr, where William Wallace had burned the barns lodging the troops of Edward I, scarcely more than half that number. There was some coal mining in the county (Ireland was an important market and the coal was shipped from Ayr and Irvine);[1] there was a sizeable army of vagrants and 'gaberlunzies';[2] for the vast majority of the population, however, earning a living meant working on the land.

To grasp just how primitive Scottish agriculture still was in the second half of the eighteenth century requires a vigorous effort of the imagination. The agrarian revolution was no rapid overturning of old ways. Certainly, after the Act of Union in 1707 the barriers to the English market were lifted, a stimulus which first became apparent in the improved trade in cattle. The year 1723 saw the foundation of the Society of Improvers in the Knowledge of Agriculture, but the effects of the 'improving movement' were patchy and the transition from subsistence farming to farming for profit was a slow one. In the 1770s and 1780s, when Andrew Wight began to publish his *Present State of Husbandry in Scotland*, the picture he painted of the common run of tenant farmers was not a flattering one: 'The bulk of our farmers are creeping in the beaten path of miserable husbandry, without knowing better or even wishing to know better.' Those who had shaken off the 'fetters of custom' found few imitators: 'so far from it, that among their slovenly neighbours they are reckoned giddy-headed projectors.'[3]

One reason for the languor of the tenantry was that many farms had traditionally been let on extremely short leases – four or even two years was not uncommon – and this was fatal to any spirit of enterprise. The 'beaten path' which they followed had two main characteristics: the division of arable land

1. The men and women who worked in Scottish mines, although their wages were relatively high, lived in conditions approximating to legal serfdom. If a pit was sold, they became the property of the new owner; infants were sometimes bound to the coalmaster for life at the time of baptism. The masters were obliged in return to keep them all their days, in sickness and old age – and to provide a coffin for their burial. This extraordinary state of affairs, sanctioned by Scots law since 1606, was not fully remedied until the last year of the century. (See Henry Grey Graham, *The Social Life of Scotland in the Eighteenth Century*, Adam & Charles Black, London, third edition, 1901, pp. 530–3.)

2. 'Gaberlunzies' were beggars licensed to operate within the bounds of a particular parish; they wore a blue gown and a small identification stamp made of lead. Maimed or deformed beggars, of whom there were many, were more prosaically referred to as 'objects'.

3. Andrew Wight, *Present State of Husbandry in Scotland. Extracted from Reports made to the Commissioners of the Annexed Estates*. 3 vols., printed for William Creech, Edinburgh, 1778–84, preface p. vii.

into what was known as 'infield' and 'outfield' and the splitting up of the cultivated fields into 'rigs' – ridges usually held by different tenants.

The infield was mainly used for growing grey oats, which gave a very poor yield, and bere, a coarse and not especially nutritious variety of barley. There was a degree of rotation, and the benefit of such manure as was produced by the farmyard. The outfield, a much larger area, was usually given over to the same crop for several years in succession, with increasingly meagre results; once the yield had diminished to the level of two seeds for every one sown, the land was left fallow for as much as seven or eight years, and then the whole miserable cycle recommenced. Expectations were not high. One old farmer in Kincardineshire was complimented on the good appearance of his crop. 'It's nae marvel,' he replied modestly, 'for it's only the auchteent crap sin' it gat gweedin' (i.e. only the eighteenth crop since it was manured).[1]

The division of arable land into rigs – a system by no means unique to Scotland – had originally been for purposes of drainage. The rigs might be anything up to a thousand yards long, and were not as a rule notably straight. The ploughman usually worked towards the middle from the edge, with the result that the soil became heaped up; it is recorded that as late as 1770 in Ayrshire, ridges were raised to an angle of almost 30 degrees.[2] Sir John Sinclair, in his *General View of the Agriculture of the Northern Counties*, noted that tenants remained jealously alert and made their ridges as high as possible to prevent good soil being lost to their neighbours.[3] 'The land,' wrote another observer, 'is like a piece of stripped cloth with banks full of weeds and ridges of corn in constant succession from one end of a field to the other . . .'[4]

An early pioneer of agricultural improvement was the hot-tempered Andrew Fletcher of Saltoun, who in the early years of the century introduced from Holland machinery for sifting grain. He is better remembered, however, as a patriot and politician and for his famous saying about the true source of civil authority: 'If a man were permitted to make all the ballads, he need not care who should make the laws of a nation.'[5] It sounds tremendous, but it didn't really mean a great deal. The only laws that people really paid attention to were those enacted by the General Assembly of the Church of Scotland. The supremacy of this national institution afforded Scotsmen massive compensation for the faint (and increasingly anglicised) voice with which their forty-five

1. Quoted in W. Alexander, *Notes and Sketches Illustrative of Northern Rural Life in the Eighteenth Century*, David Douglas, Edinburgh, 1877, p. 23.

2. See William Aiton, *General View of the Agriculture of the County of Ayr, with Observations on the Means of its Improvement*, printed by A. Napier, Glasgow, 1811, p. 72.

3. Sir John Sinclair, *General View of the Agriculture of the Northern Counties and Islands of Scotland*, printed by Colin Macrae, London, 1795, p. 20.

4. James Robertson, *General View of the Agriculture in the County of Perth, with Observations on the Means of its Improvement*, printed by order of the Board of Agriculture for James Morison, Perth, 1799, p. 393.

5. The line occurs in *An Account of a Conversation Concerning a Right Regulation of Governments for the Common Good of Mankind*, which he published in 1704.

Members spoke in the Westminster Parliament. A great many of those Members, throughout most of Burns's lifetime, would be in the pocket of Henry Dundas, later the first Viscount Melville, widely perceived as the effective ruler of Scotland. One foot planted in London, the other in Edinburgh, 'Harry the Ninth' was, for more than three decades, the most influential person north of the border. But for all that, he was, in William Ferguson's phrase, 'the uncrowned king not of Scotland but of the Scottish electors and their hangers-on';[1] even by the 1780s fewer than one person in 300 in Ayrshire was entitled to the vote.

Presbyterianism, in the form erected by John Knox on the débris of Catholicism, had done much to strengthen the national consciousness (some would say to enlarge the national ego). The notion that the Scots, like the children of Israel, were a chosen race is at least as old as the Declaration of Arbroath of 1320, in which Robert I is compared to Joshua and to Judas Maccabeus. 'Belief in the exceptional purity of the Scottish reformed church strengthened this particular form of national conceit,' as the historian Gordon Donaldson wrote drily:

Knox claimed that all other churches retained 'some footsteps of antichrist and some dregs of papistry.' . . . But it was left to the era of the Covenant to provide national conceit with a theological foundation. Samuel Rutherford had written in 1633: 'Scotland, whom our Lord took off the dunghill and out of hell and made a fair bride to Himself . . . He will embrace both us, the little young sister, and the elder sister, the Church of the Jews.'[2]

In the 1660s Presbyterianism had given way to a modified Episcopalianism. Lay patronage was revived, the covenants were declared unlawful and private conventicles were forbidden; synods and presbyteries were retained, but bishops were put in the place of the General Assembly. The story of the generation of conflict and persecution which followed has been frequently (sometimes inaccurately) told; 'Bloody Clavers' and his dragoons took fewer lives than the Cameronian version of events ('King Jesus' against 'King Charles') would have us believe.[3]

1. William Ferguson, *Scotland 1689 to the Present:* The Edinburgh History of Scotland, vol. iv, Oliver & Boyd, Edinburgh, 1968, p. 237. Dundas's long career began when he was made Solicitor-General at the age of 24 in 1766 and ended only with his impeachment for corruption in 1805 when he was Pitt's First Lord of the Admiralty. Although he was acquitted by his peers (he had been created Viscount Melville in 1802) he never held office again. Walter Scott, who had enjoyed his patronage, composed some not very good verse for a dinner held to celebrate his acquittal.

2. Gordon Donaldson, *Scotland, James V–James VII,* The Edinburgh History of Scotland, vol. iii, Oliver & Boyd, Edinburgh, 1965, pp. 315–16.

3. John Graham of Claverhouse (1648–89) was educated at the University of St Andrews. After service in the armies of France and the Netherlands, he was employed by the Scottish Privy Council to quell the militant Covenanters in the south-west of Scotland; their rebellion was crushed at the Battle of Bothwell Brig in June 1679. When William of Orange became King, Graham

The chapter which followed, opened by the landing in England of William of Orange, was every bit as violent and has been equally embroidered in the telling. What is certain is that in the winter of 1688 mobs in the counties of Ayrshire and Galloway battered down the doors of many manses. The cry was 'Strip the curate!' and when their black gowns had been torn off they and their families were turned out into the night and their books and furniture burned in the streets. More than two hundred ministers were 'outed' in this way and when the General Assembly met again in 1690, the purge which it instituted disposed of a further three hundred episcopal incumbents. They were arraigned on a wide range of charges. Some were alleged to have been gross drunkards or to have allowed Quakers to worship undisturbed; others to have played bowls on a weekday or whistled on the Sabbath.[1]

Parliament eventually cracked the whip, and the Assembly bowed sulkily to its requirement of toleration. Warfare continued by other means, however, and for several decades Presbyterian Tweedle-Dum and Episcopalian Tweedle-Dee traded venomous abuse in a stream of tracts and pamphlets. It was many years before the Church of Scotland recovered from these self-inflicted injuries. As passions over questions of church government cooled, disagreements over doctrine began to emerge. 'There hath been in some a dreadful Atheistical Boldness against God,' declared the Assembly of 1690,[2] and in the early years of the eighteenth century, in Scotland as elsewhere in Western Europe, old orthodoxies were increasingly challenged and unsettling questions posed.

What precisely, for instance, were the means of grace? Had Christ died to purchase it for all or only for the elect? There were stern evangelicals (the Reverend Ebenezer Erskine, the minister of Stirling, was one) who continued to believe, with Calvin, that predestination was strictly the business of the Almighty, and that for ordinary folk it was 'a matter with which they have no more concern than with what men are doing in Mexico or Peru.'[3] In the universities, however, and particularly in what had hitherto been the Calvinist redoubt of Glasgow, academics were beginning to savour the subversive delights of speculation, and grave men in positions of ecclesiastical authority responded with words calculated to carry an intimidatory resonance – Arminianism, Arianism, Antinomianism, Erastianism. The belief in a united national church, which had held up even through the desperate troubles of the preceding century, was gradually being sapped.

The argument which eventually triggered the Secession related to patron-

rallied to James VII, and was created Viscount Dundee in 1688. He raised a Highland army, but was killed at the Battle of Killiecrankie the following year and the uprising fizzled out.

1. For an account of these 'rabbling scenes,' see Graham, *op. cit.*, pp. 267 *et seq.*

2. *Act of Assembly, anent a Solemn National Fast and Humiliation*, reproduced in *Acts of the General Assembly of the Church of Scotland, 1638-1842* (ed. T. Pitcairn et al.), 1843.

3. Quoted in A.R. MacEwen, *The Erskines*, Oliphant, Anderson & Ferrier, Edinburgh, 1900, p. 58.

8

age, which had by now been caught up in 'political management.' The Assembly of 1732 approved an 'Act anent Calls.'

This provided that if a patron did not present a minister to a vacant charge within six months, the right of election should pass to the heritors and elders of the parish. The measure proved controversial, because it was seen by some as disregarding the wishes of the congregation. One of those who inveighed against it was Ebenezer Erskine. Such acts, he declared, were null, 'Because Zion's King never touched them with His sceptre.'[1] The following year, after a day of fasting and prayer in a small thatched cottage near Kinross, he and three others set themselves up separately in what was termed the Associate Presbytery. In 1740 they were formally deposed by the Assembly. Within two years they had twenty ministers and 36 congregations.

'It is the peculiarity of Scottish dissent that it never arose from love of change,' observed Henry Grey Graham. 'It was rather a determination to preserve more purely the creed and habits of their fathers.'[2] To attend communion and to hear the preaching of the Word, adherents would travel up to thirty or forty miles. Their Testimony of the Associate Synod not only set out the principles of the Secession at prodigious length. It also execrated Church and State for their many grievous errors, which ranged from the condonation of heresy to the repeal of the Act against witchcraft – a clear attempt to challenge the Word of God. The Associate Synod, Graham wrote, was composed of men and women 'whose consciences wound themselves round a scruple like a hedgehog round a straw.'

People who found themselves so comprehensively at odds with the world at large did not take long to fall out among themselves. The occasion arose after only nine years. Jacobite rebellion was in the air and those taking office in the cities of Edinburgh, Glasgow and Perth were required to swear a burgess oath renouncing Papistry and professing obedience to 'the true religion presently professed in this realm.' Could this be subscribed to without sin? A majority decided that the answer to this momentous question was no. The minority – it included Erskine – was cast out.

The sheep and goats resulting from this new secession became known as the Burgher or 'Associate Synod' and the Anti-burgher or 'General Associate Synod'. John Ramsay of Ochtertyre wrote in his diary that they hated each other 'worse than the Jesuits did the Jansenists.' There followed, well-nigh unbelievably, a further split among the Burgher Seceders, this time on the issue of whether ministers and members should be required to approve of civil compulsion in religious matters. A majority held that they should not. The outraged minority stormed out, declaring that they would call themselves 'Original Burghers', but they were quickly dubbed the 'Auld Lichts' – to distinguish them from those who had had the effrontery to believe that they had 'New Light' on the Solemn League and Covenant.

1. *Ibid*, p. 67.
2. Graham, *op. cit.*, p. 374.

Paradoxically, the established church derived some benefit from this bewildering cavalcade of dissent and secession. If some of the more fanatical and eccentric elements had not been siphoned off in this way they would have been the cause of infinitely more strife and disruption. The religious mainstream did not remain altogether free of turbulence, but by the middle years of the century the Moderate Party, as it had by then become known, enjoyed a general ascendancy over the Evangelicals.

In the universities, men studying for the ministry found themselves increasingly exposed to new influences, some of them scientific and philosophical. The disciplines of astronomy, physics, chemistry and botany were uncovering laws of nature which appeared compatible with a God-given dispensation. Isaac Newton, in the Preface to the second edition of his *Principia*, had written, 'We may now more clearly behold the beauties of nature and be thence incited the more profoundly to reverence and adore the Great Maker and Lord of all.' At the University of Edinburgh, in the lectures of Alexander Munro *primus*, the Professor of Anatomy, the human body figured as one of the wonderful works of the Creator, and it was not only medical students who crowded in to hear him. [1]

Even divinity students who remained within the pale of their prescribed syllabus found themselves listening to new voices. That of Archibald Campbell, for instance, who held the chair of ecclesiastical history at St Andrews between 1730 and 1756, and who brought a hornets' nest about his ears with a book called *Apostles no Enthusiasts*. Campbell had sharp things to say about those who were 'always consulting at the Throne' and taught that the law of nature was sufficient to guide rational minds to happiness. (He was hauled before the Assembly and charged with Pelagianism in 1736, but was acquitted.) In Glasgow, the Ulsterman Francis Hutcheson, Professor of Moral Philosophy from 1729 to 1746, was equally influential. He preached a Presbyterianism not far removed from Deism; one of his pupils was Adam Smith.

Although much of the controversy in the Scottish church over the years concerned ecclesiastical politics, the structure and organisation of the church remained unchanged. It rested on the broad base of the parishes (in the middle of the eighteenth century they numbered just under nine hundred) and rose to the apex of the General Assembly. In between lay Presbytery and Synod, to which each parish sent its minister and one elder as delegates, but it was at parochial level that the church made its strongest impact on people's lives.

Power lay with the Kirk Session, composed usually of the minister and two or more elders, and this lowest form of ecclesiastical court exercised functions not unlike those later assigned under totalitarian regimes to 'the Party,' from the primitive administration of poor relief to the determined pursuit of

1. Gordon Donaldson, *The Faith of the Scots*, B.T. Batsford Ltd., London 1990, p. 106. Munro (1697–1767) is known as *primus* to distinguish him from his son, Alexander Munro *secundus* (1733–1817) and his grandson, Alexander Munro *tertius*, both of whom duly succeeded him in the Chair of Anatomy. Nepotism was as common in academic life as it was in politics.

fornication. It issued certificates of good character to parishioners moving elsewhere and sent out vigilante patrols on the Sabbath in search of defectors from worship. To fodder horses or put out nets – even to be caught gazing idly out of the window – was to invite a fine. Nor were the clergy above the law. At New Machar, in Aberdeenshire, the minister was hauled before the Presbytery for powdering his wig on the Lord's Day.[1]

Such was the church into which Robert Burns was baptised in the penultimate year of the reign of George II.

> My father was a farmer upon the Carrick border O
> And carefully he bred me, in decency and order O...[2]

That, at least, was the *intention* of the poet's father. It would still, of course, be some years before the language was enriched by that well-known line about 'the best laid schemes of Mice and Men.'

1. Graham, *op. cit.*, pp. 314-34.
2. 'Song', no. 21 in James Kinsley (ed.) *The poems and Songs of Robert Burns*, 3 vols., Clarendon Press, Oxford, 1968. Cited henceforth as Kinsley.

Two

GROWING UP

BURNS'S MOTHER WAS an Ayrshire woman born and bred. Her name was Agnes Broun. She was the daughter of a tenant farmer, and the eldest of six children. When she was ten her mother died, and for a couple of years it fell to her to look after the rest of the brood. Then her father remarried, and she was sent off to live with her maternal grandmother in Maybole. She was put to work both indoors and in the fields and received little in the way of formal education; she could read from the Bible, but she never learned to write. Her youngest child, Burns's sister Isabella, remembered her as having pale red hair, dark eyes, a fine complexion and a small neat figure; she was active and industrious and of a cheerful disposition.[1]

Agnes Broun was in her mid-twenties when she met William Burnes – tall, serious-minded and twelve years her senior.[2] He too was the son of a tenant farmer, but his roots were in the north-east of Scotland. The family had fallen on hard times, and he had left his native Kincardineshire in 1748. Initially he found employment in Edinburgh as a gardener. On the south side of the city, where the old Burgh Loch and the adjacent marshes had been drained, Burnes worked for a time on the laying out of what is now the Meadows. After two years he gravitated to Ayrshire. He formed the ambition to establish himself as a nurseryman, and he eventually managed to feu a seven and a half acre plot at Alloway, although he continued working as head gardener to Provost William Fergusson of Ayr, a local man who had done well in medical practice in London and was devoting himself, in retirement, to improving the small estate of Doonholm.

In his spare time, Burnes began to build a cottage on his land, and when he and Agnes were married in December 1757 it became their first home. The

1. Robert Chambers, *The Life and Works of Robert Burns*, revised by William Wallace, 4 vols, W & R Chambers Limited, Edinburgh and London, 1896, vol. 1, p. 42n. Cited henceforth as Chambers-Wallace.

2. The family name was spelt Burnes or Burness in the north–east of Scotland and pronounced as two syllables, as it still is in those parts today. The session clerk at Ayr, as we have seen, spelt it Burns in the register; that presumably was closer to how it was pronounced in the south–west, and that is the form the poet himself eventually adopted, although he signed himself 'Robt. Burness' until he was twenty-seven.

thick walls, pierced by small windows, were washed with lime, inside and out. There was a kitchen with a concealed box bed and one other room with a fireplace and chimney. A second door in the kitchen led directly into the byre and barn. Burnes was a better gardener than he was a builder. It was not long before the gable, constructed of clay like the rest of the cottage, began to subside. The stone jambs and lintel which supported the chimney held firm, and this threw the gable off centre. A few days after the birth of their first child in January 1759, there was a storm. The events of that wild night passed into family folklore and his brother Gilbert Burns retailed the story to Burns's biographer, Dr Currie, more than forty years later: 'A little before daylight, a part of the gable fell out, and the rest appeared so shattered, that my mother, with the young poet, had to be carried through the storm to a neighbour's house, where they remained a week, till their own dwelling was adjusted.'[1]

The cottage at Alloway was Burns's home for the first seven years of his life. Gilbert, twenty months his junior, was born there in 1760 and his sisters Agnes and Arabella followed at two-yearly intervals. Little came of their father's market-gardening schemes, and he continued to work for Fergusson. After a time he sold part of his small plot of land; Agnes ran the remaining five acres as a smallholding, keeping poultry and a few cows and producing milk and cheese.

Burns's formal schooling was spasmodic. Although it is customary – especially within earshot of the English – to insist on the democratic superiority of Scottish education, the standard of instruction available in the eighteenth century does not compel unqualified admiration:

> The Church of the Reformation had framed noble plans, had urged splendid provisions, and had made admirable exertions—for it regarded education as a means to religious instruction of the people. But the scheme remained something of an ideal like the Mosaic legislation in the wilderness—a scheme of perfection to be thwarted by the deep poverty of the country, by the turbulence of parties,' by the civil and religious warfare of generations.[2]

Attempts had been made in 1633 and 1643 to remedy the ignorance of the people by legislating for the maintenance of a school in each parish, but these foundered on the unwillingness of the heritors or landlords to meet the cost.

1. Two hundred and thirty-four years later plans for rather more elaborate adjustments were announced. In January 1993, the Burns Management Trustees announced details of a £1.25 million restoration scheme. Those contributing to the cost included the Burns Monument Trustees, Enterprise Ayrshire, Kyle & Carrick District Council and the European Regional Development Fund. It was also hoped to attract grants from the Scottish Tourist Board and the Friends of Thatched Houses.

2. Graham, *op. cit.*, p. 417.

The Scottish Parliament tried again in 1696, enacting that a schoolmaster should be appointed for every parish and that 'a commodious house' should be provided for a school.

The duty of enforcement was laid on the Presbyteries, and the measure of their failure may be judged by the miserable pittance paid to the schoolmaster. The 1696 Act stipulated a maximum of 200 and a minimum of 100 merks[1], which was the equivalent of something between £5 and £10 sterling – little more than the wage of a labourer. The wretched dominie frequently had to exert himself to extract this in sums of a penny or less from anything up to a hundred tight-fisted heritors or tenants; in return he was expected to teach mathematics, Latin, grammar, arithmetic, writing and singing.

Small wonder that abler men drifted away to employment in merchant houses or sought positions as clerks in the East India Company. The less enterprising, careless of the risk of dismissal, struggled to support their families by keeping small shops or assuming additional functions within the parish. The *Statistical Account* records that even at the end of the century the dominie in the parish of Heriot was schoolmaster, precentor, clerk, beadle and gravedigger. His combined income was £8 sterling.[2]

The nearest parish school to Alloway was two miles distant at Ayr, so when they were of an age Burns and his brother were sent, at the beginning of 1765, to a little school at Alloway Mill, about a mile from home. It was run by a man called William Campbell, and from him, for a few months, they received a grounding in reading and writing. Campbell then received a better offer and went off to be Master of the Workhouse in Ayr, and William Burnes took the initiative in arranging for his sons, and the children of some of his neighbours, to be taught privately by a young man of eighteen called John Murdoch.

Murdoch, who had been a pupil at the Burgh school in Ayr and then studied at Edinburgh, has come in for some mockery because of his way with words – it was he who described the Burns's cottage as an 'argillaceous fabric' – but Gilbert testified that under him they learned 'to read English tolerably well, and to write a little.' Murdoch confirmed that the Burns brothers were apt pupils, and were 'generally at the upper end of the class, even when ranged with boys by far their seniors.' Child-centred education still lay some way in the future, however, and the syllabus Murdoch devised for his charges would make a present-day teacher of five-year olds wish to lie down in a darkened room:

The books most commonly used in the school were the Spelling Book, the New Testament, the Bible, Mason's *Collection of Prose and Verse*, and Fisher's *English Grammar*. They committed to memory the hymns, and other poems

1. This was the normal eighteenth-century Scottish spelling of the word 'mark'.
2. Sir John Sinclair, Bart., *The Statistical Account of Scotland, Drawn up from the Communications of the Ministers of the Different Parishes*, William Creech, Edinburgh, 21 vols., 1791-99, vol. xvi, p. 54.

of that collection, with uncommon facility . . . As soon as they were capable of it, I taught them to turn verse into its natural prose order; and sometimes to substitute synonimous expressions for poetical words, and to supply all the ellipses.[1]

Of the two brothers, it was Gilbert who struck Murdoch as having the livelier imagination. Rather more surprising, in view of later developments, is what he discovered when he tried to teach them a little church music: 'Here they were left far behind by all the rest of the school,' he wrote. 'Robert's ear, in particular, was remarkably dull, and his voice untunable. It was long before I could get them to distinguish one tune from another.'

Murdoch lodged in turn with each of his five employers and in later life he remembered with affection the time he had spent in William Burnes's 'tabernacle of clay'. 'In this mean cottage,' he wrote, 'I really believe there dwelt a larger portion of content than in any place in Europe.' He noted, rather touchingly, how Mrs. Burnes hung on her husband's every word:

At all times, and in all companies, she listened to him with a more marked attention than to any body else. When under the necessity of being absent while he was speaking, she seemed to regret, as a real loss, that she had missed what the good man had said. This worthy woman, Agnes Brown, had the most thorough esteem for her husband of any woman I ever knew.

Murdoch's own admiration for the head of the household was boundless. 'By far the best of the human race that ever I had the pleasure of being acquainted with,' he wrote:

He took pleasure in leading his children in the path of virtue; not in driving them, as some parents do, to the performance of duties to which they themselves are averse. He took care to find fault but very seldom; and therefore, when he did rebuke, he was listened to with a kind of reverential awe. A look of disapprobation was felt; a reproof was severely so; and a stripe with the tawz, even on the skirt of the coat, gave heart-felt pain, produced a loud lamentation, and brought forth a flood of tears.

Murdoch was greatly impressed by Burnes's ability to get on well with those who worked for him. He recorded that he only ever saw him angry twice – once with a foreman who was not reaping a field properly, on another occasion with an old man who was 'using smutty innuendoes and double entendres.'

1. These and the quotations which follow are from a letter addressed to Joseph Cooper Walker, Esq., of Dublin, dated 22 February, 1799. Quoted in James Currie, *The Works of Robert Burns; With an Account of his Life, and a Criticism on his Writings, To which are Prefixed, some Observations on the Character and Condition of the Scottish Peasantry*, 4 vols., T. Cadell, jun. and W. Davies, London, 1800, vol i, pp. 86-96. Cited henceforth as Currie.

He was equally struck by his behaviour towards those who stood higher in the social scale: 'He always treated superiors with a becoming respect; but he never gave the smallest encouragement to aristocratical arrogance.' The dominie's ear detected something else which marked William Burnes out from the common ruck: 'He spoke the English language with more propriety (both with respect to diction and pronunciation,) than any man I ever knew, with no greater advantages. This had a very good effect on the boys, who began to talk, and reason like men, much sooner than their neighbours.'

Burns's early reading was not confined to the textbooks supplied by Murdoch. Years later, in his so-called 'autobiographical letter' to Dr John Moore, he affirmed that the first two books he ever read 'in private', and which gave him more pleasure than anything he ever read again, were the life of Hannibal and the history of Sir William Wallace:

> Hannibal gave my young ideas such a turn that I used to strut in raptures up and down after the recruiting drum and bagpipe, and wish myself tall enough to be a soldier; while the story of Wallace poured a Scottish prejudice in my veins which will boil along there till the flood-gates of life shut in eternal rest.[1]

That 'Scottish prejudice' found little reinforcement from anything he read in his schoolbooks. The Scriptures had not been translated into Scots, and the biblical cadences with which he became familiar were therefore those of the Authorised Version. Nor was there anything that remotely reflected the Scottish literary tradition in Arthur Masson's *A Collection of Prose and Verse*.[2] The prose models which Masson set before his readers included Joseph Addison and, less happily, a Mrs Elizabeth Rowe; her *Letters Moral and Entertaining* exerted an influence which Burns would be slow to throw off. The verse was drawn from Shakespeare, Milton and Dryden but also from a range of eighteenth-century poets that included Gray, Shenstone and Akenside, and it was their more sentimental voices that exercised the stronger appeal. Burns had a retentive memory and got a great deal off by heart. Many of the quotations he served up in later years in his letters and his poetry had lodged in the mind of a small boy lacking any critical discernment. Masson, and Murdoch's teaching generally, were to prove a mixed blessing to him as a writer, encouraging a certain stiffness and formality which went against his true grain.

Fortunately, even at that early age, there were other influences at work:

1. Letter dated 2 August 1787, no. 125 in *The Letters of Robert Burns*, ed. J. De Lancey Ferguson, 2nd edition ed. G. Ross Roy, 2 vols, Clarendon Press, Oxford, 1985. Henceforth cited as Letters. Gilbert, who did not know of the existence of the autobiographical letter during Burns's life, disputed the accuracy of this passage in a letter to Mrs Dunlop after his brother's death. He confirmed that Murdoch lent him *The Life of Hannibal*, but maintained that he only saw *The Life of Wallace* some years later, when he borrowed it from the blacksmith who shod their horses. (See Currie, vol. i, p. 60.)
2. Burns and Murdoch both misspelt his name as 'Mason.'

> Kissin is the key o' love
> An' clappin is the lock,
> An' making o's the best thing
> That ere a young thing got –

This was earthier stuff than any of the genteel lines he had memorised from Gray or Akenside. Burns tacked it onto the end of a letter to a friend during his first stay in Edinburgh, and added its provenance – 'An auld Sang o' my Mither's.'

He had incurred another debt during his boyhood, and that too he afterwards acknowledged, not over-graciously, in his letter to Dr Moore: 'I owed much to an old Maid of my Mother's, remarkable for her ignorance, credulity and superstition.' Her name was Betty Davidson. She had been married to a cousin of his mother's, and now that she was widowed she sometimes stayed with the family and helped about the house:

> She had, I suppose, the largest collection in the county of tales and songs concerning ghosts, fairies, brownies, witches, warlocks, spunkies, kelpies, elf-candles, dead-lights, wraiths, apparitions, cantraips, giants, inchanted towers, dragons and other trumpery. – This cultivated the latent seeds of Poesy; but had so strong an effect on my imagination, that to this hour, in my nocturnal rambles, I sometimes keep a sharp look-out in suspicious places . . .

With the birth of two daughters William Burnes found that the cottage at Alloway was bursting at the seams. He had also begun to realise that if he continued as Fergusson's gardener he would be unable to bring up his sons in the way he wished:

> Had my father continued in that situation, I must have marched off to be one of the little underlings about a farm-house; but it was his dearest wish and prayer to have it in his power to keep his children under his own eye till they could discern between good and evil; so with the assistance of his generous Master my father ventured on a small farm in his estate.[1]

This was Mount Oliphant, a farm of seventy Scots acres which lay some two miles south-east of Alloway, high above the waters of the Doon.[2] William had no money to stock the farm, and failed to find a buyer for his interest in the land at Alloway,[3] but Fergusson agreed to lend him a hundred pounds and the

---

1. Letters, 125.
2. A Scots acre was 6084 square yards, an English acre 4840. By the English measure, Mount Oliphant would therefore have extended to about 90 acres.
3. The land and house were eventually bought in 1781 by the Incorporation of Shoemakers in Ayr for £160.

bargain was concluded. The lease was to run for twelve years, with a break clause at mid-term. The rent was set at forty pounds for the first six years, and was then to rise to forty-five. Burnes got the use of the land from Martinmas 1765 and the family moved in the following Whitsun. It was to be their home for the next eleven years.

The two brothers continued to be taught by Murdoch, walking the two miles to Alloway, but life at Mount Oliphant was lonelier than they had been accustomed to. 'Nothing could be more retired than our general manner of living,' Gilbert told Mrs Dunlop thirty years later. 'We rarely saw anybody but the members of our own family.' It was a harder life, too. The land was not in good heart – 'almost the very poorest soil I know of in a state of cultivation,' Gilbert wrote – and their difficulties were increased when several of his father's cattle were carried off by accident and disease:

> To the buffetings of misfortune, we could only oppose hard labour and the most rigid economy. We lived very sparingly. For several years butcher's meat was a stranger in the house, while all the members of the family exerted themselves to the utmost of their strength, and rather beyond it, in the labours of the farm.

Early in 1768, Murdoch got the chance of a teaching appointment in Dumfries and decided to move on. One evening he climbed the hill to Mount Oliphant to bid farewell to the family of his prize pupils. 'He brought us, as a present and memorial of him,' Gilbert recalled, 'a small compendium of English Grammar, and *Titus Andronicus*.' Shakespeare's earliest and bloodiest tragedy has always divided the critics. Its Restoration adapter, Edward Ravenscroft, was dismissive – 'It seems rather a heap of Rubbish than a Structure' – and nowadays it might be considered strong meat for eight-and nine-year olds. Murdoch, undeterred by any such namby-pamby considerations, began to read the play aloud. He got only as far as the stage direction to Act II, Scene 4 – *Enter the Empress' sons, Chiron and Demetrius, with Lavinia, her hands cut off and her tongue cut out, and ravished*:

> At this, in an agony of distress, we with one voice desired he would read no more. My father observed, that if we would not hear it out, it would be needless to leave the play with us. Robert replied, that if it was left he would burn it. My father was going to chide him for this ungrateful return to his tutor's kindness; but Murdoch interfered, declaring that he liked to see so much sensibility; and he left *The School for Love*, a comedy (translated I think from the French) in its place.[1]

1. Gilbert to Mrs Dunlop, quoted in Currie, vol. i, p. 62.

William Burnes was determined that Murdoch's departure should not mean the end of his sons' education. In the winter evenings he taught them (and their sisters) arithmetic by candlelight, and he was as little inclined as Murdoch had been to make concessions to their tender years:

> He conversed familiarly on all subjects with us, as if we had been men, and was at great pains, while we accompanied him in the labours of the farm, to lead the conversation to such subjects as might tend to increase our knowledge, or confirm us in virtuous habits. He borrowed Salmon's *Geographical Grammar* for us, and endeavoured to make us acquainted with the situation and history of the different countries in the world; while, from a book-society in Ayr, he procured for us Durham's *Phisico and Astro-Theology*, and Ray's *Wisdom of God in Creation*, to give us some idea of astronomy and natural history.

The children had an uncle (a brother of their mother's) who lived with them at the farm for a time and who sat in occasionally on their evening arithmetic lessons. He went off to Ayr one day in search of a ready reckoner and a manual to teach him to write letters. The bookseller misunderstood his requirements, and in place of *The Complete Letter-writer* he came home with a collection of letters by eminent writers, 'with a few directions for attaining an easy epistolary style.' Robert was delighted by his uncle's mistake. 'It inspired him,' Gilbert wrote, 'with a strong desire to excel in letter-writing, while it furnished him with models by some of the first writers in our language.' Alternatively, it might be viewed as compounding the damage done earlier by Mrs Elizabeth Rowe.

The land at Mount Oliphant was ill-drained and stony, and William Burnes's ambitions for the education of his sons came increasingly into conflict with the need to make use of their growing strength about the farm. Gilbert recalled that when his brother was thirteen or fourteen their father, concerned that they wrote so badly, sent them one summer to the nearest parish school, two or three miles away at Dalrymple, but he could so ill spare them that they went in alternate weeks.

The following year, Murdoch returned to teach English in Ayr. He sent his former pupils an edition of Pope's works and in the late summer Burns went briefly to lodge with him. Murdoch polished up his grammar and then started to teach him French. It is not certain how well equipped he was to do this – according to Gilbert Murdoch had only just begun to learn the language himself – but they both clearly enjoyed this eighteenth-century version of 'learn a foreign language in three weeks':

> Now there was little else to be heard but the declension of nouns, the conjugation of verbs, &c. When walking together, and even at meals, I was constantly telling him the names of different objects, as they presented themselves, in French; so that he was hourly laying in a stock of words, and

sometimes little phrases. In short, he took such pleasure in learning, and I in teaching, that it was difficult to say which of the two was most zealous in the business; and about the end of the second week of our study of the French, we began to read a little of the Adventures of Telemachus, in Fenelon's own words.

The season dictated that there was more pressing business elsewhere, however. Murdoch, recalling the loss of his 'very apt pupil' for Currie's benefit a quarter of a century later, switches to a key of pastoral melancholy:

> But now the plains of Mount Oliphant began to whiten, and Robert was summoned to relinquish the pleasing scenes that surrounded the grotto of Calypso, and, armed with a sickle, to seek glory by signalizing himself in the field of Ceres . . .[1]

Which is to say that he had to go home to help with the harvest.[2] He took the Fénelon with him, together with a French dictionary and grammar. Gilbert was dazzled: 'In a little while,' he told Currie, 'he had acquired such a knowledge of the language, as to read and understand any French author in prose. This was considered as a sort of prodigy.' Burns was obviously quite proud of his French – his letters are laced with the occasional French phrase. Some of the rhymes he later devised for French words in his poetry, on the other hand, raise doubts about how good a job Murdoch did on his pronunciation:

> Faites mes BAISEMAINS respectueuse,
> To sentimental Sister Susie . . .[3]

Burns also attempted to get some Latin, but with little success. At the urging of one of Murdoch's colleagues in Ayr, the writing-master at the school, he bought a copy of Thomas Ruddiman's *Rudiments of the Latin Tongue*. According to his brother he found it 'dry and uninteresting' and soon laid it aside, although it is plain from an intriguing passage in Gilbert's account that his failure to make progress irked him:

> He frequently returned to his *Rudiments* on any little chagrin or disappoint-. ment, particularly in his love affairs; but the Latin seldom predominated

---

1. Murdoch is making an allusive flourish. Fénelon's *Télémaque*, published in 1699, was a didactic novel intended for the moral instruction of his pupil the Duke of Burgundy, Louis XIV's grandson. Calypso, a character in the novel, is meant to represent Madame de Montespan, who had become Louis' mistress in 1667 and bore him seven children.
2. Gilbert's recollection was that Burns had returned home after only a week in Ayr, returning to Murdoch for a further fortnight after the harvest was in. (Currie, vol.i, p. 66.)
3. 'Epistle to Capt\. Will\. Logan at Park,' Kinsley, 129.

more than a day or two at a time, or a week at most. Observing himself the ridicule that would attach to this sort of conduct if it were known, he made two or three humorous stanzas on the subject, which I cannot now recollect, but they all ended,

'So I'll to my Latin again.'

William Burnes could no longer afford hired servants, and by the age of fifteen his elder son was the farm's principal labourer. When he looked back on his adolescence in his letter to Dr Moore he painted a sombre picture – 'the chearless gloom of a hermit with the unceasing moil of a galley slave'. Gilbert recorded that Burns suffered from almost constant headaches in the evenings and took the view that those years left a lasting mark: 'I doubt not but the hard labour and sorrow of this period of his life, was in a great measure the cause of that depression of spirits with which Robert was so often afflicted through his whole life afterwards.'[1]

The hard labour was not unrelieved. It was the Scottish custom to couple a man and woman together as partners in the harvest field. Burns told Dr Moore in his autobiographical letter how in his 'fifteenth autumn' he found himself working alongside 'a bonie, sweet, sonsie lass' a year younger than himself, and that it was she who initiated him in 'a certain delicious Passion, which in spite of acid Disappointment, gin-horse Prudence and bookworm Philosophy, I hold to be the first of human joys.'

Burns found himself unable to explain why he so much liked to loiter behind with her as they returned from the fields in the evening – 'and particularly why my pulse beat such a furious ratann when I looked and fingered over her hand, to pick out the nettle-stings and thistles.' But the girl, like his mother, sang sweetly, and it was to the tune of her favourite reel that he attempted a new set of words:

I was not so presumptive to imagine that I could make verses like printed ones, composed by men who had Greek and Latin; but my girl sung a song which was said to be composed by a small country laird's son, on one of his father's maids, with whom he was in love; and I saw no reason why I might not rhyme as well as he, for excepting smearing sheep and casting peats, his father living in the moors, he had no more Scholarcraft than I had.[2]

'Tis this in Nelly pleases me,
'Tis this enchants my soul;
For absolutely in my breast
She reigns without controul.[3]

1. Currie, vol. i, p. 70.
2. Letters, 125.
3. Kinsley, 1.

No great shakes as poetry, as Burns himself subsequently conceded, but he retained a sentimental affection for it. 'The performance is, indeed, very puerile and silly,' he wrote a decade or so later in his *Common-place Book*, 'but I am always pleased with it, as it recals to my mind those happy days when my heart was yet honest and my tongue was sincere.' The literary merit of the piece signifies as little as whether 'Handsome Nell's' name was Blair or Kirkpatrick or whether she was the daughter of a farmer or a blacksmith. Of rather greater importance is that it was the first time Burns had, as he rather archly put it to Dr Moore, 'committed the sin of RHYME.'

The chronology of Burns's long letter to Moore cannot be relied upon – he was, after all, describing events which had occurred fifteen years previously. A passage which immediately precedes his account of Nelly makes it plain that he succeeded in finding occasional relief not only from the 'unceasing moil' at Mount Oliphant but also from its hermetical gloom, although it also gives an indication of the prickliness that was such a marked characteristic: his social disposition, he tells Moore, was 'without bounds or limits – when not checked by some modification of spited pride.' He concedes, however, that his 'vicinity to Ayr' was of great advantage to him, both socially and educationally:

I formed many connections with other Youngkers who possessed superior advantages; the youngling Actors who were busy with the rehearsal of PARTS in which they were shortly to appear on that STAGE where, Alas! I was destined to druge behind the SCENES. – It is not commonly at these green years that the young Noblesse and Gentry have a just sense of the immense distance between them and their ragged Playfellows. – It takes a few dashes into the world to give the young Great man that proper, decent, unnoticing regard for the poor, insignificant, stupid devils, the mechanics and peasantry around him ... My young Superiours never insulted the clouterly appearance of my ploughboy carcase, the two extremes of which were often exposed to all the inclemencies of all the seasons ...

The lineaments of 'Scotland's first class-conscious poet' – the phrase is Christina Keith's – are already apparent.

Although William Burnes could ill-afford to be without him, he sent his elder son away for several weeks in the summer of 1775 to further his education. He went to Kirkoswald, about thirteen miles south-west of Ayr on the coast of Carrick. The local schoolmaster, Hugh Rodger, was known for his sarcastic tongue and his skill as a teacher of mathematics. Burns was set to study 'Mensuration, Surveying, Dialling, &c,' subjects in which he claimed to have made good progress, although he added that he made greater progress 'in the knowledge of mankind.' His stay in Kirkoswald, he told Dr Moore, 'made very considerable alterations in my mind and manners.' They were alterations not altogether for the better.

The coves and inlets of the Carrick shore were infested by smugglers from the Isle of Man, who carried their trade into the heart of the country. John Galt, twenty years Burns's junior and a native of Irvine, gives a memorable account of their impact on the lives of the population in his *Annals of the Parish*. 'The great smuggling trade corrupted all the west coast,' laments the novel's narrator, the Reverend Micah Balwhidder:

> The tea was going like the chaff, the brandy like well-water; and the wastrie of all things was terrible. There was nothing minded but the riding of cadgers by day and excisemen by night, and battles between the smugglers and the king's men, by both sea and land. There was a continual drunkenness and debauchery; and our Session, that was but on the lip of this whirlpool of iniquity, had an awful time o't. I did all that was in the power of nature to keep my people from the contagion: I preached sixteen times from the text, 'Render to Cæsar the things that are Cæsar's' . . . But, for all I could do, the evil got in among us, and we had no less than three contested bastard bairns upon our hands at one time, which was a thing never heard of in a parish of the shire of Ayr since the Reformation.[1]

'Scenes of swaggering riot and roaring dissipation were as yet new to me,' Burns told Moore, but he was quick to learn and there is more than a hint of swagger in his account of how he filled his time when Hugh Rodger released him from the schoolroom:

> I was no enemy to social life. – Here, though I learned to look unconcernedly on a large tavern bill, and mix without fear in a drunken squabble, yet I went on with a high hand in my Geometry; till the sun entered Virgo, a month which is always a carnival in my bosom, a charming Fillette who lived next door to the school overset my Trigonomertry [*sic*], and set me off in a tangent from the sphere of my studies.

Talk of large tavern bills is certainly swagger, but the charming Fillette was real enough. Her name was Peggy Thomson. She was thirteen years old, and Burns's trigonometry was never the same again:

> I struggled on with my Sines and Co-sines for a few days more; but stepping out to the garden one charming noon, to take the sun's altitude, I met with my Angel,

1. John Galt, *Annals of the Parish*, 1821, chapter 2. 'When very young,' Galt wrote in his autobiography, 'I wished to write a book that would be for Scotland what the *Vicar of Wakefield* is for England.' 'Wastrie' means wasteful extravagance and 'cadgers' is the colloquial term for travelling hawkers.

> – "Like Proserpine gathering flowers,
> Herself a fairer flower" –

It was vain to think of doing any more good at school. – The remaining week I staid, I did nothing but craze the faculties of my soul about her, or steal out to meet with her; and the two last nights of my stay in the country, had sleep been a mortal sin, I was innocent. –

This Kirkoswald Proserpine (Burns is showing off again – he is quoting from *Paradise Lost*) does not immediately disappear from the cast. Burns's sister, Mrs Begg, told his biographer Robert Chalmers that the 1775 affair had later been revived. Burns had struck up a friendship with one of his fellow-pupils at Kirkoswald, a boy called Thomas Orr, and they kept in touch for a number of years. None of Orr's letters to Burns survive, but three from Burns do, one of them, written in 1784, apparently an acknowledgement of the news that Peggy was about to be married:

> Dr Thomas,
> I am much oblidged to you for your last letter tho' I assure you the contents of it gave me no manner of concern. – I am at present so cursedly taken in with an affair of gallantry that I am very glad Peggy is off my hands as I am at present embarrassed enough without her, – I do'n't chuse to enter into particulars in writing but never was a poor rakish rascal in a more pitiful taking . . .[1]

Three years later, when the Kilmarnock edition of his poems was published, Burns presented Peggy with a copy and wrote an inscription on the fly leaf:

> Once fondly lov'd, and still rememb'red dear,
> Sweet early Object of my youthful vows,
> Accept this mark of friendship, warm, sincere,
> Friendship – 'tis all cold duty now allows.

This was at a time when Burns was contemplating emigration as an escape from the various complications he had made for himself, and in a second stanza he permitted himself to ham it up:

> And while you read the simple, artless rhymes,
> One friendly sigh for him – he asks no more,

---

1. Letters, 19, 11 November 1784. The particulars into which Burns was reluctant to enter were that he had seduced the servant girl Elizabeth Paton. She gave birth to his first illegitimate child six months later. (See pp. 48–9 *infra*.)

Who, distant, burns in flaming torrid climes,
Or haply lies beneath th' Atlantic roar.[1]

Burns viewed his stay in Kirkoswald with satisfaction. 'I had seen mankind in a new phasis,' he wrote, 'and I engaged several of my schoolfellows to keep up a literary correspondence with me.' He worked hard at that correspondence, sometimes using his collection of letters 'by the wits of Queen Ann's reign' as a discreet crib. He kept copies of those of his efforts which he judged the most successful, and was quietly pleased with himself – 'a comparison between them and the composition of most of my correspondents flattered my vanity.'[2]

His reading had also been extended. He had been introduced to the works of Thomson and came to know more of Shenstone. James Thomson, a fellow-Scot, was the son of the minister at Ednam in Roxburghshire. He had studied Arts at the University of Edinburgh and then Divinity, but his professor reprimanded him for the use of unintelligible language in the composition of sermons; in 1725 he abandoned his ambition to be a poet–clergyman in the manner of Isaac Watts and moved to London. There he wrote plays (one of them, the tragedy *Sophonisba*, contained the famously feeble line 'O Sophonisba, Sophonisba, O!', quickly parodied as 'O Jemmy Thomson, Jemmy Thomson, O!') He also wrote the words of *Rule Britannia* and gained the patronage of the Lord Chancellor of the day, Charles Talbot; later he was awarded a pension of £100 and the sinecure of Surveyor–General to the Leeward Islands. Notorious for his indolence, he was best known for his long poem *The Seasons*, completed in 1730. He contributed greatly to the vogue for the picturesque, but although he was seen as an early precursor of romanticism, most of the Romantics were to deplore his artifical diction. 'A great poet, rather than a good one,' wrote Coleridge; 'his style was as meretricious as his thoughts were natural.'

Thomson had died in 1748, but William Shenstone, Burns's second important discovery during that summer of 1775, had died only twelve years previously. Shenstone had been a contemporary of Samuel Johnson's at Pembroke College, Oxford. When he was not versifying, he devoted himself to 'landskip gardening.' He lived at Halesowen, then in Shropshire, later in Worcestershire, and although indifferent to the dilapidation of the family house, he ran through his inheritance (and more) in laying out the property as a *ferme ornée*, complete with vistas, cascades and a grove to Virgil. Johnson, holding him up to brief and dismissive scrutiny in *Lives of the English Poets*, was less than admiring of this 'ambition of rural elegance':

1. Kinsley, 121. 'Wrote on the blank leaf of a copy of my first Edition, which I sent to an old Sweetheart, then married –.' Burns included these verses in the first of the two manuscript volumes he prepared for his friend Robert Riddell in 1791 and added a footnote: 'Poor Peggy! Her husband is my old acquaintance and a most worthy fellow. – When I was taking leave of my Carrick relations intending to go to the West Indies, when I took farewell of her, neither she nor I could speak a syllable. Her husband escorted me three miles on my road, and we both parted with tears.'
2. Letters, 125.

Whether to plant a walk in undulating curves, and to place a bench at every turn where there is an object to catch a view; to make water run where it will be heard, and to stagnate where it will be seen; to leave intervals where the eye will be pleased, and to thicken the plantation where there is something to be hidden, demands any great power of mind, I will not enquire; perhaps a sullen and surly speculator may think such performances rather the sport than the business of human reason . . .

Shenstone wrote in a variety of forms – odes and ballads, songs and 'levities'. Burns seems to have been most taken with his elegies, which tended to the pastoral. Johnson was prepared to allow that his thoughts in this genre were 'pure and simple', but was hard put to it to find much else to approve:

The lines are sometimes, such as Elegy requires, smooth and easy; but to this praise his claim is not constant: his diction is often harsh, improper, and affected; his words ill-coined, or ill-chosen, and his phrase unskilfully inverted.

'My illustrious friend, I thought, did not sufficiently admire Shenstone,' wrote Boswell. Posterity has sided with Johnson, but Burns was not to know about that and retained his early enthusiasm, quoting from him in his *Common-place Book* and in his letters. 'My favourite authors are of the sentim'l kind,' he was to write to Murdoch in 1783, and he places Shenstone first in a catalogue that includes Thomson, Sterne and James Macpherson, the 'discoverer' of Ossian. 'These are the glorious models after which I endeavour to form my conduct,' he announces, and he is so carried away that both syntax and vocabulary become overheated:

. . . 'Tis incongruous, 'tis absurd to suppose that the man whose mind glows with sentiments lighted up at their sacred flame – the man whose heart distends with benevolence to all the human race – he 'who can soar above this little scene of things' – can he descend to mind the paulty conccerns [*sic*] about which the terrae-filial race fret, and fume, and vex themselves?[1]

On his return to Mount Oliphant from Kirkoswald, Burns had been obliged to descend to just such concerns very quickly. The farm had proved a ruinous bargain. William Burnes had tried but failed to find something better when the lease had run its first six years. Now in his fifties, he appeared to Gilbert 'broken down with the long continued fatigues of his life.' He was also burdened with an increased rent, and sometimes fell in arrears. In 1776, Provost Fergusson died. 'To clench the curse, we fell into the hands of a Factor who sat for the picture I have drawn of one in my Tale of two dogs,' Burns wrote. 'My

1. *Ibid.*, 13, dated 15 January 1783.

indignation yet boils at the recollection of the scoundrel tyrant's insolent, threatening epistles, which used to set us all in tears.'[1]

Who the 'scoundrel tyrant' was is not known – probably a lawyer in Ayr – but he has his modest immortality in the dialogue which Burns was to place first in the Kilmarnock edition of his poems. Cæsar, the rich man's dog, pictures the scene on the Laird's rent-day and shakes his head over the way 'poor tenant-bodies, scant o' cash', must endure the insolent abuse of the factor:

> He'll stamp an' threaten, curse an' swear,
> He'll *apprehend* them, *poind* their gear,
> While they maun stand, wi' aspect humble,
> An' hear it a', an' fear an' tremble![2]

'Poinding' was the seizure and sale of goods under warrant. It didn't come to that, in the event: 'My father's spirit was soon irritated, but not easily broken,' Burns wrote. 'There was a freedom in his lease in two years more, and to weather these two years we retrenched expences.' Matters were eventually settled by the Fergusson executors taking out a mortgage on the smallholding at Alloway, and at Whitsuntide 1777 the family moved to a larger farm, ten miles distant from Mount Oliphant in the parish of Tarbolton. Burns had passed his eighteenth birthday earlier in the year.

1. *Ibid.*, 125.
2. Kinsley, 71.

Three

EARLY MANHOOD

THE NAME OF THE NEW FARM was Lochlie. Halfway between Tarbolton
and Mauchline and four hundred feet above sea level, it extended to a hundred
and thirty acres. The soil was marginally better than at Mount Oliphant,
although the small loch from which it took its name was still undrained, and
the land accordingly tended to be sour and marshy. The rent, at twenty shillings
an acre, was high. The landlord was an Ayr merchant called David McClure,
and it is possible that he advanced some capital to his new tenant: 'The nature
of the bargain,' Burns wrote, 'was such as to throw a little ready money in his
hand at the commencement, otherwise the affair would have been impracticable. – For four years we lived comfortably here.'[1]

Comfortably, perhaps, but not in all respects as harmoniously as before.
Young men rarely continue to see their parents through the uncritical eyes of
childhood. There was no dramatic revolt against paternal authority, but it is
plain that Burns's admiration for his father was gradually qualified by reservations about his unbending sternness and uncertain temper. He acknowledged
his indebtedness to him for 'most of my little pretensions to wisdom,' but his
letter to Moore (he was writing three years after his father's death) makes clear
that he had come at some stage to regard him as at least the co-author of his
own misfortunes:

I have met with few who understood 'Men, their manners and their ways'
equal to him; but stubborn, ungainly Integrity, and headlong, ungovernable
Irrascibility are disqualifying circumstances: consequently I was born a very
poor man's son.[2]

Not too long after the move to Lochlie, that irascibility was provoked when
Burns decided to go for lessons to a country dancing school – 'to give my
manners a brush,' he said:

1. Letters, 125.
2. Ibid.

28

My father had an unaccountable antipathy against these meetings; and my going was, what to this hour I repent, in absolute defiance of his commands. – My father, as I said before, was the sport of strong passions: from that instance of rebellion he took a kind of dislike of me, which, I believe, was one cause of that dissipation which marked my future years.

Years later, Gilbert amplified the story for Currie's benefit. He confirmed their father's dislike of dancing schools, but said that he had so far relented after Burns's first month of attendance that he allowed other members of the family to go with him. 'I believe the truth was,' he wrote, 'that he, about this time, began to see the dangerous impetuosity of my brother's passions, as well as his not being amenable to counsel.'[1] Gilbert, for whom directness and euphemism seemed to hold equal attractions, also told Currie that it was during the Tarbolton years that the foundation was laid in his brother's character of 'certain habits' – habits, he conceded, which afterwards became 'but too prominent', but which had been unfairly exaggerated by malice and envy:

> Though when young he was bashful and awkward in his intercourse with women, yet, when he approached manhood, his attachment to their society became very strong, and he was constantly the victim of some fair enslaver. The symptoms of his passion were often such as nearly to equal those of the celebrated Sappho. I never indeed knew that he fainted, sunk, and died away; but the agitation of his mind and body exceeded any thing of the kind I ever knew in real life.

There was, it seems, one channel which was dammed against this extravagant and swirling flow of Sapphic emotion. Gilbert recorded that Burns always had a particular jealousy of anyone who was richer than himself or who 'had more consequence in life,' and that his love, therefore, 'rarely settled on persons of this description.' There was at least one occasion, however, when a scornful toss of the head at Burns's lack of 'yellow dirt'[2] was sufficient to goad him into verse. The girl was a neighbouring farmer's daughter, and Burns's revenge for the snub survives as the song 'Tibby I hae seen the day'. He relies more on the vernacular than in his earlier efforts, and this helps him to lace his indignation with humour:

> There lives a lass beside yon park
> I'd rather hae her in her sark   shift
> Than you wi' a' your thousand mark
> That gars you look sae high—[3]   makes

---

1. Currie, vol. i, p. 79.
2. 'Yellow dirt' is found in many eighteenth century Scottish songs, but also occurs in *Cymbeline* and in Pope's *An Essay on Man:* 'Is yellow dirt the passion of thy life?' (iv, 279.)
3. Kinsley, 6.

When his advances were received less haughtily, it was a very different story, and by Gilbert's account, the first casualty was objectivity:

> When he selected any one out of the sovereignty of his good pleasure to whom he should pay his particular attention, she was instantly invested with a sufficient stock of charms, out of the plentiful stores of his own imagination; and there was often a great dissimilitude between his fair captivator, as she appeared to others, and as she seemed when invested with the attributes he gave her.[1]

In the picture he later painted of himself in those early Lochlie years Burns did not flatter himself: 'I was, at the beginning of this period, perhaps the most ungainly, awkward being in the parish,' he told Moore. 'No Solitaire was less acquainted with the ways of the world.'

The deficiency was partly to be remedied by reading – 'My knowledge of modern manners, and of literature and criticism I got from the *Spectator*' – and he also mentions Pope, Shakespeare and the works of Allan Ramsay.[2] He acquired some knowledge of the ancient world from a couple of 'historical and geographical' grammars and a smattering of Greek and Roman mythology from Andrew Tooke's *Pantheon*. He read some Locke, a history of the Bible and a certain amount of theology. He was also beginning to take his farming seriously – his list of reading includes Jethro Tull's *The Horse-hoeing Husbandry*, which had appeared in the 1730s, and another agricultural manual by Adam Dickson. There was, however, in this rather mixed bag, one book – he does not identify it precisely – which meant more to Burns than any other:

> The Collection of Songs was my *vade mecum*.—I pored over them, driving my cart or walking to labor, song by song, verse by verse; carefully noting the true tender or sublime from affectation or fustian. – I am convinced I owe much to this for my critic-craft such as it is. –

Burns, by his own account, did not remain the most ungainly being in the parish for long – it is, indeed, improbable that he ever genuinely saw himself as that. 'My reputation for bookish knowledge, a certain wild, logical talent, and a strength of thought something like the rudiments of good sense, made

1. Currie, vol i, p. 72.
2. Ramsay, the father of the painter, was born in 1684. He left his native Lanarkshire in his teens and was apprenticed to an Edinburgh periwig maker. He abandoned wig-making for bookselling, established a circulating library and opened a theatre. In his younger days his sympathies were strongly nationalist and Jacobite. His first collection of poems appeared in 1721, half of them in the florid Augustan English of the day, half of them in a racy Scots vernacular. Three years later he published *The Ever Green*, an anthology of early Scottish poetry, and this was followed by *The Tea-Table Miscellany*, five volumes of traditional songs and ballads. His best-known work was *The Gentle Shepherd* (1725), a pastoral comedy which he later turned into a ballad opera and which remained popular for a hundred and fifty years. He died a year before Burns was born.

me generally a welcome guest,' he told Moore. "'Tis no great wonder,' he continued, helping himself to a verse from St. Matthew, not getting it quite right and veering in the process from the merely immodest to the mildly blasphemous, 'that always "where two or three were met together, there was I in the midst of them".'

If he was not exactly attracting disciples he was certainly beginning to attract attention, as one of the new friends he made at Tarbolton, David Sillar, later recorded:

His social disposition easily procured him acquaintance; but a certain satirical seasoning, with which he and all poetic geniuses are in some degree influenced, while it set the rustic circle in a roar, was not unaccompanied by its kindred attendant – suspicious fear. I recollect hearing his neighbours observe he had a great deal to say for himself, and that they suspected his principles.[1]

Burns's principles fell under suspicion partly because his theological reading had included a work by a man called John Taylor. It was called *The Scripture Doctrine of Original Sin Proposed to Free and Candid Examination.* That freedom and candour, mediated by Burns, was unwelcome to his new neighbours, who perceived that there had come among them someone favourable to the 'moderate side'.

The religion of the people of Tarbolton at that time was purely that of their fathers, founded on the *Westminster Confession,* and taught by one generation to another, uncontaminated by reading, reflection, and conversation; and though divided into different sectaries, the *Shorter Catechism* was the line which bounded all their controversies. The slightest insinuation of Taylor's opinions made his neighbours suspect, and some even avoid him, as an heretical and dangerous companion.[2]

Sillar, a farmer's son and a year younger than Burns, taught at the parish school for a time. He was a keen versifier and a rather more talented fiddler (Burns was moved to emulation and laid out five shillings on a fiddle of his own). Sillar, later to be the recipient of the two affectionate 'Epistles to Davie',[3] noted that his new friend drew attention to himself not only by his opinions but also by his appearance: 'He wore the only tied hair in the parish; and in the church, his plaid, which was of a particular colour, I think *fillemot,* he wrapped in a particular manner round his shoulders.' Fillemot was from the

1. David Sillar, letter to Robert Aiken, published in Josiah Walker, *Poems by Robert Burns, with an Account of his Life and Miscellaneous Remarks on his Writings,* 2 vols., printed for the Trustees of the late James Morison, Edinburgh, 1811, vol ii, p. 257.
2. *Ibid.*
3. Kinsley, 51 and 101.

French *feuillemorte*. A plaid the colour of dead leaves would certainly mark a man out from those who were content with homespun grey, and so would hair long enough to be held in a pigtail.

On Sundays, when some filled the time between church services by going to the inn, Burns and Sillar often went walking over the fields. Sillar's hopes of an elevated and extended exchange of views on matters of moment were not always realised:

> In these walks I have frequently been struck by his facility in addressing the fair sex; and many times, when I have been bashfully anxious how to express myself, he would have entered into conversation with them with the greatest ease and freedom; and it was generally a death-blow to our conversation, however agreeable, to meet a female acquaintance.[1]

Female acquaintances were allowed no opportunity of disrupting the proceedings of the Tarbolton Bachelors' Club. This exercise in sociability was dreamt up by Burns, Gilbert and five others towards the end of 1780 (Sillar, for some reason, was not admitted until six months later.) It was established 'under such rules and regulations, that while we should forget our cares and labours in mirth and diversion, we might not transgress the bounds of innocence and decorum.' It was, in fact, a debating society – Burns had heard of something similar in Ayr. He was voted into the chair for their first meeting, and for a couple of years they assembled once a month to debate such weighty questions as 'Whether is the savage man, or the peasant of a civilized country, in the most happy situation?' or 'Whether do we derive more happiness from love or friendship?' They were, Burns's American biographer Franklin Bliss Snyder was to observe, topics surprisingly like those which the young Emerson was to debate in his Harvard literary society forty years later.[2]

The constitution of the Club survives. Membership was restricted to sixteen. Any subject might be proposed for discussion, 'disputed points of religion only excepted.' Rule 6 prohibited all swearing and profane language; rule 7, somewhat masonically, enjoined members to make no mention of the club's affairs to any other person – 'and particularly if any member shall reveal any of the speeches or affairs of the club, with a view to ridicule or laugh at any of the rest of the members, he shall be for ever excommunicated from the society.'

Snyder saw in these rules and regulations 'an unusual combination of sentimentalism, decorous formality, and literary aspiration.' Their authorship is not known, but they have Burns's fingerprints all over them, especially the tenth and last:

1. Walker, *op. cit.*
2. Franklin Bliss Snyder, *The Life of Robert Burns*, Macmillan, New York, 1932, p. 70. Henceforth cited as Snyder.

Every man proper for a member of this society, must have a frank, honest, open heart; above any thing dirty or mean; and must be a professed lover of one or more of the female sex. No haughty, self-conceited person, who looks upon himself as superior to the rest of the club, and specially no mean spirited, wordly mortal, whose only will is to heap up money, shall upon any pretence whatever be admitted. In short, the proper person for this society is, a cheerful, honest-hearted lad, who, if he has a friend that is true, and a mistress that is kind, and as much wealth as genteelly to make both ends meet – is just as happy as this world can make him.[1]

Making both ends meet was never easy at Lochlie, however. 'I saw my father's situation entailed on me perpetual labour,' Burns wrote to Moore:

The only two doors by which I could enter the fields of fortune were, the most niggardly economy, or the little chicaning art of bargain-making: the first is so contracted an aperture, I never could squeeze myself into it; the last I always hated the contamination of the threshold.[2]

Contaminated or no, Burns now decided to put a tentative foot across that threshold and at the age of twenty-two he spent some months exploring an avenue of escape from the drudgery of farming. He went off in the summer of 1781 to the nearby town of Irvine to learn the trade of flax dressing. He wrote later that he went 'partly thro' whim,' but he and his brother had been growing flax for some years on the heavy clay soil at Lochlie; Gilbert later told Currie that Burns had seen it as a way of accelerating his prospects of marrying and settling down – the expense of stocking a farm of his own would have been altogether beyond him.

Flax was dressed by splitting and straightening the fibres with a pair of hand-combs known as heckles. Work in the dust-filled heckling sheds was monotonous, mechanical and every bit as hard on the hands as harvesting. Before the year was out, Burns found himself dragged down into illness and depression, but it was not just by the uncongenial nature of his new employment.

'*Vive l'amour et vive la bagatelle*, were my sole principles of action,' he was to write with airy affectation to Dr Moore six years later, but the first of his two principles had plainly not been operating at all satisfactorily: 'A *belle-fille*

---

1. Currie, vol. i, p. 367. It is interesting to note that the preamble to the Tarbolton club's rules records that the first meeting was held on the evening of 11th November 1780, 'commonly called Hallowe'en.' The introduction of the new-style Gregorian calendar, decreed by Gregory XIII in 1582, was ultimately agreed in Great Britain in 1751. It replaced the old Julian calendar the following year, prompting the public cry, 'Give us back our eleven days!'
2. Letters, 125.

whom I adored and who had pledged her soul to meet me in the field of matrimony, jilted me with peculiar circumstances of mortification.' If the *belle-fille* in question was the 'My dear E' to whom he is supposed to have addressed five letters in the course of 1781, she was a girl of good sense, because he sounds ponderously full of himself: 'I assure you, my dear,' he told her in one of them, 'I often look up to the divine disposer of events, with an eye of gratitude for the blessing which I hope he intends to bestow on me, in bestowing you.'[1]

Burns was also oppressed by domestic anxieties, and these weighed more heavily than his mortification at the hands of 'E'. Years later his brother Gilbert recalled their distress at the thought of their father, 'broken down with the long-continued fatigues of his life,' growing old. That, however, had been when William Burnes was in his fifties; now, in his early sixties, things were very much worse. 'The clouds of misfortune were gathering thick around my father's head,' Burns wrote in his letter to Moore, 'the darkest of which was, he was visibly far gone in a consumption.'

William Burnes was also becoming increasingly embroiled with his landlord, David McClure. Their agreement about the rent for Lochlie, concluded in 1777, had been a verbal one. McClure, a merchant in Ayr and a minor landowner, had incurred heavy losses when a local bank, Douglas, Heron and Company, crashed in 1772. He had managed for some years to keep his head above water but by 1781 he was in considerable straits; denying that their agreement had allowed Burnes a certain amount for improvements (the soil was acidic and required liming), he began to press for what he claimed were arrears in rent.

The exact nature of the illness which Burns himself suffered in Irvine towards the end of 1781 is not known, although we do know that by the middle of November he was unwell enough to need professional attention. Although medicine had made great strides in eighteenth-century Scotland – Edinburgh University opened its medical school in the late twenties and by the middle of the century Glasgow had followed suit – there were still physicians who preserved the mystique of their calling by resort to publications like the *Edinburgh Pharmacopoeia*, a thesaurus of advice on the curative properties of wood-lice, horse-dung, mother-of-pearl, pigeon's blood and spider's webs. Burns seems to have been relatively lucky. He was seen by a Dr Charles Fleeming, who went to see his patient – he describes him as a lint-dresser – five times in the

---

1. As is so often the case with Burns, we are in deeply speculative territory here. The originals of all these letters are now lost. Nobody has established with certainty that Burns ever actually sent any of them; it is entirely possible that they remained in his drawer in draft. Nor can it be excluded that some or all of them were composed on behalf of friends who were less ready with the pen: 'A country lad seldom carries on an amour without an assisting confident,' he told Moore. 'I possessed a curiosity, zeal and intrepid dexterity in these matters which recommended me a proper Second in duels of that kind; and I dare say, I felt as much pleasure at being in the secret of half the amours in the parish, as ever did Premier at knowing the intrigues of half the courts of Europe.' (*Letter* 125, 2 August 1787.)

course of eight days. On his first visit he prescribed ipecacuanha and a compound of rhubarb and aloes. Aloes was a purgative; used alone it tended to cause griping, and it was therefore generally administered in combination with some other substance.[1]

Ipecacuanha is made from the dried root of two plants found in South America, and its main active alkaloid is emetine. It figures as an ingredient to this day in a number of patent cough mixtures, although doctors now discount its value as an expectorant; in larger doses it is emetic, and it was formerly used in cases of acute poisoning to induce vomiting. It was also at one time favoured as a treatment for amoebiasis, which is an infection with the protozoan parasite. It is of some interest, in the light of Burns's later medical history, that it is now known to be toxic, particularly to the heart.

Dr Fleeming called again five days later and prescribed 'an anodyne,' which indicates nothing more than that there was some requirement for the relief of pain. He returned on the next three days, however, and on each occasion prescribed extremely large doses of powdered cinchona. Cinchona is a genus of evergreen native to the Andes, and its bark is the source of the quinoline group of alkaloids. We have no means of knowing how much of a pharmacologist Dr Fleeming was, but it was a fairly common treatment for a high fever.[2] Typhoid? Smallpox? (There was an epidemic in 1781.) Malaria? (Irvine was a seaport.) Dr Fleeming's day-book affords no clue to what he thought he was treating, and Burns's own later description of his illness to Dr Moore ('my hypochondriac complaint') is misleading; we not only live in a different world from Burns, but speak a different language.

He certainly was a hypochondriac in the modern sense – his letters are peppered with evidence of an excessive preoccupation with his bodily health – but that is not at all what he and his contemporaries understood by the term. Hypochondria – the word comes from the Greek – did not originally signify an illness but simply described a part of the body. It was the name given to that part of the abdomen which lies immediately under the ribs. To the ancients, and to physicians well into modern times, hypochondria served as a portmanteau diagnosis for any derangement of the organs located there: 'The liver, gall and spleen,' wrote Nicholas Culpeper in 1652, 'and the diseases that arise from them, as the jaundice and the hypochondriac.' These organs were also believed – although doctors were unable to explain how – to be the seat of melancholy. When Burns wrote to his father two days after Christmas in 1781 he clearly believed he had been quite seriously unwell, and that his illness had not been purely physical:

1. The doctor's day-book came to light in the attic of his old house as recently as 1955, and the details of how he treated Burns were published for the first time by James Mackay in his 1992 biography.
2. Quinine is still medicinally important today, even though it has been superseded for most anti-malarial purposes by synthetic compounds. Once again, it is interesting, in the light of Burns's later medical history, to note that quinidine, another of the cinchona alkaloids, is used for treating disturbances of cardiac rhythm and for its myocardial depressant effect.

The weakness of my nerves has so debilitated my mind that I dare not, either review past events, or look forward into futurity; for the least anxiety, or perturbation in my breast, produces most unhappy effects on my whole frame.

Burns still obviously has an attentive eye on that volume of 'letters by the most eminent writers, with a few sensible directions for attaining an easy epistolary style' which his uncle had brought him from Ayr. The style, as it happens, is anything but easy. Once he has filled his father in on the state of his health he embarks on a passage about his mental and spiritual condition which is as stilted as it is lugubrious:

> ... My principal, and indeed my only pleasurable enjoyment is looking backwards and forwards in a moral and religious way – I am quite transported at the thought that ere long, perhaps very soon, I shall bid an eternal adieu to all the pains and uneasiness and disquietudes of this weary life; for I assure you I am heartily tired of it, and, if I do not very much deceive myself could contentedly and gladly resign it.

This is painful stuff, but there is worse to come. He now informs his father how well he thinks of the fifteenth, sixteenth and seventeenth chapters of the Book of Revelation ('Therefore are they before the throne of God, and serve him day and night in his temple ...') and assures him that he would not exchange the 'noble enthusiasm' with which they inspire him for all this world has to offer:

> I am not formed for the bustle of the busy nor the flutter of the Gay. . . . I foresee that very probably Poverty and Obscurity await me & I am, in some measure prepared and daily preparing to meet and welcome them.

We have no means of knowing what Burns senior made of all this – it is the only letter to pass between them which survives. It is impossible to distinguish attention-seeking nonsense from literary posturing. Burns is actually appropriating, without attribution, other men's flowers; the passage just quoted is heavily derivative of Henry Mackenzie's *The Man of Feeling*, with its droopy hero Harley.

He concludes by thanking his father for his many lessons of virtue and piety – 'Lessons which were but too much neglected when they were given but which, I hope have been remembered ere it is yet too late.' He adds a brief postscript, and its unconscious bathos comes as refreshing relief: 'my meal is nearly out but I am going to borrow till I get more – '[1]

Four days after he wrote this, Burns's ambition to branch out into manufacture and retailing was snuffed out when his business premises went up in

1. Letters, 4.

flames. By the time he described the collapse of the venture to Dr Moore, he had clearly decided he was well out of it, and his tone was philosophical:

> My Partner was a scoundrel of the first water who made money by the mystery of thieving; and to finish the whole, while we were given a welcoming carousal to the New year, our shop, by the drunken carelessness of my Partner's wife, took fire and was burnt to ashes; and left me like a true Poet, not worth sixpence.

He may not have had sixpence to his name, but he somehow contrived to stay on in Irvine for several more weeks. 'From this adventure I learned something of a town-life,' he wrote cheerfully, but at Lochlie these lessons caused some pursing of lips. 'He contracted some acquaintance,' Gilbert wrote years later, 'of a freer manner of thinking and living than he had been used to, whose society prepared him for overleaping the bounds of rigid virtue, which had hitherto restrained him.'

He had, in particular, formed a close friendship there with a seafarer called Richard Brown. Six years older than Burns and a man of some education, Brown had experienced mixed fortunes; shortly before they got to know each other he had been set ashore on the west coast of Ireland by an American privateer, 'stript of everything.' Hans Hecht, Burns's German biographer, wrote that in his autobiographical letter the poet endowed Brown 'with all the virtues of the hero of a novel.'[1] The phrase captures the relationship very precisely:

> This gentleman's mind was fraught with courage, independence, Magnanimity, and every noble manly virtue. – I loved him, I admired him, to a degree of enthusiasm; and I strove to imitate him . . . His knowledge of the world was vastly superior to mine, and I was all attention to learn. – He was the only man I ever saw who was a greater fool than myself when WOMAN was the presiding star; but he spoke of a certain fashionable failing with levity, which hitherto I had regarded with horror. – Here his friendship did me a mischief . . .

'A certain fashionable failing.' If Burns had not been at such pains to impress Dr Moore with his fine phrases and his command of euphemism less ink might have been spilt over the years on what he meant by these four words. Burns's first editor, James Currie, didn't like them one little bit and substituted 'illicit love.' A century and a half later the Ayrshire-born critic Alan Dent, in a spectacularly silly chapter about four of Burns's male friendships, suggested that because Brown was a sailor the phrase could well have meant sodomy.[2]

1. Hans Hecht, *Robert Burns. Leben und Wirken des schottischen Volksdichters*, Heidelberg, 1919. An excellent translation into English by Jane Lymburn was first published by William Hodge & Co. in 1936.
2. Alan Dent, *Burns in his Time*, Nelson, London, 1966.

The truth of the matter is, in fact, embedded squarely in the text of the letter to Moore. The passage just quoted continues: 'the consequence was, that soon after I resumed the plough, I wrote the WELCOME inclosed.' What Burns enclosed was 'The Poet's Welcome to his Bastart Wean':

> Welcome! My bonie, sweet, wee Dochter!
> Tho' ye come here a wee unsought for . . .

It is one of the best and most characteristic poems of his early maturity, an affectionate and defiant welcome to the illegitimate daughter borne to him by Elizabeth Paton.[1] Brown had introduced him to nothing more fashionable than what Burns called houghmagandie and the English call fornication.

None of the half-dozen or so poems that survive from Burns's time in Irvine is of particular merit. The tone is generally sombre and they are interesting mainly as evidence of his depression and low spirits – 'To Ruin', 'Though fickle Fortune has deceiv'd me', 'A Prayer, Under the Pressure of violent Anguish'.[2] The writing is strongly derivative. One short piece, 'A Prayer, in the Prospect of Death', though cast in the measure of a Scottish metrical psalm, is closely modelled on Pope's 'Universal Prayer', and in 'Stanzas on the same Occasion' there is an echo of Young's 'Night Thoughts'. There is an insistent strain of rather remorseful religiosity:

> I tremble to approach an angry GOD.
> And justly smart beneath his sin-avenging rod.[3]

It is the only mention that God gets, although elsewhere in these poems Burns variously invokes an 'Almighty Cause' (who is ALL-GOOD), a 'Great Governor of all below' and an 'Omnipotence Divine.' This is the language not of Calvinism, but of Deism. Only in one short extempore piece does he manage to shed his despondency. In doing so he also shrugs off the constraint of formal English and lapses defiantly, almost chirpily, into the vernacular:

> O why the deuce should I repine,
>   And be an ill foreboder;
> I'm twenty-three, and five foot nine,
>   I'll go and be a sodger.   soldier
>
> I gat some gear wi' meikle care,   much
>   I held it weel thegither;

1. Burns was telescoping for effect and taking considerable liberties with chronology: the child was not born until May 1785. The poem is Kinsley, 60: 'A Poet's welcome to his love-begotten Daughter; the first instance that entitled him to the venerable appellation of Father—'.
2. Kinsley, 12, 16, 15, respectively.
3. *Ibid.*, 13 and 14.

> But now its gane, and something mair,
> I'll go and be a sodger.[1]

In fact he went back to being a farmer, but he did so with an important idea lodged in his mind. 'The great misfortune of my life was, never to have AN AIM,' he later confided in Moore. 'I had felt early some stirrings of Ambition, but they were the blind gropins [*sic*] of Homer's Cyclops round the walls of his cave.'[2] After Irvine this Ayrshire Cyclops groped his way around his cave no longer. Richard Brown may have done his impressionable young friend a mischief, but he also rendered him a service, and years later, at the height of his Edinburgh celebrity, Burns wrote to acknowledge it:

> – My will o' wisp fate, you know: do you recollect a sunday we spent in Eglinton woods? you told me, on my repeating some verses to you that you wondered I could resist the temptation of sending verses of such merit to a magazine: 'twas actually this that gave me an idea of my own pieces which encouraged me to endeavour at the character of a Poet.[3]

Shortly before he went off to Irvine, Burns had become a mason. Gilbert wrote that it was 'his first introduction to the life of a boon companion,' apparently forgetting that they had formed the Bachelors' Club some six months previously. The minute book of the combined Lodge St David in Tarbolton records that on 4th July 1781, 'Robt. Burns in Lochly was entered an Apprentice' and he travelled back from Irvine in October to be 'passed and raised'.

The eighteenth century had seen an enormous growth in freemasonry. In 1738 Pope Clement XII had forbidden Catholics to join on pain of excommunication and the Bourbons and other absolute monarchs regarded it as dangerously subversive. (Paradoxically, an important influence in some French lodges was that of Scottish Jacobites living in exile, who hoped for sympathy – and money – for the restoration of the Stuart dynasty.) In Protestant Europe, however, and in America, masonry was eminently respectable, and the notions of brotherhood and generalised benevolence which were abroad found a resonance in the masonic precepts of tolerance and free enquiry. Mozart was an ardent adherent, and so were Benjamin Franklin and George Washington; in Prussia, Frederick the Great was himself Grand Master.

In Scotland, freemasonry showed itself every bit as prone to schism as the national church. There had been a breakaway lodge in Tarbolton for some years in the 1770s, a breach healed only shortly before Burns joined, but dissension quickly broke out again and there was a further secession in the summer of 1782, of which Burns was part. The seceders constituted themselves

1. *Ibid.*, 18, 'Extempore'.
2. Letters, 125.
3. *Ibid.*, 168, 30 December 1787.

into the St James Lodge, and Burns was elected Depute Master two years later. His membership, like his association with the Bachelors' Club, gratified a strongly felt need for social contact, although the brethren were not spared Burns's sharp tongue and more than one of them live on in mock epitaphs like 'On an Innkeeper in Tarbolton':

> Here lies 'mang ither useless matters,
> A. Manson wi' his endless clatters.—[1]

Burns also honed his wit on the senior warden of the Lodge, James Humphrey. Humphrey lived on into the middle of the nineteenth century, and Allan Cunningham tracked him down when he was at work on his 1834 biography. 'This person is now grown old and infirm,' he wrote, 'but loves to talk of Burns and of the warm debates between them on Effectual Calling and Free Grace.' Burns clearly did not rate him highly as a controversialist:

> Below thir stanes lie Jamie's banes;
> O Death, it's my opinion,
> Thou ne'er took such a bleth'ran b–tch
> Into thy dark dominion![2]

Sociability was not freemasonry's sole attraction. A draft survives of a letter Burns and another member wrote to the Master of their lodge, Sir John Whitefoord. They express concern about the lodge's financial situation, which they describe as 'wretched': 'To us, Sir, who are of the lower orders of mankind, to have a fund in view on which we may with certainty depend to be kept from want should we be in circumstances of distress or old age, this is a matter of high importance.'[3]

There was precious little opportunity when he finally returned from Irvine for Burns to cultivate his new 'character of a Poet'. His father's affairs had not improved. Economic conditions generally were bleak. Foreign trade had been depressed by the outbreak of the war against the American colonies in 1775, and the livelihood of many affected by the drying up of profitable markets. The summer of 1782 was cold and stormy, and with the onset of autumn, things went from bad to worse:

On the 5th of October, when oats and barley were generally green, a frost, armed almost with the rigour of a Greenland climate, desolated, in one

1. Kinsley, 28A.
2. *Ibid.*, 33.
3. Letters, 12, thought to have been written in November 1782. Whitefoord, the third baronet, was well-known as an agricultural improver. He was later to be very helpful to Burns in Edinburgh. (see p. 106, *infra*.) Burns sent some covering lines in verse to him (Kinsley, 334A) with his 'Lament for James, Earl of Glencairn' (Kinsley, 334), 'the man to whom I owe all that I am and have!'

night, the hopes of the husbandmen. The grain, frost-bitten, immediately contracted a hoary whiteness, and ripened no more. Potatoes and turnips, dwarfish from the severity of the weather they had experienced, were also much injured by the frost . . .

Sir John Sinclair, whose account this is, recorded that in both Dumfriesshire and Ayrshire, snow fell before the corn could be cut; famine was averted only by the ending of hostilities with the American colonists and the consequent release of food supplies intended for the navy.[1] Sinclair's description of the wretched state of the country is borne out by a letter which Burns wrote the following summer to his cousin, James Burness, who was a lawyer in Montrose:

> This country, till of late was flourishing incredibly in the Manufactures of Silk, Lawn & Carpet Weaving . . . we had also a fine trade in the Shoe w[ay], but now entirely ruined & hundreds driven to a starving condition on account of it. – Farming is also at a very low ebb with us . . . Our Landholders [are] full of ideas of farming gathered from the English, and the Lothians and other rich soils in Scotland; make no allowance for the odds of the quality of land, and consequently stretch us much beyond what, in the event, we will be found able to pay. . . . In short, my d^r Sir, since the unfortunate beginning of this American war, & its as unfortunate conclusion, this country has been, and still is decaying very fast.[2]

Earlier in the letter he had reported that his father was dying. William Burnes's poor health had been exacerbated by the continuing dispute with his landlord – 'three years tossing and whirling in the vortex of Litigation,' as Burns expressed it to Moore. An attempt at arbitration failed and in May 1783, McClure, hard pressed by his own creditors, raised a Petition in the Sheriff Court at Ayr. He claimed that he was owed more than £500 in arrears of rent, alleged that Burnes was preparing to cut his losses by selling off his crops and stock and sought a warrant of sequestration. The Sheriff's officer turned up at Lochlie to make an inventory, and the town-crier did his rounds of the parish with a warning against buying any of the goods and chattels that had been impounded.

The inventory discloses that there was precious little of which to dispose – the tally of farm implements and vehicles amounted to five carts, four ploughs and two harrows. The Lochlie herd of black cattle numbered thirteen, and there were six horses, two calves, two lambs and a solitary ewe. Matters were further complicated in the autumn of 1783 when McClure was pursued by the man to whom he had mortgaged his estates and Burnes, as a debtor tenant,

---

1. Sir John Sinclair, *Analysis of the Statistical Account of Scotland*, Edinburgh, 1825, Part II, appendix No. III, 'On the Famines', pp. 40 ff.
2. Letters, 14, 21st June 1783.

found himself caught up in the action. He went twice to the Court of Session and eventually, in January 1784, Lord Braxfield, the Lord Ordinary, found in his favour. Burnes died less than three weeks later, and perhaps it was just as well, because the victory had been a costly one. 'When my father died,' Burns wrote with bitter grandiloquence three years later, 'his all went among the rapacious hell-hounds that growl in the kennels of justice.'[1]

John Mackenzie, the young doctor who attended his father in his last months, drew a sharply-etched picture of how Burns struck him at the time. His first impression was not favourable:

The poet seemed distant, suspicious, and without any wish to interest or please. He kept himself very silent in a dark corner of the room; and before he took part in the conversation, I frequently detected him scrutinising me during my conversation with his father and brother.[2]

An episode described many years later by Burns's youngest sister, Isabella, suggests that relations between father and son remained strained to the last. They were both with him on the day he died. The old man tried to comfort his daughter, enjoining her, she recalled, 'to walk in virtue's paths and shun every vice.' He then added – and repeated – that there was one member of the family for whose future conduct he feared. Burns came over to the bed and asked, 'Oh, father, is it me you mean?' When he understood that it was, he turned away to the window in tears.[3]

They took their father's body back to Alloway, the coffin slung on poles between two pack horses. William Burnes lies buried in the graveyard of the old ruined church, close to the cottage he had built for his bride.[4] The words engraved on the stone were composed by his son:

O ye whose cheek the tear of pity stains,
Draw near with pious rev'rence and attend!

1. *Ibid.*, 125. Braxfield, (1722-99) was later appointed Lord Justice Clerk and acquired the reputation of a brutal 'hanging judge.' On one occasion, having sentenced a man to death, he is said to have jeered 'he would be nane the waur o' a hangin.' He presided unsympathetically over the political trials that were held in Scotland in 1793. He is the model for Stevenson's Lord Hermiston in *Weir of Hermiston*.
2. Recorded in Walker, *op. cit.*, vol. ii, pp 261-3. Mackenzie later got to know Burns well and was enchanted by him: 'I have always thought that no person could have a just idea of the extent of Burns's talents, who had not an opportunity to hear him converse. His discrimination of character was great beyond that of any person I ever knew.' (*ibid.*)
3. Chambers-Wallace, vol. i, pp. 109-10.
4. Gilbert told Currie that when his father first went to Alloway the wall of the churchyard was broken down and cattle grazed there. Burnes and some neighbours petitioned Ayr Town Council, who were the superiors of the adjoining land, for permission to rebuild it, and raised a subscription for that purpose. 'Hence he came to consider it as his burial place,' wrote Gilbert. He also told Currie that his brother at one time had thoughts of being buried there. (Currie, vol. iii, pp. 384-5.)

Here lie the loving Husband's dear remains,
The tender Father, and the gen'rous Friend.

The pitying Heart that felt for human Woe,
The dauntless heart that fear'd no human Pride;
The Friend of Man, to vice alone a foe;
'For ev'n his failings lean'd to Virtue's side.'[1]

The last line is from Goldsmith's *The Deserted Village*. Burns would continue to borrow freely from the work of those writers he admired, particularly those 'of the sentimental kind', but either during his stay in Irvine or shortly afterwards, when he had for a time been writing very little, he encountered a poet whose influence was to be even more powerful and beneficial than that of Allan Ramsay – 'meeting with Fergusson's Scotch Poems, I strung anew my wildly-sounding, rustic lyre with emulating vigour.'[2]

Robert Fergusson, born only nine years before Burns, had died in 1774 at the age of 24. He had left St Andrews University without a degree and for the rest of his brief life supported his widowed mother and sister by copying legal documents for testamentary and matrimonial cases. Drink and dissipation brought on a rapid physical decline; he also suffered from bouts of religious melancholia. Eventually he went mad and ended his days in a straw-littered cell in the Edinburgh Bedlam.

Fergusson left only a small body of work – thirty-three poems in Scots and fifty or so in English – comic addresses, nature poems, verses on domestic and festive occasions. He wrote vigorously about the street-life of Edinburgh in 'Auld Reekie', vividly about holiday crowds in 'Leith Races'. In an epistle addressed to the Principal and Professors of his old university 'on their Superb Treat to Dr Samuel Johnson' he conjures up a witty spectacle in which the great Doctor, not known for his enthusiasm for things Caledonian, is served a feast of Scottish delicacies. Fergusson also memorably parodied Henry Mackenzie, creating in the 'Sow of Feeling' a pig of high sensibility and neo-classical inclinations. His importance to Burns was that he sapped his attachment to English Augustan models and gave him the confidence to flex his muscles in the vernacular. It was Fergusson who enabled Burns to write in 'the one true language of his mind.'[3]

Gilbert, looking back in later life on the seven years they lived in Tarbolton,

1. Kinsley, 35, 'For the Author's Father.' In his *Common-place Book* Burns called it 'Epitaph on my ever honored Father.'
2. Letters, 125.
3. The phrase is W.E. Henley's in his biographical essay *Life, Genius, Achievement*, included in the Centenary edition of Burns which he edited with Thomas F. Henderson; T.C. and E.C. Jack, Edinburgh, 1896-97, vol. iv, p. 262.

wrote that they 'were not marked by much literary improvement' on his brother's part, but Gilbert, for once, was talking nonsense. It is true that only a couple of dozen or so pieces can be dated with certainty to this period, but they show an increased assurance and a broadening of range. 'The Death and Dying Words of Poor Mailie', for instance, Burns's first substantial comic poem in Scots and one of the earliest in which Fergusson's influence is apparent, was written at this time. The poet's pet ewe, hopelessly tangled in her rope, is lying in a ditch and thinks she is dying; Hughoc, a dim-witted farm labourer, comes shambling by, and she imparts to him her mock-testament, which ranges from advice on agricultural improvement to some vaguely Rousseauesque reflections on education.[1]

'Mary Morison', one of the finest of Burns's early songs, was written at Lochlie

> Yestreen, when to the trembling string
>   The dance gaed thro' the lighted ha',   hall
> To thee my fancy took its wing,
>   I sat, but neither heard, nor saw . . .[2]

'Winter, A Dirge', with its occasional echoes of Thomson, also dates from this time:

> 'The sweeping blast, the sky o'ercast,'
>   The joyless *winter-day*,
> Let others fear, to me more dear,
>   Than all the pride of May:
> The Tempest's howl, it *soothes* my soul,
>   My *griefs* it seems to join;
> The leafless trees my fancy please,
>   Their fate resembles mine![3]

Winter held a particular attraction for Burns. 'There is,' he wrote, 'scarcely any earthly object gives me more – I don't know if I should call it pleasure, but something which exalts me, something which enraptures me – than to walk in the sheltered side of a wood or high plantation, in a cloudy, winter day, and hear a stormy wind howling among the trees and raving o'er the plain. – It is my best season for devotion . . .[4]

Towards the end of his years at Lochlie, Burns also composed the poem which begins 'On Cessnock banks a lassie dwells.' This, in spite of its stylised

---

1. Kinsley, 24.
2. *Ibid.*, 30.
3. *Ibid.*, 10. The quotation marks around the first line are Burns's own, and he attributed it in a footnote to 'Dr Young'. It is a recollection of Young's *Ocean: An Ode*.
4. First *Common-place Book*, April 1784.

and mainly English diction, gives more than a glimpse of his growing lyrical power. The imagery is sharp and bright and the poem is flooded with the brilliance of light on water. The lover seeks comparisons for the girl's beauty in a pastoral landscape, but is drawn back at the end of each stanza to her 'twa sparkling, rogueish een.'[1]

Some of these early poems were copied into what has become known as Burns's first *Common-place Book*. He started keeping it in 1783. It consisted of eleven folded folio sheets, and the first of the forty-four pages carried a lengthy (and somewhat high-flown) descriptive title:

> Observations, Hints, Songs, Scraps of Poetry &c. by Robert Burness; a man who had little art in making money, and still less in keeping it; but was, however, a man of some sense, a great deal of honesty, and unbounded good will to every creature rational or irrational.—as he was but little indebted to scholastic education, and bred at a plough-tail, his performance must be strongly tinctured with his unpolished rustic way of life . . .[2]

This is rounded off by two quotations from – who else? – William Shenstone. What follows is a jumble of original verse, homespun philosophy and critical reflection – 'I intirely agree,' says an entry dated September 1783, 'with that judicious Philosopher Mr Smith in his excellent Theory of Moral Sentiments, that remorse is the most painful sentiment that can embitter the human bosom.'[3] Six months later, he muses on the sort of company he likes to keep: 'I have often coveted the acquaintance of that part of mankind commonly known by the ordinary phrase of Blackguards, sometimes further than was consistent with the safety of my character . . .' In September 1784 he entered in it the words of 'My girl she's airy, she's buxom and gay,' one of his earliest bawdy songs:

> Her slender neck, her handsome waist,
> Her hair well buckl'd, her stays well lac'd,
> Her taper white leg with an et, and a, c,
> For her a,b,e,d, and her c,u,n,t,
> And Oh, for the joys of a long winter night!!!!![4]

1. Kinsley, 11.
2. The last known owner of the original manuscript was Sir Alfred Joseph Law, MP, who inherited it in 1913. It was still in his possession twenty-five years later and a facsimile edition was published with an introduction and notes by James Cameron Ewing and Davidson Cook (Gowans and Gray, Glasgow, 1938). The entire Law collection has now disappeared.
3. Adam Smith had published *The Theory of Moral Sentiments* in the year of Burns's birth.
4. Kinsley, 46. Burns would later succeed in being both coarse and amusing at the same time. Even as an apprentice in bawdry, however, he was nothing if not thorough; the title of the tune he specified for this song, 'Black Joke', was an eighteenth-century slang expression for the female sexual organs. His inspiration for this crude piece was the servant-girl Elizabeth Paton, (see pp. 48–9, *infra*.).

45

'A Common-place-book contains many notions in garrison, whence the owner may draw out an army into the field' – thus Thomas Fuller in 1642. Burns certainly kept 'notions in garrison' in this way, and also used his precious folio sheets to conduct exercises in style, but the mere putting of pen to paper is an act of communication and presupposes the existence of an audience of some sort. It is certainly not possible to turn the pages of this particular manuscript and believe that it was the work of a man who thought no one but himself would ever read it.

In August 1784, for instance, Burns had clearly encountered what would today be called a 'writing block' – 'The foregoing was to have been an elaborate dissertation on the various species of men,' he writes engagingly, 'but as I cannot please myself in the arrangement of my ideas, I must wait till further experience, and nicer observation throw more light on the subject.' This, however, is less artless than it sounds, because he continues: 'In the mean time I shall set down the following fragment which, as it is the genuine language of my heart, will enable any body to determine which of the Classes I belong to –' (The fragment was five verses of 'Green grow the rashes O,' which in this 'polite' version has become one of the most famous of his songs.[1])

If such internal evidence is insufficient to dispel doubts about what Burns intended or hoped for his *Common-place Book*, they are swept away by a poignant passage from something he wrote ten years later:

> ... As I was placed by Fortune among a class of men to whom my ideas would have been nonsense – I had meant that the book would have lain by me, in the fond hope that, some time or other, even after I was no more, my thoughts would fall into the hands of somebody capable of appreciating their value ...[2]

He did not have to wait as long as that. In the two years that followed his father's death, Robert Burns was to experience an explosion of creative energy which would blast him into the brief orbit of his poetic maturity.

---

1. *Ibid.*, 45. A couple of years later he was to send a friend a second version (Kinsley, 124) which was a good deal less polite.
2. This passage is printed as part of no. 487 in the Letters with a conjectural date of 1792. It appears in the Glenriddell MS as a prefatory note to an abridgement of Burns's first *Common-place Book*.

Four

LOVE AND POESY

BURNS'S DENUNCIATION OF the lawyers retained by his father contained
an element of the synthetic. 'Rapacious hell-hounds that growl in the kennels
of justice' was a splendid piece of fustian, but when he told Moore that they
had taken his father's all, he was exaggerating for effect. The two brothers
were a canny pair and had taken their precautions. 'When my father's affairs
drew near a crisis,' wrote Gilbert, 'Robert and I took the farm of Mossgiel, as
an asylum for the family in the case of the worst.'

Mossgiel lay two and a half miles south-east of Lochlie and ran to 118
acres. Their new landlord was Gavin Hamilton, a young lawyer in Mauchline,
who had originally leased the farm from the Earl of Loudoun for use as a
summer retreat. He now agreed to sub-let it at a rent of £90 per annum.
Gilbert said that it was stocked 'by the property and individual savings of the
whole family.'[1] A letter to Hamilton survives in which Burns writes of buying
cows and dairy utensils from him by private bargain. The letter is dated four
months before William Burnes's death; Burns and Gilbert had obviously seen
which way the wind was blowing.[2]

The move took place in the spring of 1784. Burns was now the head of a
household of eight – his mother, Gilbert and five younger sisters and brothers.
Gilbert's account makes plain that they had a hard time of it. The farm lay
very high, he wrote, and for the most part 'on a cold wet bottom'[3] – which is to
say that as a consequence of erosion and poor husbandry they found themselves
struggling with stubborn clay and waterlogged fields. Burns nevertheless went
to Mossgiel determined to put his back into things:

I entered on this farm with a full resolution, 'Come, go to, I will be wise!'
– I read farming books; I calculated crops; I attended markets; and in short,

---

1. These savings could not have been large, because we also know from Gilbert that during
the Lochlie years their father allowed them each £7 a year – the same wage as other labourers –
and that as a part of this, 'every article of our clothing manufactured in the family was regularly
accounted for.' (Currie, vol. i, p. 74.)
2. Letters, 15.
3. Currie, vol. i, p. 75.

47

in spite of 'The devil, the world and the flesh,' I believe I would have been a wise man; but the first year from unfortunately buying in bad seed, the second from a late harvest, we lost half of both our crops: this overset all my wisdom, and I returned 'Like the dog to his vomit, and the sow that was washed to her wallowing in the mire. –[']¹

The earthy simile which Burns employs here could not be more apposite. He is quoting from the form of words commonly used in the Church of Scotland to rebuke fornicators, a formula with which he rapidly became familiar.

In the winter before the move from Lochlie the Burns family had employed a servant girl called Elizabeth Paton, the subject of the coarse 'My Girl She's Airy'.² Whether it was before or after the move to Mossgiel that Burns seduced her is not known; she did not follow them to the new farm, but as her home was in the nearby village of Largieside, it was not difficult for Burns to continue to see her. By the autumn of 1784 she was pregnant and a child was born the following May – the 'bastart wean' whose arrival Burns celebrated in verse.³ His mother was very fond of the girl, and wanted Burns to marry her, but Gilbert and his sisters were against it:

They thought the faults of her character would soon have disgusted him. She was rude and uncultivated to a great degree; a strong masculine understanding, with a thorough (tho' unwomanly) contempt for every sort of refinement.

This is from a letter which Burns's niece Isabella wrote to Chambers when he was at work on his 1852 biography and she added: 'My mother says she does not believe that ever woman loved man with a more heartfelt devotion than that poor creature did him.'⁴ Burns repaid this heartfelt devotion by boasting about his conquest in his 'Epistle to J.R******'. John Rankine was a friend from Lochlie days, a tenant farmer twice Burns's age and what Chambers calls 'a humorist of a rather rude type'. Burns recounts how he goes out shooting and brings down a partridge:

> 'Twas ae night lately, in my fun,
> I gaed a rovin' wi' the gun,   went
> An' brought a *Paitrick* to the *grun'*,   partridge
>   A bonie *hen*,
> And, as the twilight was begun,
>   Thought nane wad ken.⁵   know

1. Letters, 125.
2. See page 45 *supra*.
3. See page 38 *supra*.
4. Chambers-Wallace, vol. i, p. 119.
5. Kinsley, 47.

The chase had provided sexual imagery in poetry since the middle ages, and in succeeding stanzas Burns elaborates the metaphor – 'The poor wee thing was little hurt;/ I straiket it a wee for sport.' The twilight had let him down, however, and his stroking did not go unobserved. Burns's skill with gun and shot came to the ears of the parish kirk session – the 'Poacher Court.' He paid his guinea fine (the 'buttock-hire') and sat for the first time on the stool of repentance, where culprits, clad in the black sackcloth gown of fornication, were obliged to take their place. Even there, however, perched high above the congregation beside his 'handsome Betsey', he found distractions from the humiliating business of the moment:

> But my downcast eye by chance did spy
> What made my lips to water,
> Those limbs so clean where I, between,
> Commenc'd a Fornicator.[1]

Burns was not entirely well during the summer and autumn of 1784. He wrote to a friend in September expressing disappointment that his 'unlucky illness on friday last' had prevented their meeting, adding that he was still 'in a kind of slow fever.'[2] In August he had copied into his *Common-place Book* a five-stanza poem headed, 'A prayer, when fainting fits, & other alarming symptoms of a Pleurisy or some other dangerous disorder, which indeed still threaten me, first put Nature on the alarm.'[3] The symptoms bear some resemblance to those he had experienced at Irvine three years previously. Many years later one of the farm-servants at Mossgiel at the time, John Blane, told Chambers that the fainting fits were most common at night. The treatment prescribed – we do not know by whom – sounds drastic: 'A barrel of water was placed near his bedside, and into this he was obliged to plunge when threatened by his ailment.'[4]

Whatever the nature of his illness, its effects were intermittent. He was certainly well enough, in the early days of August, to send a long letter to his cousin in Montrose, apologising for not writing sooner and informing him in the first paragraph that 'our family are all in health at pres'.' Most of the letter was given over to an account of a sect called the Presbytery Relief, which had become strongly established in Irvine – 'We have been surprised,' Burns wrote,

---

1. *Ibid.*, 61. Elizabeth Paton later married a farm-hand by whom she had four children. After Burns's marriage, the child Bess came to live at Mossgiel and was cared for by his mother. She later married, and died in 1817 at the age of 32.

2. Letters, 18, to John Tennant, 13th September, 1784.

3. Kinsley, 13. Kinsley thinks it probable that the poem was composed during the Irvine period. It is followed in the *Common-place Book* by a poem headed 'Misgivings in the hour of DESPONDENCY—and prospect of Death.' (Kinsley, 14.)

4. Chambers-Wallace, vol. i, p. 115.

'with one of the most extraordinary Phenomena in the moral world, which, I dare say, has happened in the course of this last Century.[1]

The central figure was a woman in her middle forties called Elspat Buchan. She was the daughter of a Banffshire publican, and the sect had come to regard her as their spiritual mother. 'Their tenets are a strange jumble of enthusiastic jargon,' Burns told his cousin:

> She pretends to give them the Holy Ghost by breathing on them, which she does with postures & practices that are scandalously indecent; they have likewise disposed of all their effects and hold a community of goods, & live nearly an idle life, carrying on a great farce of pretended devotion in barns, & woods, where they lodge & lye all together, & hold likewise a community of women, as it is another of their tenets that they can commit no moral sin.

'Luckie' Buchan as she was called gave out that she was the woman described in Revelations as being 'clothed with the sun, and the moon under her feet.' She also proclaimed that she had brought forth the man-child who was 'to rule all nations with a rod of iron' – and identified him as the Reverend Hugh White, the minister of the 'relief' congregation in Irvine, who, together with his wife, had fallen completely under her spell. The singling out of one of their number for such distinction left the local Presbytery unmoved; they charged the impressionable Mr White with heresy and deposed him. All this, Burns wrote, was eventually too much for the good people of Irvine:

> In spring last the Populace rose & mobbed the old leader Buchan, & put her out of the town; on which all her followers voluntarily quitted the place likewise, & with such precipitation, that many of them never shut their doors behind them; one left a washing on the green, another a cow bellowing at the crib without meat or any body to mind her . . .[2]

Burns, rather intriguingly, told his cousin that he was personally acquainted with most of these people. His interest in matters religious was not confined to the lunatic fringe, however, and did not only find expression in his correspondence. 'I now began to be known in the neighbourhood as a maker of rhymes,' he later wrote to Dr Moore:

1. Letters, 17, to James Burness, 3rd August, 1784.
2. The novelist John Galt, a native of Irvine, remembered the day the Buchanites left town, 'singing psalms as they went, shouting and saying they were going to the New Jerusalem.' 'I, with many other children, also accompanied her,' he wrote (he was four at the time), 'but my mother in a state of distraction pursued, and drew me back by the lug and the horn.' (John Galt, *Autobiography*, 1833.) White emigrated to the United States in 1792, abandoned his Buchanite beliefs and taught at a village school in Virginia. He 'preached occasionally to a few Universalists, but never mentioned any of his former whimsical doctrines.' See *History of the Buchanites from First to Last*, by Joseph Train, the antiquary and friend of Walter Scott. (Edinburgh, 1846.)

The first of my poetic offspring that saw the light was a burlesque lamentation on a quarrel between two rev^d Calvinists, both of them dramatis personae in my Holy Fair ... With a certain side of both clergy and laity it met with a roar of applause – Holy Willie's Prayer next made its appearance, and alarmed the kirk-session so much that they held three several meetings to look over their holy artillery, if any of it was pointed against profane Rhymers.[1]

This 'burlesque lamentation' was 'The Holy Tulzie'.[2] 'Tulzie' means quarrel or brawl, and the occasion of the poem was a dispute over parish boundaries between two 'Auld Licht' ministers. The Reverend Alexander Moodie was the minister of Riccarton – 'Singet Sawnie,' was Burns's name for him in a later poem, 'singet' meaning stunted or puny.[3] His adversary was the Reverend John Russel, a native of Morayshire and a former schoolmaster who was given to great rages – 'a large, robust, dark-complexioned man,' wrote a former pupil, 'imperturbably grave, and with a sullen expression seated in the deep folds of his forehead.' The case was thrashed out in the Presbytery of Irvine. 'There, in open court,' wrote Lockhart, 'the reverend divines, hitherto sworn friends and associates, lost all command of temper, and abused each other *coram populo*, with a fiery virulence of personal invective.'[4]

In 'Holy Willie's Prayer',[5] Burns shifts his fire from clergy to laity. Holy Willie was William Fisher, a Mauchline farmer in his late forties who had been an elder of the parish since 1772. He owes his humiliating immortality to the part he played in an extended altercation between the Mauchline kirk session and Gavin Hamilton, Burns's friend and landlord.

There was a long history of bad blood between Hamilton and the session, and their differences originally had nothing to do with religion. Between 1776 and 1778 he had acted as collector of the stent – the tax levied by the parish for purposes of poor relief. It was set at a penny for each pound of rental value, and on that basis would have raised an annual amount of just under £20. The session claimed that Hamilton had not handed over the full amount due, and pursued him intermittently over a period of years for settlement. The sum in question amounted to £6 2s 2½d; Hamilton maintained that the shortfall arose because not all those on whom the levy fell could afford to pay it.

The dispute was still spluttering on in 1784. Towards the end of that year Hamilton decided to go on the attack. He took exception to what he regarded as reflections on his character in the session minutes and accused the session of acting out of 'private pique and ill nature.' This in turn struck the session as 'highly calumnious and injurious' to their character, and they launched a

1. Letters, 125.
2. Kinsley, 52.
3. 'The Kirk of Scotland's Garland—a new Song,' Kinsley, 264.
4. J.G. Lockhart, *Life of Robert Burns*, John Murray, London, 1828, p. 78.
5. Kinsley, 53.

counter-offensive by charging Hamilton with unnecessary absences from church, breaking the Sabbath by making a journey to Carrick and 'habitual, if not total, neglect of family worship.' The litigious instincts of both sides were now thoroughly roused, and there followed an immensely tedious round of appeal and counter-appeal, first to the Presbytery of Ayr and then to the Synod of Glasgow. It was Hamilton's victory in this unedifying contest which triggered a jubilant Burns to compose 'Holy Willie's Prayer'.[1]

Many regard it as his masterpiece. Sir Walter Scott, writing in the *Quarterly Review* in 1809, pronounced it 'a piece of satire more exquisitely severe' than any Burns subsequently wrote, although it was, he added, 'unfortunately cast in a form too daringly profane to be received into Dr Currie's Collection.' (It was published in Glasgow in 1799, but only in the form of a pamphlet):

O thou that in the heavens does dwell!
Wha, as it pleases best thysel,
Sends ane to heaven, and ten to h–ll,
    A' for thy glory!
And no for ony gude or ill
    They've done before thee. –

I bless and praise thy matchless might,
When thousands thou has left in night,
That I am here before thy sight,
    For gifts and grace,
A burning and a shining light
    To a' this place. –

What was I, or my generation,
That I should get such exaltation?
I, wha deserv'd most just damnation,
    For broken laws
Sax thousand years ere my creation,   *six*
    Thro' Adam's cause!

When from my mother's womb I fell,
Thou might hae plunged me deep in hell,
To gnash my gooms, and weep, and wail,   *gums*
    In burning lakes,
Where damned devils roar and yell
    Chain'd to their stakes. –

1. For a blow-by-blow account of Hamilton's differences with the kirk session see James Mackay, *Burns*, Mainstream Publishing Company Ltd, Edinburgh, 1992, pp. 126–7 and 162–4. The 'holy beagles,' as Burns called them, did not give up easily. They pursued Hamilton again in the course of 1787 – on this occasion for causing one of his servants to dig up some potatoes in his garden on the Lord's Day.

Yet I am here, a chosen sample,
To shew thy grace is great and ample:
I'm here, a pillar o' thy temple
        Strong as a rock,
A guide, a ruler and example
        To a' thy flock. –

[O L–d thou kens what zeal I bear,   *knows*
When drinkers drink, and swearers swear,
And singin' there, and dancin' here,
        Wi' great an' sma';
For I am keepet by thy fear,   *kept*
        Free frae them a'.][1]

But yet –O L–d–confess I must –
At times I'm fash'd wi' fleshly lust;   *bothered*
And sometimes too, in wardly trust
        Vile Self gets in;
But thou remembers we are dust,
        Defil'd wi' sin. –

O L–d – yestreen – thou kens – wi' Meg –   *last night*
Thy pardon I sincerely beg!
O may't ne'er be a living plague,
        To my dishonor!
And I'll ne'er lift a lawless leg
        Again upon her.—

Besides, I farther maun avow,   *must*
Wi' Leezie's lass, three times – I trow –
But L–d, that friday I was fou   *drunk*
        When I cam near her;
Or else, thou kens, thy servant true
        Wad never steer her. –   *molest*

Maybe thou lets this fleshly thorn
Buffet thy servant e'en and morn,
Lest he o'er proud and high should turn,
        That he's sae gifted;
If sae, thy hand maun e'en be borne
        Untill thou lift it. –

1. This stanza, which is not particularly strong, is thought to be from an early manuscript, and is omitted from most editions of Burns's work.

L–d bless thy Chosen in this place,
For here thou has a chosen race:
But G–d, confound their stubborn face,
      And blast their name,
Wha bring thy rulers to disgrace
      And open shame. –

L–d mind Gaun Hamilton's deserts!
He drinks, and swears, and plays at cartes,   *cards*
Yet has sae mony taking arts   *pleasing ways*
      Wi' Great and Sma',
Frae G–d's ain priest the people's hearts
      He steals awa. –

And when we chasten'd him therefore,
Thou kens how he bred sic a splore,   *uproar*
And set the warld in a roar
      O' laughin at us:
Curse thou his basket and his store,
      Kail and potatoes. –

L–d hear my earnest cry and prayer
Against that Presbytry of Ayr!
Thy strong right hand, L–d, make it bare
      Upon their heads!
L–d visit them, and dinna spare,   *do not*
      For their misdeeds!

O L–d my G–d, that glib-tongu'd Aiken!
My very heart and flesh are quaking
To think how I sat, sweating, shaking,
      And p–ss'd with dread,
While Auld wi' hingin lip gaed sneaking
      And hid his head!

L–d, in thy day o' vengeance try him!
L– visit him that did employ him!
And pass not in thy mercy by them,
      Nor hear their prayer;
But for thy people's sake destroy them,
      And dinna spare!

But L–d, remember me and mine
Wi' mercies temporal and divine!

> That I for grace and gear may shine,   possessions
> Excell'd by nane!
> And a' the glory shall be thine!
> AMEN! AMEN!

Snyder's judgement was that this poem alone would have admitted Burns to the fellowship of Aristophanes and Swift. As a comic character Holy Willie, by turns vainglorious, lascivious and downright vicious, certainly stands comparison with Molière's Tartuffe or Shakespeare's Malvolio; and yet Burns realises him, with ferocious economy, in a mere hundred lines of dramatic monologue.

The assault on Calvinist orthodoxy continued with 'The Ordination',[1] a vigorous squib occasioned by the appointment of an Auld Licht zealot to one of the charges in Kilmarnock; as in 'Holy Willie's Prayer', Burns achieves his ironic effect by slyly affecting the standpoint of those he is concerned to pillory. In the 'Epistle to John Goldie in Kilmarnock',[2] he lays about him more directly. Goldie, forty years Burns's senior, was a miller's son who became first a cabinet maker and then a wine merchant. He speculated in canals and coal-mines, and his interests ranged from astronomy to theology. He was the author of *Essays on various Important Subjects Moral and Divine, being an attempt to distinguish True from False Religion*, which became popularly known as 'Goudie's Bible.' Goldie argued strenuously, if not always entirely coherently, against the 'lying vanities' of those who interpreted the Bible literally. This appealed strongly to Burns, and when a new edition of the work appeared in 1785 he penned a robust message of admiring solidarity:

> O Gowdie, terror o' the whigs,
> Dread o' black coats and reverend wigs!

He notes with satisfaction that 'Superstition', like 'Sour Bigotry', is in a bad way, and offers sardonic medical advice:

> Poor gapin, glowrin Superstition!
> Waes me, she's in a sad condition:
> Fye! bring Black Jock her state-physician,
>   To see her water . . .

'Black Jock' was Reverend John Russel, who had already appeared as one of his butts in 'The Holy Tulzie'. Who better to examine the patient's urine?

The most ambitious of all Burns's ecclesiastical satires is 'The Holy Fair',[3] and for many it is the most telling. Holy fairs were rural celebrations of the

1. Kinsley, 85.
2. *Ibid.*, 63.
3. *Ibid.*, 70.

Lord's Supper. In Burns's day the communion service took place not more than once a year, usually in the summer; the supreme importance which attached to it is plain from the various names by which it was known – the 'Great Work', the 'Occasion', the 'Sacred Solemnity'.

The celebration of Communion on the Sunday would be preceded and followed by several days of 'preachings'. If a particular minister had a reputation as a 'gospel' man, people would travel long miles to hear him, and the local population could be swollen many times over – in Mauchline, in 1786, there were 1,400 communicants, but only 400 of them were parishioners. These enormous open-air assemblies stirred old memories of covenanting ministers in the days of persecution. Contemporary accounts of the religious fervour generated by the 'great occasion' are curiously at odds with modern perceptions of Scottish reticence. There was much weeping, much talk of wrestling with God and of seeking light at the throne – Henry Grey Graham has a dry line about people mistaking their nerves for their conscience.

Graham also notes that the proceedings were not exclusively devotional: 'Solemn and striking as those great sacramental meetings were, there were spots in their feasts which became darker as the century went on and piety went off,'[1] and he calls in evidence a much-quoted pamphlet published anonymously in the year of Burns's birth:

I defy Italy, in spite of all its superstition, to produce a scene better fitted to raise pity and regret . . . You find a great number of men and women lying together upon the grass; here they are sleeping and snoring, some with their faces towards heaven, others with their faces turned downward, or covered with their bonnets; there you find a knot of young fellows and girls making assignations to go home together in the evening, or to meet in some ale-house . . . In a word, in this sacred assembly there is an odd mixture of religion, sleep, drinking, courtship, and a confusion of sexes, ages, and characters.[2]

It is this confusion which commands Burns's joyful attention in 'The Holy Fair':

> Upon a simmer *Sunday morn*,
>   When Nature's face is fair,
> I walked forth to view the corn,
>   An' snuff the callor air . . .   fresh

On the road he meets three 'hizzies.' Two of them, Hypocrisy and Superstition, are wearing cloaks of 'dolefu' black', but a little behind them, 'in the fashion

1. Graham, *op. cit.*, p. 312.
2. *Letter from a Blacksmith to the Ministers and Elders of the Church of Scotland, in which the Manner of Publick Worship in that Church is considered, its Inconveniences and Defects pointed out, and Methods of removing them honestly proposed*, London, 1759.

shining,' comes Fun; she drops him a low curtsey, takes his hands in hers and offers to conduct him to the Fair, and that is enough to send Burns hurrying home to put on his 'Sunday's sark'.

Noise, colour and movement are brilliantly evoked. The good humour with which Burns observes the absurdities of human nature in the congregation does not evaporate when he turns his attention to 'the lads in black' who are nominally in charge of the proceedings, although the satiric edge remains keen as each in turn is put through his preaching paces. Burns includes both New and Auld Licht clergy in his cast list, and finds room for both protagonists of 'The Holy Tulzie'. His introduction of 'Black Jock' as 'the Lord's ain trumpet' is almost affectionate; Moodie of Riccarton is handled more roughly, and it is he who falls victim to the poem's deadliest verbal ambush:

> His lengthen'd chin, his turn'd up snout,
>> His eldritch squeel and gestures,   unearthly
> O how they fire the heart devout,
>> Like cantharidian plaisters
>>> On sic a day!

Cantharides, made from the dried Spanish fly, used to be applied to the skin as a blistering agent. Taken internally, it acts as a powerful irritant on the genito-urinary tract, and was traditionally believed to be an aphrodisiac. Burns contrives a subversive and outrageous connection between the furnaces of brimstone that figured in so many sermons of the time and the fires of the flesh that have been stoked that day with small beer and toddy. As the crowds begin to straggle home, the poet casts up his ambivalent reckoning of what the 'occasion' has achieved:

> How mony hearts this day converts,
>> O' Sinners and o' Lasses!
> Their hearts o' stane, gin night are gane   by nightfall
>> As saft as ony flesh is.
> There's some are fou o' *love divine*;   drunk
>> There's some are fou o' *brandy*;
> An' monie jobs that day begin,
>> May end in *Houghmagandie*   fornication
>>> Some ither day.

The immediate models for the poem, with its eight short rhyming lines followed by a 'tag', were Fergusson's 'Hallow-Fair' and 'Leith Races', but they in turn derived from the anonymous fifteenth-century 'Chrystis Kirk of the Grene'; so Burns is reminting very old Scottish coin. Not all of his ecclesiastical satires were to appear in the Kilmarnock edition the following year, but 'The Holy Fair' did. 'It was acknowledged,' wrote Lockhart, 'amidst the sternest mutterings of wrath, that national manners were once more in the hands of a national poet.'

For the moment, however, in 1785, his fame was purely local. Versions of his poems passed by word of mouth, and sometimes he got requests for copies. One of his verse epistles that autumn was addressed to the Reverend John M'Math, a 'New Licht' moderate who was assistant to the minister of Tarbolton at the time and had asked to see 'Holy Willie's Prayer'.[1]

We also have from this time Burns's three verse epistles to John Lapraik.[2] Lapraik (1727–1807) was an elderly farmer and something of a village poet. Burns heard a song of his that he liked and sent off a friendly twenty-two stanza greeting, addressing him as 'a true, genuine, Scottish bard' and soliciting his acquaintance. The main interest of the poem lies in what it reveals of how Burns saw himself and his own work:

> I am nae *Poet*, in a sense,
> But just a *Rhymer* like by chance,
> An' hae to Learning nae pretence . . .

The modesty here is possibly a shade disingenuous. It quickly emerges that Burns is not as relaxed about his lack of learning as he would have Lapraik believe, and we get an early glimpse of what might either be applauded as democratic sentiment or deplored as a chip on the shoulder:

> A set o' dull, conceited Hashes,   *fools*
> Confuse their brains in *Colledge-classes*!
> They *gang in* Stirks, and *come out* Asses,   *bullocks*
>   Plain truth to speak;
> An' syne they think to climb Parnassus   *then*
>   By dint o' Greek!
>
> Gie me ae spark o' Nature's fire,
> That's a' the learning I desire;
> Then tho' I drudge thro' dub an' mire   *puddle*
>   At pleugh or cart,
> My Muse, tho' hamely in attire,
>   May touch the heart.[3]

1. Kinsley, 68. Chambers records that subsequently M'Math 'unhappily fell into low spirits, in consequence of his dependent situation, and became dissipated.' (Chambers-Wallace, vol. i, p. 193.n.) In 1791 he enlisted as a private soldier. He died in obscurity in Mull in 1825.

2. *Ibid.*, 57, 58, 67.

3. Later in 1785 Lapraik, who had previously suffered in the collapse of Douglas, Heron and Company, was imprisoned for debt. In 1788 he followed Burns's example and published a volume of verse, but with no great success. He eventually gave up farming and kept an inn in the village of Muirkirk, where he also became the postmaster.

Drudging through dub and mire did not exclude conviviality. Burns kept up his interest in freemasonry and was also now much in the company of two kindred spirits, both several years younger than himself. One, James Smith, kept a draper's shop in Mauchline. It is clear from the unbuttoned, somewhat rambling epistle that Burns addressed to him[1] that they had a lot in common (Smith was responsible for the pregnancy of one of his mother's servants, a woman fifteen years his senior). The epistle was written sometime in the winter of 1785–86, and in the seventh stanza Burns casually discloses that he has been fingering the idea of publishing some of his poems:

> This while my notion's taen a sklent,   turn
> To try my fate in guid, black *prent*;
> But still the mair I'm that way bent,
>   Something cries, 'Hoolie!   Softly
> 'I red you, honest man, tak tent!   heed
>   Ye'll shaw your folly.

There is another flick at those better educated than himself and a certain amount of rather pedestrian philosophising about the nature of pleasure ('This life, sae far's I understand,/Is a' enchanted fairy-land'). Towards the end of the poem a familiar Burns target comes into his sights:

> O ye, douse folk, that live by rule,
> Grave, tideless-blooded, calm and cool . . .
> Ye are sae *grave*, nae doubt ye're *wise*;
> Nae ferly tho' ye do despise   wonder
> The hairum-scairum, ram-stam boys,   reckless
>   The rattling squad . . .

The third of the ram-stam boys who made up the Mauchline rattling squad was John Richmond, the younger son of a local laird (who, the world being exceedingly small, happened to be Holy Willie's landlord). Richmond worked as a clerk in Gavin Hamilton's law office and, like Burns and Smith, had been obliged to do penance for fornication – in his case with a girl called Jenny Surgeoner, who bore him a daughter and whom, after an ungracious delay of six years, he made his wife.

We get some insight into how this trio amused themselves from the poem that has come down to us as 'Libel Summons'.[2] Chambers thought it 'full of humanity and tenderness, but too "broad" for publication'; even in 1930, when Catherine Carswell published it as an appendix to her admiring biography, she took a certain amount of flak. Burns and his friends, 'Fornicators by profession,'

1. Kinsley, 79.
2. *Ibid.*, 109.

set themselves up as a mock tribunal which parodies the disciplinary procedures of the kirk–session. They summon before them Sandy Dow, a local coachman and Clockie Brown, a watchmaker:

> First, You, JOHN BROWN, there's witness borne,
> And affidavit made and sworn,
> That ye hae bred a hurly-burly
> 'Bout JEANY MITCHEL'S tirlie-whirlie,
> And blooster'd at her regulator   stormed
> Till a' her wheels gang clitter-clatter . . .

This 'Court of Equity', however, exists to operate a code of discipline that is quite different from that of the kirk-session which it parodies – the offence to be sniffed out here is not fornication, but cowardice in owning up to it:

> YOUR CRIME, a manly deed we view it,
> AS MAN ALONE, can only do it;
> But, in denial persevering,
> Is to a SCOUNDREL'S NAME adhering.
> The BEST O' MEN, hae been surpris'd;
> The BEST O' WOMEN been advis'd:
> NAY, CLEVEREST LADS hae haen a
>   TRICK O'T,   made a habit of it
> AN', BONNIEST LASSES taen a LICK O'T.—

This is Burns in vigorous and coarsely inventive vein. He has good fun with the jargon of Scots law and his use of watchmaking terms to describe Clockie Brown's sexual marauding is clever and funny. It is one of his most ingenious essays in obscenity.[1]

Richmond was in on the conception of another and much more substantial poem written at Mossgiel, and that is 'Love and Liberty', often known as 'The Jolly Beggars'.[2] Ayrshire was overrun in those days by large numbers of vagrants, many of them from Ireland:

In the day time, they prowl through the towns, or roam in the country, begging, stealing, or swindling, as opportunity may offer. At night, they return to their miserable haunts to consume their spoils, in feasting, drinking, swearing, and carousing at the expense of the simple, whom they have duped,

1. It would have amused Burns greatly that so many of his biographers appear to believe that the 'Court of Equity' actually sat from time to time at the Whitefoord Arms in Mauchline, a rougher version of the Tarbolton Bachelors' Club. There is, as Kinsley points out, a long history of poetical 'courts'. The evidence is strongly that this one was no more than a figment of Burns's poetic imagination. See Kinsley, vol. iii, p. 1186.

2. Kinsley, 84.

or the timid whom they have terrified; and insulting and disturbing the various inhabitants. It is no way uncommon to see from ten to twenty lodgers, in one of these *hotels des vagrants*, with half a dozen tea-pots, three or four dram bottles, and several gill or half-mutchkin stoups, in rapid circulation, in their *common-hall*.[1]

There was just such an *hotel des vagrants* in Mauchline, a low tavern and lodging house called Poosie Nansie's, and it was a visit Burns paid there one night in Richmond's company that gave him his setting and his characters for 'Love and Liberty'. He called it a cantata – cantatas were all the rage in the eighteenth century, and he had encountered the form in Ramsay. Gay's 'The Beggar's Opera' is another obvious influence, although Burns was also dipping into an old tradition of vagabond literature that went back to medieval times.

Technically, it is a virtuoso performance. Metrically, the cantata is notably rich – Burns employs a different stanza form for each of its eight songs. Matthew Arnold called it 'a superb poetic success' and thought it made the celebrated scene in Auerbach's cellar, in Goethe's *Faust*, seem artificial and tame by comparison. Henley and Henderson, in their centenary edition of the poems, described it as an 'irresistible presentation of humanity caught in the act'. In this century, critics have discerned an affinity with Brecht.

The human driftwood who have found shelter in Poosie Nansie's entertain each other in song. The first to perform is an old soldier. He is a veteran of Quebec and the siege of Gibraltar with nothing but two stumps to show for it, but he retains all the swagger of a punch-drunk prize-fighter:

> I am a Son of Mars who have been in many wars,
>   And show my cuts and scars wherever I come;
> This here was for a wench, and that other in a trench,
>   When welcoming the French at the sound of the drum . . .
>
> And now though I must beg, with a wooden arm and leg,
>   And many a tatter'd rag hanging over my bum,
> I'm as happy with my wallet, my bottle and my Callet,   wench
>   As when I us'd in scarlet to follow a drum.

This battered Son of Mars is followed by his 'Callet':

> I ONCE was a Maid, tho' I cannot tell when,
> And still my delight is in proper young men:
> Some one of a troop of DRAGOONS was my dadie,
> No wonder I'm fond of a SODGER LADDIE.

1. W. Aiton, *op. cit.*, pp. 626-7.

This 'martial chuck' has been tumbled by half the regiment in her time, including the Chaplain ('He ventur'd the SOUL, and I risked the BODY'), but tonight, warmed with rough whisky, she sees only the finery of her current hero's 'auld red rags.'

Wi' USQUEBAE an' blankets warm,	whisky
She blinket on her Sodger:	glanced fondly
An' ay he gies the tozie drab	tipsy
The tither skelpan kiss,	smacking
While she held up her greedy gab,	mouth
Just like an aumous dish ...	alms

It is one of Burns's most vivid cameos – the image of the tipsy drab, hungry for the kisses of her 'sodger laddie' and holding up her greedy mouth like a begging bowl, haunts the memory.

She gives way to a Merry Andrew or jester, and he is followed by the widow of a Highlander who has been reduced to picking pockets and by a fiddler and a tinker who come to blows over her. Finally, it is the turn of a limping beggar-poet:

I AM a BARD of no regard,	
Wi' gentle folks an a' that;	
But HOMER LIKE the glowran byke,	staring crowd
Frae town to town I draw that.	

It requires only modest literary insight to see that somewhere on his travels, this particular beggar has come under the philosophical influence of Burns of Mossgiel. His performance brings the house down. Pressed for an encore, he launches into 'Jolly Mortals, fill your glasses'. His audience, we are told, was 'impatient for the chorus,' and that is unsurprising, because the song aims a cheerful and anarchical blunderbuss not merely at the authority of church and state but also at wealth, marriage and reputation:

Life is all a VARIORUM,
We regard not how it goes;
Let them cant about DECORUM,
Who have character to lose.

Chorus –

A fig for those by law protected!
LIBERTY'S a glorious feast!
Courts for Cowards were erected,
Churches built to please the PRIEST.

Freedom from social and moral obligation does not add up to a particularly elevated view of liberty, but it was certainly a fashionable one; Burns was writing, after all, within four years of the collapse of accepted authority in France and the summoning by Louis XVI of the Estates General. He is doing no more at the end of 'The Jolly Beggars' than lapse into the sort of revolutionary Esperanto that was gaining rapid currency as a European *lingua franca*.

Daily life, in the closing decades of the eighteenth century, was still intensely local, but rural communities have always been avid for news of what was going on in the next valley and beyond and impressively skilled at gleaning it – from conversation, from books and newspapers, from travellers' tales and the chit-chat of pedlars, from the yarns of sailors home from the wars, from gossip in tavern and market place and at the church door. Although by his mid-twenties Burns had travelled no further than a few miles from home, his poetry demonstrates that he was keenly alert to what went on in the wider world. 'A Fragment', for instance, a song which he wrote sometime in 1784, and which he described as a political ballad, shows a firm grasp of the events that led up to the general election of that year. He begins with a satirical account of the American war and then describes political reaction in Britain when the war began to go badly.[1]

Another piece in which Burns shows an easy familiarity with the detail of a particular political issue of the day (this time a purely domestic one), is 'The Author's Earnest Cry and Prayer'.[2] This was occasioned by the passing of the Wash Act of 1784, which was aimed at ending the favourable treatment which Scottish distillers were alleged to enjoy under the excise laws. In the 'Cry and Prayer', Burns turned to Scotland's forty-five representatives at Westminster, and he clearly thought better of some of them than of others. George Dempster, the Whig MP for Forfar Burghs, was well-known as an agricultural improver – he gets the Burns seal of approval as 'a true-blue Scot'. The Laird o' Graham, on the other hand, later to be the third Duke of Montrose, is dismissed as 'that glib-gabbet Highlan Baron'. Burns harks back to another recent provocation – Scotland, he reminds them, has been 'in crankous mood' since the rejection in 1782 of the Militia Bill, which would have provided for enlistment from the militia into the army:

> Stand forth and tell yon PREMIER YOUTH
> The honest, open, naked truth . . .

The Premier Youth is, of course, his contemporary William Pitt the Younger, Prime Minister at the age of twenty-four.

Poets, just like ploughmen and Prime Ministers, can have their off-days,

1. Kinsley, 38. It was this poem which later prompted the Reverend Hugh Blair, one of Burns's Edinburgh admirers, to remark superciliously that 'Burns's politics always smell of the smithy.'
2. *Ibid.*, 81. The full title is 'The Author's Earnest Cry and Prayer, to the Right Honorable and Honorable, the Scotch Representatives in the House of Commons.'

and there were still occasions, particularly if his subject lay nearer home, when Burns could turn a verse of doggerel with the best of them:

> O, leave novels, ye Mauchline belles,
>   Ye're safer at your spinning wheel;
> Such witching books, are baited hooks
>   For rakish rooks like Rob Mossgiel.[1]

These six 'proper young Belles' figure in another short song written in late 1784 or early 1785, and here swagger gives way to gallantry:

> Their carriage and dress a stranger would guess,
>   In Lon'on or Paris they'd gotten it a'.

They are, Burns asserts, the pride of the neighbourhood, and he parades them on the catwalk of his approval:

> Miss Miller is fine, Miss Murkland's divine,
>   Miss Smith she has wit and Miss Betty is braw;
> There's beauty and fortune to get wi' Miss Morton,
>   But ARMOUR'S the jewel for me o' them a'. —[2]

The Christian name of the 'jewel of them all' was Jean. Six years younger than Burns, she was the eldest daughter of a Mauchline stone-mason and the second oldest in a family of eleven. They lived in the Cowgate in the centre of the village, next to the Whitefoord Arms and just down the road from Poosie Nansie's. The parish records disclose that James Armour paid an annual rent of 10s 8d for his family pew; a solid citizen, therefore, and one whom 'Daddy' Auld, the Mauchline minister, could confidently number among those who shared his Auld Licht beliefs, even though he was fond of snuff and liked a good dram.

Precisely when Jean Armour first took up with Burns cannot be determined. We know from one of his later letters[3] that not long after he had made Betsey Paton pregnant (in the autumn of 1784) another of the Mauchline belles, Helen Miller, was briefly the 'Tenant of his heart' (she rebuffed him, and he worked off his resentment in the lively poem called 'The Mauchline Wedding'[4]). He was certainly in pursuit of 'Armour' by the time the 'bastart wean' was born (in May 1785); if that happy event did anything to dampen her feelings for him, the effect was purely temporary, because before the end of the year she too was pregnant.

1. *Ibid.*, 43.
2. *Ibid.*, 42.
3. Letters, 265, to Mrs Dunlop, 21st August, 1788.
4. Kinsley, 74.

Burns realised that he was in serious trouble. 'I have some very important news with respect to myself, not the most agreeable,' he wrote to his friend Richmond, who was by now working in a lawyer's office in Edinburgh.[1] That was putting it mildly. It was not just that he was in hot water over his relations with Jean Armour; at the very time her condition was becoming unmistakable to beady village eyes, Burns and Gilbert were being forced to the disagreeable conclusion that the farm at Mossgiel was simply not viable and that they must give it up.

The most straightforward account of this messy conjunction of affairs is that given by Gilbert to Currie more than a decade later:

This connexion *could no longer be concealed*, about the time we came to a final determination to quit the farm. Robert durst not engage with a family in his poor unsettled state, but was anxious to shield his partner by every means in his power from the consequences of their imprudence. It was agreed therefore between them that they should make a legal acknowledgement of an irregular and private marriage; that he should go to Jamaica to *push his fortune*; and that she should remain with her father till it might please Providence to put the means of supporting a family in his power.

Pleasing Providence would have been appreciably easier than pleasing Jean's father. The idea that his favourite daughter should enter into such an arrangement with Rab Mossgiel, the worst of the local ram-stam boys, did not commend itself to James Armour one little bit. 'He was in the greatest distress, and fainted away,' Gilbert told Currie:

A husband in Jamaica appeared to him and to his wife little better than none, and an effectual bar to any other prospect of a settlement in life that their daughter might have. They therefore expressed a wish to her, that the written papers which respected the marriage should be cancelled, and thus the marriage rendered void. In her melancholy state, she felt the deepest remorse at having brought such heavy affliction on parents that loved her so tenderly, and submitted to their entreaties. Their wish was mentioned to Robert. He felt the deepest anguish of mind. He offered to stay at home and provide for his wife and family in the best manner that his daily labours could provide for them; that being the only means in his power. Even this offer they did not approve of; for, humble as Miss Armour's station was, and great though her imprudence had been, she still, in the eyes of her partial parents, might look to a better connection than that with my friendless and unhappy brother, at that time without house or hiding place. Robert at length consented to

1. Letters, 21, 17th February, 1786.

their wishes; but his feelings on this occasion were of the most distracting nature . . .[1]

In Burns's own accounts of what happened he rather glosses over the signifi-cance of the failure of Mossgiel, but there is no mistaking the extent to which he was shaken by the turn his fortunes had taken: 'This is the unfortunate story alluded to in my printed poem, The Lament,' he later wrote to Moore:

> 'Twas a shocking affair, which I cannot yet bear to recollect; and had very nearly given [me] one or two of the principal qualifications for a place among those who have lost the chart and mistake the reckoning of Rationality.[2]

We get an insight of sorts into how he saw matters at the time in a letter written in April 1786 to a man called John Arnott – but only 'of sorts', as for much of the time Burns is simply showing off (ostensibly he was soliciting a subscription to the first edition of his poems).[3] The letter is liberally sprinkled with quota-tions from Milton, Shakespeare and the Books of Samuel and Jeremiah and although Burns had no previous acquaintance with him, he showers Arnott with a humorous analysis of the Burnsian defects of character and a racy description of his seduction of Jean couched in the language of siege warfare. First, however, in tear-jerking, mock-heroic mode, he treats him to an account of his present troubles:

> Sad & grievous of late, Sir, has been my tribulation, & many & piercing, my sorrows . . . I have lost, Sir, that dearest earthly treasure, that greatest bless-ing here below, that last, best gift which compleated Adam's happiness in the garden of bliss, I have lost – I have lost – my trembling hand refuses its office, the frightened ink recoils up the quill – Tell it not in Gath – I have lost –a–a–A WIFE!

The manner is straight out of *Tristram Shandy*. Burns presumes Arnott has already heard his story, 'with all its exaggerations,' but begs leave to tell it his own way. 'I have been all my life, Sir, one of the rueful-looking, long-visaged sons of Disappointment,' he declares:

> Still, Sir, I had long had a wishing eye to that inestimable blessing, a wife. – My mouth watered deliciously, to see a young fellow, after a few idle, common-place stories from a gentleman in black, strip & go to bed with a young girl, & no one durst say black was his eye; while I, for just doing the

---

1. Currie, vol. i, pp. 75-6.
2. Letters, 125. 'The Lament. Occasioned by the Unfortunate Issue of a Friend's Amour' is Kinsley, 93.
3. *Ibid.*, 29.

same thing, only wanting that [insignificant (*deleted*)] ceremony, am made a Sunday's laughing stock, & abused like a pick-pocket.

Then, in the brisk style of a military despatch, Burns relives for Arnott's benefit his breach of the defences of Fortress Armour and his own subsequent undoing—the passage reads like a prose précis of one of his bawdier poems:

> . . . I had found means to slip a choice detachment into the very citadel; while I had nothing less in view than displaying my victorious banners on the top of the walls – 'Heaven & Earth, must I remember'! my damned Star wheeled about to the zenith, by whose baleful rays Fortune took the alarm, and pouring in her forces on all quarters, front, flank & rear, I was utterly routed, my baggage lost, my military chest in the hands of the enemy; & your poor devil of a humble servant, commander in chief forsooth, was obliged to scamper away, without either arms or honors of war, except his bare bayonet and catridge-pouch [*sic*]; nor in all probability had he escaped even with them, had he not made a shift to hide them under the lap of his military cloak. –

This highly unusual piece of self-promotion, spirited to the point of being manic, ends on a sardonic but exuberant note of defiance:

> Already the holy beagles, the houghmagandie pack, begin to snuff the scent; & I expect every moment to see them cast off, & hear them after me in full cry: but as I am an old fox, I shall give them dodging & doubling for it; & by & bye, I intend to earth among the mountains of Jamaica.

He was right about the kirk session. Scarcely able to believe its luck, it lost no time in readying its 'holy artillery'. 'My idle wanderings,' as Burns later conceded to Moore, 'led me . . . point blank within the reach of their heaviest metal.' The first ranging shot was fired as early as April 2nd. 'The Session being informed that Jean Armour, an unmarried woman, is said to be with child,' says an entry in the minutes, 'the Session think it their duty to enquire . . .' Who better to make such an enquiry than Holy Willie? He and another elder were deputed to speak to the parents, but Mrs Armour had her story ready and was sticking to it. She did not suspect her daughter to be with child, she told them: 'She was gone to Paisley to see her friends, and would return soon.'

There is some flesh to be put on the bones of Gilbert's narrative. The paper or papers which Burns gave to Jean no longer exist, and we cannot therefore know whether they constituted, as Gilbert maintained, an acknowledgement of marriage or simply a promise. The field has been muddied by the trampling of many feet over the past two hundred years, but nobody has summarised the position more succinctly than Snyder:

If the former, if Burns and Jean had actually accepted one another as man and wife, even in the strictest privacy, and without the presence of witnesses, then they were legally though irregularly married, *per verba de presenti*. If the latter, then too, in all probability, they were man and wife; for a promise to marry, sealed by anticipatory consummation, constitutes in Scots law a true and valid marriage ... The probability, then, seems overwhelming that this fact, in conjunction with whatever acknowledgement or promise Burns gave Jean, did indeed make them man and wife.[1]

Whether the pair regarded themselves as married is a separate question. By Gilbert's account, Mr Armour certainly thought they were, and he now set about trying to have that marriage annulled. He went for advice to Robert Aiken, a convivial and cultivated lawyer and surveyor of taxes in Ayr – the same 'glib-tongued Aiken' who had acted for Gavin Hamilton in his differences with the kirk session, causing Holy Willie to sit through the Presbytery hearing 'sweating, shaking, and piss'd wi' dread'. He was a good lawyer, but it was a curious choice. It was to 'Orator Bob,' a man twenty years his senior, that Burns had submitted many of his poems for critical scrutiny; 'My chief Patron now is Mr Aiken in Ayr,' he wrote to Richmond that February, 'who is pleased to express great approbation of my works.' Burns told Richmond in the same letter that he had recently completed 'The Cotter's Saturday Night', and it is to Aiken that the poem is so warmly dedicated – 'My lov'd, my honor'd, much respected friend.'

Armour consulted Aiken on April 14th, and the legal assistance which he received seems to have taken an eccentric form – something we know from a letter Burns wrote to Gavin Hamilton the following day:

Apropos, old Mr Armour prevailed with him to mutilate that unlucky paper, yesterday. – Would you believe it? tho' I had not a hope, nor even a wish, to make her mine after her [damnable (*deleted*)] conduct; yet when he told me, the names were all cut out of the paper, my heart died within me, and he cut my very veins with the news. – Perdition seize her falsehood, and perjurious perfidy! but God bless her and forgive my poor, once-dear, misguided girl. – She is ill-advised.[2]

It all sounds very odd. It is certainly not the sort of thing the Law Society of Scotland would look kindly on today. Even in the late eighteenth century, when the concept of professional behaviour was more embryonic, a family lawyer would hesitate before doctoring important papers. What is even stranger is that Aiken would have been well aware that the paper in question had no legal validity, and that its mutilation – even its destruction – would have no effect

1. Snyder, pp. 121-2.
2. Letters, 25.

in law on the marital condition of the parties named in it. The most likely explanation is that he was trying to calm old Armour down by administering to him the legal equivalent of a placebo. The evidence is that he succeeded.

Burns, meanwhile, had persuaded himself that Jean had deserted him – by handing over 'that unlucky paper' to her parents and agreeing to be bundled off to Paisley she had annulled whatever had been agreed between them and he felt free to regard himself, and behave, as a single man. His mind was made up to cut and run; he had been pressing on with arrangements to go to the West Indies and had indeed found a position as an assistant overseer on a sugar plantation. What he lacked was money to pay for his passage, a problem which his friend and landlord Gavin Hamilton suggested he solve by publishing an edition of his poems.

Early in April, in a cordial letter to Aiken, he had told him that he was on the point of sending his 'proposals for publishing' to the press.[1] Twelve days later, immediately after hearing something of what had passed between the lawyer and Jean's father, he wrote the letter to Hamilton quoted above. Its main purpose was to send him a batch of those subscription bills, newly to hand from the printer, but there is an anxious passage which indicates his uncertainty over whether he still retained Aiken's friendship:

> I must consult you, first opportunity, on the propriety of sending my *quondam* friend, Mr Aiken, a copy. – If he is now reconciled to my character as an honest man, I would do it with all my soul; but I would not be beholden to the noblest being God ever created, if he imagined me to be a rascal. –

He was worrying unnecessarily, and he was to be considerably beholden to him – Aiken eventually collected the names of a hundred and forty-five subscribers, which was almost a quarter of the total.

The proposal, embellished by a quotation from Allan Ramsay, was brief and only slightly disingenuous:

> The work to be elegantly printed, in one volume octavo. Price, stitched, three shillings. As the author has not the most distant mercenary view in publishing, as soon as so many subscribers appear as will defray the necessary expense, the work will be sent to the press.

Burns gave his mind to farming matters only occasionally during that spring and summer of 1786. There were subscription papers to be sent out (he had ordered eight dozen of them), and decisions to be made about what to send to the printer and what to hold back. Then, early in June, Jean Armour returned to Mauchline from Paisley. A letter survives which Burns wrote a few days later to a friend called David Brice, a shoemaker who had gone off to work in

1. *Ibid.*, 24.

Glasgow. It shows that he was still in deep emotional turmoil. It is also shows an almost total disinclination to accept any of the blame for what had happened:

> ... Poor, ill-advised, ungrateful Armour came home on friday last. – You have heard all the particulars of that affair; and a black affair it is – what she thinks of her conduct now, I don't know; one thing I know, she has made me compleatly miserable. – Never man lov'd, or rather ador'd, a woman more than I did her; and [,to] confess [a] truth between you and m[e, I] do still love her to distraction after all, tho' I won't tell her so, tho I see her, which I don't want to do. – My poor, dear, unfortunate Jean! how happy I have been in her arms! – It is not the losing her that makes me so unhappy; but for *her* sake I feel most severely. – I foresee she is on the [ro]ad to, I am afraid, *eternal* ruin; and those who made so much noise, and showed so much grief, at the thought of her being *my wife*, may, some day, see her connected in such a manner as may give them more real cause of vexation. – I am su[re] I do not wish it: may Almighty God forgive her ingratitude and perjury to me, as I from my very soul forgive her! and may HIS grace be with her, to bless her in all her future life! – I can have no nearer idea of the place of eternal punishment than what I have felt in my own breast on her account. –

He describes the attempts he has made to forget her, all of them strictly conventional:

> I have run into all kinds of dissipation and riot, Mason-meetings, drinking matches, and other mischief, to drive her out of my head, but all in vain: and now for a grand cure, the Ship is on her way home that is to take me out to Jamaica, and then, farewel dear old Scotland, and farewel dear, ungrateful Jean, for never, never will I see you more![1]

On the following day, dear ungrateful Jean also wrote a letter. It was appreciably shorter, and it was addressed to 'Daddy' Auld, the Mauchline minister:

> I am heartily sorry that I have given and must give your Session trouble on my account. I acknowledge that I am with child, and Robert Burns in Mossgiel is the father. I am, with great respect, your most humble servant, Jean Armour.

Burns himself was called before the kirk session a week later, and acknowledged his part in the affair. He told his friend Richmond in a letter that he retained a 'foolish, hankering fondness' for Jean and that he had tried to see her – not with a view to reconciliation, but to enquire after her health:

1. *Ibid.*, 31.

The Mother forbade me the house; nor did Jean shew that penitence might have been expected. – However, the Priest, I am inform'd will give me a Certificate as a single man, if I comply with the rules of the Church, which for that reason I intend to do. –[1]

He might have expected to pay more dearly for his bachelor's certificate. Instead of finding himself on the penitential stool ('the Creepie chair' was his name for it), he was allowed to stand in his own place – three times, at fortnightly intervals. The Armour family – it is not clear why – wanted Jean to take her place beside him, but Dr. Auld said no. 'I am very well pleased,' Burns wrote to Brice, 'not to have her company.'

Writing a life of Burns is like restoring an old picture. Even after many layers of treacle-dark varnish have been stripped away, there remain areas of the canvas which still look as if they have been extensively overpainted. The confused and hectic months of spring and summer 1786 represent just such an area. When Burns itemised to David Brice the ways in which he had tried to drive all thoughts of Jean Armour out of his head – 'dissipation and riot, Mason-meetings, drinking matches, and other mischief' – the catalogue was incomplete. What he omitted to mention was that there was another young woman to whom he had turned for consolation; that he had indeed, as he wrote later, enjoyed 'a pretty long tract of the most ardent reciprocal attachment' with that young woman before he had any need of consolation:

> She has my heart, she has my hand,
> By secret Truth and Honor's band:
> Till the mortal stroke shall lay me low,
> I'm thine, my Highland Lassie, O![2]

The story of 'Highland Mary' bulks larger in the legend of Burns than it did in his life. In order to separate fact from fantasy, it makes sense for once to abandon the solid biographical convention of chronology and spool forward through the nineteenth century and into our own time. For some of his more romantic admirers the least-known and least knowable of Burns's conquests has become an object of near-veneration. Even Auguste Angellier, normally a model of Gallic detachment, was completely bowled over: '*La douce fille des Hautes Terres aux yeux azurés fut sa Béatrice*,' he wrote, '*et lui fit signe du bord du ciel*.'[3] Leslie Stephen, in his entry on the poet in *The Dictionary of National Biography*, wrote slyly that criticism of Burns 'is only permitted to Scotchmen

---

1. *Ibid.*, 33.
2. Kinsley, 107.
3. Auguste Angellier, *Robert Burns. La Vie. Les Oeuvres*, Hachette et Cie, Paris, 1893, 2 vols., vol. i, p. 162.

of pure blood,' but his fellow-Englishman W.E. Henley waded in regardless. The cult which had grown up round this obscure and insubstantial figure, he asserted in his penetrating centenary essay, bore witness to the existence of a national delusion:

> Little that is positive is known of Mary Campbell except that she once possessed a copy of the scriptures (now very piously preserved at Ayr), and that she is the subject of a fantasy, in bronze, at Dunoon. But to consider her story is, almost inevitably, to be forced back upon one of two conclusions: – either (1) she was something of a lightskirts; or (2) she is a kind of Scottish Mrs Harris.[1]

To the Mariolaters, those sneering words were a *casus belli*. It was mention of Mrs Harris, after all, the paragon to whom Mrs. Gamp, in *Martin Chuzzlewit*, constantly applies for corroboration of her various pronouncements, which provoked Betsey Prig to the memorable utterance, 'I don't believe there's no sich a person.'

In this case, of course, there *was* such a person – Henley was trailing his coat – but precious little is known about her. She was born in 1766 in Dunoon, a fact which allowed a twentieth-century sceptic to observe amiably that she was really no more Highland than the Cowal coast, (although in the eighteenth century that would have made her a Gaelic speaker).[2] She was the daughter of a mariner called Archibald Campbell who had bought a share in a sloop and made a living transporting coal from the Ayrshire coast to the Kintyre peninsula. She went into domestic service, first in Campbeltown and then on Arran; Burns's sister Isabella told Chambers that her brother first met the girl when she was working as a nursemaid in Gavin Hamilton's family.

The nearest thing we have to Burns's own account of their association is scanty, and can no longer be attested. According to Robert Cromek, who published his *Reliques* in 1808, Burns subsequently annotated the poem in his interleaved copy of *The Scots Musical Museum* (the leaf is now missing). 'My Highland lassie was a warm-hearted, charming young creature as ever blessed a man with generous love,' he wrote:

> After a pretty long tract of the most ardent reciprocal attachment, we met by appointment, on the second Sunday of May, in a sequestered spot by the banks of Ayr, where we spent the day in taking farewell, before she should embark for the West Highlands to arrange matters among her friends for our projected change of life.[3]

1. Henley and Henderson, *op. cit.*, vol i, p. 285.
2. See Hilton Brown, *There was A Lad, An Essay on Robert Burns*, Hamish Hamilton, London, 1949. 'To attempt a documented, intelligible and authentic account of Highland Mary,' Brown wrote, 'is one way of driving oneself mad.'
3. Robert H. Cromek, *Reliques of Robert Burns*, Cadell and Davies, London, 1808, p. 237.

'Projected change of life' sounds like marriage, or emigration, or both, but we are at once up against one of the oddest aspects of the 'Highland Mary' story, which is Burns's extraordinary reticence about it. We have two rather stilted love-songs – 'The Highland Lassie O' and 'Will ye go to the Indies, my Mary', both written in that spring or summer of 1786, which seem to confirm an intention to marry; there are three letters from the same period which appear to contain oblique references to the situation in which he found himself. His account of her concludes as economically as it began:

At the close of Autumn following she crossed the sea to meet me at Greenock, where she had scarce landed when she was seized with a malignant fever, which hurried my dear girl to the grave in a few days, before I could even hear of her illness.

Then silence. For the next three years Burns makes no reference to her either in verse or prose.

Such are the flimsy raw materials from which has been fashioned the most powerfully sentimental tradition in the Burns legend. By 1808, the fond farewell on the banks of Ayr was already being embroidered. 'The lovers stood on each side of a small purling brook,' wrote Cromek, 'they laved their hands in the limpid stream . . .'[1] In 1842 a monument was unveiled in the Old West Kirkyard at Greenock. It was paid for by public subscription, and on the marble panels inserted in the stone Grief was depicted weeping over an urn. The article on Burns for the 1876 edition of the *Encyclopaedia Britannica* was the work of John Nicholl, freethinker, professor of English Literature at Glasgow, friend of Swinburne. For him, 'Highland Mary' was the 'white rose' that 'bloomed in the midst of his passion flowers'. The merit of such formulations was that they allowed admirers of Burns to think better of him than some of them suspected they were entitled to by his record in such matters.

Not that the picture of an ideal of spiritual womanly purity went unchallenged during the nineteenth century. When Lockhart was preparing his *Life* in the 1820s, he was sent a number of memoranda by a man called Joseph Train:

Highland Mary. – Truth deprives her history of much of its charm. – Her character was loose in the extreme. – She was kept for some time by a Brother of Lord Eglinton's and even while a servant with Gavin Hamilton, and during the period of Burns's attachment it was well known that her meetings with Montgomery were open and frequent. – The friends of Burns represented to him the impropriety of his devotedness to her, but without producing any change in his sentiments. –

1. *Ibid.*, p. 238.

Malicious tittle-tattle or well-founded local gossip? Train had served his apprenticeship as a weaver and had been a soldier. He was now the Collector of Excise at Castle Douglas and a keen antiquarian – he had been helpful to Sir Walter Scott, Lockhart's father-in-law, in the writing of several of the Waverley novels. Train's information came from James Grierson of Dalgoner, a local laird whom Burns was to get to know when he moved to Dumfriesshire. Grierson was keenly interested in literature and after Burns's death began to collect material about him. He gave his source as Burns's old friend Richmond. Lockhart did not use the material, but did not destroy it, and it is preserved in the Edinburgh University Library.[1]

The small two-volume Bible which figures so prominently in the 'Highland Mary' story survives in the Burns Cottage Museum at Alloway. James Grierson records that he was shown it when he tracked down Highland Mary's sister in Ardrossan in 1817. One of her sons later took it with him when he emigrated to Canada; in 1840 a group of seventy Canadian-Scots, including the Mayor of Montreal, subscribed the sum of £25 to acquire it. It was sent to the Provost of Ayr, together with a lock of Mary's hair, and a covering letter from the editor and proprietor of the *Montreal Herald*:

> Sir – I have much pleasure in being the medium of transmitting to you the original pair of Bibles presented by our immortal national bard to Highland Mary, the object of his dearest affection, on the last occasion of their meeting in this world . . . It was the general opinion of the gentlemen who subscribed the money, that the Bibles could not be more appropriately disposed of than by depositing them in the Monument erected to the memory of Burns near Alloway Kirk, among other relics of the departed genius . . .[2]

That the Bibles had belonged to the departed genius is not in doubt, although there has been a good deal of messing about over the years with the various inscriptions they contained.[3] Each volume of the Bible is inscribed with a biblical text. In the first it is from Leviticus, chapter 19, verse 12 – 'And ye shall not swear by my name falsely, I am the Lord.' The quotation in the second volume is from St Matthew, chapter 5, verse 33 — 'Thou shalt not forswear thyself, but shalt perform unto the Lord thine oaths.' What significance attaches to the gift of the Bible remains open to speculation. A farewell present? A token sealing a promise of marriage? A romantic gesture meaning

1. The Train Manuscript, as it is known, was published in Robert T. Fitzhugh, *Robert Burns, His Associates and Contemporaries*, University of North Carolina Press, Chapel Hill, 1943.

2. Quoted in Chambers-Wallace, vol. i, pp. 477-8.

3. When he was working on his 1992 biography, James Mackay got permission from the Trustees of Burns Monument and Burns Cottage to have the volumes examined in the forensic laboratory of the Strathclyde Police and it was established that both were inscribed 'Robert Burns, Mossgavill', on the right-hand fly-leaf. He also noted that there had at one time been some writing in pencil on three blank pages at the end of one volume, but that this had subsequently been erased. The handwriting was that of Burns.

nothing very much at all? No amount of forensic examination will tell us that. We do not even know if the girl could read.

James Mackay performed a further demythologising service in the course of his extremely thorough researches – he established, by trawling through the Dunoon register of births, now in New Register House, Edinburgh, that the girl's name was not Mary but Margaret. It is true that the two names resemble each other much more closely in Gaelic than they do in English, but it was an unsettling disclosure for dyed in the wool Mariolaters, none the less. 'Highland Margaret' doesn't somehow have quite the same ring to it; it is rather like discovering that Bonnie Prince Charlie's name was really William.

To identify the girl who was Highland Mary is one thing. To establish the nature of her relationship with Burns is another. The 'malignant fever' which carried her off was almost certainly typhus – there was an epidemic in Greenock in the year of her death. The relevant Greenock registers no longer exist, but oral tradition in the town held strongly that she lay buried where the monument was erected in 1842. In 1920, the extension plans of a local shipyard led to the cemetery's closure, and it was decided that the remains should be reinterred – the matter was controversial, however, and the passage of the necessary Act through Parliament was delayed, partly because of lobbying by the Burns Federation.

The exhumation was attended by fourteen people. They included the Chief Constable and the then President of the Burns Federation, Mr Ninian McWhannell. Although the grave turned out to be only four feet deep, it became plain that the lair had been used for more than one burial. Hilton Brown was slightly carried away when he wrote that it was 'as densely populated as a modern tenement',[1] but in the course of two hours the four gravediggers did unearth three skulls, a thigh bone and a jawbone with four teeth in a good state of preservation. 'At the foot of the grave,' reported the *Greenock Telegraph*, 'the bottom of an infant's coffin was found. This while sodden was quite sound.'[2]

The contents of the grave were reburied in an oak coffin. They were subjected to no forensic examination and excited no immediate public comment. Only in the 1930s, with the biographies of Catherine Carswell and Professor Snyder, was battle joined. Possibly Mary had not just been carried off by typhus – perhaps she had died in childbirth. Mrs Carswell, indeed, saw no reason for doubt in the matter, and asserted plump and plain that 'she gave birth to a premature infant'.

This caused a predictable amount of jumping up and down in sectarian circles. In the 1932 *Burns Chronicle*, for instance, the Reverend Dr. Lauchlan Maclean Watt of Glasgow Cathedral fulminated against 'a kind of school which seems to love to unveil the sad stains upon the soul of the great.' He also wrote

1. Hilton Brown, *op. cit.*, p. 246.
2. *Greenock Telegraph*, 4th January 1921.

to the *Times Literary Supplement* to say that in a ministry of thirty-five years he had found it to be the universal custom that the dead child of a mother who had died in childbirth was buried in the same coffin – 'our largest funeral undertaker,' he added, would bear this out.

There was a similar closing of ranks on Burns's home turf. At the Ayr Burns Club in 1934 'The Immortal Memory' was proposed by Sir Thomas Oliver, a native of the town who had become an authority on industrial diseases. 'Highland Mary: Sir T. Oliver Refutes a Slander,' said a headline in the *Scotsman*. 'Baseless Assertions' ran the sub-heading. Sir Thomas had spoken to Mr Archibald McPhail, a former President of the Greenock Burns Club who had been present at the exhumation. He had told him that the floor of the infant's coffin was comparatively new, and of a different structure from that of the other pieces of wood recovered. 'In justice to the memory of a woman who had exercised an uplifting and chastening influence upon Burns,' Sir Thomas declared in his peroration, 'there is need to call a halt to the repeated publication of statements which are mere assertions, and without a vestige of proof.'[1]

'Tread softly,' a later poet wrote, 'for you tread on my dreams.' They would put it more prosily – and more aggressively – than Yeats, but a great many admirers of Burns will continue to hold the view to which Alan Bayne gave classical expression in the *Burns Chronicle* in 1906:

> Highland Mary for ever remains as the inspirer of Burns at his best, and so is linked to him eternally; and whoever seeks to defile this ideal maiden deserves the reprobation of all pure-minded men and women.[2]

The claim that this shadowy figure was 'the inspirer of Burns at his best' bears only the lightest scrutiny. With one exception, the handful of 'Highland Mary' songs, with their 'lingering stars,' 'transports past' and 'departed shades' are pretty poor stuff. Christina Keith's judgement of them was brisk but it was fair – 'choked with artificialities, stiff with exaggeration, rough with ugly forms.'[3] The Mariolaters will no doubt go on lighting candles before their icon; provoking those of a more agnostic turn of mind to reaffirm their assent to the abrasive but perceptive conclusion reached by Henley:

> That heroine-in-chief is a girl of whom scarce anything definite is known, while what may be reasonably suspected of her, though natural and feminine enough, is so displeasing to some fanatics, that, for Burns's sake (not hers) they would like to mythologise her out of being; or, at the least, to make her as arrant an impossibility as the tame, proper, figmentary Burns, the coinage

1. *Scotsman*, 26th January 1934.
2. *Burns Chronicle*, 1906, p. 108.
3. Christina Keith, *The Russet Coat. A Critical Study of Burns' Poetry and of its Background*, Robert Hale Limited, London, 1956, p. 156.

of their own tame, proper brains, which they have done their best to substitute for the lewd, amazing peasant of genius . . .[1]

The lewd amazing peasant was leading a very complicated life during the summer months of 1786. He had sent his poems to the printer on June 13th and was to and fro to Kilmarnock seeing them through the press. He was also pushing ahead with his plans for the West Indies. 'My hour is now come', he wrote somewhat melodramatically to Richmond at the end of July:

> You and I will never meet in Britain more. – I have orders within three weeks at farthest to repair aboard the *Nancy*, Cap^n Smith, from Clyde, to Jamaica, and to call at Antigua. – This, except to our friend Smith, whom God long preserve, is a secret about Mauchlin. – Would you believe it? Armour has got a warrant to throw me in jail till I find security for an enormous sum. – This they keep an entire secret, but I got it by a channel they little dream of; and I am wandering from one friend's house to another, and like a true son of the Gospel, 'have no where to lay my head.' – I know you will pour an execration on her head, but spare the poor, ill-advised Girl for my sake: tho', may all the Furies that rend the injured, enraged Lover's bosom, await the old Harridan, her Mother, until her latest hour![2]

What Mrs Armour had done to provoke this spurt of venom is not known. What her husband had done was to apply for a writ *in meditatione fugae* ('in contemplation of flight'). Burns's intention to emigrate was no secret; it had obviously occurred to Jean's father that once Burns's book of poems appeared, it ought to be possible to extract some money from him for the support of the unborn child. Burns, however, had been too quick for him. The 'channel they little dream of' could have been Jean, or perhaps it was one of his lawyer friends. At all events, eight days before writing to Richmond, Burns had put his signature to a deed of assignment.

This document had the effect of conveying all his property to his brother. It recorded that Gilbert had bound himself, in the event of Elizabeth Paton's choosing to part with Burns's natural daughter, to 'aliment, clothe and educate' the child until she was fifteen. The deed spoke of assigning 'all and Sundry Goods, Gear, Corns, Cattle, Horses, Nolt, Sheep, Household furniture, and all other moveable effects of whatever kind that I shall leave behind me on my departure from the kingdom.'[3] It was specified that Gilbert was to have the benefit of any profits arising from the publication of the poems, and Burns also conveyed the copyright, this to be held in trust for his daughter until she attained the age of fifteen.

1. Henley and Henderson, *op. cit.*, p. 289.
2. Letters, 36.
3. Nolt means cattle. For the full text of the deed, see *Letters*, 35. The original MS is preserved in the Sheriff-Clerk's office in Ayr.

The deed of assignment reflects well on Burns and perhaps even better on Gilbert. It is a generous man who undertakes to care for the natural child even of a brother 'in a suitable manner as if she was his own.' For Jean Armour, however, there was to be no provision. A passage in a letter Burns wrote to his friend James Smith shortly after signing the deed showed that though she still filled his thoughts, those thoughts were as unforgiving as they were confused:

> O Jeany thou hast stolen away my soul!
> In vain I strive against the lov'd idea:
> Thy tender image sallies on my thoughts,
> My firm resolves become an easy prey!

Against two things however, I am fix'd as Fate: staying at home, and owning her conjugally. – The first, by Heaven I will not do! the last, by Hell I will never do![1]

Burns had told Richmond, in his somewhat theatrical letter of farewell, that he wrote 'in a moment of rage, reflecting on my miserable situation, – exil'd, abandon'd, forlorn.' His life had certainly been reduced to a shambles in the twelve months since the summer of 1785, though largely through his own folly.[2] He could plead bad seed and late harvests for the straits he and Gilbert found themselves in at Mossgiel, but hardly for his humiliation before the Mauchline congregation and the yelping at his heels of the houghmagandie pack. And yet it was during that year of emotional turmoil, when he was entangled simultaneously with his Highland Lassie and Jean Armour, that he tapped his richest vein of poetic inspiration.

His *Poems, Chiefly in the Scottish Dialect* came out on the last day of July: 'I have at last made my public appearance,' he wrote to a friend, 'and am solemnly inaugurated into the numerous class of Authors.'[3] It was a notable understatement. Apart from 'Tam o'Shanter', he had completed almost all the poems on which his fame would subsequently rest. He was twenty-seven years old.

---

1. Letters, 37. De Lancey Ferguson points out that the first line is a paraphrase of one in Addison's *Cato*.
2. He had also suffered a bereavement. His youngest brother, John, ten years his junior, had died in October at the age of sixteen. We do not know the cause. The parish records disclose only that he was buried, on November 1st, 'in a second-quality mort-cloth.'
3. Letters, 38. The recipient was John Kennedy, a relative of Gavin Hamilton's wife, who was factor to the Earl of Dumfries, near Cumnock.

Five

GUID BLACK PRENT

THE KILMARNOCK EDITION, stitched in a blue paper cover, ran to two hundred and thirty-five pages of verse and a five-page glossary. Burns's preface was a cross between a manifesto and a sales-pitch and it began with what could be mistaken for a modest disclaimer:

> The following trifles are not the production of the Poet, who, with all the advantages of learned art, perhaps amid the elegances and idlenesses of upper life, looks down for a rural theme, with an eye to Theocrites [*sic*] or Virgil.

Such celebrated names were, for him, 'a fountain shut up and a book sealed'. His readers, it was implied, must take him as they found him. His subjects, he announced, were the sentiments and manners he felt and saw in himself and his 'native compeers' and he wrote of them 'in his and their native language'.

Well, almost. Between April and July the 'Scotch Poems' of the subscription proposal had been modified to *Poems, Chiefly in the Scottish Dialect*, and a handful of purely English pieces had been included, most of them triggered by his occasional descents into melancholy and depression. Possibly it was thought this would broaden the appeal of the volume. More probably it was simply that Burns still hadn't got the revered Shenstone out of his system – 'that celebrated Poet,' as he described him, 'whose divine Elegies do honor to our language, our nation, and our species.'

He acknowledged his debt to 'two justly admired Scotch Poets,' although he insisted that he had no claim to be compared with either Ramsay or Fergusson – even, as he put it, in his 'highest pulse of vanity.' After an expression of thanks to his subscribers ('not the mercenary bow over a counter, but the heart-throbbing gratitude of the Bard'), he concluded with an appeal. It begins on a decidedly obsequious note – 'He begs his readers, particularly the Learned and the Polite, who may honor him with a perusal, that they will make every allowance for Education and Circumstance of Life.' Burns quickly tires of that, however, and signs off with a sturdy request that the poems be judged on their merits:

P O E M S,

CHIEFLY IN THE

SCOTTISH DIALECT,

BY

R O B E R T   B U R N S.

THE Simple Bard, unbroke by rules of Art,
He pours the wild effusions of the heart : .
And if infpir'd, 'tis Nature's pow'rs infpire;
Her's all the melting thrill, and her's the kindling fire.

ANONYMOUS.

K I L M A R N O C K:

PRINTED BY JOHN WILSON.

M,DCC,LXXXVI.

1. 'Guid black prent.' The title page of the Kilmarnock edition.

If after a fair, candid, and impartial criticism, he shall stand convicted of Dulness and Nonsense, let him be done by, as he would in that case do by others – let him be condemned, without mercy, to contempt and oblivion.

Burns had, in fact, a pretty shrewd idea of the merit of his work. 'I weighed my productions as impartially as in my power,' he told Moore in his autobiographical letter the following year. 'I was pretty sure my Poems would meet with some applause; but at the worst, the roar of the Atlantic would deafen the voice of Censure, and the novelty of west-Indian scenes make me forget Neglect. – '[1]

The roar of the Atlantic was not required. In addition to the hundred and forty-five subscriptions secured by 'Orator Bob' Aiken, Robert Muir of Kilmarnock rustled up seventy, and so did Gilbert; James Smith was good for forty-one and Gavin Hamilton for forty. Of the 612 copies which Wilson printed, more than half went to subscribers. Before the end of August all but thirteen of the remainder had gone. Almost overnight Burns's fame had extended well beyond the borders of Ayrshire. 'They were every where received with eager admiration and delight,' wrote his first biographer, Robert Heron:

Old and young, high and low, grave and gay, learned or ignorant, all were alike delighted, agitated, transported. I was at that time resident in Galloway, contiguous to Ayrshire: and I can well remember, how that even plough-boys and maid-servants would have gladly bestowed the wages which they earned the most hardly, and which they wanted to purchase necessary clothing, if they might but procure the works of Burns.[2]

Celebrity or no, Burns, in those first weeks after the publication of his poems, was still dodging around from the house of one friend to another to avoid the service of Armour's writ. He expected at any moment to be called to Greenock to embark for the West Indies, but when he went to Ayr in the middle of August to discuss his passage with Dr Patrick Douglas, the brother of the man for whom he was going to work, he ran into difficulty on that front, too:

. . . I found the Doctor with a M^r and Mrs White, both Jamaicans, and they have derang'd my plans altogether. – They assure him that to send me from Savannah la Mar to Port Antonio will cost my Master, Charles Douglas, upwards of fifty pounds; besides running the risk of throwing myself into a pleuratic [sic] fever in consequence of hard travelling in the sun . . .[3]

1. Letters, 125
2. 'A Memoir of the Life of the Late Robert Burns', *Monthly Magazine*, Edinburgh, June 1797.
3. Letters, 40. To James Smith, Mauchline.

He was offered another sailing on September 1st, but on that date we find him back at Mossgiel and writing to Richmond that 'two days notice' had been too little to wind up his affairs – he would now be a passenger on the *Bell*, sailing at the end of the month. As he had heard about the September 1st sailing from Dr Douglas seventeen days previously it is not apparent why any further notice was necessary. It is clear, however, that the pressures on Burns were easing and perhaps it was this that was sapping his resolve to leave the country. 'I am under little apprehension now about Armour,' he told Richmond. 'The warrant is still in existence, but some of the first Gentlemen in the county have offered to befriend me; and besides, Jean will not take any step against me, without letting me know, as nothing but the most violent menaces could have forced her to sign the Petition.'

He had been to see Jean, and confessed to some anxiety about her approaching confinement. 'She would gladly now embrace that offer she once rejected,' he added, 'but it shall never more be in her power.'

Burns then turned his attention to his friend's own affairs. He had recently encountered Jenny Surgeoner, the Mauchline girl whom Richmond had seduced and abandoned, and saw nothing inconsistent in lecturing his friend about his behaviour:

> You are acting very wrong, My friend; her happiness or misery is bound up in your affection or unkindness. – Poor girl! she told me with tears in her eyes that she had been at great pains since she went to Paisley, learning to write better; just on purpose to be able to correspond with you ... Richmond, I know you to be a man of honour, but this conduct of yours to a poor girl who distractedly loves you, and whom you have ruined ... but I beg your pardon ...'tis taking an improper liberty. –[1]

Two days later the girl with whom Burns himself had taken a similarly improper liberty gave birth to twins. He dashed off another letter to Edinburgh: 'Wish me luck, dear Richmond! Armour has just now brought me fine boy and girl at one throw. God bless them poor little dears!'[2]

He was in a state of high excitement, and signed off with an inventively obscene reworking of an old song:

> Green grow the rashes O,
>   Green grow the rashes O,
> The lasses they hae wimble bores,   gimlet holes
> The widows they hae gashes O.[3]

1. *Ibid.*, 43.
2. *Ibid.*, 45.
3. Kinsley, 124.

By the end of the week he had calmed down a little. 'You will have heard that poor Armour has repaid my amorous mortgages double,' he wrote to Robert Muir in Kilmarnock. 'A very fine boy and girl have awakened a thousand feelings that thrill, some with tender pleasure and some with foreboding anguish, thro' my soul. – '[1] There is a revealing throwaway line at the end of the letter – 'I believe all hopes of staying at home will be abortive'; from this time on the impression grows that his determination to seek a new life is growing weaker by the day. 'My departure is uncertain,' he told John Kennedy at the end of the month, 'but I do not think it will be till after harvest,' and to Richmond he wrote, 'I am going perhaps to try a second edition of my book – if I do, it will detain me a little longer in the country.'[2]

One of those who had urged Burns to try his luck with a second edition was John Ballantine, a merchant and banker in Ayr to whom he had been introduced by Robert Aiken. As Dean of Guild, Ballantine had led the campaign for the narrow old bridge over the River Ayr to be replaced by a new one with an extra span, and it was to him that Burns dedicated his poem 'The Brigs of Ayr' which he wrote that autumn – a Scottish version of the ancients-versus-moderns debate in the form of a conversation between the spirits of the two bridges.[3] Ballantine, who in the following year was to become Provost of the burgh, now offered to lend Burns money, but also advised him that he would do much better to look for a publisher in Edinburgh.

As the autumn drew on, Burns had a decisive stroke of luck. His book had come to the attention of the Reverend George Lawrie, who was the minister of Loudoun, a parish a few miles east of Kilmarnock. Chambers describes him as 'an excellent specimen of the old moderate clergy – sensible, upright, kind-hearted, and with no despicable taste in literature.'[4] He numbered among his friends several notable men of letters, and to one of them, the celebrated Dr Thomas Blacklock, he sent a copy of the Kilmarnock edition.

Blacklock was a poet, a musician and a man of some classical and scientific learning. His genteel Augustan verse has not stood the test of time, even though it went through six editions in his lifetime and won the approval of Samuel Johnson. He was born in Dumfriesshire, the son of a bricklayer. At the age of six he had lost his sight from smallpox, but this had not prevented him studying for the ministry and he had been called to a charge in Kirkcudbright. When

---

1. Letters, 46.
2. *Ibid.*, 49. Burns did not date this letter, but Richmond wrote '27 Sept 1786' on it, which is presumably when he received it.
3. Kinsley, 120. There are several models for the form in Fergusson, most obviously the 'Mutual Complaint of Plainstanes and Causey.'
4. Chambers-Wallace, vol. i, pp. 412-3. Chambers also records that Mr Lawrie was a convivial soul who, 'in spite of his cloth, was partial to dancing, on the ground that it was conducive both to health and cheerfulness.' He entertained Burns at his manse on Irvine Water, and after dinner a dance was improvised. Although Burns was heavily built, he danced well; one of Lawrie's daughters said afterwards that he 'kept time admirably.' Burns left a thank-you letter in his bedroom the next morning in the form of the poem 'Lying at a Reverend Friend's house' (Kinsley, 132).

his flock complained that he could not carry out his parochial duties properly, he retired to Edinburgh on an annuity, which he and his wife supplemented by running a boarding house for students.

Blacklock was slow to reply to Lawrie, but when he did so, at the beginning of September, it was in the most enthusiastic terms:

Many instances have I seen of nature's force and beneficence, exerted under numerous and formidable disadvantages; but none equal to that, with which you have been kind enough to present me. There is a pathos and delicacy in his serious poems; a vein of wit and humour in those of a more festive turn, which cannot be too much admired, nor too warmly approved; and I think I shall never open the book without feeling my astonishment renewed and increased.[1]

Lawrie passed the letter to Gavin Hamilton, who showed it to Burns, and such unreserved praise from a man who had enjoyed the friendship of David Hume and Benjamin Franklin excited him greatly: 'The Doctor belonged to a set of Critics for whose applause I had not even dared to hope,' he later told Moore. Blacklock also offered practical advice – get a second edition out right away, and make it bigger than the first one. 'It appears certain,' he wrote, 'that its intrinsic merit, and the exertion of the author's friends, might give it a more universal circulation than any thing of the kind which has been published within my memory.'

Burns raised the question of a second edition with his printer, Wilson, when he went to Kilmarnock early in October to settle his accounts, but did not get an encouraging response. Wilson calculated that paper for a thousand copies would cost about twenty-seven pounds and the printing about fifteen or sixteen. He was prepared to meet the cost of printing if Burns would advance the money for the paper, but that was beyond him. 'So farewell hopes of a second edition 'till I grow richer!' he wrote to Bob Aiken, 'an epocha, which, I think, will arrive at the payment of the British national debt.'[2]

It is plain from this same letter to Aiken that he was still extremely unsettled. It also emerges that there had been some discussion of alternative plans for his future:

I have been feeling all the various rotations and movements within, respecting the excise. There are many things plead strongly against it; the uncertainty of getting soon into business, the consequences of my follies, which may perhaps make it impracticable for me to stay at home; and besides I have for some time been pining under secret wretchedness, from causes which you pretty well know – the pang of disappointment, the sting of pride, with

1. Quoted in Chambers-Wallace, vol. i, p. 417.
2. Letters, 53.

some wandering stabs of remorse, which never fail to settle on my vitals like vultures, when attention is not called away by the calls of society or the vagaries of the muse. Even in the hour of social mirth, my gaiety is the madness of an intoxicated criminal under the hands of the executioner. All these reasons urge me to go abroad; and to all these reasons I have only one answer – the feelings of a father. This, in the present mood I am in, overbalances everything that can be laid in the scale against it.

Towards the end of October Burns made the acquaintance of Dugald Stewart, the distinguished Professor of Moral Philosophy at Edinburgh. They were brought together by John Mackenzie, the Mauchline doctor who had attended William Burnes in his last illness, and who had become a good friend. Stewart had a country house at Catrine Bank, just south of Mauchline, and he invited Burns to dine there.

It was an important step towards recognition – Stewart was, in De Lancey Ferguson's phrase, 'the first of the real "Brahmin caste" of Scotland' to take Burns up socially. One of the other guests was Lord Daer, the second son of the Earl of Selkirk, who was one of Stewart's pupils. Daer, a strikingly tall young man a few years younger than Burns, had just returned from France, where he had met Condorcet, and was full of liberal sentiments. Burns was mightily impressed. He dashed off some extempore verses, drawing a rueful picture of himself staring and stammering in embarrassment. It was his first encounter with the nobility and he was forced to re-examine some of his prejudices:

> Then from his Lordship I shall learn,
> Henceforth to meet with unconcern,
> One rank as well's another;
> Nae honest, worthy man need care,
> To meet wi' NOBLE youthfu' DAER,
> For he but meets a BROTHER.[1]

He was very taken with Stewart, too, although less in awe of him than of the young aristocrat – 'that plain, honest, worthy man, the Professor,' he wrote to Dr Mackenzie: 'I think his character, divided into ten parts, stands thus – four parts Socrates – four parts Nathaniel – and two parts Shakespeare's Brutus.'[2]

Years later, when Currie was at work on his biography, Stewart supplied him with his recollections of that first meeting. The Professor's guest had clearly unburdened himself at the dinner table:

1. Kinsley, 127, 'Extempore Verses on Dining with Lord Daer'.
2. Letters, 53.

At this time Burns's prospects in life were so extremely gloomy, that he had seriously formed a plan of going out to Jamaica in a very humble situation, not however without lamenting, that his want of patronage should force him to think of a project so repugnant to his feelings, when his ambition aimed at no higher an object than the station of an exciseman or gauger in his own country.

His manners were then, as they continued ever afterwards, simple, manly, and independent; strongly expressive of conscious genius and worth; but without any thing that indicated forwardness, arrogance, or vanity. He took his share in conversation, but not more than belonged to him; and listened with apparent attention and deference, on subjects where his want of education deprived him of the means of information. If there had been a little more of gentleness and accommodation in his temper, he would, I think, have been still more interesting; but he had been accustomed to give law in the circle of his ordinary acquaintance; and his dread of any thing approaching to meanness or servility, rendered his manner somewhat decided and hard. Nothing, perhaps, was more remarkable among his various attainments, than the fluency and precision, and originality of his language, when he spoke in company; more particularly as he aimed at purity in his turn of expression, and avoided more successfully than most Scotchmen, the peculiarities of Scottish phraseology.[1]

The first review of the Kilmarnock edition appeared in the October issue of the *Edinburgh Magazine, or Literary Miscellany*.[2] 'Who are you, Mr Burns?' asked the author of the unsigned notice: 'At what university have you been educated? what languages do you understand? what authors have you particularly studied? whether has Aristotle or Horace directed your taste? who has praised your poems, and under whose patronage are they published?' Burns had no reason to be displeased with the responses put into his mouth in answer to this catechism: '. . . I understand no languages but my own; I have studied Allan Ramsay and Ferguson [*sic*]. My poems have been praised at many a fire-side; and I ask no patronage for them, if they deserve none. I have not looked on mankind through the spectacle of books. An ounce of mother wit, you know, is worth a pound of clergy; and Homer and Ossian, for any thing that I have heard, could neither write nor read.'

The reviewer was probably James Sibbald, the Edinburgh bookseller who was the founder of the magazine and was himself the son of a farmer. 'The author is indeed a striking example of native genius bursting through the obscurity of poverty,' he wrote:

1. Currie, vol. i, pp. 136-7
2. Published, as was then the custom, in the early days of the following month. It appeared on November 3rd.

He is said to be a common ploughman; and when we consider him in this light, we cannot help regretting that wayward fate had not placed him in a more favoured situation. Those who view him with the severity of lettered criticism, and judge him by the fastidious rules of art, will discover that he has not the doric simplicity of Ramsay, nor the brilliant imagination of Ferguson; but to those who admire the exertions of untutored fancy, and are blind to many faults for the sake of numberless beauties, his poems will afford singular gratification. His obervations on human characters are acute and sagacious, and his descriptions are lively and just. Of rustic pleasantry he has a rich fund; and some of his softer scenes are touched with inimitable delicacy. He seems to be a boon companion and often startles us with a dash of libertinism, which will keep some readers at a distance . . .

Sibbald might have been rather more than startled if he had known how much 'libertinism' Burns had judged it prudent to exclude. 'The Court of Equity' was not there, and neither was 'A Poet's Welcome to his Bastart Wean'. Burns left out several of his most bitingly effective satires – 'Holy Willie's Prayer', 'The Twa Herds' and 'The Ordination' are missing – and 'The Jolly Beggars' also failed to find a place.

There is, however, nothing particularly mysterious about these omissions. Burns was not a fool. He had in the very recent past had more than enough exposure to the processes of ecclesiastical discipline – theological liberalism could fight its own battles for a time. Nor was there any point in going out of his way to offend the aristocracy; it accordingly made sense to leave out the recently composed 'Address of Beelzebub', a savage, pamphleteering assault on Lord Breadalbane's efforts, as President of the Highland Society, to stop five hundred members of clan Macdonald emigrating to Canada.[1] There was a further consideration. The sniggers and guffaws which greeted pieces like 'The Fornicator' or the even grosser 'Brose and Butter'[2] when they were handed round in manuscript among his Ayrshire cronies were highly gratifying, but he now sought the approval of a wider, and politer, public. The selection

1. Kinsley, 108. There was rather more to the story than Burns's black and white depiction of it suggests. The meeting of the Highland Society which so incensed him had taken place in London on 23rd May 1786. Those present agreed on the desirability of improving the fisheries, agriculture and manufactures in the Highlands, and eleven of them immediately subscribed the sum of three thousand pounds for that purpose. Burns, in his introductory note to the poem, asserted that the Highlanders were emigrating 'in search of that fantastic thing – LIBERTY'.

2. *Ibid.*, 78. Although a copy of it survives in his own hand, it is not certain how much of this poem is Burns's own work. It may be one of the earliest examples of something he collected and 'improved'. The title means an abundance of semen, and the poem's five short stanzas and chorus contain a welter of sexual metaphor; there are references to the vagina, to female pubic hair and to the penis, which is variously compared to a mouse, a mole, a gardener's dibble and a rolling pin. The impenetrability of the Scots in which it is written affords almost total protection to delicate English ears. .

of poems for the Kilmarnock edition was coolly calculated to meet their taste.

The volume opens, strongly but safely, with 'The Twa Dogs', a gently satirical reflection on how the other half lives; it ends, ruefully although a shade self-regardingly, with 'A Bard's Epitaph'. ('Is there a whim-inspir'd fool,/ Owre fast for thought, owre hot for rule . . .')[1] Of recently written short poems, the outstanding example was 'To a Mouse' – Burns would be delighted that one of his occasional pieces had found a place in the memory bank of the nations, although he would also derive sardonic amusement from the burden of owlish exegesis heaped upon the back of his 'wee, sleeket, cowran, tim'rous beastie' over two centuries.[2]

He included only three songs, two of them inconsequential, the third ('It was upon a Lammas night,/When corn rigs are bonie'), one of the earliest and loveliest he ever wrote.[3] He made room, in the middle of the selection, for a rather lowering sequence made up of such poems as 'Winter, A Dirge', 'To Ruin' and 'A Prayer, in the Prospect of Death'. They are derivative, and they are gloomy, but Burns's instinct in putting them in was sound. His readers would have liked nothing better than to be reminded of their mortality – eighteenth-century gravestones were frequently adorned with the skull and crossbones, and carried epitaphs of sober reminder to those whose time was still to come: 'Death's a debt to nature due; I have paid it – so maun you.'

There was much in a more cheerful strain, however, like 'Address to the Deil' ('O Thou, whatever title suit thee!/Auld Hornie, Satan, Nick, or Clootie.')[4] and a good selection of the easy, unbuttoned epistles to friends like John Smith and John Rankine which flowed so easily from Burns's pen. The dedication, to Gavin Hamilton, is rather oddly placed half way through the book,[5] and it is immediately preceded by the jaunty 'On a Scotch Bard Gone to the West Indies':

> Fareweel, *my rhyme-composing billie!*   friend
> Your native soil was right ill-willie;   ill-disposed
> But may ye flourish like a lily,
>   Now bonilie![6]

---

1. *Ibid.*, 104.
2. *Ibid.*, 69. 'As superbly inimitable as *Hamlet*' (Snyder, p. 179); 'Can only be fully understood in the context of the Scottish Agrarian Revolution' (Thomas Crawford, *Burns: A Study of the Poems and the Songs*, 2nd ed., Oliver & Boyd, Edinburgh, 1965, p. 164); 'Burns has, then, a zoomorphic view of himself and an anthropomorphic view of the mouse' (Alan Bold, *A Burns Companion*, Macmillan, London, 1991, p. 225).
3. *Ibid.*, 8.
4. *Ibid.*, 76.
5. *Ibid.*, 103.
6. *Ibid.*, 100.

The poem in which Burns sailed closest to the political wind in the Kilmarnock edition was 'A Dream'.[1] He prefaced it with a cheeky couplet and note of explanation:

> *Thoughts, words and deeds, the Statute blames with reason;*
> *But surely* Dreams *were ne'er indicted Treason.*

On reading, in the public papers, the Laureate's Ode, with the other parade of June 4th, 1786, the Author was no sooner dropt asleep, than he imagined himself transported to the Birth-day Levee; and, in his dreaming fancy, made the following Address.

Burns's loyal salutation – 'GUID-MORNIN to your MAJESTY!' is rather different from the Laureate's Pindaric effusions on 'the Monarch's natal morn.' He notes that George III is at the receiving end of a good deal of flattery and observes that the place he occupies might perhaps be better filled by another – a thinly-veiled declaration for the House of Stuart. Then, in a phrase that has become a part of the language, he briskly tells his 'sovereign King' his fortune:

> *Facts* are cheels that winna ding,   fellows   be shifted
>   An' downa be disputed: cannot
> Your *royal nest*, beneath *Your* wing,
>   Is e'en right reft an' clouted . . .   torn and patched

This reference to the loss of the American colonies is followed by disobliging references to Pitt's ministers (who, Burns suggests, would be better suited to work in a cowshed). Then it is the turn of various junior members of the royal family – the 'young Potentate o' Wales', who spends his time gambling with Charles James Fox and 'young royal Tarry-breeks', the future William IV, who is offered coarse advice, in nautical terms, about how to proceed with a seduction. The King's younger son, Duke of York and Bishop of Osnabruck, is also offered loyal counsel (it was common knowledge that he had had as his lover the mistress of a notorious highwayman):

> Then swith! an' get a *wife* to hug,
>   Or trouth! ye'll stain the *Mitre*
>   Some luckless day.

It is a fairly safe bet that the poem which Burns intended as the centrepiece of the Kilmarnock edition was 'The Cotter's Saturday Night'.[2] It had been

1. *Ibid.*, 113.
2. *Ibid.*, 72.

composed during the previous winter – his model was almost certainly a poem of Fergusson's called 'The Farmer's Ingle'. The cotter, according to Gilbert, was an exact copy of their father 'in his manners, his family devotion, and exhortations,' and indeed much of the poem reads as if Burns were responding to a delayed impulse of filial piety: 'Robert had frequently remarked to me,' Gilbert recalled, 'that he thought there was something peculiarly venerable in the phrase, "Let us worship God," used by a decent, sober head of a family introducing family worship.'[1]

Over the years this sentimental picture of the felicities of domestic life in rural Scotland has been blown this way and that by the capricious breezes of literary taste and fashion. In Burns's own century and for most of the nineteenth, it was received with unmodified rapture. It was variously commended by early reviewers for its 'propriety and sensibility' and its 'depth of domestic joy'; Hazlitt judged it to be 'a noble and pathetic picture of human manners, mingled with a fine religious awe. It comes over the mind like a slow and solemn strain of music.'[2] By the turn of the last century, the winds of criticism had veered into another quarter – 'It is not hard to understand,' sniffed Henley, in his Centenary essay, 'that the Saturday Night was doomed to popularity from the first; being of its essence sentimental and therefore pleasingly untrue, and being, also of its essence, patriotic – an assertion of the honour and the glory and the piety of Scotland.'[3] Modern critics have been equally severe – Snyder, for instance, writing in the 1930s, found it 'astonishingly uneven' – 'the best of Burns and virtually the worst of Burns lie side by side in unseemly incongruity.'[4]

The poem certainly gets off to a wobbly start. Although some Augustan influences are apparent in Fergusson's poem, it is written entirely in broad Scots, an example Burns unwisely did not follow. He takes his epigraph, 'Let not Ambition mock their useful toil' – from Gray's *Elegy*, but in giving over his first Spenserian stanza to an extravagant dedication to his lawyer friend, Robert Aiken, he is carried away:

> To you I sing, in simple Scottish lays,
>   The *lowly train* in life's sequester'd scene;
> The native feelings strong, the guileless ways,
>   What A**** in a *Cottage* would have been;
> Ah! tho' his worth unknown, far happier there I ween!

The proposition that the convivial and worldly 'Orator Bob' would have found

1. Currie, vol. iii, pp. 384-5.
2. 'On Burns and the Old English Ballads', a lecture delivered by Hazlitt at the Surrey Institution in 1818 and published later that year in his *Lectures on the English Poets*, Taylor and Hessey, London. The text appears in *Complete Works of William Hazlitt*, ed. P.P. Howe, Hamish Hamilton, London, 1930, vol. v, pp. 127-40.
3. Henley and Henderson, *op. cit.*, pp. 276-7.
4. Snyder, p. 171.

life more congenial if his lot had been cast several rungs lower down the social
ladder and in rustic surroundings teeters between the improbable and the
ludicrous.

Burns quickly retrieves the situation with an effective setting of the winter
scene:

> November chill blaws loud wi' angry sugh;   *sound of rushing wind*
> The short'ning winter-day is near a close;
> The miry beasts retreating frae the pleugh;
> The black'ning train o' craws to their repose . . .

So long as he remains on the vernacular highroad everything bowls along very
well; when thoughts of Shenstone and other neo-classical English models cloud
his mind, he is quickly back in the ditch:

> The Parents *partial* eye their hopeful years;
> Anticipation forward points the view . . .

Nor does Burns masquerade with much success as a moralist:

> Is there, in human-form, that bears a heart –
> A wretch! a villain! lost to love and truth!
> That can, with studied, sly, ensnaring art,
> Betray sweet *Jenny's* unsuspecting youth?

From the self-appointed President of the Court of Equity this is more than a
little rich. And yet, down the years, as the whisky has flowed at Burns Suppers
in the Scottish Borders or St Andrew's Night dinners in Ulan Bator, 'The
Cotter's Saturday Night' has been fervently declaimed and as fervently
applauded – a secular hymn of national self-praise without the music. Perhaps
there is a clue to the hold it has on Scottish hearts and minds in a story told
by Cunningham in the 1830s. A friend of Burns had a housekeeper who had
rather a low opinion of the poet, and her mistress showed her 'The Cotter' in
an attempt to win her round:

> She returned the volume with a strong shaking of the head, saying, 'Nae
> doubt gentlemen and ladies think mickle o' this, but for me its naething but
> what I saw i' my father's house every day, and I dinna see how he could hae
> tauld it ony other way.'[1]

1. Allan Cunningham, *The Works of Robert Burns, with his Life*, 8 vols., Cochrane and Macrone,
London, 1834, vol. ii, p. 259.

Critical opinion has been similarly divided by 'The Vision'.[1] Burns imagines that he is visited by his native Muse. Once he has admired her tartan robe (and her shapely legs)[2] his gaze is caught by 'her Mantle large' – something it would have to be, because it appears to have been run up from an extremely large-scale Ordnance Survey map of his native Ayrshire:

> Here, DOON pour'd down his far-fetch'd floods;
> There, well-fed IRWINE stately thuds;
> Auld, hermit AIRE staw thro' his woods, crept
> On to the shore . . .

His Muse – he calls her Coila – gives him a sort of half-term report on how he is doing as a poet, and this includes some quite good advice on what not to attempt:

> 'Thou canst not learn, nor can I show,
> 'To paint with *Thomson's* landscape-glow;
> 'Or wake the bosom-melting throe,
>   'With *Shenstone's* art . . .

Her positive recommendations seem less helpful:

> 'To give my counsels all in one,
> 'Thy *tuneful flame* still careful fan;
> 'Preserve the *dignity of Man*,
>   'With Soul erect;
> 'And trust, the UNIVERSAL PLAN
>   'Will all protect.

Henley disliked the poem's sentimentality. 'It is further vitiated,' he added loftily, 'by the writer's "falling to his English," to a purpose not exhilarating to the knower of Shakespeare and Milton and Herrick.'[3] Critics disposed to look more kindly on some of the conventions of eighteenth-century poetry have thought more highly of it – Thomas Crawford, indeed, rates it one of his highest achievements: 'In this one magnificent but little-read poem, Burns attains something of Blake's visionary insight.'[4] That is surely extravagant. It is easier to assent to David Daiches' conclusion: 'There is not,' he writes, 'any

---

1. Kinsley, 62.
2. He compares their shapeliness to that of 'Bess' Paton's; in later editions, reconciled with Jean Armour, he makes a diplomatic amendment — 'And such a *leg*! my bonie JEAN/ Could only peer it.'
3. Henley and Henderson, *op. cit.*, p. 274.
4. Crawford, *op. cit.*, p. 192.

clearer example in Burns's poetry of the way in which, when he had his eye on the wrong audience, he was liable to go wrong.'[1]

The one poem above all others in the Kilmarnock edition in which Burns went triumphantly right has already been considered. 'The Holy Fair' shows him incontestably at the top of his bent – no stilted neo-classicism here. Effortless and magical, the writing casts its spell from the first stanza. An early critic wrote primly that the poem was 'entitled to every praise except that of scrupulous decency,'[2] but once again it is Henley who most truly hits the mark: 'I, for my part, would not give my Holy Fair,' he declared, 'for a wilderness of Saturday Nights.'[3]

The housekeeper who declined to be impressed by 'The Cotter's Saturday Night' was in the employ of Mrs Frances Dunlop, who in 1786 was a woman of fifty-six. Her father claimed descent from a cousin of Sir William Wallace – a distinction of which she was inclined to remind the world with some frequency. She had been married at the age of 18 to John Dunlop of Dunlop, who was twenty-three years her senior and to whom she bore six daughters and seven sons. She had been widowed the previous summer, and this had made her ill. To grief at the death of her husband had been added distress at her estrangement from her eldest surviving son, who had got into financial straits and been obliged to sell the ancestral estate. In that autumn of 1786 Frances Dunlop was in a very bad way: 'My mind was then in a state in which, had it long continued, my only refuge would inevitably have been a mad-house or a grave; nothing interested or amused me; all around me served to probe a wound whose recent stab was mortal to my peace, and had already ruined my health and benumbed my senses.'[4]

Then a friend lent her a copy of the Kilmarnock edition. Its impact – particularly 'The Cotter's Saturday Night' – was dramatic. 'She read it over with the greatest pleasure and surprise,' wrote Gilbert,

> the poet's description of the simple cottagers operating on her mind like the charm of a powerful exorcist, expelling the demon *ennui*, and restoring her to her wonted inward harmony and satisfaction. Mrs. Dunlop sent off a person express to Mossgiel, distant fifteen or sixteen miles, with a very obliging letter to my brother, desiring him to send her half-a-dozen copies of his *Poems*, if he had them to spare, and begging he would do her the pleasure of calling at Dunlop House as soon as convenient.[5]

1. David Daiches, *Robert Burns*, G. Bell and Sons Ltd., London, 1952, p. 148.
2. David Irving, *The Lives of the Scotish Poets; with preliminary dissertations on the literary history of Scotland and the early Scotish drama*, 2 vols., A. Lawrie, Edinburgh, 1804.
3. Henley and Henderson, *op. cit.*, p. 276.
4. Letter from Mrs. Dunlop to Burns dated 7th January 1790. See *Robert Burns and Mrs Dunlop, Correspondence Now Published in Full for the First Time, with elucidations by William Wallace*, Hodder and Stoughton, London, 1898, p. 232. Cited henceforth as Burns and Dunlop.
5. Letter from Gilbert, quoted in Currie, vol. i, p. 130.

Burns, who had been absent when this letter arrived, was hugely flattered at this mark of attention from so distinguished a member of the Ayrshire gentry and the next day he dashed off a long and flowery reply:

> ... I am fully persuaded that there is not any class of Mankind so feelingly alive to the titillation of applause as the Sons of Parnassus; nor is it easy to conceive how the heart of the poor Bard dances with rapture, when those, whose character in life gives them a right to be polite Judges, honor him with their approbation. –

It was the beginning of a remarkable correspondence and friendship which was to last for ten years. He wrote fulsomely about her 'illustrious ancestor, the SAVIOUR OF HIS COUNTRY'; his heart, he told her, had long glowed 'with a wish to be able to make a Song on him equal to his merits.' He could send her only five copies of his book – it was all he could lay his hands on:

> I am thinking to go to Edinburgh in a week or two at farthest, to throw off a second impression of my book: but on my return, I shall certainly do myself the honor to wait on you, and thank you in person for the oblidging notice you have been pleased to take of,
>
>
>
> Madam,
> your much indebted
> and very humble serv[t]
> Robert Burns[1]
>
>

So there it was. Our Scotch Bard was not going 'owre the Sea' to the West Indies after all. He was going the sixty or so miles to the capital to try his luck there with a second edition. Before he did so he had an encounter with another member of the Ayrshire gentry, but it was one which did less for his self-esteem than his correspondence with the chatelaine of Dunlop House.

Burns was in the habit of taking an evening stroll along the banks of the river Ayr, and this occasionally involved trespassing on the land of the Ballochmyle estate. Ballochmyle had recently changed hands, and the new owner was a returned nabob called Claud Alexander, who had made his pile as paymaster-general of the East India Company's troops in Bengal. Alexander had installed himself in the mansion house with his unmarried sister and one evening in the late spring of 1786, Wilhelmina Alexander, taking a turn in the grounds after dinner, had come upon a man leaning against a tree. 'The grounds being forbidden to unauthorised strangers – the evening being far advanced, and the encounter very sudden' she was understandably startled, but, by her own account quickly recovered herself and passed on. Wilhelmina,

1. *Letters*, 55.

a newcomer to those parts, was not to know that she had observed Burns
communing with his Muse. Now, in November, she received a letter from him:

> Madam,
>   Poets are such outré Beings, so much the children of wayward Fancy
> and capricious Whim, that I believe the world generally allows them a larger
> latitude in the rules of Propriety, than the sober Sons of Judgement and
> Prudence . . .

It was Burns at his worst. Perhaps he was a little flushed with his success as
a published poet. Possibly his head had been turned by the flattery of Mrs
Dunlop. At any event he went on at excruciating length about the evening he
had met Miss Alexander:

> 'Twas a golden moment for a poetic heart. – I listened the feathered Warb-
> lers, pouring their harmony on every hand, with a congenial kindred regard;
> and frequently turned out of my path lest I should disturb their little
> songs . . .
>   Even the hoary Hawthorn twig that shot across the way, what heart, at
> such a time, but must have been interested in its welfare, and wished it
> to be preserved from the rudely browsing Cattle, or the withering eastern
> Blast? . . .
>   Such was the scene, and such the hour, when in a corner of my Prospect
> I spyed one of the finest pieces of Nature's workmanship that ever crowned
> a poetic Landskip . . .
>   What an hour of inspiration for a Poet! It would have raised plain, dull,
> historic Prose to Metaphor and Measure![1]

He enclosed the song usually now known as 'The Bony Lass o' Ballochmyle'[2].
Perhaps, he wrote, it 'poorly answers what might have been expected of such
a scene', but might her most obedient and very humble servant have her permission to include it in the second edition of his poems?
    Miss Alexander was taken aback. She was possibly also slightly suspicious.
Who was this forward young rustic – she had taken him for a farmer – who
told her that 'Her look was like the Morning's eye' and expressed the desire
to 'strain her nightly to his bosom?' She was already into her thirties – more
likely to be thought a mature virgin than a bonnie lass. Was he making improper
advances or was he mocking her? Her family said later that she made enquiries
about her correspondent and that the opinions offered about his character were
unfavourable: 'Feeling it to be necessary to decline yielding to his request, she

1. *Ibid.*, 56.
2. Kinsley, 89.

thought that her decision would be intimated most delicately to him by allowing his letter to remain unanswered.'

Burns had a tenacious memory for snubs. Several years later, he could not resist annotating the letter: 'Well Mr Burns, & did the Lady give you the desired "Permission?"—No! She was too fine a Lady to notice so plain a compliment.' Then he directed a squirt of bile at the rest of the Alexander family:

As to her great brothers, whom I have since met in life, on more 'equal' terms of respectability, why should I quarrel their want of attention to me? – When Fate swore that their purses should be full, Nature was equally positive that their heads should be empty. – 'Men of another fashion were surely incapable of being unpolite?' – Ye canna mak a silk-purse o' a sow's lug.

Chambers has a pleasing footnote: 'Miss Alexander and her relatives learned afterwards, however, to think that the woods of Ballochmyle had been rendered classic, and herself immortal by the genius of Burns.'[1] When, years later, a question arose about the disposal of the original manuscript of the song, the lass of Ballochmyle was firm – wherever she went, it must go. She never married, and died in Glasgow in 1843, an old lady of eighty-eight. On the spot where she was supposed to have met Burns, one of her nephews built a rustic summer-house, and in it was hung a framed facsimile of the letter and the song. Known as the Fog House, it stood until 1944, when it was destroyed by vandals.

'I posted to Edinburgh without a single acquaintance in town or a single letter of introduction in my pocket.'[2] Burns's account of his descent on the capital, in his autobiographical letter to Dr Moore, is a shade impressionistic. When he sent the poem 'A Winter's Night' to his friend John Ballantine, the Ayr banker, on November 20th, it is clear from his covering letter that 'Orator Bob' at least had been active on his behalf: 'I hear of no return from Edin^r to Mr Aiken respecting my second Edition business; so I am thinking to set out beginning of next week, for the City myself.'[3]

He was in high spirits during his last days at home. He amused himself by sending off to two friends a 'nefarious, abominable, and wicked SONG or BALLAD' which he said he had discovered – presumably a recent bawdy composition of his own – enjoining them to have it burned at the Cross of Ayr. His letter to them is couched in the form of a mock writ, and he ascribes to

1. Chambers Wallace, vol. i, p. 446.
2. Letters, 125.
3. *Ibid.*, 59.

himself the title of 'POET-LAUREAT and BARD IN CHIEF in and over the Districts and Countries of Kyle, Cunningham, and Carrick, of old extent.'[1]

A friend called George Reid, a farmer at Barquharie, near Ochiltree, lent him a pony. Early on the morning of November 27th – it was a Monday – Burns pointed the beast's head eastwards and rode for the first time beyond the boundaries of those native districts and countries.

---

1. *Ibid.*, 58. The recipients were William Chalmers, who was a lawyer in Ayr, and John M'Adam, a wealthy landowner and agricultural improver. Burns addressed them as 'Students and Practitioners in the ancient and mysterious Science of Confounding Right and Wrong.'

Six

TANGENT FLIGHT

IT TOOK BURNS TWO DAYS to travel the sixty miles to Edinburgh. He had to spend the day after his arrival in bed. Chambers talks charitably of indisposition, but it is more likely that he had a hangover.

He had spent the night near Biggar in Lanarkshire. George Reid, the man who lent him his pony, had a friend there who farmed Covington Mains. Burns's fame had gone before him, and the farmers of the neighbourhood were anxious to make his acquaintance. Many years later, his host's son recalled the arrangements:

> They were all asked to meet him at a late dinner, and the signal of his arrival was to be a white sheet attached to a pitchfork, and put on the top of a cornstack in the barnyard . . . At length Burns arrived, mounted on a pownie . . . Instantly was the white flag hoisted, and as instantly were the farmers seen issuing from their houses, and converging to the point of meeting. A glorious evening, or rather night, which borrowed something from the morning, followed . . .[1]

There had been much excitement in Edinburgh on the day of Burns's arrival – not on his account, but because of the inauguration of a greatly improved service to London, with Palmer's mail-carriages offering to convey letters there in the unheard-of time of sixty hours. Edinburgh was no longer the seat of Scottish government, but it remained the chief city of North Britain, and anything that contributed to its importance as a centre of trade and commerce, not to mention learning and the arts, was grist to the mill of the City fathers.

It was more than sixty years since an Act of Parliament had sanctioned the

---

1. Letter dated 8th March 1841 from Archibald Prentice to Professor Wilson and published in the *Edinburgh Intelligencer*. Prentice, who later settled in England, and was the founder-editor of the *Manchester Times*, recalled a visit to Ayrshire in 1809 when he met a number of people who had known Burns: 'The men of strong minds and strong feelings were invariable in their expressions of admiration; but the prosy consequential *bodies* all disliked him as exceeding dictatorial. The men whose religion was based on intellect and high moral sentiment all thought well of him: but the mere professors, with their "two-mile prayers and half-mile graces," denounced him as "worse than an infidel".'

spending of money on 'narrowing the noxious lake on the north side of the said City, commonly called the North Loch.' Then, in 1752, after the sudden collapse of a six-storey building, there was published a pamphlet entitled 'Proposals for carrying on certain Public Works in the City of Edinburgh'. The document set out the inconveniences of the old part of the city:

> Placed upon a ridge of a hill, it admits but of one good street, running from east to west; and even this is tolerably accessible only from one quarter. The narrow lanes leading to the north and south, by reason of their steepness, narrowness, and dirtiness, can only be considered as so many unavoidable nuisances. Confined by the small compass of the walls, and the narrow limits of the royalty, which scarcely extends beyond the walls, the houses stand more crowded than in any other town in Europe, and are built to a height that is almost incredible.

Although the Georgian elegance of the New Town had been taking shape for some time when Burns first saw Edinburgh, it was the crowded Old Town of John Knox and Mary Queen of Scots which was still the heart of the capital. Newcomers to the city were invariably impressed. When Daniel Defoe first saw the High Street in the 1720s he thought it 'the largest, longest and finest Street for buildings and Number of Inhabitants, not in Britain only, but in the World.'[1] What was pleasing to the eye did not, however, always fall sweetly on the other senses:

> No smells were ever equal to Scotch smells. It is the school of physic; walk the streets, and you would imagine that every medical man had been administering cathartics to every man, woman and child in the town. Yet the place is uncommonly beautiful, and I am in a constant balance between admiration and trepidation –
>
> > Taste guides my eye, where'er new beauties spread
> > While prudence whispers, 'Look before you tread'.

Such was the impression which the slop-pails of Edinburgh made on the Reverend Sydney Smith, and he was writing twelve years or so after Burns first encountered them.[2] Smith was to find his first lodgings in South Hanover

---

1. Daniel Defoe, *A Tour through the Whole Island of Great Britain. Originally begun by the celebrated Daniel DeFoe, continued by the late Mr Richardson, author of Clarissa, etc., and brought down to the present time by Gentlemen of Eminence in the Literary world*, 4 vols, printed for Strahan, London, 1778. 1927 ed. vol ii, p. 708.
2. Letter to M.H. Beach, 30th June 1798, quoted in *Sydney Smith, A Biography*, by Alan Bell, Clarendon Press, Oxford, 1980, p. 15. Burns would have approved of Smith. 'I like this place extremely,' he wrote to another friend soon after his arrival in Edinburgh. 'It unites good libraries liberally managed, learned men without any system than that of pursuing truth; very good general society; large healthy virgins, with mild pleasing countenances, and white swelling breasts . . .' Letter to J.G. Clarke, 5th December 1798.

Street, in the relative salubrity of the New Town; Burns, on that evening of 28th November, 1786, made his way to the top of the Royal Mile, just below the Castle. His friend John Richmond had a room in Baxter's Close in the Lawnmarket and had offered to put him up. Richmond had been paying a rent of half-a-crown a week; when Mrs Carfrae, his landlady, heard he had a lodger, she put it up to three shillings. The room had a sanded floor and Burns's eighteen pence bought him the use of a deal table and a half-share in Richmond's chaff bed.

Burns painted for his friend Ballantine a vivid word-picture of Mrs Carfrae – 'a staid, sober, piously-disposed, sculdudery-abhoring Widow, coming on her grand climacterick' – and regaled him with an account of what went on elsewhere in Baxter's Close:

> She is at present in sore tribulation respecting some "Daughters of Belial" who are on the floor immediately above ... and as our floors are low and ill-plaistered, we can easily distinguish our laughter-loving, night-rejoicing neighbours – when they are eating, when they are drinking, when they are singing, when they are &c. ... Just now she told me, though by the by she is sometimes dubious that I am, in her own phrase, "but a rough and roun' Christian" that "We should not be uneasy and envious because the wicked enjoy the good things of this life; for these base jades who, in her own words, lie up gandygoing with their filthy fellows, drinking the best of wines, and singing abominable songs, they shall one day lie in hell, weeping and wailing and gnashing their teeth over a cup of God's wrath!"[1]

Edinburgh was no longer the decorous town Burns's father had known a generation and more earlier. One of those who tried his hand over the years at recording the passing scene was William Creech, who was to become Burns's publisher, and who in his posthumous *Edinburgh Fugitive Pieces* catalogued ways in which the life of the capital had changed between the 1760s and the 1780s. Sunday observance, he noted, particularly by men, had greatly declined, and families now 'thought it ungenteel to take their domestics to church with them.' That, however, was by no means the worst of it:

> In no respect were the manners of 1763 and 1783 more remarkable than in the decency, dignity, and delicacy of the one period, compared with the looseness, dissipation, and licentiousness of the other. Many people ceased to blush at what would formerly have been reckoned a crime ...

Creech had done his sums, and backed these assertions with statistics. In 1763, for instance, fines collected by the kirk treasure for bastard children had amounted to £154; twenty years later they amounted to £600. He also appeared

---

1. Letters, 77. The tall houses in the Old Town, piled 'close and massy, deep and high,' were generally arranged in small flats, with nobility, tradespeople and the common folk of the town living cheek by jowl within the compass of a single close or staircase.

to have done some serious fieldwork into the sort of shenanigins that kept decent folk like Mrs Carfrae awake at night in Baxter's Close:

> In 1763 – There were about five or six brothels or houses of bad fame in Edinburgh, and a very few only of the lowest and most ignorant order of females skulked about at night. A person might have walked from the Castle-hill to the Abbey, without being accosted by a single prostitute. The only one of the impure tribe who could afford a silk gown, was a Charlotte Davidson, who had been a servant maid, and afterwards died mad.

> In 1783 – The number of brothels and houses of civil accommodation are increased to some hundreds; and the *women of the town* are more than in equal proportion. Every quarter of the city and the suburbs is infested with multitudes of females, abandoned to vice, and many of them before passion could mislead, or reason teach them right from wrong. Many mothers live by the prostitution of their daughters. Gentlemen's and citizen's daughters are upon the town, who, by their dress and bold deportment, in the face of day, seem to tell us that the term WH–E ceases to be a reproach.[1]

Edinburgh was also a hard-drinking town. Robert Chambers devoted a chapter in his *Traditions of Edinburgh* to what he called 'Convivialia'. 'Tavern dissipation,' he writes, 'formerly prevailed in Edinburgh to an incredible extent, and engrossed the leisure hours of all professional men, scarcely excepting even the most stern and dignified.' It was not unusual, he adds, to find two or three of His Majesty's most honourable Lords of Council and Session 'mounting the bench in the forenoon in a crapulous state.'[2] In some private houses, a couple of sturdy Highlanders were retained to carry guests back to their quarters. E.B. Ramsay, who was Dean of Edinburgh, retailed a story he had from Henry Mackenzie:

> He had been involved in a regular drinking party. He was keeping as free from the usual excesses as he was able, and as he marked companions around him falling victim to the power of drink, he himself dropped off under the table among the slain, as a measure of precaution, and lying there, his attention was called to a small pair of hands working at his throat; on asking what it was, a voice replied, "Sir, I'm the lad that's to louse the neckcloths."[3]

It was not only Burns's reputation as a poet that had preceded him to Edinburgh. It is clear from a letter he wrote three days after his arrival that the wagging of tongues over the Armour affair had also carried well beyond the

---

1. William Creech, *Edinburgh Fugitive Pieces*, Edinburgh, 1791, p. 81.
2. Robert Chambers, *Traditions of Edinburgh*, Chambers, Edinburgh, 1824, revised edition 1868, p. 138.
3. E.B. Ramsay, *Reminiscences of Scottish Life and Character*, 5th ed., Edmonston and Douglas, Edinburgh, 1859, p. 36.

bounds of Ayrshire. He had heard that Sir John Whitefoord, the former Master of his Masonic Lodge in Tarbolton and now an Edinburgh resident, had come to his defence, and he wrote an effusive letter of thanks:

> ... I was surprised to hear that any one, who pretended in the least to the manners of the gentleman, should be so foolish, or worse, as to stoop to traduce the morals of such a one as I am, and so inhumanely cruel, too, as to meddle with that late most unfortunate, unhappy part of my story. With a tear of gratitude, I thank you, Sir, for the warmth with which you interposed in behalf of my conduct. I am, I acknowledge, too frequently the sport of whim, caprice, and passion – but reverence to GOD, and integrity to my fellow-creatures, I hope I shall ever preserve ...[1]

Whitefoord sent a friendly reply, saying he did not have much influence but that he would do anything he could to help. He also made a suggestion:

> I have been told you wished to be made a gauger; I submit it to your consideration, whether it would not be more desirable, if a sum could be raised by subscription for a second edition of your poems, to lay it out in the stocking of a small farm. I am persuaded it would be a line of life much more agreeable to your feelings, and in the end more satisfactory.[2]

Arrangements for that second edition were put in hand with impressive speed, even though Burns was plagued for a time with a bad head and some sort of stomach upset. Subscription bills were ready in little more than a week, and on December 14th it was advertised by the bookseller and publisher William Creech — 'in the press, to be published by subscription for the sole benefit of the Author.'

Creech, with his black silk breeches and powdered hair, was the leading Edinburgh publisher of the day. He sat on the town council and was Secretary of the Chamber of Commerce. He lived in Craig's Close, off the High Street. Literary Edinburgh and the printing trade mingled there each morning at what was known as Creech's Levee; those who attended were drawn more by the conversation than the grudging scale of the refreshments.[3] Canny, good natured and famously tight-fisted, Creech had raised the late settlement of accounts to

1. Letters, 61. Whitefoord had been the previous owner of the Ballochmyle estate, but had been forced to sell by the heavy losses he had incurred as a shareholder in Douglas, Heron and Co.'s bank.
2. Quoted in Chambers-Wallace, vol. ii, p. 16.
3. His shop also exercised a powerful attraction. Cockburn described it as 'this bower of the muses'. It was, he wrote, 'the natural resort of lawyers, authors, and all sorts of literary idlers, who were always buzzing about the convenient hive. All who wished to see a poet or a stranger, or to hear the public news, the last joke by Erskine, or yesterday's occurrence in the Parliament House ... congregated there.' Henry Cockburn, *Memorials of His Time*, Adam and Charles Black, Edinburgh 1856, pp. 169-70.

an art form. In the matter of the second edition he agreed essentially to act as Burns's agent. He signed up for five hundred subscription copies at five shillings (which, when sold for six shillings, would make him, in his capacity as a bookseller, a profit of £25). That was the extent of his commitment – Burns had to find his own printer and binder.

Burns produced very little poetry during the five months he stayed in Edinburgh, but he dashed off a stream of sometimes breathless letters, mostly to friends in Ayrshire, and more than forty of these have survived. 'I am in a fair way of becoming as eminent as Thomas a Kempis or John Bunyan,' he wrote jubilantly to Gavin Hamilton, little more than a week after his arrival:

> . . . you may expect henceforth to see my birthday inserted among the wonderful events, in the Poor Robin's and Aberdeen Almanacks, along with the black Monday, & the battle of Bothwel bridge . . . by all probability I shall soon be the tenth Worthy, and the eighth Wise Man, of the world.[1]

When he wrote to his friend John Ballantyne, the Ayr banker, six days later, he told him that he had been introduced 'to a good many of the noblesse.' These included the boisterous Duchess of Gordon, remembered in her younger days for riding down the Royal Mile on the back of a sow. Born Jane Maxwell, the daughter of a Wigtownshire baronet, her Grace of Gordon had good looks (captured by Reynolds), a quick wit and a coarse tongue. Twenty years of marriage to the fourth duke – she had borne him seven children[2] – had done nothing to repress her vitality; as she entered her forties she still relentlessly burned the candle at both ends. In the winter before Burns's arrival in the capital a lawyer called Drummond sent an account of her to a friend in India. 'The example of dissipation set by her Grace the Duchess of Gordon is far from showing vice her own image,' he wrote censoriously:

> It is really astonishing to think what effect a single person will have on public manners, when supported by high rank and great address. She is never absent from a public place, and the later the hour, so much the better. It is often four o'clock in the morning before she goes to bed, and she never requires more than five hours' sleep. Dancing, cards, and company occupy her whole time.[3]

1. Letters, 62. *Poor Robin's* and the *Aberdeen Almanack*, which both dated from the seventeenth century, were forerunners of *Old Moore's Almanac*. Their prophecies of future events were immensely popular and they had large circulations. Black Monday was Easter Monday, 1360. Edward III was lying before Paris with his army. The day was dark and bitterly cold, with wind and hail, and the king lost many of his horses and men. Bothwell Brig was the battle at which the Covenanters were defeated by Monmouth in 1679.
2. Her hopes that her eldest daughter would marry William Pitt were disappointed, but she did well as a matchmaker – three daughters became duchesses, one a marchioness. The fifth had to settle for a baronet.
3. Quoted in Chambers-Wallace, vol. ii, p. 72.

Tory hostess in London, arbiter of fashion in Edinburgh, the Duchess, by inviting Burns into her drawing room, ensured his admission to many others. Years later she told Sir Walter Scott that she had never met a man 'whose conversation so completely carried her off her feet.'[1]

If there were those who patronised him out of curiosity, Burns also encountered much genuine solicitude and friendship. 'I have met in Mr Dalrymple of Orangefield,' he told Hamilton, 'what Solomon emphatically calls, "a Friend that sticketh closer than a Brother".' James Dalrymple was an Ayrshire landowner and the nephew of the man who had baptised him. He performed two important services for Burns. In the week after his arrival he took him along to a meeting of the Canongate Kilwinning Lodge of Freemasons. He also introduced him to the Earl of Glencairn, who was his wife's nephew: 'The providential care of a good God placed me under the patronage of one of his noblest creatures,' Burns wrote to Moore the following year. '"*Oublie moi, Grand Dieu, si jamais je l'oublie!*"'[2]

Glencairn, a handsome bachelor ten years older than Burns, had served for four years as one of the Representative Scots peers in the House of Lords. There was already a connection of a sort, because he was also the patron of the living of Kilmarnock, and it was therefore he, in bowing the previous year to the parishioners' preference for an Auld Licht candidate, who had inspired Burns to write 'The Ordination'. That was no indication of the fourteenth Earl's own views, however. He now welcomed Burns into his home, and he and his mother, the Dowager Countess, put their names down for twenty-four copies of the poems. Even better, Glencairn got to work on his fellow-members of the Caledonian Hunt, whose interests did not normally extend beyond field sports, dancing assemblies and going to the races. 'Through my Lord's influence,' Burns wrote excitedly to Hamilton, 'it is inserted in the records of the Caledonian Hunt, that they universally, one & all, subscribe for the 2^d Edition.'[3]

The friendship of Henry Erskine was also important to Burns. Erskine, who had served as Lord Advocate in 1783 and had recently, at the age of forty, been elected Dean of the Faculty, was the second son of the tenth Earl of Buchan and was connected with Glencairn by marriage. Like so many of those who befriended Burns in Edinburgh, he was a freemason – they first met on the night of Burns's visit to the Canongate Kilwinning Lodge, of which Erskine was Past-Master. A Whig in politics, and an extremely clever lawyer, his popularity was not confined to his own class: he was affectionately known as 'Plead for all, or the poor man's lawyer.' 'Nothing was so sour,' wrote Lord Cockburn,

1. Lockhart, *op. cit.*, p. 173.
2. Letters, 125.
3. It is possible that it was Glencairn who introduced Burns to Creech. The two men had been at school together, and Creech had later accompanied Glencairn on the Grand Tour. In a letter to his friend 'Orator Bob' on December 16th, on the other hand, Burns wrote that he had found in Creech 'that honor and goodness of heart which I always expect in Mr Aiken's friends.' (Letters, 65.)

'as not to be sweetened by the glance, the voice, the gaiety, the beauty of Henry Erskine.' He was also noted for his wit. When Dr. Johnson visited Edinburgh, it was Erskine who slipped a shilling into Boswell's hand and said, 'For the sight of your bear!'

Almost a decade and a half had passed since then, however, and the Edinburgh of the late 1770s could not match the brilliance of the early years of the Enlightenment. Adam Smith still occasionally gave his celebrated 'Sunday suppers' but he was now in his middle sixties and in indifferent health.[1] The cauliflower wig and cocked hat of William Robertson were also seen less than before; Principal of the University and Moderator of the General Assembly, his *History of Scotland* had made him famous in the year of Burns's birth, but he too was now in visible decline. The plump figure of David Hume had been gone from the scene for more than a decade, and it was four years since the death of Henry Home, Lord Kames. Philosopher and judge, literary critic and agricultural improver, Kames had crossed swords impartially with the Kirk and with Voltaire. He was one of the last of the old school who spoke Scots in the courts: when the time came to bid farewell to his brother judges he did so by shaking hands all round and saying, 'Fare ye a' weel, ye auld bitches.'

Kames was not the only occupant of the Scottish bench to combine eccentricity with literary interests. There was the hard-drinking and valetudinarian Lord Gardenstone, who had fought as a volunteer against the Highland army during the '45 and narrowly escaped being hanged as a spy. He also kept a pet pigling, which followed him around like a dog and was permitted to sleep in his bed: 'When it attained the years and bulk of swinehood this was attended with inconvenience; but, unwilling to part with his companion, Lord Gardenstone, when he undressed, laid his clothes on the floor, as a bed for it, and that he might find his clothes warm in the winter mornings.'[2]

Possibly oddest of all was James Burnett, Lord Monboddo. A Lord of Session since 1767, he was for many years a close friend of James Boswell, the son of one of his colleagues on the bench; it was only recently that the younger man's rudeness and indiscretion had brought the friendship to an end.[3] People said Monboddo looked like an old stuffed monkey in judge's robes, but his appearance was not thought less strange than some of his beliefs. He published, over twenty years, a six-volume treatise entitled *Of the Origin and Progress of Language*. 'That part of it which treats of barbarous nations will be for popular use,' he wrote to a friend, 'and will tempt even the vulgar to

---

1. Mrs Dunlop provided a letter of introduction to Smith, who was then Commissioner of Customs for Scotland and could therefore have been helpful to Burns in his ambitions to enter the Excise. Smith, however, had set off for London the day before the letter arrived. He had been suffering all winter from a chronic obstruction of the bowel and had gone to consult his friend John Hunter, the eminent surgeon.

2. James Grant, *Old and New Edinburgh: Its History, its People, and its Places*. 6 vols., Cassell, Petter, Galpin and Co, London, Paris and New York, 1883, vol. i, p. 172.

3. See E. L. Cloyd, *James Burnett, Lord Monboddo*, Clarendon Press, Oxford, 1972.

look into it.'[1] The vulgar did, and greatly enjoyed his stories from Diodorus Siculus of 'insensibles' who 'lived promiscuously with other animals, and particularly with seals'; they also learned that the Nicobar Islands were inhabited by 'men with tails like those of cats, and which they moved in the same manner.'[2]

Monboddo was, for all that, a man of deep learning and singular eloquence. He also kept an excellent cellar. His house was in St. John's Street, in the Canongate, and when he entertained there, the claret was served, in Horatian style, from flasks garlanded with roses. It was not long before Burns received an invitation; the farm on which his father had been brought up in Kincardineshire was on the Monboddo estate.

Then as now, everybody in Edinburgh knew everybody else, and little passed unnoticed. Mrs Alison Cockburn, celebrated for her wit and beauty as well as for her version of 'The Flowers of the Forest', had seen sixty Edinburgh seasons come and go, and she wrote about Burns in a gossipy letter to a friend in the country:

> The town is at present agog with the ploughman poet, who receives adulation with native dignity, and is the very figure of his profession, strong and coarse, but has a most enthusiastic heart of love. He has seen Duchess Gordon and all the gay world: his favourite for looks and manners is Bess Burnet – no bad judge, indeed.[3]

Mrs Cockburn was well-informed. Burns was indeed mightily taken with Lord Monboddo's second daughter and described her rapturously to his friend William Chalmers, in Ayr: 'There has not been any thing nearly like her, in all the combinations of Beauty, Grace, and Goodness, the Great Creator has formed, since Milton's Eve on the first day of her existence.'[4]

Miss Eliza, as Burns called her, occasionally tried her hand at poetry and was generally acknowledged to be very accomplished; her new admirer worked a compliment to her into his lumbering 'Address to Edinburgh' which he composed that December:

> Fair B— strikes th' adoring eye,
> Heav'n's beauties on my fancy shine;

1. The first volume was published by Kincaid & Creech, Edinburgh, and T. Cadell, London, in 1773; the remaining five appeared under a variety of imprints between then and 1792.
2. Monboddo had read about the Nicobar Islanders in a book by a Swedish sailor called Koeping, mentioned in the works of the celebrated taxonomist Carolus Linnaeus. Monboddo wrote to Linnaeus, who sent him a copy of the book, saying that the author appeared to him to be simple and straightforward. See Cloyd, *op. cit.*, p. 43.
3. Quoted in Sarah Tytler and Jean L. Watson, *The Songstresses of Scotland*, 2 vols., H. B. Higgins, Edinburgh 1871, vol. ii, p, 180.
4. Letters, 68.

I see the *Sire of Love* on high,
And own his work indeed divine![1]

The female society he encountered in the capital was something for which Burns was quite unprepared. Robert Cromek, long underrated as an early source, records a revealing comment which he picked up on one of his early-nineteenth-century Scottish visits and attributes to Burns himself: 'Between the men of rustic life and the polite world he observed little difference,' he wrote:

> . . . In the former, though unpolished by fashion, and unenlightened by science, he had found much observation and much intelligence, – but a refined and accomplished woman was a being almost new to him, and of which he had formed but a very inadequate idea.[2]

It is plain, however, from a scrap of a letter to Gavin Hamilton, written in the first week of 1787, that an earlier emotional tie had not been entirely severed:

> . . . To tell the truth among friends, I feel a miserable blank in my heart, with want of her, and I don't think I shall ever meet with so delicious an armful again. She has her faults; and so have you and I; and so has every body.

>> Their tricks and craft hae put me daft;
>> They've ta'en me in and a' that;
>> But clear your decks, and here's the Sex,
>> I like the jads for a' that . . .

The verse he quotes is from 'The Jolly Beggars' and he is clearly referring to Jean Armour. Having done so, however, he goes on to tell Hamilton of a current pursuit:

1. Kinsley, 135. Long years later, Edinburgh opinion, never comfortable with superlatives, supplied a corrective to such extravagance. In 1834 an elderly Writer to the Signet called Alexander Young, who had been a tyro lawyer at the time of Burns's first Edinburgh visit, jotted down a memoir. 'She was remarkably handsome and a very amiable young woman,' he recalled. 'She had one great personal defect however – her teeth were much decayed and discoloured – but fortunately she had a very small mouth, and took care not to open it much in mixed company.' His friend Charles Hope, by then Lord Granton, who lived long enough to wear the robes of Lord Justice-General at the proclamation of Queen Victoria, obligingly rounded out the picture: 'She had very thick, clumsy ancles, which She was at pains to conceal by wearing her petticoats uncommonly long – and she was not a good Dancer – but take her in all she was a beautiful creature.' (Quoted in Fitzhugh, *op. cit.*, pp. 79 and 100.) It was all one to Fair Burnet. Four years after dazzling Burns, she had been carried off by consumption.
2. R.H. Cromek, *Reliques of Robert Burns*, Cadell and Davies, London, 1808, pp. 68-9.

> I have met with a very pretty girl, a Lothian farmer's daughter, whom I have almost persuaded to accompany me to the west country, should I ever return to settle there ... I had a most delicious ride from Leith to her house yesternight in a hackney coach, with her brother and two sisters, and brother's wife. We had dined all together at a common friend's house in Leith, and danced, drank, and sang till late enough. The night was dark, the claret had been good, and I thirsty ...[1]

Another letter, written at about the same time, indicates that Burns's eye roamed no less freely in Edinburgh than it had done in Ayrshire, and that his heart, as he put it later in his autobiographical letter to Moore, was no less 'compleatly tinder':

> I am so impatient to show you that I am once more at peace with you, that I send you the book I mentioned directly, rather than wait the uncertain time of my seeing you ...
>
> I know you will laugh at it, when I tell you that your Piano and you together have play'd the deuce somehow, about my heart. – I was once a zealous Devotee to your Sex, but you know the black story at home. My breast has been widowed these many months, and I thought myself proof against the fascinating witchcraft; but I am afraid you will 'feelingly convince me what I am.' – I say I am afraid, because I am not sure what is the matter with me. – I have one miserable bad symptom: when you whisper, or look kindly to another, it gives me a draught of damnation. – I have a kind of wayward wish to be with you ten minutes by yourself; though, what I would say, Heaven above knows, for I am sure, I know not. – I have no formed design in all this; but just in the nakedness of my heart write you down a meer matter-of-fact story. – You may perhaps give yourself airs of distance on this, and that will completely cure me; but I wish you would not: just let us meet if you please in the old, beaten way of friendship ...[2]

We do not know who the recipient was. Burns addresses her as 'My Dr Country-woman' – it is possible that she was a young woman called Peggy Chalmers, whose father had owned a farm near Mauchline, and who was related to Gavin Hamilton (her mother and Hamilton's stepmother were sisters). Burns may well have met her in Ayrshire and certainly encountered her in Edinburgh, where she used to sing and read for Dr Blacklock. It is known that she told Thomas Campbell, the poet, that Burns had once proposed to her, but whether this was during his time in Edinburgh or on some other occasion is unclear. When Chambers was writing his biography, an unidentified relative of Miss Chalmers furnished him with a pen-portrait of her: 'In early life, when her

1. Letters, 72.
2. *Ibid.*, 76.

hazel eyes were large and bright, and her teeth white and regular, her face must have had a charm not always the result or the accompaniment of fine features. She was little, but her figure was perfect ... She rarely talked of books, but greatly liked reading. She spoke readily and well, but preferred listening to others ...[1]

A few weeks later, in reply to a rhyming epistle from James Dalrymple, Burns tells his friend, somewhat coyly, that his relations with Cupid have recently improved:

For the blind, mischief-making little urchin of a Deity, you mention, he and I have been sadly at odds ever since some dog tricks he play'd me not half a century ago. – I have compromised matters with his godship of late by uncoupling my heart and fancy, for a slight chase, after a certain Edin^r Belle. – My devotions proceed no farther than a forenoon's walk, a sentimental conversation, now and then a squeeze of the hand or interchanging an *oeillade*, and when peculiar good humor and sequestered propriety allow –

– "Brethren, salute one another with a holy kiss." – Paul[2]

We hear no more of this uncharacteristically decorous flirtation. Nor do we read anything in the letters which survive from this period of Burns's much less decorous relationship with a young domestic servant called Margaret or May Cameron, whom he seduced in the spring of 1787. It was an involvement that was going to cause him a good deal of trouble later in the year.

Since his arrival in Edinburgh Burns had benefitted from further useful publicity in the *Edinburgh Magazine*. James Sibbald had followed up the review of the Kilmarnock edition published in his October issue by reprinting a number of the poems, and early in the New Year, Burns wrote a gracious letter of appreciation, which he embellished with a paraphrase of some lines from Othello: '– Rude am I in speech,/ 'And little blest with the set, polished phrase ...'[3]

His best letters, however – easy, unbuttoned, entertaining – were written to old and trusted friends and patrons in Ayrshire. Writing to Ballantine in the middle of January he described a masonic occasion he had attended the pre-

1. Chambers-Wallace, vol. ii, p. 207(n). On the evidence of another letter written at about this time the recipient of the 'Dear Countrywoman' letter could also have been Christina Lawrie, the daughter of his friend the minister of Loudoun: 'By far the most agreeable hours I spend in Edin" Burns wrote to Lawrie (he consistently spelt his name with an 'o'), 'must be placed to the account of Miss Lowrie and her Piano forte.' (*Letters*, 80.)
2. Letters, 84. Burns is misquoting Corinthians, 16:20.
3. *Ibid.*, 71. The speech occurs in Act 1, Scene iii.

vious evening. It had been held at St Andrew's Lodge, and a good many of the top brass of the order were present:

> The Grand Master who presided with great solemnity, and honor to himself as a Gentleman and Mason, among other general toasts gave, "Caledonia, and Caledonia's Bard, brother B–," which rung through the whole Assembly with multiplied honors and repeated acclamations. – As I had no idea such a thing would happen, I was downright thunderstruck, and trembling in every nerve made the best return in my power.

Burns told Ballantine that although he still had no idea what the future held for him, a generous friend had floated the idea of leasing a farm on an estate he had recently bought near Dumfries. The friend was Patrick Miller – his was the 'unknown hand' who had left ten guineas for him with Sibbald shortly after he arrived in town. Miller was much older than Burns. He was a brother of the President of the Court of Session and had been a director of the Bank of Scotland. He was a man of many enthusiasms – he put money into the construction of a catamaran with hand-driven paddles – and saw the run-down estate he had bought at Dalswinton as a laboratory for experiments in scientific agriculture. Burns's account of the offer to Ballantine gives the clear impression that he had reacted with proper peasant caution: 'Some life-rented, embittered Recollections whisper me that I will be happier any where than in my old neighbourhood, but Mr Miller is no Judge of land; and though I dare say he means to favour me, yet he may give me, in his opinion, an advantageous bargain that may ruin me.'[1]

That letter was written on January 14th. Unaccountably, Burns's reservations evaporated overnight. The very next morning he sat down and wrote to Miller accepting his proposition with extravagant expressions of gratitude:

> When you kindly offered to accommodate me with a Farm, I was afraid to think of it, as I knew my circumstances unequal to the proposal; but now, when by the appearances of my second edition of my book, I may reckon on a middling farming capital, there is nothing I wish for more than to resume the Plough. – Indolence and Innatention [sic] to business I have been sometimes guilty of, but I thank my God, Dissipation or Extravagance have never been a part of my character. – If therefore, Sir, you could fix me in any sequester'd romantic spot, and let me have such a Lease as by care and industry I might live in humble decency, and have a spare hour now and then to write out an idle rhyme, or wait on you, my honored Benefactor, with my grateful respects, when you were in my neighborhood – I am afraid,

1. *Ibid.*, 77.

Sir, to dwell on the idea, lest Fortune have not such happiness in store for me. – [1]

For the moment, in the depth of the Edinburgh winter, he had plenty to occupy him. By the middle of January he had corrected 152 pages of proofs. The printing of the new edition had been undertaken by William Smellie. Burns attended to his proofs perched on a stool in the printer's composing room in Anchor Close, off the High Street, although according to Smellie's son, Alexander, he was not the most diligent of authors in this regard: 'Burns would walk up and down the room three or four times, cracking a whip which he carried, to the no small surprise of the men. He paid no attention to any of his own copy that might be in hand, but looked at any other which he saw lying in the cases. One day he asked a man how many languages he was acquainted with. "Indeed, sir," replied the man, "I've enough ado wi' my ain".'[2]

Smellie, the son of a stone mason, was a man of 46 when he and Burns first met. He had printed for Fergusson and Adam Smith, translated Buffon and written many of the articles for the first edition of the *Encyclopædia Britannica*, which had appeared weekly in sixpenny numbers between 1768 and 1771. His interests included Hebrew, Scottish antiquities and botany (he had taken up the cudgels against some of the views of Linnæus). 'Old sinfull Smellie' became a trusted friend, and Burns was later to write about him with affectionate regard:

> His grisly beard just bristling in its might,
> 'Twas four long nights and days from shaving-night;
> His uncomb'd, hoary locks, wild-staring, thatch'd,
> A head for thought profound and clear unmatch'd:
> Yet, tho' his caustic wit was biting rude,
> His heart was warm, benevolent and good.[3]

The friendship between the two men lasted until Smellie's death in 1795. The flavour of their extensive correspondence can now only be guessed at. Robert Kerr, the author of a volume of biography which appeared in 1811, wrote: 'Many letters of Burns to Mr Smellie which remained, being totally unfit for publication, and several of them containing severe reflections on many respectable people still in life, have been burnt.'[4]

Burns was well aware of the importance to him of the Edinburgh literary and professional classes, and he had quickly renewed his acquaintance with

1. *Ibid.*, 78A.
2. Chambers-Wallace, vol. ii, p. 52
3. Kinsley, 335.
4. Robert Kerr, *Memoirs of the Life, Writings and Correspondence of William Smellie*, 2 vols, Edinburgh, 1811, vol.ii, p. 350.

Dugald Stewart. Within a fortnight of his arrival he could boast to Ballantine that he had met both Hugh Blair, the minister of St Giles and William Greenfield, the Professor of Rhetoric. Most exciting of all, he had been introduced to Henry Mackenzie, author of *The Man of Feeling*.

Mackenzie, an attorney in taxation by profession, was one of the most illustrious names in the polite literature of the day. *The Man of Feeling*, much influenced by Sterne, had been published anonymously in 1771, when he was 26, and enjoyed immediate success; some critics have suggested that it in turn influenced Goethe in the writing of *Werther* which appeared three years later.

In 1779–80 Mackenzie had edited the *Mirror*, a folio sheet published weekly at 3 halfpence. Some of its contents so closely resembled those of the *Spectator* that there were murmurings of plagiarism: when it failed, Mackenzie raised the plaintive cry of provincial literati down the ages, blaming 'the fastidiousness with which in a place so narrow as Edinburgh, home productions are commonly received'. Since 1785, with the same contributors, he had been editing the *Lounger*. He wrote more than half the contents himself, and he was the author of an unsigned essay which appeared in the issue of December 9 – 'Surprising effects of Original Genius, exemplified in the Poetical Productions of Robert Burns, an Ayrshire Ploughman'.

To the modern eye, the tone of the review is as intensely patronising as the title:

. . . In mentioning the circumstances of his humble station, I mean not to rest his pretension solely on that title, or to urge the merits of his poetry when considered in relation to the lowness of his birth, and the little opportunity of improvement, which his education could afford. These particulars, indeed, might excite our wonder at his productions; but his poetry, considered abstractedly, and without the apologies arising from his situation, seems to me fully intitled to command our feelings, and to obtain our applause . . .

Mackenzie detected one bar which the poet's birth and education had 'opposed to his fame' and that was the language in which most of the poems were written. This 'provincial dialect', he believed, was now read only with difficulty, and would greatly dampen the pleasure of the reader – in England, without constant reference to the glossary, it could not be read at all.

The more anodyne poems in the collection won his approval; 'The Vision' struck him as 'solemn and sublime', he thought well of the gloomier English poems and found tender and moral passages to admire in 'Man was made to mourn', 'The Cotter's Saturday Night' and 'To a Mouse'. He also singled out 'To a Mountain Daisy' – 'This last poem I shall insert, not from its superior merit, but because its length suits the bounds of my Paper.'

Mackenzie concluded by drawing the attention of his readers to Burns's 'situation and circumstances', acknowledging that in doing so he might wrong the poet's feelings, while indulging his own:

> That condition, humble as it was, in which he found content, and wooed the muse, might not have been deemed uncomfortable; but grief and misfortunes have reached him there; and one or two of his poems hint, what I have learnt from some of his countrymen, that he has been obliged to form the resolution of leaving his native land, to seek under a West Indian clime that shelter and support which Scotland has denied him. I trust means may be found to prevent this resolution from taking place; and that I do my country no more than justice, when I suppose her ready to stretch out her hand to cherish and retain this native poet, whose 'wood-notes wild' possess so much excellence.[1]

Thus was born the legend of the 'Heaven-taught ploughman'. As an essay in criticism, Mackenzie's review was truly dreadful and something of its unwitting distortion of the true nature of Burns's genius survives to the present day. As an exercise in drumming up support for a second edition, on the other hand, it was invaluable. Burns himself certainly saw nothing to complain about: 'Dugald Stewart and some of my learned friends put me in the periodical paper called the *Lounger*, a copy of which I here inclose you,' he wrote proudly to Ballantine. Yet, in the very next sentence an undertow of anxiety is present: 'I was, Sir, when I was first honored with your notice, too obscure, now I tremble lest I should be ruined by being dragged to [*sic*] suddenly into the glare of polite and learned observation.'

That was not false modesty on Burns's part. It was a note that he was to sound consistently during his months in Edinburgh. His conversation may have carried 'Dutchess Gordon' off her feet; his own feet remained stolidly where he knew a ploughman's feet belonged. He was clear that Edinburgh was no more than an interlude, that his celebrity was fragile and transitory and that the position to which it had raised him was essentially artificial. This is nowhere more clearly expressed than in a letter he wrote before he had been a month in the capital to the Reverend William Greenfield: 'Never did Saul's armour sit so heavy on David when going to encounter Goliah,' he wrote, 'as does the encumbering robe of public notice with which the friendship and patronage of some "names dear to fame" have invested me.'

Greenfield was the minister of St Andrew's Church, and when Burns arrived in Edinburgh had just been appointed Professor of Rhetoric and Belles Lettres at the university. Burns admired him, but he also trusted him (he describes him in his second *Common-place Book* as 'a steady, most disinterested

---

1. The *Lounger*, No. 97, 9th December 1786. Burns was lucky. It ceased publication the following month. Burns enclosed a copy of the last issue in a letter to his friend Mackenzie, the surgeon in Mauchline: 'I am sorry to send you the last Speech & dying words of the *Lounger*.' (Letters, 73.)

friend') and felt able to speak more frankly to him than to some of his grander new friends. 'I have long studied myself, and I think I know pretty exactly what ground I occupy, both as a Man, & a Poet,' he confided:

> ... I am willing to believe that my abilities deserved a better fate than the veriest shades of life; but to be dragged forth, with all my imperfections on my head, to the full glare of learned and polite observation, is what, I am afraid, I shall have bitter reason to repent. –
>
> I mention to you, once for all, in the Confessor style, to disburthen my conscience, and that – 'When proud Fortune's ebbing tide recedes' – you may bear me witness, when my buble of fame was at the highest, I stood, unintoxicated, with the inebriating cup in my hand, looking forward, with rueful resolve, to the hastening time when the stroke of envious Calumny, with all the eagerness of vengeful triumph, should dash it to the ground. –

If the style is embarrassingly flowery ('proud Fortune' is from his beloved Shenstone), the sentiment rings true – and he was, after all, writing to a professor of rhetoric. Later in the winter Burns's admiration for Greenfield betrayed him into a sizeable gaffe. He was a supper guest at the home of the venerable Hugh Blair. Blair had been installed as minister of the High Church of St Giles in the year after Burns was born. His ornate style as a preacher commended itself to the taste of the day – his sermons were published in five volumes, and his *Lectures on Rhetoric and Belles Lettres* (he had preceded Greenfield in the professorship) had very much set the tone for the Edinburgh literary establishment, even if his reputation had been tarnished for some by his support for the spurious 'Ossian' poems.[1] Blair was now approaching seventy, and it so happened that during Burns's stay in the city William Greenfield was to join him as an associate in the pulpit of St Giles.

It was a small party, and over supper, Blair exerted himself to draw his principal guest out. One of those present was Josiah Walker, then a young private tutor, later Professor of Humanity at Glasgow and one of Burns's earliest biographers. He had had the opportunity of observing Burns's conversational style at breakfast the previous day and his judgement had been a favourable one: 'Though somewhat authoritative, it was in a way which gave little offence, and was readily imputed to his inexperience in those modes of smoothing dissent and softening assertion which are important characteristics of polished manners.' On this second occasion, seated at Dr Blair's table, Burns's normally well-tuned antennae were not performing to their usual standard: 'Being asked from which of the public places he had received the greatest

---

1. James Macpherson, a young tutor and schoolteacher, had made his reputation in 1760 with what purported to be translations from the Ossianic tales of the third century. He was taken up by the Edinburgh literati; Goethe was also a devotee and Cesarotti's Italian translation was one of Napoleon's favourite books. Dr Johnson, on the other hand, correctly denounced the poems as forgeries – the work, he said, of a man 'who loved Scotland more than the truth'.

gratification, he named the High Church, but gave the preference as a preacher to the colleague of our worthy entertainer, whose celebrity rested on his pulpit eloquence, in a tone so pointed and decisive as to throw the whole company into the most foolish embarrassment.'

Blair, an accomplished and gracious host, tried his best to lead the company round the crater which suddenly yawned in the conversational highway, but most of his guests plainly lacked the sophistication to respond: 'The doctor, indeed, with becoming self-command, endeavoured to relieve the rest by cordially seconding the encomium so injudiciously introduced; but this did not prevent the conversation from labouring under that compulsory effort which was unavoidable, while the thoughts of all were full of the only subject on which it was improper to speak.'[1]

Burns later acknowledged his blunder and told Walker that he had been mortified by it. Edinburgh quickly discovered, however, that when he had firm views about something, the prodigy which had come among them had no great inclination to mince his words – a characteristic, as Chambers pointed out, which he shared with Thomas Carlyle. One day he was invited to breakfast by Alexander Christison, who was a teacher at the High School. A clergyman who was present was unwise enough to make some critical remarks about Gray's 'Elegy'. Burns rather menacingly invited him to be more specific and to quote some of the passages which he thought exceptionable. This the wretched cleric was unable to do, and Burns, 'with great vehemence of gesticulation,' promptly blew him out of the water: 'Sir, I now perceive a man may be an excellent judge of poetry by square and rule, and after all be a damned blockhead.' He then, rather disarmingly, turned to his hostess, who was sitting beside him with an infant on her knee. 'I beg your pardon, my little dear,' he said to the child.[2]

In February, Burns received critical attention for the first time from outside Scotland. That month's issue of the *English Review* contained an unsigned notice which while less flattering than Henry Mackenzie's was a good deal more perceptive and much more entertaining. The author was John Logan, a Scot who had abandoned the ministry in Edinburgh for the life of a man of letters in London. 'Whatever excites the jaded appetite of an epicure will be prized,' he wrote, 'and a red herring from Greenock or Dunbar will be reckoned a délice.'

Logan thought 'The Cotter's Saturday Night' the best poem in the collection, but in general judged Burns to be more at home in a satirical or humorous vein than in his serious English poems. He did not pull his critical punches:

1. Walker, *op. cit.*, p. lxxiv–lxxv. Greenfield later came a dramatic cropper. In 1796 he was elected Moderator of the General Assembly, but two years later he suddenly fled to England, assumed the name of Rutherford, and thereafter supported himself by teaching and writing. It is presumed that there was some sexual scandal – the records of the Presbytery of Edinburgh speak only of 'certain flagrant reports concerning his conduct'. He was stripped of his academic honours and excommunicated. In 1809, Sir Walter Scott introduced him to John Murray, and he became a contributor to the *Quarterly Review*. He lived until 1827.

2. Chambers-Wallace, vol. ii, pp. 76–77.

'The stanza of Mr Burns is generally ill-chosen, and his provincial dialect confines his beauties to one half of the island,' he declared:

> But he possesses the genuine characteristics of a poet; a vigorous mind, a lively fancy, a surprising knowledge of human nature, and an expression rich, various and abundant. In the plaintive or pathetic he does not excel; his love poems (though he confesses, or rather professes, a *penchant* to the *belle passion*) are execrable; but in the midst of vulgarity and commonplace, which occupy one half of the volume, we meet with many striking beauties that make ample compensation.[1]

Mackenzie, not best pleased at this deviation from critical orthodoxy, wrote to remonstrate, but Logan was unrepentant, and defended himself with spirit and a touch of malice:

> Mr Burns is a clever fellow, a Man of Observation, and a Country Libertine, but I am much mistaken if he has anything of the Penseroso in his character ... His love poems, that is his bawdy songs, are said to be execrable, which is perhaps a strong expression, but no man should avow rakery who does not possess an estate of 500£ a year. I read his works under considerable disadvantage. I received three letters from Edinburgh full of irrational and unbounded panegyric, representing him as a poetical phenomenon that owed nothing but to Nature and his own Genius. When I opened the book I found that he was as well acquainted with the English poets as I was ... When that rage and Mania which seizes Edinburgh at least once a year has subsided, I am confident that your own opinion will coincide with Mine ...[2]

No easy matter to be the object of that 'rage and Mania'. Lockhart, in his life of Scott, writes about 'the pernicious and degrading trickery of lionizing'. To outward appearance, it was a process that Burns stood up to marvellously well – infinitely better, certainly, than the lumpish and prickly Rousseau had done in London twenty years previously. But there was some attrition, both intellectual and psychological. He kept his end up with the 'noblesse', as he called them. He kept his end up – not quite so easy, this – with the literati. What he found most difficult was to keep his end up with himself.

It is Smellie who is traditionally given the credit, or blame, for introducing Burns to the Crochallan Fencibles, one of the many convivial clubs which flourished in eighteenth-century Edinburgh. The Skull, The Blast and Quaff, The Whin Bush, The Humdrum – their names varied as widely as their ceremonials and rituals. They were in some ways the forerunners of modern clubs

1. *English Review*, February 1787, ix, pp. 89–93.
2. Letter to Henry Mackenzie dated 28th February 1787, reproduced in the *Burns Chronicle* (1944), xix.

like the Rotary clubs and of the fraternal orders that flourish in North America. They drew their membership from every rank, class and profession and their activities ranged from childish high jinks at one end of the spectrum to psychopathic debauchery at the other. At the Dirty Club, nobody might appear in clean linen; members of the Odd Fellows all wrote their names upside down. It amused the wild young men who belonged to the Boar Club to regard themselves as pigs and the room in which they met as a sty; at the Facer Club, a member unable to drain a measure had to throw it in his own face.

The Crochallan Fencibles met in Anchor Close, near Smellie's printing office, in a tavern run by Daniel or 'Dawney' Douglas. When the spirit moved him, Dawney would sing an old song called 'Crochallan' ('Crodh Chailein' in the Gaelic, which means 'Colin's Cattle'); fencible regiments had been raised in many parts of the country as an auxiliary defence while the regular army was engaged with the rebellious American colonists. The office-bearers assumed mock military rank and candidates for entry were pitted against club members in a contest of wit and humour which could get quite rough; Burns said after his initiation that he had 'never been so abominably thrashed in his life'. But he was soon giving as good as he got. When the collection of bawdy folksongs now known as *The Merry Muses of Caledonia* was first printed four years after his death, it carried on the title page the words, 'Selected for use of the Crochallan Fencibles'.

A member of the Fencibles with whom Burns struck up a particularly close friendship was William Nicol, who taught Latin at the High School. Walter Scott, who had been a pupil there, left an alarming picture of him in his autobiography: 'This man was an excellent classical scholar, and an admirable convivial humourist; but worthless, drunken, and inhumanly cruel to the boys under his charge.'[1]

Nicol, fifteen years older than Burns, was the son of a tailor in Ecclefechan and had studied both for the ministry and the medical profession before winning his under-mastership at the High School in open competition. Another who endured his brutal tutelage there was Lord Cockburn, who reckoned that in four years there were not ten days in which he was not flogged. 'The beauty of no Roman word, or thought, or action ever occurred to me,' he wrote, 'nor did I ever fancy that Latin was of any use except to torture boys.'[2] Nicol did not get on with the rector of the school, Dr Adam, also a classicist, and Scott wrote that he was encouraged by the City magistrates 'in insulting his person and authority'. Things eventually got out of hand: 'He carried his feud against the Rector within an inch of assassination, for he waylaid and knocked him down in the dark.' There is no doubt that it was one of the more dangerous friendships Burns formed in Edinburgh. It was also one of the most enduring, and Burns was to name one of his sons after him.

1. Quoted in J.G. Lockhart, *Memoirs of the Life of Sir Walter Scott, Bart.*, 7 volumes, Robert Cadell, Edinburgh, John Murray and Whittaker and Co., London, 1837, vol. i, pp. 32-3.
2. Cockburn, *op. cit.*, p. 4.

The law was strongly represented in the Crochallan membership. William Dunbar, a Writer to the Signet by day, was the Fencibles' 'Colonel'; he lives on as Burns's 'Rattlin', roarin' Willie.'[1] Henry Erskine was a member, and so was the advocate Charles Hay, who served as Major and Muster-Master General. Hay, later raised to the bench as Lord Newton, is remembered for his pronouncement, 'Drinking is my occupation, law my amusement.'[2] He gazes calmly out at us today from Raeburn's classic canvas, his features almost as richly coloured as his judicial robes.[3]

It might be noted in passing that in the matter of portraits of Burns, posterity has been poorly served. Raeburn was still in Italy, Allan Ramsay had died two years previously. When Creech wanted a picture of Burns for the frontispiece, he turned to Alexander Nasmyth, a gifted pupil of Ramsay's, but essentially a painter of landscapes. He and Burns got on well. After a number of sittings at his lodgings in Wardrop's Court, Nasmyth felt he had caught a good likeness and for fear of spoiling it decided to leave the painting unfinished.

It then had to be transferred to copper: 'I am getting my Phiz done by an eminent engraver,' Burns wrote to Ballantine towards the end of February.[4] This was John Beugo, who is said, like Nasmyth, to have declined a fee. Beugo took several further sittings from the life so that he might retouch the plate. It is not known whether this reflected painstaking attention to detail on his part or some unhappiness with the original on the part of Creech. Beugo and Burns became good friends, and later took French lessons together from a Monsieur Louis Cauvin. Burns had to miss a lesson on one occasion, and the note he sent to Beugo explaining why is preserved in the National Library of Scotland: 'A certain sour faced old acquaintance called Glauber's salts hinders me from my lesson tonight. – Tomorrow night I will not fail.'[5]

The seventeenth-century alchemist Johann Glauber had been in search of the philosopher's stone when he discovered *sal mirabile*, but Burns's need for it was purgative rather than philosophical:

. . . The bucks of Edinburgh accomplished, in regard to BURNS, that in which the boors of Ayrshire had failed. After residing some months in Edinburgh, he began to estrange himself, not altogether, but in some measure, from the society of his graver friends. Too many of his hours were now spent at the tables of persons who delighted to urge conviviality to drunkenness, in the tavern, in the brothel, on the lap of the woman of pleasure. He suffered

1. Kinsley, 216. Dunbar, who was also Depute-Master of the Canongate Kilwinning Masonic Lodge at the time of Burns's visit, later became Inspector-General of Stamp Duties for Scotland.
2. Newton was known as 'The Mighty', One of his clerks declared that the best paper he had ever known his lordship dictate was done after he had put away six bottles of claret. Chambers, *op. cit.*, p. 139.)
3. The portrait is in the collection of the Earl of Rosebery at Dalmeny House. The caricature opposite is by John Kay.
4. Letters, 86.
5. *Ibid.*, 156.

2. Charles Hay, Lord Newton: 'Drinking is my occupation, law my amusement'.

himself to be surrounded by a race of miserable beings who were proud to tell; that they had been in company with BURNS; and had seen BURNS as loose and as foolish as themselves.

These are the words of Robert Heron, Burn's first biographer, and the mere mention of Heron's name is enough to make some Burnsians reach for their horse-whip. It is still widely held that he deliberately set out to blacken Burns's character and that he, along with Dr Currie, was responsible for the belief that the poet was driven to an early grave by drink. Heron's own life was certainly not especially happy or successful; he died in a London fever hospital in his early forties after being imprisoned in Newgate for debt. Five years younger than Burns, he was the son of a weaver in New Galloway. He made his way through Edinburgh University and at the time of Burns's first visit to the capital he was acting as a sort of literary assistant to Hugh Blair; his first encounter with the poet was at the house of Dr Blacklock.[1]

Heron's short essay, *A Memoir of the Life of the Late Robert Burns*, was first published in book form in 1797,[2] and it is to be noted that the indignant exception which has been taken to it down the years has always been highly selective. The well-known passage quoted in an earlier chapter about how the Kilmarnock edition was received, for instance, is frequently cited with approval, and so is the perceptive tribute in which Heron asserts that Burns exercised a greater power over the minds of men by his writings 'than has been exercised by any half-dozen of the most eminent statesmen of the present age'. If that is thought to be well observed, it is not clear, on a dispassionate view, why Heron's account of the deterioration in Burns's behaviour should be dismissed out of hand.

One must of course, set against it the testimony of men like Dugald Stewart who conveyed his recollections of Burns's time in Edinburgh in a long letter published by Currie: 'I confess, I dreaded the consequences from the first,' he wrote, 'and always wished that his pursuits and habits should continue the same as in the former part of life.' Stewart saw less of Burns than he would have liked during that first winter, but he believed that he had acquitted himself extremely well:

The attentions he received during his stay in town from all ranks and descriptions of persons, were such as would have turned any head but his own. I cannot say that I could perceive any unfavourable effect which they left on his mind. He retained the simplicity of manners and appearance which had

1. Burns seems to have offended Blacklock by being slow to call on him. 'I hear that Mr Burns is, and has been, some time in Edinburgh,' he wrote to Lawrie in the second week in December. 'These news I am sorry to have heard at second-hand; they would have come much more welcome from the bard's own mouth.' (Quoted in Chambers-Wallace, vol. ii, p. 42.)

2. Printed for T. Brown, North Bridge Street, Edinburgh, 1797. It had appeared in two parts in *The Monthly Magazine and British Register*, vol. iii, the previous year.

struck me so forcibly when I first saw him in the country; nor did he seem to feel any additional self-importance from the number and rank of his new acquaintance.[1]

Stewart was particularly impressed, as so many others were, by Burns's conversation, and by the powers of mind it seemed to him to convey:

Among the poets whom I have happened to know, I have been struck, in more than one instance, with the unaccountable disparity between their general talents, and the occasional inspirations of their more favoured moments. But all the faculties of Burns's mind were, as far as I could judge, equally vigorous ... From his conversation I should have pronounced him to be fitted to excel in whatever walk of ambition he had chosen to exert his abilities.[2]

Although Stewart is a model of discretion, he clearly did not entirely approve of Burns's conversational manners, noting in particular his inclination to sarcasm: 'His wit was ready,' he wrote, 'but, to my taste, not always pleasing or happy.' The passage in Stewart's letter which is most frequently quoted as a defence of Burns's conduct reads as follows: 'Notwithstanding various reports I heard during the preceding winter, of Burns's predilection for convivial, and not very select society, I should have concluded in favour of his habits of sobriety, from all of him that ever fell under my own observation.'

That is evidence of a gentlemanly disposition to give Burns the benefit of the doubt, but not of much else. Stewart might well have thought differently if he had followed Burns to Anchor Close and watched him taking his ease with those Henley described as 'the hard-drinking wits and jinkers' of the Fencibles.

One of the most interesting observations that has come down to us about Burns during his first winter in Edinburgh – it too is to be found in Dugald Stewart's letter to Currie – is about the way he spoke: 'Nothing, perhaps, was more remarkable among his various attainments, than the fluency, and precision, and originality of his language, when he spoke in company; more particularly as he aimed at purity in his turn of expression, and avoided more successfully than most Scotchmen, the peculiarities of Scottish phraseology.'

The question of how to get one's tongue round the King's English was one which greatly exercised many of George III's Edinburgh subjects. The days when all classes expressed themselves vigorously and unselfconsciously in broad Scots had passed. Scottish members of the Westminster Parliament were

1. Currie, vol. i, p. 138.
2. Lockhart, writing a generation later, echoed this: 'There were several of them who probably adopted in their hearts the opinion of Newton, that "poetry is ingenious nonsense," but ... every one of them whose impressions on the subject have been recorded, agrees in pronouncing his conversation to have been the most remarkable thing about him.' Lockhart, *op. cit.*, p. 163.

sometimes uncomfortably aware that their speeches fell uncouthly on southern ears. James Boswell once asked Johnson what he thought of his speech. 'Sir,' replied Johnson, squashing him with faint praise, 'your pronunciation is not offensive.'

It had taken an Irishman to see that there was money in this Caledonian complex. It was twenty-five years since Thomas Sheridan, actor, stage-manager (and the father of Richard Brinsley), had hired St Paul's Episcopal Chapel and delivered a series of twelve lectures on rhetoric and the art of speaking:

> To that consecrated but not solemnising building in the dismal Carrubber's Wynd resorted about three hundred gentlemen, nobles, judges, divines, advocates, and men of fashion. With the docility of children they gave ear to these pretentious discourses, in which the self-confident orator, in rich Irish brogue, taught pure English pronunciation to a broad-Scots-speaking assembly . . . Availing himself of the zeal of the hour, Mr Sheridan adroitly secured subscriptions for the forthcoming publication of his stimulating lectures, which only saw the light after persistent dunning by the subscribers, who got their copies when their patience and their Anglican accents were wearing away.[1]

Unsurprising, therefore, a quarter of a century on, that the thrust of much of the advice offered in Edinburgh to the author of *Poems, Chiefly in the Scottish Dialect* was that he should abandon the vernacular and write in English. In deciding what should be included and what omitted from the new edition Burns consulted Hugh Blair, still very much, in spite of advancing years, the *elegantiae arbiter* of the capital. When the Kilmarnock poems appeared, Dr Blacklock had expressed doubts about how well equipped Blair was to appreciate them: 'I will venture to assure you,' he wrote to Dr Lawrie, 'that most, if not all, of the Scots poems will fail of gaining his approbation. His taste is too highly polished and his genius too regular in its emotions to make allowances for the sallies of a more impetuous ardour.'[2]

Some notes survive of the suggestions Blair made, and it is clear from them that although he belonged to another generation – he was more than forty years Burns's senior – and indeed almost to another world, he genuinely admired a great deal of his work: 'These observations,' he wrote, 'are submitted by one who is a great friend to Mr. Burns's Poems and wishes him to preserve the fame of Virtuous Sensibility, & of humorous fun, without offence.'

He thought that the stanza in 'A Dream' beginning 'Young Royal Tarry Breeks' was coarse and should be omitted. There were some crudities which had initially gone straight over his head – he instanced the 'Epistle to John Rankine': 'The Description of shooting the hen is understood, I find, to convey

1. Graham, *op. cit.*, p. 119.
2. Letter dated 27th November 1786, quoted in Chambers-Wallace, vol. i, p. 449.

an indecent meaning: tho' in reading the poem, I confess, I took it literally, and the indecency did not strike me. But if the Author meant to allude to an affair with a Woman, as is supposed, the whole Poem ought undoubtedly to be left out of the new edition.'

Blair's own style had been moulded by the Augustan felicities of writers such as Addison and he had commended their prose to generations of pupils 'as a proper method of correcting any peculiarities of dialect.' It is comical but it is also moving to picture this eminent, rather humourless divine courteously weighing the merits of a body of work which offended against almost every canon by which he had for so long moderated the literary taste of the capital. He drew the line at 'The Jolly Beggars' ('Altogether unfit in my opinion for publication. They are by much too licentious.') and Burns accepted that. For 'Death and Dr. Hornbrook,' on the other hand, Blair was full of praise, and it was he who stopped Burns during a recitation of 'The Holy Fair' and put a shrewd finger on the phrase 'tidings of salvation'. The line, he said, 'gives just offence' and ought to be altered; Burns changed it to 'tidings of damnation,' and made it both sharper and funnier in the process.[1]

Blair did not have a great deal of time for some of Burns's political views. The poem 'When Guilford Good', which makes no attempt to conceal Burns's enthusiasm for the American revolution, had been excluded from the Kilmarnock edition on the advice of Ayrshire friends like Ballantine. Blair was unimpressed by it. 'Burns's politics always smell of the smithy,' he remarked pithily.

Burns's politics were certainly never less than moderately confused. 'In his political principles he was then a Jacobite,' Dugald Stewart wrote to Currie, 'which was perhaps owing partly to this, that his father was originally from the estate of Lord Mareschall.' He added, however, that Burns 'did not appear to have thought much on such subjects, nor very consistently'.[2] Burns quite often told versions of this story. 'My forefathers rented land of the famous, noble Keiths of Marshal,' he wrote to Dr Moore, 'and had the honor to share their fate.' Similarly, John Ramsay of Ochtertyre records that when Burns visited him in 1787 he told him that his grandfather had been 'plundered and driven out in the year 1715'. Ramsay did not detect much consistency in Burns's political and religious beliefs: 'That poor man's principles were abundantly motley,' he noted, 'he being a Jacobite, an Arminian, and a Socinian.'[3]

Burns himself apparently did not see any inconsistency between his professed attachment to the House of Stuart and his adoption in Edinburgh of the buff jacket and blue waistcoat which would normally mark a man out as a follower of Charles James Fox. Many of his patrons – Glencairn, Erskine – were Whigs, and it is possible he did it out of deference to them. Whether

1. These notes of Blair's, which are undated, were published in the *Burns Chronicle* for 1932, n.s.vii.
2. *Scotland and Scotsmen in the Eighteenth Century, from the MSS of John Ramsay, Esq., of Ochtertyre.* Edited by Alex. Allardyce, William Blackwood & Sons, Edinburgh, 1888, 2 vols, vol. 2, p. 554.
3. Currie, vol. i, p. 139.

Blair's sniffy dismissal of 'When Guilford Good' got back to Burns is not known. He certainly persisted in his search for the answer he wanted and touted the poem round quite extensively, first to Glencairn and then to Henry Erskine: 'I suspect my political tenets, such as they are, may be rather heretical in the opinion of some of my best Friends,' he wrote to the latter, although it is plain from the rest of the letter that politics was far from being an all-consuming passion: ' – I have a few first principles in Religion and Politics which, I believe, I would not easily part with; but for all the etiquette of, by whom, in what manner, &c. I would not have a dissocial word about it with any one of God's creatures; particularly, an honored Patron, or a respected Friend.'[1]

Burns was still using his new friends as a sounding board for poems he wished to include in the new edition when the process of proof-reading was far advanced. A rueful letter he wrote to Gavin Hamilton early in March 1787 makes it plain that he did not always get the response he hoped for:

> My two Songs, on Miss W. Alexander and Miss P. Kennedy were likewise tried yesterday by a jury of Literati, and found defamatory libels against the fastidious Powers of Poesy and Taste; and the Author forbid to print them under pain of forfeiture of character. – I cannot help almost shedding a tear to the memory of two Songs that had cost me some pains, and that I valued a good deal, but I must submit. – [2]

He did not always submit with such a good grace. Mrs. Dunlop had also taken to offering him advice, though from a distance, and the tone of his replies could be distinctly stiff:

> The word you object to in the mention I have made of my glorious country-man and your immortal ancestor, is indeed borrowed from Thomson; but it does not strike me as an improper epithet. I distrusted my own judgement on your finding fault with it, and applied for the opinion of some of the Literati here, who honour me with their critical strictures, and they all allow it to be proper.[3]

In another letter he choked her off with a curtness that approached the Johnsonian – 'Your criticisms, Madam, I understand very well, and could have wished to have pleased you better. – You are right in your guesses that I am not very amenable to counsel.'[4]

1. Letters, 70.
2. *Ibid.*, 88. Burns had met Margaret Kennedy at Hamilton's house in the autumn of 1785, and sent her the song as 'a small tho' grateful tribute.' She was the daughter of Hamilton's brother-in-law, factor to the Earl of Cassilis. Miss Alexander was the previously encountered sister of the laird of Ballochmyle. The songs in question were 'A Song. On Miss P— K—' (Kinsley, 65) and 'The Braes o' Ballochmyle' (Kinsley, 66).
3. *Ibid.*, 78.
4. *Ibid.*, 98.

It was through Mrs Dunlop that he began the correspondence which led to his autobiographical letter to Dr John Moore. (Mrs Dunlop was an old friend of Moore's and had sent him a copy of the Kilmarnock edition.) Moore was the son of a Scots Episcopalian minister. He had set up in medical practice in London but devoted a good deal of his time to literature. He had travelled for some years as tutor to two young Dukes of Hamilton, and the book based on his experiences, *View of Society and Manners in France, Switzerland and Germany*, had some success both at home and abroad. Burns was in considerable awe of him. 'I know his fame and character, and I am one of "the sons of little men,"' he told Mrs Dunlop: 'To write him a mere matter-of-fact affair, like a merchant's order, would be disgracing the little character I have; and to write the author of *The View of Society and Manners*, a letter of sentiment – I declare every artery runs cold at the thought. I shall try, however, to write to him tomorrow or next day.'[1]

When he plucked up courage to write, he hit on a smooth formula which committed him to nothing: 'Your criticisms, Sir, I received with reverence; only I am sorry they mostly came too late: a peccant passage or two that I would certainly have altered were gone to the Press.'[2] The correspondence shows no great critical edge on Moore's part, and he sometimes succeeds in yoking together obtuseness and good sense in one paragraph: 'It is not surprising that you improve in correctness and taste, considering where you have been for some time past. And I dare swear there is no danger of your admitting any polish which might weaken the vigour of your native powers.' He goes on to tell Burns that his youngest son, a pupil at Winchester, is translating some stanzas of his 'Halloween' into Latin verse, 'for the benefit of his comrades'.[3]

One of the more tiresome letters Burns received as the second edition was going through the press – he described it in the presumed privacy of his second *Common-place Book* as a 'bombast epistle' – came from the Earl of Buchan, the elder brother of Henry Erskine (their younger brother, Thomas, went to the English bar and became Lord Chancellor.) 'He had a desire to be a great man and a *Mecænas – a bon marché*,' wrote Sir Walter Scott. 'He was a person whose immense vanity, bordering upon insanity, obscured, or rather eclipsed, very considerable talents.'[4] Not everyone agreed about the last bit. When Buchan boasted one day to the Duchess of Gordon of the extraordinary abilities of his

1. *Ibid.*, 78.
2. *Ibid.*, 79.
3. Letter dated 28th February 1787, quoted in Chambers-Wallace, vol. ii, page 57. Moore's eldest son became Sir John Moore, the hero of Corunna.
4. Scott's diary, 29th April 1829. This was generous of Scott. When the novelist was ill in 1819, Buchan forced his way into the house intent on telling him what arrangements he had made for his funeral. As it happened, Scott lived to attend Buchan's funeral at Dryburgh Abbey: 'His body was in the grave with its feet pointing westward. My cousin, Maxpopple, was for taking notice of it, but I assured him that a man who had been wrong in the head all his life would scarce become right-headed after death.' (Lockhart, (Scott) *op. cit.*, vol. vii, p. 190.)

family, Her Grace enquired silkily 'whether the wit had not come by the mother, and been all settled on the younger branches'.[1]

'Mr Burns – I have redd with great pleasure several of your poems,' Buchan wrote:

> ... These little doric pieces of yours in our provincial dialect are very beautiful, but you will soon be able to diversify your language, your Rhyme and your subject, and then you will have it in your power to show the extent of your genius and to attempt work of greater magnitude, variety and importance ... Keep your Eye upon Parnassus and drink deep of the fountains of Helicon, but beware of the Joys that is dedicated to the Jolly God of wine ...

Buchan went on to recommend that Burns should undertake a sort of literary pilgrimage in the Borders:

> ... Visit the birth place of Thomson on the water of Rule; feed your Muse with Ethereal mildness when the spring first opens the primrose on the steep verdant margin of his parent stream; fire her in Summer with the view of Flodden Field from the summit of Mount Eildon; ripen her in Autumn with the placid chearfull scenes of harvest and the snowey fleece yielding to the happy hands of the contented shepherd ... and may the Apollo of my Nypa who sits on the fork of Eildon enable you to produce the genuine offspring of Genius, sentiment, and skill – never to die.[2]

It took Burns the best part of a week to decide how to respond to this preposterous communication, but respond he must – Buchan had begun, after all, by telling him that he had subscribed for six copies of the poems for himself and two for his wife. If the style of his reply was intended as parody, it was safe to assume that his noble correspondent would not notice: 'Your Lordship touches the darling chord of my heart when you advise me to fire my Muse at Scottish story and Scottish scenes. – I wish for nothing more than to make a leisurely Pilgrimage through my native country ...' Eventually he gets round to pointing out to Buchan that he has to earn his living, and that he must do so in the only way he knows how: 'I must return to my rustic station, and in my wonted way, woo my rustic Muse at the Ploughtail.'[3]

Buchan had planted a seed, for all that, and it would not be many weeks before Burns, with a little money in his pocket, found himself doing pretty much what the eleventh Earl had pompously proposed.

Burns had, as it happened, already made one literary pilgrimage since coming to Edinburgh, although it was a short one: he had walked down the

1. *Ibid.*, vol. iv, p. 277.
2. Letter dated 1st February 1787, quoted in Chambers-Wallace, vol. ii, pp. 46-7.
3. Letters, 82.

Royal Mile to the Kirk of the Canongate to seek out the grave of Robert Fergusson. He did not like what he found, and at the beginning of February he had written to the Bailies of the Canongate. The much corrected letter suggests that he wrote either in haste or with urgency:

> Gentlemen,
>   I am sorry to be told that the remains of Robert Ferguson [*sic*] the so justly celebrated Poet, a man whose talents for ages to come will do honor, [for ages to come, (*deleted*)] to our Caledonian name, lie in your churchyard among the ignoble Dead unnoticed and unknown [in your Churchyard (*deleted*)]. – Some memorial to direct the steps of the Lovers of Scottish Song, when they wish to shed a [grateful (*deleted*)] tear over the 'Narrow house' of the Bard who is now no more, is surely a [debt (*deleted*)] tribute due to Ferguson's memory: a [debt (*deleted*)] tribute I wish to have the honor of paying. – I petition you then, Gentlemen, for [to allow, permit me (*deleted*)] for (*sic*) your permission to lay a simple stone over his revered ashes, to remain an unalienable property to his deathless fame. –
>
> I have the honor to be, Gentlemen,
your very humble servant
ROBERT BURNS.[1]

Burns should have written not to the magistrates but to the Managers of the Kirk and Kirkyard Funds. The letter was passed to them, and they took notice of it at their next meeting:

> Thereafter the said managers, in consideration of the laudable and disinterested motion of Mr Burns, and the propriety of his request, did, and hereby do, unanimously, grant power and liberty to the said Robert Burns, to erect a headstone at the grave of the said Robert Fergusson, and to keep up and preserve the same to his memory in all time coming.[2]

Burns commissioned an Edinburgh architect (his name was Robert Burn) to design the headstone. It was made from polished Craigleith stone, and Burns composed an inscription:

> No sculptur'd marble here, nor pompous lay,
>   'No story'd urn nor animated bust;'
> This simple stone directs pale SCOTIA'S way
>   To pour her sorrows o'er her POET'S dust.[3]

1. *Ibid.*, 81.
2. Session records of the parish of Canongate, 22nd February 1787.
3. The second line is from Gray's *Elegy*. Burns later added two further stanzas to the epitaph. See Kinsley, 142.

The architect did not exert himself unduly, and the stone was not ready until the summer of 1789. He in turn had to wait for his money – the bill came to £5 10s – until 1792. Burns eventually asked a friend in Edinburgh to settle it for him, uncouthly rejecting a request for interest: 'Considering that the money was due by one Poet for putting a tombstone over another, he may, with grateful surprise, thank Heaven that he ever saw a farthing of it.'[1]

Someone who shared Burns's admiration for Fergusson was the English actor William Woods, who had come to Scotland in the early 1770s and was a stalwart of the Edinburgh stage for more than thirty years. In the middle of April 1787 he appeared at the Theatre Royal in *The Merry Wives of Windsor*. It was his benefit night, and Burns wrote a Prologue for him. It is an unremarkable piece ('Hail CALEDONIA, name for ever dear!/ Before whose sons I'm honour'd to appear!'), interesting only as one of the few things Burns ever wrote for the stage. He worked in a compliment to Henry Mackenzie and saluted the contribution made to the Enlightenment by the Edinburgh literati:

> Philosophy, no idle pedant dream,
> Here holds her search by heaven-taught Reason's beam;
> Here History paints, with elegance and force,
> The tide of Empire's fluctuating course . . .[2]

One consequence of Burns's celebrity was that all manner of people bombarded him with verse of their own, sometimes by letter, sometimes in the public prints. Most of it was predictably dreadful, but one particular piece caught his fancy. It was written by a Mrs Scot, from Wauchope, near Jedburgh, a widow in her late fifties and a niece, as it happened, of Mrs Cockburn. She flattered him by casting polite doubt on whether someone bred 'between the stilts'[3] could write so knowledgeably about Homer or make such good jokes about 'Willie Pitt' and 'Charlie Fox'. She would happily ride twenty miles 'o'er moss and muir' for the pleasure of spending an evening in his company, a much more alluring prospect, she said, than dining on turtle with dull lairds. If she knew where to find him, she would gladly make him a present of a check plaid to keep him warm in church or at the market.[4]

Burns was charmed, and replied in kind:

> For you, na bred to barn and byre,
> Wha sweetly tune the Scottish lyre,
> Thanks to you for your line . . .

1. Letters, 495. The friend was Peter Hill. He was a clerk in Creech's office when Burns first met him, but set up in business as a bookseller himself the following year. He later became Edinburgh's City Treasurer.
2. Kinsley, 151. The historical reference is to Dr William Robertson, the Principal of the University, known both for his *History of Scotland* and later for *The History of America*.
3. A stilt is the handle of the plough.
4. The text is printed in Kinsley, 147A. Mrs Scot died two years later. In 1801 her relatives published her collected poems under the title *Alonza and Cora*.

It is not one of his best poems, but he clearly took some care over it. It is the only one of his Epistles to be addressed to a woman, and apart from 'To a Haggis', the only piece he wrote in Scots during his time in the capital. He would, he told her, wear her plaid more proudly than ermine or imperial purple.[1]

The 'Guidwife of Waukhope-House' had touched a chord which had vibrated hardly at all during his stay in Edinburgh. Between Burns and almost all the women he met in 'Scotia's darling seat' there was a great gulf fixed, not only of rank but also of manners. He charmed them, certainly, and their admiration for him was no less than that to which he had become accustomed on his home turf. On that turf, however, Burns was not accustomed to matters stopping there. 'I am, you know, a veteran in these campaigns,' he wrote when he heard that his younger brother William had fallen in love. 'Let me advise you always to pay your particular assiduities and try for intimacy as soon as you feel the first symptoms of the passion.'[2] As a campaign strategy in Edinburgh it was ineffective. Here, apparently, the triumphs which he achieved so effortlessly with words did not lead on to conquests of another kind.

To the Frenchman Angellier, viewing him as if through a watchmaker's lens, it seemed as though a crucial part of the movement had ceased to function – 'un des rouages essentiels de son être ne fonctionnait plus'.[3] It is a penetrating insight. Love and Poesy had been uncoupled. Small wonder that during those months of winter and spring Burns wrote little of value or importance, or that he experienced an occasional darkening of the spirit. To one hostess who sent him an invitation he returned a reply of almost Swiftian savagery. He would, he told her, be delighted to come but only if she also asked the 'learned pig' then performing in the Grassmarket.[4]

Towards the end of his time in Edinburgh, Burns decided he must capture some of his impressions – 'Half a word fixed upon or near the spot, is worth a cart-load of recollection,' he wrote, quoting from Gray. This was the beginning of what we know as his second *Common-place Book*: 'I am determined to make these pages my Confidante. I will sketch every character that any way strikes me, to the best of my observation, with unshrinking justice.'[5] By April there had been time for first impressions to shake down, and Burns's judgement of those he had met in the preceding months was more considered. He

1. Kinsley, 147B.
2. Letters, 337.
3. Angellier, *op. cit.*, vol i, p. 237.
4. Learned pigs were all the rage, and were taught to perform various party tricks, such as picking out a particular playing card from a pack laid out on the ground. A man called Nichols made such a killing with one of these animals in the spring of 1787 that the management of the Theatre Royal felt they must get in on the act. They put on a farce called *The Learned Pig's Levée* – 'a rhiming, chiming, snorting, squeaking, grunting rhapsody.' (*Edinburgh Evening Courant*, 19th April 1787.)
5. The second *Common-place Book* was first printed in *Macmillan's Magazine* between March and July, 1879 (vols. xxxix-xl).

remained uneasily aware that he would never find himself on the same wave-length as the likes of Hugh Blair:

> ... When he kindly interests himself in my welfare, or, still more, when he descends from his pinnacle and meets me on equal ground, my heart over-flows with what is called liking: when he neglects me for the meer carcase of Greatness, or when his eye measures the difference of our points of elevation, I say to myself with scarcely an emotion, what do I care for him or his pomp either? ... Dr Blair is meerly an astonishing proof what industry and application can do. Natural parts like his are frequently to be met with; his vanity is proverbially known among his acquaintances; but he is justly at the head of what may be called fine writing ... He has a heart, not of the finest water, but far from being an ordinary one.

De Lancey Ferguson compares Burns's position in Edinburgh during the win-ter of 1786–87 with that of Benjamin Franklin at Versailles a decade earlier: 'in each place the fashionable world thought it had discovered a child of nature; in each place the newcomer had really a shrewder mind and a quicker pen-etration of character and motive than most of the élite who patronised him.'[1] The comparison is apt, but it cannot be extended to the manner in which the two men responded to their situation. The second *Common-place Book* shows that Burns was, if anything, more alive to real or imagined slights towards the end of his stay than he had been at the beginning:

> Imagine a man of abilities, his breast glowing with honest pride, conscious that men are born equal, still giving that 'honor to whom honor is due'; he meets at a Great man's table a Squire Something, or a Sir Somebody; he knows the noble landlord at heart gives the Bard or whatever he is a share of his good wishes beyond any at table perhaps, yet how will it mortify him to see a fellow whose abilities would scarcely have made an eight penny taylor, and whose heart is not worth three farthings, meet with attention and notice that are forgot to the sons of Genius and Poverty?

This outburst of jealous indignation had been prompted by an imagined lapse on the part of the man who had shown a greater awareness of Burns's sensi-tivities than any other:

> The noble Glencairn has wounded me to the soul here, because I dearly esteem respect and love him. He showed so much attention, engrossing attention, one day, to the only blockhead, as there was none but his lordship, the Dunderpate and myself, that I was within half a point of throwing down

---

1. J. De Lancey Ferguson, *Pride and Passion, Robert Burns, 1759-1796*, Oxford University Press, New York, 1939, p. 100.

my gage of contemptuous defiance, but he shook my hand and looked so benevolently good at parting – God bless him, though I should never see him more, I shall love him untill my dying day!

One of the most hospitable of the literati was Dugald Stewart's predecessor in the chair of Moral Philosophy, Dr Adam Ferguson. He lived at Sciennes Hill House, then some way out of the city – his friends referred to it jokingly as Kamtschatka, but the bleakness of the surroundings did not keep them away from his weekly conversaziones and to one of these Burns was taken by Stewart. John Home, the author of *Douglas*[1] was present, and so were James Hutton, the geologist, and Joseph Black, the great chemist and physicist. It is possible that Burns was made uneasy by the very distinction of the company; he seemed at first inclined to hold himself apart, and went round the room looking at the pictures. One print in particular seemed to hold his attention – a sentimental scene showing a soldier lying dead in the snow, a woman with a babe in arms on one side, his dog on the other. The caption was in verse:

> Cold on Canadian hills, or Minden's plain,
> Perhaps that parent wept her soldier slain –
> Bent o'er her babe, her eye dissolved in dew,
> The big drops mingling with the milk he drew . . .

Burns read the lines aloud, but before he could finish his eyes filled with tears. He then asked who the author was, but the cream of the Edinburgh literary establishment was unable to enlighten him. One or two friends of the host's young son were present, however, and after a moment one of them, a pale boy of sixteen with a limp, volunteered that they were the work of one Langhorne and occurred in a poem called 'Justice of Peace'. Burns was impressed. 'You'll be a man yet, sir,' he said. The boy's name was Walter Scott.[2]

When Scott recalled the occasion in later life, it was Burns's strong expression of sense and shrewdness that came to mind: '. . . The eye alone, I think, indicated the poetical character and temperament. It was large, and of a dark cast, which glowed (I say literally glowed) when he spoke with feeling

---

1. *Douglas*, a cross between a tragedy and a morality play, had been enthusiastically received at its first performance in Edinburgh in 1756 – 'Whaur's your Wullie Shakespeare noo?' cried a triumphant voice from the audience. It became something of a *cause célèbre* because Home was a Moderate clergyman and his more orthodox brethren attacked the piece as immoral. The issue was hotly debated in the General Assembly, and though the Moderates came off best, Home resigned his parish charge, became private secretary to the Earl of Bute and went off to write for the London stage. He was later tutor to the Prince of Wales, and on his accession as George III Home was made Conservator of the Scottish Privileges in Flanders, a sinecure worth £300 a year. He returned to Edinburgh in 1778.

2. Scott and young Ferguson gave very similar accounts of the occasion to Lockhart.

or interest. I never saw such another eye in a human head, though I have seen the most distinguished men of my time.'[1]

Scott thought that the Nasmyth portrait depicted Burns 'as if seen in perspective' and in some way diminished his features; his impression was that in life the face was 'more massive' than in any of the portraits. If he had not known who he was, he would have taken the poet for 'a very sagacious country farmer of the old Scotch school, i.e. none of your modern agriculturalists, who keep labourers for their drudgery, but the douce gudeman who held his own plough.'

Josiah Walker also remembered Burns's large dark eyes, although he confessed himself 'not much struck' with his first appearance:

> His person, though strong and well knit, and much superior to what might be expected in a ploughman, was still rather coarse in its outline. His stature, from want of setting up, appeared to be only of the middle size, but was rather above it. His motions were firm and decided . . . His countenance was not of that elegant cast which is most frequent among the upper ranks, but it was manly and intelligent, and marked by a thoughtful gravity which shaded at times into sternness . . .
>
> He was plainly, but properly dressed, in a style mid-way between the holiday costume of a farmer, and that of the company with which he now associated. His black hair, without powder, at a time when it was very generally worn, was tied behind, and spread upon his forehead. Upon the whole, from his person, physiognomy, and dress, had I met him near a seaport, and been required to guess his condition, I should have probably conjectured him to be the master of a merchant-vessel of the most respectable class.[2]

The business of seeing his poems through the press took longer than it should have done. On March 21st he told a friend that he expected to be in Edinburgh for at least another four weeks, and the following day, in a long letter to Mrs Dunlop, he announced that he had corrected the last proof sheet and that only the glossary and the list of subscribers' names remained to be printed: 'Printing this last is much against my will, but some of my friends whom I do not chuse to thwart will have it so.'[3] His displeasure was understandable. The names of the subscribers filled thirty-eight pages, and the extra printing cost fell on Burns.

The list makes fascinating reading, for all that. Fifteen hundred people subscribed, for a total of two thousand eight hundred copies.[4] There was strong

1. Lockhart, *op. cit.*, p. 153.
2. Walker, op. cit., pp. lxxi–lxxii.
3. Letters, 90.
4. Technically, there are two Edinburgh editions. Creech had only so much type, and as the number of subscriptions rose it had to be broken up and reset. The second impression was proof-read with less care than the first, (probably by Burns himself) and this has been a source of delight to bibliographers ever since. The most glaring error occurs in the 'Address to a Haggis',

support from his new patrons among the nobility – the Earl of Eglinton took forty-two copies, Glencairn and his mother twenty-four between them, the Duchess of Gordon twenty-one. Older and less grand friends also figured on the list: Robert Muir of Kilmarnock, who had taken seventy-two copies of the first edition, subscribed for forty of the second, and Archibald Prentice of Covington Mains, Burns's host when he broke his journey on the way to Edinburgh, put his name down for twenty. The subscriptions did not all come from individuals, and they did not all come from addresses in Scotland or from adherents of the reformed religion; among the more intriguing subscribers were the Benedictine Monastery at Ratisbon and the Scots Colleges at Douai, Paris and Valladolid.[1]

Because the Caledonian Hunt headed the list with its hundred copies, it seemed appropriate that the volume should be dedicated to the noblemen and gentlemen who were its members:

> . . . The Poetic Genius of my Country found me as the prophetic bard Elijah did Elisha – at the *plough*; and threw her inspiring mantle over me. She bade me sing the loves, the joys, the rural scenes and rural pleasures of my natal Soil, in my native tongue: I tuned my wild, artless notes, as she inspired. She whispered me to come to this ancient metropolis of Caledonia, and lay my Songs under your honoured protection: I now obey her dictates.

Burns's Muse may also have whispered to him that there was nothing in the rules against dedications written slightly tongue-in-cheek:

> . . . When you go forth to waken the echoes, in the ancient and favourite amusements of your Forefathers, may pleasure ever be of your party; and may Social-joy await your return! When harassed in courts or camps with the justlings of bad men and bad measures, may the honest consciousness of injured Worth attend your return to your native Seats; and may Domestic Happiness, with a smiling welcome, meet you at your gates! May Corruption shrink at your kindling indignant glance; and may tyranny in the Ruler and licentiousness in the People equally find you an inexorable foe!

The book appeared on April 17th and on that day Burns disposed of his rights in the *Poems* to Creech for the sum of a hundred guineas. He did so on the advice of Henry Mackenzie – indeed the matter was settled between the three

where the line 'Auld Scotland wants nae *skinking* ware' appears as 'Auld Scotland wants nae *stinking* ware.'

1. Burns almost certainly owed these subscriptions to the interest of the Right Reverend John Geddes (1735-99), whom he had met at Monboddo's house. Geddes, a man of great charm and learning, was the Roman Catholic Bishop of Dunkeld and had for many years been Rector of the Scots College at Valladolid. Burns was greatly impressed by him, later describing him as 'the first [i.e. foremost] Cleric character I ever saw.'

men at a meeting at Mackenzie's house. Given that Scotland seemed likely to be amply supplied by this sizeable new edition, Creech undertook to sound out Cadell, the London publisher, about acquiring a share in the book. The memorandum recorded that Burns agreed 'most cordially' the terms of the arrangement – as well he might, because he was selling to Creech something of which he had already largely disposed to his brother Gilbert.

This could have slipped Burns's mind, or it could be that he was not particularly knowledgeable about such matters. The fact is, however, that something like two-thirds of the poems which appeared in the Edinburgh edition had already been published in the Kilmarnock edition the previous year, and that rights in them had passed to Gilbert under the Deed of Assignment drawn up to stymie Jean Armour's father. A hundred guineas in 1787 would have a purchasing power today of about £30,000. The 'honest Rusticity' to which Burns laid claim in his dedication did not on this occasion serve him too badly.

Exactly how much he cleared from the whole transaction is difficult to determine. Creech told Heron that for the copyright and his subscription copies he paid Burns close on £1,100, but we do not know how much Burns's bills for printing and binding came to. Burns later told Dr Moore that he thought he would clear about £400, and to Mrs Dunlop he named a slightly higher figure. He probably did not know with any certainty. It is clear from a letter he wrote to Ballantine in Ayr the day after publication that he was neither very wise in the ways of commerce nor particularly meticulous in the keeping of accounts:

> ... I beleive Booksellers take no less than the unconscionable, Jewish tax of 25 p^r Cent. by way of agency. – I trouble you then, Sir, to find a proper person, of the mercantile folks I suppose will be best, that for a moderate consideration will retail the books to subscribers as they are called for. – Several of the Subscription bills have been mislaid, so all who say they have subscribed must be served at subscription price ...[1]

There were twenty-two poems in the Edinburgh edition which had not previously been published. Three of the rather slight epitaphs that had been included as makeweights in the earlier edition were left out. 'Death and Doctor Hornbrook',[2] 'The Brigs of Ayr'[3] and 'The Ordination'[4] now found a place, and so did 'The Calf',[5] 'Address to the Unco' Guid',[6] 'When Guilford Good our Pilot Stood'[7] and 'Tam Samson's Elegy'.[8] 'When this worthy old Sportsman

1. Letters, 95.
2. Kinsley, 55.
3. Ibid., 120.
4. Ibid., 85.
5. Ibid., 125.
6. Ibid., 39.
7. Ibid., 38.
8. Ibid., 117.

went out last muir-fowl season,' Burns wrote in a footnote, 'he supposed it was to be, in Ossian's phrase, "the last of his fields"; and expressed an ardent wish to die and be buried in the muirs. On this hint the Author composed his Elegy and Epitaph.' The old sportsman (he was a nurseryman in Kilmarnock) comes brilliantly alive, roaring up the curling rink like Jehu, terrorising the local wildlife with gun and rod. It is one of Burns's brightest canvases:

Now safe the stately Sawmont sail,	salmon
And Trouts bedropp'd wi' crimson hail,	
And Eels weel kend for souple tail,	well-known, supple
And Geds for greed,	pike
Since dark in Death's *fish-creel* we wail	
Tam Samson dead!	

Rejoice, ye birring Paitricks a';	partridges
Ye cootie Moorcocks, crousely craw;	feathery-legged, boldly
Ye Maukins, cock your fud fu' braw,	hares, backside
Withoutten dread;	
Your mortal Fae is now awa',	foe
Tam Samson's dead!	

There were also five songs (one of them was 'Green Grow the Rashes, O'[1]) and five religious poems, neo-classical and lifeless – they could have been written by anyone. Only 'To a Haggis'[2] and 'Address to Edinburgh'[3] had been written during Burns's Edinburgh stay. The new volume, bound in boards, was a more substantial affair than the Kilmarnock edition; three hundred and forty-three pages of poems as against two hundred and thirty-five and a glossary expanded from five pages to twenty-four. Poetically speaking, however, he had been marking time. The months he had spent in Ramsay's and Fergusson's Edinburgh had provided no creative stimulus.

As winter turned into spring, there are traces in his correspondence of both weariness and disillusion. To Mrs Dunlop he wrote that he had no dearer aim than to make 'leisurely pilgrimages through Caledonia,' viewing romantic rivers

1. *Ibid.*, 657.
2. *Ibid.*, 136. Fergusson's poem 'Caller Oysters' is an obvious antecedent. Burns's 'Great Chieftan o' the Puddin-race' came to be regarded as an emblem of Scottishness relatively late in the day. The earliest references to it occur in English cookery books of the fifteenth century. It remained popular south of the border until the early eighteenth century, but gradually suffered a loss of esteem. 'I am not yet Scotchman enough to relish their singed sheep's-head and haggice,' says a character in Smollett's *Humphrey Clinker*, published in 1771.
3. *Ibid.*, 135. It is not one of Burns's best efforts. Many years later, an enterprising firm that manufactured sanitary ware appropriated the name 'Edina' for their brand of lavatory pan – 'demonstrating, if somewhat crudely, real critical insight,' David Daiches wrote unkindly. (Daiches, *op. cit.*, p. 240.)

and old battlefields, musing by stately towers and venerable ruins. Then, in mid-letter, he interrupts this self-indulgent reverie:

> But these are all Utopian ideas: I have dallied long enough with life; 'tis time to be in earnest. – I have a fond, aged Mother to care for; and some other bosom-ties, perhaps equally tender ... I intend, so far as I may be said to have any intention, to return to my old acquaintance, the plough, and, if I can meet with a lease by which I can live, to commence Farmer ... The trappings and luxuries of upper stations, I have seen a little of them in Edinburgh – I can live without them ...[1]

He wrote in similar vein to Dr Moore:

> I have formed many intimacies and friendships here, but I am afraid they are all of too tender a construction to bear carriage a hundred and fifty miles. To the rich, the great, the fashionable, the polite, I have no equivalent to offer; and I am afraid my meteor appearance will by no means entitle me to a settled correspondence with any of you, who are the permanent lights of genius and literature.

Moore had sent him an admiring sonnet written by a young woman who worked for him as an amanuensis. Burns asked Moore to convey his compliments to her, and added revealingly: 'If once this tangent flight of mine were over, and I were returned to my wonted leisurely motion in my old circle, I may probably endeavour to return her poetic compliment in kind.'[2] Auld Reekie was a foreign country, and he knew it.

On the morning of Friday, May 4th, he busied himself with a batch of letters of farewell to some of his principal patrons and friends – Hugh Blair, William Dunbar, Henry Mackenzie, Glencairn. They were graciously phrased and tinged with a certain melancholy; to some he sent a proof impression on India paper of the Beugo engraving. The most formal was that to Hugh Blair ('Rev[d] & much respected Sir');[3] the most relaxed to his Crochallan Fencibles cronie William Dunbar: 'I have a strong fancy that in some future excentric Planet,' he wrote, 'you and I, among the harum-scarum Sons of Imagination and Whim, with a hearty shake of a hand, a Metaphor and a Laugh, shall

1. Letters, 90. His 'fond aged Mother' was, in fact, at 55, two years younger than Mrs Dunlop, and would live for another 33 years. In a postscript to this letter Burns told Mrs Dunlop that if he made enough money out of his book, he would not exclude the purchase of an army commission. 'Would the profits of that afford it,' he wrote, 'with rapture I would take your hint of a military life, as the most congenial to my feelings and situation of any other,' but, 'What is wanting cannot be numbered.'

2. *Ibid.*, 97. The young woman was Helen Maria Williams. In 1790 she settled in Paris, became a violent partisan of the Gironde, and ended up in prison. Later she published a novel, *Julia*, and translated Bernardin de Saint-Pierre's *Paul et Virginie.*

3. *Ibid.*, 101

recognise OLD ACQUAINTANCE.'[1] His letter to Mackenzie was particularly cordial – 'whatever is good about my heart is much indebted to Mr Harley'[2] – but his most unreserved expression of gratitude was for Glencairn:

> I came to this town without friend or acquaintance, but I met with your Lordship; and to YOU, Your good family I owe in a great measure all that at present I am and have. – My gratitude is not selfish design, that I disclaim; it is not dodging after the heels of Greatness, that is an offering you disdain; it is a feeling of the same kind with my devotion.[3]

He wrote one other short letter that morning. It was to a more recent acquaintance, and he enclosed with it not an engraving but a song:

> ... Farewel, my dear Sir! I wish to have seen you, but I have been dreadfully throng as I march tomorrow. – Had my acquaintance w^t you been a little older, I would have asked the favor of your correspondence; as I have met w^t few people whose company & conversation gave me so much pleasure, because I have met w^t few whose sentiments are so congenial to my own ... Keep the original of this Song till we meet again, whenever that may be. – [4]

The recipient was James Johnson, an engraver and music-seller. A man of little education but immense enthusiasm, Johnson had recently embarked on a highly ambitious enterprise. He proposed to collect the words and music of all the existing old Scots songs and publish them in arrangements for the pianoforte. He had engaged Burns's interest in the project. The first volume was already in the press. Burns did not know it, but his days as a poet were effectively over. He was entering on a fresh commitment that would last for the rest of his life. He never heard a symphony or a string quartet. His first teacher had thought he was tone deaf. Now, for the nine years that remained to him, almost all his creative energy was to be channelled into the new trade of songsmith.

1. *Ibid.*, 99.
2. *Ibid.*, 101A.
3. *Ibid.*, 103.
4. *Ibid.*, 104.

Seven

RURAL RIDES

WE HAVE SEEN THAT when Burns wrote to Mrs Dunlop in March he dismissed the idea of making 'leisurely pilgrimages through Caledonia' as Utopian. He had, he announced, 'dallied long enough with life'. It was time to be 'in earnest'. Six weeks later, that stern resolution had been put on ice. 'Left Edin^r.,' Burns wrote on May 5th in a newly-started journal. 'Lammermuir Hills miserably dreary, but at times very picturesque.' It was the first of four journeys he was to make during the summer and early autumn months of 1787. He was heading in a roundabout way for Mauchline, and planned on the way to inspect the farm in Dumfriesshire which Patrick Miller was dangling before him. This time there was no need to borrow a pony. He had laid out £4 on a mare of his own and given her the name of Jenny Geddes.[1]

Burns had as a travelling companion a young man called Robert Ainslie, a convivial law apprentice seven years his junior whom he had met during the winter, possibly at some Masonic affair. Their first stop was at Berrywell, near Duns, where Ainslie's father was steward to Lord Douglas. The journal Burns kept of this swing through the Borders is rather scrappy. None of his rural rides produced anything remotely comparable with the record Cobbett was to make of his perambulations through the English counties in the 1820s. The Border scenery that was to be such a rich source of inspiration for Scott and James Hogg, the Ettrick Shepherd[2], made little impression on him. Burns's knowledge of Border history was limited and his topographical interest did not extend beyond localities celebrated in ballad and song. The most interesting

1. Jenny Geddes won her place in Scottish history (or legend) on 23rd July 1637. There was certainly a riot in Edinburgh on that day, sparked by an attempt to foist Laud's episcopal prayer book on the Scottish Church. The story goes that when the service was read in St Giles and the bishop called on the dean to read the collect, Jenny Geddes, a greenwife or herbwoman who kept a stall further down the Royal Mile at the Tron Kirk, flung her cutty-stool at the dean's head.
2. James Hogg (1770–1835), the son of a failed sheep-farmer from Ettrick Forest in Selkirkshire, spent his childhood in farm service and then became a shepherd. Inspired by Burns, he resolved that he too would be a poet. He became a friend of Scott, wrote ballads and novels, contributed to *Blackwood's* and made a number of unsuccessful forays into farming. He is best remembered for *The Private Memoirs and Confessions of a Justified Sinner*, to which, in 1947, André Gide wrote an enthusiastic preface.

things in the journal are the entertaining and often barbed vignettes of people he met and the accounts he gives of his unflagging pursuit of 'the Sex'.[1]

Sitting with the Ainslies in the family pew next morning, Burns was able to indulge in the traditional Scottish Sabbath sport of sermon-tasting. He did not mark Dr Bowmaker, the minister of Duns, very highly – 'a man of strong lungs and pretty judicious remark; but ill skilled in propriety, and altogether unconscious of his want of it.' His sermon dwelt on the terrors of hellfire, and Burns noticed that Ainslie's sister, Rachel, 'attentive but agitated,' was leafing through her Bible in search of the text. Producing a pencil, he took the book from her and inscribed the blank leaf with a reassuring and flattering impromptu:

> Fair maid, you need not take the hint,
>   Nor idle texts pursue;
> 'Twas only sinners that he meant,
>   Not angels such as you.[2]

The travellers moved on and crossed briefly into England, Burns recording the day's events in a spare telegraphese: 'Cornhill – glorious river Tweed – clear & majestic – fine bridge. Dine at Cold^m. with Ainslie and Mr Foreman – beat M^r F – in a dispute about Voltaire.' Later they called at Lennel House and took tea with Patrick Brydone, a writer who had enjoyed some success with his book, *A Tour of Sicily and Malta* and whose wife was the daughter of Dr Robertson, the historian. Burns found his reception 'extremely flattering,' but had some reservations about his host:

A man of quite ordinary natural abilities, ingenious but not deep, chearful but not witty, a most excellent heart, kind, joyous & benevolent but a good deal of the French indiscriminate complaisance – from his situation past & present an admirer of every thing that bears a splendid title or possesses a large estate.

His farmer's eye noted points of difference from his own part of the world:

Climate & soil of Berwick shire & even Roxburgh shire, superiour to Ayrshire – bad roads – turnip & sheep husbandry their great improvements – M^r. M^{c}dowall at Caverton mill a friend of M^r. Ainslie's, with whom I dined today, sold his sheep, ewe & lamb together, at two guineas a piece – wash their sheep before shearing – 7 or 8lb of washen wool in a fleece – low

1. The text of the journal, edited by J. De Lancey Ferguson, is included in Fitzhugh, *op. cit.*, pp. 105-22.
2. Kinsley, 153.

markets, consequently low rents – fine lands not above 16 sh Scotch acre – Magnificence of Farmers & farm houses . . .

They spent three nights at Jedburgh, and Burns's account of breakfast with a local lawyer called Fair takes on a mildly Hogarthian note: 'A squabble between M^rs F–, a craz'd, talkative Slattern, and a sister of hers an old maid, respecting a relief Minister – Miss gives Madam the lie, & Madam by way of revenge upbraids her that she laid snares to entangle the said minister, then a widower, in the net of matrimony . . .'

Burns then found himself entangled in a walking party with these ladies, together with Mrs Fair's two daughters – 'tolerably agreable, but too much of the Mother's half-ell mouth & hag-like features.' The tedium of the occasion was lightened by the presence of two other young ladies, however, and Burns made an unsettling discovery:

> . . . Miss Lindsay a good-humor'd, amiable girl; rather short et embonpoint, but handsome and extremely graceful – beautiful hazle eyes full of spirit & sparkling with delicious moisture – an engaging face & manner, un tout ensemble that speaks her of the first order of female minds . . . Shake myself loose, after several unsuccessful efforts, of M^rs. F–r and Miss L–p and somehow or other get hold of Miss Lindsay's arm – my heart thawed into melting pleasure after being so long frozen up in the Greenland bay of Indifference amid the noise and nonsense of Edin^r . . . Nota Bene – The poet within a point and a half of being damnably in love – I am afraid my bosom still nearly as much tinder as ever.

His susceptibility did not escape the eye of the maiden aunt, and she appears to have tried to mark his card about her niece, an initiative which earned her a passage of sustained invective in Burns's journal:

> The old, cross-grained, whiggish, ugly, slanderous hag, Miss Lookup with all the poisonous spleen of a disappointed, ancient maid, stops me very unseasonably to ease her hell-rankling bursting breast by falling abusively foul on the Miss Lindsays, particularly my Dulcinea; I hardly refrain from cursing her to her face – May she, for her pains, be curst with eternal desire and damn'd with endless disappointment! Hear me, O Heavens, and give ear, O Earth! may the burden of antiquated Virginity crush her down to the lowest regions of the bottomless Pit! for daring to mouth her calumnious slander on one of the finest pieces of the workmanship of Almighty Excellence.

The next morning he rode down to Wauchope to pay his respects to his versifying correspondent, Mrs Scot. Her husband reminded him of Sancho Panza: 'Very shrewd in his farming matters,' Burns noted, 'but in other respects a compleat Hottentot.' Mrs Scot, on the other hand, seemed to him to possess 'all the sense, taste, intrepidity of face, & bold, critical decision which usually distinguish female Authors.' But he was eager to be back in Jedburgh – 'I find Miss L– would soon play the devil with me – I met with some little flattering attentions from her.' He contrived one last occasion to snatch a few minutes alone with his 'Dulcinea' in a garden: 'After some little chit-chat of the tender kind I presented her with a proof-print of my nob, which she accepted with something more tender than gratitude.'

Before he left, the local magistrates waited on him to confer the freedom of the burgh. 'Took farewell of Jedburgh with some melancholy,' he wrote in his journal:

> Jed, pure be thy chrystal streams, and hallowed thy sylvan banks! Sweet Isabella Lindsay, may Peace dwell in thy bosom, uninterrupted, except by the tumultuous throbbings of rapturous Love! That love-kindling eye must beam on another, not me; that graceful form must bless another's arms, not mine!

So they did, and sooner than Burns might have expected. To a buzz of small-town gossip, sweet Isabella Lindsay was married within the month to one Adam Armstrong, who, like many another Scot, took service with the government of the Tsar and carried his bride off to St Petersburg. She died young, leaving four children; the youngest of them rose to be a general, and became director of the Imperial Mint.

North-eastwards to Kelso, west along the Tweed to Melrose, up the Ettrick valley to Selkirk. The townspeople there are known as Souters, because from earliest times the shoemakers were a flourishing craft; in the rebellions of 1715 and 1745 they had been required to furnish the Jacobites with several thousand pairs. A royal burgh since 1113, it was in the town's Church of St Mary that Burns's hero Wallace had been proclaimed guardian of the kingdom. All the Border burghs are renowned for the sturdy opinion they entertain of their centrality in the scheme of things; when Souters assert, as they quite often do, that 'a day oot o' Selkirk's a day wasted' they are only partly joking.

Burns and Ainslie rode into the town on the evening of May 13th. Their arrival was observed by a Dr Clarkson, who was sitting over a glass with two of his cronies in Veitch's Inn, near the West Port. It was a Sunday evening. The weather had turned cold and wet. The travellers were 'just like twa droukit craws' and these Selkirk worthies, distinctly unimpressed, were not inclined to admit them to their company. The doctor asked the landlord what the men were like:

> Mr Veitch said he could not well say: the one spoke *rather* like a gentleman, but the other was a drover-looking chap; so they refused to admit them, sending them word that they were sorry they were engaged elsewhere, and

obliged to go away. The doctor saw them ride off next morning, and it was not till the third day that he knew it had been the celebrated Scottish poet whom they had refused to admit. That refusal hangs about the doctor's heart like a deadweight to this day, and will do till the day of his death, for the bard had not a more enthusiastic admirer.[1]

The bard whiled away the evening by writing to Creech, who had gone to London to discuss the details of the first English edition of the poems with Strahan and Cadell:

My honored Friend,
    The inclosed I have just wrote, nearly extempore, in a solitary Inn in Selkirk, after a miserable wet day's riding . . . I would write till I would tire you as much with dull Prose as I dare say by this time you are with wretched Verse; but I am jaded to death . . .[2]

There was nothing in the least tired or jaded about what he enclosed, which was the mock lament sometimes known as 'Willie's Awa', twelve lively stanzas deploring the publisher's absence from Auld Reekie and hymning his importance to the life of the capital:

> The brethren o' the commerce-chaumer   *chamber of commerce*
> May mourn their loss wi' doolfu' clamour;   *sorrowful*
> He was a dictionar and grammar
>   Amang them a':
> I fear they'll now mak mony a stammer,
>   Willie's awa. –
>
> Nae mair we see his levee door
> Philosophers and Poets pour,
> And toothy Critics by the score
>   In bloody raw;   *row*
> The adjutant of a' the core
>   Willie's awa. —[3]

Two days later, back at Ainslie's parents' house in Duns, Burns took up his pen again, though to less distinguished effect. He had been importuned on his first visit by a man called Simon Gray, who had retired from business in

---

1. The story is related by James Hogg in the edition of Burns which he and William Motherwell published almost half a century later (*The Works of Robert Burns*, edited by the Ettrick Shepherd and William Motherwell, 5 vols., Archibald Fullarton, Glasgow, 1838-41). Dr Clarkson, he wrote, used to tell the story "with a heavy heart and loss of all patience with himself."
2. *Letters*, 106.
3. *Kinsley*, 154.

London. Gray fancied himself as a poet and had asked Burns to look at a specimen of his work. Burns did not think much of it, and returned it with a brusque couplet:

> SYMON Gray,
> You're dull to-day.

Gray persisted and sent a second packet, to which Burns responded with a couplet only marginally more expansive than the first:

> DULNESS, with redoubled sway,
> Has seized the wits of Symon Gray.

Gray, who was either very stupid or extremely thick-skinned, made one more try, and Burns, now exasperated, blew him coarsely out of the water:

> DEAR Cimon Gray,
>   The other day,
>   When you sent me some rhyme,
> I could not then just ascertain
>   Its worth, for want of time.
>
> But now today, good Mr. Gray,
>   I've read it o'er and o'er,
> Tried all my skill, but find I'm still
>   Just where I was before.
>
> We auld wives' minions gie our opinions,
>   Solicited or no;
> Then of its fau'ts my honest thoughts
>   I'll give – and here they go.
>
> Such d——'d bombast no time that's past
>   Will show, or time to come,
> So, Cimon dear, your song I'll tear,
>   And with it wipe my [bum].[1]

Four days later, Burns and Ainslie were made Royal Arch Masons of the St Abb's Lodge at Eyemouth. The lodge minute book records that 'on account of R. Burns's remarkable poetical genius, the encampment unanimously agreed to admit him gratis.'

Several more young women have walking-on parts in the pages of the

1. *Ibid.*, 155.

Border journal – 'My bardship's heart got a brush from Miss Betsey'; 'I could grasp her with rapture on a bed of straw' (this of Ainslie's sister); 'I talk of love to Nancy the whole evening.' He was quite unable to grasp that those he drew into this compulsive game might take it for something more serious; indeed the hours he spent toying with the affections of Nancy Sherriff (she was the sister of a farmer who had entertained him to dinner) got him into something of a scrape, which he recounted with zest in a letter to Ainslie:

> ... When I returned to my horse I found Miss– ready equipp'd to escort me to Dunbar with the view of making a parade of me as a Sweetheart among her relations ... She was "bien poudré, bien frisé" in her fine cream-colored riding clothes, mounted on an old, dun carthorse that had once been fat; a broken, old side saddle, without crupper, stirrup or girth; a bridle that in former times had had buckles, and a crooked meandring hazle stick which might have borne a place with credit in a scrubbed besom. – In the words of the Highlandman when he saw the Deil on Shanter-hill in the shape of five swine – "My hair stood and my p– stood, and I swat and trembled." —Nothing could prevail with her, no distant insinuation, no broad hint would make her give over her purpose; at last, vexed, disgusted, enraged, to a high degree, I pretended a fire-haste and rode so hard that she was almost shaken to pieces on old Jolly, and, to my great joy found it convenient to stop at an uncle's house by the way: I refused to call with her, and so we quarreled & parted. – [1]

Ainslie had gone back to his law office, and Burns was missing him. 'Mon cher Compagnon de voyage,' he wrote, 'I have not had one hearty mouthful of laughter since that merry-melancholy moment we parted.' He had acquired a new travelling companion called Gilbert Ker, a friend of Ainslie's father's whom he had met at the Farmers' Club in Kelso, and they set off together for the English border. When they stopped to dine with a farmer called Thomas Hood, Burns became unwell and this, as usual, made him extremely agitated:

> I am taken extremely ill with strong feverish symptoms, & take a servant of Mr Hood's to watch me all night – embittering Remorse scares my fancy at the gloomy forebodings of death – I am determined to live for the future in such a manner as not to be scared at the approach of Death – I am sure I could meet him with indifference, but for "The Something beyond the grave."

He lived through the night. Hood agreed to accompany them if they would wait till Sunday. They visited the seat of the Duke of Northumberland at Alnwick ('furnished in a most princely manner'), moved on to Morpeth and

1. Letters, 110.

Newcastle and then struck westwards to Carlisle. Here he falls in with a girl and her married sister, and recounts 'a strange enough romantic adventure':

> ... The girl, after some overtures of gallantry on my side, sees me a little cut with the bottle, and offers to take me in for a Gretna-green affair. I, not being quite such a gull as she imagines, make an appointment with her, by way of vive la bagatelle, to hold a conference on it when we reach town. – I meet her in town and give her a brush of caressing and a bottle of cyder; but finding herself un peu trompée in her man, she sheers off.

From Carlisle he wrote a long letter to William Nicol – 'Kind, honest-hearted Willie,' as he addressed him. It gives a high-spirited account of his adventures since leaving Edinburgh, but is written in a Scots so impenetrably broad that even Chambers felt obliged to offer a translation. Burns begins with a description of Jenny Geddes:

> ... It's true, she's as poor's a Sang-maker and as hard's a kirk, and tipper-taipers when she taks the gate first, like a Lady's gentlewoman in a minuwae or a hen on a het girdle, but she's a yauld, poutherie Girran for a' that; and has a stomach like Willie Stalker's meere that wad hae disgeested tumbler-wheels, for she'll whip me aff her five stimparts o' the best aits at a down-sittin and ne'er fash her thumb. – When ance her ringbanes and spavies, her crucks and cramps, are fairly soupl'd, she beets to, beets to, and ay the hindmost hour the tightest ...

> (*It is true she is as poor as a song-maker, and as hard as a church, and totters when she takes the road, just like a lady's gentlewoman in a minuet or a hen on a hot oven; but she is an alert, spirited beast notwithstanding, and has a stomach like Willie Stalker's mare, that would have digested cart-wheels, for she'll whip me off five -eighths of a Winchester bushel of the best oats at a time, with no difficulty. When once her ill-assorted joints and spavins, her lameness and cramps, are fairly suppled, she improves by little and little, and always the last hour is her best.*)

He goes on to tell Nicol something of his amorous encounters:

> I met wi' twa dink quines in particlar, ane o' them a sonsie, fine, fodgel lass, baith braw and bonie; the tither was a clean-shankit, straught, tight, weel-far'd winch, as blythe's a lintwhite on a flowerie thorn, and as sweet and modest's a new-blawn plumrose in a hazle shaw. – They were baith bred to mainers by the beuk, and onie ane o' them has as muckle smeddum and rumblegumtion as the half o' some Presbytries that you and I baith ken. – They played me sic a deevil o' a shavie that I daur say if my harigals were turn'd out, ye wad see twa nicks i' the heart o' me like the mark o' a kail-whittle in a castock.

(I met with two fine girls in particular, one of them a fine, plump, comfortable-looking lass, well-dressed and pretty; the other a well-limbed, straight, tight, well-favoured wench, as blithe as a linnet on a flowering thorn, and as sweet and modest as a new-blown primrose in a hazel-wood. They had both acquired manners from the book, and any one of them had as much smartness and sense as the half of some of the presbyteries that you and I know. They played me such a devil of a prank, that if my inside were turned out, you would see two nicks on my heart like the mark of a knife on a cabbage-stalk.)

There wrote the best travel-writer and perhaps the finest novelist that Scotland never had. The letter is headed 'Carlisle 1st June 1787 – or I believe the 39th o' May rather,' and it is not entirely clear from the way it ends whether Burns composed it drunk or sober: 'I was gaun to write you a lang pystle. but, Gude forgie me, I gat myself sae notouriously bitchify'd the day after kail-time, that I can hardly stoiter but and ben.'[1]

He crossed back into Scotland and made for Dumfries, where he was given the freedom of the burgh.[2] Much less agreeable to him were the contents of a letter which he found waiting for him. 'Out of quarters, without friends, my situation at present is really deplorable,' he read. 'I beg, for God's sake, you will write and let me know how I am to do. You can write to any person you can trust to get me a place to stay in till such time as you come to town yourself.' It had been written on behalf of Meg Cameron, the servant girl whom he had seduced in Edinburgh, most probably in the middle of April[3] – the assumption is that she was illiterate.

Burns did write, but the letter is lost. He also wrote to Robert Ainslie. The manuscript of that letter is preserved at the Birthplace Museum, Alloway. It does not make pleasant reading:

My Dear friend,
    My first welcome to this place was the inclosed letter. – I am very sorry for it, but what is done is done. – I pay you no compliment when I say that except my old friend Smith there is not any person in the world I would trust so far. – Please call at the Jas Hog mentioned, and send for the wench and give her ten or twelve shillings, but don't for Heaven's sake meddle with her as a *Piece*. – I insist on this, on your honor; and advise her out to some country friends. – You may perhaps not like the business, but I just tax your friendship thus far. – Call immediately, [for God (*deleted*)] or at least as soon

1. Letters, 112.
2. The Dumfries magistrates do not seem to have been particularly discriminating, as they granted the honorary freedom of the burgh to thirty-eight people in that year alone. It was also possible to buy the privilege. The fee was £80 Scots, which was £6 13s 4d sterling.
3. The evidence for this is a short passage in an incomplete letter to Ainslie which is preserved in the National Library of Scotland: '. . . the Devil's Day-book only April 14 or fifteen so cannot yet have increased her growth much. I begin, from that, and some other circumstances to suspect foul play; and to tell the truth I w . . .' (Letters, 116.)

as it is dark, for God sake, lest the poor soul be starving. – Ask her for a letter I wrote her just now, by way of token. – it is unsigned. – Write me after the meeting. –

ROB^T BURNS[1]

Dalswinton was only six miles or so from Dumfries and Burns rode up Niths-dale to see what was on offer. Nothing was concluded on this first visit, though he told Nicol that he and Patrick Miller were to meet again in August: 'From my view of the lands and his reception of my Bardship, my hopes in that business are rather mended; but still they are but slender.' He also told Nicol how charmed he had been by the warmth of his reception in Dumfries: 'Mr Burnside the Clergyman, in particular, is a man whom I shall ever gratefully remember; and his wife, Gude forgie me, I had almost broke the tenth com-mandment on her account.'[2].

He reached Mauchline on the evening of June 8th. It was a low-key home-coming, and it is plain from a letter Burns wrote three days later to his friend James Smith, now settled in Linlithgow, that he was both confused and unsettled:

I date this from Mauchline, where I arrived on Friday even last. I slept at John Dows, and called for my daughter; Mr. Hamilton and family; your mother, sister and brother; my quondam Eliza, &c, all, all well. If any thing had been wanting to disgust me compleatly at Armour's family, their mean servile compliance would have done it.

Give me spirit a like my favourite hero, Milton's Satan,

"Hail, horrors! hail,
Infernal world! and thou, profoundest Hell,
Receive thy new possessor! one who brings
A mind not to be chang'd by *place* or *time!*"

I cannot settle to my mind – Farming the only thing of which I know any thing, and Heaven above knows, but little do I understand even of that, I cannot, dare not risk on farms as they are. If I do not fix, I will go for Jamaica. Should I stay, in an unsettled state, at home, I would only dissipate my little fortune, and ruin what I intend shall compensate my little ones, for the stigma I have brought on their names . . .[3]

Lucifer was still much in his mind when he wrote to Nicol a week later – 'I have bought a pocket Milton which I carry perpetually about with me, in order to study the sentiments – the dauntless magnanimity; the intrepid unyielding independance; the desperate daring, and noble defiance of hardship, in that

1. Letters, 246.
2. *Ibid.*, 114.
3. *Ibid.*, 113.

great Personage, Satan.' Although the letter began chirpily enough with news of his 'very agreable jaunt,' his underlying mood was still sombre; one passage in particular is a sour cocktail of bitterness and puzzlement: 'I never, My friend, thought mankind very capable of any thing generous; but the stateliness of the Patricians in Edin^r, and the damn'd servility of my plebeian brethren, who perhaps formerly eyed me askance, since I returned home, have nearly put me out of conceit altogether with my species.'[1]

Burns's disgust at the 'mean, servile compliance' of the Armours did not prevent him from visiting their daughter. Before his restlessness took him off on the second of his summer jaunts, Jean was once again pregnant. His 'native country' had detained him less than two weeks. He had made the painful discovery that local boys who make good often find themselves living between two worlds.

By June 24th he was in Glasgow, where he did some business with the bookseller John Smith. The firm had subscribed for twelve copies of the Edinburgh edition and also acted as agents for the distribution of copies to subscribers. According to the firm's history, Smith charged only 5 per cent for this service, and this struck Burns as agreeably modest. 'You seem a very decent sort o' folk, you Glasgow booksellers,' he exclaimed, 'but eh! they're sair birkies in Edinburgh.'[2] While he was in Glasgow he sent home to Mauchline a present of mode silk – a sufficient quantity to make a cloak and bonnet for his mother and each of his three sisters.

We have only the sketchiest idea of where he went after that and of whether he travelled alone or in company; on this short second tour he is not known to have kept a journal. On June 25th he was in Argyll and wrote to Ainslie from Arrochar, at the head of Loch Long – 'a country where savage streams tumble over savage mountains, thinly overspread with savage flocks, which starvingly support as savage inhabitants.'[3] It does not sound as if he was enjoying himself all that much, and this could have had to do with his reception at Inveraray, the seat of the Duke of Argyll. The Duke and his Duchess had subscribed to the Edinburgh edition, but if Burns had hopes of being received by them he was disappointed. The Duke was just leaving for a tour of the Hebrides on British Fishery Society business (he was the Society's President); the Castle was full of Society members who were to accompany him and so was the local inn, with the result that Burns's reception was not what he thought it should be. He let off steam in rhyme:

WHOE'ER he be that sojourns here,
I pity much his case,

---

1. *Ibid.*, 114
2. *A Short Note on a Long History, John Smith & Son*, Glasgow, 1921. Birkie means a spry, smart young fellow. It carries some suggestion of sharpness—birkie is also a Scots name for the card game 'beggar-my-neighbour.'
3. Letters, 116.

Unless he comes to wait upon
The Lord their God, his Grace.

There's naething here but Highland pride,
And Highland scab and hunger;
If Providence has sent me here,
'Twas surely in an anger.[1]

Whether Burns was so uncouth as to scratch these lines on a window pane at
the inn can no longer be verified. He certainly owned a diamond-tipped stylus
(a gift from Glencairn); the doggerel had found its way into print by early in
the nineteenth century; no such window is any longer known to exist.

He was more warmly received on the homeward journey:

. . . At a Highland gentleman's hospitable mansion, we fell in with a merry
party and danced 'till the ladies left us, at three in the morning. Our dancing
was none of the French or English insipid formal movements; the ladies
sung Scotch songs like angels, at intervals: then we flew at *Bab at the Bowster,
Tullochgorum, Loch Erroch side*, &c. like midges sporting in the mottie sun,
or craws prognosticating a storm in a hairst day. – When the dear lasses left
us, we ranged round the bowl till the good-fellow hour of six; except a few
minutes that we went out to pay our devotions to the glorious lamp of day
peering over the towering top of Benlomond.[2]

Burns spent the following day on Loch Lomond, and that evening was again
well entertained at Dumbarton: 'We dined at another good fellow's house, and
consequently push'd the bottle.' He does not say who his companions were,
but by the time they went out to their horses they were all somewhat the worse
for wear:

My two friends and I rode soberly down the Loch side, till by came a
Highlandman at the gallop, on a tolerably good horse, but which had never
known the ornaments of iron or leather. We scorned to be out-galloped by
a Highlandman, so off we started, whip and spur . . . just as I was passing
him, Donald wheeled his horse, as if to cross before me to mar my progress,
when down came his horse, and threw his rider's breekless a–e in a clipt
hedge; and down came Jenny Geddes over all, and my bardship between
her and the Highlandman's horse. Jenny Geddes trode over me with such
cautious reverence, that matters were not so bad as might well have been
expected; so I came off with a few cuts and bruises, and a thorough resolution
to be a pattern of sobriety for the future.

1. Kinsley, 159.
2. Letters, 117.

He had, in fact, taken more of a knock than he thought. A week or so later, he described his 'drunken race' in a letter to Richmond: 'I have got such a skinful of bruises and wounds, that I shall be at least four weeks before I dare venture on my journey to Edinburgh.'[1] He spent most of July at the farm, conducting a little business by post, composing a couple of elegies,[2] writing to his friends. He was in particularly exuberant form when he wrote to Ainslie, who had got a girl into trouble and, at the age of twenty-one, had just become a father: 'Give you joy, give you joy, My dear brother! may your child be as strong as Samson, as wise a man as Solomon, & as honest a man as his father. – I have double health and spirits at the news. – Welcome, Sir, to the society, the venerable Society, of FATHERS!!!'[3]

He treated Ainslie to a slightly reworked version of a metrical psalm ('L—s children are God's heritage;/The womb's fruit his reward'),[4] extracts from a couple of his own bawdy poems[5] and a few cheerful and distinctly patriarchal lines about his own brood and the prospect of its increase, both in Mauchline and Edinburgh: '. . . My ailing child is got better – and the Mother is certainly in for it again – and Peggy will bring a gallant half-Highlander – and I shall get a farm, and keep them all about my hand, and breed them in the fear of the Lord and an oatstick, and I shall be the happiest man upon earth–'

Whether Peggy – Meg Cameron – did in the event bring him his 'gallant half-Highlander' is not known. The Edinburgh parish registers for 1787 record no birth to a woman of that name. What we do know is that in the course of July Burns was served on her behalf with a writ similar to the one that had sent him scuttling for cover a year previously. Somehow again, the details are lost to us – matters were arranged, and the girl received some degree of legal satisfaction. The document which freed Burns from the restraints imposed by the writ was dated August 15th. He retained it, and with the insouciance characteristic of him in such matters, used the back of it to jot down some coarse verses that had caught his fancy.[6] Peggy Cameron passes from the scene; Burns 'meddled with her as a Piece' no more.

---

1. *Ibid.*, 119.
2. These were for Sir James Hunter Blair (Kinsley, 160) and John McLeod of Raasay (Kinsley, 162). Hunter Blair, a banker, was a native of Ayr who had been MP for Edinburgh from 1780-84 and Lord Provost of the City in 1784. He had been friendly to Burns during his stay in the capital and had entertained him at his house in Queen Street; he died at the age of forty-six. Burns did not think the elegy was the best thing he had ever done: 'The Performance is but mediocre,' he wrote, 'but my grief was sincere.' McLeod was the brother of a young woman he had met in Edinburgh the previous winter.
3. Letters, 122A.
4. Psalm 127, 3–5.
5. Kinsley, 46 and 277.
6. Chambers-Wallace, vol. ii, p. 146.

He was much flattered at this time by the attentions of Mrs Dunlop, and wrote to express his gratitude in extravagant terms: 'I am sure, Madam, you have most effectually surprized me this morning. – Send your serv' twenty miles to enquire for me!!! By all the towering flights of Pride; 'twas doing me an honor so far beyond my wildest expectation that for half a second the shadow of a Doubt eclipsed my belief, whether you might perhaps mean to burlesque me. – '[1]

Mrs Dunlop had sent him some verses, and he returned an elaborate compliment on them: 'Without any Poetic licence, I assure you upon the honor of plain, unfettered, truth-delivering Prose, they are excellent.' He also told her that he had composed his autobiographical letter to Dr Moore, and asked whether she would look it over for him before he put it in the post.

The beginning of his letter to Moore is rather mannered. 'To divert my spirits a little in this miserable fog of Ennui, I have taken a whim to give you a history of MYSELF,' he wrote:

My name has made a small noise in the country; you have done me the honor to interest yourself very warmly in my behalf; and I think a faithful account of, what character of a man I am, and how I came by that character, may perhaps amuse you in an idle moment. – I will give you an honest narrative, though I know it will be at the expense of frequently being laughed at; for I assure you, Sir, I have, like Solomon whose character, excepting the trifling affair of WISDOM, I sometimes think I resemble, I have, I say, like him "Turned my eyes to behold Madness and Folly;" and like him too, frequently shaken hands with their intoxicating friendship. –

A few days after sending this twenty-page epistle to Dunlop House, Burns paid his first visit there. Mrs Dunlop celebrated the occasion in verse ('Five months of expectation past,/The long-wish'd hour arrived at last./A face peept in just at the door . . .'), but those expectations were quickly disappointed by Burns's uncouth behaviour. She had planned an evening walk, had a thousand questions to ask him, but Burns's manner was brusque and he took his leave much sooner than she had expected: 'My crowquill wants strength to tell what joy was murdered when you bade farewell.' His lack of manners had been noticed below stairs as well as in Mrs Dunlop's drawing room, and she allows her servants to have their say in her verses:

> 'Giff that be Burns, he may hae lear   learning
> But Faith! I'm sure he has nae mair.
> He's brought his havins frae the plough,   manners
> Ne'er touched his hat nor made a bow . . .

1. Letters, 124.

This was a poor performance from the man who had so recently swept the Duchess of Gordon off her feet. 'I am, just as usual, a raking, aimless idle fellow,' he had written to Smith a few weeks earlier, and his behaviour at Dunlop House offers evidence of how unsettled and perhaps how unhappy he was. Early in August, he took himself off to Edinburgh. He had unfinished business there with Creech, who had still failed to settle accounts; he also had it in mind to see more of the Highlands.

He stayed briefly with Richmond in the Lawnmarket and then moved a few hundred yards down the Royal Mile to lodge with Nicol, who lived near the Tron Kirk. He got nowhere with Creech, and time hung heavily on his hands; a letter he wrote to Archibald Lawrie survives, and style and content both point to some reliance on the bottle:

> Here am I – that is all I can tell you of that unaccountable BEING – Myself. – What I am doing, no mortal can tell; what I am thinking, I myself cannot tell; what I am usually saying, is not worth telling. – The clock is just striking, one, two, three, four, –, –, –, –, –, –, –, twelve, forenoon; and here I sit, in the Attic story, alias, the garret, with a friend on the right hand of my standish – a friend whose kindness I shall largely experience at the close of this line – there – thank you – A friend, my dear Mr Lowrie, whose kindness often makes me blush; a Friend who has more of the milk of human kindness than all the human race put together, and what is highly to his honor, peculiarly a friend to the friendless as often as they come in his way; in short, Sir, he is, without the least alloy, [he is (*deleted*)] a universal Philanthropist; and his much beloved name is, A BOTTLE OF GOOD OLD PORT![1]

He was plainly at a low ebb. Loneliness, boredom and uncertainty about the future all clearly played a part; the Meg Cameron business may well have done so too, his breezy tone to Ainslie notwithstanding, and his unsatisfactory dealings with Creech continued to irk and frustrate him. The Edinburgh edition had been published only four short months previously, but those heady April days when his name was on every tongue might have been in another century. It is our introduction to Burns the solitary drinker.

Ten days later, he and Nicol set out for the Highlands. They travelled in a post-chaise: 'Nicol thinks it more comfortable than horse-back, to which I say Amen,' he wrote to Ainslie on the eve of their departure. His spirits had greatly improved (the Meg Cameron business had now been concluded), and in a postscript he offered Ainslie some airy advice about names for his son:

> Call your boy what you think proper, only interject Burns. – What do you [*sic*] to a scripture name; for instance –

1. *Ibid.*, 127.

Zimri Burns Ainslie

or

Achitophel, &c., &c. –

look your bible for these two heroes. – If you do this, I will repay the Compliment.[1]

The travellers drove west to Linlithgow. Burns once again kept a journal, as he had done on the Borders earlier in the year. 'The old rough palace a tolerably fine but melancholy ruin,' he wrote:

> Shown the room where the beautiful, injured Mary Queen of Scots was born – a pretty good old Gothic church – the infamous stool of repentance standing, in the old Romish way, in a lofty situation. What a poor, pimping business is a Presbyterian place of worship! dirty, narrow, squalid; stuck in a corner of old popish grandeur such as Linlithgow, and much more Melrose.

Their second day's itinerary roused Burns to a pitch of patriotic fervour: 'This morning I kneel'd at the tomb of Sir John the Graham, the gallant friend of the immortal WALLACE,' he wrote to his friend Robert Muir, 'and two hours ago, I said a fervent prayer for old Caledonia over the hole in a blue whin-stone where Robert de Bruce fixed his royal standard on the banks of Bannockburn.'[2] They had hoped to visit the famous Carron iron works, but the porter refused them admittance – not unreasonably, as it was Sunday. Burns crossed the road to the inn, and selecting a suitable window-pane, set to work with his diamond stylus:

> We cam' na here to view your warks,
>   In hopes to be mair wise,
> But only lest we gang to hell,
>   It may be nae surprise . . .[3]

---

1. *Ibid.*, 130.
2. *Ibid.*, 131.
3. Kinsley, 165. A traveller for the company copied Burns's squib into his order book and responded in kind:

> If you cam here to see our works
>   You should have been more civil
> Than give us a fictitious name
>   In hopes to cheat the devil.
>
> Six days a week to you and all
>   We think it very well,
> The other, if you go to church,
>   May keep you out of Hell.

Quoted in William Harvey, *Robert Burns in Stirlingshire*, Eneas Mackay, Stirling, 1899, pp. 7–8.

He was busy with his stylus again in Stirling. The great hall of the castle, where the old Scots parliament had sometimes sat, had fallen into ruinous disrepair. Burns made a connection between this and the Jacobite sentiments he liked to profess, and when he got back to the inn he scratched some lines of verse on the window of his room. It was an act of delinquency which subsequently caught up with him, because not content with singing the praises of the Stuarts, he also found it necessary to be offensive to the House of Hanover:

> Here Stewarts once in triumph reign'd,
> And laws for Scotland's weal ordain'd;
> But now unroof'd their Palace stands,
> Their sceptre's fall'n to other hands;
> Fallen indeed, and to the earth,
> Whence grovelling reptiles take their birth. –
> The injur'd STEWART-line are gone,
> A Race outlandish fill their throne;
> An idiot race, to honor lost;
> Who know them best despise them most. –[1]

Burns made an expedition the next day to the Devon valley, in Clackmannanshire, to visit some relatives of Gavin Hamilton's. The estate was called Harvieston, and it belonged to an Edinburgh lawyer, John Tait, who had married a sister of Margaret Chalmers's mother and Gavin Hamilton's stepmother. After the death of his wife he had invited Mrs Hamilton to preside over his household and she now lived there with her son and two daughters, Grace and Charlotte. Burns's hope was that he would see Margaret Chalmers, a close friend of her cousin Charlotte's and a frequent visitor to the house, but it turned out that she was in Edinburgh; he spent the day sightseeing and returned to Stirling that evening. He sent a long letter to Gavin Hamilton singing the family's praises and writing in particularly flattering terms of the younger of his half-sisters. 'She is not only beautiful; but lovely,' he wrote. 'Her features not regular but they have the smile of Sweetness and the settled complacency of good nature in the highest degree.' He even compared Charlotte's complexion to Miss Burnet's, and from Burns that was praise indeed.[2]

The chaise rattled on through some of the finest scenery in Scotland – over the Ochil Hills to Crieff and north again to Taymouth before turning east and following the Tay down towards Dunkeld. Burns remembered that he was a poet as well as a Jacobite and began to respond to what he saw about him; at the Falls of Moness he composed 'The birks of Aberfeldey':

1. Kinsley, 166.
2. Letters, 132. Charlotte was four years younger than Burns.

> Now Simmer blinks on flowery braes,
> And o'er the chrystal streamlets plays;
> Come let us spend the lightsome days
> In the birks of Aberfeldey ...[1]   birches

'Scottish scenes, and Scottish story are the themes I could wish to sing,' he had written to Mrs Dunlop, and now he was beginning to do so. The lyric was set to an old tune called 'The birks of Abergeldie' and appeared the following year, signed simply 'B', in the second volume of Johnson's *Scots Musical Museum*. It has remained one of the most popular of all Scots songs.

The next day, at Dunkeld, Burns met the celebrated Niel Gow, the greatest Scots fiddler of the day: 'a short, stout-built Highland figure,' he noted, 'with his greyish hair shed on his honest social brow'. Gow played for him, and Burns returned the compliment by composing 'Amang the trees'. The song is set to an old Jacobite tune called 'The King of France, he rade a race'. The words are hard work for non-Scottish ears, but repay recourse to a glossary. Burns praises the 'Pibroch, Sang, Strathspeys and Reels' of 'Auld Caledon' and takes a swipe (a somewhat outdated one, it must be said) at the *castrati* of the Italian opera:

> Their capon craws, and queer ha ha's,
> They made our lugs grow eerie, O![2]

They travelled on up the River Tummel, and through the Pass of Killiecrankie. This was where King William's English soldiers had been defeated by the insurgent Highlanders under Claverhouse in 1689; in 1746 German troops, brought north to pursue the supporters of the Young Pretender, refused to march through the pass, insisting that they had reached the last outpost of civilisation. Burns's muse was untouched; he noted laconically in his journal the 'wild grandeur' of the pass and recorded that they had visited 'the gallant Lord Dundee's stone'.[3]

Later that day they reached Blair Atholl, and from the inn Burns sent news of their arrival to Blair Castle, the seat of the Duke of Atholl. Hugh Blair had furnished him with a letter of introduction, and young Josiah Walker, whom Burns had met in Edinburgh, had recently taken up an appointment in the household as tutor to the Duke's eldest son, the Marquess of Tullibardine. The Duke was away, but the Duchess sent a cordial invitation to 'sup and sleep' at the house. In the time before supper Walker showed him the grounds:

---

1. Kinsley, 170.
2. *Ibid.*, 171. It was half a century since Hogarth, in 'The Rake's Progress', had immortalised the ecstatic lady who exclaimed, 'One God and one Farinelli!' Enthusiam for the *castrati* among the *dilettanti* was gradually diluted by irritation at their frequent arrogance and vanity.
3. 'Bonnie Dundee' did not survive the battle. The standing stone marks the spot where he is reputed to have fallen. His troops were decisively defeated three weeks later at Dunkeld.

It was already growing dark; yet the softened, though faint and uncertain, view of their beauties, which the moonlight afforded us, seemed exactly suited to the state of his feelings at the time. I had often, like others, experienced the pleasures which arise from the sublime or elegant landscape, but I never saw those feelings so intense as in Burns. When we reached a rustic hut on the river Tilt, where it is overhung by a woody precipice, from which there is a noble waterfall, he threw himself on the heathy seat, and gave himself up to a tender, abstracted, and voluptuous enthusiasm of imagination.[1]

There was as much to engage Burns's imagination in the castle itself. Athole House, as it was then called, dated from the thirteenth century. When Mary, Queen of Scots, came on a visit in 1564 six wolves were killed in a hunt in the Forest of Atholl. The house had been garrisoned in 1644 by Montrose, stormed in 1652 by Cromwell and in 1746, just before Culloden, held briefly by Cumberland. On Burns's second evening, after the Duke's return, he was entertained rather more formally. Walker later recalled the occasion for Currie, not without a touch of condescension. 'My curiosity was great to see how he would conduct himself in company so different from what he had been accustomed to,' he wrote:

His manner was unembarrassed, plain, and firm. He appeared to have complete reliance on his own native good sense for directing his behaviour. He seemed at once to perceive and to appreciate what was due to the company and to himself, and never to forget a proper respect for the separate species of dignity belonging to each. He did not arrogate conversation, but, when led into it, he spoke with ease, propriety, and manliness. He tried to exert his abilities, because he knew it was ability alone that gave him a title to be there.

Burns was a great success at the castle; toasting the younger members of the family as 'honest men and bonie lasses' went down particularly well, and he was pressed to stay longer. 'The ladies, in their anxiety to have a little more of Burns's company,' Walker told Currie, 'sent a servant to the inn, to bribe his driver to loosen or pull off a horse's shoe. But the ambush failed. *Proh mirum*! The driver was incorruptible.'

The ladies' efforts were misdirected. The obstacle was not the incorruptibility of the driver, Carnegie, but the irascibility of Nicol. Burns's travelling companion was not only coarse; he was also, in David Daiches' happy phrase, 'democratic to the point of insolence'. He had not been included in the invitation to stay at the castle. Walker found him some good fishing on the Tilt and the Garry and flattered himself that 'this quite absorbed his attention and allayed his jealousy, while the poet was made a pet of in the mansion,' but in

1. See Currie, vol. ii, pp. 99-103.

truth it did no such thing; Burns deferred to the schoolmaster's wishes and they continued on their way north.

If he had stayed a day longer, he would have met Henry Dundas, then Treasurer of the Navy. 'Though little addicted to literature,' wrote Lockhart, 'he was very especially qualified to appreciate Burns as a companion,' an elliptical observation which some have taken as a feline reference to Dundas's liking for the bottle. He undoubtedly had a prodigious amount of patronage to dispense, but it is not certain that an encounter with him would have done Burns much good. Dundas was a tolerant man with a bluff manner, but it may just have been drawn to his attention that he figured as 'a chap that's damn'd auldfarran' in one of Burns's poems and as 'slee Dundas' in another.[1] Burns had, however, been introduced to Robert Graham, the Laird of Fintry, during his stay at the castle. Graham had just been appointed a Commissioner of the Scottish Board of Excise, and it was an acquaintance that was to ripen for Burns into an important friendship.

On that first Sunday in September Burns and Nicol pushed on north through the desolation of Badenoch; in some corries the snow lay seventeen and eighteen feet deep. They dined at Dalwhinnie, crossed the Spey and viewed the barracks at Ruthven where what was left of Bonnie Prince Charlie's army had rallied briefly after Culloden. As they rattled along, Burns busied himself with a bread and butter letter with a difference – 'The Humble Petition of Bruar Water to the Noble Duke of Athole.'[2] He sent it with a covering note to Walker. 'I do not mean it was *extempore*,' he wrote, 'for I have endeavoured to brush it up as well as Mr Nicol's chat and the jogging of the chaise would allow.'[3] Soon after leaving Blair they had passed the point at which the River Bruar drops in a cascade through a steep and narrow cut:

> Here, foaming down the skelvy rocks,   ledged
>   In twisting strength I rin;
> There, high my boiling torrent smokes,
>   Wild-roaring o'er a linn: waterfall
> Enjoying large each spring and well
>   As Nature gave them me,
> I am, altho' I say 't mysel,
>   Worth gaun a mile to see.   going
>
> Would then my noble master please
>   To grant my highest wishes,

1. 'Auldfarran' can mean sagacious, but also means old-fashioned. The line occurs in 'The Author's Earnest Cry and Prayer' (Kimsley, 81). 'Slee Dundas' is in 'When Guilford good our Pilot stood' (Kinsley, 38).
2. Kinsley, 172.
3. Letters, 135.

>He'll shade my banks wi' towering trees,
>And bonie spreading bushes ...

The Duke did please. The treeless moorland was planted with firs, a walk was cut through the young forest and a number of grottoes built.

The next day, after breakfast at Aviemore ('a wild romantic spot', Burns thought) the travellers entered Strathspey. Their host at dinner was Sir James Grant, who was a half-brother of Henry Mackenzie's. Then into the valley of the Findhorn and to Cawdor Castle, which was promised to the witches by Macbeth. This may be where he murdered Duncan, and then again it may not. Burns was in any case shown the bed in which the deed was supposedly done.

The tour was proving strenuous. Burns had a letter of introduction to one of the Inverness bailies; on the evening of his arrival he had it delivered with a note of apology for not calling – he was, he wrote, 'jaded to death with the fatigues of to-day's journey'.[1] They stayed in the Highland capital two days, exploring both shores of Loch Ness; on one of their outings, at the Falls of Foyers, Burns was moved to compose the unmemorable fragment which begins 'Among the heathy hills and ragged woods/ The foaming Fyers pours his mossy floods.'[2] The next morning they crossed Culloden moor. 'Reflections on the field of battle,' Burns wrote in his journal, but he did not expand on those reflections in either verse or prose.

Burns had been looking forward to visiting the Duke and Duchess of Gordon in their castle at Fochabers. He and Nicol crossed the Spey and reached the small, orderly town (it had been laid out in 1776) on Friday, September 6th. Burns called at the castle ('fine palace, worthy of the generous proprietor') just as the family were about to sit down to dinner, and he was invited to join them. 'The Duke makes me happier than ever great man did,' he wrote in his journal. Unfortunately he was somewhat slow to mention the small man in whose company he was travelling, and by the time the Duke dispatched an invitation to Nicol to join them, the damage was done. Currie was sent an account of the episode by a local doctor:

The pride of Nicol was inflamed into a high degree of passion by the neglect to which he thought he was being subjected. He had ordered the horses to be put to the carriage, being determined to proceed on his journey alone; and they found him parading the streets of Fochabers, before the door of the inn, venting his anger on the postillion for the slowness with which he obeyed his commands.[3]

1. *Ibid.*, 133.
2. Kinsley, 174.
3. Currie, vol. i, p. 183, quoting a letter from a Dr Couper of Fochabers.

Just how exasperated and mortified Burns was by this repeat of the Blair Atholl performance is made clear in a letter he wrote some weeks later to the Duke's librarian, James Hoy:

> . . . I shall certainly, among my legacies, leave my latest curse to that unlucky predicament which hurried me, tore me away from Castle Gordon. – May that obstinate Son of Latin Prose be curst to scotch-mile periods, and damn'd to seven-league paragraphs; while Declension & Conjugation, Gender, Number and Time, under the ragged banners of Dissonance and Disarrangement eternally rank against him in hostile array!!!!!![1]

Burns and the obstinate Son of Latin Prose now made their way east along the coast of the Moray Firth and spent the night at the small port of Cullen. 'The country is sadly poor and unimproved,' Burns noted: 'The houses, crops, horses, cattle, &c., all in unison with their cart-wheels; and these are of low, coarse, unshod, clumsy work, with an axle-tree which had been made with other design than to be a resting shaft between the wheels.'

They took breakfast the following morning at Banff with Dr Chapman, the headmaster of the academy there, who was an old colleague of Nicol's. Chapman had invited one of his pupils to be present, and it is clear from his account of the occasion that neither Burns nor Nicol had yet put the Gordon Castle contretemps out of their minds:

> During breakfast, Burns played off some sportive jests at his touchy *compagnon de voyage*, about some misunderstanding which took place between them at Fochabers, in consequence of Burns having visited the castle without him; and the good old doctor seemed much amused with the way the poet chose to smoothe down the yet lurking ire of the dominie.[2]

The travellers now passed into Aberdeenshire. Near Peterhead, as Johnson and Boswell had done thirteen years previously, they viewed the oddly named Bullers of Buchan. 'Buller' comes from an old Scandinavian word meaning to roar, and this great rocky recess was probably formed by the collapse of the roof of a huge cave. A path along the edge of the cliff skirts a sheer drop of 200 ft. The sea, raging in through the natural archway, has the appearance of a cauldron on the boil.

They dined that day at Ellon. 'Lord Aberdeen's seat,' says a brief diary note. 'Entrance denied to everybody owing to the jealousy of threescore over a kept country-wench.' It is a pity that Burns was so cryptic, because there was a good story to tell – it would have made an entertaining song or poem.

1. Letters, 145. Burns enclosed a copy of the song 'Castle Gordon' which he had composed as a sign of his appreciation. (Kinsley, 175.)
2. Quoted in Chambers-Wallace, vol. ii, 172.

'Threescore' was George Gordon, the third Earl, who was now, in fact sixty-five. A shotgun marriage in his twenties to a pretty young cook had brought him two sons and four daughters, but this did not inhibit him from establishing at least three other households presided over by mistresses. The 'country-wench' was the latest of these, an English girl called Penelope Dering. She bore the elderly Earl a daughter and a son, and it was for her that he had rebuilt Ellon House between 1784 and 1787, making it in the process a good deal more comfortable than the main family seat at Haddo.[1]

Aberdeen itself Burns described as 'a lazy town,' but he spent a day there in congenial company. Lazy or no, the town boasted two universities – King's College, which had been founded by Bishop Elphinstone in 1498, and Marischal College, established almost a century later by George Keith, Earl Marischal. Burns met John Ross, the Professor of Hebrew at King's, and Thomas Gordon, 'a good-natured, jolly-looking professor', who held the chair of philosophy. He was also entertained by the editor of the *Aberdeen Journal*, James Chalmers ('a facetious fellow', he noted in his journal). Most interestingly of all he was introduced to Bishop Skinner, son of the John Skinner whom he so admired as the author of 'Tullochgorum' and other popular songs. Father and son were both ordained in the Episcopal Church, and as non-jurors, had been imprisoned in the 1750s for evading the Toleration Act. The Bishop wrote a vivid description of his meeting with Burns to his father; we even get a glimpse of Nicol scowling in the background:

> Our time was short, as he was just setting off for the south and his companion hurrying him; but we had fifty 'auld sangs' through hand, and spent an hour or so most agreeably. – 'Did not your father write the Ewie wi' the crooked horn?' – 'Yes.' – 'O, an I had the lown that did it!' said he, in a rapture of praise; 'but tell him how I love, and esteem, and venerate his truly Scottish muse.' . . . He had been at Gordon Castle, and come by Peterhead. 'Then,' said I, 'you were within four Scottish miles of *Tullochgorum's* dwelling.' Had you seen the look he gave, and how expressive of vexation; – had he been your own son you could not have wished a better proof of affection . . .[2]

Burns was now approaching his father's home territory in Kincardineshire. He had arranged to meet his cousin James Burness in Stonehaven, and he spent two agreeable days visiting aunts and cousins there, in Laurencekirk and in Montrose, which he thought a 'finely situated, handsome town.' A note from there to his cousin James, written at six o'clock in the morning, indicates that in the matter of their comings and goings it was still Nicol who was being allowed to call the tune:

---

1. See Archie Gordon, 5th Marquess of Aberdeen, *A Wild Flight of Gordons*, Weidenfeld and Nicolson, London, 1985.
2. See John Skinner, *Posthumous Works*, Aberdeen, 1809, pp. 30–33.

My dear Cousin,

Mr Nicol and Mr Carnegie[1] have taken some freak in their head and have wakened me just now with the rattling chaise to carry me to meet them at Craigie to go on our journey some other road and breakfast by the way. – I must go, which makes me very sorry . . .[2]

Three days later, with the briefest of entries, the journal closes: 'Pass through a cold, barren country to Queensferry – dine – cross the ferry, and on to Edinburgh'. They had been on the road for twenty-two days and had covered almost six hundred miles ('windings included', as he wrote with unwonted pedantry in a letter to Gilbert[3]).

The account he gives his brother of his travels is distinctly pedestrian. The letter comes alive only when he writes about the members of his father's family he had met in the north-east: 'I spent two days among our relations, and found our aunts, Jean and Isbal still alive and hale old women, John Caird, though born the same year as our father, walks as vigorously as I can; they have had several letters from his son in New York. – William Brand is likewise a stout old fellow . . .' Burns also told Gilbert he had been on the lookout for an opening for their younger brother William, then aged twenty, but that he had no great hopes of finding anything (the lad had served his time as a saddler).

He wrote a much more entertaining letter to Josiah Walker, thanking him for all his kindness during his stay at Blair Atholl and saying how gratified he was that his 'Petition for the poor naked Falls of Bruar' had been so well received. So flattered had he been by the cordial welcome he had received from the Duke and Duchess, he told Walker, that he had made a vow: if his Muse did not, within twenty-four hours, produce an appropriate poetic compliment to them, he would 'with unrelenting vengeance throw her into the House of Correction and finally banish her to Botany Bay.'[4]

Burns also wrote to Patrick Miller. 'My journey through the Highlands was perfectly inspiring,' he told him, 'and I hope to have laid in a good stock of new poetical ideas from it.' He enclosed two recent poems[5] and apologised to Miller for not having called on him at the end of August as he had promised: 'I am informed you do not come to town for a month still, and within that time I shall certainly wait on you, as by this time I suppose you will have settled your scheme with respect to your farms.'

In a flowery PS, Burns spoke of the warmth of his feelings for Miller's children: 'There is something so suspicious in the professions of attachment

1. Mr Carnegie was the driver of the chaise in which they were travelling.
2. Letters, 136.
3. *Ibid.*, 137.
4. Letters, 140.
5. These seem likely to have been 'On the Death of Sir J. Hunter Blair' (Kinsley, 160) and 'To Miss Isabella Macleod' (Kinsley, 148).

from a little man to a great man that I know not how to do justice to the grateful warmth of my heart when I would say how truly I am interested in the welfare of your little troop of angels . . .'

He also announced that he was determined not to leave Edinburgh until he had settled matters with Creech – 'which I am afraid will be a tedious business.'[1] It proved to be precisely that.

Burns's Highland tour undoubtedly provided him with more poetical raw material than his earlier jaunt through the Borders had done. There was another difference. His weeks in the north were devoid of romantic entanglements. We read of a 'jolly, frank, sensible love-inspiring widow' in Laurencekirk and of a young woman he encountered at breakfast in the last days of the tour who reminded him of Mrs Greenfield ('my bardship almost in love with her'). Burns was far from contemplating monastic vows, however. Early in October, after little more than two weeks in the capital, he set out on another journey. And what he principally had in mind on this occasion was the pursuit of Margaret Chalmers.

He travelled on this occasion with James Adair, who was a doctor. Six years younger than Burns, he had studied at both Geneva and Edinburgh. His family came from Ayr; Burns had been introduced to him by Dr Lawrie and his sister was later to marry Dr Lawrie's son, Archibald. It is from Adair's account to Currie that we have most of what is known about their journey, because Burns made no record of it.

They initially followed the same route that Burns had taken with Nicol, riding west out of the capital and passing through Linlithgow. They came to Carron, and this time the iron-works was open to visitors – Burns was reminded of the cave of the Cyclops. At Stirling, he took the opportunity of breaking the window pane on which he had scratched his imprudent verses on his last visit; the horse, as it happened, had already bolted from that particular stable, because the lines had been copied and their authorship was known. They also fell in there with a party of travellers from Edinburgh, which included Nicol, and Adair remarked on how he and Burns resembled each other – 'the same wit and power of conversation; the same fondness for convivial society, and thoughtlessness of tomorrow.'

They were heading for Harvieston where, in August, Burns's hopes of seeing Margaret Chalmers had not been realised. This time he was not disappointed. During the next eight days the two young men and their hosts made excursions into the surrounding countryside, which Adair thought 'inferior to none in Scotland in beauty, sublimity and romantic interest.' 'I am surprised that none of these scenes should have called forth an exertion of Burns's muse,' he wrote:

1. Letters, 139.

But I doubt if he had much taste for the picturesque. I well remember, that the ladies of Harvieston, who accompanied us on this jaunt, expressed their disappointment at his not expressing in more glowing and fervent language, his impressions of the Caldron Linn scene, certainly highly sublime, and somewhat horrible.

The ladies' somewhat bookish disappointment at Burns's lack of sensibility is understandable, but they did not really know their man. Although he was influenced in some respects by the literature of eighteenth-century England, the 'pre-Romantic' label pinned to him by much conventional academic criticism is almost as misleading as Henry Mackenzie's 'Heaven-taught ploughman'. Burns's best poetry came from life, not from books. He was less interested in Man than in men and women, more interested in his fellow-man than in Nature. He knew his wayside flowers and the animals of the field, but he was, like many countrymen, largely indifferent to those manifestations of nature that formed no part of his immediate experience – there is little in his verse about the sea, for instance, or about mountains.

It is possible that Burns did employ glowing and fervent language during his stay at Harvieston, but for a different purpose – it is conceivable that this was the occasion on which Miss Chalmers declined his proposal of marriage. Whatever passed between them during those early October days of 1787, they remained on friendly terms and continued to correspond until her marriage to an Edinburgh banker the following year. Adair had better fortune. He fell in love with Charlotte, of whom Burns had written so glowingly to Gavin Hamilton, and married her two years later.

During this tour Burns spent a few days at Ochtertyre, in Strathearn, as the guest of Sir William Murray, whom he had met at Blair Castle. 'I find myself very comfortable here,' he wrote to Nicol, 'neither oppressed by ceremony nor mortified by neglect.'[1] His host had a young cousin, Euphemia, renowned for her good looks (she was known locally as 'The Flower of Strathmore') and Burns made her the subject of 'Blythe, blythe and merry was she' which he composed to the tune of a popular old drinking song.[2] It was also during his stay with Murray that he wrote 'On Scaring some Water-Fowl in Loch Turit'; the result, as is often the case when Burns is striving for aesthetic correctness, teeters between the mediocre and the ludicrous:

> Why, ye tenants of the lake,
> For me your watry haunt forsake?
> Tell me, fellow creatures, why

1. *Ibid.*, 141.
2. Kinsley, 179. The tune is called 'Andro an' his cutty gun.' It turns up again in *The Merry Muses of Caledonia* where the 'cutty gun' is used as a phallic metaphor. Tradition has it that Miss Murray, later the wife of a Court of Session judge, was not best pleased to be immortalised in this way.

> At my presence thus you fly?
> Why disturb your social joys,
> Parent, filial, kindred ties? –
> Common friend to you and me,
> Nature's gifts to all are free ...[1]

Burns carried with him on this tour a letter of introduction he had been given by Dr Blacklock. It was to a man called John Ramsay. His estate, on the river Teith near Stirling, was also called Ochtertyre, and Burns visited him on two occasions. Ramsay of Ochtertyre had been called to the Scottish bar, but he had succeeded to the family estates in his twenties and they soon absorbed all his interest and energies. His voluminous diaries are an important historical source; he was also to become Scott's model for Jonathan Oldbuck in *The Antiquary*.

Ramsay had embellished his house and various parts of the property with a number of inscriptions in slightly suspect Latin; one of them expressed the wish that he might live there in peace and 'die in joyful hope,' a Horatian sentiment with which Burns was much taken. Ramsay, a bachelor in his early fifties at the time he met Burns, later gave Currie an account of his visitor. 'In a mixed company I should have made little of him,' he wrote, 'for, in the gamester's phrase, he did not always know when to play off and when to play on.' In the course of the two days they spent together, however, he had come to appreciate the formidable sparkle and penetration of Burns's conversation: 'I have been in the company of many men of genius, some of them poets, but never witnessed such flashes of intellectual brightness as from him, the impulse of the moment, sparks of celestial fire!'

Ramsay tried to persuade Burns that he should try his hand at a play, something along the lines of Allan Ramsay's *Gentle Shepherd*, and that he should attempt a Scottish 'Georgics', arguing that Thomson's 'Seasons' had by no means exhausted the genre. When he asked Burns whether the Edinburgh literati had 'mended' his poems by their criticisms, he elicited a characteristically robust response: 'Sir,' said he, 'these gentlemen remind me of some spinsters in my country, who spin their thread so fine that it is neither fit for weft or woof.' He said he had not changed a word except one, to please Dr. Blair.[2]

Burns and Adair made their way back to Edinburgh by way of Kinross and Queensferry. 'At Dunfermling we visited the ruined abbey, and the abbey church, now consecrated to Presbyterian worship,' wrote Adair:

> Here I mounted the *cutty stool*, or stool of repentance, assuming the character of a penitent for fornication; while Burns from the pulpit addressed to me

---

1. Kinsley, 180.
2. Quoted in Currie, vol. i, p. 189. The change was the one made in 'the Holy Fair'. See p. 123 *supra*.

a ludicrous reproof and exhortation, parodied from that which had been delivered to himself in Ayrshire, where he had, as he assured me, once been one of seven who mounted the *seat of shame* together.[1]

The travellers reached Edinburgh on October 20th. Burns had been offered accommodation by William Cruikshank, who, like Nicol, was a classical master at the High School. He lived in St James's Square, in the New Town, just behind the Register House, and it was here, as winter drew on, that Burns now found himself comfortably installed in two attic rooms.

1. *Ibid.*, pp. 171–2.

Eight

NYMPH AND SHEPHERD

IT WAS NOT IN BURNS'S MIND to linger unduly in the capital. He wanted to get some money out of Creech and he hoped to settle the question of how he was going to earn a living. Just as he had done the previous winter, he spent his first few days in Edinburgh in bed. He was suffering from 'a miserable cold' he wrote to Patrick Miller, 'for which the medical gentlemen have ordered me into close confinement, "under pain of Death!" the severest of penalties.' He told Miller that as soon as he was recovered, he hoped to ride down to Dumfries to see him, and he set out his latest thinking on the tenancy proposal Miller had made to him:

> I want to be a farmer in a small farm, about a plough-gang, in a pleasant country, under the auspices of a good landlord ... I only mean to live soberly, like an old-style farmer, and joining personal industry. – The banks of Nith are as sweet, poetic grounds as ever I saw; and besides, Sir, 'tis but justice to the feeling of my own heart, and the opinion of my best friends, to say that I would wish to call you landlord sooner than any landed gentleman I know ...[1]

His thoughts were not running only on farming, however; his mind was increasingly directed to the publishing project in which the engraver James Johnson had enlisted his interest earlier in the year. Although he had written little during his summer excursions, he had kept a sharp lookout for old songs. The first volume of Johnson's *Scots Musical Museum* had appeared in May, shortly after Burns had set out for the Borders, and as soon as he was back in the capital he threw himself into the work of assembling material for the second. One letter went to the Duke of Gordon's librarian, James Hoy, asking for the words of a song he had heard during his stay at the castle.[2] He also sent a lengthy letter to old John Skinner, who had written some flattering verses

---

1. *Letters*, 144. A plough-gang was a measure of arable land. It was usually taken to be 104 Scots acres, the area which could be tilled by an eight-oxen plough in a year, though statements of its extent differed widely, pointing to different local uses.
2. *Ibid.*, 145.

expressing admiration for his work and proposing that they correspond – 'You have conjured up an airy demon of vanity in my fancy,' Burns wrote in reply:

... The world may think slightingly of the craft of song-making, if they please; but, as Job says, "O! that mine adversary had written a book!" let them try. There is a certain something in the old Scotch songs, a wild happiness of thought and expression, which peculiarly marks them, not only from English songs, but also from the modern efforts of song-wrights, in our native manner and language. The only remains of this enchantment, these spells of the imagination, rests with you ... I have often wished, and will certainly endeavour, to form a kind of common acquaintance among all the genuine sons of Caledonian song. The world, busy in low prosaic pursuits, may overlook most of us; – but 'reverence thyself'. The world is not our *peers*, – so we challenge the jury. We can lash that world, – and find ourselves a very great source of amusement and happiness independent of that world.

Nothing could be more quintessentially Burnsian than that flash of contempt for the world, busy with its 'low prosaic pursuits'; lashing that world, challenging the jury, would always be favourite pastimes. He went on to describe to Skinner what he had set his hand to and to ask for contributions:

... There is a work going on in Edinburgh, just now, which claims your best assistance. An Engraver in this town has set about collecting and publishing all the Scotch Songs, with the Music, that can be found. Songs in the English language, if by Scotchmen, are admitted; but the Music must all be Scotch. Drs Beattie and Blacklock are lending a hand, and the first musician in town presides over that department. I have been absolutely crazed about it, collecting old stanzas, and every information remaining, respecting their origin, authors, &c ...[1]

The 'first musician in town' was Stephen Clarke, who at the time was organist of the Episcopal Chapel in the Cowgate, but although Burns deferred to Clarke's musicianship he exerted himself greatly to match words to music by his own efforts. When Josiah Walker called on him in St James's Square one day towards the end of October he found that he had enlisted the help of Cruikshank's twelve-year old daughter, who was a talented player: 'I found him seated by the harpsichord of this young lady, listening with the keenest interest to his own verses, which she sung and accompanied, and adjusting them to the music by repeated trials of the effect. In this occupation he was so totally absorbed, that it was difficult to draw his attention from it for a moment.'[2]

1. *Ibid*, 147.
2. Walker, *op. cit.*, vol. i, p. 81.

If Burns deferred to Clarke in matters musical, Johnson, who was not a well-educated man,[1] quickly came to defer to Burns in all that related to the words. There was no formal arrangement between them, but Burns rapidly became the editor of the enterprise in all but name, although there was never any question of financial reward.

Almost every letter which survives from those late autumn and early winter months of 1787 is shot through with his enthusiasm for the *Museum*. 'I send Charlotte the first number of the songs,' he wrote to Margaret Chalmers. 'I am determined to pay Charlotte a poetic compliment, if I could hit on some glorious old Scotch air, in number second.'[2] Within a few weeks he had married words and music to his satisfaction:

> The air is admirable: true old Highland. It was the tune of a Gaelic song
> which an Inverness lady sung me when I was there; and I was so charmed
> with it that I begged her to write me a set of it from her singing; for it had
> never been set before. I am fixed that it shall go in Johnson's next number;
> so Charlotte and you need not spend your precious time in contradicting
> me. I won't say the poetry is first-rate; though I am convinced it is very well:
> and, what is not always the case with compliments to ladies, it is not only
> *sincere* but *just*.[3]

The song was the lilting 'How pleasant the banks of the clear-winding Devon',[4] and it did indeed appear in the second volume of the *Museum* the following year. To Miss Chalmers herself Burns composed a poetic compliment that was both more direct and more personal:

> My Peggy's face, my Peggy's form,
> The frost of hermit age might warm;
> My Peggy's worth, my Peggy's mind,
> Might charm the first of human kind.
> I love my Peggy's angel air,
> Her face so truly heav'nly fair,
> Her native grace so void of art,
> But I adore my Peggy's heart . . .[5]

None of Miss Chalmers's letters to Burns has survived, but she was clearly

---

1. 'His picturesquely bad spelling,' wrote De Lancey Ferguson, 'is notable even for the eighteenth century.' Ferguson, *op. cit.*, p. 254.
2. Letters, 145.
3. *Ibid.*, 155.
4. Kinsley, 183.
5. *Ibid.*, 181.

resistant to the idea that this and another piece he sent her should be published.[1] Burns took a firm line:

> My dear Madam,
> I just now have read yours. The poetic compliments I pay cannot be misunderstood. They are neither of them so particular as to point *you* out to the world at large; and the circle of your acquaintances will allow all I have said. Besides I have complimented you chiefly, almost solely, on your mental charms. Shall I be plain with you? I will; so look to it. Personal attractions, madam, you have much above par; wit, understanding, and worth, you possess in the first class. This is a cursed flat way of telling you these truths, but let me hear no more of your sheepish timidity . . .[2]

His letters to Margaret Chalmers are some of the best that he wrote – easy, without affectation, by turns playful, entertaining and affectionate. It is clear that he saw in her a combination of qualities that he had not encountered elsewhere and that her attractions were not solely physical. 'Her heart was warm, her temper even, and her conversation lively,' wrote the relative who later offered a description of her to Chambers. 'I have often been told that her gentleness and vivacity had a favourable influence on the manner of Burns.'[3] In the matter of the two love songs, he did not entirely defer to her wishes – the less explicit of them, 'Where braving angry Winter's storms', was duly published in the second volume of the *Museum*. 'My Peggy's face', however, did not appear in print in Burns's lifetime.

Burns had told Miller that he feared the winding up of his affairs with Creech would be a tedious matter, and he was right. He did manage, on October 23rd, to get his signature to a promissory note for the hundred guineas they had agreed on for the copyright, but he failed to extract any money from him. Creech's undoubted sluggishness has been the source of some outrage over the years, but his performance was not wildly out of line with the trade practices of the day. A publisher would normally render accounts at the end of June or December, but not more than once a year, and always six months or more after the date of publication; it was also quite customary for payment to be deferred for six months beyond that. It could, of course, be argued that their agreement about copyright fell outside the scope of such arrangements and that any money which had come to him by way of subscription, in his capacity as Burns's agent, should have been handed over more speedily.

The 1787 edition of poems attracted few reviews, but interest in his work

---

1. The accompanying piece was 'Where braving angry Winter's storms', Kinsley, 182.
2. Letters, 150.
3. Chambers-Wallace, vol. ii, p. 207.

continued to grow, sometimes in ways of which Burns could know nothing. The serious-minded English poet William Cowper, for instance, was certainly familiar with it by the summer of 1787. Cowper, already known for *John Gilpin's Ride* and *The Task*, had had the poems drawn to his attention by a young friend who was a student at Glasgow University. 'I have read Burns's poems, and have read them twice,' he wrote in reply, 'and though they be written in a language that is new to me, and many of them on subjects much inferior to the author's ability, I think them on the whole a very extraordinary production ... It will be pity if he should not hereafter divest himself of barbarism, and content himself with writing pure English, in which he appears perfectly qualified to excel. He who can command admiration, dishonours himself if he aims no higher than to raise a laugh.'[1]

That the gentle and evangelically-inclined Cowper should have reservations about some of Burns's subject matter – he was, after all the author of such well-known hymns as 'God moves in a mysterious way' and 'Hark! my soul! it is the Lord' – is unsurprising. He was more concerned about the medium than about the message, however, and in a second letter to his friend it was to this that he returned:

Poor Burns loses much of his deserved praise in this country through our ignorance of his language. I despair of meeting with any Englishman who will take the pains that I have taken to understand him. His candle is bright, but shut up in a dark lantern. I lent him to a very sensible neighbour of mine; but his uncouth dialect spoiled all; and before he had half read him through he was quite *ram-feezled*.[2]

Cowper lived latterly in Norfolk. The 'uncouth dialect' of which he complained was less of an obstacle in the north of England. 'When I last wrote I forgot to thank you for those verses you were so kind as to transcribe for me' – the writer is a girl in Cumberland in her middle-teens:

My Br Wm was here at the time I got your Letter, I told him that you had recommended the book to me, he had read it and admired many of the pieces very much; and promised to get it me at the book-club, which he did.

'My Brother William' was a raw-boned youth of seventeen who had tried his own hand at poetry while he was still at the grammar school at Hawkshead

1. Letter to Samuel Rose, 24th July 1787. Published in *The Correspondence of William Cowper*, ed. Thomas. Wright, 4 vols., Hodder and Stoughton, London, 1904, vol. iii, pp. 145-6
2. Letter to Samuel Rose, 27th August 1787, *ibid*., pp. 147-8. Ramfeezled means exhausted. Cowper would have come across it in Burns's second Epistle to John Lapraik (Kinsley, 58).

and had just embarked on three undistinguished years at St. John's College, Cambridge. His surname was Wordsworth.[1]

Admiration was a commodity which Burns soon discovered to be in shorter supply during his second winter in Edinburgh than it had been in his first. Those who frequent salons and drawing rooms do not have a lengthy span of attention; no more obscure corner in the zoo than that where last year's lion has his cage. It was less than twelve months since Mrs Cockburn had written so graphically about the buzz he had created: 'No doubt he will be at the Hunters' Ball tomorrow, which has made all women and milliners mad,' she had told her friend in the country. 'Not a gauze-cap under two guineas – many ten, twelve.' This year the ladies kept their heads, obliging the milliners to do the same; the price of gauze-caps remained stubbornly deflated.[2]

Touchy as he was, Burns was enough of a philosopher not to be overly concerned by such matters, but he was clearly a good deal up and down in those early winter months. Not that he was by any manner of means idle: 'At present I have time for nothing,' he wrote to his friend Candlish in Glasgow. 'Dissipation and business engross every moment.'[3] A note he sent to Ainslie one Sunday morning towards the end of November, however, indicates that he sometimes preferred his own company. 'On looking over my engagements, constitution, present state of health, some little vexatious soul concerns, &c. I find I can't sup abroad tonight,' he wrote:

> You will think it romantic when I tell you that I find the idea of your friendship almost necessary to my existence. – You assume a proper length of face in my bitter hours of blue-devilism, and you laugh fully up to my highest wishes at my *good things* . . . I tell you this just now in the conviction that some inequalities in my temper and manner may perhaps sometimes make you suspect that I am not so warmly as I ought to be
>
> your friend
> ROB^T BURNS[4]

There is a clue to some of the causes of those 'inequalities of temper' in a letter he had written a few weeks previously to his old friend Richmond, back in Mauchline during the long weeks of the legal summer recess. Burns begins cheerfully enough with an account of his Highland jaunt, gives a brief account of his involvement with the *Museum* and enquires after Richmond's little girl (he had still not married the mother). Then, altogether too casually, this:

1. Dorothy Wordsdworth's letter was to her friend Jane Pollard. Quoted in *The Letters of William and Dorothy Wordsworth*, ed. E. de Selincourt, 2nd ed., I The Early Years, 1785-1805, rev. C.L. Shaver, Oxford University Press, 1967, p. 13.
2. A modest salute was offered to his celebrity on November 16th: he travelled on that day to Linlithgow to receive the freedom of the burgh.
3. Letters, 153A.
4. *Ibid.*, 153.

. . . By the way, I hear I am a girl out of pocket and by careless, murdering mischance too, which has provoked me and vexed me a good deal. – I beg you will write me by post immediately on receipt of this, and let me know the news of Armour's family, if the world begin to talk of Jean's appearance any way. –[1]

Burns's twins had been split between the two families, the boy going to Mossgiel, the girl staying with Jean. Nothing is known of how the child died. The language of the letter points to an accident and suggests that Burns suspected negligence. It also speaks of a good deal of anger and pain. The urgency of his request for news about Jean, by then some four months pregnant, is unmistakable, but whatever his anxieties he made no reference to her or to her condition to any of his other correspondents.

He travelled to Dalswinton to look again at what Patrick Miller had to offer, but the visit was not conclusive. 'I have been at Dumfries, and at one visit more shall be decided about a farm in that country,' he told Margaret Chalmers, but it is clear that his mind was far from made up:

I am rather hopeless in it; but as my brother is an excellent farmer, and is, besides, an exceedingly prudent, sober man, (qualities which are only a younger brother's fortune in our family,) I am determined, if my Dumfries business fail me, to return into partnership with him, and at our leisure take another farm in the neighbourhood. I assure you I look for high compliments from you and Charlotte on this very sage instance of my unfathomable, incomprehensible wisdom . . .[2]

Since the beginning of the year, scarcely a month had gone by without a letter from Mrs Dunlop. She had been assiduous from the start in her efforts to promote his interests: 'I know a gentleman in the East Indies, commanding the artillery at Patna,' she had written in her second letter, and urged him to find a way of getting a copy of the Kilmarnock edition despatched to those parts: 'I know he has taste to relish its beauties, and at my desire would be active to display them in the Eastern world . . .'[3] She also bombarded him with advice and offers of literary assistance: 'I have been told Voltaire read all his manuscripts to an old woman, and printed nothing but what she approved,' she had written in the spring. 'I wish you would name me to her office.'[4] Unabashed by Burns's failure to do so, she effectively nominated herself and persevered in it for the best part of ten years.

These letters from Mrs Dunlop did not get shorter with the passage of

1. *Ibid.*, 146.
2. *Ibid.*, 155.
3. Letter dated 9th January 1787. Burns and Dunlop, p. 6.
4. Letter dated 21st May 1787. *ibid*, p. 25.

time and Burns did not always get round to replying to them; when he did, her questions sometimes went unanswered. He had been particularly dilatory during the summer and autumn months, but that did not prevent her from writing at prodigious length in September, full of praise for his autobiographical letter to Dr Moore – 'I read your manuscript with more pleasure than Richardson or Fielding could have afforded me.'[1] She wrote again in November to forward a packet she had received from Moore. This letter was uncharacteristically brief, and its concluding sentences were distinctly acerbic: 'By the by, I am told you think no friend you have would take two hours to make your fortune. Is this sentiment the offspring of modest diffidence, small penetration, or ingratitude? For sure I am it is fraught with terrible injustice.'[2]

Burns realised he had fences to mend. He replied almost by return, and opened on a note of abject apology: 'Madam, I will bear the reproaches of my conscience respecting this letter no longer.' It is not one of his better efforts; her rebuke had clearly made him uneasy. After a couple of paragraphs of somewhat stilted flattery and not very profound philosophising he gives her the benefit of his views on a theological controversy then current in Ayr. One of the local ministers had published a book which some thought heretical, and Burns announces, in a tone disagreeably loud, that he is minded to enter the lists:

I ever could ill endure those surly cubs of "Chaos and old Night;" – these ghostly beasts of prey, who foul the hallow'd ground of Religion with their nocturnal prowlings; but if the prosecution which I hear the Erebean Fanatics are projecting against my learned and truly worthy friend, D^r M'Gill, goes on, I shall keep no measure with the savages, but fly at them with the faulcons of Ridicule, or run them down with the bloodhounds of Satire, as lawful game, wherever I start them. –[3]

Mrs Dunlop was unimpressed by such rodomontade. 'I hope the clergy will not meddle with Mr M'Gill, that you may not meddle with them,' she told him firmly when she wrote again on Christmas Day. 'Those that deserve it are too mean game for genius to hurt, and the satire too local for sale.' She also remarked drily on his non-appearance in Ayrshire: 'I am afraid Edr. has monopolised your whole time, or you calculate like Daniel by weeks of years when you are to leave it; 'tis already six weeks of our vulgar arithmetic since you said you would be west in ten days, and no news of you yet.'[4]

Burns had told her just that – had indeed announced that he would do himself the honour of calling on her at Dunlop House on his return. Two

1. Letter dated 9th September 1787. *ibid.*, p. 28.
2. Letter dated 15th November 1787, *ibid.*, p. 33.
3. *Letters*, 152A.
4. Letter dated 25th December 1787, *Burns and Dunlop*, p. 39.

things had conspired to detain him in the capital, and he wrote about the first of them to a number of people, most graphically to Margaret Chalmers:

> I am here under the care of a surgeon, with a bruised limb extended on a cushion; and the tints of my mind vying with the livid horror preceding a midnight thunder-storm. A drunken coachman was the cause of the first, and incomparably the lightest evil; misfortune, bodily constitution, hell and myself, have formed a "Quadruple Alliance" to guarantee the other.[1]

About the second he wrote only to his old friend Richard Brown, the sea captain in Irvine whose friendship, as he told Dr Moore, had done him an injury:

> Almighty Love still "reigns and revels" in my bosom; and I am at this moment ready to hang myself for a young Edin^r widow, who has wit and beauty more murderously fatal than the assassinating stiletto of the Sicilian Banditti, or the poisoned arrow of the savage African. My Highland durk, that used to hang beside my crutches, I have gravely removed into a neighbouring closet, the key of which I cannot command; in case of spring-tide paroxysms.[2]

Enter 'Clarinda.' We have arrived at one of the most celebrated episodes in the Burns story. And one of the most absurd.

Burns misinformed Richard Brown in one small particular. The young woman for whom he was ready to hang himself was only a grass widow, although it was the case that she had been separated from her husband for seven years and that three years previously, after a spell in a London debtors' prison, he had taken himself off to try his luck in Jamaica.

Agnes McLehose was several months older than Burns and was the daughter of a well-known Glasgow surgeon called Andrew Craig. Her mother had died when she was nine. At fifteen she was sent to boarding school in Edinburgh, and one of her admirers, a young lawyer called James McLehose, had the enterprising idea of booking all the other seats in the stage-coach, which meant that he could have her to himself for the best part of ten hours. The family of 'pretty Miss Nancy' did not approve of him, but McLehose was both plausible and handsome, and two months after her eighteenth birthday she had become his wife.

Four children followed in as many years, but the marriage quickly began to go off the rails. It was the conclusion of the couple's grandson, many years later, that the fault was not all on one side:

1. Letters, 160.
2. *Ibid.*, 168.

1. The Clay Biggin' – from a painting of Burns's birthplace done in the late 1830s by the Edinburgh artist David Octavius Hill.

2. Burns at the age of 28: 'When I sat to Mr Miers, I am sure he did not exceed two minutes.'

3. Ayr – the Twa Brigs. Another Hill landscape.

4. Mauchline Castle. Gavin Hamilton lived in the house on the right.

5. Edinburgh Castle as it was in Burns's day – a view from the south-east.

6. James Burnett, Lord Monboddo – a contemporary caricature.

7. Monboddo's daughter, Eliza: 'There has not been any thing nearly like her since Milton's Eve on the first day of her existence.'

8. Mrs Dunlop: 'My worthy honored Patroness.'

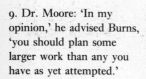

9. Dr. Moore: 'In my opinion,' he advised Burns, 'you should plan some larger work than any you have as yet attempted.'

10. Henry Mackenzie in old age: a portrait by Colvin Smith.

12. Edinburgh Cross. The building in the centre of the engraving is where Creech had his premises.

11. A portrait of William Creech by Raeburn: 'His solid sense by inches you must tell, But mete his cunning by the Scottish ell.'

13. James Cunningham, fourteenth Earl of Glencairn: 'The man to whom I owe all that I am and have.'

14. John Dowie, whose tavern in Libberton Wynd was one of Burns's haunts when in Edinburgh.

15. Henry Erskine, wit and advocate. 'No poor man wanted a friend while Harry Erskine lived,' read a plaque affixed to his birthplace.

16. William Smellie, Burns's printer: 'That old Veteran in Genius, Wit and Bawdry.'

17. Dr Thomas Blacklock, blind poet: 'The Doctor belonged to a set of Critics for whose applause I had not even dared to hope.'

18. A portrait of Niel Gow, the celebrated fiddler, by Raeburn: 'A short, stout-built Highland figure, with his greyish hair shed on his honest social brow.'

19. Margaret Chalmers: 'My Peggy's worth, my Peggy's mind, Might charm the first of human kind.'

20. Bruar Water: 'I am, altho' I say't mysel, Worth gaun a mile to see.'

Married at so early an age, before the vivacity of youth was passed, and, indeed, before it was fully developed, possessed of considerable personal attractions, a ready flow of wit, a keen relish for society, in which her conversational powers fitted her to excel, and a strong love of admiration, she appears to have displeased her husband, because she could not at once forego those enjoyments so natural to her time of life and situation.[1]

McLehose became jealous – without cause, in his grandson's view – and began to treat her with 'a severity most injudicious'. She then went home to her father, and on his death two years later moved to Edinburgh. McLehose made no provision either for her or the three surviving children (the youngest had died in infancy) and her father's estate had been sufficient only to secure an annuity of £8. Two further small annuities were arranged by friends in Glasgow, one from the Faculty of Physicians and Surgeons, the other from the Faculty of Procurators. Mrs McLehose accordingly had to make do as best she could on an income of £26 a year, supplemented occasionally by the kindness of friends and relatives.[2]

She was quite small, with delicate hands and feet; her grandson remembered lively eyes, good teeth and a soft and pleasing voice. 'Of a somewhat voluptuous style of beauty,' said an admiring contemporary; 'fluffy and bosomy,' wrote Hilton Brown in the middle of the less gallant twentieth century. All we have to go by is the Miers silhouette which she had done for Burns ('Likenesses in a style of superior excellence, with unequalled accuracy,' announced the artist on the labels of his portraits). We see her in right profile, hair curling high and tight above the forehead and crowned with a ribbon and some sort of veil. Miers has drawn a soft, full mouth, a rounded chin, a tip-tilted nose – and extremely long eyelashes. A pretty face, at once coquettish and composed.

Burns met Nancy McLehose for the first time on December 4th – she had persuaded a friend to invite him to tea. Burns then accepted an invitation to drink tea with her two days later, but something came up, and he sent his excuses; he enclosed some lines of verse, which flattered her by saying that he had heard she was 'not only a Critic but a Poetess.' She had a further disappointment on Saturday evening – he sent round a note to say that he had bruised a knee in a fall from a coach and was obliged to rest it on a cushion. 'If I don't see you again, I shall not rest in my grave for chagrin,' he wrote

---

1. *The Correspondence between Burns and Clarinda*, with a memoir of Mrs McLehose, (Clarinda) arranged and edited by her grandson, W.C. McLehose, William Tate. Edinburgh, 1843, p. 17. Cited henceforth as Burns and McLehose.

2. Notably her cousin, William Craig, who was an advocate. After McLehose settled in Jamaica and was notionally able to maintain his children, the Glasgow annuities dried up; Craig generously made up the shortfall. Thirteen years Nancy's senior, he was a friend of Henry Mackenzie's and a contributor to both the *Mirror* and the *Lounger*. He was raised to the bench as Lord Craig in 1792 and in 1795 became a judge of the Court of Justiciary. At his death in 1813 he left Nancy an annuity.

(he had previously told her that he planned to leave Edinburgh in a week's time):

> I was vexed to the soul I had not seen you sooner; I determined to cultivate your friendship with the enthusiasm of Religion; but thus has Fortune ever served me. – I cannot bear the idea of leaving Edin' without seeing you – I know not how to account for it – I am strangely taken with some people; nor am I often mistaken. You are a stranger to me; but I am an odd being: some yet unnamed feelings; things not principles, but better than whims, carry me farther than boasted reason ever did a Philosopher. –
>
> Farewel! every happiness be yours![1]

Six months previously, in a letter to his friend James Smith, Burns had described his tactics in pursuing some young woman or other who had responded coolly to his advances. 'I am an old hawk at the sport,' he boasted, 'and wrote her such a cool, deliberate, prudent reply as brought my bird from her aerial towerings, pop, down at my foot like corporal Trim's hat.' Mrs McLehose's reply now demonstrated that even with his leg on a cushion, Burns's predatory skills were unimpaired. It was the corporal's hat all over again – except that the bird was fluttering (and twittering) most gratifyingly:

> . . . Tonight I had thought of fifty things to say to you: how unfortunate this prevention! . . . You shall *not* leave town without seeing me . . . I am determined to see you; and am ready to exclaim with Yorick, 'Tut! are we not all relations?' We are, indeed, *strangers* in one sense – but of near kin in many respects: those 'nameless feelings' I perfectly comprehend, though the pen of a Locke could not define them. Perhaps *instinct* comes nearer their description than either 'principles or whims'. Think ye they have any connexion with that 'heavenly light which leads astray?' One thing I know, that they have a powerful effect upon me; and are delightful when under the check of *reason* and *religion* . . .[2]

We do not know what the verses were that Burns had sent to Mrs McLehose, but they were obviously well-judged:

> . . . Your lines were truly poetical: give me all you can spare . . . Ten years ago such lines from such a hand would have half-turned my head. Perhaps you thought it might have done so even *yet*; – and wisely premised, that 'Fiction was the native region of poetry' . . . Will you let me know, now and then, how your leg is? If I were your *sister*, I would call and see you; but 'tis a censorious world this; and (in this sense) you and I are not of the world.

1. Letters, 159.
2. Burns and McLehose, Letter III, Saturday Evening, [December 8th].

Adieu. Keep up your heart, you will soon get well, and we shall *meet* –
Farewell. God bless you. A.M.[1]

Burns, had she known it, was having not the slightest difficulty in "keeping up
his heart." A letter to Margaret Chalmers four days after the accident shows
that he was in the best of spirits:

> I have taken tooth and nail to the bible, and am got through the five books
> of Moses, and half way in Joshua. It is really a glorious book. I sent for my
> book-binder to-day, and ordered him to get me an octavo bible in sheets,
> the best paper and print in town; and bind it with all the elegance of his
> craft.
>
> I would give my best song to my worst enemy, I mean the merit of making
> it, to have you and Charlotte by me. You are angelic creatures, and would
> pour oil and wine into my wounded spirit . . .[2]

For a letter addressed on the same day to Mrs McLehose, some modulation
of tone was called for – 'I stretch a point indeed, my dearest Madam, when I
answer your card on the rack of my present agony.' She had solicited his
opinion of some verses of her own: 'Be sincere,' she had urged him, a shade
coyly, 'and own that, whatever merit it has, it has not a line resembling poetry.'
Burns, intent now on raising the emotional temperature a degree or two, was
prepared to own no such thing:

> . . . Your lines, I maintain it, are Poetry; and good Poetry; mine, were indeed
> partly fiction, and partly a friendship which had I been so blest as to have
> met with you *in time*, might have led me – God of love only knows where.
> – Time is too short for ceremonies – I swear solemnly (in all the tenor of
> my former oath) to remember you in all the pride and warmth of friendship
> until – I cease to be! –
>
> Tomorrow, and every day till I see you, you shall hear from me. –
> Farewell! May you enjoy a better night's repose than I am likely to have.[3]

Burns's instinct for the right stops was unerring: 'How could you tell me that
you were in "agony"?' came the reply. 'I hope you would swallow laudanum, and
procure some ease from sleep.' Convention demanded a mild reproof, however:

---

1. *Ibid.*
2. Letters, 160.
3. *Ibid.*, 161. the original manuscript of this letter, now in the Birthplace Museum, Alloway, no
longer contains the last sentence, although it appears in Burns and McLehose. In later life, Clarinda
hacked the correspondence about a good deal, sometimes apparently to oblige autograph hunters,
but she also erased or snipped out most proper names and some of the more ardent passages in
Burns's letters.

When I meet you, I must chide you for writing in your romantic style. Do you remember that she whom you address is a married woman? or, Jacob-like, would you wait seven years, and even then, perhaps, be disappointed, as he was? No; I know you better: you have too much of that impetuosity which generally accompanies noble minds. To be serious, most people would think, by your style, that you were writing to some vain, silly woman to make a fool of her – or worse.[1]

Well, yes, most people probably would; and their suspicions would not have been lessened by the Tartuffian assurance of Burns's reply:

Your last, my dear Madam, had the effect on me that Job's situation had on his friends, when "they sat down seven days and seven nights astonied, and spake not a word." – "Pay my addresses to a married woman!" [I] started, as if I had seen the ghost of him I had injur'd: I recollected my expressions; some of them indeed were, in the law phrase, "habit and repute," which is being half guilty. – I cannot positively say, Madam, whether my heart might not have gone astray a [little]; but I can declare upon the honor of a Poet that the vagrant [has] wandered unknown to me. I have a pretty handsome troop of Follies of my own; and, like some other people's retinue, they are but undisciplined blackguards: but the luckless rascals have something of honor in them; they would not do a dishonest thing . . .[2]

The damage to his knee could still be moderately milked for sympathy: 'My limb now allows me to sit in some peace; to walk I have [yet] no prospect of, as I can't mark it to the ground.' To Margaret Chalmers, the previous day, he had written in less doleful vein:

For the first time, yesterday I crossed the room on crutches. It would do your heart good to see my bardship, not on my *poetic*, but on my *oaken* stilts; throwing my best leg with an air! and with as much hilarity in my gait and countenance, as a May frog leaping across the newly harrowed ridge, enjoying the fragrance of the refreshed earth after the long-expected shower![3]

His correspondence and his Bible-reading did not leave much time for poetic composition, but in the middle of December, on the death of Lord Arniston, the Lord President of the Court of Session (and half-brother of Henry Dundas), Burns tried his hand at an elegy:

1. Burns and McLehose, Letter V, *Sunday, Noon*, [December 16.]
2. Letters, 163. The edge of the original manuscript, now in the Birthplace Museum, is frayed, and the words in brackets have been lost.
3. *Ibid.*, 162.

O heavy loss thy Country ill could bear!
A loss these evil days can ne'er repair!
Justice, the high viceregent of her God,
Her doubtful balance ey'd and sway'd her rod;
Hearing the tidings of the fatal blow,
She sunk abandon'd to the widest woe. –[1]

It was not a brilliant effort, and Burns knew it: 'These kind of subjects are much hackneyed,' he wrote to his friend the advocate Charles Hay, 'and besides, the wailings of the rhyming tribe over the ashes of the Great, are damnably suspicious, and out of all character for sincerity. – These ideas damp'd my Muse's fire.'[2] He may not have been very proud of it, but he sent it with a covering letter to Arniston's son, who was Solicitor-General for Scotland at the time, and he was hugely indignant when there was no acknowledgement. He had a long memory for a grievance; a letter he wrote four years later to his friend Cunningham showed that the slight still rankled:

His Solicitorship never took the smallest notice of the Letter, the Poem, or the Poet. – From that time, highly as I respect the talents of their family, I never see the name, Dundas, in the column of a newspaper, but my heart seems straitened for room in my bosom; & if I am obliged to read aloud a paragraph relating to one of them, I feel my forehead flush, & my nether lip quivers.[3]

He put much more of himself into two other compositions that date from this period. One of them was a song inspired by Charlotte, the daughter of Prince Charles Edward and his mistress Clementina Walkinshaw, who had recently been legitimised and adopted the style of Duchess of Albany:

This lovely maid's of noble blood,
    That ruled Albion's kingdoms three;
But Oh, Alas, for her bonie face!
    They hae wrang'd the lass of ALBANIE! —

Burns contrived to combine this effusion of Jacobite sentiment with some insulting lines about the Prince of Wales:

But there is a youth, a witless youth,
    That fills the place where she should be,
We'll send him o'er to his native shore,
    And bring our ain sweet ALBANIE. —[4]

1. Kinsley, 186.
2. Letters, 164. Burns had written the poem at Hay's suggestion.
3. *Ibid.*, 441.
4. Kinsley, 188.

It is a better poem, for all that, than the truly dreadful ode which Burns composed later in the month to mark the sixty-seventh birthday of Charlotte's father:

> AFAR th' illustrious exile roams,
>> Whom Kingdoms on this day should hail!
> An Inmate of the casual shed;
>> On transient pity's bounty fed . . .[1]

Burns ranted on in this vein for almost sixty lines, working in a couple of disobliging references to 'usurping Brunswick.' Kinsley describes it as 'another of Burns's calamitous attempts at the Pindaric ode' (his first had been 'A Winter Night', written the previous year, 'When biting Boreas, fell and doure . . .').[2] This second attempt had been occasioned by an invitation to a dinner to celebrate the birthday of the 'King over the Water' which fell on the last day of the year. The host, James Steuart, lived in Cleland's Gardens, which was just round the corner from Burns's lodgings. Burns's acceptance was distinctly high-flown: 'Monday next is a day of the year with me hallowed as the ceremonies of Religion, and sacred to the memory of the sufferings of my King and my Forefathers.'[3] He enclosed with it two stanzas from one of his earlier expressions of Jacobite enthusiasm, and the first line has the distinction of being incontestably the most ludicrous that Burns ever wrote:

> Tho' something like moisture conglobes in my eye,
>> Let no man misdeem me disloyal;
> A poor friendless wand'rer may well claim a sigh,
>> Still more if that Wand'rer were royal.[4]

The Royal Wanderer died in Rome a month later.

Meanwhile the game of amorous battledore and shuttlecock continued. In some of the more intense rallies the players each launched two letters in the course of a single day; before it ended the correspondence would amount to some eighty letters. The postal connection between Burns's lodgings in St James's Square and Potterow, where Nancy lived, was assured by the Edinburgh Penny Post, which, from nine in the morning till nine at night offered an hourly service 'within an English mile of the cross of Edinburgh'.

By the end of the year, Mrs McLehose was no longer 'My dear Madam' and Burns had ceased to be 'her humble servant.' 'I like the idea of Arcadian names in a commerce of this kind,' he wrote on December 28th. 'You cannot

---

1. *Ibid.*, 189.
2. *Ibid.*, 130.
3. Letters, 165.
4. 'Epistle to Mr Tytler of Woodhouselee, Author of a Defence of Mary Queen of Scots –', Kinsley 152.

imagine, Clarinda, how much store I have set by the hopes of your future friendship.'[1] It was the nymph, however, not the shepherd, who had conceived the conceit of transposing their relationship into this more rustic key. 'I have proposed to myself a more pastoral name for you,' she had written the previous week, 'although it be not much in keeping with the shrillness of the Ettrick Pipe. What say you to Sylvander?' She added archly, 'I feel somewhat less restraint when I subscribe myself CLARINDA.'[2]

The 'commerce' between them was not yet a month old and they had met only once, but an intriguing indication survives of what Burns already hoped the outcome might be. Sometime in late December (the accompanying note is undated) he sent a parcel to a jeweller called Francis Howden who had a shop in Parliament Square. The parcel contained a small miniature. 'Set it just as you did the others you did for me,' Burns wrote, 'both to answer as a breastpin and with a ring to answer as a locket.' He was in a tearing hurry to get the work done. 'It goes a hundred miles into the country,' he told Howden, and unless he had it by five the next evening he would be unable to send it:

Do, despatch it; as it is, I believe, the pledge of Love, and perhaps the prelude to ma-tri-mo-ny . . .

The Parties, one of them at least, is a very particular acquaintance of mine; the honest lover. – He only needs a little of an advice which my grandmother, rest her soul! often gave me, and I as often neglected –"Leuk twice or ye loup ance!" –

Let me conjure you, my friend, by the bended bow of Cupid; by the unloosed cestus of Venus; by the lighted torch of Hymen, that you will have the locket finished by the time mentioned![3]

The tone is playful, but the urgency of the request is unmistakable. Some biographers have assumed that it was a wedding present for a friend, but that does not square with 'perhaps the prelude to matrimony'; nor is it clear how a profile of Burns himself could serve as a pledge of love for somebody else. It seems much more likely that the 'honest lover' in question was Sylvander; and we know from their correspondence that his Clarinda left Edinburgh on the last weekend of the year to spend several days in the country. 'Let me know how long your stay will be out of town,' Burns wrote. 'I shall count the hours till you inform me of your return.'

At the end of that same letter he assured her he was incapable of dissimulation. 'I despise Design because I want either coolness or wisdom to be capable

1. Letters, 166.
2. This letter is not included in the published correspondence, although extracts from it were circulating in print within a few years of Burns's death. It is conjecturally dated December 20th. See the article by J.C. Ewing in the *Burns Chronicle* for 1934.
3. Letters, 167.

of it. – I may take a fort by storm, but never by Siege. – '[1] The truth of the matter was that his siege engines were now cunningly drawn up on all sides, and her reply shows that they had reduced the fort's sole inhabitant to a state of tremulous rapture:

> . . . Good night; for Clarinda's 'heavenly eyes' need the earthly aid of sleep. Adieu.
> P.S.– I entreat you not to mention our corresponding to one on earth. Though I've conscious innocence, my situation is a delicate one.'[2]

They corresponded about literature, and they corresponded about religion. Burns had read some of her verse to 'a gentleman for whose character, abilities and critical knowledge I have the highest veneration.' This was Dr James Gregory, the Professor of Physick at the University. Gregory was a large and powerful man, something of a Latin scholar and the inventor of Gregory's Powder, which was a popular laxative. The *Dictionary of National Biography* records that he 'wasted his great powers on temporary and irritating controversies,' (he once took his stick to a colleague, and was fined for defamation) but for Clarinda's verse he had nothing but praise: 'My learned friend,' Burns told her, 'seriously protested that he did not believe any young woman in Edin[r] was capable of such lines.'[3]

Clarinda was all of a flutter:

> . . . I have not time to answer yours as it deserves; nor, had I the age of Methusalem, could I answer it in kind. I shall grow vain. Your praises were enough, – but those of a Dr Gregory superadded! Take care: many a 'glorious' woman has been undone by having her head turned . . .[4]

When religious questions arose, the author of 'Holy Willie's Prayer' quickly realised that some parts of the keep were more heavily fortified than others. Religion, Clarinda told him, had been her balm in every woe. 'O! could I make her appear to you as she has done to me! Instead of ridiculing her tenets, you would fall down and worship her very semblance wherever you found it!'[5] Burns rose to the occasion: 'You are right, my dear Clarinda: a friendly correspondence goes for nothing, except one write their undisguised sentiments,' he assured her:

> . . . Your religious sentiments, Madam, I revere. – If you have, on some suspicious evidence, from some lying oracle, learnt that I despise or ridicule

1. *Ibid.*, 166.
2. Burns and McLehose, Letter VIII, Friday Evening, [December 28th].
3. Letters, 166.
4. Burns and McLehose, Letter VIII, Friday Evening [December 28th].
5. *Ibid.*

so sacredly important a matter as real Religion, you have, my Clarinda, much misconstrued your friend . . .

My definition of Worth is short: Truth and Humanity respecting our fellow-creatures; Reverence and Humility in the presence of that Being, my Creator and Preserver, and who, I have every reason to believe, will one day be my Judge. – The first part of my definition is the creature of unbiassed Instinct; the last is the child of after Reflection. –

Burns then judges that he may safely prepare to tack about: 'I can easily enter into the sublime pleasures that your strong imagination and keen sensibility must derive from Religion,' he writes:

> . . . but I own I cannot without a marked grudge, see Heaven totally engross so amiable, so charming a woman as my friend Clarinda; and should be very well pleased at *a circumstance* that would put it in the power of Somebody, happy Somebody! to divide her attention, with all the delicacy and tenderness of an earthly attachment . . .[1]

Burns announced towards the end of this letter that he proposed the following evening to hire a sedan chair and venture out to visit friends: 'If I could be sure of finding you at home,' he told her, 'I would spend from five to six o'clock with you, as I go passt. I cannot [do] more at this time, as I have something on my hand [tha]t hurries me much.'

The short letter which Burns dashed off at noon two days later indicates that the hour from five to six had been a success: 'Some days, some nights, nay some *hours*, like the "ten righteous persons in Sodom," save the rest of the vapid, tiresome, miserable months and years of life. – One of these hours, my dear Clarinda blesst me with yesternight [*sic*] –' He appears to have told her something of his relations with Jean Armour and to have spoken of his little son, and he now followed this up by sending her a copy of his letter to Dr Moore: 'It is truth, every word of it; and will give you the just idea of a man whom you have honor'd with your friendship.'[2]

Burns's thoughts were not totally taken up with Clarinda in those early days of 1788. When he told her that he had a matter in hand 'which hurries me much' he was almost certainly referring to his revival of interest in becoming an exciseman, and on January 7th he wrote to solicit the patronage of Robert Graham of Fintry, lately appointed an Excise Commissioner, whom he had met briefly the previous summer at Blair Atholl:

1. *Letters*, 170.
2. *Ibid.*, 171.

You know, I dare say, of an application I lately made to your Board, to be admitted an Officer of Excise. – I have, according to form, been examined by a Supervisor, and today I give in his Certificate with a request for an Order for instructions . . . I had intended to have closed my late meteorous appearance on the stage of Life, in the country Farmer; but after discharging some filial and fraternal claims, I find I could only fight for existence in that miserable manner, which I have lived to see repeatedly throw a venerable Parent in the jaws of a Jail; where, but for the Poor Man's last and often best friend, Death, he might have ended his days . . .[1]

The certificate which Burns mentions was the necessary first step for admission to the excise. A candidate had to be between the ages of twenty-one and thirty and, if married, to have no more than two children. He had to declare that he understood the first four rules of 'vulgar and decimal arithmetick' and that he belonged to the Church of Scotland. The applicant also had to supply the names of two securities to answer to £200 'for the due execution of his office'. If his application was approved by the Board of Commissioners, an order would be issued for him to receive instruction by a nominated officer. He would then, after examination by a supervisor, be admitted to the service as an 'expectant' – placed, that is to say, on the waiting list for the next vacancy.

Excisemen were not loved. When Johnson had weighed the word 'excise' for his *Dictionary* thirty years previously he did not arrive at one of his more dispassionate definitions – 'a hateful tax levied upon commodities and adjudged not by the common judges of property but by wretches hired by those to whom the excise is paid.' The fact that so many young men jostled to become 'gaugers' was explained by the conditions of service. The work might be arduous (and sometimes dangerous) but the salary was good, and it was paid regularly – a ride officer started at £50 a year.[2] There were promotion prospects, and there was security of tenure – anyone who kept his nose clean had a job for life. Posts were pensionable, and there was a fund for widows and orphans. Officers were also entitled to a share of the proceeds from the sale of smuggled goods. A man lucky enough to be present at a couple of sizeable tobacco seizures could come close to doubling his salary.[3] Once admitted, promotion, to supervisor, and perhaps collector, was based largely on merit. To get across the

1. *Ibid.*, 172.
2. Scotland was divided for excise purposes into twenty areas, known as 'collections'. These were divided into 'districts' and districts were further divided into 'stations', which were the basic units of administration. In towns, where the work was concentrated in a small area, a station was known as a 'foot-walk'. Rural stations covering larger areas were known as 'itineraries' and contained a number of 'rides'. New entrants to the service were normally appointed to a ride and would then progress to a foot-walk, where the number and variety of excise traders would generally be greater.
3. William Younger, the founder of the Edinburgh brewing dynasty, was an exciseman from 1753 until his death in 1770. His good fortune in tobacco seizures was important to the success of the brewery he had established in Leith in 1747.

threshold, however, demanded, like so much else in the eighteenth century, the interest of a person of influence; the tone of Burns's letter to Graham was no more than the convention of the age required:

> ... When Lear, in Shakespeare, asks old Kent why he wished to be in his service, he answers, "Because you have that in your face I could like to call Master" ...
>
> I know, Sir, that to need your goodness is to have a claim on it: may I therefore beg your Patronage to forward me in this affair till I be appointed to a Division; where, by the help of rigid Economy, I shall try to support that Independance so dear to my soul, but which has too often been so distant from my situation. –

Clarinda had by now digested Burns's letter to Dr Moore. 'Some parts of it did beguile me of my tears,' she told him:

> Nothing is so binding to a generous mind as placing confidence in it. I have ever felt it so. You seem to have known this feature in my character intuitively; and, therefore, intrusted me with all your faults and follies. The description of your first love-scene delighted me. It recalled the idea of some tender circumstances which happened to myself, at the same period of life – only mine did not go so far ...

She had been hurt, however, by his avowal of being an enemy to Calvinism:

> I guessed it was so by some of your pieces; but the confirmation of it gave me a shock I could only have felt for one I was interested in. You will not ·wonder at this, when I inform you that I am a strict Calvinist, *one or two* dark tenets excepted, which I never meddle with.

She gave him an account of her own religious formation. She had been bred by her father 'in the Arminian principles'. Her mother, a Calvinist, had died 'triumphing in the prospect of immortality,' and her pious precepts and example had often risen in her mind 'amidst the giddiness and adulation of Miss in her teens.' Her present principles had been formed since coming to Edinburgh: they were those of a dear, valued friend, in whose judgement and integrity she had entire confidence – 'Conviction of understanding, and peace of mind, were the happy consequences.' She urged Burns to give her an account of his chief objections to Calvinism:

> Ah, Sylvander! Heaven has not endowed you with such uncommon powers of mind to employ them in the manner you have done. This long, serious subject will, I know, have one of *three* effects: either to make you laugh in derision – yawn in supine indifference – or set about examining the

hitherto-despised subject. Judge of the interest Clarinda takes in you when she affirms, that there are but few events could take place that would afford her the heartfelt pleasure of the latter.[1]

This put Burns on the spot, and he realised that he must find some high ground on which to stake out some sort of position. He began on a note of flattering condescension: 'I am delighted, charming Clarinda, with your honest enthusiasm for Religion.' Then, professing himself 'deeply interested' in her good opinion, he laid before her the outlines of his belief. 'He, who is our Author and Preserver, and will one day be our Judge, must be the object of our reverential awe and grateful adoration,' he asserted, and he followed this with a misquotation from St John: 'He is not willing that any should perish, but that all should come to everlasting life':

> Consequently, it must be in every one's power to embrace His offer of "everlasting life"; otherwise He could not, in justice, condemn those who did not. A mind pervaded, actuated and governed by purity, truth and charity, though it does not *merit* heaven, yet is an absolutely necessary pre-requisite, without which heaven can neither be obtained nor enjoyed; and, by Divine promise, such a mind shall never fail of attaining "everlasting life": hence, the impure, the deceiving, and the uncharitable, extrude themselves from eternal bliss, by their unfitness for enjoying it. The Supreme Being has put the immediate administration of all this, for wise and good ends known to himself, into the hands of Jesus Christ, a great Personage, whose relation to Him we cannot comprehend, but whose relation to us is a Guide and Saviour; and who, except for our own obstinacy and misconduct, will bring us all, through various ways and by various means, to bliss at last.

With this somewhat sketchy account of the relationship between the first two persons of the Trinity, Burns concluded his credo, judging that he might now safely descend again to the plains:

> These are my tenets, my lovely friend; and which, I think, cannot be well disputed. My creed is pretty nearly expressed in the last clause of Jamie Dean's grace, an honest weaver in Ayrshire; "Lord grant that we may lead a gude life! for a gude life maks a gude end, at least it helps weel!"[2]

Clarinda replied at length the following evening, but wrote of other matters: 'I am not in a humour to answer your creed tonight.' She told him that her sleep had been disturbed; her younger son 'has been for some time in a crazy state of health, but has been worse these two days past.' She had been puzzling

1. Burns and McLehose, Letter XIV, Monday Night, [January 7th].
2. Letters, 174.

over a rambling passage in his last letter about someone whose name was 'indelibly written in my heart's core':

> I first thought it your Jean; but I don't know if she now possesses your 'tenderest, faithfulest friendship.' I can't understand that bonny lassie: her refusal, after such proofs of love, proves her to be either an angel or a dolt. I beg pardon; I know not all the circumstances, and am no judge therefore. I love you for your continued fondness, even after enjoyment: few of your sex have souls in such cases.[1]

It is not certain that Burns himself had been clear whom he was writing about – '*Don't guess at these ravings*,' he had enjoined her. He had scrawled the closing paragraphs of the letter at one o'clock in the morning: 'I am just risen from a two-hours bout after supper, with silly or sordid souls, who could relish nothing in common with me – but the Port.' The next day, he was ruefully aware that it had been a hard night: 'What I said in my last letter, the Powers of fuddling sociality only know for me;' but then he made matters worse by an unguarded phrase in which he railed against 'the coarse tie of human laws which keep fast what Common Sense would loose.'[2]

Clarinda was unimpressed by this, and there was an edge to her reply:

> Your 'ravings' last night, and your ambiguous remarks upon them, I cannot, perhaps ought not to comprehend. I am your friend, Sylvander: take care lest virtue demand even friendship as a sacrifice.[3]

It was not a hugely credible threat. Mrs McLehose had taken to walking in St James's Square in the hope of catching a glimpse of Burns at his attic window: 'I am laughing to myself at announcing this for the third time,' she told him.[4] 'I am certain I saw you, Clarinda; but you don't look to the proper story for a poet's lodging,' came the reply. 'I could almost have thrown myself over for very vexation.'[5]

January 12th was a Saturday. Burns wrote two letters on that day, the second of them in reply to one from Clarinda which is now lost:

> You talk of weeping Clarinda; some involuntary drops wet your lines as I read them. – Offend me, my dearest Angel! you cannot offend me: you never offended me! If you had ever given me the least shadow of offence; so pardon me, my God, as I forgive Clarinda – I have read yours again: it has blotted

1. Burns and McLehose, Letter XVI, Wednesday 10pm. [January 9th].
2. Letters, 175.
3. Burns and McLehose, Letter XVIII, Thursday Eve, [January 10th].
4. *Ibid.*, Letter XVI, Wednesday 10pm. [January 9th], Thursday Morning.
5. Letters, 175.

my paper. – Tho' I find your letter has agitated me into a violent headach, I shall take a chair and be with you about eight . . .[1]

It was only their third meeting. Clarinda enjoyed it so much that by the time she picked up her pen on Sunday evening, she was experiencing some twinges of Calvinist conscience:

> I will not deny it, Sylvander, last night was one of the most exquisite I ever experienced. Few such fall to the lot of mortals! Few, extremely few, are formed to relish such refined enjoyment. That it should be so, vindicates the wisdom of Heaven. But, though our enjoyment did not lead beyond the limits of virtue, yet today's reflections have not been altogether unmixed with regret.

She was bothered by three things. The first, she wrote, was that their encounter, if known, could have been the cause of pain to a friend to whom she was bound 'by the sacred ties of gratitude, (no more)'. This must have been a reference either to her cousin William Craig, who helped her financially, or to Dr John Kemp, who was her minister at the Tolbooth Church and kept an eye on her spiritual and moral bank balance.[2] Her second concern – one sees Burns's black brows arching in disbelief – was 'the opinion Sylvander may have formed from my unreservedness'. Above all, however, she was troubled by 'some secret misgivings that Heaven may not approve, situated as I am'. These, she told Burns, 'procured me a sleepless night; and, though at church, I am not at all well.'

Well enough, however, to dilate on one of the themes that ran most insistently through their correspondence: 'I intended to resume a little upon your favourite topic, the "Religion of the Bosom",' she told him:

> Did you ever imagine that I meant any other? Poor were that religion and unprofitable whose seat was merely in the brain. In most points we seem to agree: only I found all my hopes of pardon and acceptance with Heaven upon the merit of Christ's atonement, – whereas you do upon a good life . . .
>
> If my head did not ache, I would continue the subject . . . My God! Sylvander, why am I so anxious to make you embrace the Gospel? I dare not probe too deep for an answer . . .[3]

---

1. *Ibid.*, 177.
2. Kemp was also Secretary of the Society in Scotland for Propagating Christian Knowledge. He was three times married, and towards the end of his life was touched with scandal. He became a sort of father-confessor to Lady Colquhoun of Luss, an association which eventually prompted her husband to raise an action for divorce. Sir James Colquhoun and Kemp both died before the proceedings were completed.
3. Burns and McLehose, Letter XXI, Sunday Evening [January 13th].

She held this letter over until noon on Tuesday, and Burns became restive: 'Why have I not heard from you Clarinda? Today I expected it.' When he did hear, he immediately dashed off a reproachful reply:

> O, Clarinda, why will you wound my soul by hinting that last night must have lessened my opinion of you! True; I was "behind the scenes with you;" but what did I see? A bosom glowing with honour and benevolence; a mind ennobled by genius, informed and refined by education and reflection, and exalted by native religion, genuine as in the climes of heaven; a heart formed for all the glorious meltings of friendship, love and pity . . .
> . . . Oh, my angel! how soon must we part! and when can we meet again! I look forward on the horrid interval with tearful eyes! What have I lost by not knowing you sooner . . .[1]

He was eager to get behind the scenes again as soon as possible: 'If I can't walk all the way, I'll take a chair to Nicolson's square, or so; and walk the rest.' She was equally eager to receive him, although alive to what the neighbours might think:

> Come to tea if you please; but eight will be an hour less liable to intrusions. I hope you'll *come afoot*, even though you take a chair home. A chair is so uncommon a thing in our neighbourhood, it is apt to raise speculation – but they are all asleep by ten . . .[2]

The long letter which he composed the following day shows Burns at his most tedious – quotations from Thomson and Young, and a great deal of nonsense about his life reminding him of a ruined temple – 'what strength, what proportion in some parts! what unsightly gaps, what prostrate ruins in others!' There is much tiresome religiosity and a flowery and totally unconvincing evocation of the delights he had savoured the previous evening:

> What luxury of bliss I was enjoying this time yesternight! My ever-dearest Clarinda, you have stolen away my soul: but you have refined, you have exalted it; you have given it a stronger sense of Virtue, and a stronger relish for Piety . . .
> Clarinda, when a Poet and Poetess of Nature's making, two of Nature's noblest productions! when they drink together of the same "cup of Love and Bliss" – Attempt not, ye coarser stuff of Human-nature, profanely to measure enjoyment ye never can know![3]

1. Letters, 179.
2. Burns and McLehose, Letter XXIV, Wednesday Morning, [January 16th].
3. Letters, 181.

Nancy, too, was busy reviewing and analysing what had passed between them the previous evening. The letter she wrote was a sober and troubled one: 'I am wishing, Sylvander, for the power of looking into your heart,' she began. 'It would be but fair – for you have the key to mine.' It was the letter of a woman disturbed by the dawning realisation that she was getting herself into a situation that she did not fully understand and which she feared might be dangerous. It was a very honest letter, and one that displayed a surprising degree of self-knowledge:

Last night must have shown you Clarinda not 'divine' – but as she really is. I can't recollect some things I said without a degree of pain. Nature has been kind to me in several respects; but one essential she has denied me entirely: it is that instantaneous preception of fit and unfit, which is so useful in the conduct of life. No one can discriminate more accurately afterwards than Clarinda. But when her heart is expanded by the influence of kindness, she loses all command of it, and often suffers severely in the recollection of her unguardedness ... I would have given much for society to-day; for I can't bear my own ...

She told him that she had, for many years, sought a male friend endowed with sentiments like his:

one who could love me with tenderness, yet unmixed with selfishness: who could be my friend, companion, protector, and who would sooner die than injure me. I sought – but I sought in vain! Heaven has, I hope, sent me this blessing in my Sylvander! Whatever weaknesses may cleave to Clarinda, her heart is not to blame ... If she dare dispose of it – last night can leave you at no loss to guess the man.

She enclosed a poem called 'To a Blackbird':

It was written to soothe an aching heart. I then laboured under a cruel anguish of soul, which I cannot tell you of. If I ever take a walk to the Temple of H[ymen], I'll disclose it; but you and I (were it even possible) would 'fall out by the way' ...[1]

She took up her pen again the following evening. 'I would have given much, Sylvander,' she told him, 'that you had heard Mr Kemp this afternoon.' Kemp had taken as his text 'Let me live the life of the righteous, and my latter end be like his.' For Mrs McLehose it had been an elegant exposition of her own beliefs, and she now treated Burns to an extended résumé.

1. This letter is numbered XXXV in Burns and McLehose and dated February 2nd. Wallace assigns it to January 19th, which seems more likely.

Suddenly, after a thousand words or so of this she realises that she may not be holding his attention: 'Forgive me, Sylvander, if I've been tedious upon my favourite theme.' And equally suddenly, that tedium is arrestingly dispelled by a remarkable outburst of raw feeling:

I met the Judges in the morning, as I went into the Parliament Square, among whom was Lord Dreghorn, in his new robes of purple. He is my mother's cousin-german, the greatest real honour he could ever claim; but used me in a manner unfeeling, harsh beyond description, at one of the darkest periods of my chequered life. I looked steadfastly in his sour face; his eye met mine. I was a female, and therefore he stared; but, when he knew who it was, he averted his eyes suddenly. Instantaneously these lines darted into my mind:

"Would you the purple should your limbs adorn,
Go wash the conscious blemish with a tear."

The man, who enjoys more pleasure in the mercenary embrace of a courtezan, than in relieving the unfortunate, is a detestable character, whatever his bright talents may be.

I pity him! Sylvander, all his fortune could not purchase half the luxury of Friday night![1]

It had not, in Burns's book, been especially luxurious. He had also become briefly unwell. While Clarinda's pen ran on in Potterow, Sylvander was holed up in his attic in St James's Square feeling sorry for himself:

The impertinence of fools has joined with a return of an old indisposition, to make me good for nothing today ... What a creature is man! A little alarm last night and today that I am mortal, has made such a revolution on my spirits! There is no Philosophy, no Divinity, comes half so home to the mind ...

I can no more, Clarinda; I can scarce hold up my head ...

By the following morning he was rather less hung-over and hypochondria had given way to 'a horrid languor on my spirits.' Employing Locke, Pope and the Book of Samuel as literary crutches, Burns maundered on to Clarinda about friendship, inconstancy and the mysteries of the imagination.[2] It is clear from

1. *Ibid*. Dreghorn, newly raised to the bench, was John McLaurin; his father had been Professor of Mathematics at the University and a friend of Isaac Newton's. The son (1734-96) was a friend of James Boswell's and had literary and historical interests: in 1790 he conducted a learned correspondence with Lord Monboddo and Le Chevalier, Talleyrand's future secretary, on the site of Troy. He lived for a time in David Hume's old house in St Andrew Square. His fondness for the company of prostitutes to which Mrs McLehose refers did not endure; in 1789 Dreghorn had much to do with a drive to clean up the city and close its brothels.
2. Letters, 182.

what he wrote to other correspondents that he was at a low ebb. 'They have been six horrible weeks,' he wrote to Mrs Dunlop, in his first letter for almost three months. 'Anguish and low spirits made me unfit to read, write, or think. I have a hundred times wished that one could resign life as an officer resigns a commission.'[1]

It is unclear whether he had once again seriously thought about an army career, but in a despondent letter to Margaret Chalmers he sustained the military imagery: 'You must not desert me! Your friendship I think I can count on, though I should date my letters from a marching regiment. Early in life, and all my life, I reckoned on a recruiting drum as my forlorn hope . . .'

Earlier in the same letter there occurs an obscure passage, embellished with a quotation from *Othello*, which suggests that his emotional life was even more complicated than it seemed:

"I wish that I were dead, but I'm no like to die!" I had lately "a hairbreadth 'scape in th'imminent deadly breach" of love too. Thank my stars I got off heart-whole, "waur fleyd than hurt." – Interruption.

I have this moment got a hint . . . I fear I am something like – undone – but I hope for the best . . .[2]

The original of this letter no longer exists. It is generally believed to have been written in late January. If the reference is to his relations with Clarinda, it reflects extremely ill on him and means that everything he wrote to her after this date was insincere and even cynical. Alternatively, it is the first indication we have that although Clarinda retained the starring role in the pastoral comedy being played out in Edinburgh that winter, there may also have been a sub-plot, in which the story-line was cruder and the characters behaved more coarsely.

Burns's patience with Creech had now worn paper-thin. 'I have broke measures with him,' he told Margaret Chalmers, 'and last week I wrote him a frosty, keen letter.' Eight short months previously, at the inn in Selkirk, he had dashed off the affectionate 'Willie's Awa'. 'May never wicked men bamboozle him,' he had written in the last stanza, but that line now had an ironical ring to it:

Sir,
    when a business, which could at any time be done in a few hours, has kept me four months without even a shadow of anything else to do but wait

---

1. Letters, 184. Mrs Dunlop replied at great length and not altogether sympathetically: 'I don't know how to comfort you under the pressure of such terrible guilt but by recommending you to the Jesuits.' She also retailed a startling rumour: 'We are told you are in prison for writing not only Jacobite but blackguard verses against the King,' and she added: 'Perhaps it had been as well so. Pain is a hard jailer, and a prison might have saved you a crutch.' (Undated letter, conjecturally dated January 1788, Burns and Dunlop, pp. 41-43.)
2. *Ibid.*, 185.

on it, 'tis no very favourable symptom that it will be soon done, when I am
a hundred miles absent. – At any rate, I have no mind to make the experiment, but am determined to have it done before I leave Edin^r. – But why
should I go into the country? till I clear with you, I don't know what to do
or what I have in my power to do . . .[1]

Burns signed off with a peremptory flourish: 'I shall expect to hear from you
tomorrow, or next day,' but Creech was not moved to reply. Burns's 'why
should I go into the country?' was rhetorical, but answers to it were multiplying.
Such news as came to him from Ayrshire was not good. Gilbert was in financial
difficulties and was asking for help; a letter survives – internal evidence suggests
it was to John Ballantine – in which Burns asks for money due to him from
book sales to be handed over: 'Should he want half a dozen pounds more, dare
I ask you to accommodate him?'[2] Even more disturbing were the reports that
reached him about the Armour family. 'I have heard melancholly enough
accounts of Jean,' he wrote to his friend Richmond: ''tis an unlucky affair.'[3]
James Armour, enraged by the discovery that his daughter was once again
pregnant, had turned her out of doors.

Mrs McLehose received Burns again at Potterow on January 23rd. The
terms in which she wrote to him the following morning make it plain that the
evening had not been without its torrid passages:

Sylvander, the moment I waked this morning, I received a summons from
Conscience to appear at the Bar of Reason. While I trembled before this
sacred throne, I beheld a succession of figures pass before me in awful
brightness! Religion, clad in a robe of light, stalked majestically along, her
hair dishevelled . . . Reputation followed: her eyes darted indignation . . .

Eventually, she abandoned allegory for plain speaking:

Sylvander, to drop my metaphor, I am neither well nor happy to-day: my
heart reproaches me for last night. If you wish Clarinda to regain her peace,
determine against everything but what the strictest delicacy warrants.
    I do not blame you but myself. I must not see you on Saturday, unless
I find I can depend on myself acting otherwise . . . Remember Clarinda's
present and eternal happiness depends upon her adherence to Virtue . . .
Alas! I feel I cannot serve two masters. God pity me!!

When she continued that evening she was still in a state of some agitation. 'Do
not be displeased,' she told him, 'when I tell you I wish our parting was over.

1. *Ibid.*, 185 A.
2. *Ibid.*, 173.
3. *Ibid.*, 196.

At a distance we shall retain the same heartfelt affection . . . but absence will mellow and restrain those violent heart-agitations which, if continued much longer, would unhinge my very soul . . .'[1]

Burns, for his part, was hugely pleased with himself, and wrote a fanciful, swaggering note in which he makes Clarinda the subject of a conversation between Nature and Fortune:

> I was vain enough to think that Nature, who has a great deal to say with Fortune, had given the coquettish goddess some such hint as, "Here is a paragon of Female Excellence, whose equal, in all my former compositions, I never was lucky enough to hit on, and despair of ever doing so again; you have cast her rather in the shades of life; there is a certain Poet, of my making; among your frolicks, it would not be amiss to attach him to this master-piece of my hand, to give her that immortality among mankind which no woman of any age ever more deserv'd, and which few Rhymesters of this age are better able to confer."

That evening, at 9, he added a less poetic footnote:

> I am here, absolutely unfit to finish my letter – pretty hearty after a bowl, which has been constantly plied since dinner, till this moment. I have been with Mr. Schetki, the musician, and he has set it finely. – I have no distinct ideas [of] any thing, but that I have drunk your health [tw]ice tonight, and that you are all my soul holds [dea]r in this world. –[2]

These two very different letters crossed, and now it was Burns's turn to be agitated – or give a good impersonation of being so:

> Clarinda, my life, you have wounded my soul . . . if in the moment of fond endearment and tender dalliance, I perhaps trespassed against the *letter of* Decorum's law; I appeal, even to you, whether I ever sinned in the very least degree against the *spirit* of her strictest statute . . .
>
> O Love and Sensibility, ye have conspired against My Peace! I love. to madness, and I feel to torture![3]

The Man of Feeling could not have put it better. Clarinda relented, and he was permitted to call again the next evening and introduce his friend Ainslie.

---

1. Burns and McLehose, Letter XXVII, Thursday Forenoon, [January 24th].
2. Letters, 186. The piece Burns mentions was 'Clarinda, mistress of my soul,' (Kinsley, 217). Johann Georg Christoff Schetky, by now in his late forties, had first come to Edinburgh from Hesse-Darmstadt sixteen years previously when he was engaged as first cellist for the concerts at St Cecilia's Hall. He married the daughter of an Austrian musician and remained in Scotland for the rest of his life; one of his sons became marine painter to George IV and Queen Victoria.
3. *Ibid.*, 187.

It is clear from the long letter she wrote him the following day that Ainslie had taken his leave early and left the lovers alone:

> . . . Last night we were happy beyond what the bulk of mankind can conceive. Perhaps the 'line' you had marked was a little infringed, – it was really; but, though I disapprove, I have not been unhappy about it . . . Yet we must guard against going to the verge of danger . . . May those benevolent spirits, whose office it is to save the fall of Virtue struggling on the brink of Vice, be ever present to protect and guide us in right paths!

She was writing on Sunday evening. She had, she told him, had the benefit of an hour's conversation with just such a benevolent spirit that very day in the person of her minister, Mr Kemp:

> I confessed I had conceived a tender impression of late – that it was mutual, and that I had wished to unbosom myself to him, (as I always did,) particularly to ask if he thought I should, or not, mention it to my friend? I saw he felt for me, (for I was in tears;) but he bewailed that I had given my heart while in my present state of bondage; wished I had made it friendship only; in short talked to me in the style of a tender parent, anxious for my happiness.

The friend in question was clearly her cousin, William Craig, and Kemp had advised her to say nothing – it could only make him uneasy:

> This has eased me of a load which has lain upon my mind ever since our intimacy. Sylvander, I wish you and Mr Kemp were acquainted, – such worth and sensibility! If you had his piety and sobriety of manners, united to the shining abilities you possess, you'd be 'a faultless monster which the world ne'er saw' . . . I wish our kind feelings were more moderate; why set one's heart upon impossibilities? Try me merely as your friend (alas, all I ought to be.) Believe me, you'll find me most rational. If you'd caress the 'mental intelligence' as you do the corporeal frame, indeed, Sylvander you'd make me a philosopher. I see you fidgeting at this violently, blasting rationality . . .[1]

Burns, as it happened, was fidgeting much more violently at the recollection of an interview to which he had submitted that day in the furtherance of his excise ambitions. He had been sent to see 'a great person' called Mrs Stewart, and the encounter had raised his hackles to such an extent that he told Mrs McLehose he was minded to abandon the whole idea: 'Why will Great people

1. Burns and McLehose, Letter XXXI, Sunday, Eight Evening [January 27th]. The line about 'a faultless monster' is from Sheffield's *Essay upon Poetry*. John Sheffield, (1648–1721), Duke of Buckingham, Lord Privy Seal and Lord President of the Council under Queen Anne was a friend of Pope and a patron of Dryden.

not only deafen us with the din of their equipage, and dazzle us with their fastidious pomp, but they must also be so very dictatorially wise? I have been question'd like a child about my matters, and blamed and schooled for my Inscription on Stirling window . . .'[1]

Mrs McLehose was only mildly sympathetic: 'I am half glad you were schooled about the Inscription; 'twill be a lesson, I hope, in future. Clarinda would have lectured you on it before, "if she dared".'[2] Two days later he had calmed down and wrote to Lord Glencairn to enlist his help:

'I know your Lordship will disapprove of my ideas in the request I am going to make to you,' he wrote:

. . . I am told your Lordship's interest will easily procure me the grant from the Commissioners; and your Lordship's Patronage and Goodness which have already rescued me from obscurity, wretchedness and exile, embolden me to ask that interest. – You have put it in my power to save the little HOME that sheltered an aged mother, two brothers and three sisters, from destruction. – My brother's lease is but a wretched one, though I think he will probably weather out the remaining seven years of it. – After what I have given and will give him as a small farming capital to keep the family together, I guess my remaining all will be about two hundred pounds. – Instead of beggaring myself with a small dear farm, I will lodge my little stock, a sacred deposite, in a banking-house. – Extraordinary distress, or helpless old age have often harrowed my soul with fears; and I have one or two claims on me in the name of father: I will stoop to any thing that honesty warrants to have it in my power to leave them some better remembrance of me than the odium of illegitimacy . . .[3]

The letter is postmarked February 1st. Burns enclosed a copy of 'Holy Willie' and proposed calling on Glencairn at the beginning of the following week, 'as against then I hope to have settled my business with M' Creech.' A letter written six days later to his friend John Tennant, however, shows that he had not abandoned his earlier option: 'I go, on my return home to take the decisive look of a farm near Dumfries; where, if you will do me the favour to accompany me, your judgem' shall determine me.'[4]

He had persuaded Mrs McLehose to sit to Miers for her silhouette. 'Urge him, for necessity calls, to have it done by the middle of next week,' he wrote: 'I want it for a breast-pin, to wear next my heart. – I propose to keep sacred set times to wander in the woods and wilds for meditation on you.'[5]

1. Letters, 189. All that is known of Mrs Stewart is that she was a friend of Miss Nimmo, at whose house Burns and Clarinda had first met.
2. Burns and McLehose, Letter XXXI, Monday Morning.
3. Letters, 192.
4. *Ibid.*, 197
5. *Ibid.*, 195.

As his departure loomed, her emotions ran the gamut from dread to resignation:

> Alas! I shudder at the idea of an hundred miles distance. You'll hardly write
> me once a-month, and other objects will weaken your affection for Clarinda.
> Yet I cannot believe so ... At all events, Sylvander, the storms of life will
> quickly pass, and 'one unbounded spring encircle all'. There, Sylvander, I
> trust we'll meet. Love, there, is not a crime. I charge you to meet me there
> – Oh, God! – I must lay down my pen ...[1]

In spite of Kemp's advice, she was still much exercised by whether she should
tell William Craig about her relations with Burns. The question was complicated by the fact that his feelings for her were not simply those of a cousin:

> When I had hardly a friend to care for me in Edinburgh, he befriended me.
> I saw, too soon, 'twas with him a warmer feeling: perhaps a little infection
> was the natural effect ... I esteem him as a faithful friend; but I can never
> feel more for him. I fear he's not convinced of that ... I cannot bear to
> deceive one in so tender a point, and am hurt at his harbouring an attachment
> I never can return. I have thoughts of owning my intimacy with Sylvander;
> but a thousand things forbid it.[2]

At this point there are tantalising gaps in the correspondence and a number
of letters from Clarinda have gone missing. Whether she spoke to her cousin
is not known. What is certain is that the following week, possibly from Craig
but more probably from her minister, Kemp, she received a letter of admonition
and that she sent it round to Sylvander.

It was not a good moment – 'I make a numerous dinner party wait while I
read yours and write this' – but having scanned the enclosure he dashed off a
first, snarling response:

> I have not patience to read the puritanic scrawl. – Vile sophistry! – Ye
> heavens! thou God of nature! thou Redeemer of mankind! ye look down
> with approving eyes on a passion inspired by the purest flame, and guarded
> by truth, delicacy and honour: but the half-inch soul of an unfeeling, cold-
> blooded, pitiful presbyterian bigot, cannot forgive any thing above his dun-
> geon bosom and foggy head ...[3]

By midnight the dinner party had dispersed, and he fired off a second salvo:
'Madam, After a wretched day, I am preparing for a sleepless night.' The tone

1. Burns and McLehose, Letter XXXIII, Wednesday Evening, Nine. McLehose gives the date
as January 30th, but Wallace places it a week later, and February 6th seems more probable.
2. *Ibid.*
3. Letters, 199.

now was more considered, but he was plainly still in a very considerable rage: 'I have read over your friend's haughty, dictatorial letter ... Who gave any fellow creature of yours a right to catechize, scold, undervalue, abuse and insult, wantonly and inhumanly to insult you thus? ... It is not mouthing every thing sacred; it is not vague, ranting assertions; it is not assuming, haughtily and insultingly assuming, the dictatorial language of a Roman Pontiff, that must dissolve a union like ours ...'[1]

He dashed off two further letters to her the following day. The tone of the first is remorseful, that of the second more sober and considered. In each there is some recognition that he has damaged her interests by depriving her of the comfort and protection of friendship: 'How shall I comfort you who am the cause of the injury? Can I wish that I had never seen you? that we had never met? No: I never will! But have I thrown you friendless? there is almost distraction in that thought.'[2]

He went to her that evening, wrote to her again the following morning – the thirty-first time he had done so. 'When matters, My Love, are desperate, we must put on a desperate face ...' It was an unimpressive beginning; it did not greatly improve in the middle and he did not succeed in rising above a shabby ending:

I am yours, Clarinda, for life ... Be comforted, my Love! the present moment is the worst; the lenient hand of Time is daily and hourly either lightening the burden, or making us insensible to the weight. – None of these friends, I mean M^r–[3] and the other gentleman can hurt your worldly support; and for their friendship, in a little time you will learn to be easy, and by and by, to be happy without it. – A decent means of livelyhood in the world, an approving God, a peaceful conscience and one firm trusty friend – can any body that has these, be said to be unhappy? These are yours. –

Tomorrow evening I shall be with you about eight: probably for the last time, till I return to Edin^r – In the mean time, should any of these two *unlucky* friends question you respecting me, whether I am *the Man*; I do not think they are entitled to any information. – As to their jealousy and spying, I despise them. – Adieu! my dearest Madam!'[4]

'I do not think they are entitled to any information.' Thus did the Man hope to tiptoe out of trouble. Close behind him we glimpse another figure. Clarinda, forlorn in the emotional wreckage he has created round her, will not grasp the fact for some time, but Sylvander too has started to tiptoe away.

---

1. *Ibid.*, 200.
2. *Ibid.*, 201.
3. Burns wrote only an initial – K? – and someone later blotted it out.
4. *Ibid.*, 204.

------◄○►------

Nine

THE RETURN OF THE NATIVE

PENNY PLAIN, TWOPENCE TECHNICOLOURED. In what might be called the Hollywood version of Burns's second winter in Edinburgh, his relentless campaign to breach Mrs McLehose's defences drives all else to the margin. This is partly because the letters exchanged with Clarinda have come down to us so fully, effectively swamping his other correspondence; partly it is because of the exaggerated terms in which he writes about himself to others: 'I am the luckless victim of mad tornadoes, which blow me into chaos,' he told his friend Richard Brown.[1] His mind may engage fleetingly with questions of farming or the excise; certainly, when he remembers to, he darts the occasional venomous thought towards his publisher; but the image most insistently offered to us is of a man gripped by some obsessional, elemental disorder: 'I am sure the soul is capable of disease, for mine has convulsed itself into an inflammatory fever.'[2]

It was not in the least like that. Philandering for Burns was a frequent pastime but never a full-time pursuit. For much of the time that he sat with his leg on a chair in Cruikshank's attic, he was absorbed by something quite different. Four days before he left Edinburgh, the second volume of Johnson's *Scots Musical Museum* was published. It contained songs by Ramsay, Fergusson, Smollett and 'Ossian'; Burns had a hand in almost forty of them.

He had also written the preface, an imperious and muscular statement of editorial intention shorn of the shopkeeper accents in which Johnson had introduced the first volume the previous year:

> In the first Volume of this work, two or three Airs not of Scots composition have been inadvertently inserted; which, whatever excellence they may have, was improper, as the Collection is meant to be solely the music of our own Country – The Songs contained in this volume, both music and poetry, are all of them the work of Scotsmen . . .
>
> Ignorance and Prejudice may perhaps affect to sneer at the simplicity of

1. *Letters*, 168.
2. *Ibid.*, 175.

the poetry or music of some of these pieces; but their having been for ages the favorites of Nature's Judges – the Common People, was to the Editor a sufficient test of their merit . . .[1]

Burns's contributions ranged from very early pieces like 'I dream'd I lay where flowers were springing', written when he was seventeen, to 'Clarinda, mistress of my soul', the song which Schetky had set to music for him only weeks before. (Schetky, presumably, constitutes a proving exception to Burns's rule that everything in the *Museum* must be the work of Scotsmen.) His summer jaunts, particularly those in the north, had produced a solid return, both in words and music. His tribute to Charlotte Hamilton, for instance, 'How pleasant the banks of the clear-winding Devon,'[2] was set to an air he had picked up in Inverness. There are revisions of popular songs ('A' the lads o' Thornie-bank/ When they gae to the shore o' Bucky'[3]) and pieces cobbled together from traditional fragments, such as 'Hey tuti tatey'.[4]

In one or two cases Burns took an old chorus and added verses of his own. A strikingly successful example of this is 'McPherson's Farewell':[5]

> Farewell, ye dungeons dark and strong,
>> The wretch's destinie!
> McPherson's time will not be long,
>> On yonder gallows-tree.

McPherson, the son of a gentleman by a gypsy mother, was the leader of a gang of cattle-thieves. He was also a musician, and the story went that on the day he was to be hanged at the market-cross in Banff he walked to the scaffold from prison playing his fiddle. When he came to the gallows, he offered the instrument to the crowd; when none would accept it, he broke it across his knee and tossed the pieces among them.

Burns rejected the moralising tone of his ballad models ('Therefore, good people all, take heed') preferring simply to depict the defiant barbarism of the man:

> Sae rantingly, sae wantonly,
>> Sae dauntingly gae'd he:
> He play'd a spring, and danc'd it round
>> Below the gallows-tree.

1. *The Scots Musical Museum*, vol. ii, Printed and sold by James Johnson, Engraver, Bells Wynd. The preface is dated March 1st, 1788, but Burns sent a copy to the Reverend John Skinner on February 14th and said in his covering letter that it was published that day. (Letters, 203.)
2. Kinsley, 183.
3. *Ibid.*, 178.
4. *Ibid.*, 206.
5. *Ibid.*, 196.

The lines were to make a powerful impression on Thomas Carlyle: when he came to review Lockhart's *Life of Burns*, he wrote of a 'wild stormful Song'. He also told Edward Fitzgerald of a visit from Tennyson: 'An unforgettable day. He stayed with us till late, we dismissed him with *McPherson's farewell*. Alfred's face grew darker and darker and I saw his lips slightly quivering.'[1]

One of the best examples of Burns's 'mending' of old material is 'To daunton me', in which, like Boccaccio and Chaucer and Dunbar before him, he treats the age-old theme of the elderly man and the youthful bride:

> To daunton me, and me sae young,   subdue
> Wi' his fause heart and his flattering tongue,
> That is the thing you never shall see
> For an auld man shall never daunton me.—[2]

One of Burns's models for this was an old Jacobite song in which love was expressed in political terms, and several of his other contributions to this volume of the *Museum* contain sentimental professions of attachment to the House of Stuart of a conventional sort – 'Come boat me o'er, come row me o'er,/ Come boat me o'er to Charlie.'[3]

It is possible to make too much of Burns's Jacobitism: the evidence is that he used it as a sort of poetic fashion-accessory – it was a minor form of exhibitionism rather than a matter of conviction. He himself rather gave the game away in a note about the man who composed the tune for another of his Jacobite pieces, 'Strathallan's Lament'.[4] His name was Allan Masterton, and he was an Edinburgh schoolmaster. 'As he and I were both sprouts of Jacobitism,' Burns wrote, 'we agreed to dedicate the words and air to that cause. To tell the matter of fact, except when my passions were heated by some accidental cause, my Jacobitism was merely by way of, *Vive la bagatelle*.'[5]

One or two of the songs – 'There was a lass, they ca'd her Meg,'[6] is an example – are sanitised versions of older, earthier originals; Burns seems to have picked this one up during his Border tour. 'Duncan Grey'[7] is in the same category – 'Like *Green Grow the Rashes O* and *John Anderson my jo, John*,' writes Donald Low, 'an example of a lively tune with bawdy associations which

---

1. Quoted in James C. Dick, *The Songs of Robert Burns*, Henry Frowde, London, Edinburgh, Glasgow and New York, 1903, p. 477.

2. Kinsley, 209.

3. *Ibid.*, 211, 'O'er the water to Charlie –'

4. *Ibid.*, 168 Viscount Strathallan fell at Culloden. The subject of the poem is his eldest son, James Drummond, who escaped to France and died there in 1765.

5. The remark occurs on the interleaved copy of *The Scots Musical Museum* which Burns subsequently annotated and presented to Robert Riddell, p. 27. His notes are reproduced in Chambers-Wallace, vol. iv, pp. 371–412.

6. Kinsley, 202, 'Duncan Davison'.

7. *Ibid.*, 204. Burns wrote his second, better-known set of words to this tune four years later (Kinsley, 394) 'Duncan Grey', he wrote, 'is that kind of light-horse gallop of an air, which precludes sentiment. – The ludicrous is its ruling feature.' (Letters, 523.)

acquired non-bawdy words when Burns was in the mood for polite song-writing.'[1]

Special interest attaches to 'To the Weaver's gin ye go'. Kinsley places it in the tradition of love-songs related – 'with varying degrees of impropriety' – to the crafts:

> A bonie, westlin weaver lad   west-country
> Sat working at his loom;
> He took my heart as wi' a net
> In every knot and thrum.[2]

The thrum is an end of warp-thread left unwoven on the loom when the web is cut off; the girl's account of how she was seduced is cleverly couched in the language of the weaver's trade. Burns himself considered that this song had no particular merit; he appears, indeed, from a later note, to have regarded much of what he did in this line as little more than journey-work: 'Here, once for all, let me apologise for many silly compositions of mine in this work. Many beautiful airs wanted words; in the hurry of other avocations, if I could string a parcel of rhymes together anything near tolerable, I was fain to let them pass. He must be an excellent poet indeed, whose every performance is excellent.'[3]

'Written for this work by Robert Burns' – only 'Clarinda, mistress of my soul' was fully identified as his. Some songs were unsigned; about a dozen were identified by the letter R or B; old verses which he had corrected or made additions to carried the letter Z. Towards the end of the collection, over the signature M, appears 'To a Blackbird. By a Lady'. This was one of the poems Clarinda had sent him: 'I am just going to take your Blackbird', he had told her, 'the sweetest, I am sure that ever sung, and prune its wings a little,'[4] but he had revised it hardly at all:

> Go on, sweet bird, and soothe my care,
> Thy tuneful notes will hush Despair;
> Thy plaintive warblings void of art
> Thrill sweetly thro' my aching heart . . .[5]

While Clarinda nursed her aching heart in Edinburgh, Burns had made his way westward to Glasgow. He wrote to her on his first evening at the Black Bull Inn, telling her that he had found the attraction of love to be in an inverse proportion to the attraction of the Newtonian philosophy: '. . . In my system,

1. Donald A. Low, *The Songs of Robert Burns*, Routledge, London, 1993, p. 249.
2. Kinsley, 194.
3. Notes to *The Scots Musical Museum*, p. 24.
4. Letters, 183.
5. Kinsley, 214, [Revision for Clarinda].

every milestone that marked my progress from Clarinda, awaked a keener pang of attachment to her. – How do you feel, my Love? is your heart ill at ease? I fear it. – God forbid that these Persecutors should harass that Peace which is more precious to me than my own . . .[1]

He had finally stopped dithering about his future; so at least he had assured Margaret Chalmers on the eve of his departure from Edinburgh. 'You will condemn me for the next step I have taken,' he told her: 'I have entered into the excise. I stay in the west about three weeks, and then return to Edinburgh for six weeks instructions; afterwards, for I get employ instantly, I go *où il plait a Dieu, – et mon Roi* . . .'

He was anxious for her to know that he had not compromised himself: 'I got this without any hanging on, or mortifying solicitation; it is immediate bread, and though poor in comparison of the last eighteen months of my existence, 'tis luxury in comparison of all my preceding life . . .'[2]

Richard Brown, now master of a ship making ready to sail for Grenada, had come up from Greenock to meet him. They were joined by Burns's brother William, and the three spent a convivial evening together: 'Adieu, My Clarinda! I am just going to propose your health by way of grace-drink.'[3]

He moved on to Paisley, and then to Stewarton, where he was a guest for two days at Dunlop House. The dry opening of a letter Mrs Dunlop wrote to him a week later suggests that his manners had not been of the best:

Trusting to your aversion for the foppish fashions fetched from France, I flattered myself we should have had the pleasure of seeing you at breakfast, and that you would also have despised a French leave. I had a vision ready for your morning entertainment, but when William told you had been gone two hours, it wholly escaped me in the surprise and disappointment . . .[4]

'I hear there is a book come out against you,' she added, 'but I have not seen it' – evidence that Burns was already provoking a groundswell of adverse criticism. Gossip about his morals, dislike of his politics, class-prejudice and good old-fashioned jealousy all contributed to this – 'The encouragement that fellow has met with is a perfect disgrace to the nation,' grumbled John Home, the author of *Douglas*.[5] The book mentioned by Mrs Dunlop was probably one published in that year by a man called James Maxwell, a poet of sorts who lived in Paisley. It was called *Animadversions on Some Poets and Poetasters of the Present Age ... With a Contrast of Some of the Former Age*, and it contained a tum-ti-tum sequence 'On the Ayrshire Ploughman Poet, or Poetaster, R.B':

1. Letters, 208.
2. *Ibid.*, 207.
3. *Ibid.*, 208.
4. Letter dated February 30th, 1788. Burns and Dunlop, p. 46.
5. See *The Burns Chronicle*, (1940), new series, xv, p. 16.

Of all British poets that yet have appear'd,
None e'er at things sacred so daringly sneer'd,
As he in the west, who but lately is sprung
From behind the plough-tails, and from raking of dung.
A champion for Satan, none like him before,
And his equal, pray God, we may never see more;
For none have like him, been by Satan inspir'd,
Which makes his rank nonsense by fools so admir'd . . .[1]

Burns's performance as a correspondent fell short of what he had promised before leaving Edinburgh, and Clarinda was cast down:

I wish you had given me a hint, my dear Sylvander, that you were to write me only once in a week. Yesterday I looked for a letter; to-day, never doubted it; but both days have terminated in disappointment. A thousand conjectures have conspired to make me most unhappy . . . If I don't hear tomorrow, I shall form dreadful reasons. God forbid! . . .[2]

Life had not been easy for her since Burns's departure. Her minister, Kemp, had called, and had given her a hard time. When she thanked him for coming, he told her that it was 'merely to hide the change in his friendship from the world.' She was mortified, and close to tears. 'He did not name you,' she wrote to Burns, 'but spoke in terms that showed plainly he knew.' She was also anxious about her son, Willie, whose leg had to be lanced: 'I shall be fluttered till the operation is fairly over.'[3]

Burns had by now reached Mauchline, and he wrote to thank Mrs McLehose for her present to his 'sweet, little Bobbie' (she had sent 'twa wee sarkies'). The rest of the letter makes less pleasant reading:

Now for a little news that will please you. – I, this morning as I came home, called for a certain woman. – I am disgusted with her; I cannot endure her! I, while my heart smote me for the prophanity, tried to compare her with my Clarinda: 'twas setting the expiring glimmer of a farthing taper beside the cloudless glory of the meridian sun. – Here was tasteless insipidity, vulgarity of soul, and mercenary fawning; there, polished good sense, heaven-born genius, and the most generous, the most delicate, the most tender Passion. – I have done with her, and she with me.[4]

1. Maxwell, described by Chambers as 'a prolific rhymester,' had published some years previously *A new version of the whole Book of Psalms in Metre*. He frequently signed himself 'James Maxwell, S.D.P.,' which stood for 'Student of Divine Poetry.'
2. Burns and McLehose, Letter XLIX, Edinburgh, Friday Evening [22nd February].
3. *Ibid.*, Letter XLVII, 'Edinburgh, Tuesday Evening, Nine o'clock' [19th February.]
4. Letters, 210.

Less than two weeks later he worked up a cheerful nautical metaphor to give his friend Richard Brown a very different version of his homecoming:

> I found Jean – with her cargo very well laid in; but unfortunately moor'd, almost at the mercy of wind and tide: I have towed her into convenient harbour where she may lie snug till she unload; and have taken the command myself – not ostensibly, but for a time in secret. – I am gratified by your kind enquiries after her; as after all, I may say with Othello –
>
> "Excellent wretch!
"Perdition catch my soul but I do love thee!"[1]

There is no period in his short life when it is so hard to read Burns as in those early spring months of 1788. Nor is there a time at which it is so difficult to observe his behaviour with any degree of sympathy or understanding. Jean, now eight months pregnant, had found shelter with a family called Muir, old friends of the Burnses' who had the mill at Tarbolton. Burns brought her back to Mauchline – the 'convenient harbour' he had found for her was the house of his old friend John Mackenzie, the local doctor. His letters to Mrs McLehose were naturally silent on these arrangements, but Burns judged that his friend Ainslie, whom he had so recently introduced to Clarinda, would be diverted by an account of how he had renewed his relations with Jean. 'I have reconciled her to her fate, and I have reconciled her to her mother,' he wrote:

> . . . I have taken her to my arms. I have given her a mahogony bed. I have given her a guinea, and I have f—d her till she rejoiced with joy unspeakable and full of glory. But, as I always am on every occasion, I have been prudent and cautious to an astonishing degree. I swore her privately and solemnly never to attempt any claim on me as a husband, even though anybody should persuade her she had such a claim (which she had not), neither during my life nor after my death. She did all this like a good girl, and I took the opportunity of some dry horse litter, and gave her such a thundering scalade that electrified the very marrow of her bones. Oh, what a peacemaker is a guid weel-willy p—le! It is the mediator, the guarantee, the umpire, the bond of union, the solemn league and covenant, the plenipotentiary, the Aaron's rod, the Jacob's staff, the prophet Elisha's pot of oil, the Ahasuerus' Sceptre, the sword of mercy, the philosopher's stone, the Horn of Plenty, and Tree of Life between Man and Woman . . .[2]

Jean Armour's 'joy unspeakable' was not of long duration. Early in March she went into labour and once again gave birth to twins, this time both girls. There

1. *Ibid.*, 220.
2. *Ibid.*, 215.

is no reference in Burns's correspondence to this second confinement. The Mauchline burial register records that one child died on March 10th, the other twelve days later. Neither infant had been baptised.

Jean's confinement was subsequently chronicled by Saunders Tait, the eccentric Tarbolton tailor and doggerel-monger. He and Burns had been feuding for years, and Tait embraced this new opportunity to level the score with scabrous glee:

> The wives they up their coats did kilt,
> And through the streets so clean did stilt, prance
> Some at the door fell wi' a pelt blow
> Maist broke their leg,
> To see the Hen, poor wanton jilt!
> Lay her fourth egg.

Arcady was never like this.

Clarinda continued to be displeased by the infrequency of his letters. 'I fear, Sylvander, you overvalue my generosity,' she wrote on March 5th:

> Believe me, it will be some time ere I can cordially forgive you the pain your silence has caused me! Did you ever feel that sickness of heart which arises from "hope deferred"? That, the cruelest of pains, you have inflicted on me for eight days by-past. I hope I can make every reasonable allowance for the hurry of business and dissipation . . .

The news conveyed in his letter went some way to mollify her: '. . . I am happy that the farming scheme promises so well. There's no fickleness, my dear Sir, in changing for the better. I never liked the Excise for you; and feel a sensible pleasure in the hope of your becoming a sober, industrious farmer . . .'[1]

Burns had been down in Dumfriesshire taking yet another look at Patrick Miller's Dalswinton farms. He had persuaded his father's old neighbour, John Tennant, to go with him. Tennant, who had been one of the witnesses at Burns's own baptism, farmed at Glenconner, and had for some years been the Countess of Glencairn's factor at Ochiltree; Burns valued his friendship and respected his advice.

There were three farms on offer, two on low ground on the east bank of the Nith, the third on higher, stonier ground on the river's west bank. It was called Ellisland, and this was the one which Burns finally chose. He seems to the last to have been in two minds about it. He told Nicol he was well pleased with the prospect;[2] to Ainslie he wrote that Tennant's advice 'has staggered

1. Burns and McLehose, Letter LI, Edinburgh, March 5th, 1788.
2. Letters, 222A.

me a good deal'.[1] The two men were accompanied on their tour of inspection by Miller's factor: 'Mr Burns,' he is supposed to have said, 'you have made a poet's, not a farmer's choice.'[2]

Miller himself had bought the Dalswinton estate unseen, and conceded, many years later, that it had been 'in the most miserable state of exhaustion'. This had obviously not escaped Tennant, and Burns dwelt on it in the tough and businesslike letter he wrote to his prospective landlord about the terms of the lease:

> . . . It is usual, I understand, to make the entries to leasses in your neighbour-hood, at Whitsunday.—This will not do at Ellisland; the farm is so worn out, and every bit of it, good for any thing, is this year under tillage; at least the fields are so intersected with pieces under crop, that four horses which I will need this summer for driving lime and materials for building, with a cow for a married servant perhaps the first year, and one for myself as I must be on the spot, will eat up the whole pasture . . .[3]

Burns went on to make a number of proposals about the rent and the length of the lease and announced that he would call on Miller in Edinburgh at the beginning of the following week.

Back in Mauchline, he was obliged to give his mind to Gilbert's difficulties at Mossgiel, and in doing so he appears to have done grave injury to his friendship with Gavin Hamilton. Hamilton's legal papers do not survive, but he clearly suggested to Burns that he should guarantee his brother for a considerable sum. Burns did not think it prudent to agree to this, and told Hamilton so in admirably sturdy terms:

> Sir,
> The language of refusal is to me the most difficult language on earth, and you are the man of the world, excepting One of the R[t] Hon[ble] designation, to whom it gives me the greatest pain to hold such language. – My brother has already got money, and shall want nothing in my power to enable him to fulfil his engagement with you; but to be security on so large a scale even for a brother, is what I dare not do, except I were in such circumstances of life as that the worst that might happen could not greatly injure me. – I never wrote a letter which gave me so much pain in my life, as I know the unhappy consequences; I shall incur the displeasure of a Gentleman for whom I have the highest respect, and to whom I am deeply oblidged. –[4]

1. *Ibid.*, 215.
2. The factor's name was Cunningham. The story is told by his son Allan in the *Life of Burns* he published in 1834. 'Anything that Cunningham says may be true,' wrote Snyder; 'nothing that he says should be believed without corroborating testimony.' (Snyder, p. 489.)
3. Letters, 214 A.
4. *Ibid.*, 222.

He dashed off a number of other letters on the day that he wrote to Hamilton – to Clarinda, to Mrs Dunlop, to Richard Brown. He also wrote to his old friend Robert Muir, the wine merchant in Kilmarnock who had exerted himself so strenuously over both editions of the poems. Muir was seriously ill with consumption: 'I trust the Spring will renew your shattered frame and make your friends happy,' Burns wrote. It is a thoughtful and sober letter, but also delicate and almost tender. 'You and I have often agreed that life is no great blessing,' he reminded Muir. 'But an honest man has nothing to fear:

If we lie down in the grave, the whole man a piece of broke machinery, to moulder with the clods of the valley, – be it so; at least there is an end of pain, care, woes and wants: if that part of us called Mind, does survive the apparent destruction of the man – away with old-wife prejudices and tales! . . . a man, conscious of having acted an honest part among his fellow creatures; even granting that he may have been the sport, at times, of passions and instincts; he goes to a great unknown Being who could have no other end in giving him existence but to make him happy; who gave him those passions and instincts, and well knows their force . . .

It becomes a man of sense to think for himself; particularly in a case where all men are equally interested, and where indeed all men are equally in the dark . . .[1]

Burns, who could be so monstrously coarse, was also possessed of a keen, almost feminine, sensibility; perhaps he sensed that his friend was for the dark. The spring did nothing for him and he was dead before April was out.

In the second week in March, Burns had set out for Edinburgh again – to settle the terms of his lease with Miller, to try once more to flush out Creech, to advance matters on the excise front, to see Clarinda.

The capital was awash with rumour. The most sensational story going the rounds concerned William Brodie, Deacon of the Wrights and Masons, a prosperous cabinet maker and highly respected member of the Town Council with a secret passion for gambling. During the winter, the city had been startled by a series of robberies, the most outrageous of them at the Excise Office in Chessel's Court as recently as March 5th. Now one of those involved had decided to turn king's evidence, and led the police to a cache of keys intended for future operations. Deacon Brodie had disappeared, and the king's messenger for Scotland was said to be pursuing him in England, and possibly abroad.[2]

1. *Ibid.*, 221.
2. Brodie was eventually arrested in Amsterdam in August, on the eve of his departure for America. He was arraigned in the High Court of Justiciary (his counsel was Henry Erskine) and hanged on October 1st – 'the *first* to know the excellence of an improvement he had formerly made on that identical gibbet – the substitution of what is called the *drop*, for the ancient practice of the double ladder.' (Grant, *op. cit.*, vol. 1, p. 115).

3. William Brodie: Deacon of the Wrights and Masons by day, gambler and felon by night – a double life terminated on 1st October 1788 when he was hanged at the west end of the Luckenbooths.

Another rumour – this one touched Burns closely – was that Creech had been making a dishonest penny by quietly putting out a new edition of the poems. He was said to have approached Beugo for the engraved plate which had been used as the frontispiece; Beugo had let him have it, but only after putting a distinguishing mark on it: 'Report addeth that numberless copies of the Poems afterwards appeared with this private mark upon the portrait.'[1] Burns could easily have established the facts of the matter, because Beugo was a friend. There is no direct reference to it in what survives of his correspondence, although a note which he scribbled to Clarinda shows that his exasperation was at a high pitch:

> I have just now written Creech such a letter, that the very goose-feather in my hand shrunk back from the line, and seemed to say, "I exceedingly fear and quake!" I am forming ideal schemes of vengeance. O for a little of my will on him![2]

A week later he told Richard Brown he had been 'racking shop accounts with Mr Creech' and that for a good part of the day he had been 'convuls'd with rage'.[3] Burns was to nurse his indignation for quite some time. 'I cannot boast of Mr Creech's ingenuous fair-dealing to me,' he told Dr Moore the following January, adding sourly, 'but what am I that I should speak against the Lord's annointed Bailie of Edinburgh?'[4] Even then, as will be seen, Burns would still be obliged to return to the charge over the hundred guineas that had been agreed for the copyright.

With Miller, matters were swiftly arranged; Burns concluded a bargain with him on March 13th. 'I begin at Whitsunday to build a house, drive lime, &c.' he wrote to Margaret Chalmers, 'and heaven be my help! for it will take a strong effort to bring my mind into the routine of business.'[5]

He saw Clarinda several times in the course of that week, and also directed at her a flow of extravagant written protestations. Her replies do not survive, but from the letter Burns dashed off to her at nine o'clock on Friday evening, she could reasonably have drawn only one conclusion about his intentions:

> Life, my Clarinda, is a weary, barren path; and wo be to him or her that ventures on it alone! For me, I have my dearest partner of my soul: Clarinda and I will make out our pilgrimage together. Wherever I am, I shall constantly let her know how I go on, what I observe in the world around me, and what adventures I meet with. Will it please you, my love, to get, every week, or,

1. The words quoted are from the Train Manuscript in the Edinburgh University Library. See Fitzhugh, *op. cit.*, p. 57.
2. Letters, 222B.
3. *Ibid.*, 228.
4. *Ibid.*, 294.
5. *Ibid.*, 223.

at least, every fortnight, a packet, two or three sheets, full of remarks, non-sense, news, rhymes, and old songs?

Will you open, with satisfaction and delight, a letter from a man who loves you, who has loved you, and who will love you to death, through death, and for ever? . . .[1]

He sent round a further note at noon the following Monday. 'Excuse me, my dearest angel, this hurried scrawl and miserable paper; circumstances make both,' he wrote: 'My Excise affair is just concluded, and I have got my order for instructions: so far good.'[2] He told her that he was engaged to join 'some of the principals of the Excise' for supper later in the week and that he was also to dine with one of the Commissioners.

He presented her, on parting, with two drinking glasses and four of the least distinguished stanzas he ever wrote:

> Fair Empress of the Poet's soul,
>   And Queen of Poetesses;
> Clarinda, take this little boon,
>   This humble pair of Glasses . . .[3]

He wrote her one last note the following morning, just as he was hurrying off 'to wait on the Great Man' – possibly Graham of Fintry:

. . . My imagination, like a child's favorite bird, will fondly flutter along with this scrawl till it perch on your bosom. – I thank you for all the happiness you bestowed on me yesterday. – The walk – delightful; the evening – rapture. – Do not be uneasy today, Clarinda; forgive me . . .[4]

This suggests Burns may have made one final attempt to establish where the boundaries of delicacy were drawn. Clarinda's thoughts about the evening are lost to us, but the glasses were carefully preserved. In time they passed to her grandson, and we know from him that they were often taken down from the open cupboard in her parlour and shown to strangers.[5]

Burns now once again returned to Ayrshire by way of Glasgow. His immediate concern was to get his instruction for the excise over and done with. It had originally been arranged that this should take place in Edinburgh under an officer called Dickson, but now that he had gone firm on Ellisland he sought

1. *Ibid.*, 224.
2. *Ibid.*, 225.
3. Kinsley, 219.
4. Letters, 226.
5. Burns and McLehose, p. 258.

Graham of Fintry's help in negotiating the bureaucratic obstacles which stood in the way of a change of plan:

> I have been lucky enough to find an Excise Off^r here who is exceedingly clever, and who enters with the warmth of a friend in my ideas of being instructed. − I got M^r· Dickson, the Officer whom formerly I chose for my Instructor, to assign over his Order to this gentleman; but it seems the supervisor in Ayr, who must examine me, is superstitiously strict, and to make all things fast I must trouble you, as you were so very good as to give me permission, to order the Secretary to make out a new Order for my instruction, and direct it to M^r· James Findlay, Excise Off^r at Tarbolton, Ayr District. −[1]

Graham obliged very promptly − the new order of instruction was dated March 31st. Findlay was enjoined to instruct Burns 'in the art of gauging and practical dry gouging casks and utensils; and that you fit him for surveying victuallers, rectifiers, chandlers, tanners, tawers, maltsters etc'. Findlay was a single man two years older than Burns, with seven years' experience in the service. Burns repaid him by introducing him to Jean Markland, one of the six 'Mauchline belles'; they were married the following September.

For the present, Burns explained to Mrs Dunlop, his excise commission would be tucked into his back pocket as a sort of insurance policy: 'I thought five & thirty pounds a year was no bad dernier resort for a poor Poet, if Fortune in her jade tricks should kick him down from the little eminence to which she has lately helped him up.'[2] All the time he could spare from his instruction was given over to preparations to his entry to Ellisland: 'I am so harrassed with Care and Anxiety about this farming project of mine, that my Muse has degenerated into the veriest prose-wench that ever picked cinders, or followed a Tinker.'[3] He needed money, and he wrote, in surprisingly cordial terms, to Creech; indeed, in the light of what had so recently passed between them the accommodating tone of the letter is baffling:

> As I am seriously set in for my farming operations, I shall need that sum your kindness procured me for my Copyright. − I have sent the line to M^r· John Sommerville, a particular friend of mine, who will call on you; but as I do not need the sum, at least I can make a shift without it till then, any time between [now] and the first of May, as it may suit your convenience to pay it, will do for me. −[4]

1. Letters, 228B.
2. *Ibid.*, 238.
3. *Ibid.*, 230. Burns was writing to Robert Cleghorn, who farmed at Corstorphine, then on the outskirts of Edinburgh, and was a fellow-Crochallan Fencible.
4. *Ibid.*, 231.

He was no businessman, and Creech knew it. Burns, indeed, knew it well enough himself, and to old friends like William Dunbar he was prepared to concede it:

> . . . I am earnestly busy to bring about a revolution in my own mind. – As, till within these eighteen months, I never was the wealthy master of ten guineas, my knowledge of business is to learn; add to this my late scenes of idleness and dissipation have enervated my mind to an alarming degree . . . I have dropt all conversation and all reading (prose reading) but what tends in some way or other to my serious aim. Except one worthy young fellow, I have not one single Correspondent in Edin^r . . .[1]

Clarinda, certainly, was not getting those regular packets 'full of remarks, nonsense, news, rhymes, and old songs' which she had been promised. Burns gave the first hint of the reason why to Margaret Chalmers in the first week in April: 'I have lately made some sacrifices for which, were I *viva voce* with you to paint the situation and recount the circumstances, you would applaud me.'[2] This may have intrigued Miss Chalmers, but can hardly have enlightened her. Three weeks later, to his friend James Smith in Linlithgow, he was more explicit: 'There is, you must know, a certain clean-limb'd, handsome bewitching young Hussy of your acquaintance to whom I have lately and privately given a matrimonial title to my Corpus.' If Burns had felt any distress at the death of the twins the previous month, he had quickly got over it; he now appeared to regard Jean Armour's fecundity as a matter for self-congratulation:

> . . . I hate to presage ill-luck; and as my girl in some late random trials has been *doubly* kinder to me than even the best of women usually are to their Partners of our Sex, in similar circumstances; I reckon on twelve times a brace of children against I celebrate my twelfth wedding-day . . .
>
> Now for business. – I intend to present Mrs Burns with a printed shawl, an article of which I dare say you have variety; 'tis my first present to her since I have *irrevocably* called her mine, and I have a kind of whimsical wish to get her the said first present from an old and much valued friend of hers & mine . . .[3]

He found it more difficult to confide in newer friends. By the end of May, he had still not got round to telling Mrs Dunlop: 'I did not know how to tell her,' he wrote lamely to her son Andrew. 'I am afraid that perhaps she will not entirely enter into the motives of my conduct.'[4] The news did not take long to travel to Haddington, where Mrs Dunlop was staying with another of her sons.

1. *Ibid.*, 236.
2. *Ibid.*, 235.
3. *Ibid.*, 237.
4. *Ibid.*, 245.

She had grumbled in an earlier letter about hearing of Burns's Ellisland venture at second-hand; now she pronounced herself staggered: 'I am told in a letter that you have been a month married. I am unwilling to believe so important an era in your life has past, and you have considered me as so very little concerned . . .' Her indignation quickly gave way to her underlying motherly concern: 'Allow me, however, married or unmarried, to wish you joy, which I assure you I do most sincerely in every situation in which yourself or Providence can put you.'[1]

Burns's reasons for deciding to marry Jean Armour were complex and must be pieced together from what he told friends and what he wrote in his *Commonplace Book*. There are interesting variations in those accounts. To Ainslie, at that time the friend in whom he probably felt most able to confide, he was sober and frank: 'It has indeed added to my anxieties for Futurity but it has given a stability to my mind & resolutions, unknown before.'[2] In a letter to James Johnson of the *Scots Musical Museum* (and the Crochallan Fencibles) he puts on more of a performance:

> I am so enamoured with a certain girl's prolific twin-bearing merit, that I have given her a *legal* title to the best blood in my body; and so farewell Rakery! To be serious, my worthy friend; I found I had a long and much-loved fellow-creature's happiness or misery among my hands; and tho' Pride & seeming Justice were murderous King's Advocates on the one side, yet Humanity, Generosity & Forgiveness were such powerful such irresistible Counsel on the other side, that a Jury of old Endearments & new attachments brought in a unanimous verdict – *NOT GUILTY!*[3]

The 'much-loved fellow-creature' line served as a model for what he later wrote both to Mrs Dunlop and her son.[4] In his *Common-place Book*, he looked in the glass more steadily and wrote with greater candour:

> Wedlock, the circumstance that buckles me hardest to Care, if Virtue and Religion were to be anything with me but mere names, was what in a few seasons I must have resolved on; in the present case it was unavoidably necessary. Humanity, Generosity, honest vanity of character, Justice to my own happiness for after-life, so far as it could depend, which it surely will a great deal, on internal peace, all those joined their warmest suffrages, their most powerful sollicitations, with a rooted Attachment, to urge the step I

1. Letter dated 4th June 1788, Burns and Dunlop, pp. 63–6.
2. Letters, 243.
3. *Ibid.*, 242.
4. *Ibid.*, 245 and 247.

have taken. Nor have I any reason on her part to rue it. I can fancy how, but have never seen where, I could have made it better.[1]

The form which Burns's marriage took has never been established; this part of the legend is richly encrusted with conflicting 'traditions.' The Train Manuscript says that they were married privately by a magistrate in Gavin Hamilton's office; in other versions the ceremony is variously located in a Mauchline tavern and a local dance hall. Legally, a simple declaration in the presence of two witnesses would have constituted a valid union; indeed lawyers might well have held that Burns had been a married man since the spring of 1786. The church saw matters differently, and it was not until later in the year that Burns and his bride were formally readmitted to the paths of righteousness.

When he wrote to Mrs Dunlop's son Andrew at the end of May, he was philosophical about his changed circumstances:

Do you know that except from your Mother and the good family, my existence or non-existence is now of as little importance to that Great World I lately left, as the satelites of the Georgium Sidus is to a parcel of your Ditchers. – I foresaw this from the beginning. – Ambition could not form a higher wish than to be wedded to Novelty; but I retired to my shades with a little comfortable pride and a few comfortable pounds.[2]

Those 'few comfortable pounds' could not be spent twice, however. Whitsunday was upon him. There were farm-servants to hire and other outgoings. When he wrote to James Johnson on May 25th, it was not only to boast about 'a certain girl's prolific twin-bearing merit':

I am really uneasy about that money which Mr Creech owes me p^r Note in your hand, and I want it much at present as I am engaging in business pretty deeply both for myself & my brother. A hundred guineas can be but a trifling affair to him, and 'tis a matter of most serious importance to me. – Tomorrow I begin my operations as a farmer, and God speed the Plough! –[3]

1. Entry dated 14th June 1788.
2. Letters, 245.
3. Ibid., 242.

Ten

THE ELBOW OF EXISTENCE

WHITSUNTIDE CAME AND WENT. Burns, never the slave of time, took a turn up to Glasgow before making his way down to Nithsdale; the Almighty was not called upon to speed the plough at Ellisland for several weeks. On June 13th, the new tenant decided he must mend some private fences and wrote a long letter to Mrs Dunlop:

> This is the second day, my honored Friend, that I have been on my farm. – A solitary inmate of an old smoky 'SPENCE'; far from every object I love or by whom I am belov'd, nor any acquaintance older than yesterday except Jenny Geddes the old mare I ride on; while uncouth Cares and novel Plans hourly insult my awkward Ignorance & bashful Inexperience . . .[1]

A spence is a small inner room. There was no farmhouse at Ellisland, and for his first five months there Burns was given shelter by the outgoing tenant and his wife, a mile or so down the river from the farm. 'This hovel that I shelter in,' he told Margaret Chalmers, 'is pervious to every blast that blows, and every shower that falls; and I am only preserved from being chilled to death, by being suffocated with smoke.'[2]

The terms of his lease with Patrick Miller appear generous. It was to run for seventy-six years, nineteen at a time. The rent, payable in equal instalments at Whitsunday and Martinmas, was set at fifty pounds for the first three years, rising thereafter to seventy. Miller agreed to pay Burns the sum of three hundred pounds, which was to be spent on the construction of a house and farm buildings and on the enclosure of the fields. Miller reserved two acres of land for his own use for planting; he also undertook to plant both the river bank and a twenty-foot belt of land dividing Ellisland from the neighbouring property belonging to Captain Riddell of the Carse. Burns, for his part, agreed 'to labour and manure the lands hereby let in a proper manner'. The lease also stipulated

1. Letters, 247.
2. *Ibid.*, 272.

that he should make no encroachments on the river Nith – 'by making any Caul, pier, or embankment, throwing in stones or rubbish, or by driuing piles or in any other manner of way whateuer.' The parties agreed that in the event of non-performance there should be a penalty of one hundred pounds sterling.[1]

During the spring and summer months of 1788, Burns shuttled to and fro between Ellisland and Mauchline, a distance of about forty-five miles, spending eight or ten days in each place. It was an unsettling routine, and he did not find it easy to come to terms with his new life: 'My farm gives me a good many uncouth Cares and Anxieties,' he wrote to Ainslie, although he would also have had his young friend believe that he was a reformed character and intended to rise to the challenge:

> I have all along, hitherto, in the warfare of life, been bred to arms among the light-horse – the piquet-guards of fancy; a kind of Hussars and Highlanders of the *Brain*; but I am firmly resolved to *sell out* of these giddy battalions, who have no ideas of a battle but fighting the foe, or of a siege but storming the town. Cost what it will, I am determined to buy in among the grave squadrons of heavy-armed thought, or the artillery corps of plodding contrivance.[2]

Burns quickly established that in Robert Riddell he had a congenial and convivial neighbour. Four years older than Burns, Riddell had studied at St Andrews and Edinburgh and later served in the Royal Scots and the Eighty-Third Regiment, the Prince of Wales Light Dragoons. Retiring on half-pay, he had settled at Friars' Carse and devoted himself to music, to coin-collecting and to other antiquarian pursuits.

His mansion stood at a bend of the Nith on a rocky promontory. The land hereabouts had once belonged to Melrose Abbey and the house was on the site of an old monastic retreat. It had pleased Riddell to build a 'Hermitage' in the grounds, to instal a baptismal font salvaged from a ruined church in his entrance hall and to construct a reproduction of a druidical stone circle. One episode in his family history was calculated to appeal strongly to Burns – during the northward retreat of the Jacobite army in 1745, Riddell's father, together with the Provost of Dumfries, had been held hostage by the Young Pretender as security for the levy laid on the town.

The two men were soon on friendly terms. Indeed within a fortnight of his arrival in Dumfriesshire, Burns had been given a key to the Hermitage and composed some verses there:

> Thou whom chance may hither lead,
> Be thou clad in russet weed,

1. The text of the lease is reproduced as an appendix in Snyder, pp. 503-10.
2. Letters, 249.

> Be thou deckt in silken stole,
> Grave these maxims on thy soul. –

Poetically it is a rather stilted piece; its interest lies in the strong impression that we are listening to the voice of a man who has lowered his sights and expects less of life than he formerly did:

> Happiness is but a name,
> Make CONTENT and EASE thy aim. –
> Ambition is a meteor gleam,
> Fame a restless, airy dream . . .

And again:

> Follies past, give thou to air;
> Make their consequence thy care:
> Keep the name of MAN in mind,
> And dishonor not thy kind. –[1]

There is a first cryptic reference in that last week in June to the consequence of a folly of his own from a past still uncomfortably recent. Some months later, when he briefly resumed his correspondence with Mrs McLehose he was to depict his conduct towards her during his second winter in Edinburgh as that of an honest man, 'struggling successfully with temptations the most powerful that ever beset humanity'. He had, he asserted, preserved 'untainted honor in situations where the austerest Virtue would have forgiven a fall'.[2] He had, it now emerged, been engaged simultaneously in another struggle where he had been less successful. Holy Willie would have understood:

> But yet – O L–d – confess I must –
> At times I'm fash'd wi' fleshly lust:
> And sometimes too, in wardly trust
>   Vile Self gets in . . .

Robert Ainslie later judged it prudent to retrieve and destroy his letters to Burns, but we know that the one which reached Ellisland on June 30th contained unwelcome news, even if Burns dismissed it in one sentence: 'I am vexed at that affair of the girl, but dare not enlarge on the subject until you send me your direction, as I suppose that will be altered on your late Master and Friend's death.'[3]

---

1. Kinsley, 223
2. Letters, 320.
3. *Ibid.*, 252. Samuel Mitchelson, in whose office Ainslie was a law student, had just died.

There were still also one or two matrimonial loose ends to be tied up, and Burns now wrote to enlist the help of James Smith:

> I have waited on M^r. Auld about my Marriage affair, & stated that I was legally fined for an irregular marriage by a Justice of the Peace. – He says, if I bring an attestation of this by the two witnesses, there shall be no more litigation about it. – As soon as this comes to hand, please write me in the way of familiar Epistle that, "Such things are".[1]

Snyder took the view that Burns was inventing what he called 'a pious fiction'. If that is what it was, his letter to Smith constituted an appeal to his friend to commit perjury. Whether he obliged is not known. The matter was in any event resolved, apparently to everyone's satisfaction, when Burns was back in Mauchline early in August. 'Compeared Robert Burns with Jean Armour, his alledged Spouse,' reads an entry in the Kirk Session minutes:

> They both acknowledged their irregular marriage, and their Sorrow for that irregularity, and desiring that the Session will take such steps as may seem to them proper, in order to the solemn confirmation of said marriage.
> The Session, taking this affair under their consideration, agree that they both be rebuked for their acknowledged irregularity, and that they be taken solemnly engaged to adhere faithfully to one another as husband and wife all the days of their life.
> In regard the Session have a tittle in Law to some fine for behoof of the Poor, they agree to refer to Mr Burns his own generosity.
> The above sentence was accordingly executed, and the Session absolved the said parties from any scandal on this acct.

The minute was signed by Dr Auld in his capacity as Moderator of the Session. Unusually, he required the newly-weds to do the same. A sentence added beneath the signatures states, 'Mr Burns gave a guinea note for behoof of the poor.'

Mr Burns also decided that celebrations were called for, and that his bride must have a wedding present. That evening he picked up his pen and wrote, not without difficulty, to Mr Robert McIndoe, a Glasgow silk merchant: 'This is the night of our Fair, and I, as you see, cannot keep well *in a line.*' He wanted some black silk, and promised payment – 'and a more coherent letter' – on the carrier's next journey:

> To be brief, send me fifteen y^ds black lutestring silk, such as they use to make gowns & petticoats of, and I shall chuse some sober morning before

1. *Ibid.*, 251.

breakfast, & write you a sober answer, with the sober sum which will then be due you . . .[1]

Mrs Dunlop, still in Haddington, was eager to know all, but her curiosity was laced with candour:

Your picture of the character and disposition ought to make a rational man happy, if fairly drawn, and properly accompany'd, but much depends on the man as well as on the poor female, from whom you men generally require all, and to whom a great many of you give nothing . . .[2]

Burns sent an expansive and revealing reply:

In housewife matters, of aptness to learn and activity to execute she is eminently mistress; and during my absence in Nithsdale, she is regularly & constantly apprentice to my Mother & Sisters in their dairy & other rural business. – In short, I can easily *fancy* a more agreable companion for my journey of Life, but, upon my honor, I have never *seen* the Individual Instance! . . .

He also glanced, with almost brutal frankness, at what might have been:

Circumstanced as I am, I could never have got a female Partner for life who could have entered into my favorite studies, relished my favorite Authors, &c. without entailing on me at the same time, expensive living, fantastic caprice, apish affectation, with all the other blessed, Boarding-school acquirements which (pardonnez-moi, Madame!) are some times to be found among females of the upper ranks, but almost universally pervade the Misses of the Would-be-gentry . . .[3]

Burns absent-mindedly dated this letter August 10th, although he wrote it in the middle of July. This earned him an interminable reply, almost by return. 'Yours was Agt,' she wrote under the date, 'How fast time flies when a man is married!' She took the liberty – her own word – of sending him a wedding present: ' 'Tis a Scots superstition to believe a bargain always turns out much the better for being followed with a luckpenny.' She knew how prickly he was, and that she might well incur his displeasure; she sought to avert it by drawing on her apparently inexhaustible fund of bizarre anecdotes:

1. *Ibid.*, 262.
2. Letter dated 24th June 1788, Burns and Dunlop, pp. 70-3.
3. Letters, 254.

. . . I have ventured, even at the risk of it, to send you a £5 card from the Thistle Bank. I am wrong, as Lord Bankton said when his fourth wife mist one napkin of a dozen fine ones in a parcel. 'My dr., when my last wife was buried, I forgot to draw it out in putting her corpse into the coffin. I shall behave better next time.'[1]

She had judged her man shrewdly, and he did no more than go through the motions of being offended: 'I am indeed seriously angry with you at the Quantum of your "Luckpenny"; but vexed and hurt as I was, I could not help laughing very heartily at the noble Lord's apology for the miss'd Napkin. – '[2]

Marriage plainly agreed with him. When his friend Peter Hill, formerly Creech's assistant, but now in business as a bookseller on his own account, reproached him for being a poor correspondent, Burns sent a racily suggestive reply; in Nithsdale he was building a house, and in Kyle he had a young wife to keep him busy:

Good God, Sir, could my dearest BROTHER expect a regular correspondence from me! – I who am busied with the sacred Pen of Nature, in the mystic Volume of Creation, can I dishonor my hand with a dirty goose feather, on a parcel of mash'd old rags?

He wanted Hill to get some books for him – 'the cheapest way, the best; so you may have to hunt for them in the evening Auctions,' he wrote:

I want Smollet's works, for the sake of his incomparable humor. – I have already Roderick Random & Humphrey Clinker. – Peregrine Pickle, Lancelot Greaves & Ferdinand Count Fathom, I still want; but as I said, the veriest ordinary Copies will serve me. – I am nice only in the appearance of my Poets.[3]

He was not writing a great deal of poetry; when he sent Mrs Dunlop a copy of the 'Lines in Friars Carse Hermitage', he told her, 'They are almost the only favors the Muses have conferred on me in that Country.'[4] He did, however, find time to keep James Johnson supplied with offerings for the third volume of the *Museum*. 'I send you here yet another cargo of Songs. I long to know whether you are begun yet, & how you come on.' He reported that he was still working on a good number of Dr Blacklock's songs, but that they required 'sad hacking & hewing'. He was also at work on a collection of Highland airs that Johnson had given him in Edinburgh: 'I have had an able Fiddler two days

1. Letter dated 22nd July 1788, Burns and Dunlop, pp. 75-9. Lord Bankton was William McDouall, a Lord of Session, who wrote *Institute of the Law of Scotland*.
2. Letters, 260.
3. *Ibid.*, 255.
4. *Ibid.*, 260.

already on it, & I expect him every day for another review of it. – I have got one most beautiful air out of it that sings to the measure of Lochaber.'[1]

Two of the songs that date from this period were, as he put it, 'composed out of compliment to Mrs Burns.' The best-known of them is 'Of a' the airts', though some critics have admired it more than others – Christina Keith, for example, thought that for a honeymoon song it was 'remarkably cool'.[2] Burns set it to a lively tune called *Miss Admiral Gordon's Strathspey*, written by the Duke of Gordon's butler:

> Of a' the airts the wind can blaw,   directions
>   I dearly like the West;
> For there the bony Lassie lives,
>   The Lassie I lo'e best:
> There wild-woods grow, and rivers row,
>   And mony a hill between;
> But day and night my fancy's flight
>   Is ever wi' my Jean. –[3]

Although it is less celebrated, 'O, were I on Parnassus Hill' also has a number of fine lines, which some have seen as heralding the emotional directness of the Romantics:

> Tho' I were doomed to wander on,
> Beyond the sea, beyond the sun,
> Till my last, weary sand was run;
>   Till then – and then I love thee.[4]

Burns also tried his hand at a mildly satirical political ballad in the summer of 1788. He called it 'The Fête Champetre', and the occasion was the coming of age of a young man called William Cunninghame of Enterkine. Cunninghame was the owner of two mansion houses, but as they both happened to be under repair, he had some temporary structures put up on the banks of the Ayr, beautified them with trees and shrubs and invited all the best families in the county to a grand supper and ball. As the dissolution of Parliament was expected, Cunninghame was suspected – unjustly, as it turned out – of preparing the ground for his candidacy. James Boswell was also thought to be a possible runner, and Burns works into the first stanza a reference to his bear-leading Johnson round the Highlands fifteen years previously:

> O wha will to Saint Stephen's house,
>   To do our errands there, man;

1. *Ibid.*, 258.
2. Keith, *op. cit.*, p. 151.
3. Kinsley, 227.
4. *Ibid.*, 228.

> O wha will to Saint Stephen's house,
>   O' th' merry lads of Ayr, man?
> Or will we send a Man-o'-law,
>   Or will we send a Sodger?
> Or him wha led o'er Scotland a'
>   The meikle Ursa Major?[1]   great

'The Fête Champetre' was one of a number of pieces that Burns set to the tune Gilliecrankie, but although it goes with an agreeable swing, it altogether lacks the edge and attack of his great ecclesiastical satires.

In addition to the songs that he wrote or mended for Johnson's *Museum*, Burns was a keen collector of unprintable material, and was in the habit of circulating examples to his friends for their amusement. He enclosed a selection with a short note that he dashed off one evening during the summer to a new friend called William Stewart, who was the factor of the Closeburn estate: 'I go for Ayrshire tomorrow, so cannot have the pleasure of meeting you for some time; but anxious for your "Spiritual welfare & growth in grace," I inclose you the Plenipo.'[2]

This was a piece later included in *The Merry Muses of Caledonia* and is, in effect, an eighteenth-century forerunner of the 'The Ball of Kirriemuir'.[3] It was the work of a Captain Morris, an ornament, it seems, of the Carlton House set, and author of *Songs Drinking, Political and Facetious*. The Plenipotentiary in question had been despatched to the Court of St James by the Dey of Algiers, and this 'great-pintled Bashaw' from the Barbary shore was an immediate sensation:

> A Duchess whose Duke made her ready to puke,
> With fumbling and f— all night, sir,
> Being first for the prize, was so pleased with its size,
> That she begged for to stroke its big snout, sir.

1. *Ibid.*, 224. Burns was eager to meet Boswell, and later in the year he sent a copy of the ballad to an Ayrshire landowner called Bruce Campbell, hoping it would lead to an introduction: 'As I had the honor of drawing my first breath almost in the same parish with Mr Boswell, my Pride plumes itself on the connection,' he wrote, adding that to have been acquainted with such a man, 'I would hand down to my Posterity as one of the honors of their Ancestor.' Boswell does not appear to have responded. (Letters, 284.)

2. Letters, 253.

3. James Barke, co-editor with Sydney Goodsir Smith of the the edition of *The Merry Muses* published by W.H. Allen in 1965, says that *The Ball* had its origins in an orgiastic barn dance held in Perthshire in the 1880s. Embroidered by generations of farm-hands and by servicemen in two World Wars, the ballad now runs to hundreds of verses and innumerable variants. When the Highland Division paraded before Winston Churchill in Tripoli after their victories in the North African campaign, they broke into a spirited rendering of it as they marched past. The Prime Minister's initial puzzlement did not last long, and it was reported that the descendant of Marlborough soon broke into a broad grin. This historic event was broadcast, but the recording unfortunately does not survive.

My stars! cried her Grace, its head's like a mace,
'Tis as high as the Corsican Fairy;
I'll make up, please the pigs, for dry bobs and frigs,
With the great Plenipotentiary.

Although accredited to the Court, the Plenipo was no snob, and made his services freely available at all levels of society:

The next to be tried was an Alderman's Bride,
With a c– that would swallow a turtle,
She had horned the dull brows of her worshipful spouse,
Till they sprouted like Venus's myrtle.

Whores and housemaids, ladies of high breeding, boarding-school mistresses and school marms from France – it was all one to the great Turk. He also carried all before him in the theatre and the opera house, where, with a political correctness well in advance of his time, he exercised no discrimination between the sexes:

The nymphs of the stage did his ramrod engage,
Made him free of their gay seminary;
And Italian Signors opened all their back doors
To the great Plenipotentiary.[1]

With such *samizdat* material did Burns seek to divert his friends.

Towards the end of August Burns wrote to Ainslie about what he termed 'a vexatious business'. Mrs McLehose, it seems, had entertained a low opinion of his friend Nicol and had retailed some disobliging story or other about him. Burns, gossiping with his landlord Cruikshank, had passed it on, although without disclosing the source; he had also let slip his suspicion that the story originated with the Rector of the High School, Dr Adam, with whom Nicol was perpetually at daggers drawn. The story, unsurprisingly, had got back to Nicol (he and Cruikshank were both members of Adam's staff). Nicol and Adam were now involved in legal proceedings, and Nicol had been pressing Burns for the name of the lady in the case. 'I have refused this,' he told Ainslie, '& last post Mr N– acquaints me, but in very good natured terms, that if I persist in my refusal, I am to be served with a summonds to compear & declare the fact. –'

Burns, caught between the devil and the deep blue sea, appealed to Ainslie

1. For the complete text see *The Merry Muses of Caledonia*, ed. James Barke and Sydney Goodsir Smith, W.H. Allen, London, 1965, pp. 199–203.

to act as a go-between. He had written to Mrs McLehose to tell her this, and proposed to inform Nicol 'that I will not give up my female friend till farther consideration'. He begged Ainslie to call on the irascible schoolmaster – '& give up the name or not, as Your & M^{rs} M^c—se's prudence shall suggest'.[1] On that feeble note, the story come to a ragged end. The assumption must be that Ainslie hit upon an appropriately diplomatic form of words, because Burns's friendship with Nicol continued unimpaired.

September came, and Burns was busy with his first harvest – 'without good-weather when I may have Reapers,' he complained to Mrs Dunlop, 'and without Reapers when I may have good weather'.[2] He was still hard at it ten days later, and was grateful to Robert Riddell for sending a boy over to help: 'Dare I ask him for tomorrow? I dare not ask more: I would not ask even that one, did not staring Necessity compel me.'[3]

Later in the year, readers of the *Edinburgh Advertiser* were given a progress report on the fortunes of the man so recently lionised in their city. 'Burns, the Ayrshire Bard, is now enjoying the sweets of retirement at his farm,' they were told:

Burns, in thus retiring, has acted wisely. Stephen Duck, the *Poetical Thresher*, by his ill-advised patrons, was made a parson. The poor man, hurried out of his proper element, found himself quite unhappy; became insane; and with his own hands, it is said, ended his life. Burns, with propriety, has resumed the *flail* – but we hope he has not thrown away the *quill*.[4]

Journalists, then as now, could get it badly wrong. The vision of Horatian ease conjured up by the *Advertiser* was at almost total variance with the facts. The bad weather, slow progress on the house and the loneliness of Burns's life in Nithsdale combined to drag his spirits down: 'For all that most pleasurable part of life called, Social Communication, I am here at the very elbow of Existence' (this in a letter to the engraver John Beugo):

The only things that are to be found in this country, in any degree of perfection, are Stupidity and Canting. – Prose, they only know in Graces, Prayers, &c. and the value of these they estimate as they do their plaiding webs – by the Ell; as for the Muses, they have as much idea of a Rhinoceros as of a Poet.

1. *Ibid.*, 266.
2. *Ibid.*, 267.
3. *Ibid.*, 271.
4. *Edinburgh Advertiser*, 28th November 1788. Stephen Duck (1705-56) began life as a Wiltshire farm labourer. Lord Macclesfield brought his verse to the attention of Queen Caroline, and he was given a pension and made a Yeoman of the Guard. He took Holy Orders in his early forties, but ten years later, in a fit of despondency, drowned himself.

He also urged Beugo to marry, although he contrived to do so in terms that were profoundly insulting to his own wife:

> Depend upon it, if you do not make some damned foolish choice, it will be a very great improvement on the Dish of Life. – I can speak from experience; tho' God knows, my choice was as random as Blind-man's-buff. I like the idea of an honest country Rake of my acquaintance, who, like myself, married lately. – Speaking to me of his late Step, "L—d, man" says he, "a body's baith cheaper and better sair't!" –[1]

If he considered himself well-served by Jean, a letter he wrote in the middle of his harvest to Robert Graham showed that he was beginning to have second thoughts about his recent transaction with Patrick Miller:

> My farm, now that I have tried it a little, tho' I think it will in time be a saving bargain, yet does by no means promise to be such a Pennyworth as I was taught to expect. – It is in the last stage of worn-out poverty, and will take some time before it pay the rent. –

Burns explained that his small surplus had gone to the support of his family in Ayrshire, and that if that support were withdrawn, Gilbert would be ruined. He then put to Graham a scheme by which he might be extricated from this embarrassment:

> I live here, Sir, in the very centre of a country Excise-Division; the present Officer lately lived on a farm which he rented in my nearest neighbourhood; and as the gentleman, owing to some legacies, is quite opulent, a removal could do him no manner of injury . . .

If Burns could sometimes appear egotistical and unfeeling in his dealings with others, he was never thick-skinned, and on reading over his letter he realised that it was pretty cool to suggest that a serving officer should be shunted out to suit his convenience: 'I shudder at my own Hardiesse,' he added. 'Forgive me, Sir! I have told you my situation. – If asking anything less could possibly have done, I would not have asked so much.' He went on to tell Graham that he saw another advantage in what he proposed:

> If I were in the Service, it would likewise favor my Poetical schemes. – I am thinking of something, in the rural way, of the Drama-kind. – Originality of character is, I think, the most striking beauty in that Species of Composition,

1. Letters, 268.

and my wanderings in the way of business would be vastly favorable to my picking up the original traits of Human nature. –[1]

He had clearly been giving some thought to possible new literary directions; he touched on the subject again a few days later in the first letter he had written for several months to Margaret Chalmers:

> I very lately, to wit, since harvest began, wrote a poem, not in imitation, but in the manner of Pope's Moral Epistles. It is only a short esssay, just to try the strength of my Muse's pinion in that way ... I have like wise been laying the foundation of some pretty large Poetic works: how the superstructure will come on I leave to that great maker and marrer of projects – TIME.

The 'pretty large Poetic works' came to nothing. His experiment in the manner of Pope was an adulatory epistle, running to just under a hundred lines, which he had enclosed with his letter to Robert Graham:

> When Nature her great Masterpiece designed,
> And framed her last, best Work, The Human Mind,
> Her eye intent on all the mazy Plan,
> She forms of various stuff the various Man ...[2]

He sent several copies of it to friends for their opinion – to Margaret Chalmers, to William Dunbar and, of course to Mrs Dunlop. She thought well of it – 'there is great variety of finely fancied epithets' – and Burns was hugely gratified: 'Your Criticisms, my honored Benefactress, are truly the work of a FRIEND. – They are not the blasting depredations of a canker-toothed caterpillar-Critic.'[3] Later critics have been less admiring. Kinsley points out that Mrs Dunlop's response was the last thing he needed because it encouraged him, as some of the criticism he got in Edinburgh had done, in a misconceived attempt to write 'Augustan' poetry.[4]

The letter which he wrote to Miss Chalmers on this occasion contains a passage that has been much quoted but also much misconstrued:

> When I think of you – hearts the best, minds the noblest, of human kind – when I think I have met with you, and have lived more of real life with you in eight days, than I can do with almost any body I meet with in eight years – when I think on the improbability of meeting you in this world again – I could sit down and cry like a child![5]

1. *Ibid.*, 269.
2. Kinsley, 230.
3. Letters, 275.
4. Kinsley, vol. iii, p. 1280.
5. Letters, 272.

He is harking back to the days he spent at Hervieston the previous summer. It is an odd sentiment, perhaps, for a man so newly married, but it is certainly not, as has sometimes been made out, the anguished cry of a man who has suddenly realised he has chosen the wrong woman. 'Hearts the best, minds the noblest': Burns is here addressing not only Miss Chalmers but also her sister, Lady McKenzie – indeed he mentions them both by name in the preceding sentence. Snyder makes the point that for much of the time Burns, unconsciously and without hypocrisy, lived a sort of double life. Burns, the tenant farmer, he writes, intent upon making 'a happy fireside clime,' was one person. Burns the poet, eager to broaden his intellectual horizon to compensate for the cramped conditions of his physical existence – this Burns was someone entirely different: 'Before Burns married Jean, she was in no way connected with his inner life. After marriage he felt an affection for her, but an affection which was not in any sense strong enough to bind him firmly to her, and which never seems to have carried over into the realm of the spirit.'[1]

This is largely borne out by the manner in which Burns writes about 'my Jean' later in that same letter to Margaret Chalmers. He concedes that he may not have married her 'in consequence of the attachment of romance' but goes on to say that he has no cause to repent it. There is an echo of what he had previously told Mrs Dunlop:

> If I have not got polite tattle, modish manners, and fashionable dress, I am not sickened and disgusted with the multiform curse of boarding-school affectation; and I have got the handsomest figure, the sweetest temper, the soundest constitution, and the kindest heart in the country.

He also had an uncritical admirer:

> Mrs Burns believes, as firmly as her creed, that I am *le plus bel esprit, et le plus honnete homme* in the universe; although she scarcely ever in her life, except the Scriptures of the Old and New Testament, and the Psalms of David in metre, spent five minutes together on either prose or verse. – I must except also from this last, a certain late publication of Scots poems, which she has perused very devoutly; and all the ballads in the country, as she has (Oh the partial lover! you will cry) the finest 'wood note wild' I ever heard.[2]

To Burns's somewhat importunate letter about the excise, Graham of Fintry sent a prompt and encouraging reply. Burns was ill when it arrived ('I am scarce able to hold up my head with this fashionable Influenza'), but wrote an

---

1. Snyder, p. 307.
2. He is referring to Jean's voice. It is a phrase he often used. He had found it in Milton: 'Then to the well-trod stage anon,/If Jonson's learnèd sock be on,/Or sweetest Shakespeare's fancy child,/Warble his native wood-notes wild . . .' (*L'Allegro.*)

effusive letter of thanks. He repeated that he would like, if possible, to make a start in the excise at the beginning of the following summer and proposed a variation on his plan for creating a vacancy:

> I was thinking that as I am only a little more than five miles from Dumfries, I might perhaps officiate there, if any of these Officers could be removed with more propriety than Mr Smith; but besides the monstrous inconvenience of it to me, I could not bear to injure a poor fellow by outing him to make way for myself: to a wealthy Son of good-fortune like Smith, the injury is imaginary, where the propriety of your rules admit. –[1]

Burns had bound himself, under the terms of his lease, to complete the building of the farmhouse 'during the course of the ensuing summer,' but the work had fallen far behind. As autumn drew on, he made other arrangements. 'You must get ready for Nithsdale as fast as possible,' he wrote to Jean:

> I have an offer of a house in the very neibourhood with some furniture in it, all which I shall have the use of for nothing till my own house be got ready . . . I am extremely happy at the idea of your coming to Nithsdale, as it will save us from these cruel separations.[2]

We have only four short letters from Burns to Jean. His correspondence with Mrs Dunlop, on the other hand, fills a plump volume. He sometimes heard from her twice in a month. Her letters were not only extremely long, but also largely innocent of punctuation. Her spelling resembled Winnie-the-Pooh's a century and a half later – 'It's good spelling, but it Wobbles, and the letters get in the wrong place.' Clarinda's letters are shot through with hopeless passion; Mrs Dunlop's are permeated with an almost motherly anxiety. She is concerned for his well-being and for his reputation. The receipt of a letter from him was an event of major importance – she pored over what he had written and commented on it almost line by line. She bombarded him with news of her health ('I must tell you I have drunk two pounds of hemp seed boiled in small beer, and am greatly better'); she quizzed him about his use of the language ('Dear Burns, will you allow me to ask, is "Each pleasure riches give" a proper English expression?'); she occasionally performed the useful service of allowing him to see himself as others saw him ('If ever he was good for anything, he is the damnedest bundle of self-conceit and insolence I ever saw.')

He teased her with a confession that he was not the most systematic of correspondents: 'When I write to you, Madam, I do not sit down to answer every paragraph of yours, by echoing every sentiment – like, The faithful Commons of

1. *Letters*, 273.
2. *Ibid.*, 278.

Great Britain, in parliament assembled, answering a speech from the best of Kings."[1] But he also rewarded her with the first sight of some of the most beautiful things he ever wrote:

> I gaed a waefu' gate, yestreen,   went, sorrowful, way
>   A gate, I fear, I'll dearly rue;
> I gat my death frae twa sweet een,   eyes
>   Twa lovely e'en o' bonie blue! . . .[2]

Towards the end of 1788 he also wrote to her about an old song and tune 'which has often thrilled thro' my soul'. He sent the words of five verses and the chorus – Light be the turf on the breast of the heaven-Inspired Poet who composed this glorious fragment!' he wrote:

> Should auld acquaintance be forgot,
>   And never thought upon?
> Let's hae a waught o' Malaga,
>   For auld lang syne. –[3]

Burns later called it 'the old Song of the olden times' (although he thought the air 'mediocre.')[4] For two hundred years now the words have been sung, and not infrequently mangled, in most of the world's languages. When it eventually appeared in print in the *Scots Musical Museum* it was signed 'Z', denoting 'old verses, with corrections or additions'; Burns himself wrote that he 'took it down from an old man's singing' and there is no reason to doubt that. It remains a famous piece of tinkering.[5]

The onset of winter also gave him leisure to try his hand (much less success-fully) at what was for him a new literary genre – he wrote a letter to a newspaper. The occasion was the centenary of the landing of William of Orange at Torbay. The General Assembly of the Church of Scotland had appointed November 5th as 'a day of solemn thanksgiving for that most glorious event – the Revolution'. Ellisland was in the parish of Dunscore, and the local minister, the Reverend Joseph Kirkpatrick, preached a sermon whose Whiggish sentiments were not remotely to Burns's taste.

---

1. *Ibid.*, 254.
2. Kinsley, 232. Burns unfortunately set this lyric to a tune by his friend Captain Riddell, who was a keen but amateur musician. It is singable only by prodigies whose voice can encompass two octaves.
3. Letters, 290.
4. Letters, 586.
5. Burns sent in the same letter the words of two other pieces of inspired tinkering: 'Tam Glen' (Kinsley 236) and 'My bony Mary' (Kinsley, 242) – 'Go fetch to me a pint o' wine,/And fill it in a silver tassie . . .'

He addressed himself to the editor of the *Edinburgh Evening Courant*:

... I went last Wednesday to my parish church, most cordially to join in grateful acknowledgements to the Author of all Good, for the consequent blessings of the Glorious Revolution ... Bred and educated in revolution principles, the principles of reason and common sense, it could not be any silly political prejudice that made my heart revolt at the harsh abusive manner in which the Reverend Gentleman mentioned the House of Stuart ...

He prudently doffed his cap to the House of Hanover, 'the ruling features of whose administration have ever been, mildness to the subject, and tenderness of his rights,' but argued that allowance must be made for the manners of the times:

The Stuarts have been condemned and laughed at for the folly and impractibility of their attempts, in 1715 and 1745. That they failed, I bless my God most fervently; but cannot join in the ridicule against them ...

It was a long letter, the rhetorical style at the opposite pole from the racy immediacy and directness of his best private manner. As he approached his peroration, he glanced across the Atlantic at a more recent revolution:

... I dare say, the American Congress, in 1776, will be allowed to have been as able and as enlightened, and, a whole empire will say, as honest, as the English Convention in 1688; and that the fourth of July will be as sacred to their posterity as the fifth of November is to us ...[1]

Burns did not put his name to the letter, signing himself only 'A BRITON.' He returned to the theme the following week in a letter to Mrs Dunlop, and there he expressed himself a good deal less circumspectly:

Is it not remarkable, odiously remarkable, that tho' manners are more civilized, & the rights of mankind better understood, by an Augustan Century's improvement, yet in this very reign of heavenly Hanoverianism, & almost in this very year, an empire beyond the Atlantic has had its REVOLUTION too, & for the very same maladministration & legislative misdemeanours in the illustrious & sapientipotent Family of H— as was complained of in the 'tyrannical & bloody house of STUART.'—[2]

Mrs Dunlop was eager for another visit from him, but was full of scruples about taking him away from his 'now complicated cares,' as she called them:

1. Letters, 283. His letter appeared in the paper on November 22nd.
2. *Ibid.*, 285.

> If I may judge by what I have seen of late, a farmer has no time almost at liberty; at least I have never in seven months seen my son able to afford one day's absence, seldom two hours, without finding something neglected and wrong at his return.[1]

Burns took a much more grasshopperish view of things than that and cheerfully disabused her:

> You miscalculate matters widely, when you forbid my waiting on you lest it should hurt my wordly [sic] concerns. – My small scale of farming is exceedingly more simple & easy than what you have lately seen at Moreham mains. – But be that as it may, the heart of Man, and the fancy of the Poet are the two grand considerations for which I live: if miry ridges & dirty dunghills are to engross the best part of the functions of my soul immortal, I had better been a rook or a magpie all at once . . .

He gave fuller answers to some of her questions than to others. When she announced, in her direct and uninhibited way, that she would like to know who the song 'Clarinda, mistress of my soul' was addressed to, he fobbed her off with an airy reply that would have created outrage in Potterow – 'It was un petit egaremen du coeur during my last stay in Edin^r.'[2]

There had, as it happened, been another small *égarement* during his last stay in Edinburgh. To describe it as an affair of the heart would be to resort to the most extreme poetic licence, but its consequences now began to claim Burns's attention, and early in the New Year he began to plan a visit to the capital. His friend Robert Ainslie, although still only twenty-two, had just become a Writer to the Signet, and Burns wrote to congratulate him. Seventeen months previously, when he heard that Ainslie had fathered an illegitimate child, he had sent him a verse from an indecent old song – 'Robin, silly body/ He gat me wi' bairn.' Now, by way of sly compliment, he enclosed a 'brushed up' version of it 'with a view to your worship'. Then, at the end of the letter he became serious:

> I shall be in town in about four or five weeks, & I must again trouble you to find & secure for me a direction where to find Jenny Clow, for a main part of my busin[ess] in Edin^r is to settle that matter with her, & free her hand of the process. –[3]

It is the first time the name is mentioned in any of Burns's letters that are extant. Another piece of the jigsaw slots into place – this was the vexing affair on which Burns had not initially dared to enlarge to Ainslie during the summer.

---

1. Letter franked 3rd December 1788, Burns and Dunlop, pp. 119-21.
2. Letters, 290.
3. *Ibid.*, 295. The manuscript is torn at the word 'business'.

Jenny Clow was a servant girl. She came from Newburgh in Fife, she was twenty years old and in the course of the previous winter she had proved an easier conquest than Clarinda. She had given birth to a son in November – the assumption must be that Burns had news of this from Ainslie. And she had now, like Meg Cameron before her, issued a writ. It is not the most elaborate of sub-plots, and of how it developed during Burns's brief visit to Edinburgh we have no knowledge. The curtain will rise briefly on it one last time.

Burns's arrangements were always liable to a generous degree of slippage. Although it was in the middle of October that he had urged Jean to make ready to move as soon as possible, she was not in the event installed at Ellisland until early December. His aim of being in Edinburgh in early February went similarly adrift, but he was there by the twentieth and reached home again on the last day of the month. Of how he spent his time in the capital next to nothing is known. He had written to a number of friends – they included Henry Erskine, Dr John Geddes and Willie Dunbar[1] – to announce his arrival and he was eager to have Robert Cleghorn's advice about his schemes for enclosure.[2] He later told Mrs Dunlop that he had gone in hopes of securing an excise division for himself, but that certain regulations of the Board had prevented it, Graham of Fintry's 'warmest exertions' notwithstanding.[3] He undoubtedly gave some attention to the affairs of the *Museum*. He had kept up a steady flow of songs to Johnson, telling him, in the middle of November, that he was preparing 'a flaming Preface' for the third volume.[4] In a later letter he expressed the hope that when they met they might 'overhaul the whole Collection and report progress.'[5]

He certainly saw Creech. 'I have settled matters greatly to my satisfaction,' he wrote to Jean. 'He is certainly not what he should be, nor has he given me what I should have, but I am better than I expected.'[6] To Mrs Dunlop he wrote at greater length. 'I love the social pleasures in moderation,' he told her, 'but here I am impressed into the service of Bacchus.' He also gave her a piece of family news:

> I hope to be a father again in about two or three months, and I had resolved and indeed had told Mrs Burns, that the said child should be christened by the name of FRANCES-DUNLOP, if a girl, or FRANCIS &c. if a boy . . .

1. *Ibid.*, 299, 308 and 309.
2. *Ibid.*, 302.
3. *Ibid.*, 324.
4. *Ibid.*, 288. He enclosed with this letter 'Whistle o'er the lave o't' and 'Tam Glen' (Kinsley, 235 and 236).
5. *Ibid.*, 303. With this he enclosed the song 'There was on a time, but old Time was then young' (Kinsley, 253).
6. *Ibid.*, 315. A month later he gave Mrs Dunlop a rather different account. Creech, he wrote, 'has at last settled amicably & fully as fairly as could have been expected with me, I clear about 440 or 450£.' (Letters, 324.)

It occurred to him that if it did turn out to be a boy, she might wish to wait 'for one of your own Sex'. She should be reassured: 'I have not the smallest doubt of being very soon able to accommodate you in that way too.'[1]

The delay in setting out for Edinburgh had been due in part to family reasons. In one of his infrequent letters to his cousin James in Montrose ('For goodness sake don't take example by me, but write me soon') Burns wrote that an old uncle had died, and that he had taken in his daughter and one of his sons.[2] He was also increasingly exasperated by the slow progress in building operations at the farm. 'I see at last, dear Sir, some signs of your executing my house within the current year,' he wrote sarcastically to the architect, Thomas Boyd:

> I am distressed with the want of my house in a most provoking manner. It loses me two hours work of my servants every day, besides other inconveniences. For G—d's sake let me but within the shell of it![3]

He had to chivvy Boyd again on his return from Edinburgh: 'I was a good deal surprised at finding my house still lying like Babylon in the prophecies of Isiah. – I beg, dear Sir, for humanity's sake, that you will send me out your hands tomorrow.'[4]

All in all, however, domestic concerns did not weigh unduly heavily on him. 'In the first great concern of life, the means of supporting that life, I think myself tolerably secure,' he wrote in a letter to Glencairn's sister, Lady Elizabeth Cunningham. He told her about his excise commission:

> This last is comparitively a poor resource, but it is a luxury to any thing the first five & twenty years of my life taught me to expect; and I would despise myself if I thought I were not capable of sacrificing any one little liquorish gratification on the altar of Independance. –

It is plain from what he told her about his writing that his mind was by no means exclusively taken up with his commitment to the *Museum*:

> I muse & rhyme, morning noon & night; & have a hundred different Poetic plans, pastorals, georgic, dramatic, &c. floating in the region of fancy, somewhere between Purpose and resolve.—[5]

He reminds Lady Elizabeth of his devotion to her brother. He had two silhouettes of him, both by Miers, the larger hanging over the chimney-piece in his parlour, the smaller set in a gold breast-pin with the words 'Mon Dieu et

---

1. *Ibid.*, 316.
2. *Ibid.*, 314.
3. *Ibid.*, 313.
4. *Ibid.*, 317. 'It shall never be inhabited, neither shall it be dwelt in from generation to generation.' Isaiah, Chapter xiii, verse 20.
5. *Ibid.*, 298.

toi' engraved on the shell. When, in conclusion he comes to pay his compliments to their mother, we get a poignant glimpse of the gulf Burns saw set between himself and those in the great world with whom his fame had brought him briefly in contact:

> I have often, during this hard winter, wished myself a Great-man, that I might, with propriety in the etiquette of the world, have enquired after Lady Glencairn's health. – One of the sons of little men as I am, I can only wish fervently for her welfare ...

Riding up to Ayrshire on a wild January night that winter Burns was subjected to one of the humiliations which sometimes come the way of the sons of little men. He described the occasion both to Dr Moore and to Mrs Dunlop:

> As I came to Sanquhar on Saturday evening – the landlord & landlady are my particular acquaintances – I had just dispatched my dinner, and was sitting in a family way over a friendly bowl, glad that my weary body & soul had found out so comfortable a place of rest – when lo, the quondam Mrs Oswald wheeled into the courtyard with an immense retinue, and the poor Bard is obliged amid the shades of night, bitter frost howling hills & icy cataracts to goad his jaded steed twelve miles farther on to another stage. – O for a muse, not of heroic fire but satiric aquafortis, to gnaw the iron pride of unfeeling greatness![1]

The good lady whose funeral cortège deprived Burns of his night's lodging was the widow of one Richard Oswald, a London merchant who had made his pile during the Seven Years' War and bought the Ayrshire estate of Auchencruive from Lord Cathcart in 1764. Burns, who knew her by reputation, told Moore that Mrs Oswald had been cordially detested by her servants and tenants. He rode on over the moors, nursing his indignation: 'When a good fire at New Cumnock had so far recovered my frozen sinews, I sat down and wrote the enclosed Ode.'[2]

> ... Keeper of Mammon's iron chest,
> Lo, there she goes, unpitied and unblest,
> She goes, but not to realms of everlasting rest! ...[3]

It is a savage piece of work, another of Burns's unsuccessful attempts at the Pindaric form. No doubt he felt better once he had got it down on paper. He sent it off at the next post-office to the *Edinburgh Courant*. The editor refused

1. *Ibid.*, 305.
2. *Ibid.*, 322.
3. Kinsley, 243.

it, which was Burns's good luck. Unfortunately he later sent it to the *London Star* with two covering letters, one of which disclosed his identity; the editor obligingly printed the lot.[1]

Burns had by now acquired a taste for writing to the papers and on February 9th the *Edinburgh Courant* published an open letter from him addressed to William Pitt. The king's insanity and controversy over the question of regency were widely believed to threaten the Prime Minister's position. Sheltering behind the signature 'John Barleycorn,' Burns judged it a good moment to have a go at what he saw as the government's recent unfair treatment of the Scottish distillers; appointing himself their spokesman, he offered Pitt 'fraternal condolence' on his impending political eclipse:

> If fame say true, and omens be not very much mistaken, you are about to make your exit from that world where the sun of gladness guilds the paths of prosperous men: permit us, great Sir, with the sympathy of fellow-feeling, to hail your passage to the realms of ruin ...[2]

It was not a very good letter. It was also, particularly for a man with an excise commission burning a hole in his pocket, exceedingly rash, and he knew it: 'I inclose you a piece of my prose,' he wrote to Mrs Dunlop, 'which, for obvious reasons I send you for your sole amusement: it is dangerous ground to tread on.' He enclosed in the same letter the words of 'Afton Water', one of the most beautiful lyrics he ever wrote, and one of the best-loved:

> Flow gently, sweet Afton, among thy green braes,
> Flow gently, I'll sing thee a song in thy praise;
> My Mary's asleep by thy murmuring stream,
> Flow gently, sweet Afton, disturb not her dream.[3]

Burns also had to find an answer to a charge of indecency which Mrs Dunlop, with characteristic directness, had levelled at him: 'I heard a man say lately he had seen a poem of yours so grossly indelicate he was ashamed to read it alone on a brae side.' She hoped that this was 'one of the follies long cast to air and polished off by mine, if not by better company'.[4]

The defendant pleaded misattribution, but felt that he had better also offer an alternative defence, embroider it with one or two extenuating circumstances and confuse the issue with a short burst of moral righteousness:

1. He got low marks for it from Mrs Dunlop. 'You should, instead of a holly garland, get a birch rod as a reward for your Ode,' she wrote, 'since it was torturing the living to be avenged of the senseless dead.' (Letter conjecturally dated 22nd January 1789, Burns and Dunlop, pp. 136-9.)
2. Letters, 311.
3. Kinsley, 257.
4. Letter conjecturally dated 22nd January 1789. Burns and Dunlop, pp. 136-9.

I am very sorry that you should be informed of my supposed guilt in composing, in some midnight frolic, a stanza or two perhaps not quite proper for a clergyman's reading to a company of ladies. – That I am the author of the verses alluded to in your letter, is what I much doubt. – You may guess that the convivial hours of *men* have their mysteries of wit and mirth; and I hold it a piece of contemptible baseness, to detail the sallies of thoughtless merriment or the orgies of accidental intoxication, to the ear of cool Sobriety or female Delicacy. –[1]

Burns had his young brother William on his hands for several months during his first winter in Dumfriesshire. The boy had been apprenticed as a saddler, but it had not proved easy to find an opening for him. Burns had exerted himself in Edinburgh on his return from his Highland tour two years previously; more recently he had responded gratefully to an offer of help from Ainslie: 'If I get him into a first rate shop, I will bind him a year or two, I almost do not care on what terms.'[2] Early in 1789 the boy found work near Carlisle. He wrote asking for some of his things to be sent on, and he was plainly somewhat in awe of his famous and worldly-wise brother:

As I am now in a manner only entering the world, I begin this our correspondence with a view of being a gainer by your advice ... I know not how it happened, but you were more shy of your counsel than I could have wished, the time I stayed with you: whether it was because you thought it would disgust me to have my faults freely told while I was dependent on you, or whether it was because you saw that, by my indolent disposition, your instructions would have no effect, I cannot determine ...

'My small knowledge & experience of the world is heartily at your service,' Burns assured him in reply. He *did* have advice to offer; he prefaced its bluntness with a brotherly pat on the back:

I am indebted to you for one of the best letters that has been written by any Mechanic-lad in Nithsdale or Annandale or any Dale on either side of the Border this twelvemonth ...

I intended to have given you a sheetful of counsels, but some business has prevented me. – In a word, Learn Taciturnity: let that be your motto. – Though you had the wisdom of Newton, or the wit of Swift, garrulousness would lower you in the eyes of your fellow-creatures.—[3]

Burns reinforced his theme in a further letter to William the following week:

1. Letters, 310.
2. *Ibid.*, 266.
3. *Ibid.*, 318.

'What mischiefs daily arise from silly garrulity or foolish confidence! There is
an excellent Scots Saying, that "A man's mind is his kingdom." – It is certainly
so; but how few can govern that kingdom with propriety. – '[1]

He had recently been reminded that his own performance in that area was
not outstanding. For the first time in nine months he had heard from Mrs
McLehose. After Burns's death she persuaded his trustees to return her letters,
and this one no longer exists. We do not know whether she had yet found out
about Jenny Clow; she certainly called him a villain and accused him of treach-
ery – that much is clear from Burns's reply. The manuscript, (now in the
Collection of the Rosenbach Museum & Library in Philadelphia) also shows
that Sylvander addressed his 'dear Clarinda' as 'Madam' and left the letter
unsigned:

> ... As I am convinced of my own innocence, and though conscious of high
> imprudence & egregious folly, can lay my hand on my breast and attest the
> rectitude of my heart; you will pardon me, Madam, if I do not carry my
> complaisance so far, as humbly to acquiesce in the name of, Villain, merely
> out of compliment even to YOUR opinion; much as I esteem your judgement,
> and warmly as I regard your worth. –

Warming to his theme, he invited her to recall the scenes that had passed
between them and to consider how manfully he had struggled against temptation:

> – Situations that I will dare to say, not a single individual of all his kind,
> even with half his sensibility and passion, could have encountered without
> ruin; and I leave you to guess, Madam, how such a man is likely to digest
> an accusation of perfidious treachery!
> Was I to blame, Madam, in being the distracted victim of Charms which,
> I affirm it, no man ever approached with impunity? – Had I seen the least
> glimmering of hope that these Charms could ever have been mine – or even
> had not iron Necessity – but these are unavailing words. –

Ainslie, it seems, had kept her fully posted about his comings and goings:

> I would have called on you when I was in town, indeed I could not have
> resisted it, but that M^r A— told me that you were determined to avoid your
> windows while I was in town, lest even a glance of me should occur in the
> Street. –
> When I have regained your good opinion, perhaps I may venture to solicit

1. *Ibid.*, 321.

your friendship: but be that as it may, the first of her Sex I ever knew, shall always be the object of my warmest good wishes.[1]

If he could not count on Mrs McLehose's friendship, he continued to have proof of Mrs Dunlop's pretty well every other week. In the middle of March she announced her intention of presuming on her acquaintance with Graham of Fintry to lobby him on Burns's behalf:

> It is a cruel tax malevolence lays on talents to depreciate the moral character of those who incontestably possess them, and force one's friends, in resentment of underhand massacres, to repeat truths that speak plain enough themselves to all who are unprejudiced by malicious whisperers. Should such earwigs have crawled towards Fintry, I would like to brush them off.[2]

She obligingly enclosed a draft of what she proposed to say to Graham (she thought her plea would carry greater weight if it were buttressed by some verses, so she enclosed these too.) Burns was entirely happy that she should deal with the 'earwigs,' but was alive to the possibility that she might say too much: 'As for your writing Mr Graham, it is what pleases me above all things; but no plans in it if you please,' he wrote. 'When I tell you the narrative of my situation, plans in life, &c. you will see the propriety of altering the scope of your epistle.'

It is plain that although he was less than a year into his lease, he was already beginning to regard his situation at Ellisland as untenable; but the account he gave to Mrs Dunlop of how he came to be in that situation was distinctly revisionist:

> You remember, Madam, I had two plans of life before me; the Excise and farming. – I thought, by the glimmering of my own prudence, the Excise was my most eligible scheme; but all my Great friends, and particularly You, were decidedly & therefore decided me, for farming. – My master, Mr Miller, out of real tho' mistaken benevolence, sought me industriously out, to set me this farm, as he said to give me a lease that would make me comfortable & easy. – I was a stranger to country, the farm and the soil, and so ventured on a bargain, that instead of being comfortable, is & will be a very, very hard bargain, if at all practicable. – I am sorry to tell you this Madam, but it is a damning truth; though I beg, as the world think that I have got a pennyworth of a farm, you will not undeceive them. –

This was rough on Miller. Burns had, after all, had the benefit of John Tennant's advice about the farm's potential. The lease had acknowledged the need

1. *Ibid.*, 320.
2. Letter conjecturally dated 18th March 1789, Burns and Dunlop, pp. 152-5.

for improvements and made provision for them. And if Miller himself was at that stage a well-meaning improver without much practical experience, the same cannot be said for Burns's new friend and neighbour Robert Riddell, who had been farming next door for six years and was later to have his achievements recognised by the award of a silver medal from the Dumfriesshire Agricultural Society.[1]

Burns disclosed more of his plans to Mrs Dunlop than he wanted the rest of the world to know:

> My brother's lease is near expiring, he may be able to live by my lease as he can with propriety do things that I *now* can not do; I will plant him in this farm & throw myself on the Excise at large, where I am sure of immediate & constant bread. –
> Let these matters lie between you & I only. –[2]

What these things were that only Gilbert could do with propriety is not clear. If Burns had looked over his lease more carefully he would in any case have seen that the idea was a non-starter; sub-tenancies were excluded, and although he was allowed the power of assignation, it was specified that this might take effect only after his death. Miller had not intended his benevolence to be open-ended. The plain fact seems to be that for all his professed attachment to his 'rustic shades' Burns was unable to muster the single-minded resolve that would have made Ellisland something more than a marginal enterprise. His literary fame, such as it was, had both made him and undone him; the divisions which had opened within him would remain for the rest of his life.

His grip on the flail might be slackening, but his quill was as busy as ever. With a pen in his hand and a mental line open to a trusted friend, he was at his happiest and best. At the beginning of April he wrote a long, free-wheeling letter to Peter Hill, the bookseller, but before stating his business, he treated him, for no particular reason, to a sparkling, inventive parenthesis about the capital's City Fathers:

> (. . . How they hunt down a [Shop (*deleted*)] housebreaker with the sanguinary perseverance of a bloodhound – how they outdo a terrier in a badger-hole, in unearthing a Resettor of stolen goods – how they steal on a thoughtless troop of Night-nymphs as a spaniel winds the unsuspecting Covey – or how they riot o'er a ravaged B—dy-house as a cat does o'er a plundered Mouse-nest – how they new-vamp old Churches, aiming at

---

1. Riddell also wrote the introduction to the *Agricultural Account of Dumfriesshire* which appeared in 1812, and in which he stressed the benefits of liming.
2. Letters, 324.

appearances of Piety – plan Squares and Colledges, to pass for men of taste and learning &c. &c. &c.

Change the accent, and it is like hearing the rich voice of Dylan Thomas a century and a half before his time. Burns wanted books. He always wanted books: 'I want a Shakespear – let me know what plays your used Copy of Bell's Shakespear wants: I want likewise an English dictionary, Johnson's I suppose is best. – These and all my *Prose* commissions, the cheapest is always the best for me. –' He also told Hill about a scheme he and Riddell had for a library:

Captn R— gave his infant society a great many of his old books, else I had written you on that subject; but one of these days I shall trouble you with a Commission for "the Monkland friendly Society." – A copy of the Spectator, Mirror & Lounger, Man of feeling, Man of the world, Guthrie's Geographical grammar, with some religious pieces, will likely be our first order. –[1]

Although Riddell gave the Society his patronage and acted as its President, it was Burns who did the donkey-work. The membership was made up of tenants of Riddell's and other farming neighbours. There was an entry fee of 5s, and members paid a further 6d each time they met, which was every fourth Saturday. They eventually assembled a library of about 150 volumes. First choice went by rotation, and a system of fines operated if books were not returned. The account of the Monklands Library which appeared in Sinclair's *Statistical Account* was contributed by Burns himself: 'A peasant who can read and enjoy such books,' he wrote, '"is certainly a much superior being to his neighbour, who, perhaps, stalks beside his team, very little removed, except in shape, from the brutes he drives."[2]

He was still drawn, moth-like, to the flame of politics. 'I have this moment finished the following political Squib,' he wrote to Mrs Dunlop, 'and I cannot resist the temptation of sending you a copy of it.' This was his 'Ode to the departed Regency-bill – 1789'.[3] George III, having gone mad in November, had regained his sanity three months later and resumed his powers, putting paid to Fox's hopes of coasting to power on the coat-tails of the Prince of Wales. 'Politics is dangerous ground for me to tread on,' Burns wrote, 'and yet I cannot for the soul of me resist an impulse of any thing like Wit.'

Wit is the last thing that can be claimed for the piece, which is turgid to a degree ('Daughter of Chaos' doting years,/Nurse of ten thousand hopes and fears . . .'); Burns was completely out of his depth. He sent it, for all that, to

1. *Ibid.*, 325.
2. Sir John Sinclair, *op. cit.*, vol. 3, p. 599.
3. Kinsley, 258.

a London newspaper, the *Star*, and it appeared there on April 17th, though in a mangled form.

His touch was much more assured with a second poem which he sent to the *Star* on April 25th.

> O, sing a new Song to the L—!
>   Make, all and every one,
> A joyful noise, ev'n for the king
>   His Restoration. —[1]

This was 'A new Psalm for the Chapel of Kilmarnock, on the thanksgiving-day for his Majesty's recovery,' and here he brought considerable wit to bear in a clever parody of a Presbyterian metrical psalm.

Burns was soon to discover that journalism was a murky trade. Unknown to him his name had already appeared in the columns of the *Star* several weeks previously in an item about the Duchess of Gordon. He was described as 'Mr Burns, the ploughing poet'; the writer of this anonymous communication asserted that he owed much of his good fortune to her Grace's 'critical discernment and generous patronage' and reproduced an 'elegant stanza' about the Duchess which he attributed to Burns:

> She was the mucklest of them aw;   greatest
>   Like SAUL she stood the Tribes aboon;   above
> Her gown was whiter than the snaw,
>   Her face was redder than the moon.

Four days later, a second correspondent gravely disputed the authenticity of this verse and submitted three others as a 'specimen of Mr Burns's performance'. The *Star* then entered the lists editorially by disclosing that the initiator of the correspondence had called at their office to supply evidence in support of his claim. He had even volunteered his name, and given them freedom to publish it – 'he styles himself Dr Theodore Theobald Theophilus Tripe'.

Dr Tripe declined to leave the full text of his 'Burns' poem with the newspaper, but allowed them a further tantalising glimpse – he had, he assured them, had it from the author's own hand in Mauchline the previous summer:

> But frae thy mow, O Gordon fair!   mouth
>   Could I but get as kiss sae frisky,
> For a' the sharney queans in Ayr   dung-smeared wenches
>   I wadna gi' a glass of whisky.

1. 'A new Psalm for the Chapel of Kilmarnock, on the thanksgiving-day for his Majesty's recovery –' Kinsley, 260.

The *Star* confessed itself perplexed by these problems of exegesis, and could see only one solution – it appealed to Burns himself to write to them and 'remove the anxiety of the Public'. Poor Burns, however, was oblivious of all this tomfoolery and remained so until the story was picked up by another newspaper, the *Gazetteer*; there it was spotted by a friend and drawn to his attention.

He wrote to both papers to expostulate: 'Had you only forged dullness on me, I should not have thought it worth while to reply: but to add ingratitude too, is what I cannot in silence bear.'[1] The *Gazetteer* printed this a week later, but in an accompanying note the editor gave the story a new and somewhat startling twist. Burns could be assured, he wrote smoothly, that the Duchess of Gordon acquitted him 'both of the ingratitude and the dullness':

> She has, with much difficulty, discovered that the *Jeu d'Esprit* was written by the Right honourable the Treasurer of the Navy, on her Grace's dancing at a ball given by the Earl of Findlater; this has been found out by the industry and penetration of Lord Fife. The lines are certainly not so dull as Mr Burns insinuates, and we fear he is jealous of the poetical talents of his rival, Mr Dundas.[2]

A senior member of Pitt's administration moonlighting as a Grub Street hack? Politics was quite as rough a trade in the eighteenth century as it is today. Members of the Lords and Commons snigger over *Private Eye* in the late twentieth century, after all; it cannot be excluded that their more robust predecessors occasionally contributed snippets to its eighteenth-century equivalents. There is no record of any disclaimer by Dundas – but then politicians had thicker hides in those days. Whether the lines were his or not, the suggestion alone was an unsettling one for Burns. Dundas had no direct influence in excise matters at the level at which he hoped to enter the service, but hostility in high places was something one could do without. And the Treasurer of the Navy was still 'the Pharos of Scotland' (the phrase is Lord Cockburn's): 'Who steered upon him was safe; who disregarded his light was wrecked. It was to his nod that every man owed what he got, and looked for what he wished.'[3]

With the *Star – Stuart's Star, and Evening Advertiser*, as it was properly called at that time – Burns fared better. It was run by Peter Stuart, who was about the same age as Burns and was the second of three brothers who had left Edinburgh in the 1770s to try their luck in London, initially as printers[4]. Stuart had been one of a group who had founded the paper the previous spring, and it had become the first London evening paper to appear regularly. Early in

1. *Letters*, 327.
2. *The Gazetteer and New Daily Advertiser*, London, 17th April 1789.
3. Cockburn, Henry, *Life of Francis Jeffrey*, 2 vols., Adam and Charles Black, Edinburgh, 1852, vol. i, p. 77.
4. Charles, the eldest, had been a school-fellow of Robert Fergusson's.

1789, however, he had quarrelled with his fellow-proprietors over their pro-Pitt policy; he set up in opposition (in editorial support, that is to say, of the Prince of Wales) and brought out a paper which was not only identical in appearance to the *Star* but even initially appropriated its name.

When Burns wrote to set the record straight, Stuart felt he was onto a good thing. 'The Printer feels himself exceedingly proud of the receipt of the following Letter,' he wrote, describing Burns as 'a very ingenious Poet, whose productions are now the delight and admiration of every Reader of Taste'. In a further note at the end of the letter he added that he had 'the happiness of flattering himself with an assurance of the future correspondence of Mr Burns'.[1]

Stuart then proposed that he should pay Burns a salary in return for regular contributions, but Burns preferred to keep their arrangement on an occasional basis, accepting the offer of a free subscription to the paper in lieu of payment. 'Any alterations you think necessary in my trifles, make them and welcome,' he told Stuart, and he gave an assurance of his conformity to the paper's line: 'In political principles, I promise you I shall be seldom out of the way; as I could lay down my life for that amiable, gallant, generous fellow, our heir apparent.'

He was anxious to preserve his anonymity:

I must beg of you never to put my name to any thing I send, except where I myself set it down at the head or foot of the piece. I am charmed with your paper. I wish it was more in my power to contribute to it; but over and above a comfortable stock of laziness, of which, or rather *by* which I am possessed, the regions of my fancy are dreadfully subject to baleful eastwinds, which, at times, for months together, wither every bud and blossom, and turn the whole into an avid [*sic*] waste . . .[2]

Burns turned down a quite different suggestion for employment in that spring of 1789. Mrs Dunlop, always eager to blunt his interest in the excise, drew his attention to a forthcoming vacancy in Edinburgh:

. . . I forgot that I meant to bid you read your friend Creech's advertisement in the Edr. Courant for proposals about a professor of Agriculture. I would have you give this a little serious attention, since I do not believe there is a man in the kingdom who might so properly blend the theoretical and practical knowledge that plan would seem to require . . . Edina would not be so irksome when one was not from home there, nor would a grave member of the College be so oft the prey of jolly Bacchus as an exciseman, at least against his will . . .

1. *Stuart's Star, and Evening Advertiser*, 16th April 1789.
2. Letters, 339.

Creech was involved through his membership of the town council, which had received a gift of £1,250 to endow the chair. The benefactor's name was William Pulteney, and he intended to retain the first presentation in his own hands. The terms of appointment required the professor to deliver a set of lectures 'respecting the nature of soils and manures; the modes of cultivation; the succession of crops; the construction of the implements of husbandry; the best and most successful known practices; the manner of instituting experiments to ascertain the effect of any proposed practice in any soil or climate; and the best manner of introducing or training skilful labourers and country artificers, where these may be wanting.'

Blissfully unaware of just how eccentric a suggestion it was and unconscious of any irony in what she was saying, Mrs Dunlop rattled on in the same letter about a recent encounter with Gilbert's landlord, Claud Alexander of Ballochmyle:

> I said I wondered he had quit you for a tenant. He said he had kept a much better man for his purpose; your brother was a much better farmer, one he would be really sorry to lose, and who had ten times the sense of you . . .[1]

Burns made no comment on this unflattering testimonial, but he knew himself well enough not to waste any time on Mrs Dunlop's hare-brained idea. 'I believe the Professorship you mention will be an idle project,' he told her; 'but whatever it may be, I, or such as I, am quite out of the question.'[2]

His brother William had now moved on to Newcastle-on-Tyne. He had found work, but he was once again in need of advice, this time in an area where Burns could pronounce *ex cathedra*:

> Your falling in love is indeed a phenomenon. To a fellow of your turn it cannot be hurtful. I am, you know, a veteran in these campaigns, so let me advise you always to pay your particular assiduities and try for intimacy as soon as you feel the first symptoms of the passion: this is not only best, as making the most of the little entertainment which the sportabilities of distant addresses always gives, but is the best preservative for one's peace. I need not caution you against guilty amours – they are bad and ruinous everywhere, but in England they are the very devil.[3]

It had been an occasional habit of Burns to put together manuscript collections of what he judged to be his best pieces and present them to friends or patrons.

1. Letter dated 1st April 1789, Burns and Dunlop, pp. 158-61.
2. Letters, 330. In spite of his lack of enthusiasm, both Mrs Dunlop and Dr Moore took it upon themselves to mention Burns's name to Pulteney as a possible candidate. This emerges from a later letter to Mrs Dunlop (Letters, 351).
3. *Ibid.*, 337.

Sometime in the spring of 1789, he made a start on such a collection for Robert Riddell: 'I wish from my inmost soul it were in my power to give you a more substantial gratification & return for all your goodness to the Poet, than transcribing a few of his idle rhymes.'[1] This, however, was to be a more ambitious enterprise than any previously undertaken, and was to be much more handsomely presented.

Burns was equipped with two quarto volumes bound in calf – the assumption is that they were provided by Riddell. Each had an impression of the Beugo engraving pasted on the frontispiece, and the Glenriddell arms were stamped on the boards. One volume was to be for poetry, the other for prose. The first poem to be entered was 'The Belles of Mauchline'. Under the last line – 'But Armour's the jewel for me o' them a'' Burns added, 'Note. Miss Armour is now known by the designation of Mrs Burns.' A further note, in what looks like another hand, reads 'who has the finest foot & leg. & *had* the finest waist.'

Burns also had the idea of presenting a small book of unpublished manuscript poems to the wife of Graham of Fintry. He wrote to tell him so in the middle of May:

> That is *one* reason of my troubling you with this – another motive I have is a hackneyed subject in my letters to you. – God help a poor devil, who carries about with him a load of gratitude, of which he can never hope to ease his shoulders but at the expence of his heart! –

Graham, when he had previously told Burns that even Commissioners could not bend the rules, had undertaken to write a letter of introduction to the collector in Dumfries, and Burns had now met him. His name was John Mitchell, and Burns told Graham that although it had been Collection day, Mitchell had received him 'with the utmost politeness' and suggested he should call again soon. 'As I don't wish to degrade myself to a hungry rook gaping for a morsel,' Burns wrote, 'I shall just give him a hint of my wishes.'[2]

Burns's moods appear to have been more than usually volatile during the late spring and early summer. At one moment, dashing off a letter to his friend Richard Brown, whose ship was at Port Glasgow, he was in high spirits:

> . . . Wishing Mrs Brown and your little ones as few of the evils of this world as is consistent with humanity – wishing you & she were to make two at the ensuing lying-in with which Mrs Burns threatens very soon to favor me – wishing that I had longer time to write you at present . . .[3]

1. *Ibid.*, 340.
2. *Ibid.*, 341.
3. *Ibid.*, 344.

That was written towards the end of May. A month later, it is plain from a long letter to Mrs Dunlop (it was the first for two months) that he was once again wrestling with an old enemy. 'Will you take the effusions, the miserable effusions, of low spirits, just as they flow from their bitter spring?' he asked:

> I know not of any particular cause for this worst of all my foes besetting me; but for some time my soul has been beclouded with a thickening atmosphere of evil imaginations and gloomy presages.

He went on to tell her that her 'little *dear* namesake' had not yet made his appearance, but it is unlikely that his worries included Jean's forthcoming confinement – Burns's attitude to such matters tended to the agricultural. Whatever the causes of his dejection, the effect of letter-writing was therapeutic, and he assured Mrs Dunlop in a concluding flourish that his spirits were a good deal the lighter.[1]

In spite of Burns's wish not to appear as 'a hungry rook gaping for a morsel,' the 'hint of his wishes' which he had given to John Mitchell, the Dumfries Collector, must have been a broad one. At the end of July he was able to describe to Graham the measure of that official's amenability. 'The language of Gratitude,' he began, 'has been so prostituted by servile adulation and designing flattery, that I know not how to express myself,' but he managed well enough. What it boiled down to was that he and Mitchell had now discussed the removal of the incumbent, and in the Collector's view it would be 'productive of at least no disadvantage to the Revenue, and may likewise be done without any detriment to him'. Having succeeded in engineering a vacancy, Burns coolly proposed himself to fill it:

> Should the Honorable Board think so, and should they deem it eligible to appoint me to officiate in his present place, I am then at the top of my wishes. – The emoluments of my Office will enable me to carry on and enjoy those improvements in my farm, which, but for this additional assistance, I must in a year or two have abandonded [*sic*].

The letter is a painful mixture of the frank and the servile. Burns told Graham that if the Board judged it improper to accommodate him in that division, he would consider giving up farming altogether and taking a place in the excise wherever one could be found:

> The worst of it is, I know that there are some respectable Characters who do me the honor to interest themselves in my welfare & behaviour, and as leaving the farm so soon may have an unsteady, giddy-headed appearance, I had perhaps better lose a little money than hazard such people's esteem. –

1. *Ibid.*, 350.

You see, Sir, with what freedom I lay before you all my little matters – little indeed to the World, but of the most important magnitude to me. – You are so good, that I trust I am not troublesome. –[1]

Although farming matters and his hopes for the excise preoccupied him greatly, he always found time for poetry and song. 'What are you doing,' he wrote to James Johnson in the middle of June, 'and what is the reason that you have sent me no proof sheets to correct? Though I have been rather remiss in writing you, as I have been hurried, puzzled, plagued & confounded with some disagreable matters, yet believe me, it is not owing to the smallest neglect or forget of you, my good Sir, or your patriotic work.'[2] A couple of days later he sent Patrick Miller a copy of the poem inspired by the sight of a wounded hare ('Inhuman man! curse on thy barb'rous art,/And blasted be thy murder-aiming eye . . .')[3] In July of 1789 he sounded a note which had not been heard from him for some time:

> Orthodox, Orthodox, who believe in John Knox,
>   Let me sound an alarm to your conscience;
> A heretic blast has been blawn i' the West –
>   That what is not Sense must be Nonsense, Orthodox,
>   That what is not Sense must be Nonsense. –[4]

'The Kirk's Alarm' (it is sometimes known as 'The Kirk of Scotland's Garland') satirises a theological storm that had arisen in Ayr. The 'heretic blast' had been blown by Dr William McGill, who was one of the ministers there and had been a friend of Burns's father. Three years previously he had published *A Practical Essay on the Death of Jesus Christ*, and some of his arguments had been branded as Arian or Socinian: 'Upon the whole,' he had written, 'to suffer many indignities in the world, and to die on the cross, were not the chief and ultimate ends of our saviour's mission.' The controversy had rumbled on ever since, and formal charges of heresy had eventually been laid in the synod of Glasgow and Ayr.

When Burns had fingered the idea of entering the lists on McGill's behalf two years previously he had been dissuaded by Mrs Dunlop, but now he was determined to let fly: 'Several of these reverend lads, his opponents, have come thro' my hands before; but I have some thoughts of serving them up again in a different dish.'[5] Mrs Dunlop once again argued strongly against the idea:

. . . My dr. Burns, I am now in the last evenings of my life; the bright torch of your genius is perhaps the last I shall ever see lighted, and I grudge

1. *Ibid.*, 353.
2. *Ibid.*, 348.
3. Kinsley, 259.
4. *Ibid.*, 264.
5. Letters, 352.

extremely to see it wasted singeing muketoes [mosquitos] in a corner, instead of being set on a hill where it cannot be hid, and giving light to the world ... Yet should your ballad lead the puppies full cry a heretic-hunting, you'll wish you had bit your tongue rather than given the view-hollo, and cast off a whole pack of blood-hounds against a poor little white rabbit.[1]

Mrs Dunlop seems at least to have persuaded him that it would be foolish to print 'The Garland'; when he sent a manuscript copy of it to John Logan, a friend of Gavin Hamilton's and a subscriber to the Kilmarnock edition, he requested him to read it only to 'a few of us,' and enjoined him not to let any copies be made:

If I could be of any service to D^r M^{c}gill, I would do it though it should be at a much greater expence than irritating a few bigotted Priests; but as I am afraid, serving him in his present embarras is a task too hard for me, I have enemies enow, God knows, tho' I do not wantonly add to the number.[2]

The poem lacks the subtlety of the powerful ecclesiastical satires of earlier years, and is so local in its references that it can only be made comprehensible today by detailed annotation.

While Burns was working himself into a lather over these parochial concerns, the wider world was becoming uneasily aware of a much louder 'heretic blast'. Between May and August 1789 the French people turned the rejection of their national past into a revolutionary principle. The month in which Burns composed 'The Kirk's Alarm' was the month in which Louis XVI dismissed his liberal ministers. In Paris, on July 12th, soldiers of the Garde Française joined the rioting citizenry. The following day, a human wave smashed the hated tolls and there was looting of gunsmiths' shops. At dawn on July 14th the mob invaded the Hôtel des Invalides, seized 32,000 muskets and marched on the Bastille. The governor of the legendary prison surrendered in mid-afternoon; his head was struck off and paraded on a pike to the Palais Royal.

There would come a time when these stirring events would intrude uncomfortably into Burns's own life, but in those summer months of 1789 he had to content himself with lesser excitements. 'About two hours ago I welcomed home your little Godson,' he wrote to Mrs Dunlop in the middle of August. 'He is a fine squalling fellow with a pipe that makes the room ring.' Jean's safe delivery he recorded more matter-of-factly – 'His Mother as usual.' There was a second important event to announce:

1. Letter dated 1st August 1789, Burns and Dunlop, pp. 193-7.
2. Letters, 356.

I mentioned to you my Excise hopes and views. – I have been once more a lucky fellow in that quarter. – The Excisemen's Salaries are now £50 per Ann. and I believe the Board have been so oblidging as fix me in the Division in which I live; and I suppose I shall begin doing duty at the commencement of next month. – I shall have a large portion of country, but, what to me and my studies is no trifling matter, it is a fine, romantic Country.–[1]

1. *Ibid.*, 359.

Eleven

DIRTY PONDS AND
YEASTY BARRELS

THERE WERE ONE OR TWO formalities. Burns had to obtain a certificate, signed by a Minister and witnesses, that he had received the sacrament 'according to the usage of the Church of Scotland'. There were also various oaths to be sworn, and he appeared for this purpose before the Dumfries Quarter Sessions at the end of October. (The taker of the minutes nodded; he recorded that Burns had taken the oath of allegiance 'to His Majesty King George the Second', although that monarch had been in his grave for the best part of thirty years.) Burns further swore to defend the sovereign against 'all traitorous Conspiracies and attempts, which shall be made against his person'. Officers were obliged to keep this certificate about their person, and might be required to produce it by a superior.

The Dumfries district was divided into twelve 'stations', and Burns was assigned to the largest of them. Known as the Dumfries First Itinerary, it covered ten parishes and consisted of five separate 'rides'. He was supposed to survey one full ride each day, but was enjoined to retain an element of surprise by avoiding set patterns and varying his starting point.

Spirits, beer and malt accounted for more than half the amount collected by the excise in late-eighteenth century Scotland, but the text of Burns's Commission spelt out for him the whole bewildering range of goods and commodities and processes on which duty must be levied:

> . . . upon making of Soap, Paper, Pasteboard, Millboard, and Scaleboard, respectively; and upon printing, painting, or staining of Paper; and upon printing, painting, staining, or dying of Silks, Callicoes, Linens, and Stuffs respectively; and upon the making of Starch, and of Gilt and Silver Wire respectively; and upon tanning, tawing, or dressing of Hides and Skins, and pieces of Hides and Skins; and upon the making of Vellum and Parchment respectively; and upon Silver-plate and Manufactures of Silver respectively; and of the Inland Duties upon Coffee, Tea, and Chocolate respectively; and upon making Malt, and making and importing Mum, Cyder, and Perry,

respectively; and of the Duties upon Glass . . . and upon every Coach, Berlin, Landau, Chariot, Calash, Chaise-marine, Chaise, Chair, and Caravan, or by what Name soever such Wheel Carriages now are or hereafter may be called or known . . .[1]

Because duty was mostly charged during manufacture, surveillance was a time-consuming business, involving visits at all hours of the day and night – candle-makers, for instance, had to be inspected every six hours, soap-boilers every four. Many articles attracted several different rates of duty – tanners had to reckon with fourteen different rates, depending on the size and weight of skins and on whether they had been dressed in oil or soaked in alum and salt; paper-makers had to contend with no fewer than seventy-eight rates of duty. No officer would be likely to encounter the full range of dutiable manufactures, but in his first station Burns found himself himself dealing with a catholic sample – he had twenty-one spirit-dealers, twenty-seven tobacconists, two tanners, fifteen tea-dealers and eleven maltsters. These last took up a disproportionate amount of time. The malting process – the drying out of barley that has been allowed to germinate in water – consisted of four stages and could last for up to two weeks; during that time an officer would be expected to make at least five visits.

The work extended his vocabulary. His instructions included a glossary of trade terms – to keep his end up at his two tanneries he would need to know the meaning of words like 'pates', 'randings' and 'wooze'. Each skin and hide had to be weighed and marked with an excise seal – on each flank for horse skins, but for dog skins just above the tail. Some of the processes with which he had to be familiar were more agreeable than others: clout-leather, for instance, which was used for mending shoes, was first tanned and then placed in a hole and covered with horse dung – this apparently hardened it and improved the colour.[2]

There was an enormous amount of paper-work. Burns had to write up a daily journal, with details of visits made, work done and distances travelled, and this had to be available for regular inspection. There were calculations to be made of the quantities of beer or malt produced and duty vouchers to be made out for each trader. There was also a 'specimen book', kept on the trader's premises, and in this he had to enter details of the gauges and dips; these would be regularly inspected by the supervisor.

It was unusual for officers to be appointed, as Burns had been, to the district in which he lived – anything conducive to over-cosy relations between poacher and gamekeeper was deemed undesirable. (This was also why officers

1. The full text of the Commission (it occupied one printed sheet measuring 16 inches by 13) is reproduced as an appendix in Snyder, pp. 507-10. Mum was a strong beer, originally brewed in Brunswick and largely imported in the seventeenth and eighteenth centuries.
2. Graham Smith, *Robert Burns the Exciseman*, Alloway Publishing, Ayr, 1989, p. 55. Further information about Burns's excise duties are to be found in 'Burns's Excise Duties and Emoluments', by R.W. MacFadzean, in the *Burns Chronicle* for 1893.

4. A page from Burns's excise book.

were generally moved on after three years or so.) One dodge which supervisors had to be on the look-out for was what was known as 'stamping' a survey. It was easy enough for an experienced officer to make an educated guess about what the state of a brewing process would be some days thence and make a bogus entry in the specimen book – thus saving himself a journey, and possibly earning himself a bottle or two. A quarter of a century earlier a careless young English exciseman called Tom Paine had been discharged from the service for 'stamping' not just one survey but a whole ride.

Burns had to be in the saddle four and sometimes five days a week, and by the time he got back to Ellisland he had frequently ridden thirty or forty miles. It was a routine that did not leave much time for the farm, but it allowed him to keep a sensitive finger on the pulse of local politics. In September 1789 a contest got under way for parliamentary representation of the Dumfries-shire burghs; 'In this country we are just now Election-mad,' he told Mrs Dunlop:

Sir Ja[s] Johnston, the present Member for the Boroughs, has now opposite interests to the Great Man of this place, Queensberry. – His Grace is keenly attached to the Buff and blue Party: renegadoes and Apostates are, you know, always keen. – My Landlord's Son, a young Officer of twenty, is his Grace's creature, and is supported by the Foxites; Sir James, on the other hand, is backed by Ministerial influence. The Boroughs are much divided, and veer about with much uncertainty ...[1]

1. Letters, 363.

The constituency was made up of the five Dumfriesshire burghs – Dumfries, Lochmaben, Annan, Kirkcudbright and Sanquhar, and Burns set the scene for the contest in 'The Five Carlins', a political ballad in which the burghs are portrayed as five old beldams squabbling over the merits of the two candidates:

> Now wham to chuse, and wham refuse,   whom
>   At strife thir Carlins fell;   these
> For some had Gentle Folk to please,
>   And some wad please themsel. –[1]

There is little indication in this first salvo of Burns's own leanings, but as the campaign gathered leisurely momentum (it went on for several months) we see a weakening of his normally Whiggish preferences and a shift to the Tory side. This was partly because he was unimpressed by young Miller, his landlord's son ('entre *nous*, a youth by no means above mediocrity in his abilities,' he wrote to Graham of Fintry, 'and is said to have a huckster-lust for shillings, pence & farthings.'[2]) The main reason, however, was that he detested the Earl of Queensberry. In an intemperate passage in a letter to Dr Moore, he compared him unfavourably to Judas Iscariot: 'His Grace is a man of thirty thousand a year, & come to that imbecille period of life when no temptation but Avarice can be supposed to affect him. – '[3] Burns also attacked Queensberry (though privately) in verse, savaging him for his failure to support George III during the crisis over the Regency Bill:

> The turn-coat Duke his King forsook,
>   When his back was at the wa', man: wall
> The rattan ran wi' a' his clan   rat
>   For fear the house should fa', man.[4]   fall

Although Burns told Graham of Fintry that he regarded himself as 'too little a man to have any political attachments' his correspondence is full of references to the Dumfriesshire contest, and a vivid and entertaining picture emerges of how elections were conducted. Politicians like Fox might inveigh against it – 'so monstrous and absurd, so ridiculous and so revolting' – but there was nothing out of the ordinary about aristocratic control of parliamentary representation. 'Dumfries & Sanquhar are decidedly the Duke's, "to let or sell",' Burns wrote:

> So Lochmaben, a city containing upwards of fourscore living souls that cannot discern between their right hand and their left – for drunkenness,

1. Kinsley, 269.
2. Letters, 373.
3. *Ibid.*, 437
4. The verse occurs in an early version of 'The Laddies by the Banks o' Nith' (Kinsley, 270). Neither version was published in Burns's lifetime.

has at present the balance of power in her hands. – The Hon[ble] Council of that ancient borough are fifteen in number; but alas! their fifteen names indorsing a bill of fifteen pounds, would not discount the said bill in any banking-house.[1]

As the campaign drew to a close, he described to Mrs Dunlop how he had been required by his landlord to turn out on polling day and do his bit in the Whig interest:

> I have just got a summons to attend with my men-servants armed as well as we can, on Monday at one o'clock in the *morning* to escort Capt[n] Miller from Dalswinton in to Dumfries . . . On Thurday last, at chusing the Delegate for the boro' of Lochmaben, the Duke and Capt[n] Miller's friends led a strong party, among others, upwards of two hundred Colliers from Sanquhar Coalworks & Miners from Wanlock-head; but when they appeared over a hill-top within half a mile of Lochmaben, they found such a superiour host of Annandale warriors drawn out to dispute the Day, that without striking a stroke, they turned their backs & fled with all the precipitation the horrors of blood & murther could inspire. – What will be the event, I know not. – I shall go to please my Landlord, & to see the Combustion; but instead of trusting to the strength of Man, I shall trust to the heels of my horse, which are among the best in Nithsdale. –[2]

In the late autumn of 1789 Burns was witness to a contest of a more convivial nature:

> I sing of a Whistle, a Whistle of worth,
> I sing of a Whistle, the pride of the North,
> Was brought to the court of our good Scottish king,
> And long with this Whistle all Scotland shall ring.[3]

The whistle was currently the property of his neighbour Robert Riddell, and Burns prefaced his ballad with a prose note of its history:

> In the train of Anne of Denmark, when she came to Scotland with our James the Sixth, there came over also a Danish gentleman of gigantic stature and great prowess, and a matchless champion of Bacchus. He had a little ebony Whistle, which, at the commencement of the orgies, he laid on the table; and whoever was last able to blow it, every body else being disabled by the

1. Letters, 373.
2. *Ibid.*, 403.
3. Kinsley, 272.

potency of the bottle, was to carry off the Whistle as a trophy of victory. – The Dane produced credentials of his victories, without a single defeat, at the courts of Copenhagen, Stockholm, Moscow, Warsaw, and several of the petty courts in Germany; and challenged the Scots Bacchanalians to the alternative of trying his prowess, or else of acknowledging their inferiority.

Riddell decided to brighten an October evening by inviting two neighbouring landowners to contend with him for this curious trophy. One of them, Sir Robert Lowrie of Maxwelton, was a direct descendant of the man who after three hard days and nights had won an early gold medal for Scotland by drinking the Great Dane under the table. Riddell also decided that the events of the evening must be recorded:

> A bard was selected to witness the fray,
> And tell future ages the feats of the day;
> A bard who detested all sadness and spleen,
> And wished that Parnassus a vineyard had been . . .

More than half a century later, Chambers prodded the memory of an old man called William Hunter who had been a servant at Friars' Carse at the time. His recollection was that when dinner was over, Burns was installed at a side table to see fair play. He took no part in the claret drinking, but had placed before him a bottle of rum and another of brandy:

> Six bottles a-piece had well wore out the night,
> When gallant Sir Robert, to finish the fight,
> Turned o'er in one bumper a bottle of red,
> And swore 'twas the way that their ancestor did . . .

The contestants were put to bed, and Burns 'walked home without any assistance, not being the worse of drink'.[1]

He quickly got the measure of his excise work and did it well; a letter in which he thanks his Dumfries Supervisor for a favourable report sent to the office in Edinburgh is dated less than two months after he had started his rides. There were, for all that, traces of lingering sensitivity about his new employment. 'I know how the word, Exciseman, or still more opprobrious, Gauger, will sound in your ears,' he wrote to Ainslie:

I too have seen the day when my auditory nerves would have felt very delicately on this subject, but a wife & children are things which have a wonderful power in blunting these kind of sensations . . . For the ignominy

1. Chambers-Wallace, vol. iii, p. 108, n.

of the Profession, I have the encouragement which I once heard a recruiting Sergeant give to a numerous if not a respectable audience in the Streets of Kilmarnock – "Gentlemen, for your farther & better encouragement, I can assure you that our regiment is the most blackguard corps under the crown, and consequently with us an honest fellow has the surest chance for 'preferment'." –[1]

His health was not of the best that winter. Early in November he had a heavy cold; he was, he wrote to Mrs Dunlop, 'in the stupid, disagreeable predicament of a stuffed, aching head and an unsound, sickly crasis'.[2] He went on to ask her opinion of the song which begins 'Thou lingering star with lesser ray',[3] telling her that he was 'too much interested in the subject of it, to be a Critic in the composition'. The subject was, of course, 'Highland Mary' and the song appears to have been written close to the third anniversary of the day Burns received the news of her death. Jean Burns later recalled that as evening came on he had seemed 'very sad about something'; she had found him stretched out on straw in the barn-yard, gazing at the stars, and it had been difficult to persuade him to come into the house. He seems to have been composing in his head. When he did finally go indoors he called for his desk and committed the song to paper 'with all the ease of one copying from memory'.[4]

Mrs Dunlop professed herself 'charmed' by it: 'But oh! my good friend,' she added, 'I hope it is only a fancy piece for your sake'. Burns's reply made plain that it was no such thing. 'I am groaning under the miseries of a diseased nervous System,' he wrote:

> For now near three weeks I have been so ill with a nervous head-ach, that I have been obliged to give up for a time my Excise-books, being scarce able to lift my head, much less to ride once a week over ten muir Parishes.[5]

The letter is a rambling, stilted affair in which he maunders on in rather grisly fashion about the existence of an after-life ('when the cold, stiffened, unconscious ghastly corse is resigned into the earth, to be the prey of unsightly reptiles . . .'). 'What a flattering idea, then, is a World to come!' he continues: 'There should I, with speechless agony of rapture, again recognise my lost, my ever dear MARY, whose bosom was fraught with Truth, Honor, Constancy & Love –'

1. Letters, 367.
2. *Ibid.*, 371.
3. Kinsley, 274.
4. Chambers-Wallace, vol. iii, p. 110. Some biographers have been sceptical about this episode. Snyder is especially severe: 'If Burns wrote a poem to the morning star ("that lovest to greet the rising morn") while lying on a mass of straw in his barnyard during the early evening, he was making himself unnecessarily and inappropriately ridiculous.' (Snyder, pp. 309-10.)
5. Letters, 374.

> My Mary! dear, departed Shade!
>   Where is thy place of heavenly rest?
> Seest thou thy Lover lowly laid?
>   Hear'st thou the groans that rend his breast![1]

Then, an extraordinary invocation:

> Jesus Christ, thou amiablest of characters, I trust thou art no Impostor, &
> that thy revelation of blissful scenes of existence beyond death and the grave,
> is not one of the many impositions which time after time have been palmed
> on credulous mankind ...

He is in a bad way, and he knows it:

> I am a good deal inclined to think with those who maintain that what are
> called nervous affections are in fact diseases of the mind. – I cannot reason,
> I cannot think; & but to You, I would not venture to write any thing above
> an order to a Cobler. – You have felt too much of the ills of life not to
> sympathise with a diseased wretch who is impaired more than half of any
> faculties he possessed. – Your goodness will excuse this distracted scrawl
> which the Writer dare scarcely read, and which he would throw into the fire,
> were he able to write any thing better, or indeed any thing at all.

He signed himself 'le pauvre Miserable', but by the time another week had
gone by the black mood had lifted, and we find him writing to Robert Maxwell,
the Provost of Lochmaben, in very different vein. He had described Maxwell to
Graham of Fintry as 'one of the soundest headed, best hearted, whisky-drinking
fellows in the south of Scotland,' and he addresses him as he would one of his
Crochallan familiars in Edinburgh:

> ... To make the matter short, I shall betake myself to a subject ever fertile
> of themes, a Subject, the turtle-feast of the Sons of Satan, and the delicious,
> secret Sugar-plumb of the Babes of Grace; a Subject, sparkling with all the
> jewels that Wit can find in the mines of Genius, and pregnant with all the
> stores of Learning, from Moses & Confucius to Franklin & Priestly – in
> short, may it please Your Lordship, I intend to write BAUDY!

> I'll tell you a tale of a Wife,
>   And she was a Whig and a Saunt;   saint
> She liv'd a most sanctify'd life,
>   But whyles she was fash'd wi' her — —   troubled with

---

1. The poem, Kinsley 274, begins with the line 'Thou lingering Star with lessening ray' and
has become known as 'To Mary in Heaven'.

The 'wife' takes her problem to the priest, who reassures her: it is well-known that Beelzebub attacks the pure in heart by aiming his darts at a lower part of their anatomy – she, as one of the elect, has nothing to fear:

> And now with a sanctify'd kiss
> Let's kneel and renew covenant:
> It's this – and it's this – and it's this –
> That settles the pride o' your —.–[1]

The tradition of satire on puritan hypocrisy is a very old one and the theme of lecherous priests improving on the purely verbal pronouncement of absolution was common long before the Reformation. All bawdy is crude; 'I'll tell you a tale of a Wife' is savage as well. Catherine Carswell, who characterised the song as 'infamous and ludicrous' thought that Burns may have been venting the rage he felt at his failure to possess Clarinda. There have been wilder speculations.

Burns had not abandoned the idea of breaking fresh ground in his writing. Just before Christmas, 1789, he wrote a long letter to Glencairn's sister, Lady Elizabeth Cunningham:

> I am aware that though I were to give the world Performances superiour to my former works, if they were productions of the same kind, the comparative reception they would meet with would mortify me. – For this reason I wish still to secure my old friend, Novelty, on my side, by the *kind* of my perform- ances: I have some thoughts of the Drama . . . I have got Shakespeare, and begun with him; and I shall stretch a point & make myself master of all the Dramatic Authors of any repute, in both English and French, the only langauages which I know. –[2]

His interest in drama had been stimulated by the presence in Dumfries of a theatre company. Jogging home to Ellisland on the next to last night of the year, he passed the time by cobbling together in his head a rhyming prologue, and he sent it the next day to George Sutherland, the company's manager – 'the first crude suggestions of my Muse, by way of bearing me company in my darkling journey,' he wrote[3]:

> No song nor dance I bring from yon great city,
> That queens it o'er our taste – the more's the pity:
> Tho' by the bye, abroad why will you roam?
> Good sense and taste are natives here at home;

1. Letters, 378. The poem is Kinsley, 277.
2. Letters, 379.
3. *Ibid.*, 380.

But not for panegyric I appear,
I come to wish you all a good new year![1]

Burns told Gilbert that Sutherland had 'spouted [it] to his Audience with great applause' and the two men struck up a friendship. The rest of the letter to his brother makes less cheerful reading:

My nerves are in a damnable State.—I feel that horrid hypochondria pervading every atom of both body & Soul. – This Farm has undone my enjoyment of myself. – It is a ruinous affair on all hands. – But let it go to hell! I'll fight it out and be off with it. –[2]

By the end of the month his spirits had lifted once again: 'My health is greatly better, and I now begin once more to share in satisfaction and enjoyment with the rest of my fellow-creatures'. (This to Mrs Dunlop. He was writing on his thirty-first birthday.) He told her that he was arranging to have her 'little Godson' inoculated – there was a lot of smallpox about. 'By the way, I cannot help congratulating you on his looks & spirit,' he added:

Every Person who sees him acknowledges him to be the finest, handsomest child they have ever seen. – I am myself delighted with the manly swell of his little chest, and a certain miniature dignity in the carriage of his head & the glance of his fine black eye, which promises the undaunted gallantry of an Independant Mind. –[3]

He had still not brought all his friends up to date about his changed circumstances. When he wrote to the bookseller Peter Hill in early February he was still a shade defensive about the excise, but he had recaptured all his old jauntiness:

No! I will not say one word about apologies or excuses for not writing you. – I am a poor, damn'd rascally Gager, condemned to gallop at least 200 miles every week to inspect dirty Ponds and yeasty barrels, and where can I find time to write to, or importance to interest, any body?

He was eager for news of the town: 'What is become of the Borough Reform, or how is the fate of my poor Namesake, Madamoisselle Burns, decided?' His enquiry related to a young woman called Mathews, a native of Durham. She had come to Edinburgh the previous year and adopted the name Burns for professional reasons, the profession in question being the oldest. She and

1. Kinsley, 278.
2. Letters, 381.
3. *Ibid.*, 385.

another young whore called Sally Sanderson kept a disorderly house in Rose Street; the neighbours objected, and had succeeded in having them 'banished forth of the city and liberties for ever'.

The case had occasioned much interest and some hilarity; malicious tongues put it about that some of those on the bench and on the city council who were now proceeding with such severity against Burns's 'poor Namesake' (they included Bailie Creech and Mrs McLehose's relative Lord Dreghorn) had been visitors to her place of business. Burns the gauger was no more inclined than Rab the Rhymer to give authority the benefit of the doubt: 'Which of their grave Lordships can lay his hand on his heart and say that he has not taken the advantage of such frailty?' he enquired rhetorically of Hill:

As for those flinty-bosomed, puritannic Prosecutors of Female Frailty & Persecutors of Female Charms – I am quite sober – I am dispassionate . . . May Woman curse them! May Woman blast them! May Woman damn them! May her lovely hand inexorably shut the Portal of Rapture to their most earnest Prayers & fondest essays for entrance! And when many years, and much port and great business have delivered them over to Vulture Gouts and Aspen Palsies, *then* may the dear, bewitching Charmer in derision throw open the blissful Gate to tantalize their impotent desires which like ghosts haunt their bosoms when all their powers to give or receive enjoyment, are for ever asleep in the sepulchre of their fathers!!!
Now for business. – Our book Society owe you still £1–4– . . .[1]

His correspondence with Mrs McLehose flickered briefly into life again early in 1790. The exchange appears to have been initiated by her, but we no longer know for what reason – she appears to have heard that he had been ill. Burns confirmed to her that incessant headaches and depression of spirits had made dreadful havoc of his 'health and peace' during the winter, but the one letter and fragment of another which survive are mainly taken up with defending himself against whatever it was she had reproached him with:

I cannot, will not, enter into extenuatory circumstances; else I could show you how my precipitate, headlong, unthinking conduct leagued, with a conjuncture of unlucky events, to thrust me out of a possibility of keeping the path of rectitude; to curse me, by an irreconcileable war between my duty and my nearest wishes, and to damn me with a choice only of different species of error and misconduct.

1. *Ibid.*, 387. Creech found himself in a no-win situation over the Mademoiselle Burns affair. A London paper reported that he was 'about to lead the beautiful and accomplished Miss Burns to the hymeneal altar'. Creech threatened to sue and got a retraction, but of the sort which made matters much worse: 'We now have the authority of the gentleman to say that the proposed marriage is not to take place, matters having been otherwise arranged to the mutual satisfaction of both parties and their respective friends.' (Chambers-Wallace, vol. iii, p. 164, n.)

'I dare not trust myself further with this subject,' he wrote, but, ever eager for an audience, he did trust himself to send her one of his latest productions:

> Thine am I, my faithful fair,
>   Thine, my lovely Nancy;
> Ev'ry pulse along my veins,
>   Ev'ry roving fancy.[1]

During that same month of February Burns had the satisfaction of knowing that a great many more of his 'productions' were now before a larger public. It was a largely private satisfaction, because contributions to the *Scots Musical Museum* continued in the main to be identified by the same cryptic system of initials as before. Burns had been particularly prolific in the period since his move to Ellisland, and the third volume is full of good things. He once again contributed a preface, and once again he did not go out of his way to ingratiate himself with his readership:

> ... As this is not one of those many Publications which are hourly ushered into the world merely to catch the eye of Fashion in her Frenzy of a day, the Editor has little hope or fear from the herd of readers ...

He had, as before, tinkered to powerful and magical effect with many old songs:

> O, cam ye here the fight to shun,
>   Or herd the sheep wi' me, man,
> Or were ye at the Sherra-moor,
>   Or did the battle see, man.[2]

The battle of Sheriffmuir, which effectively ended the first Jacobite uprising, had been fought in November 1715 between Government forces led by the Duke of Argyll and the rebels under the Earl of Mar. Neither side won, and yet both claimed victory, a circumstance which over the years had invited much satiric comment. Burns skilfully tightened up an earlier and much slacker song on the same theme; for his sardonic narrator, the only certain thing was that once upon a time there had been a battle—and that both sides had run away:

> Now wad ye sing this double flight,
> Some fell for wrang and some for right,
> And mony bade the warld gudenight;
> Say pell and mell, wi' muskets knell

---

1. *Letters*, 388. The song was never published in this form. Burns, however, was not one to discard serviceable material, and some years later, when his interest was fixed on a young woman called Jean Lorimer, he revised the words and changed 'Nancy' to 'Chloris'. (Kinsley, 434.)
2. Kinsley, 308.

How Tories fell, and Whigs to h-ll
Flew off in frighted bands, man.

Burns also dusted down an old Jacobite ballad about the defeat of the Hanover-
ian general Sir John Cope at Prestonpans in 1745. Some of the rhyming is
rather slipshod, and Burns himself did not much like the air to which it was
set, but it is a catchy tune, and his contemptuous portrayal of the hapless Cope
and the song's mocking refrain have guaranteed its popularity down the years:

> But when he saw the Highland lads
> Wi' tartan trews and white cockauds, cockades
> Wi' swords and guns and rungs and gauds, cudgels
> O Johnie he took wing in the morning.
>   Hey Johnie Cope are ye wauking yet, awake
>   Or are ye sleeping I would wit;
>   O haste ye get up for the drums do beat,
>   O fye Cope rise in the morning.[1]

Another skilful piece of mending was 'My heart's in the Highlands', which
Burns set to a fine old Gaelic tune called *Failte na miosg – The Musket Salute*.
What he did here was to gut a none-too-distinguished old stall song called
'The strong walls of Derry', adding two stanzas of his own and retaining only
one from the original:

> My heart's in the Highlands, my heart is not here;
> My heart's in the Highlands a chasing the deer;
> Chasing the wild deer, and following the roe;
> My heart's in the Highlands, wherever I go.—[2]

There were numbers of love songs, some of them of an exquisite simplicity:

> Lang hae we parted been,
>   Lassie my dearie;
> Now we are met again,
>   Lassie lie near me.
>
> A' that I hae endur'd,
>   Lassie my dearie,
> Here in thy arms is cur'd,
>   Lassie lie near me.[3]

1. Kinsley, 297.
2. *Ibid.*, 301.
3. *Ibid.*, 290.

'My love she's but a lassie yet' appeared for the first time in Volume III, as
did 'Tibbie Dunbar', 'Jamie come try me' and 'I love my Love in secret'.[1] The
volume was also distinguished by a supreme example of Burns's poetic virtu-
osity. He took by the scruff of the neck a traditional bawdy monologue in
which a wife grumbles about her husband's declining sexual powers and boldly
transformed it into a tender love-song for old age in which passion has given
way to gentle reflection on companionship and fidelity:

John Anderson my jo, John,	sweetheart
When we were first acquent;	
Your locks were like the raven,	
Your bony brow was brent;	unwrinkled
But now your brow is beld, John,	bald
Your locks are like the snaw;	
But blessings on your frosty pow,	head
John Anderson my Jo.	
John Anderson my jo, John,	
We clamb the hill the gither;	climbed, together
And mony a canty day, John,	cheerful
We've had wi' ane anither:	one another
Now we maun totter down, John,	must
And hand in hand we'll go;	
And sleep the gither at the foot,	
John Anderson my Jo.[2]	

Burns's brother William was on the move again. He had decided to try his
luck in London, and he wrote asking for the address of Burns's old teacher,
John Murdoch – and for further advice about the ways of the world: 'You
promised me some instructions about behaviour in companies rather above my
station,' he reminded Burns:

To these instructions pray add some of a moral kind, for though (either
through the strength of early impressions or the frigidity of my constitution)
I have hitherto withstood the temptation to those vices to which young fellows
of my station and time of life are so much addicted, yet I do not know if my
virtue will be able to withstand the more powerful temptations of the metropolis; yet, through God's assistance and your instructions, I hope to weather
the storm.[3]

1. *Ibid.*, 293, 285, 295 and 284 respectively.
2. *Ibid.*, 302. The traditional, unsanitised version later found its way into *The Merry Muses of Caledonia*.
3. Chambers-Wallace, vol. iii, p. 168.

Burns, uninhibited by the fact that he himself had never actually been there, marked his brother's card about the temptations lying in wait for unsuspecting country boys in the metropolis: 'London swarms with worthless wretches who prey on their fellow-creatures' thoughtlessness or inexperience. – Be cautious in forming connections with comrades and companions,' he warned him:

> Another caution; I give you great credit for you [sic] sobriety with respect to that universal vice, Bad Women. – It is an impulse the hardest to be restrained, but if once a man accustoms himself to gratifications of that impulse, it is then nearly or altogether impossible to restrain it. – Whoring is a most ruinous expensive species of dissipation; is spending a poor fellow's money with which he ought clothe & support himself nothing? Whoring has ninety nine chances in a hundred to bring on a man the most nauseous and excrutiating diseases to which Human nature is liable; are disease & an impaired constitution trifling considerations? All this is independant of the criminality of it. –[1]

His mind was still running on writing for the theatre. At the beginning of March, when he sent an order to Peter Hill on behalf of the Monklands Friendly Society, he also listed some requirements of his own:

> I want likewise for myself, as you can pick them up, second-handed, or any way cheap copies of Otway's dramatic works, Ben Johnson's D. [for Ditto?] Dryden's, Congreve's, Wycherly's, Vanburgh's, Cibber's, or any dramatic works of the more Moderns, Mackline Garrick, Foote, Colman, or Sheridan's. – A good Copy too of Moliere in French I much want. – Any other good Dramatic Authors, in their native language I want them; I mean Comic Authors chiefly, tho' I should wish Raci[ne,] Corneille & Voltaire too.[2]

As the theatre company's Dumfries season drew to a close, Burns tried his hand at a second prologue, this time for Sutherland's wife's benefit night. Once again, he sounded a patriotic note, opening with a plea for the recognition of home-grown talent:

> What needs this din about the town o' Lon'on?
> How this new Play, and that new Sang is comin?
> Why is outlandish stuff sae meikle courted?   much
> Does Nonsense mend, like Brandy, when imported –
> Is there nae Poet, burning keen for Fame,
> Will bauldly try to gie us Plays at hame?[3]   boldly

1. Letters, 391.
2. *Ibid.*, 395. Mackline was Charles Macklin, (?1699-1797), an Irish-born actor famous for his interpretation of Shylock and the author of a number of plays. The most successful was *Love à la Mode* (1759), which has a character called Sir Archy MacSarcasm.
3. Kinsley, 315.

Two days before it was to be performed, he judged it prudent to send a copy of the prologue to the Provost of Dumfries. 'There is a dark stroke of Politics in the belly of the Piece,' he wrote, 'and like a faithful loyal Subject, I lay it before You, as the chief Magistrate of the Country ... that if the said Poem be found to contain any Treason, or words of treasonable construction, or any Fama clamosa or Scandalum magnatum, against our Sovereign lord the King, or any of his liege Subjects, the said Prologue may not see the light ...'[1]

It is possible that Burns was merely showing off. If not, then he was making extraordinarily heavy weather of his exciseman's oath of allegiance. He cannot seriously have believed that the flag-waving of his introductory lines was open to objection. It is true that later on he writes of 'the lovely hapless Scottish queen' and refers disobligingly to Elizabeth Tudor as '*a vengeful woman*', but that falls some way short of incitement to sedition.

It is also possible that Burns's thinking was coloured at this time by his historical reading – when ordering books for the Monklands Library from Peter Hill he had asked for a particular book about the Jacobite rising of 1715[2] and 'any good history of the Rebellion 1745'. Whatever the reason, it is plain from a letter that he wrote to Mrs Dunlop in the second week in April that he still had a mildly chauvinist bee buzzing round inside his bonnet:

> Alas! have I often said to myself, what are all the boasted advantages which my Country reaps from a certain Union, that can counterbalance the annihilation of her Independance, & even her very Name! ... Nothing can reconcile me to the common terms, "English Embassador, English Court, &c.["] And I am out of all patience to see that [e]quivocal Character, Hastings, empeached by "the Commons of England." – Tell me, my friend, is this weak prejudice?[3]

A little later he sent Mrs Dunlop a copy of 'Lament of Mary Queen of Scots on the Approach of Spring'.[4] Thomas Crawford has dismissed this song, which Burns set to a slow lament, as 'a perfect example of the sentimental *boudoir* poem':

> Now Nature hangs her mantle green
>   On every blooming tree,
> And spreads her sheets o' daisies white
>   Out o'er the grassy lea ...

1. Letters, 394.
2. Peter Rae, *History of the Late Rebellion Rais'd against ... King George*, Dumfries, 1718; 2nd ed. enlarged, London, 1746.
3. Letters, 397.
4. Kinsley, 316.

That is certainly an unpromising start (Burns later disclosed to another correspondent that it 'was begun while I was busy with Percy's Reliques of English
Poetry'.[1]) Gradually, however, he slips out of this lifeless, neo-classical mode
and moves into a key reminiscent of the old ballads:

> I was the Queen o' bonie France,
>   Where happy I hae been;
> Fu' lightly rase I on the morn,   rose
>   As blythe lay down at e'en:
> And I'm the sovereign of Scotland,
>   And mony a traitor there;
> Yet here I lie in foreign bands,
>   And never ending care.

Burns's excise duties did not allow him time for half the literary projects he
dreamt up as he rode about the countryside. Dr Moore had sent him a copy
of his novel *Zeluco*, which had been published in 1786 and had enjoyed a
certain success. Zeluco is a repulsive Sicilian nobleman who crushes a pet
sparrow, has a slave beaten to death in the West Indies and kills his own child;
light relief is provided by two Scottish servants, Buchanan and Targe, who are
unable to agree about the character of Mary Queen of Scots. Burns was much
enthused by this savage and improbable tale, and he whiled away the idle
moments of a Collection Day in the Dumfries Excise Office by writing to
Moore about it:

> You were pleased to express a wish for my opinion of the Work, which so
> flattered me that nothing less would serve my over-weening fancy than a
> formal criticism on the Book. In fact, I have gravely planned a Comparative
> view of You, Fielding, Richardson & Smollet, in your different qualities &
> merits as Novel-Writers. – This, I own, betrays my ridiculous vanity, and I
> may probably never bring the business to bear . . .[2]

Nothing ever came of it. It was, in truth, an ambition every bit as improbable
as the plot of *Zeluco*. Burns the literary critic, together with Burns the dramatist,
hovers eternally in the wings – two characters in search of an author.

Burns had made up his mind as early as the spring of 1790 that he must leave
Ellisland, although in this, as in so much else, he initially confided only in Mrs
Dunlop. 'At Martinmass 1791, my rent rises 20£ per annum,' he told her, '&
then, I am, on the maturest deliberation, determined to give it up . . . So much

1. Letter to Dr Moore, 28th February 1791 (Letters, 437).
2. Letters, 404.

for Farming! Would to God I had never engaged in it!' He had plotted his escape route with some precision:

> I can have in the Excise-line what they call a foot-walk whenever I chuse; that is an appointment to a Division where I am under no necessity of keeping a horse. – There is in every Sea-port town, one or two Officers, called Port-Officers, whose income is at least seventy pounds per ann. – I will petition Mr Graham & stretch all my interest, to get one of these; and if possible on Clyde. – Greenock & Port-Glasgow are both lucrative places in that way, & to them my views are bent . . . One word more, & then to have done with this most ungracious subject; all this business of my farm, &c. is for your most private ear: it would be of considerable prejudice to me to have it known at present. –[1]

William Burns had gone to London by sea. He had still not found anything permanent, but had got temporary work in a shop in the Strand. Things were proving harder than he had imagined:

> There are such swarms of fresh hands just come from the country that the town is quite overstocked, and except one is a particularly good workman (which you know I am not, nor, I am afraid, ever will be) it will be hard to get a place.

He asked for his best linen shirts – 'I wish one of my sisters could find as much time as to trim my shirts at the breast, for there is no such thing to be seen here as a plain shirt.' He also hoped Gilbert might spare him a cheese: 'The cheese I could get here; but I will have a pride in eating Ayrshire cheese in London.'[2] He did not have long to enjoy either and had small need of the advice he had received from his worldy-wise brother. Before the summer was out he was dead of a fever – had, in Murdoch's excruciating phrase, 'bid an everlasting farewell to all sublunary things'.[3]

Burns's excise duties and writing left little time for the farm, and the oversight of what had to be done there fell increasingly to Jean. They kept nine or ten cows, four horses, a number of young cattle and several pet sheep. Four farm servants were employed, two women and two men; a ploughman called William Clark, who was employed at Ellisland for six months, remembered Burns as a kind and indulgent master, although he could flare up and become 'gey guldersome' (the word 'gulder' describes the angry growl of a dog). Once, one of the women-servants was careless while feeding potatoes to the cows, and one of the beasts almost choked – it was the only time Clark saw Burns

1. *Ibid.*, 396.
2. Letter dated 21st March 1790, Chambers-Wallace, vol. iii, pp. 177-8.
3. *Ibid.*, p. 203.

really angry. He occasionally took a turn at the plough, and at seed-time he would still sometimes be out early with his sowing-sheet before riding off on gauging business. When he was about the farm he wore corduroy breeches, dark-blue stockings and 'cootikens' (gaiters), a long-tailed coat that was either drab or blue and a broad blue bonnet.[1]

Burns was intensely sociable, and did not always head straight for Ellisland after a day in the saddle. One favourite port of call was the manse at Loch-maben, where the minister was Andrew Jaffray – it was his daughter, Jean, who inspired the lovely song 'I gaed a waefu' gate yestreen'. Thirty years later, when she was widowed and living in New York, she reminisced about how Burns would appear on a cold wet night after a long ride over the moors:

> On such occasions one of the family would help to disencumber him of his dreadnought and boots, while others brought him a pair of slippers and made him a warm dish of tea. It was during these visits that he felt himself perfectly happy, and opened his whole soul to us, repeated and even sang many of his admirable songs, and enchanted all who had the good fortune to be present with his manly, luminous observations and artless manners.[2]

On other occasions Burns took his ease after a long day in the saddle not at the house of friends but at some hostelry or other, as often as not at the Globe Inn in Dumfries. There too his artless manners were employed to good effect:

> Yestreen I had a pint o' wine,
>   A place where body saw na;
> Yestreen lay on this breast o' mine
>   The gowden locks of Anna. –   golden
> The hungry Jew in wilderness
>   Rejoicing o'er his manna,
> Was naething to my hiney bliss   honey
>   Upon the lips of Anna. –[3]

Ann Park was a relative of the landlady at the Globe, and worked there as a barmaid. She was the daughter of an Edinburgh coachmaker, and when Burns first met her she was a girl of nineteen. Allan Cunningham's description of her, when he published his *Life of Burns* more than forty years later, was succinct: 'She was,' he wrote, 'accounted beautiful by the customers, when wine made them tolerant in matters of taste'.[4]

It is true that Cunningham was only six at the time, and that his biography is not generally regarded as a by-word for accuracy. It is equally the case, however, that his father was Burns's neighbour at Ellisland and knew him

1. *Ibid*, p. 198.
2. *Ibid.*, p. 138. A dreadnought was a thick coat worn in inclement weather.
3. Kinsley, 320.
4. Cunningham, *op. cit.*, vol iv, p. 337.

extremely well; if a certain glancing malice is apparent in Cunningham's choice of words, there is no reason to call in question his account of how Ann Park was seen in the town. Burns himself later wrote that he thought it the best love-song he had ever composed in his life, although he conceded that in its original state it was 'not quite a lady's song':

> Ye Monarchs take the East and West,
> Frae Indus to Savannah!
> Gie me within my straining grasp
> The melting form of Anna. –
> There I'll despise Imperial charms,
> An Empress or Sultana,
> While dying raptures in her arms
> I give and take with Anna!!!

The frankness of the language leaves no doubt about the nature of the relationship. Kinsley points out that dying is in common metaphorical use in English poetry to mean orgastic, and offers examples from both Shakespeare and Dryden.[1]

From time to time Burns entertained visitors at home. Ramsay of Ochtertyre was touring in the south-west in the summer of 1790. Catching a glimpse of Burns on the road, he left a note for him at a nearby inn and then made his way to Ellisland:

> I was much pleased with his *uxor Sabina qualis* and the poet's modest mansion, so unlike the habitation of ordinary rustics. In the evening he suddenly bounced in upon us and said, as he entered, 'I come, to use the words of Shakespeare, *stewed in haste.*' In fact, he had ridden incredibly fast after receiving my note. We fell into conversation directly, and soon got into the *mare magnum* of poetry. He told me that he had now gotten a story for a drama, which he was to call *Rob Macquechan's Elshon*, from a popular story of Robert Bruce being defeated on the water of Cairn, when the heel of his boot having loosened in his flight, he applied to Robert Macquechan to fit it, who, to make sure, ran his awl nine inches up the king's heel.[2]

Burns had retained the friendship of Nicol, and they continued to see something of each other. The schoolmaster's wife had recently come into some money, and in the spring of 1790 they bought a 340-acre farm in Dumfriesshire which Burns inspected for them and reported on favourably – 'an exceeding

---

1. Kinsley, vol iii, p. 1347. The Shakespearean references are to *Much Ado* and *Lear*. Dryden uses the word in his song 'Whilst *Alexis* lay prest'.
2. Chambers-Wallace, vol iii, pp. 199-200. Ramsay's compliment to Jean is from Horace; Burns's quotation from Shakespeare is from *King Lear*.

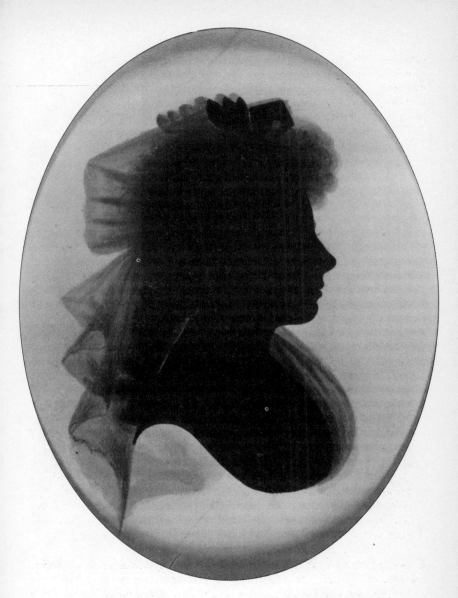

21. A silhouette of Nancy McLehose by John Miers.

22. General's Entry, Potterow. Mrs McLehose's apartment was on the first floor.

23. Robert Ainslie in later life.

24. The Reverend Dr. John Kemp, Mrs McLehose's minister at the Tolbooth Church: 'There's not one on earth has so much influence on me, except – Sylvander.'

25. William Craig, Mrs McLehose's cousin, raised to the bench as Lord Craig in 1792.

THE *British Antiquarian*

27. Captain Francis Grose:
'If you discover a chearful-looking grig
of an old, fat fellow, the precise figure
of Dr Slop, wheeling about your avenue
in his own carriage with a pencil and
paper in his hand, you may conclude:
"Thou art the man!"'

26. '*Kirk-Alloway* was drawing nigh,
   Whare ghaists and houlets nightly cry.'

28. A portrait of Maria Riddell by Lawrence: 'Thou first of Friends, and most accomplished of Women; even with all thy little caprices!!!'

29. Friars' Carse.

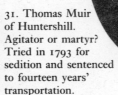

31. Thomas Muir
of Huntershill.
Agitator or martyr?
Tried in 1793 for
sedition and sentenced
to fourteen years'
transportation.

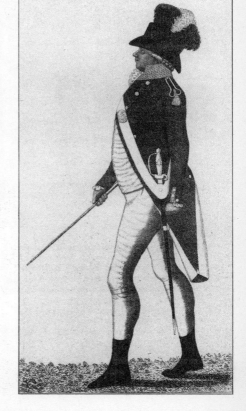

30 Margaret Burns, lady of the town:
'Cease, ye prudes, your envious railing,
Lovely Burns has charms – *confess*;
True it is, she has one failing,
Had ae woman ever less?'

32. Henry Dundas, Viscount Melville:
'Harry the Ninth' in the uniform of
the Royal Edinburgh Volunteers.

Dear Brother

It will be no very pleasing news to you to be told that I am dangerously ill, & not likely to get better. — An inveterate rheumatism has reduced me to such a state of debility, & my appetite is totally gone, so that I can scarce stand on my legs. — I have been a week at sea-bathing, & I will continue there or in a friend's house in the country all the summer — God help my wife & children, if I am taken from their head! — They will be poor indeed. — I have contracted one or two serious debts, partly from my illness these many months & partly from too much thoughtlessness as to expence when I came to town that will cut in too much on the little I leave them in your hands. — Remember me to my Mother. — Yours

July 10th 1796.   R Burns

33. Burns's last letter to his brother Gilbert.

34. John Syme:
   'Who is proof to thy personal
      converse and wit,
   Is proof to all other temptation.'

35. George Thomson: 'You
cannot imagine how much this
business of composing for your
publication has added to my
enjoyment.'

36. Burns's funeral cortège from a painting by the Victorian
artist W.E. Lockhart.

GRAND BURNS' FESTIVAL—BROWN ENTERTAINS HIS FRIEND WI' A HAGGIS!

37. *Punch* cartoon, 1859.

38. Sir James Crichton-
Browne, fervent Burnsian,
loyal son of Dumfries,
Lord Chancellor's Visitor
in Lunacy, 1875–92:
'It was rheumatism that
was the undoing of Burns.'

cheap purchase'.[1] In the autumn, in an amusing letter to Ainslie, Nicol reported
– inaccurately, as it happens – on Burns's rapid progress in the excise:

> As to Burns, poor folks like you and I must resign all thoughts of future
> correspondence with him. To the pride of applauded genius is now super-
> added the pride of office. He was lately raised to the dignity of an Examiner
> of Excise, which is a step preparative to attaining that of a *supervisor*. There-
> fore we can expect no less than his language will become perfectly Horatian
> – 'odi profanum vulgus et arceo'. However, I will see him in a fortnight
> hence; and if I find that Beelzebub had inflated his heart like a bladder with
> pride, and given it the fullest distension that vanity can effect, you and I will
> burn him in effigy, and write a satire, as bitter as gall and wormwood, against
> government for employing its *enemies*, like Lord North, to effect its purposes.
> This will be taking all the revenge in our power.[2]

It is interesting to learn how Nicol viewed Burns's politics, but he was wrong
about his progress in the excise – all that had happened in the summer of 1790
was that he had been appointed to Dumfries Third Foot-Walk Division. This
meant a dramatic reduction in the amount of travelling he had to do. Instead
of ten parishes, his new area covered only about a third of the burgh of Dumfries, which involved walking a distance of no more than four miles. The move
represented unusually rapid promotion. Burns had been in the service little
more than six months, and an officer would normally have expected to spend
up to three years in an out-ride before he was considered experienced enough
to take on a town division. Burns owned his advancement in this instance
solely to John Mitchell, the Dumfries Collector, who transferred the incumbent, an officer called William Johnston, to the neighbouring district of
Wigtown.

Burns's transfer involved a shift in the emphasis of his duties. His new area
was known as 'the tobacco district' – he now had to keep an eye on more than
fifty tobacco dealers and retailers. Tobacco smuggling had been big business
ever since James I had tried to tax the 'obnoxious weed' out of existence in
the early seventeenth century.[3] Pitt had introduced new legislation the previous
year which the trade regarded as unduly restrictive, and it was the excise officer
on the ground who bore the brunt of their antagonism. When Burns tired of
the complaints of the tobacco trade, he could turn for relief to his other charges,
who included a brickmaker, a chandler and nine victuallers.

The evidence is that he was a more assiduous exciseman than he was a
farmer. In March 1790 he asked Peter Hill to find him three copies of *An
Index to Excise Laws now in Force*, a massive compendium produced by an excise

1. Letters, 398A.
2. Chambers-Wallace, vol. iii, p. 200.
3. The tax in 1602 was 6s 8d a pound, which represented a duty by value of approximately
1,000%.

lawyer – 'If this book is now to be had, cheap or dear, get it for me.'[1] If he did not always do things by the book, his methods seems to have achieved results that gave satisfaction all round. 'I took, I fancy, rather a new way with my Frauds,' he informed Graham of Fintry:

> I recorded every Defaulter; but at the Court, I myself begged off every poor body that was unable to pay, which seeming candour gave me so much implicit credit with the Hon. Bench that with high Compl[nts] they gave me such ample vengeance on the rest, that my Decreet is double the amount of any Division in the District. –[2]

It was a shrewd and effective way of playing the system. It did him no harm to be popular, in a mildly Robin Hoodish way, with petty defaulters. He lost nothing on the swings and he gained handsomely on the roundabouts. His 'decreet' constituted a valuable supplement to his salary, as he was entitled to half of any fines imposed by the courts and half of any sums realised by seizures. He told Graham he believed it would amount to between fifty and sixty pounds.

He did not, of course, enjoy a monopoly of shrewdness, and was much irritated on one occasion when he thought he was in danger of being outsmarted by a man called Thomas Johnson, who farmed at Mirecleugh. Johnson had been fined £5 for 'making fifty-four bushels of malt, without entry, notice or licence,' but had appealed to the justices of the peace, who included Riddell of Glen Riddell, and who instructed Mitchell to suspend proceedings while they reviewed the case.

Burns wrote a lengthy rebuttal of Johnson's petition. He plainly suspected the man's good faith. He mentioned that he was a seceder; he pointed out that he had refused to swear in court that he had intended no fraud but that he had now announced that he was willing to swear after all. 'He has been excercising his Conscience in private,' Burns wrote sarcastically, '& will perhaps stretch a point.'[3] Mitchell apparently asked him to call on Riddell, presumably to talk him through the excise case. Burns complied, but with some sourness: 'I wish & pray that the goddess of Justice herself would appear tomorrow among our Hon[ble] Gentlemen,' he wrote, 'merely to give them a word in their ear, that "Mercy to the Thief, is Injustice to the Honest Man".'[4]

Patronage of the sort Burns himself had enjoyed from Glencairn or Graham was one thing; he clearly regarded that as enlightened and unexceptionable. That a local farmer should attempt to key into the old-boy net to avoid the rigour of the law struck him as something quite different; his letter to Mitchell conveys the measure of his indignation:

1. *Letters*, 395.
2. *Ibid.*, 419.
3. *Ibid.*, 418.
4. *Ibid.*, 417.

I have broke my horse's wind, & almost broke my own neck, besides some injuries in a part that shall be nameless, owing to a hard-hearted stone of a saddle; & I find that every Offender has so many Great Men to espouse his cause, that I shall not be surprised if I am committed to the strong Hold of the Law tomorrow for insolence to the dear friends of the Gentlemen of the Country.—

Before he had been two months in his new post, he was eyeing the next rung on the ladder. 'I will petition Mr Graham & stretch all my interest,' he had told Mrs Dunlop in the spring, and that is precisely what he now did. 'I do not like to be an incessant beggar from you,' he wrote:

If ever I am so fortunate as to be called out to do business as a Supervisor, I would then chuse the North of Scotland; but untill that Utopian period, I own I have some wayward feelings at appearing as a simple Gauger in a Country where I am only known by fame. – Portglasgow, Greenock, or Dumfries, Ports, would be in the mean time my ultimatum. –[1]

He was now no longer keeping it to himself that he intended to give up Ellisland. He said as much to Graham, and when Ainslie came to see him in the middle of October he told him, too. Ainslie immediately passed on this, and much else, in a letter to Mrs McLehose: 'You desired that I should let you hear every thing regarding him & his family and how I was pleased,' he wrote:

This is a difficult question as my short room here will not permitt me to be so full as I might – and part of the question admitts of Double Answers – I was pleased with Burns' hearty welcome of me – and it was an addition to his pleasure, that my arrival was upon his *Kirn* night [harvest-home], when he Expected some of his friends to help make merry, but much displeased with the Company when they arrived – They consisted of a Vulgar looking Tavern keeper from Dumfries; and his Wife more Vulgar – Mr. Miller of Dalswinton's Gardener and his wife – and said Wife's Sister – and a little fellow from Dumfries, who had been a Clerk – These were the strangers, and the rest of the Company who are inmates of the house were Burns' Sister, and Mrs Burns' Sister, who are Two common looking Girls who act as their servants – and 3 Male and female cousins who had been Shearing for him.

They had spent the evening, Ainslie told Clarinda, 'in the common way on Such occasions of Dancing, and Kissing the Lasses at the end of every dance.' He was very sniffy about Jean – and about her house:

With regard to the helpmate She seems Vulgar and Common-place in a considerable degree – and pretty round & fat – She is however a kind Body

1. *Ibid.*, 419.

in her Own way, and the husband Tolerably Attentive to her – As to the house, it is ill-contrived – and pretty Dirty, and *Hugry Mugry* –

Then Ainslie came to what Clarinda most wanted to know:

Tho' last, not least our Friend himself is as ingenious as ever, and Seem'd very happy with the Situation I have described – His Mind however now appears to me to be a great Mixture of the poet and the Excise Man – One day he Sitts down and writes a Beautiful poem – and the Next he Seizes a cargo of Tobacco from some unfortunate Smuggler – or Roups out some poor Wretch for Selling liquors without a License. From his conversation he Seems to be frequently among the Great – but No Attention is paid by people of any rank to his wife . . .

In conclusion Ainslie treated Mrs McLehose to a snivelling paragraph about himself. 'That Cursed melancholy, which I was complaining of, has been daily increasing,' he wrote, 'and all Burns' Jokes cannot dispell it – I sit silent & frail even amidst Mirth . . . I know of no Sufficient reason for Such Misery.' Possibly the betrayal of friendship was reason enough.

On the Saturday, he and Burns went out to an inn and drank Clarinda's health – '& to settle the matter Got both Exceedingly drunk.'[1]

As, famously, did Tam o' Shanter and Souter Johnnie – and it was in that same autumn of 1790 that Burns conjured his fuddled hero from the national folk-memory and wrote one of the comic masterpieces of Scottish literature. 'I shall give the beginning of it,' announced Hazlitt, when he lectured on Burns in 1818, 'but I am afraid I shall hardly know where to leave off'[2]:

When chapman billies leave the street,	pedlars
And drouthy neebors, neebors meet,	thirsty neighbours
As market-days are wearing late,	
An' folk begin to tak the gate;	road
While we sit bousing at the nappy,	ale
And getting fou and unco happy,	drunk, very
We think na on the lang Scots miles,	
The mosses, waters, slaps, and styles,	gaps in walls
That lie between us and our hame,	
Whare sits our sulky sullen dame,	

1. See Robert T. Fitzhugh, 'Burns at Ellisland', *Modern Language Notes*, LII (November 1938), pp. 525–6.
2. Hazlitt's fears were justified, and he did not leave off until he got to the end of the poem. The lecture, 'On Burns, and the Old English Ballads' was delivered at the Surrey Institution in 1818 and published in his *Lectures on the English Poets* the same year. The text appears in *Complete Works of William Hazlitt*, ed. P.P. Howe, Hamish Hamilton, London, 1930, vol. v, pp. 127–40.

Gathering her brows like gathering storm,
Nursing her wrath to keep it warm . . .[1]

Burns wrote his most famous tale for a colourful character called Captain
Francis Grose. They had met at Riddell's house the previous year, and Burns
had described him enthusiastically to Mrs Dunlop: 'If you discover a chearful-
looking grig of an old, fat fellow, the precise figure of Dr Slop, wheeling about
your avenue in his own carriage with a pencil & paper in his hand, you may
conclude: "Thou art the man!" '[2]

Grose, a jovial man in permanently reduced circumstances, had tried his
hand at most things. The son of a Swiss jeweller, he had been a soldier, had
studied art and had also, in his time, served as Richmond Herald in the College
of Arms and as Paymaster and Adjutant of the Surrey Militia. He was the
author of *The Antiquities of England and Wales*, which had appeared in six
volumes between 1773 and 1787, and he had come north to collect material
for an equivalent work on Scotland. Burns took to him at once, and celebrated
their friendship in a sparkling piece which he sent off to one of the Edinburgh
papers:

Hear, Land o' Cakes, and brither Scots,
Frae Maidenkirk to Johny Groats! –
If there's a hole in a' your coats,
    I rede you tent it: advise, look to
A child's amang you, taking notes,   fellow
    And, faith, he'll prent it.[3]   print

Burns filled Grose in on what was worth seeing in Ayrshire, and suggested
a drawing of Alloway kirk; it was not only the burial place of his father, but
the scene of many a good story of witchcraft. Grose agreed, on condition that
Burns furnish him with a suitable tale to accompany the engraving. Burns
originally sent him three short prose sketches in the summer of 1790, and
turned one of them into verse later in the year – he recited part of it to Ainslie
during his visit. 'Should you think it worthy a place in your Scots Antiquities,'
he wrote modestly to Grose, 'it will lengthen not a little the altitude of my
Muse's pride.'[4]

Grose thought it a 'pretty tale' and printed it the following April in his
second volume, which carried a generous acknowledgement 'to my *ingenious*

1. Kinsley, 321.
2. Letters, 352.
3. Kinsley, 275. 'On the Late Captain Grose's Peregrinations thro' Scotland, collecting the
Antiquities of that Kingdom', first appeared in the *Edinburgh Evening Courant* on 27th August,
1789 and was reprinted in four other periodicals before being published in the 1793 edition of
Burns's poems.
4. Letters, 427A. The poem appeared in the second volume of *The Antiquities of Scotland*, which
was published the following April. It was also printed in the March issue of the *Edinburgh Magazine*.

friend Mr Robert Burns'. Written partly in English and partly in the vernacular, it is by turns sophisticated and simple, comic and grotesque. It is the only narrative poem of the kind that Burns ever wrote, and more's the pity. He knew that he had never done anything better; he told Mrs Dunlop that it had 'a finishing polish that I despair of ever excelling'.[1]

Burns had been ill again during the autumn of 1790. Early in October he wrote to his friend Alexander Dalziel, who was the factor on Lord Glencairn's estate at Finlayston in Renfrewshire. 'I suppose that by this time & long before this time, your Indignation has given me over to as many devils as chuse to accept of me,' he wrote:

A few days after I received yours I was seized with a slow, illformed Fever, from which I am just risen out of the weary bed of Sickness; & if this is not apology enough, I must inform you farther that I have likewise had a most malignant Squinancy which had me very near the precints of the Grave. – I am now got greatly better, though by no means in a confirmed state of health. –[2]

So Burns had been suffering from suppurative tonsillitis, but as 1790 gave way to 1791 he had recovered both his health and his spirits. 'I am not gone to Elysium, most noble Colonel,' he wrote jauntily to Willie Dunbar, his Crochallan crony, 'but am still here in this sublunary world, serving my God by propagating his image, and honoring my king by begetting him loyal subjects.'[3] Ainslie's coldly appraising eye had registered in October that Jean was 'pretty round and fat,' but he had not adduced a reason – he was perhaps indifferent, or possibly merely obtuse. She was, in fact, once more pregnant. Now, in the early weeks of 1791, she was six months gone.

Burns's release from the punishing routine of his early months in the excise gave him more time for reading. (He had some weeks of enforced leisure, too; late in January he broke his right arm and damaged his hand in a fall – 'not from my horse but with my horse' as he told Mrs Dunlop.[4]) An order placed in January for the Monklands Friendly Society library included *Joseph Andrews*, *Don Quixote* and *The Arabian Nights*. He also got to grips with *Essays on the Nature and Principles of Taste*. He had been presented with a copy by the author, the Reverend Archibald Alison. This was altogether new territory for him. 'I own, Sir, that at first glance, several of your propositions startled me as paradoxical,' he wrote:

1. *Ibid.*, 443.
2. *Ibid.*, 422. The letter now forms part of the Berg Collection in the New York Public Library.
3. *Ibid.*, 431.
4. *Ibid.*, 435.

That the martial clangor of a trumpet had something in it vastly more grand, heroic & sublime, than the twingle-twangle of a jews-harp; that the delicate flexure of a rose-twig, when the half-blown flower is heavy with the tears of the dawn, was infinitely more beautiful & elegant than the upright stub of a burdock ... these I had set down as irrefragable, orthodox truths, untill perusing your book shook my faith. – In short, Sir, except Euclid's elements of Geometry, which I made a shift to unravel by my father's fire-side, in the winter-evenings of the first season I held a plough, I never read a book which gave me such a quantum of information & added so much to my stock of ideas ...[1]

He also re-read, not for the first time, Moore's *Zeluco*, and was moved to give the author the benefit of his views on the Virgin Queen:

What a rocky-hearted, perfidious Succubus was that Queen Elizabeth! – Judas Iscariot was a sad dog to be sure, but still his demerits shrink to insignificance, compared with the doings of the infernal Bess Tudor. –[2]

Burns had recently had news of the death of Lord Glencairn. Although only in his early forties, he had been in failing health since the previous autumn, and on medical advice had gone to Lisbon; returning to England at the end of January he had died as the boat docked at Falmouth. This was a severe blow to Burns. Glencairn, he wrote, had been 'the Patron from whom all my fame & good fortune took its rise.' He was engagingly frank with Moore:

Independant of my grateful attachment to him, which was indeed so strong that it pervaded my very soul, & was entwined with the thread of my existence; so soon as the Prince's friends had got in, (& every dog you know has his day) my getting forward in the Excise would have been an easier business than otherwise it will be. –

He was, for all that, much affected by Glencairn's death. 'God knows what I have suffered, at the loss of my best Friend,' he wrote to Alexander Dalziel:

I will be exceedingly oblidged to you indeed, to let me know the news of the Noble Family, how the poor Mother & the two sisters support their loss ... Dare I trouble you to let me know privately before the day of interment, that

1. *Ibid.*, 436. Alison was the son-in-law of Dr John Gregory, and two years older than Burns, who had met him in Edinburgh in February 1789. He had been educated at Glasgow University and Balliol College, Oxford and ordained in the Church of England.
2. *Ibid.*, 437.

I may cross the country & steal among the croud, to pay a tear to the last sight of my ever revered Benefactor? –[1]

On April 9th, Jean gave birth to a son. Mrs Dunlop was the first of his correspondents to have the news – 'a fine boy, rather stouter but not so handsome as your God-son at his time of life was. – Indeed I look on your little Namesake to be my chef d'œuvre in that species of manufacture, as I look on "Tam o' Shanter" to be my standard performance in the Poetical line.'[2] He did not mention to Mrs Dunlop that it was his second production 'in that species of manufacture' in little more than a week – nine days previously Ann Park had presented him with an illegitimate daughter. The son was given the names William Nicol. Ann Park's child was christened Elizabeth.

It was the first time Burns had written to Mrs Dunlop for more than two months. He pleaded his broken arm, although that had not prevented him writing to a good many other friends. Possibly he had been offended at her initial lack of enthusiasm for 'Tam o' Shanter', but more probably he was simply idle. Mrs Dunlop, however, had devised her own method for dealing with his dilatory ways. 'I should have had still more pleasure in receiving your last,' she told him briskly, 'had it not been preceded by one from your brother, who forestalled all your good news.'[3] Anxious for news of Burns's arm, she had simply written to Gilbert.

When Burns put his mind to it, nobody could offer excuses with a more winning grace. 'I am the most indolent of all human beings,' he announced to another correspondent at this time, 'and when I matriculate in the Herald's office, I intend that my supporters shall be two sloths, my crest a slow-worm, and the motto, "Deil tak the foremost." '[4]

He was the very reverse of indolent if a friend was in trouble, and in the summer of 1791 he exerted himself considerably on behalf of a man called James Clarke, who for the past five years had been the principal schoolmaster at Moffat. Accusations of cruelty were being bandied about, and there was a move to unseat him. The patronage of the school rested with the magistrates and town council of Edinburgh, and when the matter was referred to them, Burns wrote to enlist the support of Alexander Cunningham. Clarke, he told him, was 'suffering severely under the persecution of one or two malicious but powerful individuals of his employers' (these included Lord Hopetoun, who was the principal heritor of the parish):

He is accused of harshness to some perverse dunces that were placed under

1. *Ibid.*, 439.
2. *Ibid.*, 443.
3. Letter dated 30th April 1791, Burns and Dunlop, pp. 314-17.
4. Letters, 454. The correspondent has not been identified.

his care. – God help the Teacher, a man of genius & sensibility, for such is my friend Clarke, when the blockhead Father presents him his booby son, & insists on having the rays of science lighted up in a fellow's head whose scull is impervious & inaccessible by any other way than a positive fracture with a cudgel! –[1]

Burns also drafted a letter for Clarke to send to the Lord Provost of Edinburgh – a robust statement of his case, and a dignified plea for proper procedures to be observed:

> ... A fair hearing, my Lord, is what above all things I want; & what I greatly fear, will be attempted to be denied me. – It is to be insinuated, that I have vacated my place; that I never was legally appointed; with I know not how many pretences more, to hinder the business from coming properly before your Lordship & the other Patrons of the School: all of which I deny; & will insist on holding my appointment untill the dignified Characters who gave it to me, shall find me unworthy of it ...[2]

The dispute rumbled on for some time, and was eventually decided in the schoolmaster's favour. A note at the bottom of another letter Burns drafted for him reads, 'Bravo! Clarke. – In spite of Hopeton & his myrmidons thou camest off victorious! –'[3] Clarke stayed on at Moffat until 1794, when he became master of the burgh school at Forfar. Although Burns's financial situation was by no means easy at the time ('O the supreme curse of making three guineas do the business of five!' he groaned to Hill) his friendship to Clarke also extended to lending him quite a lot of money.

There had been another instance of Burns's generosity earlier in the year, when he was approached for help in publishing a new edition of the work of the poet Michael Bruce. Bruce, the son of a weaver in Kinross, had died of consumption a quarter of a century earlier at the age of twenty-one. He had matriculated at Edinburgh University and studied for the ministry of Ebenezer Erskine's Secessionist Church. Although most of his poetry was juvenilia, a collection had been published three years after his death. His mother was still alive, and it was proposed that the profits of a new subscription edition should go to her.

Burns, approached by the Reverend George Husband Baird, the minister of Dunkeld,[4] responded immediately: 'Why did you, my dear Sir, write to me

1. *Ibid.*, 456.
2. *Ibid.*, 459.
3. *Ibid.*, 470.
4. The following year Baird became minister of Greyfriars Kirk, Edinburgh, and in 1800 he was chosen as Moderator of the General Assembly. He also had a distinguished academic career, becoming joint Professor of Oriental Languages at the University, and subsequently succeeding Robertson as Principal.

in such a hesitating style on the business of poor Bruce?' He had been asked only to look over the manuscript and agree to write a few lines by way of introduction, but he offered Baird the choice of all his own unpublished poems for inclusion in the volume:

> I only ask that some prefatory advertisement in the Book, as well as the Subscrip^n bills, may bear, that the Publication is solely for the behoof of Bruce's Mother: I would not leave Ignorance the least room to surmise, or Malice to insinuate, that I clubbed a share in the work from mercenary motives.—[1]

Ironically, Burns's offer of his own work was not taken up. Baird consulted both Dr Blair and Dr Moore; their advice was that 'from the moral tendency of Bruce's poetry, the insertion of Burns's "Alloway Kirk" would be as gross a violation of propriety as the exhibition of a farce after a tragedy'.[2]

The generosity of Burns's impulses towards others went hand in hand with an extraordinary blindness to where his own interest lay. He had sent Dr Moore a proof-sheet of 'Tam o' Shanter'. Moore's reply offered some fairly conventional criticism of the piece, but also tendered some excellent advice:

> I cannot help thinking you imprudent in scattering abroad so many copies of your verses. It is most natural to give a few to confidential friends, particularly to those who are connected with the subject or who are perhaps themselves the subject; but this ought to be done under promise not to give other copies. Of the poem you sent me on Queen Mary, I refused every solicitation for copies; but I lately saw it in a newspaper. My motive for cautioning you on this subject is that I wish to engage you to collect all your fugitive pieces not already printed, and after they have been re-considered and polished to the utmost of your power, I would have you publish them by another subscription; in promoting of which I will exert myself with pleasure.[3]

Burns paid no attention. There was an element of caution in this – there floated always at the back of his mind the thought that a second volume might be pronounced inferior to the first, and that would be intolerable. Mainly, however, it had to do with how he saw his 'bardship'. The idea of accepting money for writing poetry was quite simply alien to him; he would as soon think of offering a fee to a thrush singing in a thorn bush.

The year 1791 was a thin one, as it happens – he attempted an elegy on

1. Letters, 438.
2. Chambers-Wallace, vol. iii, p. 240. Publication of the new edition of Bruce did not in the event take place until 1799.
3. *Ibid.*, p. 238.

Miss Burnett, Lord Monboddo's daughter, who had died the previous year, but was not very pleased with it.[1] (Nor was Mrs Dunlop: 'I find one great fault with it,' she wrote damningly, 'which is that it begins at the wrong end.')[2] Burns also tried his hand at a lament for Glencairn, but that too has a smell of the lamp.[3] He did, however, loyally keep Johnson supplied with contributions for the fourth volume of the *Museum* which was now in preparation. In the late spring or early summer he sent him thirteen songs: 'I have besides many other Songs on the stocks,' he wrote, 'so you need not fear a want of materials.'[4] One of the best-loved of them was 'The Banks of Doon'. The imagery of the rose and the thorn is as old as medieval court poetry, but Burns employed it with a simple poignancy that has seldom been matched:

> Oft hae I rov'd by bonie Doon,
>   To see the rose and woodbine twine;
> And ilka bird sang o' its Luve,   every
>   And fondly sae did I o' mine. –
> Wi' lightsome heart i pu'd a rose,   pulled
>   Fu' sweet upon its thorny tree;
> And my fause Luver staw my rose,   stole
>   But, ah! he left the thorn wi' me. –[5]

During the summer he received an invitation from the Earl of Buchan to attend a ceremony in commemoration of the poet Thomson. Buchan proposed to unveil a bust on Ednam Hill on his estate in Roxburghshire, and hoped that Burns might be inspired to compose an ode for the occasion. This would have involved Burns in a journey of seventy miles or more in the middle of his harvest, and he begged to be excused, although he obliged with a twenty-line address of no particular distinction.[6] He clearly thought the whole business rather ridiculous, because he wrote (but sensibly did not send) a second piece which would have gone down like a lead balloon:

> Dost thou not rise, Indignant Shade,
>   And smile wi' spurning scorn,
> When they wha wad hae starv'd thy life,
>   Thy senseless turf adorn . . .[7]

In the event, things got slightly out of hand. During the local race week in September there occurred what Buchan described as 'a midnight frolic'; the

---

1. Kinsley, 324.
2. Letter dated 13th February 1791, Burns and Dunlop, pp. 303-5.
3. Kinsley, 334.
4. Letters, 452.
5. Kinsley, 328 B.
6. *Ibid.*, 331.
7. *Ibid.*, 332.

bust – it had been cast from the one in Westminster Abbey – was broken, and on the day of the planned coronation he had to make do with placing a laurel wreath on a copy of *The Seasons*.

Burns did, however, travel to Ayrshire during the summer. Gilbert, now thirty-one, had decided to get married – the bride, Jean Breckenridge, was a native of Kilmarnock, and the ceremony took place there on June 21st. Burns was careful to clear his absence with the Dumfries collector, John Mitchell, in writing – 'I shall remember that three days are all that I can expect'.[1] He made a brief call on his way to Kilmarnock on Mrs Dunlop.

Shortly after his return Burns was rapped over the knuckles by his Supervisor, Alexander Findlater. He had recorded the amount of stock incorrectly on a brewery visit and he had failed to survey the premises in the way that his instructions required. It was the first time that he had been admonished, and the tone in which he responded indicates that he was flustered. He made an apology of sorts, but at the same time tried to exculpate himself by blackening the character of the owner of the premises, a tenant farmer called William Lorimer:

I am both much surprised & vexed at that accident of Lorimer's Stock. – The last survey I made prior to Mr Lorimer's going to Edinr I was very particular in my inspection & the quantity was certainly in his possession as I stated it. – The surveys I have made during his absence might as well have been marked '*key absent*' as I never found any body but the lady, who I know is not mistress of keys, &c. to know any thing of it, and one of the times it would have rejoiced all Hell to have seen her so drunk. – I have not surveyed there since his return. – I know the gentleman's ways are, like the grace of G—, past all comprehension; but I shall give the house a severe scrutiny tomorrow morning, & send you in the naked facts. – I know, Sir, & deeply regret, that this business glances with a malign aspect on my character as an Officer; but as I am really innocent in the affair, & as the gentleman is known to be an illicit Dealer, & particularly as this is the *single* instance of the least shadow of carelessness or impropriety in my conduct as an Officer, I shall be peculiarly unfortunate if my character shall fall a sacrifice to the dark maneouvres of a Smuggler. –[2]

Below his signature, he added, 'I send you some rhymes I have just finished which tickle my fancy a little.' How they appealed to Findlater we do not know. With or without the tail-wagging postscript, it was not a very creditable letter. Burns appears to have been given the benefit of the doubt, and we hear no more of the matter.

Mrs McLehose now enters the picture once again. She wrote to him twice during the summer of 1791; she also, ominously, sent him some verses, and

1. Letters, 457.
2. *Ibid.*, 460.

eventually she squeezed a reply out of him. 'I have rec^d both your last letters, Madam, & ought & would have answered the first long ago,' he wrote:

> But on what subject shall I write you? How can you expect a Correspondent should write you, when you declare that you mean to preserve his letters with a view, sooner or later, to expose them on the pillory of derision & the rack of criticism? This is gagging me compleatly as to speaking the sentiments of my bosom ...

The gag was very loosely tied, however, and he was quickly able to lapse into the familiar routine: 'I have perused your most beautiful but most pathetic Poem – do not ask me how often, or with what emotions.' He was constitutionally incapable of addressing a woman, on paper or in the flesh, without placing a hand on her thigh:

> You know that, "I dare to *sin*, but not to *lie*." – Your Verses wring the confession from my inmost soul that – I will say it – expose it if you please – that – I have more than once in my life been the victim of a damning conjuncture of circumstances; & that to me you must be ever
>
> 'Dear as the light that visits those sad eyes.'[1]

'Pop, down at my foot.' It was Corporal Trim's hat all over again:

> You surely mistake me, Sir – 'Expose your letters to criticism!' Nothing could be further from my intention: read my letters and you will find nothing to justify such an idea. But I suppose they are burned, so you can't have recourse to them. In an impassioned hour I once talked of publishing them, but a little cool reflection showed me its impropriety: the idea has been long abandoned and I wish you to write me with that confidence you would do to a person of whom you entertained a good opinion and who is sincerely interested in your welfare. To the 'every day children of the world' I well know one cannot speak the sentiments of the bosom ...[2]

'Mrs B— & family have been in Ayrshire these many weeks,' Burns wrote to an acquaintance in Manchester in the early autumn. Judging by the rest of his news it was perhaps just as well:

> I sold my crop on this day se'ennight past, & sold it very well: a guinea an acre, on an average, above value. – But such a scene of drunkenness was hardly ever seen in this country. – After the roup was over, about thirty

---

1. *Ibid.*, 462. The line quoted is from Gray's *The Bard*.
2. This letter, dated August 2nd, 1791, was not published by Clarinda's grandson. It was first printed in William Scott Douglas's *The Complete Works of Robert Burns*, William Paterson, Edinburgh, 1833, and also appears in Chambers-Wallace, vol iii, pp. 273-4.

people engaged in a battle, every ma [*3 or 4 letters illegible*] his own hand, &
fought it out for three hours. – Nor was the scene much better in the house.
– No fighting, indeed, but folks lieing drunk on the floor, & decanting, untill
both my dogs got so drunk by attending them, that they could not stand. –
You will easily guess how I enjoyed the scene as I was no farther over than
you used to see me. –[1]

Mrs Dunlop visited Jean while she was in Mauchline and thought better
of her than Ainslie had done. 'Mrs Burns I found in all the rosy bloom of
health and beauty,' she wrote to Burns. 'I was delighted with the cheerful
openness of her countenance, the intelligence of her eyes, and her easy, modest,
unaffected manners.'[2] Burns did not distinguish himself in her absence. In a
surviving fragment of another letter from this time – it was to Alexander Cunningham – he breaks off in the middle of a rambling passage about Glencairn
to announce, 'I am so completely nettled with the fumes of wine, that I cannot
write anything like a letter.' As if to make amends, he concludes by offering
his friend instead the words of a song about pubic hair – to be sung, he
informed him, to the tune 'The Quaker's wife'.[3]

Drunken coarseness could alternate with elaborate gallantry. His friend
Riddell was related to a Dr Davies, who came from Tenby in Pembrokeshire.
Davies had a daughter called Deborah, and Burns, charmed by her vivacity
and her *petite* good looks, made her the subject of some verses which he
enclosed in a letter full of elaborate compliments: 'When I meet with a person
"after my own heart," I positively feel what an orthodox Protestant would call
a species of idolatry, & which acts on my mind like inspiration, & I can no
more resist rhyming on the impulse, than an Eolian harp can refuse its tones
to the streaming air.'[4] He described the song in question, 'Lovely Davies'[5] as
'the unfinished production of a random moment,' and it would certainly have
benefitted from a little polishing. Later, however, Miss Davies was the inspiration for something much more beautiful:

> Bonie wee thing, canie wee thing,   pleasant
>   Lovely wee thing, was thou mine;
> I wad wear thee in my bosom,
>   Least my Jewel I should tine. –   lose

1. Letters, 466.
2. Letter dated 27th August 1791, Burns and Dunlop, pp. 329-30.
3. Letters, 463. Kinsley thinks the song may be a variant of 'when Mary cam over the Border'
(Kinsley 435) which Burns sent to his friend Cleghorn some years later as an example of his
'violent propensity to Bawdy'. (Letters, 592.)
4. *Ibid.*, 472A.
5. Kinsley, 333.

There is another intriguing instance at this time of Burns's susceptibility to charm, whether in men or women. We have seen in what low regard he held the Duke of Queensberry. Now, an evening spent in His Grace's company obliged him to modify that opinion – 'he treated me with the most distinguished politeness, and marked attention'. He decided to present him with a copy of 'The Whistle' – Queensberry was acquainted with all three contestants – and it was accompanied by a covering letter in his most obsequious mode:

> ... When I first thought of sending my poem to your Grace, I had some misgivings of heart about it. – Something within me seemed to say – "A Nobleman of the first rank & the first taste, & who has lived in the first Court of Europe, what will he care for you or your ballad? Depend upon it that he will look on this business as some one or other of the many modifications of that servility of soul, with which Authors, & particularly you Poets, have ever approached the Great." No! said I to myself: I am conscious of the purity of my motives. – And as I never crouch to any man, but the man I have wronged; nor even him, except he forgives me; I will approach his Grace with tolerable upright confidence, that even were I & my ballad poorer stuff than we are, the Duke of Queensberry's polite affability would make me welcome . . .[1]

When he transcribed the letter into one of the Glenriddell volumes, he obviously felt a word of explanation was called for in case he should be thought either inconsistent or insincere: 'though I am afraid his Grace's character as a Man of worth is very equivocal, yet he certainly is a Nobleman of the first taste, & a Gentleman of the first manners. –'

He did not write many more letters from Ellisland. One of the last was to his friend Hill, the bookseller, and once again he had an accident to report – the third that year, the fourth since he had moved to Nithsdale in 1788: 'A poor devil nailed to an elbow chair, writhing in anguish with a bruised leg, laid on a stool before him, is in a fine situation truly for saying bright things.' There was more important news than the state of his leg, however:

> I may perhaps see you about Martinmass. – I have sold to my Landlord the lease of my farm, & as I roup off every thing then, I have a mind to take a week's excursion to see old acquaintances.[2]

Burns's renunciation of the lease, written in his own hand at the end of the original document, is dated September 10th. Patrick Miller had been approached by the laird of the neighbouring estate of Laggin, John Morin, and had agreed to sell him Ellisland for £1,900. A brief aside in his letter to Hill

1. Letters, 471.
2. Ibid., 475.

seems to indicate that relations with his landlord were no longer what they had been: 'Mr Miller's kindness,' he wrote sourly, 'has been just such another as Creech's was.' That seems ungenerous. He can scarcely have believed that Miller regarded him as a model tenant, yet he told Cleghorn that he had got 'some little consideration' for his lease[1] and informed Mrs. Dunlop that he had got rid of his farm 'with little, if any loss'.[2]

Burns sold off his stock and implements early in November. Jean's recollection in later years was that the roup had attracted a large crowd and had gone well: 'A cow in her first calf brought eighteen guineas, and the purchaser never rued his bargain. Two other cows brought good prices. They had been presented by Mrs Dunlop of Dunlop.'[3]

The hand-over to Morin, on the other hand, was less than amicable. He and Burns were unable to agree about the value of the manure left on the farm; Morin also felt that the state of the fences and some of the farm buildings left something to be desired, and that they should be put in order by the outgoing tenant. On the day of the flitting, Burns's temper was up. Jean's young brother Adam was there to lend a hand, and that night he was sent back to Ellisland on a curious and demeaning mission. Burns, with the aid of the diamond stylus he had been given by Glencairn, had embellished a number of window panes at the farm; Adam was instructed to return and smash them.[4]

Morin decided to settle the matter of what repairs were necesssary by recourse to the services of two 'barleymen' – a court of neighbours used for the settling of local disputes. They visited the farm in the middle of January:

> We went this day and viewed the Houses upon Ellisland lately possessed by Mr Robert Burns, and find that the byre and stable will take ten shillings for thatch and workmanship, the Barn thirteen shillings for thatch and workmanship, the dwellinghouse for Glass six shillings, for sclate and workmanship five shillings. This we give as our opinion to put the House in a tenantable condition.[5]

The late tenant, meanwhile, had installed his wife and three children in Dumfries. As at Ellisland, they were still close to the River Nith, but the surroundings were less picturesque and the accommodation more cramped – they rented three small rooms and a kitchen on the first floor of a tenement building. Cavart's Vennel was one of a number of small alleyways that ran down from

1. *Ibid.*, 473.
2. *Ibid.*, 491.
3. Quoted in P. Hately Waddell, *Life and Work of Robert Burns*, David Wilson, Glasgow, 1867, 2 vols. vol. ii, Appendix, xxi.
4. Chambers-Wallace, vol. iii, p. 296 n.
5. Mackay, *op. cit.*, p. 445.

the High Street to the river; it was known popularly as the Stinking Vennel because of the filth which coursed down it into the Nith.

Burns had brought one cow with him, but there was nowhere for it to graze and it had to be sold. The 'Heaven-taught ploughman' would be plagued by the drudgery of farm work no longer.

Twelve

INCAUTIOUS PLACEMAN

I HAVE NOT TIME to write you at large, but wish much to hear from you, & to know whether I could venture to write you by post without any risk of the letter being read by any body but yourself. – In so many words, I may perhaps have occasion to tell you somewhat & ask a little advice too, which I would not wish even Mrs Cleghorn to see, & I believe the Good Women in general take a freedom to break up or peep into their husband's letters.— This is indeed all a perhaps; but let me hear from you. –[1]

Thus Burns in a letter to his friend Robert Cleghorn shortly before he left Ellisland. Cleghorn, who farmed at Saughton Mills just outside Edinburgh and was a fellow Fencible, was a regular recipient of Burns's less printable compositions; it would be understandable that he should not want the sight of those to bring a blush to Mrs Cleghorn's cheek. The tantalising question is what he wanted advice about. Not about Ellisland or anything connected with farming – by that time the lease had been disposed of and he was making his preparations to move to Dumfries.

It is possible that he wanted to sound out Cleghorn about some business which awaited him in Edinburgh. A letter he received during November indicated its pressing nature:

Sir,
– I take the liberty of addressing a few lines in behalf of your old acquaintance, Jenny Clow, who, to all appearance, is at this moment dying. Obliged, from all the symptoms of a rapid decay, to quit her service, she is gone to a room almost without common necessaries, untended and unmourned. In circumstances so distressing, to whom can she so naturally look for aid as to the father of her child, the man for whose sake she has suffered many a sad and anxious night, shut from the world, with no other companions than guilt and solitude? You have now an opportunity to evince you indeed possess those fine feelings you have delineated, so as to claim the just admiration of

1. Letters, 473.

288

your country. I am convinced I need add nothing farther to persuade you to act as every consideration of humanity as well as gratitude must dictate. I am Sir, your sincere well-wisher,

A.M.

Although Burns was within a few days of setting off for the capital, he sent Mrs McLehose an immediate reply. He did not find it easy, and as the first stiff, fumbling paragraph shows, he did not make a very good job of it:

It is extremely difficult, my dear Madam, for me to deny a lady anything; but to a lady whom I regard with all the endearing epithets of respectful esteem and old friendship, how shall I find the language of refusal? I have, indeed, a shade of the lady, which I keep, and shall ever keep, in the *sanctum sanctorum* of my most anxious care . . .

He has heard, either in a letter from her which is lost, or from someone like Ainslie, that she is planning to visit her husband in the West Indies, and expresses anxiety about the voyage – 'I pray God my fears may be groundless.' Only after this extended process of throat-clearing does he get down to the matter in hand – choosing in doing so, what's more, to persist in the curious device of addressing her indirectly, and affecting to refer to her letter as if it had come from some third party. She has touched a very exposed nerve; he is quite clearly floundering; what is well-nigh incredible is that in his search for appropriate words of concern, he is unable to resist sarcasm:

By the way, I have this moment a letter from her, with a paragraph or two conceived in so stately a style, that I would not pardon it in any created being except herself; but, as the subject interests me so much, I shall answer it to you, as I do not know her present address. I am sure she must have told you of a girl, a Jenny Clow, who had the misfortune to make me a father, with contrition I own it, contrary to the laws of our most excellent constitution, in our holy Presbyterian hierarchy.

Whether this sneering parenthesis was intended to embrace Mrs McLehose as well as the church is not clear. He has at any rate now discerned roughly where he ought to be heading, and he blunders on to a conclusion:

Mrs M— tells me a tale of the poor girl's distress that makes my very heart weep blood. I will trust that your goodness will apologise to your delicacy for me, when I beg of you, for Heaven's sake, to send a porter to the poor woman – Mrs M., it seems, knows where she is to be found – with five shillings in my name; and, as I shall be in Edinburgh on Tuesday first, for certain, make the poor wench leave a line for me, before Tuesday, at Mr Mackay's, White Hart Inn, Grassmarket, where I shall put up; and before I am two hours in town, I shall see the poor girl, and try what is to be done for her relief. I would have taken my boy from her long ago, but she would never consent . . .[1]

Six shillings to repair the shattered windows at Ellisland, five shillings to provide some common necessaries for the dying Jenny Clow. Burns did not have to lay out a great deal more on her, because by January she was dead.

Little is known of what else Burns did during what he airily described to Mrs Dunlop as 'a ten day jaunt into Edin''. He certainly saw Clarinda, and for a short period after his return to Dumfries he wrote to her almost every day – 'My dearest Nancy,' 'my ever dearest of women'. It was quite like old times; although he had not played Sylvander for some years, he was still word-perfect:

. . . By the bye, this is the sixth letter that I have written you, since I left you; & if you were an ordinary being, as you are a creature very extraordinary, an instance of what God Almighty in the plenitude of his power & the fullness of his goodness can make!! I would never forgive you for not answering my letters. –

I have sent in your hair, a part of the parcel you gave me, with a measure, to Mr Bruce the Jeweller in Prince's Street, to get a ring done for me. – I have likewise sent in the verses on Sensibility, altered to –

> Sensibility how charming
> Dearest, Nancy, thou canst tell – &c,

in to the Editor of the Scots Songs, of which you have three volumes, to set to a most beautiful air; out of compliment to the first of women, my ever beloved, my ever sacred Clarinda. –

I shall probably write to you tomorrow. – In the mean time, from a man who is literally drunk, accept and forgive! ! ![2]

The song about sensibility had originally been composed the previous July and sent to Mrs Dunlop. 'Allow me, my dear Friend, to dedicate them to you, as a Relique at the shrine of friendship,' he had written. 'If ever I print it, permit me to prefix your name . . .'[3]

There was however, no question of a recycled dedication to one of the songs he sent to Clarinda two days after Christmas:

> Ae fond kiss, and then we sever;
> Ae fareweel, and then for ever! . . .

There is a song by the English poet, Robert Dodsley, which Burns was probably familiar with ('One fond kiss before we part,/Drop a Tear and bid adieu'), but

1. *Ibid.*, 483.
2. Letters 485. The verses he refers to are Kinsley, 317.
3. Letters, 411.

as so often in his song-making, he works a subtle alchemy on his raw material and makes of it something that is unmistakably his own. It is not the most even of his love lyrics – 'heart-wrung tears' and 'dark despair' suggest momentary surrender to the auto-pilot – but it owes its fame to the four short lines of the fourth stanza:

> Had we never lov'd sae kindly,
> Had we never lov'd sae blindly!
> Never met – or never parted,
> We had ne'er been broken-hearted.[1]

The stanza 'contains the essence of a thousand love tales,' wrote Sir Walter Scott, and the Wizard of Abbotsford knew about such things.

Burns and Mrs McLehose continued to correspond, but they never met again. Early in February 1792 she sailed from Leith for the West Indies in an attempt to be reconciled with her husband. The ship was the *Roselle*, in which Burns was to have gone to Jamaica four long years previously. She dashed off a hurried note to him before embarking, full of exclamation marks and moral injunctions:

And now, my dearest Sir, I have a few things to say to you, as the last advice of her, who could have lived or died with you! I am happy to know of your applying so steadily to the business you have engaged in; but, oh remember, this life is a short, passing scene! Seek God's favour, – keep his Commandments, – be solicitous to prepare for a happy eternity! There, I trust, we will meet, in perfect and never-ending bliss. Read my former letters attentively: let the religious tenets there expressed sink deep into your mind; meditate on them with candour, and your accurate judgement must be convinced that they accord with the words of Eternal Truth! Laugh no more at holy things, or holy men . . .[2]

It was not the sort of advice to which Burns was especially amenable. A letter he wrote at the time to Ainslie indicates that he was not finding it altogether easy to settle into his new style of life in Dumfries:

Can you minister to a mind diseased? Can you, amid the horrors of penitence, regret, remorse, head-ache, nausea, and all the rest of the d—d hounds of hell, that beset a poor wretch, who has been guilty of the sin of drunkenness – can you speak peace to a troubled mind?

Miserable perdu that I am! I have tried every thing that used to amuse me, but in vain . . . My wife scolds me! my business torments me, and my

1. Kinsley, 337.
2. Burns and McLehose, letter LXVII, 25th January 1792.

sins come staring me in the face, every one telling a more bitter tale than his fellow . . .[1]

When Burns wrote that he had tried everything to chase away his black mood, he was not exaggerating. The remedies he had sampled, he informed Ainslie, included singing a particularly crude bawdy song to himself – 'I began *Elibanks and Elibraes*, but the stanzas fell unenjoyed and unfinished from my listless tongue.'[2]

That his wife should scold him is entirely understandable; why, on the other hand, he should write 'my business torments me' is obscure. The patronage of Graham of Fintry was not the only advantage Burns enjoyed in excise matters. He had also secured the sympathetic interest of a man called John Corbet, who was one of the two Supervisors-General of Excise in Edinburgh (this thanks to the indefatigable Mrs Dunlop, who knew his wife), and now, in February 1792, he was able to tell Mrs Dunlop that her intervention looked like paying off:

> . . . As to M[r] Corbet, I have some faint hopes of seeing him here this season: if he come, it will be of essential service to me. – Not that I have any immediate hopes of a Supervisorship; but there is what is called, a Port Division, here, &, entre nous, the present incumbent is so obnoxious, that M[r] C—s presence will in all probability send him adrift into some other Division, & with equal probability will fix me in his stead.[3]

That is precisely what happened. He was formally appointed to the Dumfries First Foot-Walk towards the end of April and took up his new duties early in May. He was now responsible for excise goods at the port, and for the town brewery. He worked hard for the extra £20 in salary which the post brought him. Alexander Findlater's Supervisor's diary for a six-week period in June and July of 1792 is still in existence, and shows that on June 11th he spent the whole day with Burns. In the course of the ten hours or so the men spent together they visited the brewery, eight victuallers, the same number of wine and spirit dealers, three chandlers, a dealer in tea, two tanners and two tawers (tawing is the preparation of white leather).

The Supervisor discovered that his new Port Officer was not yet fully up to speed, and noted one or two irregularities; at one victualler's he had failed to record a reduction in dutiable stock, for instance, and for this he was formally

---

1. Letters, 482.
2. Burns had mentioned the song in the journal of the Border tour he made with Ainslie in 1787: 'Come to Inverleithing a famous Spaw, & in the vicinity of the palace of Traquair . . . saw Elibanks and Elibraes so famous in baudy song today – on the other side of the Tweed.' The song appears in *The Merry Muses of Caledonia.*
3. Letters, 493.

admonished. The two men were good friends – Findlater had been presented with fresh eggs and the occasional impromptu verse during the Ellisland days – but the excise was an admirably professional service, and the requirement to provide an assessment of an officer's performance was not something to be taken lightly: 'Mr Burns had but lately taken charge of this Division,' Findlater wrote, 'and from that cause, and his inexperience in the Brewery branch of business, has fallen into these errors but promises, and I believe will bestow, due attention in future, which indeed he is rarely deficient in.'

Shortly before his transfer, Burns was involved in the capture of a smuggling schooner in the Solway Firth, although the Errol Flynn-like role assigned to him by Lockhart is unhistorical. The action was spread out over several days at the end of February. The operation was conducted by the excise riding officer for Dumfries collection, one Walter Crawford. He had been recruited only a month previously from the South Fencibles in Edinburgh. Based in Annan, it was his business to patrol the coast between Dumfries and Gretna, getting to know what he could about the routes favoured by the smugglers and gleaning intelligence about proposed runs.

Crawford recorded in his journal that he was initially outnumbered. He and one other officer, supported by a party of thirteen dragoons, made a first attempt to board the vessel, which was lying in shallow water, but they were armed only with pistols and withdrew when the crew threatened to open fire. Rather oddly, Crawford was then allowed to go on board, and established that there were twenty-four men under arms and that each had fifteen rounds of shot. He sent both to Dumfries and Ecclefechan for reinforcements, and by nine o'clock the next morning he was able to muster a force of forty-four dragoons, 'fully accoutered and on horse-back'.

By this time, however, the schooner had slipped a mile or so down the firth. There was a heavy current running, and Crawford judged it impossible to get at the vessel either on foot or on horseback. When they started a search for boats, they quickly discovered that the locals on this smuggling coast were one step ahead of them and had stove them all in, 'the vessel in the mean time keeping up a fire of grape shott and musquetry'.

There were quicksands, and that ruled out the use of horses: there was nothing for it but to make an attempt on foot. Crawford drew up the military in three divisions, aiming to attack the vessel fore and aft and broadside. The first party was commanded by a quartermaster of dragoons, the second by Crawford himself, the third by Burns:

> Our orders to the Millitary were to reserve there fire till within eight yards of the vessel, then to pour a volley and board her with sword & Pistol. The vessel keept on firing thou without any damage to us, as from the situation of the ship they could not bring their great guns to bear on us, we in the mean time wading breast high, and in Justice to the party under my Command I must say with great alacrity; by the time we were within one hundred yards

of the vessel the Crew gave up the cause, gott over side towards England which shore was for a long way dry sand.

Before hot-footing it to the safety of the English shore, carrying with them most of what was movable, the smugglers loosed off a six-pounder carronade through the hull of the vessel.

> The deil cam fiddlin thro' the town,   devil
> And danc'd awa wi' th' Exciseman,
> And ilka wife cries, auld Mahoun,   every   the devil
> I wish you luck o' the prize, man![1]

Although it was the occasion of one of Burns's liveliest songs, the encounter was no more remarkable than a hundred others along that smuggler-infested coast. There are those, however, who believe it had a sequel of some significance. In addition to Crawford's journal two other documents survive relating to the capture of this particular schooner (she turned out to be the *Rosamond*, of Plymouth, master Alexander Patty). The first, mainly in Burns's hand, records the detail of the expenditure incurred in guarding the vessel, refloating it and having it repaired (this was done on the Nith estuary at Kelton). He recorded the cost of maintaining the fishermen, carpenters and dragoons involved (and 'one & often two Excise offrs. aboard') as £17 10s.

The second is an inventory of the ship and her 'furniture'. This was prepared by Burns's Dumfries fellow-officer John Lewars, and lists fifty-three items. The sale was advertised in newspapers in Dumfries, Whitehaven and Edinburgh, and took place in the Coffee House, Dumfries, in the middle of April. It realised a sum of £166 16s 6d. The expenses of preparation came to £45 15s 4d. This left a sum of £121 1s 2d, of which half went to the Crown.

One of the weightiest items in the inventory – it tipped the scale at 33cwt, which is 1,680 kilos – consisted of four four-pounder carronade guns, complete with carriages and a certain amount of grape shot. They were sold at half a crown a hundredweight. Every Scottish schoolboy knows that they were bought by Burns and despatched as a gesture of admiration and solidarity to the French Convention – but there are those who believe that every Scottish schoolboy has been misinformed.

When Lockhart first recounted the *Rosamond* story in 1828 he had at his disposal certain documentary evidence supplied to him by his father-in-law. Scott's source was his friend Joseph Train, a keen antiquarian, and himself a member of the excise, who had in turn acquired the documents in question from Lewars's widow.[2] By Train's account, this material included, in addition

---

1. Kinsley, 386.
2. Train was Supervisor of Excise at Castle Douglas and later at Dumfries, where he succeeded Lewars in 1825.

to the three items mentioned above, a copy of the sale catalogue and a journal belonging to Lewars. The catalogue carried a note in Burns's hand recording his purchase of the carronades, the journal contained some details of the transaction.

This was all of intense interest to the author of *The Antiquary*. Train told a correspondent (a Dr Robert Carruthers of Inverness) that Scott had spent some time trying to test the accuracy of the story by scanning French newspaper files. Failing to find any confirmation of the receipt of the guns in Paris, he approached the Custom House authorities in London, who searched the files and told him that the guns had been seized at Dover.

Allan Cunningham questioned the Lockhart version as early as 1834, and a century later opinion had hardened still further against him: 'The whole thing,' wrote the gentle and dispassionate Snyder, 'would do full justice to Gilbert and Sullivan.' Lockhart did rather ask for it. The role he assigned to Burns had a decided whiff of Hollywood about it, and he was also not above pressing the fast-forward button for dramatic effect – in his account, for instance, the *Rosamond* was sold by auction on the day after the encounter. Worst of all, for some, was that he had Burns offering a gift to the French Convention several months before that body had been called into existence.[1]

Train's involvement also excited suspicion. Lockhart, in the *Life*, described him as 'able and amiable' and said that his services to Scott had been 'of high importance to him . . . in the prosecution of his literary labours'.[2] That was undoubtedly so, but his main usefulness to Scott had been as a supplier of ballads and old tales from that misty region where the boundary between tradition and legend can be fluid. Customs records, on the other hand, were meticulously kept; it was the practice to copy all correspondence, incoming and outgoing, into a bound letter book; a search of the Dover files has not produced evidence of an enquiry from Scott. That the *Rosamond* episode is nowhere mentioned in Burns's correspondence is not conclusive evidence that it did not happen; what seemed to many to nail the coffin of Lockhart's credibility firmly shut was that since his day not a soul seemed to have clapped eyes on any of the documents on which he had based his account.

Then, in 1934, two years after Snyder had sternly called for the *Rosamond* affair to be 'absolutely deleted from any account of Burns's life,' a great quantity of unsorted papers was transferred from Abbotsford to the National Library of Scotland. Among them were discovered Crawford's journal, Lewars's inventory of the sale and, on the back of two blank excise receipt forms, Burns's account of the cost involved in making the vessel ready for auction. The find did not completely put Lockhart together again – Lewars's journal and the sale catalogue were not in the Abbotsford haul and have still not surfaced, which means that the carronade part of the story remains unauthenticated.

1. The first meeting of the Convention was on 21st September 1792.
2. Lockhart, *Life*, vol. iii, p. 306.

Exaggeration is a less serious offence than fabrication, however. Crawford's journal demonstrated that Lockhart had some of his father-in-law's instinct for a good story, but it was no longer reasonable to dismiss the carronade chapter as a fiction. *Non è vero* had at the very least been softened to *ben trovato*.

'Everything rung, and was connected with the Revolution in France,' wrote Henry Cockburn; 'which, for above 20 years, was, or was made, the all in all. Everything, not this or that thing, but literally everything, was soaked in this one event.'[1] It had initially been regarded with general benevolence. The British political class was certainly not opposed to anything which did an injury to the House of Bourbon; when Burke published his *Reflections on the Revolution in France* in 1790 he was at first dismissed as somewhat hysterical. The intoxicating simplicities of Tom Paine's *Rights of Man*, (the first part had been published in 1791) were infinitely more popular – particularly in Scotland; cheap abridgements were on sale at twopence, and it appears even to have penetrated the Highlands in a rough Gaelic translation.[2]

Paris became for a time the lodestar of progressive aspiration. One Scottish visitor was Thomas Christie, son of the Provost of Montrose and editor of the *Analytical Review*; the National Assembly requested him to translate the French Constitution into English. Another was Professor John Anderson, of the University of Glasgow. 'Jolly Jack Phosphorus' to his students, Anderson was a versatile man who had held the chairs both of Oriental Languages and Natural Philosophy. He had also invented a shock-absorbing gun-carriage. When the British government showed no interest in it, he took it to France; a model was hung in the Hall of the Convention, and the inscription read, 'The gift of science to liberty.'[3]

In Scotland, as in England, dinners were held annually to commemorate the fall of the Bastille. At one in Glasgow in 1791 the toasts had included one to 'The standing army of France who, in the duties of soldiers, lost not the feelings of citizens'; guests were also invited to raise their glasses to 'May every civil government be founded on the natural rights of man'.[4] Henry Dundas, now Home Secretary, received lists of the names of those who celebrated Bastille Day in this fashion from the Lord Provost of Edinburgh.

A similar dinner, organised on the same day by the Constitutional Society of Birmingham, had ended badly for Joseph Priestley, the chemist and nonconformist minister. Priestley, a foreign associate of the French Academy of Sciences, was known to sympathise with the Revolution. A mob took advantage of the occasion to burn down his chapel and sack his house, destroying his

1. Cockburn, *op. cit.*, p. 80.
2. P.A Brown, *The French Revolution in English History*, ed. J.L. Hammond, C. Lockwood & Son, London, 1918, p. 90.
3. J.G. Alger, *Englishmen in the French Revolution*, Sampson, Low & Co., London, 1889, p. 52.
4. *Edinburgh Herald*, 18th July 1791.

possessions and the work of many years. From then on, 'King and Church' mobs were not discouraged from demonstrating to dissenters and radicals the error of their ways.

North of the border, reformers and conservatives glowered at each other with particular bitterness. There had been a rapid growth in the number of newspapers. In 1782, there had been only eight in the whole of Scotland. By 1790 there were 27, most of them lining up on one side or the other of the political divide – after 1792 the government made payments to some of those who toed the party line. There had also been an increase in the number of debating societies and political associations, and by the early 1790s conservative opinion was beginning to learn from the radicals and organise accordingly. An important model was the London Corresponding Society, which had been founded by a Scottish shoemaker called Thomas Hardy.

It was against such a background that Burns, in the spring of 1792, despatched his putative thirty-three hundredweight of gun-metal to France. It would not have been an isolated gesture. In the west of Scotland support for the revolution was especially strong. In January, the *Glasgow Mercury* reported that a fund had been opened in the city 'to aid the French in carrying on the war against the emigrant princes or any foreign power by whom they may be attacked'. A sum of £1,200 had already been subscribed. The foreign powers in question were the German principalities and the Austrian Empire, to which the majority of French émigrés had fled – the emperor, after all, was Marie Antoinette's brother.

The sale of the *Rosamond* had taken place on April 19th. The following day, on the proposal of Louis XVI, the French Assembly voted to declare war on the 'king of Bohemia and Hungary' (who happened also to be the Emperor of Austria – the Assembly hoped by this form of words to avoid the involvement of Prussia and the Empire). The first engagements, near Lille, went badly for the French. They could certainly have found a use for Burns's four-pounders.

Mrs Dunlop continued to follow all Burns's activities with the closest attention. She too, she told him playfully, occasionally went in for hunting smugglers, but to no great effect, 'for I have never been able to obtain intelligence of one pint of brandy, spite of all my assiduity'.[1] That was something Burns could easily remedy. A Port Division did not only mean an extra twenty pounds a year; it also brought in 'as much rum & brandy as will easily supply an ordinary family'. So far as smugglers were concerned, he had, he announced with a flourish, 'hunted these Gentry' to better purpose than she had: 'as a servant of my brother's goes from here to Mauchline tomorrow morning, I beg leave to send you by him a very small jar, sealed full of as genuine Nantz as ever I tasted . . .'[2]

1. Letter dated 25th January 1792, Burns and Dunlop, pp. 338–43.
2. Letters, 493.

'Nantz' was so called because much of it came from Nantes, on the Loire. It is not clear how Burns came by the brandy. Smuggled goods were generally either destroyed or sold off. There was no rule against officers bidding at auction, but they were not allowed to retain contraband as a perquisite, and the handling of smuggled goods could result in dismissal. Possibly the rule was sometimes honoured in the breach.

Mrs Dunlop, uncharacteristically, did not acknowledge this gift of 'hippocrene' until mid-April. Burns, for his part, did not write again for many months. There was a new woman in his life: 'I sit down, my dear Sir, to introduce a young lady to you, & a lady in the first ranks of fashion,' he announced to his Edinburgh printer, Smellie:

> What a task! You, who care no more for the herd of animals called, "Young Ladies," than for the herd of animals called – "Young Gentlemen" . . . M[rs] Riddel who takes this letter to town with her, is a Character that even in your own way, as a Naturalist & a Philosopher, would be an acquisition to your acquaintance. – The Lady too, is a votary of the Muses; and as I think I am somewhat of a judge in my own trade, I assure you that her verses, always correct, & often elegant, are very much beyond the common run of the Lady Poetesses of the day . . .[1]

Maria Riddell was the sister-in-law of Riddell of Friars' Carse, a young married woman who had recently given birth to her first child. (Burns described her to Smellie as 'a lively West-Indian girl of eighteen,' but she was in fact almost twenty.) She had spent two years in the West Indies, where her father had been Governor and Captain-General of St Kitts and the Leeward Islands. There she had met Walter Riddell, a widower eight years her senior with an estate in Antigua. They were married in 1790 and returned to London shortly afterwards. Early in 1792 Riddell bought the estate of Goldilea, near Dumfries. Maria's maiden name was Woodley, and the property was renamed Woodley Park in her honour.

'She is a great admirer of your Book,' Burns told Smellie (he had brought out the first volume of *The Philosophy of Natural History* two years previously):

> To be impartial, however, the Lady has one unlucky failing; a failing which you will easily discover, as she seems rather pleased with indulging it; & a failing which you will as easily pardon, as it is a sin that very much besets yourself: – where she dislikes, or despises, she is apt to make no more a secret of it – than where she esteems & respects. –

Before setting out for Edinburgh the Riddells made up a party to visit Wanlockhead. An outing in February to the highest village in Scotland (Wanlockhead

1. *Ibid.*, 492.

lies at 1370 ft) is not everybody's idea of fun. The attraction was the old mine workings there – they had produced not only lead, but also silver and gold, including that used in the crown of James V and his queen. Maria prevailed upon her sister- and brother-in-law to go with them. Burns went too, a tribute either to her charm or her powers of persuasion; he was not an early riser and on that morning they rode off from Friars' Carse two hours before dawn, breakfasted at Sanquhar and continued from there in a chaise.

'The interesting remarks and fascinating conversation of our friend Burns, not only beguiled the tediousness of the road,' Maria wrote, 'but likewise made us forget its danger.' If the road was tedious, the mine workings were downright disagreeable. Holding tapers, they had to make their way bent almost double; water dripped continually from the roof, and they waded through muddy water that came half-way up their legs. The pit props were slimy; Maria held onto the walls for support and her gloves were soon in ribbons. After about a mile of this they, or at least Burns, had had enough:

> The damp and confined air affected our fellow adventurer Burns so much, that we resolved to turn back, after I had satisfied my curiosity by going down one of the shafts. This you will say was a crazy scheme – assailing the Gnomes in their subterranean abodes! Indeed there has never been but *one* instance of a *female* hazarding herself thither.[1]

It was also Mrs Riddell's first visit to Edinburgh. What she wanted was Smellie's advice about a literary project. She had kept a diary during her time in the West Indies and done some sketching, and now she wanted to turn them into a privately-printed book. Smellie was bowled over, both by Maria and by her manuscript:

> When I considered your youth, and still more, your sex, the perusal of your ingenious and judicious work, if I had not previously had the pleasure of your conversation, the devil himself could not have frightened me into the belief that a female human creature could, in the bloom of youth, beauty and, consequently, of giddiness, have produced a performance so much out of the line of your ladies' works. Smart little poems, flippant romances, are not uncommon. But science, minute observation, accurate description and excellent composition are qualities seldom to be met with in the female world.[2]

The first letter that we have from Burns to Mrs Riddell dates from February, 1792, shortly after her return from Edinburgh. He addresses her as 'My

---

1. Angus McNaghten, *Burns's Mrs Riddell*, Volturna, Peterhead, 1975, pp. 30-32.
2. The correspondence between Mrs Riddell and Smellie is to be found in Robert Kerr, *Memoirs of the Life, Writings and Correspondence of William Smellie*, 2 vols., Edinburgh, 1811.

Dearest Friend'. The tone – unusual for him when addressing a woman – is a mixture of the sober, the affectionate, the respectful and the solicitous. She has fallen ill, and he is concerned for her: 'God grant that now when your health is reestablished, you may take a little, little more care of a life so truly valuable to society and so truly invaluable to your friends!' She had written to him from Edinburgh. The letter does not survive, but he refers to it in a way which suggests that she may have undertaken some commission concerning his daughter by Ann Park – 'I shall answer it in its own way sometime next week; as also settle all matters as to little Miss. Your goodness there is just like your kindness in everything else.' He also expresses his concern for her own six-month-old daughter:

Apropos has little Mademoiselle been inoculated with the Small-pox yet? If not let it be done as soon as it is proper for her habit of body, teeth, &c.

Once more, let me congratulate you on your returning health. God grant that you may live at least while I live, for were I to lose you it would leave a Vacuum in my enjoyments that nothing could fill up.[1]

Burns now became a frequent visitor at Woodley Park. There was a fine library there, with foreign as well as English books, but that was plainly not the principal attraction.

Dumfries brought him other new friends. John Syme, who enjoyed the sinecure of Distributor of Stamps for Dumfries and Galloway, lived at Ryedale, a house on the Kirkcudbrightshire side of the Nith, but had his office directly below the Burns apartment in the Stinking Vennel. Syme, four years older than the poet, was the son of a local laird. He had practised as a Writer to the Signet in Edinburgh, served for a time as an ensign in the 72nd Regiment and then retired to run his father's estate at Barncailzie in Kirkcudbrightshire. The family was hard hit by the failure of the Ayr Bank, and they had to sell up. Syme had come to Dumfries in 1791. He found life in the town dull; he and Burns were soon close friends, and the poet frequently submitted his verses to him for his judgement.

Long after Burns was dead, Syme gave an account of his appearance and manner in those Dumfries years:

The poet's expression varied perpetually, according to the idea that predominated in his mind; and it was beautiful to remark how well the play of his lips indicated the sentiment he was about to utter. His eyes and lips – the first remarkable for fire, and the second for flexibility – formed at all times an index to his mind, and, as sunshine or shade predominated, you might have told, *a priori*, whether the company was to be favoured with a scintillation of wit, or a sentiment of benevolence, or a burst of fiery indignation . . .

1. Letters, 497.

Robert Chambers, who had a conversation with Syme in 1826, remembered him as 'essentially a Scottish gentleman of "the old school" – a well-bred *bon-vivant*, with a rich fund of anecdote':

> He expatiated on the electric flashes of the poet's eloquence at table, and on the burning satiric shafts which he was accustomed to launch at those whom he disliked or who betrayed any affectation or meanness in their behaviour. I particularly remember the old gentleman glowing over the discomfiture of a too considerate Amphitryon, who, when entertaining himself, Burns, and some others, lingered with screw in hand over a fresh bottle of claret, which he evidently wished to be forbidden to draw – till Burns transfixed him by a comparison of his present position with that of Abraham lingering over the filial sacrifice.[1]

Dumfries in Burns's day was a small county town with a population of between five and six thousand. It had been made a royal burgh by William the Lion in 1186, and could claim a respectable share in the bloody history of the nation. It was in the chapel of the Minorite Convent there, in 1305, that a quarrel broke out between Robert the Bruce and Comyn, the representative of Balliol, the rival claimant to the crown. Bruce stabbed him, and rushed out, saying, 'I doubt I have slain the Comyn.' One of his supporters was Roger Kirkpatrick, a man with a properly Scottish disinclination to leave anything to chance. 'I'll mak siccar,' he announced dourly, and marching into the building, finished the Comyn off.

Dumfries had been sacked or burned by the English in 1448, 1536 and 1570. When the Young Pretender was retreating north in 1745 he established his headquarters in the Blue Bell Inn. In Burns's day the town boasted a hospital, a poorhouse, several boarding schools for the education of young ladies, a weekly newspaper, two libraries and branches of three Scottish banks. There were regular horse and cattle fairs, and daily mail coaches to and from London, Edinburgh and Port Patrick. The Nith was navigable to within a few miles of the town, and something like two hundred small vessels came and went each year, plying a coastal trade and importing coal, potatoes, wine and tobacco.

Burns went to live there in the year the census was made for Sinclair's *Statistical Account*. There were seven Incorporated Trades, of which the Shoemakers, with two hundred and thirty-six Guild members, were the most numerous. Carpenters and Joiners (Squaremen) came next, with two hundred and twenty, followed by the Tailors with eighty-five. There were seventy Hammermen, fifty-nine Weavers, thirty-three Fleshers and twenty-three Skinners and Glovers. The needs of the town were also served by thirty stocking-weavers,

---

1. Chambers-Wallace, vol. iv, pp. 217-8.

fifty gardeners and thirty lawyers. The town's one physician, three surgeons and four apothecaries all did good business – 'consumptions and rheumatisms are frequent here,' the *Account* acknowledged. In summer the weather could be humid and oppressive; Dumfries is low-lying, and in the late eighteenth century was still surrounded by extensive tracts of undrained marshland.

The burgh was prosperous, and not a little stagnant. 'Like most small towns of its type,' wrote Chambers, 'it was cursed rather than blessed by the partial or entire idleness of large classes of its inhabitants – men living in retirement on competencies, well-to-do professional men, and tradesmen whose professional duties did not occupy much of their time.'[1] In his contribution to the *Statistical Account*, Dr William Burnside, the minister of the Second or New Church, saw his flock in a kindlier light:

> In their private manners they are social and polite; and the town, together with the neighbourhood a few miles around it, furnishes a society among whom a person with a moderate income may spend his days with as much enjoyment, perhaps, as in any part of the kingdom whatever.

Dr Burnside was also quietly proud of what he described as the 'Gaierties' of the town: 'During our Circuits in Spring and Autumn the Assembly rooms will often exhibit 150 or 200 people as genteel and fashionable as are to be seen in any provincial town anywhere.' Those 'Gaierties' were enhanced when the Revolutionary Wars brought military garrisons to the town.

The town was well supplied with watering holes – there were three large inns, several taverns and a coffee house; seventy-five smaller premises were licensed for the sale of liquor and there were twenty or so prosecutions each year for selling it illegally. One of the taverns, the Coach and Horses, was next door to Burns's apartment in Cavart's Vennel; upstairs a woman called Margaret Hog kept a brothel, and Burns reworked a traditional bawdy song in her honour:

> Amang our young lassies there's Muirland Meg,
> She'll beg or she work, and she'll play or she beg,   before
> At thretteen her maidenhead flew to the gate,   thirteen
> And the door o' her cage stands open yet. –[2]

Burns was methodical in the interest he took in collecting and adding to bawdy folk songs. He kept them in a special notebook, which he sometimes lent out. One friend thus favoured in the late winter of 1792 was John McMurdo, who, as his father had been before him, was chamberlain to the Duke of Queensberry at Drumlanrig Castle:

1. *Ibid*., vol. iii, p. 298.
2. Kinsley, 608.

I think I once mentioned something to you of a Collection of Scots songs I have for some years been making: I send you a perusal of what I have gathered. – I could not conveniently spare them above five or six days, & five or six glances of them will probably more than suffice you ... There is not another copy of the Collection in the world, & I should be sorry that any unfortunate negligence should deprive me of what has cost me a good deal of pains. –[1]

So far as Burns's printable work was concerned, there had over the past months been some rather inconclusive discussion about a new edition. The thoughts he entertained about his old publisher were still far from cordial. 'By the way, I have taken a damned revenge of Creech,' he had written to Peter Hill the previous autumn:

He wrote me a fine, fair letter, telling me that he was going to print a third Edition; & as he had a brother's care of my fame, he wished to add every new thing I have written since, & I should be amply rewarded with – a copy or two to present to my friends! He has sent me a copy of the last Ed^n to correct, &c. – but I have as yet taken no notice of it; & I hear he has published without me ...[2]

It was Burns at his most foolish; a striking example of his ability to stand in his own light. He was mistaken, as it happens – Creech had published nothing, but he must have renewed his proposition, and by the time Burns got round to apologising for his 'criminal indolence' as a correspondent in the middle of April, he had changed his tune:

... Now, to try a language of which I am not half master, I shall assume as well as I can, the man of business. – I suppose, at a gross guess, that I could add of new materials to your two volumes, about fifty pages. – I would also correct & retrench a good deal ... A few Books which I very much want, are all the recompence I crave, together with as many copies of this new edition of my own works as Friendship or Gratitude shall prompt me to *present* ...[3]

He was busy throughout the summer correcting proofs, both of his own poems and of the fourth volume of the *Museum*. There was a certain stop–go quality to work on the musical side of the latter. Stephen Clarke could be every bit as indolent as Burns himself, and Burns sometimes had to chivvy him. During the summer of 1792 he undertook to get him to spend some time at Drumlanrig

1. Letters, 499A.
2. Letters, 475.
3. *Ibid.*, 502.

to give singing lessons to two of McMurdo's daughters. When Clarke failed to respond, Burns felt that a less direct approach was called for:

Mr Burns begs leave to present his most respectful Compl^{nts} to Mr Clarke – M^r B— some time ago did himself the honor of writing M^r C— respecting coming out to the country to give a little Musical instruction in a highly respectable family where M^r C— may have his own terms, & may be as happy as Indolence, the Devil, & the Gout will permit him . . . M^r B– is deeply impressed with, and awefully conscious of, the high importance of M^r C–'s time, whether in the winged moments of symphonious exhibition at the keys of Harmony, while listening Seraphs cease their own less delightful strains; – or in the drowsy hours of slumbrous repose, in the arms of his dearly beloved elbow-chair . . . but half a line conveying half a meaning from M^r C– would make M^r B the very happiest of mortals. –[1]

The Misses McMurdo got their lessons.

The new edition of his poems was delayed until the following year, but Volume IV of the *Museum* appeared in August. Burns once again wrote the Preface, and he once again indicated to his readers that they must take it as they found it:

All our Songs cannot have equal merit. Besides, as the world have not yet agreed on any unerring balance, any undisputed standard, in matters of Taste, what to one person yields no manner of pleasure, may to another be a high enjoyment.

Something like two-thirds of the pieces in the new volume were by Burns. There was once again a sprinkling of Jacobite songs – 'Frae the friends and Land I love', 'Cock up your Beaver', and 'Bonie laddie, Highland laddie'[2]; Burns also included (though he prudently left it unsigned) 'Such a parcel of rogues in a nation',[3] a powerful assault on the thirty-one Parliamentary Commissioners who took Scotland into the Union in 1707:

> Fareweel to a' our Scotish fame,
>   Fareweel our ancient glory;
> Fareweel even to the Scotish name,
>   Sae fam'd in martial story! . . .

1. *Ibid.*, 504.
2. Kinsley 341, 344 and 353 respectively.
3. *Ibid.*, 375.

> The English steel we could disdain,
>> Secure in valor's station;
> But English gold has been our bane,
>> Such a parcel of rogues in a nation!

There were some notable love lyrics: 'The lea-rig',[1] 'Craigieburn-wood',[2] 'The Posie', for which he took down the air from his wife's singing ('O luve will venture in where it daur na weel be seen,/O luve will venture in where wisdom ance has been . . .')[3] and a revision of an old song which Burns set to the Gaelic air *Rinn m'eudial mo mhealladh*:

> As I was a wand'ring ae midsummer e'enin,   evening
>> The pipers and youngsters were makin their game,
> Amang them I spyed my faithless fause luver,   false
>> Which bled a' the wounds o' my dolour again. –[4]

There was humour and no lack of earthy realism, as in 'What can a young lassie do wi' an auld man.' There is nothing novel in either the young woman's situation or the sentiments she expresses about it, but Burns puts his own vigorous stamp on both:

> He's always compleenin frae mornin till e'enin,
>> He hosts and he hirpls the weary day lang: coughs, hobbles
> He's doyl't and he's dozin, his blude it is frozen,   confused
>> O, dreary's the night wi' a crazy auld man![5]

Another familiar theme, in 'Kellyburnbraes', is that of the wife who is such a harpie that not even the devil can do anything with her:

> The d–v–l he swore by the kirk and the bell,
>> Hey and the rue grows bonie wi' thyme;
> He was not in wedlock, thank Heaven, but in h–,
>> And the thyme it is wither'd and rue is in prime . . .[6]

One of the more unusual songs in the fourth volume of the *Museum* is one Burns set to the tune 'The Slave's Lament':

1. *Ibid.*, 392.
2. *Ibid.*, 340.
3. *Ibid.*, 372. Burns told Thomson a couple of years later that the tune was well known in the West of Scotland, adding matter-of-factly, 'but the old words are trash'. (Letters, 644.)
4. Kinsley, 359.
5. *Ibid.*, 347.
6. *Ibid.*, 376.

It was in sweet Senegal that my foes did me enthrall
   For the land of Virginia-ginia O;
Torn from that lovely shore, and must never see it more,
   And alas! I am weary, weary O![1]

The abolition of slavery was one of the big issues of the day. The columns of the newspapers bristled with notices announcing the holding of meetings and the passing of resolutions. In the space of a few weeks early in 1792, for instance, an attentive reader of the *Edinburgh Mercury* would have become familiar with the views of the Incorporation of Bakers of Canongate, the nine Incorporated Trades of Paisley, the farmers and tradesmen of the parish of Kirkliston and the Gaelic Congregation of Edinburgh. (Their views, as it happens, were indistinguishable. They were unanimous that the trade was 'cruel, inexpedient, contrary to the laws of God, and subversive of the rights of man'.) Henry Erskine took the chair at a public meeting to consider the presentation of a petition to Parliament, and the theatre-goers of the capital were offered 'A Grand, Serious PANTOMIMIC BALLET, called THE AFRICAN SLAVES! OR FREEDOM'S CAUSE.' Patrons were promised 'Several Real and Striking SCENES, Particularly the Mode of Enslaving and Selling these unhappy People.'[2]

The burden I must bear, while the cruel scourge I fear,
   In the lands of Virginia-ginia O;
And I think on friends most dear with the bitter, bitter tear,
   And alas! I am weary, weary O!

Burns's song is a sentimental ballad of no great poetic merit, but its inclusion is an interesting reflection of the political mood of the day.

There is some evidence that Burns was drinking a good deal during the spring and summer of 1792. 'I am just now devilish drunk,' he had written to Cunningham in April. 'If you doubt it, ask a Mr Campbell, whom I have just met with by lucky accident.'[3] To the testimony of Mr Campbell might be added the tone – and the syntax – of several of his letters, some of which are notable more for their exuberance than their coherence. Early in September he wrote to Cunningham again, apologising on this occasion not only for a long silence, but for his rudeness in not acknowledging the honour done to him several months previously by his admission to the Royal Company of Archers, the

---

1. *Ibid.*, 378.
2. *Caledonian Mercury*, 5 March 1792.
3. Letters, 502A.

sovereign's ceremonial bodyguard in Scotland. He had meant to, of course, and in rhyme . . .

> . . . Well then, here is to your good health! for you must know, I have set a nipperkin of TODDY by me, just by way of SPELL to keep away the meikle horned Deil, or any of his subaltern Imps who may be on their nightly rounds . . .

He confesses himself 'quite jaded in the attempt to share half an idea among half a hundred words,' but he rambles on for four quarto pages, treating Cunningham to an extended anatomy of Nonsense: 'Nonsense, auspicious name! – Tutor, Friend & Finger-post in the mystic mazes of Law; the cadaverous paths of Physic; & particularly in the sightless soarings of SCHOOL DIVINITY.' By now the toddy is really doing its work. Of all nonsense, he asserts, religious nonsense is the most nonsensical:

> Only, by the bye, will you, or can you tell me, my dear Cunningham, why a religioso turn of mind has always a tendency to narrow & illiberalize the heart? They are orderly; they may be just; nay, I have known them merciful: but still your children of Sanctity move among their fellow-creatures with a nostril snuffing putrescence, & a foot spurning filth, in short with that conceited dignity which your titled Douglases, Hamiltons, Gordons or any other of your Scots Lordlings of seven centuries standing, display when they accidentally mix among the many-aproned Sons of Mechanical life. – I remember, in my Plough-boy days, I could not conceive it possible that a noble Lord could be a Fool, or that a godly Man could be a Knave. – How ignorant are Plough-boys! – Nay, I have since discovered that a *godly woman* may be a —! – But hold – Here's t'ye again – this Rum is damn'd generous Antigua, so a very unfit menstruum for scandal. –

It is impossible to judge whether any very precise meaning attaches to these last few savage and appalling words. He sounds very drunk. He had not known all that many godly women. Clarinda, 'the first of all God's works,' a whore? Or did the 'generous Antigua' make him rail against her because she had refused to behave like one?

The letter offers a good example of the extreme volatility which was one of Burns's most pronounced characteristics. From one paragraph to the next there is a lightning change; Swiftian bile is replaced by a mood of sunny playfulness. 'I am a Husband of older standing than you, & I shall give you *my* ideas of the Conjugal State,' he announces to his friend:

> The scale of Good-wife-ship I divide into ten parts. – Good-Nature, four; Good-Sense, two; Wit, one; Personal Charms, viz. a sweet face, eloquent eyes, fine limbs, graceful carriage, (I would add a fine waist too, but that is

so soon spoilt you know) all these, one: as for the other qualities belonging to, or attending on, a Wife, such as, fortune, connections, education, (I mean education extraordinary) family-blood, &c. divide the two remaining degrees among them as you please; only, remember that all these minor properties must be expressed by *fractions*; for there is not any one of them, in the aforesaid scale, entitled to the dignity of an *integer*. –[1]

The autumn of 1792 saw the beginning of a second important collaboration for Burns. Early in September there came from Edinburgh a letter which interested him greatly. The writer, one George Thomson, announced that for some years past he and one or two friends had employed their leisure hours in collating and collecting 'the most famous of our national melodies' with a view to publication. They had engaged Pleyel (whom he described as 'the most agreeable composer living'[2]) to compose accompaniments and instrumental preludes and conclusions:

> To render this work perfect, we are desirous to have the poetry improved wherever it seems unworthy of the music; and that it is so, in many instances, is allowed by every one conversant with our musical collections. The editors of these seem in general to have depended on the music proving an excuse for the verses; and hence some charming melodies are united to mere nonsense and doggerel, while others are accommodated with rhymes so loose and indelicate as cannot be sung in decent company. To remove this reproach would be an easy task to the author of 'The Cotter's Saturday Night'; and, for the honour of Caledonia, I would fain hope that he may be induced to take up the pen.[3]

Thomson seems not to have realised that by writing in such terms he was running a certain risk. The author of 'The Cotter' was certainly all for the honour of Caledonia, but he was also the editor in all but name of the *Scots Musical Museum* – was this one of the publications in which Thomson and his friends found charming melodies 'united to mere nonsense and doggerel'? If Burns detected any such reflection, he was content to let it pass; he may well also have savoured the irony of an invitation to deck out traditional indelicacies

---

1. *Ibid.*, 506.
2. Ignaz Pleyel, the twenty-fourth child of a village schoolmaster in Lower Austria, was a pupil of Haydn's. In 1791, when he was Kapellmeister at the Cathedral in Strasbourg, he was invited to London to run the following season's Professional Concerts. On his return to France he was denounced as an enemy of the Republic and was forced for a time into exile. He eventually returned to Paris and established himself successfully as a music seller and pianoforte maker.
3. Chambers-Wallace, vol. iii, p. 330. The friends Thomson mentions as being involved in the enterprise with him included the Hon. Andrew Erskine, who was the brother of the Earl of Kellie. Erskine was an eccentric character who had served as a captain in the old 71st and was a friend of Boswell's. His involvement did not last long. He incurred heavy gambling debts, and the following year drowned himself in the Firth of Forth.

in more respectable attire. He appears at all events to have been flattered, and he accepted with alacrity:

> I have just this moment got your letter. – As the request you make to me will positively add to my enjoyments in complying with it, I shall enter into your undertaking with all the small portion of abilities I have, strained to their utmost exertion by the impulse of Enthusiasm. – Only, do n't hurry me: "Deil tak the hindmost" is by no means the Crie de guerre of my Muse . . . Àpropos, if you are for *English* verses, there is, on my part, an end of the matter. – Whether in the simplicity of *the Ballad*, or the pathos of *the Song*, I can only hope to please myself in being allowed at least a sprinkling of our native tongue. –

Thomson had said that they would reward his assistance by paying 'any reasonable price you shall please to demand for it,' a suggestion which Burns dismissed with a characteristic blend of the lofty and the forthright:

> As to any remuneration, you may think my Songs either *above*, or *below* price; for they shall absolutely be the one or the other.—In the honest enthusiasm with which I embark on your undertaking, to talk of money, wages, fee, hire, &c. would be downright Sodomy of Soul![1]

Years later, when he sent the letter to Currie for his biography, Thomson still winced at the phrase: 'I presume Dr C— will think it right to substitute some other word for *Sodomy*,' he wrote. He presumed correctly: Currie substituted 'prostitution.'

About Burns's attitude to remuneration there can be more than one view. For some it is proof of an almost saintly lack of commercial acumen, for others merely evidence of plain silliness. Donald Low has offered a startlingly graphic comparison. When the poet Tom Moore began to work on Irish Melodies for Sir John Stevenson in 1807, he was paid a hundred guineas for a song. By the time publication ceased in 1834, he had received a total of £12,810.[2]

George Thomson, two years older than Burns, was a schoolmaster's son. He had trained as a lawyer's clerk but was now employed by the grandly named Board of Trustees for the Encouragement of Art and Manufacture in Scotland.[3] A keen amateur of music, he was a competent violinist and a frequent concertgoer; he told Chambers many years later that it was the St Cecilia concerts which had fired him with enthusiasm for the idea of the collection:

1. Letters, 507.
2. Donald Low, *The Songs of Robert Burns*, Routledge, London, 1993, p. 16
3. The Board, whose function was to promote Scottish trade, had been set up under the Act of Union. It received funds voted by Parliament in return for Scotland's assumption of a share of the English national debt and in compensation for losses incurred in the Darien scheme.

I heard Scottish songs sung in a style of excellence far surpassing any idea which I had previously had of their beauty, and that, too, from Italians, Signor Tenducci the one, and Signora Domenica Corri the other . . . Tenducci's singing was full of passion, feeling, and taste, his articulation of the words was no less perfect than his expression of the music.[1]

When Burns accepted Thomson's invitation he added a postscript: 'I have some particular reasons for wishing my interferance to be known as little as possible.' It was plain that before very long the course of the *Museum* would be run, but although his response to the new challenge was eager, he was anxious not to hurt the loyal and undemanding Johnson. The two projects were very different, and so would Burns's relations be with their respective editors.

As a piece of book-making, the *Museum* was hardly in the first flight; the paper was shoddy, the engravings were crude, the printing undistinguished; Thomson appeared to promise better things. Burns told him, as he had told Johnson, that he would lay claim to no editorial prerogatives in the work. He would, he wrote, leave to Thomson and his associates 'the undoubted right of Publishers, to approve, or reject, at your pleasure'. Unlike Johnson, Thomson took him at his word, and kept up a frequent correspondence with Burns about his contributions. His comments were not always particularly apt, but they performed an important service; fifty-seven letters from Burns to Thomson have survived and they provide what is in effect a running commentary on how he operated as a songsmith.

Although the tone of the correspondence is generally good-natured, it is plain that Burns occasionally found Thomson's suggestions irksome. 'Let me tell you, that you are too fastidious in your ideas of Songs & ballads,' he wrote at the end of October[2], and in a further letter a couple of weeks later he is clearly exasperated:

If you mean, my dear Sir, that all the Songs in your Collection shall be Poetry of the first merit, I am afraid you will find difficulty in the undertaking more than you are aware of. – There is a peculiar rhythmus in many of our airs, a necessity of adapting syllables to the emphasis, or what I would call, the *feature notes*, of the tune, that cramps the Poet, & lays him under almost insuperable difficulties. –[3]

1. Quoted in J. Cuthbert Hadden, *George Thomson: The Friend of Burns: his life and correspondence*, J.C. Nimmo, London, 1898, p. 20. The extensive Corri family had been prominent in Edinburgh musical life since the early 1770s as performers, teachers, concert promoters and music publishers. Giusto Tenducci, a native of Siena, was a male soprano and composer. He had first come to Edinburgh in 1768 at the age of thirty, having eloped two years previously in Limerick with a fifteen-year-old Irish pupil. He was noted for his vanity and extravagance, and for a time was forced out of the country by his debts. Grove records that he sang with success 'as long as his voice lasted, and even when it had almost disappeared.'
2. Letters, 511.
3. *Ibid.*, 514.

In his next letter he accepted Thomson's view that the words originally set to the tune 'Lady Catherine Ogie' were poor stuff. He had failed to mend them to his satisfaction and offered in their place a composition of his own. 'I think it is in my happiest manner,' he wrote. 'The Subject of the Song is one of the most interesting passages of my youthful days; & I own that I would be much flattered to see the verses set to an Air which would insure celebrity':[1]

> Wi' mony a vow, and lock'd embrace,
>   Our parting was fu' tender;
> And pledging aft to meet again,
>   We tore oursels asunder:
> But Oh, fell Death's untimely frost,
>   That nipt my Flower sae early!
> Now green's the sod, and cauld's the clay,
>   That wraps my Highland Mary!
>
> O pale, pale now, those rosy lips
>   I aft hae kiss'd sae fondly!
> And clos'd for ay, the sparkling glance,
>   That dwalt on me sae kindly!
> And mouldering now in silent dust,
>   That heart that lo'ed me dearly!
> But still within my bosom's core
>   Shall live my Highland Mary.[2]

It was the only time he called her by that name, and he wrote of her no more.[3]

Politically it had been what a later age would call a long hot summer. Events in France continued to exert a feverish gravitational pull and to muddy the waters of domestic debate about burgh and parliamentary reform. The publication in February of the second part of *The Rights of Man* had prompted the government to draw up an indictment for treason; Paine, tipped off by William Blake that he was about to be arrested, prudently slipped across the Channel, where, not unnaturally, he was warmly received and, later in the year, elected by the department of Calais to the French Convention. His political career did not prosper, however. He spoke no French and quickly found himself at cross-purposes with the Jacobins. Robespierre had him thrown into prison; he

---

1. Letters, 518.
2. Kinsley, 389.
3. Thomson suggested changes to the first of the song's four verses, but Burns dug his heels in. 'I cannot alter it without injuring the poetry in proportion as I mended the perspicuity,' he wrote, 'so, if you please, we will let it stand as it is.' (Letters, 535.)

languished there for ten months and was lucky to escape an appointment with Madame Guillotine.[1]

Robespierre was the subject of a celebrated witticism by Mirabeau: 'He will go far, because he believes everything he says.' What he said to the Jacobins in a powerful speech on 29th July was that the king should be deposed and that a Convention should be elected by universal suffrage; on 10th August there was a popular insurrection in the capital and the Bourbon monarchy was finally overthrown.

The British government took the view that the growing unrest in Scotland in 1792 had been whipped up by the reformers, but there were other reasons, too. A severe winter had been followed by a wet summer; the price of corn had not been so high for ten years. At Aberdeen and at Leith, sailors and colliers registered their feelings about low pay and poor conditions by going on strike; in Rossshire there were fears that the landowners intended to drive out people in favour of sheep, and the crofters rioted.

On 21st May, the government had issued a proclamation against seditious meetings and publications. This immediately boosted sales of *The Rights of Man* (not everyone knew its name – it was enough to ask for 'the book that was forbidden to be sold'). Otherwise, the measure had little effect. In Dundee and Aberdeen, in Perth and Peebles, Henry Dundas was burnt in effigy, and just before the King's Birthday on 4th June anonymous handbills circulated in Edinburgh urging demonstrations in favour of democracy. Troops were called out, and it took them three days to get the mob off the streets; one of those brought to trial for rioting was sentenced to fourteen years transportation.[2]

While the poor demonstrated in the hope of improving their economic lot, the 'middling classes' continued to join the reform societies. Senior Foxite Whigs like Burns's friend Henry Erskine, who were convinced burgh reformers, hesitated to add their voices to the clamour for parliamentary reform; younger professional men with more radical views – they included the advocate Thomas Muir of Huntershill – became impatient, and on July 26th formed the Edinburgh Society of the Friends of the People. A retired army captain called Johnston was elected President, and young Lord Daer, who had so impressed Burns at Dugald Stewart's house, also joined. The bulk of the membership, however, came from lower reaches of the social scale – shopkeepers, schoolmasters, tailors, brewers.

1. Pitt's niece, Lady Hester Stanhope, used to maintain that her uncle was quite prepared to concede many of the arguments contained in *The Rights of Man*, but that he would add, 'What am I to do? As things are, if I were to encourage Tom Paine's opinions we should have a bloody revolution.' Part II outlined Paine's schemes for social reform, which included allowances for the old, the very young and the poor, free education and a progressive income tax. These ideas, however, attracted less attention than his proposals for the redistribution of property and the abolition of titles and primogeniture. The book was also notable for the virulence of the abuse it heaped on George III and his ministers.

2. His name was Alex Lockie, described in the indictment as a 'servant.' The authorities appear to have had doubts about the sentence; it was remitted in February 1793 and Lockie was released.

The formation of national societies was technically illegal, so the tactic was to maintain liaison with other societies by correspondence, each group electing delegates to sit on co-ordinating committees. Four separate groups were formed in Perth, and others sprang up in Dundee, Stirling, Musselburgh, Dunfermline, Strathaven and Wigtown. 'That keenness of political enquiry which for a long time seemed to be confined to England,' reported the *Caledonian Mercury*, 'has now reached this northern clime and extended its influence with rapid strides, so that it now pervades the whole of Caledonia.'[1]

Burns, an avid newspaper reader, was well informed about the course of events. He was certainly aware of what was going on in France, and what he gleaned from the public prints was supplemented from a private source. Mrs Dunlop had a widowed daughter there (her French husband had died in the summer of 1789, leaving her four months pregnant). By September 1792 her situation was desperate:

My poor Susan, after all her sufferings, is at this moment doomed to struggle with a severe, perhaps a fatal fever in a foreign country, torn with perpetual alarms, overrun with adverse foes on every side, and hourly threatened with still-increasing dangers . . .[2]

Burns was full of solicitude, and replied, most unusually, by return. 'I have this moment, my dear Madam, yours of the twenty third,' he wrote:

All your other kind reproaches, your news, &c. are out of my head when I read, & think on poor Mrs Henri's situation. – Good God! a heart-wounded, helpless young woman – in a strange, a foreign Land, & that Land convulsed with every horror that can harrow the human feelings – sick – looking, longing for a Comforter, but finding none –[3]

Mrs Dunlop's son had just become a father again. 'I suppose he means to go on,' Burns wrote cheerfully, 'untill he shall count his children as one does wine – by the dozen.' He was doing quite well in that department himself:

. . . I cannot leave Mrs B– untill her nine-month race is run, which may perhaps be in three or four weeks. – She, too, seems determined to make me the Patriarchal leader of a band. – However, if Heaven will be so obliging as let me have them in the proportion of three boys to one girl, I shall be so much the more pleased. – I hope, if I am spared with them, to shew a set of boys that will do honor to my cares & name; but I am not equal to

1. *Caledonian Mercury*, 30 September 1792.
2. Letter dated 23 September 1792, Burns and Dunlop, p. 362-4.
3. Letters, 510. His next letter to Mrs Dunlop (512) was one of condolence. Susan had died in the middle of September.

the task of rearing girls. – Besides, I am too poor: a girl should always have a fortune. –[1]

Burns wrote those words in late September. He was extremely fortunate that he did not very quickly find himself very much poorer, because in the closing months of 1792 he did a number of things which were foolish to the point of recklessness.

The first was to write a letter to William Johnston. This was the retired military man who had recently been elected President of the Edinburgh Society of the Friends of the People, and who had now decided to start a newspaper to promote its aims. Burns was impressed. 'I have just read your Prospectus of the Edin[r] Gazetteer,' he wrote:

If you go on in your Paper with the same spirit, it will, beyond all comparison, be the first Composition of the kind in Europe. – I beg leave to insert my name as a Subscriber; & if you have already published any papers, please send me them from the beginning . . .

Go on, Sir! Lay bare, with undaunted heart & steady hand, that horrid mass of corruption called Politics & State-Craft! Dare to draw in their native colors these

"Calm, thinking VILLAINS whom no faith can fix"–

whatever be the shiboleth of their pretended Party. –[2]

For an officer of the excise to subscribe to such a publication was to say the least indiscreet; he now formed the ambition to contribute to it as well. The occasion soon presented itself. Burns had had some involvement in the building of the new theatre which had recently opened in Dumfries. He was not himself a subscriber, but the founding deed had been drafted in the name of Robert Riddell, Thomas Boyd, who had built Ellisland, was the architect and Burns's friend Alexander Nasmyth, the painter, had been commissioned to design the interior.[3]

There had been a gala opening at the end of September, and Burns was currently at the feet of Louisa Fontenelle, the company's diminutive leading lady. 'To you, Madam, on our humble Dumfries boards,' he wrote to her, 'I have been more indebted for entertainment, than ever I was in prouder Theatres. – Your charms as a woman would insure applause to the most indifferent Actress, & your theatrical talents would secure admiration to the

---

1. It was a girl, for all that. She was born on November 21st, and christened Elizabeth Riddell.
2. Letters 515. The quotation is from Pope's *The Temple of Fame*, line 410.
3. Boyd's plans were a scaled-down version of the Theatre Royal in Bristol. It is possible that Nasmyth owed his commission, which was worth a hundred guineas, to Burns. His enthusiasm for reform and for the French Revolution were not to the taste of fashionable Edinburgh, and he was not getting a great deal of work.

plainest figure.'[1] He went on to offer her a prologue for her benefit night, which fell on November 26th, and the following day he sent it off to Johnston, signing himself 'Your fervent wellwisher.'

Eighteenth-century theatregoers got their money's worth. Miss Fontenelle's big night opened with a performance of Wycherley's *Country Girl*, in which she played the lead. This was followed by a re-enactment of Drake's victory over the Spanish Armada, complete with fire-ships. Only then did Miss Fontenelle return to the stage to declaim the lines Burns had written for her:

> While Europe's eye is fixed on mighty things,
> The fate of Empires and the fall of Kings;
> While quacks of State must each produce his plan,
> And even children lisp The Rights of Man;
> Amid this mighty fuss, just let me mention,
> The Rights of Woman merit some attention. −[2]

Just how allusive Burns was trying to be cannot now be established. Paine's name was certainly on everybody's lips, but what about Mary Wollstonecraft's? She had published *A Vindication of the Rights of Woman* earlier that year, but whether it had swum into Burns's ken is something we do not know. The three rights which he had Miss Fontenelle claim for her sex turned out to be Protection, Decorum and Admiration, so the Prologue can scarcely be represented as a precocious toot on the feminist trumpet − indeed it reads rather simperingly. Burns later told Graham of Fintry's wife that the piece had been 'written in haste on the spur of the occasion'. It might well have sunk without trace − if he had not, in the last four lines, yielded to the twin temptations of showing off his French and advertising his political proclivities:

> But truce with kings, and truce with Constitutions,
> With bloody armaments, and Revolutions;
> Let MAJESTY your first attention summon,
> Ah, ça ira! THE MAJESTY OF WOMAN!!!

'ÇA IRA.' The hymn of the Revolution, ferocious and unmetrical, all about stringing up aristocrats − sung to *Le Carillon national*, a tune which, ironically, Marie Antoinette was for ever strumming on her harpsichord.

> Ah! ça ira, ça ira, ça ira!
> Les aristocrat' à la lanterne;
> Ah! ça ira, ça ira, ça ira!
> Les aristocrat' on les pendra . . .[3]

1. Letters, 519.
2. Kinsley, 390.
3. *Ça Ira* had quickly caught on in Britain − it was incorporated in an opera at Covent Garden as early as 1790. It remained popular after the outbreak of war with France, and was even adopted, in 1793, as the quickstep of the 14th Regiment (later the West Yorkshire Regiment).

It was a catchy melody, but Burns would come to have his fill of it. He had thought well enough of his lines for the enchanting Miss Fontenelle to send them to Mrs Dunlop for her approval, copying them out at the end of a lengthy letter to her early in December:

> . . . I see you are in for double Postage, so I shall e'en scribble out t'other sheet. – We, in this country, here have many alarms of the Reform, or rather the Republican spirit, of your part of the kingdom. – Indeed, we are a good deal in commotion ourselves, & in our Theatre here, "God save the king" has met with some groans and hisses, while Ça ira has been repeatedly called for. – For me, I am a *Placeman*, you know; a very humble one indeed, Heaven knows, but still so much so as to gag me from joining in the cry. – What my private sentiments are, you will find out without an Interpreter. –[1]

On the same day that he wrote this to Mrs Dunlop, his private sentiments on a more personal matter suddenly came bubbling to the surface. In her last letter before sailing for the West Indies, Mrs McLehose had enjoined him not to compromise her there: 'As you value my peace, do not write me to Jamaica, until I let you know you may with safety. Write Mary often.'[2] Burns did, but clearly did not find her the most diligent of correspondents:

> I have written so often to you and have got no answer, that I had resolved never to lift up a pen to you again, but this eventful day, *the sixth of December*, recalls to my memory such a scene! Heaven and earth! when I remember a far distant person! – but no more of this, until I learn from you a proper address, and why my letters have lain by you unanswered, as this is the third I have sent you . . .[3]

The jinx on his correspondence with Miss Peacock was not immediately removed. This time she did reply, but her letter arrived when Burns was away, was mislaid, and came to light only some months later.

In the middle of December he travelled to Ayrshire and spent several days with Mrs Dunlop; he was not to know it, but it was his last visit to Dunlop House. Once again he appears to have behaved if not with uncouthness certainly with some lack of ceremony; possibly because he was not entirely well. Mrs Dunlop herself had not been well enough to be up and about on the morning of his departure and in her next letter there is a note of reproach: 'It was no cordial for my disappointment in not seeing you when I heard from Keith how much you were complaining yourself,' she wrote. 'Yet I hoped we should have

---

1. Letters, 524.
2. Letter LXVII, 25th January 1792. Mary was Mary Peacock, a close friend of Clarinda's who knew all about her relations with Burns.
3. Letters, 525.

had a line from your brother's to say you were better, or to ask for me, as I surely would for you had I been able.'

She had clearly not much liked the look of him. Later in the letter she suddenly breaks off in the middle of a passage about various family misfortunes:

But why do I surfeit you with this yellow melancholy which discolours my own imagination, and can only jaundice yours too, if that is not too much the case already – a circumstance it distresses me to believe, but too possible from what I saw, and yet more from what I know of the natural effects of your changed habits of life – deprived of that free air and wholesome labour, the portion of your early, thoughtless days.

She wraps it up quite a bit, with references to 'the prescription of the wise King Solomon,' but she plainly thinks he drinks too much: 'Yet I am no fair judge, since among other aversions that haunt me just now is a strong one for the bottle.' (She had been suffering from both gout and jaundice.) Towards the end of the letter – a long one even by her standards – she turns to the subject yet again: 'I think more just now of your health than of all your writing, or even of the talents that first inspired them,' she writes; 'and when I see you ill, I forget the poet to regret the friend, the father, the man and the husband.' Then, touchingly, this:

Have you still a horse? If so, ride him frequently; if you have not a little garden, get one, not for the convenience, but for the amusement and the wholesome labour it would afford. Manual exertions and the smell of the red earth are sovereign specifics in complaints like yours, especially in the spring of the year and the morning of the day ... A man had better plant potatoes than have his peace wrecked with relaxation and vapours for which he may in vain drain all the volumes of Galen and Hippocrates or the deceiving potions of their successors ...[1]

Burns broke his journey to or from Ayrshire at Sanquhar, and from there he scribbled a note to his friend Cleghorn, a favoured recipient of his coarser verses: 'I send you a song, just finished this moment.'[2]:

> When Princes and Prelates and het-headed zealots
>   All Europe hae set in a lowe,   blaze
> The poor man lies down, nor envies a crown,
>   And comforts himsel with a mowe. –
>   Chorus

1. Letter dated 30 December 1792, Burns and Dunlop, pp. 370-5.
2. Letters, 527.

> And why shouldna poor folk mowe, mowe, mowe,
> And why shouldna poor folk mowe:
> The great folk hae siller, and houses and lands,   money
> Poor bodies hae naething but mowe. –

To mowe means to copulate. When Burns favoured another correspondent with a copy a month later he sent it to him 'sealed up, as it is not every body's reading' and described it as 'a tippling Ballad . . . sung one convivial evening'.[1] Judging by the handwriting on the holograph it must have been a very convivial evening indeed, and yet the song, set to the old Jacobite air 'The Campbells are comin', contrives to be much more than a defiantly drunken celebration of the levelling power of sexual intercourse.

The first of the 'Princes and Prelates' to whom Burns directs his attention is George III's brother-in-law the Duke of Brunswick, who had led the Prussian and Austrian armies against the French earlier in the year but had been defeated on September 20th by General Dumouriez at the battle of Valmy:

> Bauld Br-nsw-c's great Prince wad hae shawn better sense,
> At hame with his Princess to mowe. –

Catherine the Great, who was notorious for her immorality, comes in for even rougher handling. She had set her lover, Stanislaus Poniatowski, on the Polish throne thirty years previously, had partitioned Poland with the Prussians in 1772 and was to snuff out Polish independence in a second dismemberment in 1793. In four economical lines Burns chronicles her misdeeds and suggests appropriately crude retribution:

> Auld Kate laid her claws on poor Stanislaus,
> And Poland has bent like a bow:
> May the deil in her a— ram a huge pr-ck o' brass!
> And damn her in h-ll with a mowe!

He turns in conclusion to the House of Hanover, and proposes, tongue only slightly in cheek, a benevolent if slightly unusual royal toast:

> But truce with commotions and new-fangled notions,
> A bumper I trust you'll allow:
> Here's George our gude king and Charlotte his queen,
> And lang may they tak a gude mowe![2]

It was the last day of the year before Burns picked up his pen to write a bread

1. *Ibid.*, 530. The recipient was Graham of Fintry.
2. Kinsley, 395.

and butter letter to Mrs Dunlop. He told her that he had found on his return to Dumfries 'a hurry of business, thrown in heaps by my absence,' but that the days he had spent under her 'genial roof' were four of the pleasantest he had ever enjoyed. His recollection of that enjoyment was rudely interrupted, however; he wrote no more to his kindly hostess that day, because it suddenly became a matter of imperative urgency that he should communicate with Graham of Fintry:

Sir,
I have been surprised, confounded & distracted by Mr Mitchel, the Collector, telling me just now, that he has received an order from your Honble Board to enquire into my political conduct, & blaming me as a person disaffected to Government. –

The letter reads like a sustained sob of panic:

Sir, you are a Husband – & a father – you know what you would feel, to see the much-loved wife of your bosom, & your helpless, prattling little ones, turned adrift into the world, degraded & disgraced from a situation in which they had been respectable & respected, & left almost without the necessary support of a miserable existence. – Alas, Sir! must I think that such, soon, will be my lot! And from the damned, dark insinuations of hellish, groundless Envy too! – I believe, Sir, I may aver it, & in the sight of Omnipotence, that I would not tell a deliberate Falsehood, no, not though even worse horrors, if worse can be, than those I have mentioned, hung over my head; & I say, that the allegation, whatever villain has made it, is a Lie! To the British Constitution, on Revolution principles, next after my God, I am most devoutly attached! –

He concluded with an appeal to Graham's humanity and the generosity of his friendship – 'Heaven knows how warmly I have felt the obligation, how gratefully I have thanked you.' Even after two hundred years the abject tone of the letter makes painful reading:

To your patronage, as a man of some genius, you have allowed me a claim; & your esteem, as an honest Man, I know is my due: to these, Sir, permit me to appeal; & by these may I adjure you to save me from that misery which threatens to overwhelm me, & which, with my latest breath I will say it, I have not deserved. –
Pardon this confused scrawl. – Indeed I know not well what I have written.[1]

1. Letters, 528.

That was not strictly true – he had taken time to try his hand at a draft[1] – but as 1792 guttered out he waited for Graham's reply in a state of agitated suspense.

1. Burns's draft – it was written on Excise paper – at one time formed part of the Gribbel Collection. Its present whereabouts are not known.

Thirteen

AND THIS IS LAW
I WILL MAINTAIN

IT COULD HAVE BEEN very much worse. The reply he received from Graham
on January 5th was friendly and reassuring. While waiting for it he had resumed
his letter to Mrs Dunlop, and to her he had played down his difficulties very
considerably, saying only, 'Some envious malicious devil has raised a little
demur on my political principles.' Now he was able to add a final instalment:

> ... You see my hurried life, Madam: I can only command starts of time. –
> However, I am glad of one thing; since I finished the other sheet, the political
> blast that threatened my welfare is overblown ... I have the pleasure of
> informing that all is set to rights in that quarter. – Now as to these inquisi-
> torial Informers, Spies, Persecutors, &c. may the d-vil & his angels be let
> loose to – but hold! I was praying most fervently in my last sheet, & I must
> not so soon fall acursing in this. –[1]

Graham had gone into some detail about the accusations that had been made,
and it is plain from Burns's detailed response that he had been comprehensively
denounced by someone who knew quite a lot about him. The first charge was
that he not only belonged to but was the head of a 'disaffected party' in
Dumfries. This he flatly, and scornfully, denied: 'If there exists such an association, it must consist of such obscure, nameless beings, as precludes any possibility of my being known to them, or they to me.'

About his devotion to 'Reform Principles' he was frank. Although he
claimed to regard the arrangements brought about in 1688 as 'the most glorious
Constitution on earth, or that perhaps the wit of man can frame,' he believed
there had been some deviation from its original principles, particularly in the
matter of relations between the executive and the Commons, which had become

1. Letters, 529.

corrupt: 'This is the Truth, the Whole truth, of my Reform opinions; opinions which, before I was aware of the complection of these innovating times, I too unguardedly (now I see it) sported with: but henceforth I seal up my lips.'

He also denied that he had spoken ill of the monarch: 'I never uttered any invectives against the king,' he told Graham. 'I always revered, & ever will, with the soundest loyalty, revere, the Monarch of Great-britain, as, to speak in Masonic, the sacred KEYSTONE OF OUR ROYAL ARCH CONSTI-TUTION' – quite a rich claim, this, from the author of 'A Dream', in which George III had been ridiculed as a usurper. (The line about the Hanoverians being 'an idiot race, to honor lost,' scratched on an inn window in Stirling, also seem to have slipped his mind.[1])

When it came to his dealings with Captain Johnston, Burns's memory again appeared to operate somewhat selectively:

Of Johnston, the publisher of the Edin[r] Gazetteer, I know nothing. – One evening in company with four or five friends, we met with his prospectus which we thought manly & independant; and I wrote to him, ordering his paper for us. – If you think that I acted improperly in allowing his Paper to come addressed to me, I shall immediately countermand it. –

He owned to having sent Johnston the prologue he had written for La Fontenelle and some stanzas commemorating Thomson – 'both these I will subjoin for your perusal. – You will see that they have nothing whatever to do with Politics.' He did not, however think to subjoin another set of verses from his pen which had found their way onto Johnston's pages:

> . . . It's gude to be merry and wise,
> It's gude to be honest and true,
> It's gude to support Caledonia's cause,
> And bide by the Buff and the Blue.

> Here's a health to them that's awa,
> Here's a health to them that's awa;
> Here's a health to Charlie, the chief of the clan,
> Altho' that his band be sma' . . .[2]

A clever piece of song-mending, and political twice over, the Charlie in question being, of course, not Charles Edward Stuart but Charles James Fox.

One paragraph in Burns's letter to Graham has been picked over more than any other:

1. See page 154 *supra.*
2. Kinsley, 391.

I was in the playhouse one night, when Çà ira was called for. – I was in the middle of the pit, & from the Pit the clamour arose. – One or two individuals with whom I occasionally associate were of the party, but I neither knew of the Plot, nor joined in the Plot; nor ever opened my lips to hiss, or huzza, that, or any other Political tune whatever. – I looked on myself as far too obscure a man to have any weight in quelling a Riot; at the same time, as a character of higher respectability, than to yell in the howlings of a rabble. –

This is a fuller version of what Burns had told Mrs Dunlop a month previously, but only the whole truth is wholly true, and it remains open to doubt whether Burns was telling Graham the full story. There is, as it happens, another piece of evidence to be weighed. Many years after the death of the poet, Charles Kirkpatrick Sharpe wrote to Allan Cunningham to say that he thought he did an injustice to human nature to contend that when the talk was about politics, there were malicious people who laid traps for Burns. 'I know he was most woefully indiscreet on that point, and I remember one proof,' he wrote:

The play was *As You Like It*, Miss Fontenelle, Rosalind, when 'God save the King' was called for and sung; we all stood up uncovered, but Burns sat still in the middle of the pit with his hat on his head. There was a great tumult, with shouts of 'Turn him out! – Shame Burns!' which continued a good while. At last he was either expelled or forced to take off his hat – I forget which; nor can my mother remember. This silly conduct all sensible persons condemned.[1]

That sounds remarkably like an account of the same evening. Theatre audiences at that time had something of the aggressive herd instinct characteristic of modern football supporters. Political opinion had become polarised, and opportunities to provoke confrontation were eagerly sought. 'Ça ira' and 'God Save the King' had both in effect ceased to be expressions of loyalty or political commitment and degenerated into tribal war-cries. If that is what Burns was trying to convey to Graham, depicting himself as reluctant to descend into the political gutter, he was naïve: fastidious people who do not wish to be pinned down by crossfire should avoid the company of ruffians. It is not, in any case, a reading which squares with what he had previously said to Mrs Dunlop in describing the 'Ça ira' episode and letting slip that his position as a placeman gagged him 'from joining in the cry'.

It is fairly plain that in divining his views, his 'Inquisitorial Informers' had as little need of an Interpreter as Mrs Dunlop. They came spilling out all too easily, with or without the assistance of the punch-bowl. Burns's intense sociability, his hunger for an audience and his powerful gifts of raillery and repartee frequently combined to make him his own worst enemy.

1. Quoted in Chambers-Wallace, vol. iii, p. 384, n.

It is a measure of how well Burns thought he had defended himself to Graham that he felt able to conclude his letter with a request for further preferment: 'If, Sir, I have been so fortunate as to do away these misapprehensions of my conduct & character, I shall with the confidence which you were wont to allow me, apply to your goodness on every opening in the way of business.' He then, as he had done on a previous occasion, coolly suggested himself for the place of a colleague:

Mr Mcfarlane, Supervisor of the Galloway District is & has been for some time, very ill. – I spoke to Mr Mitchel as to his wishes to forward my application for the job, but though he expressed & ever does express every kindness for me, he hesitates, in hopes that the disease may be of short continuance.

Burns himself had no such inhibitions, and pressed his case with a directness as engaging as it was eccentric:

However, as it seems to be a paralytic affection, I fear that it may be some time ere he can take charge of so extended a District. – There is a great deal of fatigue, & very little business in the District; two things suitable enough to my hardy constitution, & inexperience in that line of life. –[1]

A good try, but an unsuccessful one; Burns stayed put in Dumfries. To all outward appearance he was, as he approached his thirty-fourth birthday, a man in his vigorous prime, but the hardy constitution of which he boasted to Graham was severely tested from time to time. To Mrs Dunlop's concern for his health he had responded reassuringly, but also with an admission:

. . . I am better, though not quite free of my complaint. – You must not think, as you seem to insinuate, that in my way of life I want exercise. – Of that I have enough; but occasional hard drinking is the devil to me. – Against this I have again & again bent my resolution, & have greatly succeeded. – Taverns, I have totally abandoned: it is the private parties in the family way, among the hard drinking gentlemen of this country, that does me the mischief – but even this, I have more than half given over. –[2]

In a letter from this time to his friend John McMurdo he offers a wry apology for a lapse from this new rule:

I believe last night that my old enemy, the Devil, taking the advantage of my being in drink (he well knows he has no chance with me in my sober hours) tempted me to be a little turbulent. – You have too much humanity to heed

1. Letters, 530.
2. *Ibid.*, 529.

the maniac ravings of a poor wretch whom the powers of Hell, & the potency of Port, beset at the same time . . .[1]

He was well aware of his reputation as a tippler. One of the estates where he was made welcome was Arbigland, the property of a family called Craik whom he had met at Friars' Carse. A fellow guest at dinner there in March 1793 was a young Englishwoman called Anna Dorothea Benson, the daughter of a York wine-merchant and in later life a friend of the Carlyles. Burns was much taken with her good looks, and wrote to her in flattering and roguish terms enclosing a sonnet;[2] Allan Cunningham published her recollection of the occasion in 1834:

> . . . He was witty, drank as others drank, and was long in coming to the tea-table. It was then the fashion for young ladies to be busy about something – I was working a flower. The poet sat down beside me, talked of the beauty of what I was imitating, and put his hand so near the work that I said: 'Well, take it and do a bit yourself.' 'O ho!' said he, 'you think my hand is unsteady with wine. I cannot work a flower madam; but' – he pulled the thread out of the needle and re-threaded it in a moment. 'Can a tipsy man do that?' He talked to me of his children, more particularly of his eldest son, and called him a promising boy. 'And yet, madam' he said, with a sarcastic glance of his eye, 'I hope he will turn out a glorious blockhead, and so make his fortune.'[3]

Burns's concern for his children is well attested, most notably by James Gray, who, when Burns first moved to the town, was the Latin master at what later became Dumfries Academy. 'He superintended the education of his children with a degree of care that I have never seen surpassed by any parent in any rank of life whatever,' he wrote:

> In the bosom of his family, he spent many a delightful hour in directing the studies of his eldest son, a boy of uncommon talents. I have frequently found him explaining to this youth, then not more than nine years of age, the English poets, from Shakespeare to Gray, or storing his mind with examples of heroic virtue, as they live in the pages of our most celebrated English historians.[4]

1. *Ibid.*, 542 A.
2. *Ibid.*, 541.
3. Cunningham, *op cit.*, vol. i, pp. 363–4. When Miss Benson saw her anecdote in print she had second thoughts, and wrote to Cunningham to dispute the phrase 'drank as others drank'. Her worship of Burns 'continued fervent,' Carlyle wrote in his *Reminiscences*, 'her few recollections always a jewel she was ready to produce'.
4. Gray, who had subsequently become Rector of the Academy, wrote this in a long letter about Burns's character which he sent to Alexander Peterkin in September 1814. Peterkin included it in his edition of the *Works* which he published the following year. Gray later took holy orders, went off to India as a chaplain and translated sections of the Bible into Cutchee.

It occurred to Burns early in 1793 that there was a way in which he might capitalise on the honorary freedom of the burgh which had been conferred on him six years previously. The children of burgesses benefited from reduced school fees; Burns now wrote to the Lord Provost and Council, drawing attention to his large family and 'very stinted' income, to ask whether for that purpose he might be made a real Freeman. He began his letter with an appropriate reference to the town's 'literary taste & liberal spirit'. He ended by reminding them that he had recently done the burgh a favour – the removal of an anomaly relating to the duty on beer had been at his suggestion and the burgh revenue had already been increased by almost £10 as a result.[1] He pointed out that he had been the only excise officer to interest himself in the matter, adding somewhat crudely, 'except Mr Mitchell, whom you pay for his trouble'. The request was granted.

News of his difficulties with the Board of Excise had quickly become known to his friends in Edinburgh. The best letter he received, and the best advice, came from William Nicol. 'Dear Christless Bobbie,' he wrote:

What is become of thee? Has the Devil flown off with thee, as the gled [kite] does with a bird? If he should do so there is little matter, if the reports concerning thy *imprudence* are true. What concerns it thee whether the lousy Dumfriesian fiddlers play 'Ça Ira' or 'God save the King?' Suppose you *had* an aversion to the King, you could not, as a gentleman, wish God to use him worse than He has done. The infliction of idiocy is no sign of Friendship or Love; and I am sure damnation is a matter far beyond your wishes or ideas. But reports of this kind are only the insidious suggestions of ill-minded persons; for your good sense will ever point out to you, as well as to me, a bright model of political conduct who flourished in the victorious reign of Queen Anne, viz., the Vicar of Bray, who, during the convulsions of Great Britain which were without any former example, saw eight reigns, in perfect security; because he remembered that precept of the *sensible, shrewd, temporising* Apostle, 'We ought not to resist the Higher Power.'[2]

Burns was grateful, and managed a reply in his best vein:

... How infinitely is thy puddle-headed, rattle-headed; wrong-headed, round-headed slave indebted to thy supereminent goodness, that from the luminous path of thy own right-lined rectitude, thou lookest benignly down on an erring Wretch, of whom the zig-zag wanderings defy all the powers

1. The duty, a relic of pre-Union days, was popularly known as the 'twa pennies on ale' and was levied only on beer brewed within the burgh. This gave brewers just outside the town – in Bridgend, for instance, on the west bank of the Nith – a competitive advantage: most of their beer was sold in Dumfries, but they escaped the duty paid by their competitors, as did any English traders who sold ale or porter in the town.

2. Letter dated 10 February 1793, quoted in Chambers-Wallace, vol. iii, pp. 394–5.

of Calculation, from the simple copulation of Units up to the hidden mystery of Fluxions! . . . For me, I am a beast, a reptile, & know nothing. – From the cave of my ignorance, amid the fogs of my dulness & pestilential fumes of my Political heresies, I look up to thee, as doth a toad through the iron-barred lucarne of a pestiferous dungeon to the cloudless glory of a summer sun! . . .[1]

The tone of a letter which he wrote on the same day to Cunningham, however, is much sourer; he subjects his friend to an ironic catechism on the nature of politics – 'a science wherewith, by means of nefarious cunning, & hypocritical pretence, we govern civil Polities for the emolument of ourselves & our adherents':

Quere, What is a Minister?
Answer, A Minister is an unprincipled fellow, who by the influence of heredi-tary, or acquired wealth; by superiour abilities; or by a lucky conjuncture of circumstances, obtains a principal place in the administration of the affairs of government. –
Q. What is a Patriot?
A. An individual exactly of the same description as a Minister, only, out of place. –[2]

If Burns believed that his letter to Graham had disposed of his difficulties with his superiors in the excise, he was over-sanguine; he was not yet entirely out of the wood. When the letter was placed before the full Board, some exception was taken to his remarks about corruption, and it was decided that William Corbet should be despatched to Dumfries to enquire into Burns's conduct.

Findlater, his Supervisor, proved a good friend, testifying that Burns was 'exact, vigilant and sober' and describing him as one of the best officers in the district.[3] The proceedings do not appear to have been too formally judicial. Burns's friend Syme later told Alexander Peterkin that he had joined Findlater, Burns and Corbet for dinner once or twice during the latter's visit, and that Corbet had admonished Burns, 'but found no grounds, save some witty sayings'. Such excise records as survive disclose no reprimand. Findlater, in a letter to Johnston's *Edinburgh Magazine* in February 1834, wrote: 'Had Burns been subjected to a Board's recorded censure, I must *ex-officio* have known of it, as it could not have been concealed from me . . . All such censures are transmitted to the respective supervisors to be registered, and delivered to the officers, who must give written receipts for them.'[4]

1. Letters, 537.
2. *Ibid.*, 536.
3. John Sinton, *Burns: Excise Officer and Poet. A Vindication*, 2nd edition, Kilmarnock, 1896, p. 28.
4. Quoted in Appendix no. III to Chambers-Wallace, vol. iii, p, 452.

Burns's own version was that Corbet had been instructed to remind him 'that my business was to act, not to think; & that whatever might be Men or Measures, it was my business to be silent & obedient'. Burns gave this account to John Erskine of Mar, a friend of Glenriddell's. He had picked up a rumour that Burns had been dismissed, and wrote to Riddell for confirmation; if it were true, he proposed to get up a subscription for the poet's benefit. Erskine, later the twenty-seventh Earl of Mar, was the grandson of the Jacobite earl who had forfeited his titles for his part in the '15'. Burns had never met him, but when Riddell read him a paragraph of his letter, in the middle of April, he wrote at once to Erskine to express his gratitude. He also gave him a lengthy account of the whole affair, and it is plain that after little more than three months Burns's view of what had happened, and why, had become distinctly revisionist.

He began with a warm tribute to Graham of Fintry. Without his exertions, he believed, he would have been turned adrift 'without so much as a hearing, or the smallest previous intimation'. Then, rather grandly, he added what reads suspiciously like a retrospective embellishment:

Had I had any other resource, probably I might have saved them the trouble of a dismissal; but the little money I gained by my Publication, is almost every guinea embarked, to save from ruin an only brother; who, though one of the worthiest, is by no means the most fortunate of men. –

Burns then rehearsed the accusations that had been made against him, summarised his defence and gave his own assessment of where he now stood: 'I have been partly forgiven: only, I understand that all hopes of my getting officially forward are blasted.'

That sounds like the natural end to the letter: a conventional salutation, preceded, perhaps, by a brief reiteration of gratitude is all that seems called for. But Burns has now cranked himself up to a rare pitch of excitement, and launches headlong into an extended and quite extraordinary flight of rhetoric. He is addressing a complete stranger, and yet it is difficult to think of anything he ever wrote which is psychologically more revealing:

Now, Sir, to the business in which I would more immediately interest you. – The partiality of my Countrymen has brought me forward as a man of genius, & has given me a Character to support. – In the Poet, I have avowed manly & independant sentiments, which I trust will be found in the Man. – Reasons of no less weight than the support of a wife & children have pointed out as the eligible, & indeed the only eligible line of life for me, my present occupation. – Still, my honest fame is my dearest concern; & a thousand times have I trembled at the idea of the degrading epithets that Malice, or Misrepresentation may affix to my name. – I have often, in blasting anticipation, listened to some future hackney Magazine Scribbler, with the heavy malice of savage stupidity, exulting in his hireling paragraphs that "Burns, notwithstanding the fanfaronade of independance to be found in his works, & after having been held forth to Public View & Public Estimation as a man of some genius, yet, quite destitute of resources within himself to support this borrowed dignity, he dwindled into a paltry Exciseman; & slunk out the rest of his insignificant existence in the meanest of pursuits & among the vilest of mankind." –

In your illustrious hands, Sir, permit me to lodge my strong disavowal & defiance of these slanderous falsehoods. – BURNS was a poor man, from birth; & an Exciseman, by necessity: but – I will say it! – the sterling of his honest worth, no poverty could debase; & his independant British mind, Oppression might bend, but could not subdue! – Have not I, to me, a more precious stake in my Country's welfare than the richest Dukedom in it? – I have a large family of children, & the probability of more. – I have three sons, whom, I see already, have brought with them into the world souls ill qualified to inhabit the bodies of Slaves. – Can I look tamely on, & see any machination to wrest from them, the birthright of my boys, the little independant Britons in whose veins runs my own blood? – No! I will not! – should my heart stream around my attempt to defend it!

Does any man tell me, that my feeble efforts can be of no service; & that it does not belong to my humble station to meddle with the concerns of a People? – I tell him, that it is on such individuals as I, that for the hand of support & the eye of intelligence, a Nation has to rest. – The uninformed mob may swell a Nation's bulk; & the titled, tinsel Courtly throng may be its feathered ornament, but the number of those who are elevated enough in life, to reason & reflect; & yet low enough to keep clear of the venal Contagion of a Court; these are a Nation's strength. –

He had almost done:

One small request more: when you have honored this letter with a perusal, please commit it to the flames. – BURNS, in whose behalf you have so generously interested yourself, I have here, in his native colours, drawn *as he is*; but should any of the people in whose hands is the very bread he eats, get the least knowledge of the picture, it would ruin the poor Bard for ever. –[1]

This remarkable, confessional shout of pain was wrenched out of Burns in the spring of 1793. The political weather was by now even wilder than it had been at the close of the previous year. In December, Paine had been tried in London *in absentia*, and found guilty of seditious libel.[2] In the same month the

1. Letters, 558.
2. Paine had been defended by Thomas Erskine, brother of Henry, and the future Lord Chancellor.

Friends of the People in Scotland had held their first General Convention in Edinburgh. Muir of Huntershill, already a marked man, insisted on reading out an inflammatory address from the Society of United Irishman; he was arrested on January 2nd, and from then on the law officers of the Crown initiated a series of sedition trials clearly designed to discredit the reform movement and intimidate its supporters. They were not hindered in their efforts by events in France; on the morning of 21st January 1793 Louis XVI was led to the guillotine in what is today the Place de la Concorde but was then the Place de la Révolution. Three days earlier, a club known as the Loyal Natives had been founded in Dumfries. Although they mainly expressed their political views by making a lot of noise over dinner at a local hostelry, it seemed prudent for Burns to heed Nicol's advice; after the Convention declared war on Great Britain on February 1st it seemed more prudent still.

Happily, he had less controversial matters to occupy his mind. 'I understand that my Book is published,' he wrote to Creech at the end of the month. 'I beg that you will, as soon as possible, send me twenty copies of it.' They were intended, he said, for 'a few Great Folks whom I respect, & a few Little Folks whom I love,' and he was busy throughout March sending them out. 'A mark of my gratitude to you as a Patriot,' he wrote to Patrick Miller, 'who, in a venal, sliding age, stands forth the champion of the liberties of my Country.'[1] Another copy went to Glencairn's brother: 'Fame belies you, my Lord, if you possess not the same Dignity of Man, which was your noble brother's characteristic feature.'[2] In the inscription to Mrs Graham of Fintry gratitude is jostled by immodesty: 'It is probable, Madam, that this page may be read when the hand that now writes it, is mouldering in the dust.'[3] To Mrs Riddell he showed off his French, but was careless with his accents: 'Un gage d'Amitié le plus sincére.'[4] With the 'Little Folks' whom he loved there was no need to strike attitudes. One of them was 'dear-bought Bess,' his illegimate daughter by Elizabeth Paton. The girl was now approaching her eighth birthday and lived still at Mossgiel in the care of Burns's mother. In her copy he wrote simply, 'To Elizabeth Burns – her Father's gift – The Author.'[5]

1. Letters, 545.
2. *Ibid.*, 546. John, the fifteenth Earl, born in 1750, had served in the 14th Dragoons and was later ordained in the Church of England. He married a sister of Henry Erskine's, but had no children, and with his death in 1796 the earldom became extinct.
3. *Ibid.*, 547.
4. *Ibid.*, 550A. In Mrs Riddell's case, the gift of his poems represented not simply a token of friendship but an exchange of compliments between authors. Several months previously she had sent him a copy of her *Voyages to the Madeira and Leeward and Caribee Islands*, which Smellie had just published. 'Be assured I shall ever keep it sacred,' Burns wrote in a note of thanks, 'as a boasted testimony how much I have the honour to be your highly obliged humble servt' (Letters, 517.)
5. *Ibid.*, 547A.

One set of the new edition made the return journey to Edinburgh accompanied by a long covering letter:

> I suppose, my dear Madam, that by your neglecting to inform me of your arrival in [Europe], a circumstance which could not be indifferent to me, as indeed no occurrence relating to you can – you meant to leave me to guess & gather that a correspondence I once had the honor & *felicity* to enjoy, is to be no more . . .

Mrs McLehose's attempt at a reconciliation with her husband had lasted less than three months. When James Grierson went to see her many years later he recorded that she had come home because 'she was so much anoyed with muiskitos & the Climate,' but there had also, as Grierson's editor points out, been the small matter of her husband's 'ebony mistress and mahogony children'.[1] Burns now congratulated her on her return, expressed concern for her health and indicated an interest in renewing their correspondence – on certain conditions:

> Shall I hear from you? – But first, hear me! – No cold language – no prudential documents – I despise Advice, & scorn Controul – If you are not to write such language, such sentiments, as you know I shall wish, shall delight to receive; I conjure you, By wounded Pride! By ruined Peace! by frantic disappointed Passion! By all the many ills that constitute that sum of human woes – A BROKEN HEART! – To me be silent for ever! ! ! – If you insult me with the unfeeling apothegms of cold-blooded Caution, May all the – but hold – a Fiend could not breathe a malevolent wish on the head of *MY* Angel! –
>
> Mind my request!—If you send me a page baptised in the font of sanctimonious Prudence—By Heaven, Earth & Hell, I will tear it into atoms![2]

It was one of the more preposterous letters he ever wrote, but that did not prevent him from copying it into the appropriate Glenriddell volume. 'I need scarcely remark,' he added in an untruthful footnote, 'that the foregoing was the fustian rant of enthusiastic youth'. We no longer know whether Mrs McLehose favoured it with a reply.

Burns was particularly busy in the spring of 1793 on work for Thomson's *Collection.* Kinsley describes their collaboration as 'this uneasy alliance between a true artist in folk-song and a stiff-necked "refiner",' but that seems a little hard. 'Ballad-making is now so compleatly my hobby-horse, as ever Fortification was Uncle Toby's,' Burns wrote cheerfully to Thomson at the beginning

---

1. Fitzhugh, *op. cit.,* p. 41, n.
2. Letters, 544.

of April, 'so I'll e'en canter it away till I come to the limit of my race, (God grant that I may take the right side of the winning-post!).'[1] The evidence of the letters is that he rather enjoyed their exchanges and found them stimulating; if he occasionally felt strongly about something, he found no difficulty in saying so:

> Give me leave to criticise your taste in the only thing in which it is in my opinion reprehensible: (you know I ought to know something of my own trade) of pathos, Sentiment & Point, you are a compleat judge; but there is a quality more necessary than either, in a Song, & which is the very essence of a Ballad, I mean Simplicity – now, if I mistake not, this last feature you are a little apt to sacrifice to the foregoing. –

Thomson was planning a visit to London, and Burns tried to persuade him to go by way of Dumfries:

> I have still several M.S.S. Scots airs by me, which I have pickt up, mostly from the singing of country lasses. – They please me vastly; but your learned lugs would perhaps be displeased with the very feature for which I like them. – I call them Simple; you would pronounce them Silly.[2]

He reverted to musical matters in another letter towards the end of the month: 'Whatever Mr Pleyel does, let him not alter one iota of the original Scots Air,' he wrote firmly. 'Let our National Music preserve its native features. – They are, I own, frequently wild, & unreduceable to the more modern rules; but on that very eccentricity, perhaps, depends a great part of their effect.'[3]

The preface to *A Select Collection, Original Scotish Airs* is dated 1st May 1793. This first part – the only part, indeed, to appear in Burns's lifetime – contained twenty-five songs, of which six were his.[4] Quite the best of them was his reworking of the old ballad 'Open the door to me Oh,' with its justly celebrated third stanza:

> The wan moon sets behind the white wave,
>   And time is setting with me, Oh:
> False friends, false love, farewell! for mair
>   I'll ne'er trouble them, nor thee, Oh.[5]

1. *Ibid.*, 557.
2. *Ibid.*, 554.
3. *Ibid.*, 559.
4. Burns maintained a steady flow of material to Thomson and when the work was eventually complete in five volumes it was advertised as including 'upward of a hundred new songs by BURNS'; what he would have thought of Thomson's 'improvements' can only be guessed.
5. Kinsley, 403.

When Burns wrote to thank Thomson for his copy he was full of praise for the quality of the work: 'Never did my eyes behold, in any Musical work, such elegance & correctness.' He had been less pleased to discover that Thomson had enclosed with the book a £5 note:

> I assure you, my dear Sir, that you truly hurt me with your pecuniary parcel. – It degrades me in my own eyes. – However, to return it would savour of bombast affectation; But, as to any more traffic of that D^r & C^r kind, I swear by that HONOUR which crowns the upright Statue of ROB^t BURNS'S INTEGRITY! – On the least motion of it, I will indignantly spurn the bypast transaction, & from that moment commence entire Stranger to you![1]

Burns's resolution to steer clear of trouble held up pretty well. Those 'pestilential fumes of my Political heresies' of which he had written to Nicol seem not to have tickled his nostrils in those early months of 1793. In the spring, indeed, he found an occasion to demonstrate his patriotism and political soundness. Ten years previously, on April 12th, Admiral Rodney's victory over the French off Dominica had saved Jamaica, dented France's naval prestige and, as the war with America drew to a close, done something for Britain's \attered national pride. The anniversary was celebrated in Dumfries at a dinner in the King's Arms; Burns, called on for a song, offered instead some extempore verses:

> Instead of a song, boys, I'll give you a toast,
> Here's the memory of those on the twelfth that we lost;
> That we lost, did I say, nay, by heav'n that we found,
> For their fame it shall last while the world goes round.
> The next in succession, I'll give you the King,
> Whoe'er wou'd betray him, on high may he swing;
> And here's the grand fabric, our free Constitution,
> As built on the base of the great Revolution . . .[2]

That more recent and continuing revolution on the other side of the English Channel was never far from his mind, however. War with France played havoc with trade, with consequences both serious and frivolous. The scope for an excise officer to augment his income by seizures was seriously curtailed; the flow of imports virtually dried up. For fashionable ladies like Maria Riddell the prospect of life without gloves from France was well-nigh unbearable; Burns decided he must exercise himself on her behalf:

> . . . You must know that FRENCH GLOVES are contraband goods, &

1. Letters, 569.
2. Kinsley, 402.

expressly prohibited by the laws of this wise-governed Realm of ours. – A Satirist would say, that this is one reason why the ladies are so fond of them; but I, who have not one grain of GALL in my composition, shall alledge, that it is the PATRIOTISM of the dear Goddesses of man's idolatry, that makes them so fond of dress from the LAND OF LIBERTY & EQUALITY...

He had, he informed her, recently been involved in a search through the town for French gloves, and as a result three of Dumfries's principal merchants had been subpœnaed to appear before the Court of Exchequer:

Still, I have discovered one Haberdasher, who, at my particular request, will clothe your fair hands as they ought to be, to keep them from being profaned by the rude gaze of the gloting eye, or – Horrid! – from perhaps A RAPE by the unhallowed lips, of the Satyr Man. – You will remember, though, that you are to tell no body, but the ladies of your acquaintance, & that only on the same condition so that the secret may be sure to be kept, & the poor Haberdasher not ruined by his kindness...[1]

Just occasionally Burns's sympathy for the 'Land of Liberty and Equality' was too strong for his new-found discretion. The French general Charles François Dumouriez ('a most shifty wiry man,' wrote Carlyle, 'one of Heaven's Swiss') had briefly served the Revolution both as minister of foreign affairs and minister of war. After inflicting a severe defeat on the Austrians at Jemappes in November 1792 he was himself defeated at Neerwinden four months later. When commissaries appeared to invite him to appear at the bar of the Convention, he arrested them and handed them over to the Austrians.

Dumouriez then tried to persuade his troops to march on Paris and overthrow the government; when this attempt failed he went over to the enemy camp, taking with him the duc de Montpensier and his brother the duc de Chartres (later King Louis-Philippe). When someone expressed satisfaction at these proceedings in Burns's presence, he was provoked into a bitter riposte, which took the form of a parody of the traditional song 'Robin Adair':

> You're welcome to Despots, Dumourier;
> You're welcome to Despots, Dumourier. –
>   How does Dampiere do?
>   Aye, and Bournonville too?
> Why did they not come along with you, Dumourier?
>
> I will fight France with you, Dumourier, –
> I will fight France with you, Dumourier: –

1. *Letters*, 554 A.

I will fight France with you,
I will take my chance with you;
By my soul I'll dance a dance with you, Dumourier.

Then let us fight about, Dumourier;
Then let us fight about, Dumourier;
    Then let us fight about,
    'Till freedom's spark is out,
Then we'll be d-mned no doubt – Dumourier.[1]

The apartment which Burns and his ever-increasing family occupied in the Wee Vennel was now bursting at the seams, and at Whitsun 1793 they moved to a larger property in what was then known as Mill Hole Brae.[2] It was a stone-built house on two floors, and it belonged, like the flat in the Vennel, to Hamilton of Allershaw. The rent was set at £8 a year (Burns had previously paid £6) and he laid out a certain amount on fittings – a new fire-grate cost him £1 8s. His son Robert, six years old at the time of the move, recalled in later years what he had seen with the clear eyes of childhood:

> There was much rough comfort in the house, not to have been found in those of ordinary citizens; for besides the spoils of smugglers, the poet received many presents of game and country produce from the rural gentle-folk, besides occasional barrels of oysters from Hill, Cunningham, and other friends in town . . .

He remembered the house as well furnished and carpeted; when there was company, 'the hospitable board which they surrounded was of a patrician mahagony.'[3]

Jean was to live out the rest of her long life in the Mill Hole Brae house. Many years after Burns's death a local man called John McDiarmid prodded her memory about their domestic routines. Burns, she volunteered, 'was not an early riser, except when he had anything particular to do in the way of his profession':

> The family breakfasted at nine. If he lay long in bed awake he was always reading. At all his meals he had a book beside him on the table. He did his

---

1. Kinsley, 401. The marquis de Dampierre was one of Dumouriez's generals, whom he had hoped would desert with him. The marquis de Beurnonville, Minister of War and leader of the deputation despatched by the Convention, similarly disappointed him. Dumouriez eventually settled in England and was an adviser to the War Office during the struggle with Napoleon. He died at Henley-on-Thames in 1823.

2. It later became Millbrae Vennel, and is today known as Burns Street.

3. Mackay, *op. cit.*, p. 532.

work in the forenoon, and was seldom engaged professionally in the evening. He dined at two o'clock when he dined at home; was fond of plain things, and hated tarts, pies, and puddings. When at home in the evening he employed his time in writing and reading, with the children playing about him. Their prattle never disturbed him in the least.[1]

There is a suggestion here that Jean did not always command a place in the forefront of Burns's attention, but that must be set beside other evidence – the recollections, for instance, of Jessy Lawers, whose father and brother both served with Burns in the excise:

He was always anxious that his wife should be well and neatly dressed, and did his utmost to counteract any tendency to carelessness – which she sometimes excused by alleging the duties of a nurse and mother – not only by gentle remonstrance, but by buying for her the best clothes he could afford. He rarely omitted to get for her any little novelty in female dress. She was, for instance, one of the first persons in Dumfries to wear a dress of gingham – stuff which was at its first introduction rather costly, and used almost exclusively by the well-to-do.[2]

That his marriage to Jean was essentially stable and contented seems to me conclusively demonstrated by a throwaway passage, light-hearted but revealing, in a letter written about this time to Robert Aiken. 'Ah! there is nothing like matrimony for setting a man's face Zion-ward!' he wrote:

Whether it be that it sublimes a man above this visible, diurnal sphere – or whether it tires him of this Sublunary state – or whether the delicious morsel of happiness which he enjoys in the conjugal yoke gives him a longing for the feasts above – or whether a poor Husband thinks he has every chance in his favour, as should he go to H-ll he can be no worse – I shall leave to a weel-waled Presbytery of Orthodox Ayrshire priests.[3]

Jean's view of their marriage is less well-documented. She may have joked to a Mauchline friend that 'Oor Robin should hae had twa wives'; the words may, on the other hand, have been put in her mouth by one of the many hagiographers who beat a track to her door during the thirty-eight years of her widowhood. What cannot be questioned are her reserves of tolerance and generosity; in 1791 or 1792 she took in the child which Burns had fathered on Ann Park and brought it up as her own.

The publication of Thomson's first volume had clearly been a stimulus, and

1. John McDiarmid, *Reminiscences of Mrs Burns*, Dumfries, 1827.
2. Quoted in Chambers-Wallace, vol. iv, p. 119.
3. Letters, 570. Weel-waled means well-chosen.

throughout the summer Burns kept up a frequent correspondence with him, sending new or reworked songs, responding good-humouredly to criticism or advice ('What you think a defect, I esteem as a positive beauty: so you see how Doctors differ. – ').[1] It was a period as creative as any since the *annus mirabilis* at Mossgiel when he was feverishly minting the gold of the Kilmarnock edition.

Very occasionally, there was an eruption of political passion:

> Have you ever, my dear Sir, felt your bosom ready to burst with indignation, on reading of, or seeing, how these mighty villains who divide kingdom against kingdom, desolate provinces & lay Nations waste out of the wantonness of Ambition, or often from still more ignoble passions? ... If I have done any thing at all like justice to my feelings, the following song, composed in three-quarters of an hour's lucubrations in my elbow chair, ought to have some merit.[2]

This outburst seems to have been prompted more by Burns's agitation at the general course of events in Europe than by any particular episode. The desertion of Dumouriez had left the way clear for the Austrians and the British to invade France, and at the end of May they had stormed the French camp at Famars. Burns was writing at the end of June. At the beginning of that month, *sansculotte* agitators in Paris had surrounded the Tuileries and expelled the Girondins from the Convention; much of the country was in a state of civil war; in the Vendée and elsewhere the soldiers of the Republic were frequently defeated by the organised peasantry. Abroad, revolutionary propaganda had united the powers of Europe as nothing else could; with the exception of Russia and of such minor states as Denmark, Sweden and Venice, France was now at war with virtually the entire continent.[3]

The result of Burns's 'lucubrations' was the sentimental and unremarkable ballad beginning 'O Logan, sweetly didst thou glide,' in which a young wife bewails her husband's absence at the wars:

> O wae upon you, Men o' State,
> That brethren rouse in deadly hate!
> As ye make mony a fond heart mourn,
> Sae may it on your heads return![4]

Generally, however, Burns's morale was high in the summer of 1793; if for any reason it temporarily sagged, he rapidly wrote himself back into better spirits:

1. *Ibid.*, 567.
2. *Ibid.*, 566.
3. Sweden, Denmark and Venice had declared themselves neutral. Catherine the Great explained her failure to send an army or a fleet against the Republic by pointing out that she was engaged in dealing with Jacobins in Poland.
4. Kinsley, 409.

I am d-mnably out of humour, my dear Ainslie, & that is the reason why I take up the pen to *you* . . .

I rec^d your last, & was much entertained with it; but I will not at this time, nor at any other time, answer it. – Answer a letter? I never could answer a letter in my life! – I have written many a letter in return for letters I have received; but then – they were original matter – spurt – away! zig, here; zag, there; as if the Devil that, my grannie (an old woman *indeed*!) often told me, rode on Will-o'-wisp, or, in her more classic phrase, S P U N K I E, were looking over my elbow. – A happy thought that idea has ingendered in my head! S P U N K I E – thou shalt henceforth be my Symbol, Signature, & Tutelary Genius! Like thee, hap-step-&-lowp, here-awa-there-awa, higglety-pigglety, pell-mell, hither-&-yon, ram-stam, happy-go-lucky, up-tails-a'-by-the-light-o'-the-moon, has been, is, & shall be, my progress through the mosses & moors of this vile, bleak, barren wilderness of a life of ours. –

Come, then, my Guardian Spirit! like thee, may I skip away, amusing myself by & at my own light: and if any opaque-souled lubber of mankind complain that my elfine, lambent, glimmerous wanderings have misled his stupid steps over precipes, or into bogs; let the thick-headed blunderbuss recollect, that he is not S P U N K I E – that

> 'S P U N K I E' S wanderings could not copied be;
> Amid these perils none durst walk but he'[1]

Mrs Dunlop, to whom he had not written since his troubles with the excise during the winter, was also the beneficiary of this spell of summer sunshine; he sent her an epigram on 'a stupid, money-loving dunderpate of a Galloway laird'[2] and the extempore 'On being asked why God had made Miss Davies so little and M^rs S— so big':

Miss D— you must know, is positively the least creature ever I saw, to be at the same time unexceptionably, & indeed uncommonly, handsome & beautiful; & besides has the felicity to be a peculiar favorite of mine. – On the contrary M^rs S— is a huge, bony, masculine, cowp-carl, horse-godmother, he-termagant of a six-feet figure, who might have been bride to Og, King of Bashan; or Goliah of Gath. –

Epigram
Ask why God made the G E M so small,
And why so huge the Granite?
Because, God meant mankind should set
That higher value on it. –[3]

1. Letters, 561. The couplet is paraphrased from Dryden's *Prologue to The Tempest*.
2. Kinsley, 411 A.
3. Letters, 563. The identity of the generously-proportioned Mrs S is not known.

Towards the end of July, Burns and Syme went off together on a short tour of Galloway, Burns riding a grey Highland pony which his friend had provided for him. For three days they were entertained by John Gordon at Kenmure Castle, the seat of the Gordons of Lochinvar. The family had played host to Mary, Queen of Scots, during her western tour in 1563; after the rout of her army at Langside five years later, it was Lochinvar who provided the clothing in which she disguised herself. Gordon's grandfather, the sixth Lord Kenmure, had raised the Jacobite standard at Lochmaben in 1715, marched south with the rebel army, was taken prisoner at Preston and beheaded on Tower Hill two months later.

'Here is a genuine baron's seat,' wrote Syme. 'Burns thinks so highly of it that he meditates a description of it in poetry.' More immediately, however, the bard was required to sing for his supper by composing an epitaph for Mrs Gordon's recently deceased lapdog, Echo. 'This was setting Hercules to the distaff,' Syme later told Currie. 'He disliked the subject, but, to please the lady, he would try.'[1] And so he did, to singularly dire effect:

> In wood and wild, ye warbling throng,
>   Your heavy loss deplore;
> Now, half extinct your powers of song,
>   Sweet Echo is no more . . .[2]

John Gordon kept a barge. He proposed to his guests an excursion on Loch Ken, and they sailed down the loch as far as the Airds Hill. The barge ran aground shortly before reaching the intended landing place; the party included the local minister, who was elderly; Burns coaxed him onto his shoulders and waded ashore. This struck Syme as extremely funny. 'Well, Burns,' he called out, 'of all the men on earth, you are the last that I could have expected to see priest-ridden.' Burns did not join in the general laughter.

The next day, as they headed across the moors from Kenmure to Gatehouse the weather turned bad: 'The sky,' Syme wrote, 'was sympathetic with the wretchedness of the soil.' Burns enjoyed the wind and the rain and the thunder and lightning, but when they reached their destination three hours later insisted that they should have their revenge by getting 'utterly drunk'.

Burns had kitted himself out for the journey with a pair of new riding boots. They had smart white tops and had set him back £1 2s. These jemmy boots, as they were called, did not stand up well to their immersion in the loch and their exposure to the elements, and once they had dried out Burns was unable to get them on again. 'The brawny poet tried force and tore them to shreds,' Syme recorded:

1. Currie, vol. i, p. 202.
2. Kinsley, 416. Burns, gritting his teeth, composed two versions, each of two stanzas. It is difficult to say which is the more dreadful.

A whiffling vexation of this sort is more trying to the temper than a serious calamity. We were going to St Mary's Isle, the seat of the Earl of Selkirk, and the forlorn Burns was discomfited at the thought of his ruined boots. A sick stomach and a headache lent their aid, and the man of verse was quite *accablé*. I attempted to reason with him. Mercy on us, how he did fume and rage! Nothing could reinstate him in temper. I tried various expedients, and at last hit on one that succeeded. I showed him the house of Garlieston, across the Bay of Wigton. Against the Earl of Galloway, with whom he was offended, he expectorated his spleen and regained a most agreeable temper.

Syme told Alexander Cunningham that Burns had reeled off 'about half a dozen of capital extempores'. The four which survive are all equally disobliging:

> What dost thou in that mansion fair,
>   Flit, G—! and find
> Some narrow, dirty, dungeon cave,
>   The picture of thy mind. —[1]

What John Stewart, the seventh Earl of Galloway, had done to deserve this unpleasant spurt of venom is obscure. He was unknown to Burns, noted for his piety, a lover of music and a kindly and generous landlord – perhaps he gave offence by his Tory politics. When told that Burns had exercised his poetic skills on him, he remarked that 'it would not become him, when his good old master The King despised and disregarded the paltry attacks of a Peter Pindar, to feel himself hurt by those of a licentious, rhyming plough-man'.[2]

The travellers reached Kirkcudbright in the early afternoon and put up at the Heid Inn. Syme recorded that Burns 'had not absolutely regained the milkiness of good temper'; when they set out in the evening for St Mary's Isle he reflected sourly more than once that like Garlieston, it was the seat of a Lord. The Earl of Selkirk's politics were much more to his liking, however; he was, after all, the father of the progressive and francophile Lord Daer whom he had met at Dugald Stewart's house seven years previously.

They arrived about eight. The company was at tea and coffee. 'We found all the ladies of the family (all beautiful) at home,' wrote Syme, 'and some strangers, and among others who but Urbani.' Pietro Urbani, a native of Milan, had settled in Edinburgh in 1784 and pursued a career as teacher, singer and

---

1. Kinsley, 415.
2. Galloway's riposte is recorded in the manuscript *Memoir of the lawyer Alexander Young of Harburn*, reproduced in Fitzhugh, *op. cit.*, pp. 61-93. 'Peter Pindar' was John Wolcot (1738-1819). Boswell, in his *Life of Johnson*, describes him as 'a contemptible scribbler [who], having disgraced and deserted the clerical character ... picks up in London a scanty livelihood by scurrilous lampoons under feigned name.'

composer. He and the daughters of the house sang, and Burns recited 'Lord Gregory':

> O mirk, mirk is this midnight hour,
>   And loud the tempest's roar:
> A waefu' wanderer seeks thy tower,
>   Lord Gregory ope thy door . . .[1]

'Such was the effect that a dead silence ensued,' wrote Syme. 'The poet was delighted with his company. The lion that had raged so violently in the morning was now as mild and gentle as a lamb.' The next day they returned to Dumfries.

Throughout August, Burns deluged Thomson with letters – no fewer than nine survive. One of them took the form of a deed of assignment of copyright.[2] In others he transmitted a whole sheaf of new offerings for the *Collection* – these included 'Phillis the fair', 'O poortith cauld, & restless love' and 'Had I a cave on some wild, distant shore'.[3] He also sent the lovely song 'Let me in this ae night':

> O lassie, art thou sleeping yet,
>   Or art thou wakin, I would wit,
> For love has bound me, hand and foot,
>   And I would fain be in, jo.[4]

There was one letter into which he injected a shrewd touch of ginger:

Is, Whistle & I'll come to you, my lad – one of your airs? – I admire it much; & yesterday I set the following verses to it. – Urbani, whom I have met with here, begged them of me, as he admires the air much; but as I understand that he looks with rather an evil eye on your WORK, I did not chuse to comply. – However, if the song does not suit your taste, I may possibly send it to him. – He is, éntre nous, a narrow, contracted creature; but he sings so delightfully, that whatever he introduces at your concert, must have immediate celebrity. –[5]

Urbani had begun to publish *A Selection of Scots Songs* the previous year. The accompaniments were elaborate and each volume was dedicated to a lady of title. The arrangements were generally much admired, although Thomson, unappreciative of the prospect of competition, spoke of 'a water-gruel collec-

---

1. Kinsley, 399.
2. Letters, 574 A.
3. Kinsley, 418, 398 and 419 respectively.
4. *Ibid.*, 485.
5. Letters, 578.

tion'. So far as 'O whistle, and I'll come to ye, my lad' was concerned he had
the good sense to snap it up quickly for himself.

The chorus is traditional, and five years previously Burns had sent it, with
a single verse of his own, to Johnson for the *Scots Musical Museum*. He considered the expanded version he now offered to Thomson one of his best
efforts, and he was right. The words fit the tune like a glove, and are every bit
as lively. The song is essentially a variation on the theme of a night visit to a
girl, which is as old as folk music itself, but Burns contrives for the young
singer a marvellous range of mood and colour:

> But warily tent, when ye come to court me,   take care
> And come nae unless the back-yett be a-jee;   -gate, ajar
> Syne up the back-style and let naebody see,   then
>   And come as ye were na comin to me.—
>
> At kirk, or at market whene'er ye meet me,
> Gang by me as tho' that ye car'd nae a flie;
> But steal me a blink o' your bonie black e'e,
>   Yet look as ye were na lookin at me.—[1]

Burns was not above having a spot of gentle fun at Thomson's expense from
time to time. 'You know that my pretensions to musical taste, are merely a few
of Nature's instincts, untaught and untutored by Art,' he wrote towards the
end of August:

> For this reason, many musical compositions, particularly where much of the
> merit lies in Counterpoint . . . affect my simple lug no otherwise than merely
> as melodious Din. – On the other hand, by way of amends, I am delighted
> with many little melodies, which the learned Musician despises as silly &
> insipid. – I do not know whether the old Air, "Hey tutti taitie," may rank
> among this number . . .[2]

It was a tune, he wrote, which had often filled his eyes with tears. There was
a tradition, which he had encountered in many parts of Scotland, that Robert
Bruce's men had marched to it at the battle of Bannockburn; now he offered
Thomson some words to it, in the form of an ode on liberty and independence:

> SCOTS, wha hae wi' WALLACE bled,
> SCOTS, wham BRUCE has aften led,
> Welcome to your gory bed,—
>   Or to victorie.—

1. Kinsley, 420.
2. Letters, 582.

Burns added a postscript to his letter – he had shown the tune to Urbani, he told Thomson, and it was he who had begged him 'to make soft verses for it'. He also let slip that he had not found his inspiration solely in Scottish history: the recollection of Bannockburn was associated in his mind 'with the glowing ideas of some other struggles of the same nature, *not quite so ancient*'.

Thomson was bowled over: 'Your Heroic ode is to me the noblest Composition of the kind in the Scottish language'. His enthusiasm for the words did not extend to the music, however, and he told Burns that a party of friends with whom he had dined the previous evening had been equally lukewarm, judging it to be 'totally devoid of interest or grandeur'. What about the air called 'Lewie Gordon'? This was an altogether more insipid affair, but to Thomson and his fellow-arbiters of musical taste in the capital it had 'more of the grand than the plaintive'. All Burns would have to do would be add a foot to every fourth line of the song ... Thomson had one other small reservation:

> I think, with great deference to the poet, that a prudent general would avoid saying anything to his soldiers which might tend to make death more frightful than it is. 'Gory' presents a disagreeable image to the mind; and to tell them, 'Welcome to your gory bed,' seems rather a discouraging address, notwithstanding the alternative which follows ... I would suggest –
>
> > Now prepare for honour's bed,
> > Or for glorious victory.[1]

Burns's response to most of these fatuous suggestions was remarkably patient. 'I am happy, my dear Sir, that my Ode pleases you so much,' he wrote on September 8th. 'Your idea, "honour's bed," is, though a beautiful, a hacknied idea; so, if you please, we will let the line stand as it is.' By the middle of the month, however, although his tone remained unruffled, he had plainly had enough. 'Who shall decide, when Doctors disagree?' he wrote, wheeling out one of his favourite quotations from Pope's *Moral Essays*:

> My Ode pleases me so much that I cannot alter it. – Your proposed alterations would, in my opinion, make it tame ... I have scrutinized it over & over; & to the world some way or other, it shall go as it is. –[2]

And so in the end it did. Thomson initially persisted in his preference for 'Lewie Gordon' but eventually, five years after Burns's death, he recanted, acknowledging that the poet's choice of melody 'gave more energy to the words'.[3] It has been sung ever since – not just in Scots, but in Czech and

---

1. Letters dated 5th and 12th September 1793, quoted in Chambers-Wallace, vol. iv, pp. 40 and 48-9.
2. Letters, 587.
3. *A Select Collection* (1801), p. 133.

German, in French and Swedish, in Welsh and Italian, in Hungarian and in Latin. And with no less energy and passion than that other patriotic marching song, 'La Marseillaise', which had been composed the year before.[1]

Burns's bombardment of Thomson by letter continued through September; there cannot have been much time for excise work:

> I dare say, my dear Sir, that you will begin to think my correspondence is persecution. – No matter – I can't help it – a Ballad is my hobby-horse; which, though otherwise a simple sort of harmless, idiotical beast enough, has yet this blessed headstrong property, that when once it has fairly made off with a hapless wight, it gets so enamoured with the tinkle-gingle, tinkle-gingle of its own bells, that it is sure to run poor Pilgarlick, the bedlam Jockey, quite beyond any useful point or post in the common race of MAN. –[2]

Thomson had sent Burns a list of a hundred airs. He did not intend to go beyond that number, partly on grounds of cost, partly on grounds of quality: 'I find my list contains every fine air that is known of the serious and pastoral kind,' he wrote, 'all diamonds of the first water'. He was frank about his reliance on Burns: 'I certainly have got into a scrape if you do not stand my friend,' he confessed. 'A couple of stanzas to each air will do as well as half a dozen; and to an imagination so infinitely fruitful as yours this will not be a Herculean labour.'[3]

Burns gave the list his immediate attention. His immensely long and detailed reply, pithy, practical, authoritative, gives a marvellous insight into the working of a first-class editorial mind:

> N° 11th Bonie Dundee – Your objection of the stiff line, is just; but mending my colouring would spoil my likeness; so the Picture must stand as it is . . .
>
> N° 24 . . . 'Cruel joys,' is a d—d stupid expression . . .
>
> N° 34. Gill Morice – I am unalterably, for leaving out altogether. – It is a plaguey length, which will put you to great Press-expence; the air itself, is never sung . . .
>
> N° 53. Banks of the Dee – Leave it out entirely – 'tis rank Irish . . . why 'tis no more like a Scots air, than Lunardi's balloon is like Diogenes' tub . . .
>
> 59. Dainty Davie, – I have heard sung, nineteen thousand, nine hundred

---

1. In April 1792 the Mayor of Strasbourg had deplored the fact that the young soldiers of the Revolution had no patriotic song to sing. Claude Joseph Rouget de Lisle, a captain of engineers and amateur violinist then stationed in the town, returned to his lodgings and in one night wrote the words and music of his 'Chant de guerre pour l'armée du Rhin'.

2. Letters, 583.

3. Letter dated 20th August 1793, quoted in Chambers-Wallace, vol. iv, pp. 28-9.

& ninety nine times, & always with the chorus to the low part of the tune; & nothing, since a Highland wench in the Cowgate once bore me three bastards at a birth, has surprised me so much, as your opinion on this Subject . . .

The letter is also important because of the well-known digression in which Burns describes his own working methods: 'Untill I am compleat master of a tune, in my own singing, (such as it is) I never can compose for it,' he told Thomson:

> My way is: I consider the poetic Sentiment, correspondent to my idea of the musical expression; then chuse my theme; begin one Stanza; when that is composed, which is generally the most difficult part of the business, I walk out, sit down now & then, look out for objects in Nature around me that are in unison or harmony with the cogitations of my fancy & workings of my bosom; humming every now & then the air with the verses I have framed: when I feel my Muse beginning to jade, I retire to the solitary fireside of my study, & there commit my effusions to paper; swinging, at intervals, on the hind-legs of my elbow-chair, by way of calling forth my own critical strictures, as my pen goes on. –
> Seriously, this, at home, is almost invariably my way. – What damn'd Egotism![1]

Although Burns had schooled himself to keep his head down publicly, there was a small incident in the autumn of 1793 which showed that he had not changed his political spots. A public library had been established in Dumfries by public subscription the previous September, and Burns had presented it with a copy of his *Poems*. In March 1793, 'out of respect and esteem for his abilities as a literary man,' the committee offered him a free share in the library, thus exempting him from the admission charge, which then stood at 10s 6d, and the quarterly subscription of 2s 6d, and a few months later he was elected to the committee.

At the end of September, Burns made a presentation to the library of four books. Two of them were novels – Smollett's *Humphrey Clinker* and *Julia de Roubigné*, a sentimental work by Henry Mackenzie. The other two volumes were much weightier affairs – John Knox's *History of the Reformation* and an analysis of the British constitution by a Swiss called Jean Louis De Lolme. Burns, not always able to resist the temptation to show off, decided that he must adorn this last tome with an inscription: 'Mr Burns presents this book to the Library, & begs they will take it as a creed of British Liberty – untill they find a better. R.B.' Overnight, discretion reasserted itself as the better part of radical valour. Very early the next morning the man with whom the books had

1. Letters, 586.

been left awoke to find an anxious Burns at his bedside. He feared that he had written something in the De Lolme 'which might bring him into trouble'. The inscription had been written on the back of the frontispiece; it was quickly pasted over with the adjoining fly-leaf.

The book is preserved today in the Robert Burns Centre, and the leaves are once again separate. The words no longer sound particularly inflammatory, but circumstances alter cases; four weeks before Burns wrote them, Thomas Muir of Huntershill had been sentenced to fourteen years' transportation for sedition.

One of the main charges of the indictment was that he had advised and exhorted people 'to purchase and peruse seditious and wicked publications'. Annie Fisher, a former scullery maid in his parents' house, testified that Muir often told country people coming to his father's shop that *The Rights of Man* was a very good book. She also said that Muir frequently read French law books . . . She offered the court some learned comments on Constantin Volvey's book *Les Ruines, ou méditations sur les révolutions des empires*, a speculative essay on the philosophy of history covering a span of six thousand years and another of the wicked publications cited in the indictment.

It was an impressively erudite performance, even for a Scottish scullery maid, but then bribery and rehearsal can achieve much. Before leaving the witness box, she said that Muir had once sent her out to ask a street organist to play a tune called 'Ça ira', and this was the Lord Advocate's cue to assert that this was employed in France 'as a signal for blood and carnage'. Perhaps it was sensible of Burns to get up so early on the morning of October 1st and paste those pages of De Lolme's book together.

He found time, in the rare intervals of his correspondence with Thomson, to keep up with old Edinburgh friends. 'I have just bought a quire of Post,' he wrote at the end of October, '& I am determined, my Dear Cleghorn, to give you the maidenhead of it.' He was feeling distinctly fragile: 'From my late hours last night, & the dripping fogs & damn'd east-wind of this stupid day, I have left me as little soul as an oyster.'[1] His main purpose, as so often when writing to Cleghorn, was to show off his latest essays in obscenity, and on this occasion he favoured him with two. One of them describes a vigorous if improbable sexual encounter between 'Bonie Mary' and 'wanton Wattie':

And was nae Wattie a Clinker,	lively rogue
He m-w'd frae the Queen to the tinkler,	copulated with
Then sat down, in grief, like the Macedon chief	
For want o' mae warlds to conquer.—	more

Chorus
Come cowe me, minnie, come cowe me;   crop
Come cowe me, minnie, come cowe me;

1. Letters, 592.

The hair o' my a— is grown into my c—t,
And they canna win to, to m—we me[1]   manage to

'Bawdry written round the theme of pubic hair,' notes Kinsley, rather wearily, 'is common in Scots.'

Burns also sent Cleghorn 'Act Sederunt of the Session – A Scots Ballad'. This, however, was not one of his own efforts. Always scrupulous about his sources, he later noted that it was composed by a whore from Kilmarnock called Jean Glover: 'I took [it] down . . . from her singing as she was strolling through the country, with a slight-of hand blackguard.'[2] In Scots law an Act of Sederunt was an ordinance for regulating the forms of procedure before the Court of Session; here it is used more loosely to mean the judgement of a court of law:

> Chorus
> Act Sederunt o' the Session,
>   Decreet o' the Court o' Session,
> That standing pr-cks are fauteors a',   (sexual) defaulters
>   And guilty of a high transgression.
>
> And they've provided dungeons deep,
>   Ilk lass has ane in her possession;
> Untill the wretches wail and weep,
>   They there shall lie for their transgression . . .[3]

To Alexander Cunningham, a few weeks later, he sent a very different sort of composition. He described it as 'a simple old Scots song which I had pickt up in this country' and which Urbani had promised to set for him. He would, he told Cunningham, most gladly have sent it to Thomson, but was convinced that they would disagree about it: 'What to me, appears the simple & the wild, to him, & I suspect to you likewise, will be looked on as the ludicrous & the absurd.'[4]

Posterity has sided with Burns:

> O my Love's like the red, red rose,
>   That's newly sprung in June:
> My Love's like the melodie
>   That's sweetly play'd in tune. –
>
> As fair art thou, my bonie lass,
>   So deep in love am I;
> And I can love thee still, my Dear,
>   Till a' the seas gang dry. –

1. Kinsley, 435.
2. The note occurs in Burns's interleaved copy of the *Scots Musical Museum*, p. 57.
3. Kinsley, 436.
4. Letters, 593 A.

Till a' the seas gang dry, my Dear,
  And the rocks melt wi' the sun:
I will love thee still, my Dear,
  While the sands o' life shall run. –

And fare thee weel, my only Love,
  O fare thee weel a while!
And I will come again, my Love,
  Tho' 'twere ten thousand mile. –[1]

Scholars have burrowed their way through hundreds of chapbooks and ballad collections over the years and pounced on echoes of many popular songs in this beautiful lyric. It is for all that a striking instance of what Thomas Crawford describes as 'the perfection of the old achieving the shock and immediacy of the new'.[2]

Burns was still powerfully attracted by the glare of the footlights and the smell of greasepaint. 'We have had a brilliant Theatre here, this season,' he told Mrs Dunlop, 'only, as all other business has, it experiences a stagnation of trade from the epidemical complaint of the Country – "WANT OF CASH". Then he came clean: "I mention our Theatre, merely to lug in an occasional Address which I wrote for the Benefit-Night of one of the Actresses.'[3] Burns had sent the Address to the delectable Miss Fontenelle, together with a high-flown (and much-corrected) letter –

> . . . Were I a man of gallantry & fashion, strutting & fluttering in the foreground of the picture of Life, making the speech to a lovely young girl might be construed to be one of the doings of All-powerful Love; but you will be surprised, my dear Madam, when I tell you, that it is not Love, nor even Friendship, but sheer Avarice . . .'[4]

This was probably some way above Miss Fontenelle's pretty head; Burns found a better range with 'On seeing Miss Fontenelle in a Favourite Character', which was much shorter and a good deal less elaborate:

Sweet naïveté of feature,
  Simple wild, enchanting elf,
Not to thee, but thanks to nature,
  Thou art acting but thyself . . .[5]

1. Kinsley, 453.
2. Crawford, op. cit. p. 278.
3. Letters, 605.
4. Letters, 599.
5. Kinsley, 440. The 'Address' is Kinsley 439.

Burns was acting, too – his gallantries to Louise Fontenelle were no more than an agreeable game. With Maria Riddell, on the other hand, his emotions were much more seriously engaged. None of her letters to him has survived, but we have more than twenty of his, because she docketed and numbered them. He admired her, and he respected her judgement. In one letter she is 'thou first & fairest of Critics' and 'Thou most amiable & accomplished of Thy Sex'.[1] In the next he asks her to accept a new song: 'It is a trifling present, but – "Give all thou canst",' he writes:

> Were my esteem for a certain Lady to be measured by a musical offering, that could not be less than the music of the Spheres in Score, or the Haleluias of the Hierarchies with all their accompaniments.—[2]

The war had turned Dumfries into a garrison town, but Burns did not share the view that the officers of the regiments stationed there added a welcome touch of colour to local society – not, at least, when he found them competing for the attention of Mrs Riddell at the theatre (her husband had gone off to the West Indies and was away for several months). He dashed off a jealous little note:

> I meant to have called on you yesternight, but as I edged up [to] your Box-door, the first object which greeted my view was one of these lobster-coated PUPPIES, sitting, like another dragon, guarding the Hesperian fruit . . . [3]

He obviously received a reply that mollified him: 'On the conditions & capitulations you so obligingly make,' he wrote, 'I shall certainly make my plain, weather-beaten, rustic phiz a part of your box furniture on Tuesday.'[4]

Her birthday fell early in November, and Burns sent her an impromptu, in which he imagines Winter grumbling to Jove about having drawn the short straw in the matter of weather:

> Now, Jove, for once be mighty civil;
> To counter balance all this evil;
> Give me, and I've no more to say,
> Give me MARIA'S natal day!
> That brilliant gift will so enrich me,
> Spring, Summer, Autumn, cannot match me.[5]

He was more than a little in love with her. Not since the days of his intimacy with Peggy Chalmers had there been anyone of the opposite sex with whom

---

1. *Letters*, 595.
2. *Ibid.*, 595 A.
3. *Ibid.*, 594.
4. *Ibid.*, 595.
5. Kinsley, 438.

he felt able to be so open and direct (Mrs Dunlop, who was old enough to be his mother, was a special case). In Maria Riddell he recognised not only an intellectual equal but a kindred spirit; with her he could lower his guard, and some of his deepest frustrations – and longings – came tumbling out without inhibition:

> I will wait on you, my ever-valued Friend; but whether in the morning, I am not sure. – Sunday closes a period of our cursed revenue business, & may probably keep me employed with my pen until Noon. – Fine employment for a Poet's pen! There is a species of the Human genus that I call, the Gin-horse Class: what enviable dogs they are! – Round, & round, & round they go – Mundell's ox that drives his cotton-mill, their exact prototype – without an idea or wish beyond their circle; fat, sleek, stupid, patient, quiet & contented: – while here I sit, altogether Novemberish, a damn'd mélange of Fretfulness & melancholy; not enough of the one to rouse me to passion; nor of the other to repose me in torpor; my soul flouncing & fluttering round her tenement, like a wild Finch caught amid the horrors of winter & newly thrust into a cage. –[1]

He was still deep in winter depression when he wrote to Mrs Dunlop the following month, but to her he disclosed a reason more serious than the tedium of his excise work:

> As I am in a compleat Decemberish humour, gloomy, sullen, stupid, as even the deity of Dullness herself could wish, I will not drawl out a heavy letter with a number of heavier apologies for my late silence. – [he had not written since August.] Only one I shall mention, because I know you will sympathise in it: these four months, a sweet little girl, my youngest child, has been so ill, that every day, a week or less threatened to terminate her existence. –

His anxiety about the child had affected his sleep, and had set him brooding on his own mortality:

> I see a train of helpless little folks; me, & my exertions, all their stay; & on what a brittle thread does the life of man hang! If I am nipt off, at the command of Fate; even in all the vigour of manhood as I am, such things happen every day – Gracious God! what would become of my little flock! – 'Tis here that I envy your people of fortune. –[2]

Burns had again been drinking heavily in the autumn of 1793. 'Forgive this

---

1. Letters, 600. A. James Mundell was a retired naval surgeon who had a medical practice in Dumfries. He also had an interest in a small cotton mill, powered by an ox on a treadmill.
2. *Ibid.*, 605.

wicked scrawl,' he had written at the end of his letter to Cleghorn. 'Thine, in all the sincerity of a brace of honest Port.' Some weeks later, on an evening in early December, he encountered a Major William Robertson of the Perthshire Fencibles, who was a friend of Glenriddell's. The long letter he wrote to him the next day, enclosing a copy of 'Scots Wha Hae', indicates an awareness that he had not made a good impression: 'Sir, – heated as I was with wine yesternight, I was perhaps rather seemingly impertinent in my anxious wish to be honored with your acquaintance. – You will forgive it: twas the impulse of heart-felt respect ...'[1]

Robertson did forgive it, as it happened, and the two men corresponded further, but at the turn of the year Burns found himself caught up in an evening of drunken debauchery which had infinitely more painful consequences. The close of 1792 had found him in a state of agitation as the Board of Excise prepared to enquire into his political conduct and he had taken up his pen to Graham of Fintry: 'I adjure you to save me from that misery that threatens to overwhelm me.' A year later, the misery was of a more personal nature. The threat now was not that he should lose his livelihood but that he should forfeit the esteem of a family with whom he had enjoyed the closest ties of friendship.

The morning after the night before is not always a good time to write letters, but this one could not wait:

Madam,
    I daresay this is the first epistle you ever received from this nether world. I write you from the regions of Hell, amid the horrors of the damned. The time and manner of my leaving your earth I do not exactly know, as I took my departure in the heat of a fever of intoxication, contracted at your too hospitable mansion; but, on my arrival here, I was fairly tried, and sentenced to endure the purgatorial tortures of this infernal confine for the space of ninety-nine years, eleven months, and twenty-nine days, and all on account of the impropriety of my conduct yesternight under your roof. Here am I, laid on a bed of pityless furze, with my aching head reclined on a pillow of ever-piercing thorn, while an infernal tormentor, wrinkled and old, and cruel, his name I think is *Recollection*, with a whip of scorpions, forbids peace or rest to approach me, and keeps anguish eternally awake. Still, Madam, if I could in any measure be reinstated in the good opinion of the fair circle whom my conduct last night so much injured, I think it would be an alleviation to my torments. For this reason I trouble you with this letter. To the men of the company I will make no apology. – Your husband, who insisted on my drinking more than I chose, has no right to blame me; and the other gentlemen were partakers of my guilt. But to you, Madam, I have much to apologize. Your good opinion I valued as one of the greatest acquisitions I had made on earth, and I was truly a beast to forfeit it. There was a Miss I—,

1. *Ibid.*, 600.

too, a woman of fine sense, gentle and unassuming manners – do make, on my part, a miserable d—d wretch's best apology to her. A Mrs. G—, a charming woman, did me the honour to be prejudiced in my favour; this makes me hope that I have not outraged her beyond all forgiveness. – To all the other ladies please present my humblest contrition for my conduct, and my petition for their gracious pardon. O, all ye powers of decency and decorum! whisper to them that my errors, though great, were involuntary – that an intoxicated man is the vilest of beasts – that it was not in my nature to be brutal to any one – that to be rude to a woman, when in my senses, was impossible with me – but –

* * * * * *

Regret! Remorse! Shame! ye three hell-hounds that ever dog my steps and bay at my heels, spare me! spare me!

Forgive the offences, and pity the perdition of, Madam,
Your humble slave,[1]

1. *Ibid.*, 608.

Fourteen

LOW SPIRITS AND
BLUE DEVILS

THE 'LETTER FROM HELL' is a text-book example of how not to grovel.
In the first place it is far too long. The temptation to show off was always
strong when Burns had his pen in his hand, and what begins as an apology
quickly runs away with him and turns into a literary exercise, by turns mannered, flippant and lumbering. It contains an excellent description of what it
feels like to have a hangover; as an expression of contrition it is less than
well-judged and might quickly have an offended hostess's fingers drumming
on the table.

But what exactly was he apologising for? And to whom? Neither question
can be answered with certainty. We are groping our way through yet another
of those tantalising episodes in Burns's life which it is well-nigh impossible to
document, the scanty range of ascertainable fact richly garlanded in impen-
etrable 'tradition'.

'The men sat too long over their wine,' wrote Chambers in the nineteenth
century:

Some madcap with the flowers in his hair seems to have suggested a wild
rush to the drawing room and a romp with the ladies. The story goes that
every man seized a lady and kissed her, and that the hostess fell to Burns.
There is no room for the suggestion that the frolic went further; the presence
of the host himself renders such a suggestion preposterous . . .[1]

Writing in the more politically conscious 1930s, Catherine Carswell elabor-
ated a theory of conspiracy. She argued that the idea of improvising a re-
enactment of the rape of the Sabines was not just country-house high jinks
but an officer-class ploy to put the radical ploughman-poet turned gauger in
his place. In this version, Burns descends on the ladies like an accomplished
method actor, while his fellow-Romans slyly stop short, sniggering and hic-

1. Chambers-Wallace, vol. iv, p. 76.

cuping in the doorway as they savour his humiliation and disgrace. (*'Without*
D.H. LAWRENCE, MY FRIEND, AND DONALD CARSWELL, MY HUS-
BAND,' reads Mrs Carswell's dedication, *'this book could not have been.'*)

The 'letter from Hell' was first published in the 1803 edition of Currie's
biography, but the manuscript has now disappeared. Currie certainly edited it
(the asterisks towards the end are his) and he may well have doctored it, too;
he printed no signature or date and identified the addressee only as Mrs
R*****. It was assumed for many years that Burns was apologising to Maria,
but his reference in the letter to his hostess's husband makes nonsense of that,
because at the time Walter Riddell was still in the West Indies. The plea for
reinstatement was therefore addressed to the other Mrs Riddell, Glenriddell's
wife, Elizabeth, after whom Burns had named his daughter; the disastrous
evening took place not at Woodley Park, but at Friars' Carse – the scene of
the more auspicious Whistle contest four years previously.

The break with Friars' Carse was total and final. Elizabeth Riddell did not
choose to forgive her 'humble slave,' and no more did her husband – there
was, in truth, little time for him to do so, because within four months, at the
age of thirty-nine, the amiable and hard-drinking Robert Riddell was dead. A
year later the estate was sold and his widow went to live with her father and
an unmarried sister in Edinburgh; she eventually moved to Bath, and was to
die there in 1801.

Whether Maria had witnessed Burns's humiliation at Friars' Carse is not
known, but it is plain that she had taken her sister- and brother-in-law's part,
and in the early days of 1794 we see Burns, tail miserably between his legs,
trying frantically to salvage his friendship with her. He sent her a copy of
Werther: 'Truly happy to have any, the smallest, opportunity of obliging you,'
he wrote pathetically:

'Tis true, Madam, I saw you once since I was at W[oodley] p[ark]; and that
once froze the very life-blood of my heart. – Your reception of me was such,
that a wretch, meeting the eye of his Judge, about to pronounce sentence of
death on him, could only have envied my feelings & situation. –[1]

A few days later he tried again, this time in verse:

To Maria –
    Epigram – on Lord Buchan's assertion, that 'Women ought always to be
flattered grossly, or not spoken to at all' –

                'Praise woman still!' his Lordship says,
                  'Deserved, or not, no matter,'
             But thee, Maria, while I praise,
               There Flattery cannot flatter. –

1. Letters, 609.

> Maria, all my thought and dream,
> Inspires my vocal shell:
> The more I praise my lovely Theme
> The more the truth I tell. –

R.B.[1]

It was no use. The pained formality of a third letter, dated January 12th, is a clear acknowledgement of defeat:

Madam

I return your Common Place Book. – I have perused it with much pleasure, & would have continued my criticisms; but as it seems the Critic has forfeited your esteem, his strictures must lose their value. –

If it is true, that "Offences come only from the heart;" – before you, I am guiltless: – To admire, esteem, prize and adore you, as the most accomplished of Women, & the first of Friends – if these are crimes, I am the most offending thing alive. –

In a face where I used to meet the kind complacency of friendly confidence, *now* to find cold neglect & contemptuous scorn – is a wrench that my heart can ill bear. – It is however some kind of miserable good luck; that while De-haut-en-bas rigour may depress an unoffending wretch to the ground, it has a tendency to rouse a stubborn something in his bosom, which, though it cannot heal the wounds of his soul, is at least an opiate to blunt their poignancy –

With the profoundest respect for your exalted abilities; the most sincere esteem & ardent regard for your gentle heart & amiable manners; & the most fervent wish & prayer for your welfare, peace & bliss –[2]

Burns, hurt and angry, now turned extremely nasty – an intention he had signalled in his letter with the passage about 'De-haut-en-bas rigour'. The 'stubborn something in his bosom' was not slow to show itself and it took the form of a powerful desire to wound:

> How cold is that bosom which folly once fired,
> How pale is that cheek where the rouge lately glistened;
> How silent that tongue which the echoes oft tired,
> How dull is that ear which to flattery listened. –[3]

'Monody on Maria' runs to six stanzas, each of them shot through with malice. One line – 'Here Vanity strums on her idiot lyre' – is buttressed by a sneering

1. *Ibid.*, 610 A.
2. *Ibid.*, 611.
3. Kinsley, 443.

footnote: 'N.B. the lady affected to be a Poetess.' Nor was he content, having vented his venom in this way, to let the piece lie in a drawer. A copy went to Mrs Dunlop: 'How do you like the following verses, which I wrote the other day on a fantastical, fine-fashioned Dame of my acquaintance?' he enquired cockily.[1]

He was also rather pleased with himself over the four-line squib 'Pinned to Mrs R—'s carriage –', and enclosed it in a letter to young Patrick Miller, the local MP. 'How do you like the following clinch?' he asked. 'If your friends think this worth insertion, they are welcome.'[2]

> If you rattle along like your Mistress's tongue,
>   Your speed will outrival the dart:
> But, a fly for your load, you'll break down on her road,
>   If your stuff be as rotten's her heart. –[3]

The friends in question were the proprietors of the London *Morning Chronicle*. They were discriminating enough to decline the offer.

Burns had mauled many people in his time, but however ferocious the ridicule there was usually a hint of a smile, a suggestion that he had something in reserve and remained in command. These pieces on Mrs Riddell are different. They have about them an unfamiliar feline quality which is not only disagreeable but disturbing.

Burns also felt obliged to have a go at Maria's husband:

> So vile was poor Wat, such a miscreant slave,
> That the worms even damn'd him when laid in his grave.
> 'In his scull there is famine!' a starv'd reptile cries;
> 'And his heart it is poison!' another replies.[4]

As he surveyed the ruins of his friendship with both branches of the Riddell family, he thought wistfully back to happier days. 'How is old sinfull Smellie coming on with this world?' he enquired in a letter to Peter Hill:

> If you meet with my much-valued old friend, Colon¹ Dunbar of the Crachal-lan Fencibles, remember me most affection [*sic*] to him. – Alas! not infrequently, when my heart is in a wandring humor, I live past scenes over again – to my mind's eye, you, Dunbar, Cleghorn, Cunningham, &c – present their friendly phiz; my bosom achs with tender recollections!

Although France was now in the grip of the Terror and the Revolution was

1. Letters, 620 A.
2. *Ibid.*, 620 B.
3. Kinsley, 448.
4. *Ibid.*, 452.

rapidly devouring its own children, Burns was at no pains to disguise from old friends like Hill how much he still felt himself to be at odds with the times:

> How do you weather this accursed time? – God only knows what will be the consequence; but in the mean time, the country, at least in our part of it, is still progressive to the devil. – For my part, "I jouk & let the jaw flee o'er." – As my hopes in this world are but slender, I am turning very rapidly, Devotee, in the prospect of sharing larger in the world to come.[1]

He had, as it happens, been giving some thought to his 'hopes in this world'. Early in January he had written to Graham of Fintry to recommend a streamlining of the excise structure in Dumfries. 'I am going to venture on a subject which I am afraid may appear, *from me*, improper,' Burns wrote, 'but as I do it from the best of motives, if you should not approve of my ideas, you will forgive them.' His proposal had a certain surgical simplicity – 'Let the second Division be annihilated; & be divided among the others.' This would allow one Officer to be made redundant ('Economy of the Public Monies is, I know, highly the wish of your Honorable Board').

He urged Graham to be discreet: 'I must beg of you, Sir, should my plan please you, that you will conceal my hand in it.' He thought that his Supervisor, Findlater, ('one of the worthiest fellows in the universe and one of my most intimate friends') would feel hurt, and that his 'warm and worthy friend' Mr Corbet might think him 'an impertinent meddler in his department'. He added a postscript, recommending to Graham's 'humanity and justice' the unfortunate colleague who would become surplus to requirements under the Burns plan: 'He is a very good Officer, & is burdened with a family of small children, which, with some debts of early days, crush him much to the ground.'[2]

Whether Graham responded to this freelance foray into management consultancy is not known, but a few weeks later he heard from Burns again – 'The language of supplication is almost the only language in which I have it in my power to approach you,' he wrote. This time he made a direct proposal for his own advancement. He had heard that Corbet and Findlater might both soon be promoted:

> Could it be possible then, Sir, that an old Supervisor who may still be continued, as I know is sometimes the case, after they are rather too infirm for much DUTY, could not such an Officer be appointed to Dumfries, & so let the OFFICIATING JOB fall to my share?[3]

1. Letters, 614. To jouk means to dodge or duck or swerve.
2. *Ibid.*, 610. The colleague in question not only had a large number of children but had been widowed some years previously. He had been in the service for twenty-two years – and was to continue in it until his death in 1811.
3. *Ibid.*, 615 A.

If Graham made a response to this rather pushy suggestion, it has not been traced; Burns's correspondence contains no further reference to it. Such letters as have survived from those early months of 1794 tell an all too familiar story:

> You should have heard from me long ago; but, over & above some vexatious share in the pecuniary losses of these accursed times, I have, all this winter, been plagued with low spirits & blue devils, so that I have almost hung my harp on the willow trees. –[1]

That was to James Johnson in February. Later in the same month, in a long letter to Cunningham, he wrote not only of money troubles but also of 'domestic vexations,' although he was no more specific than that. In his opening sentence he echoed Macbeth:

> Canst thou minister to a mind diseased? Canst thou speak peace and rest to a soul tost on a sea of troubles without one friendly star to guide her course, and dreading that the next surge may overwhelm her?

For two months, he told Cunningham, he had not been able to lift a pen. He had exhausted, in reflection, every topic of comfort. 'I was like Judas Iscariot preaching the gospel; he might melt and mould the hearts of those around him, but his own kept its native incorrigibility':

> I do not remember, my dear Cunningham, that you and I ever talked on the subject of religion at all. I know some who laugh at it, as the trick of the crafty FEW, to lead the undiscerning MANY; or at most as an uncertain obscurity, which mankind can never know any thing of, and with which they are fools if they give themselves much to do. Nor would I quarrel with a man for his irreligion, any more than I would for his want of a musical ear. I would regret that he was shut out from what, to me and to others, were such superlative sources of enjoyment. It is from this point of view, and for this reason, that I will deeply imbue the mind of every child of mine with religion . . .[2]

That other Edinburgh friend, William Nicol, would have been hard put to it to recognise his 'dear Christless Bobbie' in those sober lines. He would have had less difficulty with a pathetic note which Burns dashed off one morning to a young Dumfries solicitor of his acquaintance called Samuel Clark:

> My dear Sir,
>   I recollect something of a drunken promise yesternight to breakfast with you this morning. – I am very sorry that it is impossible. – I remember too, your very oblidgingly mentioning something of your intimacy with Mr Corbet

1. *Ibid.*, 616.
2. *Ibid.*, 619.

our Supervisor General. – Some of our folks about the Excise Office, Edin[r], had & perhaps still have conceived a prejudice against me as being a drunken dissipated character. – I might be all this, you know, & yet be an honest fellow, but you know that I am an honest fellow and am nothing of this. – You may in your own way let him know that I am not unworthy of subscribing myself

My dear Clarke, YOUR FRIEND
R. BURNS[1]

By early March, the blue devils were in retreat. 'Thank Heaven, I feel my spirits buoying upwards with the renovating year,' he wrote to Cunningham, and the result is a long, discursive letter in his best old style, enlivened with snatches of song, an anecdote about a drunken carrier in Ayr and his equally drunken 'Cara Sposa' and some philosophical musings on the effect of wealth:

> What, my dear Cunningham, is there in riches, that they narrow & encallous the heart so? – I think, that were I as rich as the sun, I would be as generous as day; but as I have no reason to imagine my soul a nobler one than every other man's, I must conclude that wealth imparts a bird-lime quality to the Possessor, at which the man, in native poverty, would have revolted . . .[2]

Sometime in March Burns had the chance of employment with a London newspaper. Patrick Miller Jr had spoken to James Perry, the proprietor and editor of the *Morning Chronicle* (and an Aberdonian). Miller later told Walter Scott that Perry had offered Burns five guineas a week as an occasional correspondent; alternatively he proposed that he should settle in London and work for the paper as a reporter and general contributor. Burns was flattered, but told Miller he felt he must decline:

> Your offer is indeed truly generous, & most sincerely do I thank you for it; but in my present situation, I find that I dare not accept it. – You well know my Political sentiments; & were I an insular individual, unconnected with a wife & a family of children, with the most fervid enthusiasm I would have volunteered my services: I then could & would have despised all consequences that might have ensued. –

Burns said he would be happy to supply Perry with the occasional 'bagatelle' – 'if he will give me an Address & channel by which any thing will come safe from these spies with which he may be certain that his correspondence is beset.'

---

1. *Ibid.*, 618. Clark, ten years younger than Burns, appears to have been a man of some social standing. He is described on his tombstone in St Michael's churchyard as 'conjunct Commissary Clerk, and Clerk of the Peace for the County of Dumfries'.
2. *Ibid.*, 620. His harp was not entirely out of commission; he told Johnson he was sending him forty-one songs for his fifth volume.

He told Miller that he had long had it in mind to try his hand 'in the way of little Prose Essays,' but these never saw the light of day.[1]

Robert Riddell's death in April affected Burns deeply, and he immediately composed a sonnet, which was printed two days later in the *Dumfries Journal* – 'a small heart-felt tribute to the memory of the *man I loved*.'[2] He also, if the sometimes fanciful Cunningham is to be believed, made his way one last time to the hermitage in the grounds of Friars' Carse and scratched an epitaph to his friend on a window pane.[3]

Shortly afterwards he decided he would like to retrieve the first volume of the Glenriddell Manuscripts (the second volume, containing a selection of his letters, was unfinished, and had not been handed over). Feeling inhibited from approaching his friend's widow, he wrote instead to one of Riddell's unmarried sisters – not, he asserted, 'to oppose those prejudices which have been raised against me,' but to request, as a favour, the return of this 'collection of all my trifles':

> They are many of them local, some of them puerile and silly, and all of them unfit for the public eye. As I have some little fame at stake, a fame that I trust may live, when the hate of those who "watch for my halting," and the contumelious sneer of those whom accident has made my superiors, will, with themselves, be gone to the region of oblivion; I am uneasy now for the fate of those manuscripts – will Mrs.— have the goodness to destroy them, or return them to me?[4]

'Unfit for the public eye' was a curious description for a body of work that included 'Tam o' Shanter', but Elizabeth Riddell agreed to the request, even though the handsome calf-bound volume, stamped with the Glenriddell arms, was now indisputably her property. Burns repaid her generosity by copying into it the disobliging 'Pinned to Mrs R—'s carriage' which he had written about her sister-in-law.

Towards the end of June, Burns set out on a second brief tour of Galloway. Holed up alone in a small inn at Castle Douglas (he had an arrangement to meet Syme the following morning), he picked up his pen to Mrs Dunlop:

> Here, in a solitary inn, in a solitary village, am I set by myself, to amuse my brooding fancy as I may. – Solitary confinement, you know, is Howard's

---

1. *Ibid.*, 620 B. It was in this letter that he offered the *Chronicle* his 'Extempore, pinned to a Lady's coach'.

2. The sonnet is Kinsley 445. Burns sent it on the day of Riddell's death to an acquaintance called John Clarke, who was the laird of Lockerwoods, an estate some six miles outside Dumfries on the road to Brow. (Letters, 621.)

3. Kinsley, 446.

4. Letters, 624. 'Watch for my halting' is from Jeremiah, 20:10.

favorite idea of reclaiming sinners; so let me consider by what fatality it happens that I have so long been exceeding sinful as to neglect the correspondence of the most valued Friend I have on earth. – To tell you that I have been in poor health, will not be excuse enough, though it is true. – I am afraid that I am about to suffer for the follies of my youth. – My Medical friends threaten me with a flying gout; but I trust they are mistaken.[1]

He wanted to try out on her the first sketch of a poem he had been working up on the road: 'The Subject is, LIBERTY: you know, my honored friend, how dear the theme is to me. I design it as an irregular Ode for Gen¹ Washington's birth-day.'[2] The first two stanzas are a hymn of praise to the American colonists in their War of Independence:

> See gathering thousands, while I sing,
> A broken chain, exulting, bring,
>   And dash it in a tyrant's face!
> And dare him to his very beard,
> And tell him, he no more is feared,
>   No more the Despot of Columbia's race . . .

Burns was not one to keep his political enthusiasms in watertight compartments. He had demonstrated in 'Scots Wha Hae' that a patriotic struggle from one epoch and a revolutionary conflict from another could flow together in his mind without much hindrance; a similar easy confluence occurs in his 'Ode for Washington's Birthday'. Having saluted 'Columbia's offspring, brave as free,' he turns his attention from the new world to the old, and in the contemporary struggle with France he finds little to enthuse about:

> Beneath her hostile banners waving
> Every pang of honor braving,
> England in thunders calls – 'The Tyrant's cause is mine!'

Poetic licence now allows Burns to unscramble the Union between England and Scotland and to offer (to the descendant of Wallace) an oblique but unmistakable comment on the state of politics north of the border: 'After having mentioned the degeneracy of other kingdoms,' he tells Mrs Dunlop, 'I come to Scotland thus –'

> Thee Caledonia, thy wild heaths among,
> Famed for the martial deed, the heaven-taught song,

1. *Ibid.*, 628. John Howard, the English philanthropist and prison reformer, (born 1726) had died four years previously. His *The State of the Prisons in England and Wales* had appeared in 1777. He was also known for his *State of Prisons* (1780) and his *Account of the Principal Lazarettos in Europe* (1789). He died of camp fever while visiting military hospitals in Russia.
2. He was either rather late or very early: Washington was born on February 22nd.

To thee, I turn with swimming eyes. –
Where is that soul of Freedom fled?
Immingled with the mighty Dead!
Beneath that hallowed turf where WALLACE lies![1]

Burns's letter went astray, and he had to wait until September to hear Mrs
Dunlop's verdict on this ode to liberty. She read him a brisk lesson in political
realism. She had detected that he was rather pleased with his composition, and
'enthusiastically fond of the theme'. 'So was I once,' she told him, 'but your
goddess has behaved in such a way as to injure her reputation. She is too much
attached of late to the society of butchers to be admitted among ladies.'[2]

Burns had time on his hands on that summer evening at the Carlinwark
Inn at Castle Douglas. He employed it to write a second letter. It too was to
a lady, and it was a good deal longer than the first:

Before you ask me why I have not written you; first let me be informed of
you, *how* I shall write you? "In Friendship," you say; & I have many a time
taken up my pen to try an epistle of "Friendship" to you; but it will not do:
'tis like Jove grasping a pop-gun, after having wielded his thunder. – When
I take up the pen, Recollection ruins me. – Ah! my ever dearest Clarinda!
– Clarinda? – What a host of Memory's tenderest offspring crowd on my
fancy at that sound! – But I must not indulge that subject: – you have forbid
it. –

He mentions his old friend Ainslie, who has been attentive to her:

Tell him that I envy him the power of serving you. – I had a letter from him
a while ago, but it was so dry, so distant, so like a card to one of his Clients,
that I could scarce bear to read it, & have not yet answered it . . . Though
Fame does not blow her trumpet at my approach *now*, as she did *then*, when
he first honored me with his friendship, yet I am as proud as ever; & when
I am laid in my grave, I wish to be stretched at my full length, that I may
occupy every inch of ground which I have a right to. –

He tells her that if she could see him she would laugh – 'would to Heaven
you were here to laugh with me, though I am afraid that crying would be our
first employment'. A solitary hermit, in a solitary room, in a solitary inn – he
repeats the formula he has used to Mrs Dunlop but enlarges it, because he
now has for a companion a solitary bottle of wine: 'Here am I set, as grave &

1. Kinsley, 451.
2. Letter dated 8th September 1794. Burns and Dunlop, pp. 406–9. Mrs Dunlop also retailed
in this letter a rumour that he had lost his place in the excise and gone to London.

stupid as an owl – but like that owl, still faithful to my own song; in confirmation of which, my dear Mrs Mack, here is your good health!'

The tone is one of resigned wistfulness – there was not quite enough in his solitary bottle to make him maudlin:

> You must know, my dearest Madam, that these now many years, whereever I am, in whatever company, when a married lady is called as a toast, I constantly give you; but as your name has never passed my lips, even to my most intimate friend, I give you by the name of Mrs Mack. – This is so well known among my acquaintances , that when my married lady is called for, the toast-master will say – "O, we need not ask him who it is – here's Mrs Mac!"

He concludes by giving her his epigram on Mrs Riddell's coach and by asking her opinion on the 'Monody'. 'The subject of the foregoing is a woman of fashion in this country, with whom, at one period, I was well acquainted,' he told her. 'By some scandalous conduct to me, & two or three other gentlemen here as well as me, she steered so far to the north of my good opinion, that I have made her the theme of several illnatured things.'[1]

Politically speaking, Burns himself continued to steer to the north of the good opinion of many of his fellow-townsmen, and one Sunday morning during the summer he was obliged once again to make an urgent call on the good offices of Samuel Clark:

> I was, I know, drunk last night, but I am sober this morning. – From the expression Captn Dods made use of to me, had I had nobody's welfare to care for but my own, we should certainly have come, according to the manners of the world, to the necessity of murdering one another about the business. – The words were such as generally, I believe, end in a brace of pistols; but I am still pleased to think that I did not ruin the peace welfare [sic] of a wife & family of children in a drunken squabble.

Burns was in a muck sweat. 'You know that the report of certain Political opinions being mine, has already once before brought me to the brink of destruction,' he told Clark. 'I dread lest last night's business may be misrepresented in the same way.' The 'business' had arisen when Burns, called on for a toast, had given, 'May our success in the present war be equal to the justice of our cause.' He protested disingenuously to Clark that it was 'a toast that the most outrageous frenzy of loyalty cannot object to,' but Captain Dods had clearly detected an ironical second meaning.

Burns was asking quite a lot of Clark – he urged him to call on everyone who had been present the previous evening and smoothe things over. 'The

1. Letters, 629.

least delay may be of unlucky consequence,' he wrote, adding, rather loftily, 'I am truly sorry that a man who stood so high in my estimation as Mr Dods, should use me in the manner in which I conceive he has done.'[1]

The affair blew over, but it was not the only brush Burns and his friends had with those whose ideas of loyalty differed from theirs. Syme seems broadly to have shared Burns's political outlook, as did a lawyer called William McCracken and the doctor, James Mundell. Another medical man figured prominently in this liberal circle. Before studying medicine at Edinburgh, William Maxwell, who was a year younger than Burns, had been educated by the Jesuits in France and later practised there – indeed it was only in 1794 that he had returned to Dumfries. His political credentials were impeccably romantic. He was the son of a notable Jacobite. While he was in France, his republican sympathies had led him to join the National Guard. He had witnessed the execution of Louis XVI. Burns admired him inordinately. 'Maxwell is my most intimate friend,' he told Mrs Dunlop, 'and one of the first characters I ever met with; but on account of his Politics is rather shunned by some high Aristocrates, though his Family & Fortune entitle him to the first circles.'[2]

The liberal, anti-government views of this circle were well-known in Dumfries, and a member of the Loyal Natives directed a political squib at them:

> Ye sons of sedition, give ear to my song,
> Let Syme, Burns and Maxwell pervade every throng,
> With Craken the attorney, and Mundell the quack
> Send Willie the monger to hell with a smack.

Not from the higher slopes of Parnassus, perhaps, but no more was the extempore which Burns lobbed back at them:

> Ye true 'Loyal Natives', attend to my song,
> In uproar and riot rejoice the night long;
> From *envy* and *hatred* your corps is exempt;
> But where is your shield from the *darts of contempt?*[3]

Whether because of his ill-concealed political views and the relish with which he expressed them, whether because of gossip about what had happened at Friars' Carse, Burns was subjected at this time to a good deal of social ostracism. One witness to this was a young friend called David McCulloch who, like Maxwell, had seen something of the Revolution in France at first hand; he had been in Paris at the fall of the Bastille and had returned to the family

1. *Ibid.*, 631.
2. *Ibid.*, 638. Maxwell had also figured in a speech of Burke's in the House of Commons on 28th December 1792 when he mentioned a gentleman who had ordered three thousand daggers in Birmingham.
3. Kinsley, 450.

home at Ardwell in Kirkcudbrightshire only late the previous summer. He was a fellow-mason, and he had a good tenor voice – Burns said he had not fully appreciated the beauty of some of his songs until he heard McCulloch sing them. Lockhart wrote that he had heard the story from McCulloch more than once, and there is no reason to doubt it:

> He was seldom more grieved, than when riding into Dumfries one fine summer's evening, about this time, to attend a county-ball, he saw Burns walking alone, on the shady side of the principal street of the town, while the opposite side was gay with successive groups of gentlemen and ladies, all drawn together for the festivities of the night, not one of whom appeared willing to recognise him. The horseman dismounted and joined Burns, who, on his proposing to him to cross the street, said, 'Nay, nay, my young friend, – that's all over now.'[1]

Burns always firmly believed that there were certain times of the year when he wrote better than others. 'Now, & for six or seven months,' he had told Thomson in May, '*I shall be quite in song*, as you shall see by & by.' The war was hindering progress with the *Collection*, however: 'I am quite vexed at Pleyel's being cooped up in France,' he had grumbled in the same letter, 'as it will put an entire stop to our work.'[2] Two months later, the composer was still incommunicado, and Burns's restiveness found expression in a bitterly ironical thrust at the allies:

> Is there no news yet, my dear Sir, of Pleyel? – Or is your work to be at a dead stop untill these glorious Crusaders, the Allies, set our modern Orpheus at liberty from the savage thraldom of Democratic Discords? – Alas the day! And woe is me! That auspicious period, pregnant with the happiness of Millions – that golden age, spotless with Monarchical innocence & Despotic purity – That Millenium, of which the earliest dawn will enlighten even Republican turbulence, & shew the swinish multitude that they are but beasts, & like beasts must be led by the nose & goaded in the backside – these days of sweet chords & concords seem by no means near![3]

He kept up a steady stream of material to Thomson, for all that. 'Making a poem is like begetting a son,' he told him cheerfully in September, 'you cannot know whether you have a wise man or a fool, untill you produce him to the world & try him. – For that reason, I send you the offspring of my brain, *abortions* & all.'[4]

---

1. Lockhart, *op. cit.*, pp. 236-7. There was a family connection: Lockhart was Scott's son-in-law and McCulloch's sister married Scott's brother.
2. Letters, 625.
3. *Ibid.*, 632.
4. *Ibid.*, 636.

In the summer and autumn of 1794 quite a number of his songs had a single inspiration. 'Do you know, my dear Sir, a blackguard Irish song called, "OOnagh's waterfall, or The lock that scattered OOnagh's p-ss?" ' he enquired of Thomson in September. 'Our friend Cunningham sings it delightfully. – The air is charming, & I have often regretted the want of decent verses to it.' (This was understandable. Una, a milkmaid, is pursued by a village swain called Darby; a twentieth-century psychotherapist turning the pages of *The Merry Muses* would recognise an eighteenth-century description of urolagnia, a deviant practice in which sexual gratification is derived from urination.) 'You may be pleased to have verses to it that you may sing it before Ladies,' Burns suggested – and helpfully provided them:

> Sae flaxen were her ringlets,
> Her eyebrows of a darker hue,
> Bewitchingly o'erarching
> Twa laughing een o' bonie blue. – . . .

> Like harmony her motion;
> Her pretty ancle is a spy,
> Betraying fair proportion,
> Wad make a saint forget the sky. – . . .[1]

It was not the first of Burns's songs to 'Chloris' – she had been the inspiration for 'Poortith Cauld' which he had sent to Thomson at the beginning of 1793 – but over the next few months he was to produce a whole cluster of them, celebrating her most famously in 'Lassie wi' the lintwhite locks', rather less happily in such effusions as 'On Chloris being ill'.('Can I cease to care,/Can I cease to languish,/while my darling Fair/Is on the couch of anguish.')[2]

Her unpoetical name was Jean Lorimer. Burns had first known her three years previously when she was a young girl in her teens, the daughter of a neighbouring farmer at Ellisland. At that time he was one of the few excisemen in Dumfries not besotted with her – when he wrote the first version of the song 'Craigieburn-wood' it was to help a fellow-officer called John Gillespie to woo her. Miss Lorimer would have none of him, and in March 1793 eloped to Gretna Green with an Englishman called Whelpdale. The honeymoon was of the briefest. Whelpdale's creditors were soon at his heels, causing him to abandon his bride and flee to his native Cumberland; Mrs Whelpdale resumed her maiden name and went home to keep house for her father. The thirty-five-year-old Burns was renewing an acquaintance with a woman who was not quite nineteen.

In the middle of October we find him trying to persuade Thomson to accept the words he had written to 'Craigieburn Wood':

1. Kinsley, 457.
2. Kinsley, 466 and 489 respectively.

The Lady on whom it was made, is one of the finest women in Scotland; & in fact (entre nous) is in a manner to me what Sterne's Eliza was to him – a Mistress, or Friend, or what you will, in the guileless simplicity of Platonic love. – (Now don't put any of your squinting construction on this, or have any clishmaclaiver about it among our acquaintances) – I assure you that to my lovely Friend you are indebted for many of your best songs of mine.[1]

Having filled Thomson in on the nature of his relationship with his Eliza, Burns entrusted him with some of the secrets of inspiration and composition:

Do you think that the sober, gin-horse routine of existence could inspire a man with life, & love, & joy – could fire him with enthusiasm, or melt him with pathos, equal to the genius of your Book? – No! No! ! ! – Whenever I want to be more than ordinary *in song*; to be in some degree equal to your diviner airs; do you imagine I fast & pray for the celestial emanation? – Tout au contraire! I have a glorious recipe, the very one that for his own use was invented by the Divinity of Healing & Poesy when erst he piped to the flocks of Admetus. – I put myself in a regimen of admiring a fine woman; & in proportion to the adorability of her charms, in proportion you are delighted with my verses. –

    The lightning of her eye is the godhead of Parnassus, & the witchery of her smile the divinity of Helicon!

Burns's previous interest in platonic friendship had not been strong, and there is more than one view about the true nature of his relations with Jean Lorimer. If they were as chaste as he wished Thomson to believe, there is evidence that this was not achieved without a struggle. A cryptic but suggestive letter survives which he wrote that September to his Supervisor, Alexander Findlater:

I have been among the Angelic World, this forenoon.—Ah!

        "had ye but been whare I hae been,
        "Ye wad hae been sae canty, O!"

But don't be afraid: I did not dare to touch the ark of the Covenant; nor even to cast a prophane eye to the mercy-seat, where it is hid among the feathered Cherubim. – I am in the clouds elsewhere –

        "Ah, Chloris, could I now but sit
          "As unconcerned as when
        "Your infant beauty could beget
          "Nor happiness nor pain."[2]

1. Letters, 644.
2. *Ibid.*, 639. The couplet is adapted from Burns's own song 'Killiecrankie', Kinsley, 313.

Burns is quoting here from Sir Charles Sedley's *The Mulberry Garden*, a comedy published in 1668 which drew on Molière's *L'Ecole des maris*, and it is likely that this is what gave him the idea of using the name. For the Greeks, Chloris was the goddess of flowers and the husband of Zephyr, but it was not, as James Mackay has pointed out, the happiest of choices. Sedley's friend Rochester, the favourite of Charles II who, in Johnson's phrase, 'blazed out his youth and his health in lavish voluptuousness,' also has a Chloris; she was a shepherdess who achieved orgasm by wallowing in a pigsty.

About the charms of this modern Chloris, Thomson remained sceptical. 'I am sensible, my dear friend,' he told Burns, 'that a genuine poet can no more exist without his mistress than his meat'. He also wrote, however, that he could 'scarce conceive a woman to be a beauty, on reading that she had lint-white locks'. Burns was undismayed:

I like you for entering so candidly & so kindly into the story of Ma chere Amie. – I assure you, I was never more in earnest in my life, than in the account of that affair which I sent you in my last. – Conjugal-love is a Passion which I deeply feel, & highly venerate; but somehow it does not make such a figure in Poesy as that other species of the Passion –

"Where Love is liberty & Nature law.—"

Musically speaking, the first is an instrument of which the gamut is scanty & confined, but the tones are inexpressibly sweet; while the last, has powers equal to all the intellectual Modulation of the Human Soul. –[1]

Chloris subsequently gravitated to Edinburgh, drifting for some years between domestic service, mendicancy and prostitution. Eventually she found work as a housekeeper; she lived till 1831. The poet James Hogg remembered a meeting with her: 'She was the ruin of a fine woman, of a fair complexion, and well-made, and I heard by her voice that she had once sung well.'[2] He also recorded that she kept a lock of Burns's hair in a box.

'I am so poorly today as to be scarce able to hold my pen, & so deplorably stupid as to be totally unable to hold it to any purpose' – this to Mrs Dunlop in September. 'I know you are pretty deep read in Medical matters, but I fear you have nothing in the Materia Medica which can heal a diseased SPIRIT.'[3] He was in financial straits, too. During the summer he had been obliged to write an embarrassed note to his landlord, Captain Hamilton: 'You are the

1. *Ibid.*, 646. Burns is quoting from Pope's *Eloisa to Abelard*.
2. Hogg and Motherwell, *op. cit.*, vol. v, pp. 364-5. 'Perhaps the worst life of Burns written before the twentieth century,' wrote the judicious Snyder.
3. Letters, 638.

only person in Dumfries or in the world, to whom I have *run in debt*.'[1] Now he confided some of his troubles to his old friend Mrs Dunlop: 'I think that the Poet's old companion, Poverty, is to be my attendant to my grave,' he wrote wearily:

> You know that my brother, poor fellow! was on the brink of ruin, when my good fortune threw a little money among my hands which saved him for a while. – Still his ruinous farm threatens to beggar him, & though, a bad debt of ten pounds excepted, he has every shilling I am worth in the world among his hands, I am nearly certain that I have done with it for ever. – This loss, as to my individual self, I could hold it very light; but my little flock would have been the better for a couple of hundred pounds: for *their* sakes, it wrings my heart! –

He had a piece of family news for her, but he conveyed it casually, almost as an afterthought: 'A propos, the other day, Mrs Burns presented me with my fourth son, whom I have christened James Glencairn; in grateful memory of my lamented Patron. – I shall make all my children's names altars of gratitude.'[2]

Mrs Dunlop's reply is missing, but a passage in Burns's next letter to her, written only a month later, suggests she may have sent him money: 'Something else that was in your letter, I do not know how to mention,' he wrote. 'My plaintive epistle, & the contents of your answer, give me, on my part, so much the air of mendicant insinuation, that I do not know how to lift up my head under it. – I know not how to be the object of Pity.'

The Caledonian Hunt had been in Dumfries for the past fortnight, but he had clearly taken little pleasure in their presence, reporting on their antics to Mrs Dunlop with something approaching puritan disdain:

> Of course we have had a roar of Folly & Dissipation. – Most of our fashionable young men have all that Profligacy & Outrage which have sometimes accompanied Superior Understanding & brilliant Wit – but without those bright talents which might throw a kind of veil over mischievous Folly & unprincipled Wickedness. –[3]

One ray of light pierced his October gloom. Stephen Kemble, Mrs Siddons' brother, had brought his theatre company down from Edinburgh and Burns had seen their performance of *Inkle and Yarico*, George Colman the younger's romantic tale of an English merchant and a beautiful savage. Yarico was played by Kemble's wife, Elizabeth; she was not in the same class as her famous sister-in-law, but Burns was entranced, and presented her with a signed extempore:

1. Letters, 633.
2. *Ibid.*, 638.
3. *Ibid.*, 645.

> Kemble, thou cur'st my unbelief
> Of Moses and his rod:
> At Yarico's sweet notes of grief
> The rock with *tears* had flow'd. —[1]

Towards the end of 1794, there were signs that Burns's broken friendship with Maria Riddell might be on the mend. Things had not been going well for her. In April, her husband had been obliged to give up Woodley Park – he had gone to the West Indies partly in search of funds to complete the purchase of the estate, and he had failed. The conventional way of saving money was to go abroad, but the successes of the French armies on the continent ruled that out. They returned north, and for a time lived at Tinwald House, between Dumfries and Lochmaben – 'a crazy, rambling, worm-eaten cob-web hunting chateau of the Duke of Queensberry,' she wrote to Smellie.

Extraordinary as it seems, Mrs Riddell appears to have had no knowledge of the disobliging manner in which Burns had been writing about her – she seems not to have realised it even as late as 1800; when she saw the 'Monody' in print in Currie's biography, she averred that she had never read it before and thought it 'very well written in its way'.[2]

Late in December, or possibly in the first days of 1795, she made an overture, and Burns responded – rather stuffily at first, and in the third person:

Mr Burns's Compliments to Mrs Riddell – is much obliged to her for her polite attention in sending him the book. – Owing to M^r B—s's being at present acting as Supervisor of Excise, a department that occupies his every hour of the day, he had not that time to spare which is necessary for any Belle Lettre pursuit; but, as he will, in a week or two, again return to his wonted leisure, he will then pay that attention to M^rs R—'s beautiful Song "To thee, loved Nith", which it so well deserves.

He had a favour to ask her:

When "Anarcharsis Travels" come to hand, which Mrs Riddell mentioned as her gift to the Public Library, M^r B— will thank her for a reading of it, previous to her sending it to the Library, as it is a book M^r B— has never seen, & wishes to have a longer perusal of than the regulations of the Library allow.

P.S. Mr. Burns will be much obliged to Mrs Riddell if she will favour him with a perusal of any of her poetical pieces which he may not have seen.[3]

1. Kinsley, 463.
2. A batch of letters written by Mrs Riddell to Currie was sold at Sotheby's in 1918 and published in the *Burns Chronicle* in 1923.
3. Letters, 650.

It looked as if the friendship might be put together again. Things were looking up.

Burns would not know it for some time, but with another letter which he had written a few days previously, a much older friendship had been destroyed for ever.

Fifteen

THE DYING OF THE LIGHT

BURNS WAS ACTING AS Supervisor because Findlater was ill. It was only a temporary appointment, but he was quite excited about it: 'I look forward to an early period when I shall be appointed in full form,' he told Mrs Dunlop, 'a consumation devoutly to be wished! – My Political sins seem to be forgiven me. –'

That was on December 29th. He laid the letter aside, picking it up again on the first day of the New Year to send her seasonal greetings. He was in philosophical mood:

> May life, to you, be a positive blessing while it lasts, for your own sake; & may it yet be greatly prolonged, is my wish for my own sake & for the sake of the rest of your friends! – What a transient business is life! – Very lately I was a boy; but t'other day I was a young man; & I already begin to feel the rigid fibre & stiffening joints of Old Age coming fast o'er my frame . . . :

Mrs Dunlop was in London, and Burns knew that she intended to see Dr Moore. He sent his good wishes; he had just been re-reading ('I dare say for the hundred & fiftieth time') Moore's *View of Society and Manners*, and read it still 'with unsated delight'. He was less impressed, however, with a more recent work. In 1792 Moore had gone travelling with Lord Lauderdale, and over the next two years had published his *Journal during a Residence in France*. In the second volume he had quoted from 'Tam o' Shanter' and written some flattering words about its author: 'He has paid me a pretty compliment,' Burns told Mrs Dunlop, 'though I must beg leave to say, that he has not written this last work in his usual happy manner.'

If he had left it at that, no great harm would have been done; what was to prove disastrous was the opinionated manner in which he ploughed on:

> Entre nous, you know my Politics; & I cannot approve of the honest Doctor's whining over the deserved fate of a certain pair of Personages. – What is there in the delivering over a perjured Blockhead & an unprincipled Prostitute into

372

the hands of the hangman, that it should arrest for a moment, attention, in an eventful hour . . .

Having disposed of Louis XVI and Marie Antoinette, he reverted to Dr Moore, contriving in one short sentence both to patronise him and impugn his integrity:

. . . Our friend is already indebted to People in power, & still looks forward for his Family, so I can apologise for him; for at bottom I am sure he is a staunch friend to liberty. – Thank God, these London trials have given us a little more breath, & I imagine that the time is not far distant when a man may freely blame Billy Pit, without being called an enemy to his Country. –[1]

His letter – it was an extended, portmanteau affair – finally went off on January 12th – the same day, as chance would have it, on which Mrs Dunlop sat down in her daughter's house in London to compose the last letter she would ever write to him. She began, as she had not infrequently had occasion to do, with a gentle reproach – 'I write you from this Lethe of the world, you who seemed to forget me before I quitted the Land of Cakes . . .'

She too wrote about Pitt, and with a good deal less ceremony than he had done; the freedom of conversation in the capital, she told him, 'stretched far beyond those limits Scots decorum now allows':

Indeed it is ordinary to send our Premier to Coventry with as much ease and as little ceremony as you could do any other man who went half seas over every morning by the hour of breakfast amongst *sans-culottes*: nor does any one seem inclinable to lend the poor man an assisting arm in his staggering state, which appears an unanswerable apology for all the stumbles he can make; and grievous ones he does make at almost every step.

No quarrel then, over embattled, tipsy 'Billy Pit'. And probably no more than passing irritation over Burns's rudeness about Moore. Mrs Dunlop herself was not entirely uncritical of the good doctor; she had seen a few chapters of the new book he was working on, she wrote: 'I believe it will be interesting, but more in the style of a Grumbletonian than I could have expected.'[2]

The fact is that the breach with Mrs Dunlop was an accident waiting to happen. She had reacted sharply more than once to Burns's tendency to broadcast his political views with a blunderbuss; the uncritical and unmodulated tone in which he regularly proclaimed his attachment to democratic principles without any regard to political context were an offence to her intelligence.

1. Letters, 649.
2. 'Grumbletonian' was a nickname for members of the Country Party in English politics after the Revolution of 1688. They were accused by the Court Party of being actuated by unsatisfied personal ambition.

But there was something else. Burns was not uninformed about Mrs Dunlop's family situation – their correspondence is full of it. Four of her sons and one of her grandsons were or had been army officers. One daughter, Susan Henri, was the widow of a Frenchman; another, Agnes Perochon, was married to a Royalist refugee. It was obtuse of Burns not to consider how strongly his old friend's views must be coloured by such connections, liberal-minded though she might be. When he did, belatedly, begin to suspect that something was amiss, his attempts to establish the nature of his offence would be met with stony, unforgiving silence.

Burns's acting supervisorship lasted for four months but added only £12 to his normal salary. He found himself so hard pressed in January 1795 that he was obliged to swallow his pride and solicit a loan. 'This [is] a painful, disagreeable letter; & the first of the kind I ever wrote,' he told his friend William Stewart, the factor of the Closeburn estate:

> I am truly in serious distress for three or four guineas: can you, my dear Sir, accommodate me? – it will indeed truly oblige me. – These accursed times, by stopping up Importation, have for this year at least lopt off a full third part of my income: &, with my large Family, this is to me a distressing matter. –[1]

Stewart sent him three guineas, and Burns used them to reduce his arrears in rent. 'It is needless to attempt an apology for my remissness to you in money-matters,' he wrote to his landlord. 'My conduct is beyond all excuse.' He told Hamilton that the sluggish state of commerce in the town had reduced his income by £20.[2]

Harrassed as he was, he did not neglect his correspondence with Thomson. He told him that some years previously, 'when I was young, & by no means the saint I am now,' a friend had offered him a wager that he could not produce an original ode to spring. Burns had risen to the challenge and now offered Thomson the result:

> When maukin bucks, at early f—s,   buck-hares
> In dewy glens are seen, Sir . . .[3]

Having regaled Thomson with this vigorous piece of mock-pastoral bawdy, he switched with disconcerting swiftness into a completely different key:

1. Letters, 652.
2. Ibid., 653.
3. Kinsley, 481. The letter is no. 651.

374

Now for decency. – A great critic, Aikin on songs, says, that love & wine are the exclusive themes for song-writing. – The following is on neither subject, & consequently is no Song; but will be allowed, I think, to be two or three pretty good *prose* thoughts, inverted into rhyme. –

There followed some of the best-known words he ever wrote – forty short lines which explain much of the extraordinary appeal Burns has exercised over the years around the globe and across the barriers of language. More than any other of his songs or poems, they occupy, as Kinsley so well puts it, 'a central place in the psalmody of radicalism':

Is there, for honest Poverty	
That hings his head, and a' that;	hangs
The coward-slave, we pass him by,	
We dare be poor for a' that!	
For a' that, and a' that,	
Our toils obscure, and a' that,	
The rank is but the guinea's stamp,	
The Man's the gowd for a' that. –	gold

What though on hamely fare we dine,	simple
Wear hoddin grey, and a' that.	coarse homespun
Gie fools their silks, and knaves their wine,	
A Man's a Man for a' that.	
For a' that, and a' that,	
Their tinsel show, and a' that;	
The honest man, though e'er sae poor,	
Is king o' men for a' that. –	

Ye see yon birkie ca'd, a lord,	conceited fellow
Wha struts, and stares, and a' that,	
Though hundreds worship at his word,	
He's but a coof for a' that.	fool
For a' that, and a' that,	
His ribband, star and a' that,	
The man of independant mind,	
He looks and laughs at a' that. –	

A prince can mak a belted knight,	
A marquis, duke, and a' that;	
But an honest man's aboon his might,	above
Gude faith he mauna fa' that!	must not lay claim to
For a' that, and a' that,	
Their dignities, and a' that,	

> The pith o' Sense, and pride o' Worth,
> Are higher rank than a' that. –
>
> Then let us pray that come it may,
> As come it will for a' that,
> That Sense and Worth, o'er a' the earth
> Shall bear the gree, and a' that.   come off best
> For a' that, and a' that,
> Its comin yet for a' that,
> That Man to Man the warld o'er,
> Shall brothers be for a' that. —[1]

Angellier, writing almost a century later, was full of Gallic admiration for the pride and energy the song displayed, describing it as 'a sort of Marseillaise of Equality'. Burns's savage contempt for rank certainly lingers powerfully in the mind. Set as it is to a lively reel tune[2] it undoubtedly makes a good song, although as David Daiches has observed, not everyone regards slogan poetry as the highest form of literary art.

For the 'two or three pretty good prose ideas' which Burns wrote about to Thomson, he was clearly indebted to *The Rights of Man*. Here and there he echoes not only Paine's sentiments, but his actual words.[3] Even 'the rank is but the guinea's stamp' has a pedigree. Five years earlier, Burns had ordered the plays of Wycherley from his friend Peter Hill. 'I weigh the man, not his title,' says a character in *The Plain Dealer*, ''tis not the king's stamp can make the metal better or heavier'.

None of which hugely matters. On 'For a' that, and a' that,' as on so much else, there stands out from the pages of Chambers-Wallace the judgement which still rings most true – 'the chosen hymn of all high-hearted dreamers of a better day'.

It was hard work acting in Findlater's place as Supervisor, with long days in the saddle. Part of Burns's official diary for the period survives. Two days before Christmas a visit to Sanquhar division, the most northerly in the district, had meant a five o'clock start and a fourteen-hour day; on Christmas Eve he rode another forty miles and visited the premises of twenty traders. It was an exceptionally severe winter, with hard frosts and heavy snowfalls. 'You cannot have any idea of the predicament in which I write you,' he announced cheerfully to Thomson early in February:

1. Kinsley, 482.
2. The tune, *For a' that, an' a' that*, had been popular since the middle of the eighteenth century. Burns had used it once before for a rather different sort of radical song, 'I am a Bard of no regard', in *Love and Liberty – A Cantata*.
3. See Chambers-Wallace, vol. iv, p. 186, n. and Crawford, *op. cit.*, p. 365.

I came yesternight to this unfortunate, wicked little village. – I have gone forward – but snows of ten feet deep have impeded my progress: I have tried to "gae back the gate I cam again," but the same obstacle has shut me up within insuperable bars. – To add to my misfortune; since dinner, a Scraper has been torturing Catgut, in sounds that would have insulted the dying agonies of a Sow under the hands of a Butcher – and thinks himself, *on that very account*, exceeding good company. – In fact, I have been in a dilemma, either to get drunk, to forget these miseries; or to hang myself, to get rid of these miseries: – like a prudent man (a character congenial to my every thought, word & deed) I, of two evils have chosen the least, & am very drunk – at your service! –[1]

The 'wicked little village' in which he had chosen the lesser of two evils was Ecclefechan, in Annandale. Later that same year it would become the birthplace of Thomas Carlyle.

The struggle with France was not going well for the allies. Howe had won his famous naval victory off Ushant the previous summer, certainly, and several of France's rich sugar islands in the West Indies had fallen to the British, although at a price: between 1794 and 1796, 40,000 British troops died in the West Indies. On land, reeling from the successive victories of generals Pichegru, Jourdan and Moreau, the coalition was crumbling. The French, having overrun Holland in 1794, compelled her at the beginning of 1795 to go to war with the United Kingdom, forcing the British to maintain a separate fleet in the North Sea to guard against invasion from the Texel.

At the outbreak of the war with France, the only force in the United Kingdom capable of providing civil defence had been the militia, and then only in England and Wales; there would be no militia in Scotland until 1797 when the provisions of the previous year's Supplementary Militia Act were extended. Ever-growing fears of a French invasion prompted the authorities to encourage the raising of local volunteer corps of infantry or cavalry.

The first meeting to organise such a body in Dumfries had taken place on January 31st. The Loyal Natives comprised an obvious reservoir for recruitment – one of the first to put his name forward was Francis Shortt, town clerk of Dumfries, secretary of the Natives and the author of the lampoon on Burns and his friends quoted earlier. He came forward at the second meeting of the Volunteers on February 3rd. Burns, together with Syme and Mundell, had beaten him to it in the loyalty stakes, however – their names appear in the minute book among those present at the inaugural meeting three days previously.

After that second meeting, the number who had expressed interest in joining

1. Letters, 657.

377

stood at sixty-three. The Provost and his two bailies had answered the call, and so had Burns's landlord, Captain Hamilton, and William Hyslop, the landlord of Burns's 'howff,' the Globe. Several of Burns's excise colleagues had come forward, as had Thomas Boyd, who had built the farmhouse at Ellisland, and his friend McMurdo from Drumlanrig. A retired military man called Colonel de Peyster was appointed Major Commandant – he was married to the daughter of a former Provost, and had recently bought an estate just outside Dumfries. The Volunteers elected their own officers and a Committee of Management, one of whose functions was to vet applications for membership. Not everyone went through on the nod, but there is no record of any opposition to Burns's candidacy, his liberal views notwithstanding.

No government money was made available to these bodies – those who volunteered to serve did so without pay and undertook to find their own clothing. This meant that decisions about what sort of uniforms should be worn were made locally, a circumstance which opened up a rich vein for the cartoonists of the day. For his corps of yeomen cavalry at Petworth the Earl of Egremont designed an ensemble that was richly operatic – white waistcoat and breeches, green jacket lined with white, dark-blue cloak edged with scarlet, plumed and cockaded bearskins ornamented with gilt. A patriotic Sussex yeoman eager to be seen in such finery could not expect much change out of £40.

In Dumfries they managed things much more economically but still contrived to put on a colourful show. The uniforms were provided by a tailor called David Williamson, himself a member of the corps; Burns's account for his amounted to £8 7s. 'Odd but not ungraceful,' was how Allan Cunningham remembered it: 'white kerseymere breeches and waistcoat; short blue coat, faced with red; and round hat, surmounted by a bearskin, like the helmets of our Horse-guards.'[1]

The Volunteers turned out several times a week for drill and target practice in the Dock Park, a spectacle which drew large crowds. A Dumfries merchant called William Grierson, then a young man in his early twenties, recorded their progress in his diary: 'Went to the Dock to see the Volunteers go through their exercise,' he noted in the middle of April. 'Not very proficient yet.'[2]

Burns was quickly in action not only with his musket but with his pen:

> Does haughty Gaul invasion threat,
>   Then let the louns bewaure, sir,   rascals
> There's WOODEN WALLS upon our seas
>   And VOLUNTEERS on shore, Sir:
> The Nith shall run to *Corsincon*,
>   And *Criffell* sink in *Solway*,

---

1. Cunningham. *op. cit.*, vol. i, p. 319.
2. *Apostle to Burns. The Diaries of William Grierson*, edited by John Davis, William Blackwood, Edinburgh, 1981, p. 35. The manuscript diaries are in the Dumfries Museum. In later life Grierson, with Syme, was instrumental in the erection of the Burns mausoleum.

E'er we permit a Foreign Foe
On British ground to rally.[1]

Burns set the words to the tune *Push about the jorum*, which was a particular favourite of his (it bobs up three times in the *Merry Muses*). The song achieved more than local popularity, appearing in the *Edinburgh Evening Courant* and the *Caledonian Mercury*; it is good rousing stuff, in the genre of 'The British Grenadiers', and it rattles on through four stanzas to a suitably jingoistic close. Anyone thinking back to the 'Ça ira' episode might consider the ending came close to apostasy, although there is a schizophrenic twist in the last line:

> Who will not sing, GOD SAVE THE KING,
>   Shall hang as high's the steeple;
> But while we sing, GOD SAVE THE KING,
>   We'll ne'er forget THE PEOPLE!

Behind Burns the patriot one can still make out Burns the democrat, crossing his fingers like a child in the old game.

His relations with Maria Riddell were much improved. A long chatty letter survives from this time in which he thanks her for the loan of the Anacharsis book, sends her a number of songs and brings her up to date about the progress of his work with Thomson:

> Pleyel is still in statu quo. – In a little time, however, we will have all the work. – He is still in Strasbourg; but the Mess[rs] Coutts, the London bankers, have been so obliging as to allow my friend Thomson, the Editor, the channel of their correspondence in Switzerland, through which medium the business is going forward. – Thomson has enlarged his plan. – The hundred pathetic airs are to be as proposed, only he means to have four plates, instead of two. – He likewise has increased his number of facetious songs & lively airs & proposes adorning them here and there with vignettes.

He also told her that he was sitting for a miniature: 'I think he has hit by far the best likeness of me ever was taken,' he wrote:

> When you are at any time so idle, in town, as to call at Reid's painting-room, & mention to him that I spoke of such a thing to you, he will shew it to you;

1. Kinsley, 484.

else he will not; for both the Miniature's existence & its destiny, are an inviolable secret, & therefore very properly trusted in part *to you*. —[1]

There was a by-election campaign in the spring of 1795. The Member of Parliament for the Stewartry of Kirkcudbright had died during the winter and Burns threw himself into the fray on the side of the Whig candidate, Patrick Heron, whom he had met during his tour of Galloway the year before. With 'Is there for honest poverty' still running fresh in his mind, his first contribution was a ballad set to the same tune:

> Wham will we send to London town,
> To Parliament, and a' that . . .

Heron he describes as 'The independant Patriot, The Honest Man'; his Tory opponent, the nephew of another MP who was an extremely wealthy landowner, is dismissed as an inexperienced carpet-bagger:

> Yon beardless boy comes o'er the hills,
> Wi's uncle's gowd, and a' that . . .[2]   gold

Burns sent this and another ballad to Heron with an effusive covering letter: 'In order to bring my humble efforts to bear with more effect on the foe, I have privately printed a good many copies of both ballads, and have sent them among friends all about the country.'

He had reason to cultivate the candidate. Syme had shown him a letter from Heron in which there had been a suggestion that he might be able to advance Burns's career in the excise. Burns responded appreciatively, and gave Heron a frank account of how he saw his promotion prospects and of his ambitions:

I am on the supervisor's list, and as we come on there by precedency, in two or three years I shall be at the head of that list, and be appointed, *of course*. *Then*, a FRIEND might be of service to me in getting me into a place of the kingdom which I would like.

Although this would mean an income of between £120 and £200 a year, his recent experience had taught him that a supervisor's lot was not entirely happy: 'The business is an incessant drudgery, and would be nearly a compleat bar

1. Letters, 658. It is not known for whom the picture was intended. It is generally presumed to be the one now in the Scottish National Portrait Gallery in Edinburgh, although the provenance is patchy. See *Burns: Authentic Likenesses*, by Basil C Skinner (2nd edition), Alloway Publishing, Darvel, 1990.
2. Kinsley, 491.

bar to every species of literary pursuit.' Beyond that, however, he could discern the sunny uplands:

> The moment I am appointed a supervisor, in the common routine, I may be nominated on the collector's list; and this is always a business purely of political patronage. A collectorship varies much, from better than two hundred a year to near a thousand. They also come forward by precedency on the list; and have besides a handsome income, a life of compleat leisure. A life of literary leisure with a decent competence, is the summit of my wishes.[1]

The savage tone of Burns's electioneering efforts for Heron was not universally admired. Young of Harburn, who was the law agent for his opponent, thought well of Heron, even though he did not share his politics:

> A most amiable & excellent person he was, well entitled to represent in parlt. either the Stewartry or shire of Galloway, his native country; but not likely to be aided in the attainment of that object by the libels and lampoons of Burns, on all those who did not support, or were opposed to, Mr. Heron's political interests, with which Burns had no more to do than he had with the affairs of the man in the moon.[2]

The second political ballad which Burns enclosed with his letter to Heron, 'Fy, let us a' to K[irkcudbright],/For there will be bickerin there',[3] is so full of local references and allusions as to be largely incomprehensible (as is the piece he wrote a little later to celebrate Heron's victory.) They are no worse, but they are not better, than the general run of ephemera thrown up at election time in every age. Their circulation as broadsheets no doubt provided a brief and local addition to the gaiety of the nation but it is unlikely that they did much to influence the handful of people who in the late eighteenth century were entitled to vote.

On this occasion, however, one of the targets of Burns's invective was provoked to retaliate. He had taken a swipe in passing at two members of the local clergy:

> Whase haly Priest-hoods nane could stain,
> For wha can dye the BLACK. –[4]

The Reverend James Muirhead was the minister of Urr. He was also a land-owner and chief of the Muirheads. Young of Harburn described him as 'of

1. Letters, 660.
2. Fitzhugh, *op. cit.*, p. 65.
3. Kinsley, 492.
4. Kinsley, 493.

the *irritable genus,* and nowise disposed to submit to the abuse and sarcastic ballads of Burns.' He found the ammunition for his revenge in Martial:

> Vacerra, shabby son of whore,
> Why do thy patrons keep thee poor?

The Latin original is laced with words like 'calumniator,' 'fraudator' and 'fellator,' and the free translation which Muirhead directed against Burns is every bit as scurrilous:

> Who conscience – hadst thou that – would sell,
> Nay, lave the common shores of Hell
> For whiskey – Eke, most precious imp,
> Thou art a rhymester, *gauger,* pimp:
> Whence comes it then, Vacerra, that
> Thou still art poor as a church rat?

Muirhead had this and other promptings of his muse printed in Edinburgh and they circulated in the constituency. Young was not alone in thinking that the reverend gentleman had gone too far in repaying Burns in his own coin, and finding an occasion to remonstrate with him asked how he could prove that Vacerra like Burns, was a gauger. 'Martial calls him Fellator,' came the smooth reply, 'which means a Sucker or a man who drinks from the cask.' Although Young disapproved of Muirhead's descending to his attacker's level, he was in no doubt that he had found his mark: 'No publication in answer to the scurrilities of Burns ever did him so much harm in public opinion or made Burns himself feel so sore.'[1]

Burns also kept an eye on proceedings on the larger political stage. Since 1788 Warren Hastings, the first governor-general of British India, had been defending himself at the bar of Parliament against charges of 'high crimes and misdemeanours'. The trial had come to an end at the close of the session of 1794. In May 1795, the House of Lords pronounced a verdict of not guilty on all charges laid against him. The prime mover in the impeachment proceedings had been Edmund Burke. Burns produced an epigram 'On Mr Burke by an opponent and a friend to Mr Hastings':

> Oft I have wonder'd that on Irish ground
> No poisonous Reptile ever has been found:
> Revealed the secret stands of great Nature's work:
> She preserved her poison to create a Burke![2]

1. Fitzhugh, *op. cit.,* p. 87.
2. Kinsley, 478.

It is poor stuff, and plainly owes more to Burns's hostility to Burke's views on the French Revolution than to an informed interest in the affairs of India.

The late spring found him in good spirits and in productive vein, and he kept up a strong flow of material to both Johnson and Thomson. 'I am just now in a high fit of Poetizing, provided that the strait-jacket of Criticism don't cure me,' he wrote to the latter:

> If you can in a post or two administer a little of the intoxicating potion of your applause, it will raise your humble servant's phrenzy to any height you want. – I am at this moment "holding high converse" with the Muses, & have not a word to throw away on such a Prosaic dog as you are. –[1]

One of the fruits of this 'high converse' was the ballad that begins 'Last May a braw wooer cam doon the lang glen,'[2] This is not only a lively song about the comedy of love and courtship; it also illuminates to subtle effect a particular trait of the Scottish character.

The pride he took in his epigrams was disproportionate to their merit, a fact only imperfectly disguised by the false modesty he affected on the subject. At the end of May he sent off a batch of them to Peter Hill in Edinburgh:

> I do not pretend there is much merit in these Morceaux, but I have two reasons for sending them; primo, they are mostly ill-natured, so are in unison with my present feelings while fifty troops of infernal Spirits are riding post from ear to ear along my jaw-bones; & secondly, they are so short, that you cannot leave off in the middle, & so hurt my pride . . .[3]

He also managed to be amusing about his toothache in verse:

> My curse on your envenom'd stang,   sting
> That shoots my tortur'd gums alang,
> An' thro' my lugs gies mony a bang   ears
>   Wi' gnawin vengeance;
> Tearing my nerves wi' bitter twang,
>   Like racking engines . . .[4]

Maria Riddell had moved again, and was now living at a house called Halleaths, a couple of miles east of Lochmaben. She had sent him some of her writing; she also sought Burns's advice about finding an opening for a young man of her acquaintance in the customs or excise, and Burns read her a short lesson on the workings of patronage. His tone of easy familiarity makes it plain that

1. Letters, 665.
2. Kinsley, 503.
3. Letters, 671.
4. Kinsley, 500.

the breach between them was now completely healed. 'The Commissioners of both Boards are people quite in the fashionable circle, & must be known to many of your friends,' he wrote:

> I was going to mention some of your Female acquaintance who might give you a lift, but, on recollection, your interest with the WOMEN is, I believe, but a sorry business. – So much the better! 'tis God's judgement upon you for making such a despotic use of your sway over the MEN. – *You* a Republican! – You have an Empire over us; & you know it too: but the Lord's holy name be praised, you have something of the same propensity to get giddy – (intoxi-cated is not a lady's word) with power; & a devilish deal of aptitude to the same blind, undistinguishing FAVORITISM, which makes other Despots less dangerous to the welfare & repose of mankind than they otherwise might be. –
>
> So much for scolding you.[1]

June 4th was the King's birthday. Church bells were rung at intervals through-out the day and bonfires were lit. At twelve o'clock the Volunteers were drawn up in Queensberry Square. Colours were presented, and Colonel de Peyster pointed out to his men that their device was St. Michael, the tutelary saint of the town:

> As the saint is here portrayed tramping the serpent under his feet, so I trust the Royal Dumfries Volunteers will in support of the civil power trample on all who shall offer to disturb the peace and good order of this town and its neighbourhood, as shall dare to raise their heads against the King and Constitution.

The colours were then consecrated by Dr William Burnside, now, appropriately enough, the minister of St Michael's church. (This was the same Dr Burnside for whose wife Burns had conceived such an extravagant admiration eight years previously and on whose account he had 'almost broke the tenth command-ment.') Burnside's message to the Volunteers was uncompromising and did not make comfortable listening to those who in the not so distant past had been beguiled by the strains of 'Ça Ira'. He spoke of 'a nation long the rival of ours in the arts of peace and war,' and he laid at its door the guilt for miseries 'unequalled in the history of civilised society':

> Under a pretended seal of liberty, and in pursuit of an equality which no political establishment upon earth will ever be able to realise, they have employed means which no end however wise or sacred could justify . . . Not satisfied with overturning all law and all religion, all property and all security,

1. Letters, 673 A.

all liberty and all happiness within their own dominions, they have aimed at the dissolution of the same plans and principles among surrounding nations. Unhappily individuals have not been wanting even in this island who, misled by ignorance if not by evil passions, have shown too much inclination to countenance these principles – principles which if permitted to produce their full effect could not fail to overturn every institution, human and divine, and to produce amongst us such scenes of anarchy, of plunder and of bloodshed as have been seen upon the continent . . .

Later the Volunteers dined together at the King's Arms, and at 6 o'clock they went with the Magistrates to the court house to drink His Majesty's health. The day's arrangements were the cause of some disgruntlement among the townspeople. 'There was none of the inhabitants invited to the Court House as was customary,' William Grierson noted in his diary, 'which offended the people very much, it being such an old custom.'[1]

Whatever his private thoughts, Burns kept his head down and was a regular attender throughout the summer at the Volunteers' parades. Not everyone was so conscientious. The minute book shows that his old Loyalist adversary, Shortt, who had been made a lieutenant, was fined 7s 6d for failing to attend parades. His landlord, Captain Hamilton, was also a defaulter, but he escaped with a fine of 2s 6d.[2] These penalties were imposed on August 24th. Two days previously, Burns had been elected to the Management Committee of the Corps.

His correspondence shows that he was busy with song-writing for much of August. Then for a period of many weeks all letters to him went unanswered. Only in October or November did he take up his pen again; the few sentences which he got off to Mrs Riddell were unlike any she had ever received from him:

A severe domestic misfortune has put all literary business out of my head for some time past. – Now I begin to resume my wonted studies. – I am much correspondence in your debt: I shall pay it soon . . .

1. Grierson, *op. cit.*, p. 36.
2. Grierson's diary gives an illustration of the ferocity with which discipline was enforced in regular military formations at the time. The Strathspey or Grant's Fencibles had been quartered in Dumfries and earned golden opinions for their behaviour. Just before they were due to leave, a soldier sentenced to confinement for talking in the ranks was freed by his fellow Highlanders. Charges of mutiny were brought; four men were condemned to death, and one was sentenced to receive five hundred lashes. Grierson deplored the severity of the sentences, which he attributed to a desire 'to gratify the pride and spleen of an officer'. Two of the men were pardoned at the place of execution, two were shot. 'Fraser behaved at the time of execution rather turbulent,' Grierson wrote, 'but the other submitted with calmness to his hard fate.'

That you, my friend, may never experience such a loss as mine, sincerely prays –

RB[1]

So dazed was he with grief that he omitted to say that the loss he had suffered was the death of his three-year-old daughter. Not only that, but he had been unable to attend the funeral – the child had been at Mauchline and had died very suddenly; Burns was prevented from making the journey by illness.

From that time forward, Burns's own health went into ominous decline. On the last day of the year, he composed a verse epistle to John Mitchell, his superior in the excise. It was a light-hearted affair, in which he expressed seasonal wishes and requested the advance of a guinea against his next salary payment, but from the postscript which he added it is clear that he had been seriously ill:

Ye've heard this while how I've been licket,	stricken
And by fell Death 'maist nearly nicket;	seized
Grim loon! he gat me by the fecket,	waistcoat
And sair he sheuk;	shook me sorely
But by good luck, I lap a wicket,	leaped over gate
And turn'd a neuk.[2]	corner

When he wrote to Robert Cleghorn in the early weeks of 1796, he was more sober and more specific:

Since I saw you, I have indeed been much the child of disaster. – Scarcely began to recover the loss of an only daughter & darling child, I became my self the victim of a rheumatic fever, which brought me to the borders of the grave. – After many weeks of a sick-bed, I am just beginning to crawl about. –[3]

He wrote in similar terms about his daughter and his illness to Mrs Dunlop. He had still not fathomed her silence – 'These many months you have been two packets in my debt,' he complained. 'What sin of ignorance I have committed against so highly a valued friend I am utterly at a loss to guess.' He described his fever as 'most severe,' adding '& long the die spun doubtful'. He also gave a bleak account of economic conditions in Dumfries (the 1795 harvest had been disastrous):

I know not how you are in Ayr-shire, but here, we have actual famine, & that too in the midst of plenty. – Many days my family, & hundreds of other

1. Letters, 685.
2. Kinsley, 514. Salaries were paid in arrears eight times a year, at the end of each collecting round.
3. Letters, 687.

families, are absolutely without one grain of meal; as money cannot purchase it. – How long the *Swinish Multitude* will be quiet, I cannot tell: they threaten daily. –[1]

The 'Swinish Multitude' remained quiet only for another few weeks. William Grierson recorded in his diary that March 10th was a day 'appointed by the King for a general fast over Scotland'. Two days later, when the supplies of meal being sold by the Magistrates at the Trades Hall proved inadequate, serious rioting broke out. The mob seized several cartloads of meal and fifteen cartloads of potatoes; later they broke open the granaries at the Town Mills and got their hands on further large quantities of meal.

The following day was a Sunday, and passed quietly, but there were reports that the mob intended to reassemble once the Sabbath was over and go foraging for further supplies in the countryside. The authorities accordingly called out the Volunteers, the Angus Fencibles and Colonel McDoual's Light Cavalry, and they patrolled the streets until well into the morning. As soon as they dispersed, the mob reassembled on the bridge and succeeded in unearthing a good deal more meal. In the afternoon there were rumours that property was being destroyed in the surrounding countryside; the alarm drum was beaten and the town was in an uproar. The military were once again called out and remained under arms throughout the next two nights, but there were no further disturbances. Grierson took an extremely relaxed view of the affair:

> I think a mob never took place that did less real mischief. They seemed to have no other object in view except bringing in meal, which there was an absolute necessity for as the farmers seemed to be determined to starve the town as they would not bring it in nor sell it at any price – but now there appears to be plenty of meal.[2]

There was a good deal of more general discontent in the country in those early months of 1796, some of it attributable to the additional restrictions on the freedom of speech and assembly imposed by the previous year's Sedition Bill. The measure had been vigorously opposed by the Whigs, and Burns's old friend and patron Henry Erskine had taken the chair at a protest meeting in an Edinburgh theatre. This did not please his colleagues at the Scottish bar, who for the most part were Tories, and there was a move to oppose his re-election as Dean of the Faculty of Advocates. The election took place once a year. Erskine, who enjoyed great personal popularity, had been Dean for ten years, but on January 12th 1796 he could attract only 38 votes while Robert Dundas, the Lord Advocate, mustered 123.

Erskine felt the rebuff deeply – so deeply that he took a coal-axe to his own front door and hacked off the brass plate. Burns was equally incensed,

1. *Ibid.*, 688.
2. Grierson, *op. cit.*, p. 57.

THE MODERN CAIN'S LAMENT

O Harrie whether shall I fly: I am this day A Murderer / of thousands Every one that finds me will count me his / Enemy and Slay me.

5. Pitt and Dundas: a Kay cartoon suggesting that the Prime Minister, having led the country into war with France, was now developing cold feet.

especially as there was a Dundas in the case, and worked off his indignation in 'The Dean of Faculty – A new Ballad –':

> This HAL for genius, wit and lore
>   Among the first was number'd;
> But pious BOB, 'mid Learning's store,
>   Commandment the tenth remember'd.
> Yet simple BOB the victory got,
>   And wan his heart's desire;
> Which shows that Heaven can boil the pot
>   Though the devil piss in the fire.—[1]

1. Kinsley, 515.

388

Burns's condition had by now become a cause of concern to his friends. Thomson tried to rally him:

> O Robby Burns, are ye sleeping yet?
> Or are ye wauken, I would wit?

The pause you have made, my dear Sir, is awful! Am I never to hear from you again? I know, and I lament how much you have been afflicted of late; but I trust that returning health and spirits will now enable you to resume the pen, and delight us with your musings . . .[1]

He did return to his excise duties, but he was far from well. 'When I get a little more health,' he wrote wearily to Johnson towards the end of February, 'you shall hear from me at large on the subject of the songs.' He had put a small printing job in Johnson's way – Hyslop, the landlord of The Globe, needed some bills – but poor Johnson's spelling had not improved with the years, and Burns returned the proof to him with a gentle indication of what needed to be put right:

I am highly pleased with Hyslop's bill, only you have, in your usual luck, mispelt two words. – The article – "Postages & porter" – you have made, "*Porterages & porter*" – pray, alter that. – In the article – "Pipes & Tobacco" – you have spelt Tobacco thus – To*bb*acco – whereas it is spelt with a single b, thus – "Tobacco". –[2]

Spring brought no improvement to his health. 'Alas, my dear Thomson, I fear it will be sometime ere I tune my lyre again!' he wrote in April:

Almost ever since I write you last, I have only known Existence by the pressure of the heavy hand of SICKNESS; & have counted Time by the repercussions of PAIN! Rheumatism, Cold & Fever, have formed, to me, a terrible Trinity in Unity, which makes me close my eyes in misery, & open them without hope. – I look on the vernal day, & say with poor Ferguson –

> "Say, wherefore has an all indulgent Heaven
> Light to the comfortless & wretched given?" –[3]

He was painfully changed in appearance. Grace Aiken, the daughter of his old friend 'Orator Bob,' the Ayr lawyer, happened to pass through Dumfries that spring. Chambers recounts that on her way to visit a friend she encountered 'a tall, slovenly-looking man, of sickly aspect'. As she passed, he uttered an exclamation, causing her to turn:

1. Letter dated 5th February 1796. Quoted in Chambers-Wallace, vol. iv, p. 259.
2. Letters, 690.
3. *Ibid.*, 693. He is quoting from Ferguson's *Job, Chap. III, Paraphrased*.

It was Burns, but so changed from his former self that she could hardly have recognised him, except by his voice. When she asked him playfully if he had been going to pass her without notice, he spoke as if he felt that it was proper for him, nowadays, to let his old friends be the first to hold forth the hand of friendship.[1]

He still had literary projects in mind, however. In a letter in May he told Thomson that he had it in mind to publish a cheap collection of all the songs he had written for him and for Johnson – or rather, he added, of all those of which he wished to be known as the author: 'I do not propose this so much in the way of emolument, as to do justice to my Muse, lest I should be blamed for trash I never saw, or be defrauded by other claimants of what is justly my own.'[2]

The late spring of that year was exceptionally fine. 'The whole country is covered with green and blossoms,' the young Francis Jeffrey wrote to his brother, 'and the sun shines perpetually through a light east wind, which would have brought you here from Boston since it began to blow.'[3] The perpetual sunshine did little for Burns. By early summer, his correspondence carries an unmistakable note of valediction. 'You are a good, worthy, honest fellow, & have a good right to live in this world,' he wrote to Johnson:

Many a merry meeting this Publication has given us, & possibly it may give us more, though, alas! I fear it. – This protracting, slow, consuming illness which hangs over me, will, I doubt much, my ever dear friend, arrest my sun before he has well reached his middle carreer, & will turn over the Poet to far other & more important concerns than studying the brilliancy of Wit or the pathos of Sentiment. –[4]

Maria Riddell invited him to accompany her to the celebrations marking the King's birthday on June 4th, but he wasn't up to it: 'I am in such miserable health as to be utterly incapable of showing my loyalty in any way,' he wrote:

Rackt as I am with rheumatisms, I meet every face with a greeting like that of Balak to Balaam – "Come, curse me Jacob; & come, defy me Israel!" – So, say I, Come, curse me that East-wind; & come, defy me the North!!! Would you have me in such circumstances copy you out a Love-song? No, if I must write, let it be Sedition, or Blasphemy, or something else that begins with a B, so that I may grin with the grin of iniquity, & rejoice with the rejoicing of an apostate Angel.

1. Chambers-Wallace, vol. iv, p. 262.
2. Letters, 695.
3. Letter dated 20th May 1796, quoted in Cockburn, *op. cit.*, vol. i, pp. 21–4.
4. Letters, 696.

—"All good to me is lost;
"Evil, be thou my good!"[1]

If he was disinclined to copy out a love-song for Mrs Riddell, that study of
'the pathos of Sentiment' of which he had written to Johnson had not been
totally laid aside:

> I mourn thro' the gay, gaudy day,
>   As, hopeless, I muse on thy charms;
> But welcome the dream o' sweet slumber,
>   For then I am lockt in thy arms – Jessy.[2]

Jessy Lewars was a girl of eighteen in 1796. Her father, who had died seven
years previously, had been the Supervisor of Excise at Dumfries and her brother
John was also in the service. Burns had found in him a kindred spirit. 'A young
fellow of uncommon merit,' he told Thomson, 'indeed, by far the cleverest
fellow I have met with in this part of the world.' – 'His only fault is – D-m-cratic
heresy.'[3]

Jessy lived with her heretical brother in Mill Vennel, just across the road
from Burns, and since he had become ill she had taken a hand in helping Jean
to care for him and look after the children. She sometimes played the harpsichord for him, and it pleased the dying man to fancy that he was in love with
her. He wrote several fragments of verse to her, and presented her with an
inscribed set of the *Scots Musical Museum*. She was also the inspiration for one
of his loveliest songs – not quite the last thing he wrote, but of all his lyrics
one of the most tender:

> Oh wert thou in the cauld blast,
>   On yonder lea, on yonder lea;   pasture
> My plaidie to the angry airt,   cloak,   direction
>   I'd shelter thee, I'd shelter thee:
> Or did misfortune's bitter storms
>   Around thee blaw, around thee blaw,
> Thy bield should be my bosom,   refuge
>   To share it a', to share it a'.
>
> Or were I in the wildest waste,
>   Sae black and bare, sae black and bare,
> The desart were a paradise,
>   If thou wert there, if thou wert there.

1. *Ibid.*, 697. Burns is quoting from *Paradise Lost*, Bk. iv, lines 109-10 and earlier from the
Book of Numbers, chapter 23, verse 7.
2. Kinsley, 518.
3. Letters, 694.

> Or were I monarch o' the globe,
>   Wi' thee to reign, wi' thee to reign;
> The brightest jewel in my crown,
>   Wad be my queen, wad be my queen.[1]

The tenderness is matched by poignancy. The black and bare waste of which Burns wrote in 'Oh wert thou in the cauld blast' was not conjured solely from his imagination. In that last fevered summer of his life, the idea grew on him that he was about to be overwhelmed by the hated threat of penury; that he stood in the same cold blast which had hastened his father's death twelve years previously.

The regulations of the day provided that if an excise officer was off sick, his salary was reduced by half (the difference was paid to whoever stood in for him). Excise records preserved in the Scottish Record Office in Edinburgh show that in 1796 Burns received a full payment of £6 for the period ended March 3rd, but only half that amount for the ensuing period. He obviously struggled back to work again after that, because he was paid a further £6 on June 2nd. The last recorded payment, however, made on July 14th, shows that his salary had once again been halved. The decline in his condition is graphically attested by his signature on the receipts. Still bold and clear in the spring, by July it has become a palsied squiggle.

Viewed objectively, his financial difficulties were not great. There were undoubtedly many people close at hand who would gladly have come to his assistance, but that was something his pride would not permit; in his desperation, he began to cast about in ways that seem pathetically ineffective. His first thought was to turn to James Clarke, the schoolmaster friend to whom he had behaved so generously some years previously. Clarke was now satisfactorily installed at the burgh school at Forfar, miles away on the other side of Scotland. It is clear that he had responded to an earlier request; now at the end of June, Burns launched a second, as urgent as it was pathetic:

My dear Clarke,
    Still, still the victim of affliction, were you to see the emaciated figure who now holds the pen to you, you would not know your old friend. – Whether I shall ever get about again, is only known to HIM, the Great Unknown, whose creature I am. – Alas, Clarke, I begin to fear the worst! – As to my individual Self, I am tranquil; I would despise myself if I were not: but Burns's poor widow! & half a dozen of his dear little ones, helpless orphans, there I am weak as a woman's tear. – Enough of this! 'tis half my disease! –

1. Kinsley, 524. The theme is traditional. There are echoes of Gay's song 'Were I laid on Greenland's Coast', from the first act of *The Beggar's Opera*. Burns set the words to the old air 'Lenox love to Blantyre'. Almost half a century later they were to catch the sensitive ear of Felix Mendelssohn, and he composed new music for them.

I duly rec^d your last, enclosing the note. – It came extremely in time, &
I was much obliged to your punctuality. – Again I must request you to do
me the same kindness. – Be so very good as *by return of post* to inclose me
another note. – I trust you can do it without much inconvenience, & it will
seriously oblige me . . .[1]

He was in truth doing no more than call in an old debt, but delicacy permitted
only that he should seem to be asking a favour.

Early in July Burns travelled to Brow, a small scattering of cottages on the
Solway Firth about ten miles from Dumfries. He was in a very bad way. 'Beside
my inveterate rheumatism,' he wrote to Thomson, 'my appetite is quite gone;
& I am so emaciated as to be scarce able to support myself on my own legs.'
His mind, however, remained doggedly engaged on what he had set his hand
to: 'I am still anxiously willing to serve your work; & if possible shall try: – I
would not like to see another employed, unless you could lay your hand upon
a poet whose productions would be equal to the rest.'[2]

He had gone to Brow on doctor's orders: 'The Medical folks tell me that
my last and only chance is bathing & country quarters & riding,' he wrote to
Cunningham:

> The deuce of the matter is this . . . What way, in the name of thrift, shall I
> maintain myself & keep a horse in Country-quarters – with a wife & five
> children at home, on 35£? I mention this, because I had intended to beg
> your utmost interest & all friends you can muster to move our Commiss^{rs}
> of Excise to grant me the full salary. – I dare say you know them all personally.
> – If they do not grant it me, I must lay my account with an exit truly en
> poete, if I die not of disease I must perish with hunger.

He also gave Cunningham a piece of family news:

> Mrs Burns threatens in a week or two, to add one more to my Paternal
> charge, which, if of the right gender, I intend shall be introduced to the
> world by the respectable designation of Alex^r Cunningham Burns. My last
> was James Glencairn, so you can have no objection to the company of
> Nobility. –[3]

Brow, or Brow-Well, as it was generally called, was not a place to lift the spirits.
On a fine day, certainly, the view across the firth, to Saddleback and Skiddaw
and Helvellyn, was impressive, but the hinterland was flat and windswept.
There was a spring, strong in iron, but Burns's treatment consisted mainly in

1. Letters, 698.
2. *Ibid.*, 699.
3. *Ibid.*, 700.

wading out chest deep into the Solway. The beach, slimy with mud, was uninviting. At low tide the water receded so far as to be out of sight; in those northern parts the water temperature at that time of year rarely rises above 50°F.

Burns did not invest much confidence in this appalling routine. 'I have now been a week at salt water,' he wrote on July 10th, '& though I think I have got some good by it, yet I have some secret fears that this business will be dangerous if not fatal.' This pessimistic bulletin formed part of one of the very few letters he ever wrote to his father-in-law. His main purpose in writing was to beg for the despatch of Mrs Armour to be with Jean – 'it is ten thousand chances to one that I shall not be within a dozen miles of her when her hour comes.'[1]

There were certain matters to be put in order. Another letter which went off from Brow that day made no pleas for assistance. Nor did it request any explanation of Mrs Dunlop's continued silence; it was a brief attempt, dignified and only fleetingly literary, to tie up a puzzling and still painful loose end:

Madam
I have written you so often without rec.g any answer, that I would not trouble you again but for the circumstances in which I am. – An illness which has long hung about me in all probability will speedily send me beyond that bourne whence no traveller returns. – Your friendship with which for many years you honored me was a friendship dearest to my soul. – Your conversation & especially your correspondence were at once highly entertaining & instructive. – With what pleasure did I use to break up the seal! The remembrance yet adds one pulse more to my poor palpitating heart!
Farewell!!![2]

To Gilbert he was brief and to the point – no allusions to Hamlet here: 'Dear Brother,' he wrote, 'It will be no very pleasing news to you to be told that I am dangerously ill, & not likely to get better.' He gave a matter-of-fact account of his total loss of appetite and general debility and in effect consigned Jean and the children to his care:

God help my wife & children, if I am taken from their head! – They will be poor indeed. – I have contracted one or two serious debts, partly from my illness these many months & partly from too much thoughtlessness as to expense when I came to town that will cut in too much on the little I leave them in your hands. – Remember me to my Mother. –[3]

Burns seems at this point to have had no immediate plans to return to Dumfries, because he told Gilbert that he would spend the whole summer at Brow 'or

1. *Ibid.*, 701.
2. *Ibid.*, 702.
3. *Ibid.*, 703.

in a friend's house in the country'. It is possible that the friend was Mrs Riddell. She too had been unwell and had been recuperating not far from Brow. Hearing of his arrival she had invited him to dinner and sent her carriage to collect him. 'The stamp of death was imprinted on his features,' she wrote to a friend. 'He seemed already touching the brink of eternity.' Mortal illness had not deprived Burns of his taste for the theatrical, however, and he made a good entrance: 'Well, madam,' he enquired, 'have you any commands for the other world?'

At table he ate little or nothing. He expressed concern at how ill his hostess looked. 'He looked in my face with an air of great kindness,' she told her friend. 'He spoke of his death without any of the ostentation of philosophy.' Burns told her how proud he was of his children: 'His anxiety for his family seemed to hang heavy upon him, and the more perhaps from the reflection that he had not done them all the justice he was so well qualified to do.'

He also told Mrs Riddell how deeply he regretted not having put his papers in order, but that the exertion was now beyond him:

He said he was well aware that his death would occasion some noise, and that every scrap of his writing would be revived against him to the injury of his future reputation: that letters and verses written with unguarded and improper freedom, and which he earnestly wished to have buried in oblivion, would be handed about by idle vanity or malevolence when no dread of his resentment would restrain them or prevent the censures of shrill-tongued malice or the insidious sarcasms of envy from pouring forth all their venom to blast his fame.

For all the anxieties that weighed on him, Burns seems to have kept his end up rather better than Mrs Riddell. 'There was frequently a considerable degree of vivacity in his sallies,' she recorded, 'and they would probably have had a greater share, had not the concern and dejection I could not disguise damped the spirit of pleasantry he seemed not unwilling to indulge.'[1]

During his stay at Brow, Burns also visited a Mrs Craig, the widow of the minister of the village of Ruthwell. He called on an evening of brilliant sunshine and as they sat drinking tea Mrs Craig's daughter, fearing that the light might be too much for him, made as if to lower the blinds. 'Thank you, my dear, for your kind attention,' said Burns, 'but oh, let him shine: he will not shine long for me!'[2]

By July 12th, Burns was in a state of great agitation about his financial position and sent an anguished letter to James Burness, his cousin in Montrose,

1. Chambers-Wallace, vol iv, pp. 275-7.
2. *Ibid.*, p. 283. Chambers was relying on John McDiarmid's 'Affecting circumstances connected with the history of the family of Burns', published in the *Dumfries Monthly Magazine* in 1825. McDiarmid had the story from Miss Craig, later Mrs Henry Duncan.

who had clearly been informed of his difficulties: 'When you offered me money-assistance little did I think I should want it so soon,' he wrote;

> A rascal of a Haberdasher to whom I owe a considerable bill taking it into his head that I am dying, has commenced a process against me & will infallibly put my emaciated body into jail. – Will you be so good as to accomodate me, & that by return of post, with ten pound. – O, James! did you know the pride of my heart, you would feel doubly for me! Alas! I am not used to beg![1]

The haberdasher was David Williamson, who had supplied the Volunteers with some of their uniforms the previous year. There is no reason to believe that he was in the least rascally – all he had done was ask a lawyer to chase up a number of bills that were outstanding, and Burns had presumably received the sort of stiff letter that lawyers are paid to send out on such occasions. The sum in question was £7 4s. It is possible that Burns was facing demands for the settlement of other debts; in his reduced state, away from family and friends, the prospect of imprisonment for debt, however far-fetched, took on a nightmarish reality, and he dashed off a second frenzied appeal for help. 'After all my boasted independance, curst necessity compels me to implore you for five pounds,' he wrote to Thomson. 'Forgive me this earnestness, but the horrors of a jail have made me half distracted.' (The measure of his distraction is apparent in the wildness of his language – the unfortunate Williamson is promoted from 'rascal' to 'cruel scoundrel'.) Burns offered the friend he had never met a pathetic and improbable assurance: 'I do not ask all this gratuitously; for upon returning health, I hereby promise & engage to furnish you with five pounds' worth of the neatest song genius you have seen.'[2]

After Burns's death, uncashed drafts for the sums he had requested from both men were found among his papers. Thomson, who was never particularly flush, had to borrow the money from a friend, but wrote a warm and generous letter by return. He told Burns that he had frequently thought of suggesting a financial arrangement but had been deterred by the recollection of what he had once written on the subject and the fear of offending his independent spirit: 'Would I were Chancellor of the Exchequer but for one day, for your sake!'

The good-hearted Thomson also offered a practical suggestion. 'Pray, my good Sir, is it not possible for you to muster a volume of poetry?' he asked:

> If too much trouble to you in the present state of your health, some literary friend might be found here, who would select and arrange from your manuscripts and take upon him the task of editor. In the meantime, it could be

1. *Letters*, 705.
2. *Ibid.*, 706.

advertised to be published by subscription. Do not shun this mode of obtaining the value of your labour; remember Pope published the *Iliad* by subscription. Think of this, my dear Burns, and do not reckon me intrusive with my advice . . .[1]

The author of the Kilmarnock and Edinburgh editions was quite knowledgeable about publishing by subscription, as it happened, but the time for that was past. Thomson's letter is dated July 14th; on that same day in Brow, Burns wrote the last of the very few letters he had ever written to his wife:

My dearest Love,
    I delayed writing until I could tell you what effect sea-bathing was likely to produce. It would be injustice to deny that it has eased my pains, and, I think, has strengthened me; but my appetite is still extremely bad. No flesh nor fish can I swallow; porridge and milk are the only things I can taste. I am very happy to hear, by Miss Jess Lewars, that you are all well. My very best and kindest compliments to her, and to all the children. I will see you on Sunday.

> Your affectionate husband,
> R.B.[2]

He returned home in a friend's gig. Syme went to see him the next morning and felt it his duty to write at once to Alexander Cunningham in Edinburgh. 'I believe it is all over with him,' he wrote:

Dr Maxwell told me yesterday he had no hopes – today the hand of Death is visibly fixed upon him. I cannot dwell on the scene – It overpowers me – yet Gracious God were it thy will to recover him! He had life enough to acknowledge me – and Mrs. Burns said he had been calling on you and me continually – He made a wonderful exertion when I took him by the hand – with a strong voice he said, 'I am much better today, – I shall soon be well again for I command my spirits & my mind. But yesterday I resigned myself to death' – Alas it will not do.
    My dear friend Cunningham, we must think on what can be done for his family. I fear they are in a pitiable condition . . .[3]

News spreads quickly in small towns. 'Dumfries was like a beseiged place,' wrote Allan Cunningham. 'It was known he was dying, and the anxiety, not of the rich and the learned only, but of the mechanics and peasants, exceeded all belief.' So that there might be quiet in the house, the children were sent across

1. Letter dated 14th July 1796. Quoted in Chambers-Wallace, vol. iv, p. 282.
2. Letters, 708.
3. 'Syme-Cunningham Correspondence (2)' in *Burns Chronicle*, x (1935), p. 40.

the street to stay with the Lewars family. Findlater and other friends sat for a time at his bedside. One of them, a fellow-Volunteer called Gibson, could not hold back his tears. Burns smiled at him and said, 'John, don't let the awkward squad fire over me.'

Towards the end he became delirious: by Jean's account he 'was scarcely himself for half an hour together'. The day before he died he twice called out Gilbert's name, 'very quickly and with a hale voice'. Maxwell watched by his bed for the greater part of the last night. He died at five o'clock on the morning of July 21st.

They buried him four days later. 'Showery forenoon, pleasant afternoon, wet evening and night,' William Grierson noted prosaically in his diary. 'In respect to the memory of such a genius as Mr Burns, his funeral was uncommonly splendid.'

Most of the arrangements had been made by Syme. The body had been previously carried from Burns's house to the Town Hall, and the half-mile route from there to the churchyard was lined by troops from the Angusshire Fencibles and the Cinque Ports Cavalry, both then quartered in the town. At the head of the procession, with arms reversed, a funeral party drawn from the Volunteers; behind them, and immediately in front of the bier, the military band of the Cavalry. The church bells of the town tolled at intervals. To muffled drums and the sombre beat of Handel's 'Dead March' from *Saul*, the procession moved forward – magistrates, townsfolk, neighbouring gentry. At the gate of the churchyard, the Volunteers formed two lines and rested their heads on their firelocks, pointed to the ground; the corpse was borne between them and carried to the graveside.

Burns would have relished the small ironies of the day – it was the sort of occasion he would have itched to celebrate in sardonic verse. Tradition has it that he was buried in the Volunteer's uniform for which, in his lordly fashion, he had so long neglected to pay. The presence of the Cinque Ports Cavalry meant that the principal mourners included a future Tory Prime Minister – they were commanded that day by a young MP called Jenkinson, later the second Lord Liverpool. As the first shovelful of earth sounded on the coffin lid, the firing party from the Volunteers, the awkward squad, loosed off three straggling and ragged volleys.

Gilbert was the only close member of Burns's family to attend the funeral. At the house in Mill Vennel, a young widow of thirty-one lay struggling to give birth to her ninth child.[1]

---

1. It was a boy. Jean, presumably knowing nothing of the compliment Burns had intended to pay Cunningham in the matter of names, decided on a gesture of gratitude to another friend and had him christened James Maxwell. He was a sickly child, and was to die before his third birthday.

Sixteen

NIHIL NISI VERUM

YOUNG WILLIAM GRIERSON confided to his diary that he had found Burns's funeral 'solemn, grand and affecting'; a spectacle which accorded with the general sorrow and regret felt in the town at the loss of a man 'whose like we can scarce see again'. He did not, however, lapse into hagiography:

As for his private character and behaviour, it might not have been so fair as could have been wished but whatever faults he had I believe he was always worst for himself and it becomes us to pass over his failings in silence, and with veneration and esteem look to his immortal works which will live for ever. I believe his extraordinary genius may be said to have been the cause of bringing him so soon to his end, his company being courted by all ranks of people and being of too easy and accommodating a temper which often involved him in scenes of dissipation and intoxication which by slow degrees impaired his health and at last totally ruined his constitution.[1]

In the taverns and drawing rooms of Dumfries that would not be controversial. In Edinburgh, however, Alexander Cunningham had lost no time in arranging for more conventional things to be said; as soon as he had been alerted by Syme that the end was near he went into action and he was able to report on what might be expected from the newspapers three days before the funeral took place: 'Mr Thomson has kindly undertaken to announce the Death to the Public. It will appear perhaps tomorrow or Monday, and I dare say from his pen something elegant will be said.'[2]

The result appeared in both the *Edinburgh Evening Courant* and the *Glasgow Mercury* two days after Burns's death and was later picked up by many other papers, not only in Scotland, but also in London and the English provinces. The choice of Thomson turned out to be less than inspired:

1. Grierson, *op. cit.*, p. 63.
2. Correspondence between Syme and Cunningham, published in the 1935 *Burns Chronicle*, p. 43.

His poetical compositions, distinguished equally by the force of native humour, by the warmth and tenderness of passion, and by the glowing touches of a descriptive pencil, will remain a lasting monument of the vigour and the versatility of a mind guided only by the lights of nature and the inspirations of genius. The public . . . will learn with regret that his extraordinary endowments were accompanied with frailties which rendered them useless to himself and his family. The last months of his short life were spent in sickness and indigence; and his widow, with five infant children and in the hourly expectation of a sixth, is now left without any resource but what she may hope from the regard due to the memory of her husband.

It may be that Thomson, knowing that a fund was to be set up for Jean and her children, was trying to be helpful. Cunningham certainly saw nothing to take exception to, describing it to Syme as 'a short Panageric to the Memory of Poor Burns,'[1] but Syme and some of Burns's other friends in Dumfriesshire were affronted, finding the reference to 'frailties' indelicate and unfeeling:

Pardon this bluntness − I mean no personal application, for I am ignorant of its author, but I cannot help saying that it was improper to wake the idea of his irregularities while the melancholy subject of his death was announced. Maxwell, McMurdo, and others were extremely wounded by it.[2]

With a view to redressing the balance, Syme appealed to Mrs Riddell to write something for the local *Dumfries Journal*. She was at first reluctant, but eventually agreed on condition that it should be anonymous. Syme did not at all like what she first showed to him. 'I found it quite impossible,' he told Cunningham. 'I wrote her a note, a free note, searing the whole with a red hot iron.'[3] A number of the offending passages were toned down, and some of them were none the worse for it: 'a penchant for the joy-inspiring bowl' became 'the frolic spirit of the flowing bowl,' which was a gain in subtlety. Mrs Riddell's 'sketch,' as she called it, subsequently had a wide circulation, in a variety of versions, in numerous newspapers and periodicals.

It may not have served Syme's purpose quite in the way he had hoped but it is without question one of the most perceptive and rounded of contemporary portraits of Burns to come down to us. Mrs Riddell begins, almost provocatively, by declaring that it would be an injustice to Burns to dwell exclusively on his talent as a poet: 'Poetry was actually not his *forte*.' It is a bold assertion, but it offers to posterity precious corroboration of the testimony of the letters:

Many others perhaps may have ascended to prouder heights in the region of Parnassus, but none certainly ever outshone Burns in the charms − the sorcery, I would almost call it, of fascinating conversation, the spontaneous

1. *Ibid.*, letter dated 24th July 1796.
2. *Ibid.*, letter dated 26th July 1796.
3. *Ibid.*, letter dated 18th August 1796.

eloquence of social argument, or the unstudied poignancy of brilliant repartee; nor was any man, I believe, ever gifted with a larger portion of the '*vivida vis animi*'.

Mrs Riddell signed herself 'Candidior,' and there are some notably forthright passages:

> The keenness of satire was, I am almost at a loss whether to say his *forte* or his foible; for though nature had endowed him with a portion of the most pointed excellence in that dangerous talent, he suffered it too often to be the vehicle of personal, and sometimes unfounded, animosities.

That suggests that she may by then have caught up with some of the unpleasant things he had written about her after the breach between them; if so, she was intelligent and witty enough to settle the score with no more than a slightly feline display of magnanimity:

> The suppression of an arch and full-pointed bon-mot from a dread of offending its object, the sage of Zuric very properly classes as a virtue *only to be sought for in the Calendar of Saints*; if so, Burns must not be too severely dealt with for being rather deficient in it. He paid for this mischievous wit as dearly as any one could do. "'Twas no extravagant arithmetic" to say of him, as was said of Yorick, 'that for every ten jokes he got an hundred enemies.'

She was very acute about his emotional extremism:

> He acknowledged in the universe but two classes of objects, those of adoration the most fervent, or of aversion the most uncontrollable; and it has been frequently a reproach to him, that unsusceptible of indifference, often hating, where he ought only to have despised, he alternately opened his heart and poured forth the treasures of his understanding to such as were incapable of appreciating the homage; and elevated to the privilege of an adversary, some who were unqualified in all respects for the honor of a contest so distinguished.

In a robust sequence towards the end she declares that although she declines to play the role of apologist, she believes that genius 'never was free from irregularities':

> It is perfectly evident that the world had continued very stationary in its intellectual acquirements, had it never given birth to any but men of plain sense ... besides, the frailties that cast their shade over the splendor of superior merit, are more conspicuously glaring than where they are the

attendants of mere mediocrity. It is only on the gem we see the dust, the pebble may be soiled and we never regard it.[1]

In the matter of attending to the needs of the family Cunningham and Syme moved swiftly, and within a few days they had raised 70 guineas. Jean was faced immediately only with the settlement of Burns's debts, which stood at £14 15s and with meeting the modest expenses of the funeral – 5s for the tolling of the bells, 2s 6d for the grave, 3s for the mort-cloth. Gilbert owed something over £180, Burns's library was valued at £90 and there were drafts to the value of £15. Pauperdom had been a phantom.

Cunningham had formed the view that they must not only raise a subscription for Jean and her brood but also arrange for the sale of all Burns's post-humous work to a London bookseller. He had sketched out his ideas urgently to Syme even before their friend was dead: 'We must do the thing instan-taneously and while the pulse of the Public will beat at the name of Burns.'[2]

The beat of the public pulse was not uniformly strong. Indeed in Scotland's capital city it was downright sluggish. 'The truth is, my dear Syme,' Cunning-ham wrote on August 9th, 'the poor Bard's *frailties* – excuse this vile word – were not only so well known here, but often I believe exaggerated, that even the admirers of Genius cannot be prevailed on to do what we all ought – to forget and forgive.'[3] Lewis Hay, Margaret Chalmers' husband, and a partner in Sir William Forbes's banking house, was helpful, and so was Patrick Heron; Stephen Kemble, the manager of the Theatre Royal, arranged a benefit night; Erskine of Mar, Dugald Stewart and George Thomson, on the other hand, all proved broken reeds. 'All help short of actual assistance' seemed to be the general line – it was certainly the device of Sir John Sinclair, to whose *Statistical Account* Burns had contributed material on the Monklands Friendly Society. Sinclair declined to broach with Dundas the possibility of an annuity and by way of assistance for Jean offered one guinea – Cunningham, incensed, coldly advised him to enter himself for that princely sum in the public subscription lists. William Nicol had been devastated by Burns's death – 'social joy is blighted to me, for ever,' he wrote to John Lewars – but Cunningham was not receptive to the idea that he should harness his energies; he was, he told Syme, 'constantly besoted and Drunk,' and indeed cirrhosis of the liver carried him off the following April.

By that time, the sum raised in the Athens of the North totalled £171 19s 6d. The response in Ayrshire had been equally dismal, and Syme expressed himself forcibly to Cunningham:

Those friends in Ayr etc. whom the Bard has immortalized have not contrib-

---

1. The passages quoted are taken from the revised text printed in Currie's 2nd edition of 1801.
2. Letter dated 20th July 1796, 'Syme-Cunningham Correspondence (2)', in *Burns Chronicle*, x (1935), p. 41.
3. 'Syme-Cunningham Correspondence (3)', published in *Burns Chronicle*, 1936, 39.

uted a sous!!! By heavens, they should be as immortally d—d, and a list of the d—d should be made out."[1]

In Dumfries, Syme himself, assisted by friends like Maxwell and McMurdo, had done rather better, although they too had their disappointments, notably the way in which they felt Patrick Miller was sitting on his hands.[2] By the spring, however, the Dumfries figure was close to £500, with the promise of more to come; Jean had in addition received a payment of £25 from the recently inaugurated Royal Literary Fund.[3]

Money was also donated in England. The London appeal brought in £700 and in Liverpool, a Scottish doctor called James Currie succeeded in raising £73. Currie, a son of the manse, had been born in Dumfriesshire and had gone to school with Robert Riddell. He was related to the McMurdo family and was a close friend of one of Dr Moore's sons. Now a man of forty, Currie's early life had been adventurous. Apprenticed as a boy to one of the great Glasgow tobacco companies, he had spent five years in Virginia. Forced to serve in the Colonial Army, he eventually gained his freedom after sailing a hundred and fifty miles in an open boat; only then did he return home and embark on his medical studies at Edinburgh. He had done well enough as a doctor to buy the small estate of Dumcrieff, near Moffat (Syme, another friend of long standing, acted as his factor), and on a visit to Dumfries in 1792 he had, very briefly, met Burns.

Shortly after Burns's funeral, Syme received a long letter from Currie. 'I assure you, I lament over his early fate,' he wrote, adding that even in the few minutes of conversation he had had with him, he had distinguished a 'bold, powerful and ardent mind'. Currie did not write solely to offer condolences, however. 'What did Burns die of? What family has he left – and in what circumstances?' he enquired:

By what I have heard, he was not very correct in his conduct; and a report goes about that he died of the effect of habitual drinking . . . As you knew this singular man, of whom much will now be said, and much enquired in future times, I wish you would give me as much of his character and of his private life as you can without inconvenience, in addition to the points I have enquired into; and I will endeavour, in one way or another, to turn it to some account.[4]

1. Letter dated 7th March 1797. Quoted in 'Syme-Cunningham Correspondence (4)', *Burns Chronicle*, xiii (1938), 48.

2. Miller not only took a back seat in Dumfries but declined to lend his support to an approach to Dundas to request an annuity. Without the backing of prominent Dumfriesshire figures, the Lord Advocate's willingness to forward a petition to Dundas went for very little.

3. This was on the initiative of an Englishman called Thomas White, a good friend of Burns's who taught locally and had been a fellow-Volunteer. White had contributed an obituary notice to the *Dumfries Journal* on the day after Burns died.

4. Quoted in D. McNaught, 'Dr Currie and his Biography of Burns', *Burns Chronicle*, 1919, pp. 11-12.

Currie's words seem to convey not only curiosity about Burns as a case history but also an interest in writing something about him. When he wrote again two and a half weeks later, however, the emphasis was different:

> Roscoe and I are also very anxious to hear who are to be the editors of his posthumous works, and who is to be Burns's biographer. It is a national concern that this be done with care and skill, and I earnestly entreat you to consider well of this point. All his remains should be carefully collected, but not all published; and his life should be written by one who feels the charms of his genius, and who can express what he feels. By this time such points are probably settled. I should be happy to hear that you are Burns's biographer yourself; and if you undertake it, you may command our assistance, if we can assist you.[1]

Syme's reply is now lost, but he must have written at some length about Mrs Riddell's 'Candidior' sketch, and in terms that suggested the biography might be entrusted to her. Currie reacted sharply. 'I agree with you in thinking the subject of his life delicate as well as important in its nature,' he wrote:

> I should, however, be very sorry if there were not a superior hand employed to that you mention; for though I have seen some productions of that person, which convey a favourable notion of her taste and fancy, yet I can never suppose her equal to a conception of the character of this great and masculine genius.

Currie repeated the offer of his own services, adding that he had some connections with booksellers in London, and that he was confident of being able to command a larger sum from them than could be had in Edinburgh:

> That an authorised biographer should be fixed soon, seems to me the more necessary, because it is to be feared that volunteers may appear, attracted by the popularity of a subject which they may deform and disgrace.[2]

Syme now seems to have given Currie to understand that Dugald Stewart was a likely candidate. That went down much better – 'certainly a man as well qualified as any in the Island, and to whose superior genius I bow'. Stewart, however, declined, and by the time Currie received a formal invitation from the executors at the beginning of September, he was beginning to have cold

---

1. Letter dated 12th August 1796, *Ibid.*, p. 13. William Roscoe, the Liverpool friend whose assistance Currie was volunteering along with his own, was the son of a market-gardener and publican. He carved out for himself a varied career as a lawyer, a banker, a Member of Parliament and a writer – his *Life of Lorenzo de' Medici* had appeared the previous year, and had, as it happened, contained a handsome compliment to Burns in a footnote.
2. Letter dated 15th August 1796, *Ibid.*, pp. 14-15.

feet: 'My objections (w^h you will justly say ought to have been considered first) arise from various considerations,' he wrote to Syme:

> Every day of my life, I am at least four hours on horseback & two on foot, and this bodily exertion is attended with incessant exertion of mind – My only leisure is from two to four after my forenoon calls are over & an hour or two in the evening. But at such times I am generally fatigued, & when I attempt to write after my morning calls, as at present, I am obliged to stimulate my jaded nerves by large quantities of Coffee – The little leisure I have, finds me almost constantly disposed to sleep, & without Coffee I am ready to yawn & tumble back on my sopha.[1]

Although Currie was also badly behind with a long-projected medical publication, he realised that he had all but committed himself. If no other 'competent hand' could be found, he told Syme, 'I will not draw back from any expectation I have excited,' and he sketched out one or two preliminary ideas on how the work should proceed.

By the middle of September, the matter was agreed. By modern standards, the time scale proposed for the work was hair-raising – 'As it will not be required for some ten or twelve months I can accomplish it,' Currie wrote, although he had obviously been led to expect that some of the material was going to be sifted for him: 'I am glad that our friend Cunningham is to have the papers in his charge,' he told Syme; 'I know his excellent heart':

> He will, of course, be very cautious whom he trusts with a sight of the naked effusions of poor Burns; for there are many that would, from mere curiosity, wish to inspect them; and several who, I fear, would be glad of an opportunity of finding in them food for their malevolence.[2]

Currie later maintained that only Syme's modesty had prevented him from undertaking the biography himself, but it is much more likely that Syme was deterred by the enormity of the undertaking. A public appeal for the loan of manuscripts had met with a healthy response, but many of the poems with which the committee was deluged were already in the public domain. Letters proved tricky in a different way. This was partly because Burns's own papers were in such disorder, partly because some of his correspondents were extremely eager to get their hands on the letters they had written to him.

Syme and Maxwell, on first looking through the confused mass of Burns's papers, had come across what Syme described to Cunningham as 'a considerable packet of a peculiar description':

> We paused before we ventured to read. We consulted whether to seal them

---

1. Besterman Papers, pp. 3-7. Quoted in R.D. Thornton, *James Currie: The Entire Stranger and Robert Burns*, Oliver & Boyd, Edinburgh and London, 1963, pp. 347-9.
2. McNaught, *op. cit.*, pp. 19-20.

up and deliver them to the person, who, if alive, must have an anxious, a distracted heart. We resolved to be a Court of honour and delicacy, and to examine what the letters contained. We read three or four, and were rapt and astonished at the inconceivable merits of the authoress. But Love, such Love as Eloise flames on St. Preux, is the inexhaustible fountain. Heavens! were it possible to get his letters to that person ... What shall be done with these letters?[1]

The authoress herself was in no doubt about what should be done with them and wrote to Cunningham requesting their return. (In doing so Mrs McLehose made an extraordinary slip which would have roused Burns and his fellow-Crochallan Fencibles to extremes of lewd hilarity – by way of identifying the letters, she said they had been written 'under the Signature of Clitander'.)

Cunningham did not immediately comply with this request, and found himself in consequence badgered by an unwelcome visitor:

I have today had another call from a Mr. Ainslie, W.S., *whom I suspect does Mrs McLehose's business*, demanding her Letters. He wished very much to introduce me to her, which I declined for two reasons. I never accept of an invitation from any Man without intending to make the retort corteous; and his manners and behaviour seem quite opposite to what I would wish to meet with even in a common acquaintance, besides involving me in an introduction to a Woman who for aught I know may be as chaste as Diana, but who bears a quisquis character in the World, and which might lead to many perplexities.[2]

It was as easy to acquire a 'quisquis character' in the small world of Edinburgh two hundred years ago as it is today – there would have been raw material enough to hand in Mrs McLehose's marital misfortunes alone, even if she had never met Burns. There were also those who believed that Ainslie had become more than her 'man of business' – a letter from him survives in the National Library of Scotland in which he writes to her of the 'end of the week which you appointed as the Termination of my Banishment'.[3]

Whatever the nature of their relationship, they deployed between them an effectively threatening range of weaponry to get what they wanted; Clarinda's surviving letters to Syme, with their blend of coyness and flattery, suggest that she and Ainslie had stumbled on a highly effective tactic – an eighteenth-century version of the 'nice cop, nasty cop' routine so beloved of twentieth-century television directors:

What can have impressed such an idea upon you, as that I ever conceived the most distant intention to destroy these precious memorials of an acquaint-

1. Letter dated 31st July 1796, quoted in 'Syme-Cunningham Correspondence (3)', *Burns Chronicle*, ix (1936), p. 40.
2. 'Syme-Cunningham Correspondence (4)', *Burns Chronicle*, xiii (1938), p. 44.
3. National Library of Scotland,. MS 587 (1181).

ance, the recollection of which would influence me were I to live till four-score! Be assured I will never suffer one of them to perish. This I give you my solemn word of honour upon; – nay, more, on condition that you send me my letters, I will select such passages from our dear bard's letters as will do honour to his memory, and cannot hurt my own fame, even with the most rigid. His letters, however, are really not literary; they are the passionate effusions of an elegant mind – indeed, too tender to be exposed to any but the eye of a partial friend. Were the world composed of minds such as yours, it would be cruel even to bury them: but ah! how very few would understand, much less relish, such compositions! The bulk of mankind are strangers to the delicate refinements of superior minds . . .

In the face of arguments like these, Syme and his superior mind were defence-less. Mrs McLehose accepted his surrender with gracious skittishness:

Dear Sir,
– I am much obliged to you for the speedy return you made to my last letter. What could induce you to spend New Year's Day in so solitary a manner? Had I not heard *other things* of you, I should have imagined you in the predicament of Hamlet, when he exclaims, 'Man delights me not, nor woman neither'.[1]

She was happy, she told him, that he had at last consented to the return of her letters:

You must pardon me for refusing to send B.'s. I never will. I am determined not to allow them to be out of my house; but it will be quite the same to you, as you shall see them all when you come to Edinburgh next month . . . I hold them sacred – too sacred for the public eye; and I am sure you will agree they are so when you see them. If any argument could have prevailed on me, (and Mrs R. exhausted all her eloquence could dictate,) the idea of their affording pecuniary assistance was most likely. But I am convinced they would have added little to this effect . . .[2]

If Mrs Riddell's powers of persuasion had failed with Clarinda, they were entirely adequate when it came to defending her own interests. Details of the transaction are unknown, but to this day not one of her letters to Burns has been known to pass through a sale room. The presumption must be that she persuaded Syme to allow her to retrieve them all and that she destroyed them.

1. By a strange chance Burns had quoted the same line in his last letter to Maria Riddell. (Letters, 697.)
2. Letter dated 9th January 1797. Burns and McLehose, pp. 72-6. Almost half a century would go by before the complete correspondence was published by Mrs McLehose's grandson.

Not a few people whose lives had touched that of Burns at some point had reason to be apprehensive as to how their names might figure in a posthumous edition of his work. Cunningham floated before Syme the idea of playing on this sensitivity to the benefit of the general subscription:

> By the way, can it be possible for us to *extort* something from Lonsdale, Queensbury, etc., whom he has satiryzed, without incurring a Lybel? A hint of a broad kind might induce them to *purchase* Silence.[1]

Syme, sensibly, took the view that he and his fellow-executors had enough problems without courting prosecution for blackmail. He continued to assemble what material he could and to extract the occasional promise from Maxwell and McMurdo that they would do some preparatory work on it. By the end of the year, five months after Burns's death, he had to recognise that nothing further was going to be accomplished in Scotland, and in the first week of 1797 he despatched everything that had been assembled to Liverpool. Currie, normally the most assiduous of correspondents, took almost a month to acknowledge receipt of 'the remains of poor Burns':

> I viewed the huge and shapeless mass with astonishment! Instead of finding, as I expected, a selection of his papers, with such annotations as might clear up any obscurities – of papers perused and approved by his friends as fit for publication – I received the complete sweepings of his drawers and of his desk (as it appeared to me), even to the copy-book on which his little boy had been practising his writing. No one had given these papers a perusal, or even an inspection; the sheep were not separated from the goats; and – what has, perhaps, not happened before since the beginning of the world, – the manuscripts of a man of genius, unarranged by himself, and unexamined by his family or friends, were sent, with all their sins on their heads, to meet the eye of an entire stranger![2]

The astonishment with which poor Currie viewed this biographer's dream was laced with dismay. Although he was a man of wide literary interests, his only previous excursion into print (apart from the odd medical article) had been a pamphlet, published under a pseudonym in 1793, urging Pitt not to go to war with France.[3] For much of 1797 he was obliged to busy himself with the first edition of his *Medical Reports*, a study of the effects of water upon fevers (he thought somebody else was going to beat him to it); throughout the time he worked on his life of Burns he was almost never well, struggling, as he had

---

1. 'Syme-Cunningham Correspondence (4)', *Burns Chronicle*, xiii (1938), 44.
2. . McNaught, *op. cit.*, p. 22.
3. *A Letter, Commercial and Political, addressed to the Rt. Hon. William Pitt: in which the Real Interests of Britain, in the Present Crisis, are Considered, and some Observations are Offered on the General State of Europe by Jasper Wilson*, Liverpool, 1793.

done for most of his life, with the consumption that was eventually to kill him. It is a great marvel that he accomplished what he had undertaken to do in as little as three years, and not in the least surprising that he was not first in the field.

That distinction fell to Robert Heron, who scrambled into print just six months after the death of his subject. 'Original Memoirs of the Late Robert Burns' began to appear in serial form in the *Monthly Magazine and British Register* in January 1797, and was republished in book form in Edinburgh later in the year. It is conventional to abuse Heron for being the first to say in print what many said behind their hand. 'He seems to have taken great delight in blackening the poet's character,' wrote Snyder, 'and by so doing furnished the starting point for the tradition of alcoholism and debauchery.'

I do not detect the delight. Certainly, Heron pictures Burns and Nicol 'as dead drunk as ever Silenus was'; but he also observes that whatever the subject of his verse, Burns 'seems still to grasp it with giant force'. It is true that in describing the 'morals of the town' in Dumfries he writes that Burns 'did not escape suffering by the general contamination'; but he also has a passage in which he notes his 'quick and correct DISCERNMENT of the distinctions between RIGHT and WRONG, between TRUTH and FALSEHOOD'. And to say of a poet that he demands to be ranked not with the Ramsays, but with the Miltons, the Popes and the Grays is hardly to damn with faint praise.

Heron's *Memoir* was written in some haste and contained rather less than 14,000 words. Currie laboured for three years over Burns's 'sweepings' and when his *Life* made its appearance in the autumn of 1800 it ran to four volumes and was published in an edition of 2,000 copies.

On the social and political questions of the day, the biographer and his subject would have found little to quarrel about. Currie was vehement in his denunciation of the slave trade; to Dr Moore's son Graham he wrote of the late war with America as 'a long journal of disgrace';[1] when Joseph Priestley's home was destroyed by the Birmingham mob in 1791, it was Currie who composed the public address sent to him by Liverpool Dissenters. Above all, Burns would have approved of Currie's opposition to the war with France – 'this desperate crusade of despotism and superstition against anarchy and enthusiasm,' as he described it in his pamphlet addressed to Pitt.

In late eighteenth-century Britain, biography as we know it today was still in its infancy. Izaak Walton had pointed the way a hundred and fifty years previously with his *Life of Donne*, and there had been the spectacularly unmethodical John Aubrey – 'I now set things down tumultuarily, as if tumbled out of a Sack.' Boswell's *Life of Johnson* had appeared in 1791, although that extraordinary work, like its author, was very much *sui generis*; Currie himself greatly admired Johnson's *Lives of the Poets*, and in one of his letters to Syme

1. Quoted in William Wallace Currie, (ed.), *Memoir of the Life , Writings, and Correspondence of James Currie, M.D., F.R.S., of Liverpool,* 2 vols., London, 1831, vol ii, p. 152.

he had proposed that he should work to the same plan – a narrative of the life followed by an appreciation of the writings.

Johnson believed that biography had a moral purpose, but it was very far from his intention simply to produce a moral effect. His aim was neither didactic nor improving. It was his special concern to establish as honestly as he could the nature of the difficulties with which his subjects had had to contend, not only in the world around them but in their own natures. 'If nothing but the bright side of characters should be shown,' he said to Edmond Malone, the Shakespearean scholar, 'we should sit down in despondency, and think it utterly impossible to imitate them in *anything*.' A funeral oration was one thing, an essay in biography something quite different – 'If a man is to write a Panegyrick, he may keep vices out of sight, but if he professes to write a life, he must represent it really as it was.'

The main consequence of Currie's admiration for Johnson is that posterity has pinned him down in a critical crossfire. He has been blamed for saying both too much and too little, for paying undue attention to Burns's frailties but also for being mealy-mouthed about them. About the man and the poet alike Currie has many admiring things to say, but for readers avid for unrestrained panegyric that has never been enough, and there are passages which even today make them stir indignantly.

These passages are mostly about the the demon drink, a subject on which Currie was something of an expert. As a younger man he had himself been quite an accomplished tippler; now, in middle life, he had developed a professional interest in the subject – his *Medical Reports* which began by examining the merits of water as a remedy for fever, went on to consider 'the Effects of Opium, Alcohol, and Inanition'. Alcohol and poetry, Currie insisted, did not mix:

> In proportion to its stimulating influence on the system (on which the pleasurable sensations depend) is the debility that ensues; a debility that destroys digestion, and terminates in habitual fever, dropsy, jaundice, paralysis or insanity. As the strength of the body decays, the volition fails; in proportion as the sensations are soothing and gratified, the sensibility increases; and morbid sensibility is the parent of indolence, because, while it impairs the regulating power of the mind, it exaggerates all the obstacles to exertion. Activity, perseverance, and self-command, and the great purposes of utility, patriotism, or of honourable ambition, which had occupied the imagination, die away in fruitless resolutions, or in feeble efforts . . .

It is true that several pages later Currie writes that 'to apply these observations to the subject of our memoirs, would be a useless as well as a painful task,' but by then all but his dullest readers have done just that. Currie now seems to sense that he has said enough and that it is time to move on, but in the attempt he ceases to be entirely clear and fashions the two sentences which, more than any others, have been held against him down the years: 'He who suffers the pollution of inebriation, how shall he escape other pollution?' he enquires rhetorically. 'But let us refrain from the mention of errors over which delicacy and humanity draw the veil.'

By taking refuge in 'delicacy and humanity' Currie is, of course, disregarding the Johnsonian injunction to 'represent it really as it was'. What is he suggesting – a touch of the clap? If he believed Burns had contracted venereal disease, he should have said so, and given his reasons. It is this aspect of the *Life* which exposes the opposite flank, attracting the charge of sanctimoniousness and irritating those modern readers who are able to regard Burns's various frailties and shortcomings with a degree of detachment. The same instinct led to the occasional doctoring of what Burns had actually written: the phrase 'sodomy of soul' which Burns employed in a letter to Thomson, for instance, was sanitised, and 'sodomy' became 'prostitution'.

And yet none of this is particularly surprising. Currie must be seen in his time. We are not considering the work of an agnostic investigative journalist living in a modern democracy but of an eighteenth-century Scots doctor living among English Dissenters at the time of the Napoleonic Wars. He was extremely clear-sighted, both about Burns and about what he had undertaken on his behalf. He never forgot that he was engaged, not in a dilettante literary exercise, but in an attempt to swell the subscription for Burns's widow and children; he recognised that there were constraints – and he recognised it, as one of his letters to Syme makes plain, before he had even seen the material:

> I suspect that many of his effusions, and probably some of the best of them, have such strong parts in them of different kinds, that I am not willing, even with Roscoe's assistance, to take the responsibility of editing them. . . . It appears to me that everything that is now printed should be as free of exceptions as may be; but that a future volume may contain such things as are now too vehement, but which yet may stand the test of time.[1]

His own volumes also stand that test, although not everyone admired them when they first appeared. 'Have you seen the new edition of Burns?' Charles Lamb enquired in a letter to Coleridge – 'very confusedly and badly written, and interspersed with dull pathological and *medical* discussions'.[2] Currie proved a better judge of public taste than the author of *Elia*; no fewer than twenty editions appeared in the United Kingdom over the next two decades, and the work was extensively pirated in Scotland, Ireland and the United States.

1. Letter dated 31st December 1796, quoted in McNaught, *op. cit* pp. 21-2. Currie was also very careful politically, as he made plain in his dedication to Dr Moore's son, Graham: 'All topics are omitted in the writings, and avoided in the life of Burns, that have a tendency to awake the animosity of party.'

2. Letter dated 28th July 1800. *The Letters of Charles Lamb, to which are added those of his Sister, Mary Lamb,* ed. E.V. Lucas, 2 vols., J. M. Dent & Sons Ltd., London 1912, vol i, p. 193.

Currie did not live to see this. His health held up until the winter of 1803, but from then on he suffered increasingly frequent bleedings. He sought relief in the milder climate of the south-west of England; he died at the small watering-place of Sidmouth, in Devon, in August 1805.

His efforts had added the sum of £1200 to the Trust Fund for Burns' family. And it was also thanks to James Currie that within two decades of his death, the name of Robert Burns was known throughout the English-speaking world.

Seventeen

APOTHEOSIS

THE STRONG ATTACHMENT which Scots profess to democratic principles does nothing to moderate the passion with which they debate matters of precedence. When did the first Burns Club come into existence? And where? The Burns Club of Greenock claims to have been founded in 1801, but the minute book for its first ten years is lost; a likely tale, retort the Burnsians of Paisley, and produce with a flourish a minute book dating back to 1805. Certainly, by the early years of the nineteenth century, the vogue for Burns Suppers was well-established, with recitations of the 'Address to a Haggis' and the proposing of numerous toasts. In 1826 the members of the Dumfries club were invited to raise their glasses thirty-four times; the toasts included Homer, Milton and the cause of Greek independence.

Not everyone was yet prepared to drink to 'the Immortal Memory', however.[1] There were still those who nursed aggrieved memories of wounds inflicted by Burns. One such was the Reverend William Peebles, Minister of Newton-upon-Ayr and would-be poet, who had sustained multiple injuries in 'The Twa Herds', 'The Holy Fair' and 'The Kirk's Alarm':

> O'er Pegasus' side ye ne'er laid a stride,
> Ye only stood by where he shit ...

That coarse reflection on Peebles' abilities as a versifier still rankled after more than twenty years, and 'Poet Willie' could now have his revenge on the 'irreligious profligate' who had penned it without fear of retaliation. This took the form of the grandly-titled *Burnomania; the Celebrity of Robert Burns Considered: In a Discourse Addressed to All Real Christians of Every Denomination*:

> – His race is run: the hero dies:
> What heaving breasts! what streaming eyes!

1. The first recorded reference to the now traditional form of words dates from the inaugural meeting of the Paisley Club at the Star Inn, when the toast was proposed by a William McLaren.

413

The collegies Ambubaiarum
O'er Scotland sound the sad alarum,
Thro' many an elegiac strain,
We ne'er shall see his like again . . .
What call you this? Is it Insania?
I'll coin a word, 'tis Burnomania.
His Greenock friends we therefore dub
The Annual Burnomanian Club.

When Dorothy and William Wordsworth visited Dumfries in 1803, they found Burns's grave unmarked. The Immortal Bard's mortal remains lay under a plain stone slab in St Michael's churchyard until 1815, but in that year they were disinterred and moved, with those of two of his sons, to a vault under a new mausoleum.

A public subscription had been opened two years previously. The committee included the Duke of Buccleuch, the Marquess of Queensberry and several Members of Parliament; Syme was a member, and so was Colonel de Peyster, still going strong at seventy-seven; William Grierson acted as one of two secretaries. The committee considered that it had long been a matter for regret – a reflection, indeed, on their country – that no public tribute of respect had yet been paid to the memory of the man 'who employed his remarkable powers in giving grace and dignity to the lowland language of Scotland, and in illustrating the manners and character of the Scottish peasantry'. It was resolved to seek contributions by writing to friends and admirers of Burns 'in the United Empire, the East and West Indies and America'.[1]

The money came rolling in – £32 6s from Huddersfield, £23 from Lisbon, £81 from Montreal. The Committee also heard that a sum of £300 had been subscribed in Bombay – it transpired that for the past two years an expatriate admirer of Burns had been raising money to build a monument there.[2] In Edinburgh, Walter Scott prevailed on Henry Siddons to hold a benefit night. 'We had by no means a crowded, but a very genteel audience,' Scott told Grierson, and this swelled the subscription by a further £39 14s.

There was also a benefit night at the theatre in Dumfries. The celebrated Mrs Jordan was in town. She was now, in her mid-forties, acting only intermittently, but the fact that she had been the Duke of Clarence's mistress for twenty years and borne him ten children always guaranteed a good house. Mrs Jordan professed herself highly gratified by the Committee's request, 'as it will allow her to become (though an humble) yet most zealous promoter of so interesting and liberal a design and one so worthy the feelings of Scotia's Sons'. She played the part of Widow Belmure in a comedy called *The Way to Keep*

1. The minutes of the Mausoleum Committee are reproduced in Grierson, *op. cit.*, pp. 259-99.
2. John Forbes Mitchell, the Scot who had collected this sum in Bombay, later announced that he was not disposed to give it to Dumfries; in his view it ought to be applied to the building of a national monument on the Calton Hill in Edinburgh. (*Ibid.*, p. 284.)

Him. It was one of her last performances. She died in poverty in Paris two years later.

The design competition for the mausoleum attracted fifty entries, and was won by Thomas Frederick Hunt of London; he also won golden opinions in the burgh by declining the prize of £10 and furnishing working drawings free of charge. A commission to produce a marble group went to Peter Turnerelli, an Irishman of Italian extraction, and taking his cue from the dedication of the Kilmarnock edition he depicted the Muse of Poetry discovering Burns at the Plough.

Turnerelli, who had named a figure of 750 guineas as a fee, proved to be more commercially minded than Hunt. At one stage he told the Committee that he would settle for whatever remained of the subscription money after the mausoleum had actually been built, but that was after a good dinner at the King's Arms at which the freedom of the burgh was conferred on him; after two years' work in his London studio, his mood was less benign. Artists do not generally like to have patrons looking over their shoulder. Turnerelli had conceived of his work as an allegory in the classical manner, and is unlikely to have taken kindly to the sort of advice recorded in the committee's minutes:

> The plough in Mr Turnerelli's model not being considered anything like the plough used in Scotland it was judged proper to have a model of a proper plough made by Mr Small in Edinburgh to be sent to the sculptor in London.[1]

The disinterment was carried out very early in the morning. It had been hoped that Burns's remains could be transferred to the vault with a minimum of disturbance, but it turned out that the coffin was not made of oak, and it had to be opened. A number of accounts have come down to us; a modern American scholar has observed that the nineteenth century's fascination with the details of physical decay rivalled that of the Elizabethans:[2]

> There lay the remains of the great poet, to all appearances entire, retaining various traces of recent vitality, or, to speak more correctly, exhibiting the features of one who had recently sunk into the sleep of death. The forehead struck every one as beautifully arched, if not so high as might reasonably have been supposed, while the scalp was rather thickly covered with hair, and the teeth perfectly firm and white. Altogether, the scene was so imposing that the commonest workmen stood uncovered, as the late Dr Gregory did at the exhumation of the remains of King Robert Bruce, and for some moments remained inactive, as if thrilling under the effects of some undefin-

1. Minute dated 23rd March 1816, *ibid*, p. 279. When Turnerelli insisted on reverting to the original terms, the Committee was obliged to place a number of advertisements in the press to make up the deficiency. (Minute dated 28th January 1819, p. 297.)

2. Carol McGuirk, 'Burns and Nostalgia', in *Burns Now*, edited by Kenneth Simpson, Canongate Academic, Edinburgh, 1994, p. 48.

able emotion while gazing on all that remained of one 'whose fame is wide as the world itself'. But the scene, however imposing, was brief; for the instant the workmen inserted a shell beneath the original wooden coffin, the head separated from the trunk, and the whole body, with the exception of the bones, crumbled into dust.[1]

The coffin was opened a second time on the night before Jean's funeral in 1834. On that occasion a Dumfries surgeon called Archibald Blacklock was present. 'The cranial bones were perfect in every respect,' he noted:

> ... even the delicate bones of the orbits, with the trifling exception of the *os unguis* in the left, were sound, and uninjured by death and the grave. The superior maxillary bones still retained the four most posterior teeth on each side, including the dentes sapientiae, and all without spot or blemish; the incisores, cuspidati, &c., had in all probability recently dropped from the jaw, for the *alveoli* were but little decayed. The bones of the face and palate were also sound. Some small portions of black hair, with a very few gray hairs intermixed, were observed while detaching some extraneous matter from the occiput. Indeed, nothing could exceed the high state of preservation in which we found the bones of the cranium, or offer a fairer opportunity of supplying what has so long been desiderated by phrenologists – a correct model of our immortal poet's head ...[2]

The pseudo-science of phrenology was all the rage. The notion that the configuration of the skull – the 'arrangement of the bumps' – was indicative of the moral and intellectual qualities of the individual had been formulated by the anatomist and physiologist Franz Joseph Gall. The lectures on phrenology on which he embarked in Vienna in 1796 were a *succès fou* – in 1802 the government banned them as dangerous to religion. Gall's followers included an Edinburgh man called George Combe, who had originally trained as a lawyer, and was married to a daughter of the actress Mrs Siddons. The plaster cast of Burns's skull told Combe that its owner had been a highly creative individual, perhaps even a professional writer. How this squared with a rating of 'uncertain' for Language is unclear; his bumps did, on the other hand, indicate a high rating for Adhesiveness, Combativeness and Philoprogenitiveness.

By the time of Jean's death in 1834, those who had known Burns in the flesh were becoming thin on the ground. Cunningham had died as early as 1812, Gilbert in 1827, and Syme in 1831. Ainslie was still about; he had

---

1. John McDiarmid, 'St Michael's Churchyard, Disinterment of Burns', in *Sketches from Nature*, Dumfries, 1830.
2. Blacklock's account was published in *Phrenological Development of Robert Burns, from a cast of his skull moulded at Dumfries, the 31st day of March, 1834*, with remarks by George Combe, author of 'A system of Phrenology', etc. W. and A.K. Johnson, Edinburgh, 1859.

become pious with advancing years, and taken to writing religious tracts with titles like *Reasons for the hope that is in us.*

Hope was also important to Mrs. McLehose. She had been widowed in 1812, and her cousin, Lord Craig, had died the following year. Walter Scott met her once at Craig's house, and remembered her as 'old, charmless and devout'. 'When later years thinned the ranks of her friends,' wrote her grandson, 'it was with great difficulty she became reconciled to a more retired mode of life'. She showed Burns's letters to visitors until the paper hardly held together. Here and there she had taken her scissors to them; some names had been inked over, and in one or two places she appeared to have used chemicals. She still took her favourite walk round Calton Hill, and continued, when her memory allowed, to write up her journal. 'This day I never can forget,' ran the entry for 6th December 1831. 'Parted with Burns, in the year 1791, never more to meet in this world. Oh, may we meet in Heaven!'[1]

The critics had continued to give as much attention to the defects of Burns's moral character as to the qualities of his poetry. The publication of Cromek's *Reliques of Robert Burns* in 1808 had occasioned two influential unsigned reviews – that by Francis Jeffrey in the *Whig Edinburgh Review*, and that by Walter Scott in the first issue of the *Quarterly Review*, recently established as a rival Tory voice. Jeffrey, who was later to begin his demolition of Wordsworth's *The Excursion* with the notorious 'This will never do!' was alive to the value of a provocative opening:

Burns is certainly by far the greatest of our poetical prodigies – from Stephen Duck down to Thomas Dermody. *They* are forgotten already; or only remembered for derision. But the name of Burns, if we are not mistaken, has not yet 'gathered all its fame'; and will endure long after those circumstances are forgotten which contributed to its first notoriety . . .

Burnsians who succumbed to apoplexy at this early point missed much that was judicious and discriminating, because it was Jeffrey's contention that to regard their hero as a prodigy was to derogate from his merits: 'We can see no propriety in regarding the poetry of Burns chiefly as the wonderful work of a peasant, and thus admiring it much in the same way as if it had been written with his toes.' Behind the acerbic and sometimes patronising manner, an informed critical intelligence was at work. Jeffrey, who stood in the urbane tradition of Addison and Johnson, was critical of what he termed the 'undisciplined harshness and acrimony' of Burns's invective, although that was not the most severe criticism he had to offer:

1. Burns and McLehose, p. 53.

The leading vice in Burns's character, and the cardinal deformity, indeed, of all his productions, was his contempt, or affectation of contempt, for prudence, decency and regularity; and his admiration of thoughtlessness, oddity, and vehement sensibility; – his belief, in short, in *the dispensing power* of genius and social feeling, in all matters of morality and common sense ... This pitiful cant of careless feeling and eccentric genius, accordingly, has never found much favour in the eyes of English sense and morality. The most signal effect which it ever produced, was on the muddy brains of some German youth, who are said to have left college in a body to rob on the highway! because Schiller had represented the captain of a gang as so very noble a creature ...

These were robust strictures, but Jeffrey was not less incisive in what he had to say about the humour, the pathos and the animation which he found in Burns. He paid particularly close attention to the songs. They were, he said, 'written with more tenderness, nature, and feeling than any other lyric compositions that are extant' and were likely to outlive all his other work. His judgement that Burns was 'entitled to the rank of a great and original genius' was unqualified.[1]

Scott, in his review for the *Quarterly* a month later,[2] did not think that Cromek had performed much of a service either to the poet or the public: 'The contents of the volume before us are more properly gleanings than reliques, the refuse and sweepings of the shop, rather than the commodities which might be deemed contraband.' Like Jeffrey, he thought highly of the songs – 'No poet of our tongue ever displayed higher skill in marrying melody to immortal verse' – although he also took the view that Burns's devotion to compiling and composing for musical collections was so much time and talent frittered away and a diversion from 'his grand plan of dramatic composition'.

For Scott, Burns was 'the child of passion and feeling'. The tone of his review is kindlier than Jeffrey's, but he shakes his head no less reprovingly over his recklessness:

The extravagance of genius with which this wonderful man was gifted, being in his later and more evil days directed to no fixed or general purpose, was, in the morbid state of his health and feelings, apt to display itself in hasty sallies of virulent and unmerited severity: sallies often regretted by the bard himself; and of which, justice to the living and to the dead, alike demanded the suppression.

Scott's social and political conservatism did nothing to blunt his literary judgement, however – he dwelt at length, for instance, on the merits of that

1. *Edinburgh Review*, xiii (January 1809), pp. 249-76.
2. *Quarterly Review*, i, (February 1809), pp. 19-36.

riotously subversive piece 'The Jolly Beggars' – 'for humorous description and nice discrimination of character, [it] is inferior to no poem of the same length in the whole range of English poetry'. He also had a keen eye for the strengths and weaknesses of Burns's prose style, pointing impartially to the 'meretricious ornaments' to be found in his letters to Clarinda and the mastery of the vernacular he displayed in one of his letters to William Nicol – 'an attempt to read a sentence of which, would break the teeth of most modern Scotchmen'.[1]

By the time Scott's son-in-law, John Gibson Lockhart, tried his hand at a biography in 1828, he felt the need to placate the reader with a defensively worded preface: 'Some apology must be deemed necessary for any new attempt to write the *Life of Burns*.' By then Wordsworth, Coleridge and Hazlitt had all had their say and so, in *English Bards and Scotch Reviewers*, had Byron; there is even a short passsage referring to Burns in *Sanditon*, the novel which Jane Austen left unfinished at her death.

Lockhart had, in fact, correctly identified the need for something less monumental than the successive editions of Currie, and his book was well received. 'All people applaud it,' Scott told him in a letter, 'a new edition will immediately be wanted'. Scott was right. The style is mellifluous and Lockhart's *Life* ran into many editions; it was only in the 1930s that it came under the beady scrutiny of modern academic scholarship: 'Inexcusably inaccurate from beginning to end, at times demonstrably mendacious,' wrote Snyder. He allowed one thing in its favour – it was the occasion of a famous review by Thomas Carlyle.[2]

Carlyle, thirty-two years old and still struggling to establish himself, had just abandoned Edinburgh for the bleak solitude of Craigenputtoch. He saw Burns's life as a tragedy of potential unfulfilled and opportunity squandered, but argued that he must for all that be ranked 'not only as a true British poet, but as one of the most considerable British men of the eighteenth century':

An educated man stands, as it were, in the midst of a boundless arsenal and magazine, filled with all the weapons and engines which man's skill has been able to devise from the earliest time; and he works, accordingly, with a strength borrowed from all past ages. How different is *his* state who stands on the outside of that storehouse, and feels that its gates must be stormed, or remain forever shut against him! His means are the commonest or rudest; the mere work done is no measure of his strength. A dwarf behind his steam-engine may remove mountains; but no dwarf will hew them down with the pickaxe; and he must be a Titan that hurls them abroad with his arms.

Carlyle's own origins and associations were not so very different from those of Burns and nobody before or since has written about him with such passionate

---

1. Letters, 112. This is the letter written from Carlisle in June 1787. See pp. 145–6 *supra*.
2. Snyder, p. 488.

insight. He paid scant attention to Lockhart's text – what he produced was not really a review at all but an extended essay in biography. For him, Burns's writing was 'no more than a poor mutilated fraction of what was in him, broken glimpses of a genius that could never show itself complete'. He notes, however, the tonic effect of his work on Scottish literature as a whole: 'For a long period after Scotland became British, we had no literature ... Theologic ink, and Jacobite blood, with gall enough in both cases, seemed to have blotted out the intellect of the country.'

The merits of the poetry interest Carlyle less than the psychological complexities of the man who wrote it:

> There is but one era in the life of Burns, and that is the earliest. We have not youth and manhood, but only youth ... With all that resoluteness of judgement, that penetrating insight, and singular maturity of intellectual power, he never attains to any clearness regarding himself.

He acknowledges that Burns was unfortunate in some of the 'fashionable danglers after literature' he fell in with along the way, but contemplates the various difficulties he encountered in his life with a complete lack of sentimentality; in Carlyle's view, the world treated him no worse than it did Tasso or Galileo or Camoens. 'It is his inward, not his outward misfortunes that bring him to the dust.' Burns, he declares, like Byron, never came to 'moral manhood'.

His conclusion is that the Burnses, the Swifts and the Rousseaus of this world are sometimes tried 'at a tribunal far more rigid than that where the Plebiscita of common civic reputations are pronounced,' and that the result is often a condemnation that is both blind and cruel:

> Granted, the ship comes into harbour with shrouds and tackle damaged; the pilot is blameworthy; he has not been all-wise and all-powerful; but to know how blameworthy, tell us first whether his voyage has been round the Globe, or only to Ramsgate and the Isle of Dogs.[1]

Jeffrey, still editing the *Review* after twenty-six years, considered the article too long and diffuse and did not admire its author's Germanic English. When Carlyle received the proofs, he found that he had been drastically pruned – 'the body of a quadruped with the head of a bird,' he grumbled to his wife; 'a man shortened by cutting out his thighs, and fixing the Knee-pans on the hips!' He restored the cuts and returned the proofs to Jeffrey, telling him he was free to drop the article but not to mutilate it; rather surprisingly, his editor

1. *Edinburgh Review*, xlviii, no. xcvi, December 1828.

acquiesced.[1] As things turned out, Carlyle's views on Burns carried a good deal further than either the Isle of Dogs or Ramsgate; Goethe thought so highly of the article that he translated long passages from it and published them in his collected works.

Language was initially something of a barrier to the spread of Burns's fame beyond the English-speaking world. There were several translations into French between 1825 and 1840 and articles about him began to appear in the Russian periodical press in the 1820s. (Appropriately enough there is an early translation of 'Ae Fond Kiss' by Mikhail Lermontov, himself the descendant of a Scottish adventurer called Learmont who had entered the Russian service in the seventeenth century.) Burns's work was also greatly admired in Scandinavia, and one of the first to translate him was Henrik Wergeland, the outstanding Norwegian lyric poet of the nineteenth century.

In Canada and the United States, Burns's egalitarianism and his identification with the colonial cause had gone down well from the start. There were also many expatriate Scots who needed no prompting either to promote the work or foster the legend. Emigrant sons of Caledonia might quickly shed their Scottish accents after a few years in the land of the free, but they remained in the grip of a powerful nostalgia for the real or imagined Scotland they had left behind. From Pittsburgh, in 1852, the young Andrew Carnegie wrote home to an uncle:

Although I cannot say sow crae just as broad as I once could I can read about Wallace, Bruce and Burns with as much enthusiasm as ever and feel proud of having been a son of old Calodonia, [sic] and I like to tell people when they ask, 'Are you native born?' 'No sir, I am a scotchman,' and I feel as proud as I am sure as ever Romans did when it was their boast to say, 'I am a Roman citizen.'[2]

In 1859, the hundredth anniversary of Burns's birth was widely celebrated in North America. In New York City, a centenary oration was given by the Reverend Henry Ward Beecher, then at the height of his fame as a congregational minister and moral crusader. Until his death, he told his audience, Burns's life had been a failure: 'Ever since it has been a marvelous success.' In Boston, there was a lavishly eloquent tribute from Ralph Waldo Emerson:

Not Latimer, nor Luther struck more telling blows against false theology

1. The two men were very good friends. 'A beautiful little man,' Carlyle wrote of Jeffrey in his *Reminiscences*, 'and a bright island to me and mine in the sea of things.'
2. Letter to George Lauder dated 30th May 1852, now in the Carnegie papers in the Library of Congress. Quoted in Joseph Frazier Wall, *Andrew Carnegie*, Oxford University Press, New York, 1970, p. 101.

than did this brave singer. The Confession of Augsburg, the Declaration of Independence, the French Rights of Man, and the 'Marseillaise', are not more weighty documents in the history of freedom than the songs of Burns.

Emerson drew heady comparisons with Rabelais, Shakespeare and Cervantes. 'If I should add another name,' he continued, 'I find it only in a living country-man of Burns.' (He was a great friend and admirer of Carlyle's.) The genius of Burns was exceptional, and for a curious reason:

> The people who care nothing for literature and poetry care for Burns ... Yet how true a poet he is! And the poet, too, of poor men, of gray hodden and the guernsey coat and the blouse ... And as he was thus the poet of the poor, anxious, cheerful, working humanity, so had he the language of low life ... It seemed odious to Luther that the devil should have all the best tunes; he would bring them into the churches; and Burns knew how to take from friars and gypsies, blacksmiths and drovers, the speech of the market and the street, and clothe it with melody ...[1]

Celebrations took place in fifty-nine other locations in the United States. We know this because they were chronicled in meticulous detail by an Edinburgh artist and man of letters called James Ballantine. England did slightly better with seventy-six meetings, the Colonies notched up forty-eight and Ireland ten; the occasion was also marked by Burnsians in Copenhagen. Ballantine recorded proudly that in Scotland itself the day was celebrated by six hundred and seventy-six events:

> The utmost enthusiasm pervaded all ranks and classes. Villages and hamlets, unnoticed in statistical reports, unrecorded in Gazetteers, had their dinners, suppers, and balls. City vied with clachan, peer with peasant, philanthropist with patriot, philosopher with statesman, orator with poet, in honouring the memory of the Ploughman Bard.[2]

The Centenary Banquet held in the City Hall in Glasgow was a particularly strenuous affair. The reply to 'The Immortal Memory' was given by Burns's

---

1. E.W. Emerson, (ed.) *Complete Works of Ralph Waldo Emerson*, Centenary Edition, Boston and New York, 1911, vol. xi, pp. 440–3. Margaret Fuller, Emerson's associate on the transcendentalist magazine the *Dial*, waxed even more rhapsodical: 'Since Adam,' she wrote, 'there has been none that approached nearer fitness to stand up before God and angels in the naked majesty of manhood than Robert Burns.' (Quoted in Franklyn Bliss Snyder, *Robert Burns, His Personality, His Reputation and His Art*, University of Toronto Press, 1936, p. 77.)

2. James Ballantine (comp. and ed.) *Chronicle of the Hundredth Birthday of Robert Burns*, A. Fullarton & Co., Edinburgh, 1859, p. 430. Ballantine (1808–77) began life as a house-painter. He later became interested in the revival of glass-painting, and was commissioned to execute the stained-glass windows in the House of Lords. He was also one of the so-called Whistle-binkie poets, who published collections of sentimental songs and poems.

son, William Nicol, who had risen to the rank of Colonel in the East India Company and was now living in retirement in Cheltenham; there were twenty-two further toasts and fifteen replies, interspersed by musical items. The evening had begun with 'Scots Wha Hae'; the final item on the programme reads 'Solos, "Auld Lang Syne" – the Vocalists – Chorus by the Company, standing, accompanied by Band and Organ.'

South of the border, there were those who permitted themselves to view the festivities with less than total seriousness. The Crystal Palace Company had offered a prize of fifty guineas for a Burns Centenary Ode, and this attracted more than six hundred entries. *Punch*, in a parody of Tennyson's 'Charge of the Light Brigade', extended its sympathy to the judges:

> Rhymesters to right of them,
> Rhymesters to left of them,
> Rhymesters behind them,
>   Volleyed and thundered,
> Stormed at with shout and yell,
> They that had given the bell,
> Pale on the judgement seat,
> Wished themselves off again,
> Ere they had dared to sell
> Thirty score bards save one,
>   Out of six hundred!

When it was announced that the winner of the competition was a woman, Isabella Craig Knox, *Punch* printed a letter from one Thalestris Hardlines:

I feel *doubly* the *triumph* of our sex, in that it has been won in doing honour to a *bard*, who, whatever his *errors* and *imprudences*, had a proper *esteem* for *women*.[1]

Burns carries many posthumous burdens. One of the heaviest ought in fairness to be borne equally by Henry Mackenzie, who first hung the 'ploughman poet' tag around his neck. From quite early in the nineteenth century a legion of versifiers – blacksmith poets, policeman poets, engine-driver poets, ratcatcher poets – vied with each other to demonstrate that there was nothing special about being a ploughman. The fact that their work was uniformly execrable did not prevent an enthusiast who lived near Dundee from publishing a collection of it in sixteen volumes – complete with a break-down of the contributors by occupation. The palm was effortlessly carried off by William McGonagall, son

---

1. *Punch*, 5th February 1859, p. 51. Editors of *Punch* in the nineteenth century assumed that their readers had a classical education. Thalestris was the Amazonian Queen who descended on Alexander the Great with a retinue of three hundred women, hoping that together they might raise a race of Alexanders.

of an immigrant Irish cotton weaver and self-styled 'poet and tragedian'. His public performances often ended in his being pelted with refuse; he became a national figure of fun; he was memorably described (by the writer William Power) as 'the Ossian of the ineffably absurd'.

Punch also used the occasion of the Burns centenary festivities to have a sly dig at Queen Victoria. Her passion for the Highlands was well-known. Albert had bought Balmoral for her seven years previously, and the house's conversion to the Scottish baronial style had been completed in 1855: 'Every year,' she wrote in her journal, 'my heart becomes more fixed in this dear Paradise.'

A *Punch* cartoon depicted a dinner party. 'GRAND BURNS FESTIVAL,' reads the caption. 'BROWN ENTERTAINS HIS FRIEND WI' A HAGGIS!' The allusion is obvious. The chief guest at the table is portrayed as small and plump and is wearing what could just be a coronet. The host (he is having difficulty in serving the haggis, which for some reason is exploding like a mortar bomb) is clearly John Brown, Victoria's favourite Highland servant. The innuendo would have been plain enough to *Punch* readers. What is intriguing is that Victoria's supposed relations with Brown did not become the stuff of common gossip until later in the following decade. The cartoon suggests that tongues were wagging round London dinner tables long before that – and two years before the death of the Prince Consort in 1861.[1]

Politicians also found ways of exploiting Burns. When Gladstone came out of retirement in 1879 and made the iniquities of Turkish rule the occasion for an onslaught on Disraeli's foreign and imperial policies, Burns found himself posthumously press-ganged into supporting the Liberal Party. (He was in distinguished company – the Liberals took it for granted that Wallace would be on their side, too.)

Gladstone made his challenge in Midlothian, standing against the sitting member, Lord Dalkeith, son and heir of the Duke of Buccleuch. 'Gentlemen of Midlothia,' said one of his posters, 'the spirits of Burns and Wallace stand by my side, and we appeal to you to be jealous of liberties bequeathed to you by your forefathers and to hand them down to your children unsullied and untarnished by the withering hand of Imperialism and Tyranny.' (Imperialism got a mention because Gladstone was opposed to Disraeli's proposal that Queen Victoria should be styled Empress of India.)

The poster artist has depicted Gladstone, tall and erect, haranguing the electors of 'Midlothia', and ghostly representations of Burns and Wallace do indeed stand at his shoulder, the former looking rather as Nasmyth painted him, the latter vaguely resembling Genghis Khan. At the bottom, Gladstone's spin-doctors have taken liberties with both the words and the metre of 'Scots Wha Hae':

1. See Tom Cullen, *The Empress Brown: The Story of a Royal Friendship*, Bodley Head, London, 1969.

Scots whose sires wi' Wallace bled,
Scots to truth and justice wed,
Prepare for a servile bed,
　　Or a victory!

Now's the day and now's the hour,
See the front o' battle lour,
See advance proud jingo's power,
　　Chains and slavery!

Gladstone–Wallace–Burns – an unusual triple ticket, but an effective one. The Liberals made a net gain of one hundred and three seats at the polls. Gladstone, at the age of seventy, formed his second administration; Disraeli, old and ill, found leisure in the year of life that remained to him to complete *Endymion* – and to take philosophical satisfaction from what was at that time the largest advance ever extracted from a British publisher for a work of fiction.[1]

As the nineteenth century drew to a close, the apotheosis of Burns was well-nigh accomplished. In March 1885, a marble bust was placed in Poets' Corner in Westminster Abbey. It was unveiled by Gladstone's successor as Prime Minister, Lord Rosebery, and the name of the Prince of Wales stood at the head of the subscription list. The sculptor was the Aberdonian Sir John Steell, who had executed the marble figure for the Scott Monument in Edinburgh and who had been awarded a commission some years previously for a statue of Burns in New York's Central Park – the first outside Scotland. Bronze casts of this were made, one for Dundee, one for Dunedin, one for the Thames Embankment. This too had been unveiled by Rosebery, who delivered a speech arrestingly free of the sentimentality that was so often the hallmark of such occasions:

It was not much for him to die so young; he died in noble company, for he died at the age which took away Raphael and Byron, the age which Lord Beaconsfield has called the fatal age of 37. After all, in life there is but a very limited stock of life's breath; some draw it in deep sighs and make an end; some draw it in quick draughts and have done with it; and some draw it placidly through four-score quiet years; but genius as a rule makes quick work with it. It crowds a lifetime into a few brief years, and then passes away, as if glad to be delivered of its message to the world, and glad to be delivered from an uncongenial sphere.[2]

1. Longmans offered £10,000.
2. Robert Rhodes James, *Rosebery*, Weidenfeld and Nicolson, London, 1963, p. 213.

In the heyday of Victorian prosperity a small army of likenesses in stone and bronze sprang up in Great Britain, North America and the southern hemisphere – not only statues, but plaques and roundels, panels in high and low relief, busts in bronze and plaster and wood and Sicilian marble. James Mackay, indefatigable auditor of the world's store of Burnsiana, believes that only Christopher Columbus and (in his day) Lenin have been more widely commemorated.

A bust had been installed in the Mercantile Library in St Louis, Missouri, in 1866; on Labour Day, 1877, a statue was unveiled by the Scottish community in the Australian gold-rush town of Ballarat. Burns attracted the attention of a number of nineteenth-century Italian sculptors. Fidardo Landi, a professor in the Academy of Fine Arts in Carrara, produced several busts – one of them found its way to the public library of Fall River in Massachussets. In the Scottish capital, the statue in marble commissioned from John Flaxman in 1824 took some time to find a permanent home. Originally sited in the Burns monument on Calton Hill, it was subsequently transferred to the University Library. The Principal, however, Dr John Lee, took exception to this on the ground that Burns was not a graduate. After some wrangling it was moved to the National Gallery of Scotland; finally, in 1889, it came to rest in the entrance hall of the newly-opened National Portrait Gallery, and that is where it stands today.

Burns seated, Burns standing to attention, Burns leaning on a stick, Burns sprawled on the fork of a tree. Life-size in Adelaide, eleven feet tall in San Francisco. Burns in plaid and breeches, Burns in the Fox livery of buff and blue; bare-headed and shirt-sleeved in Barre, Vermont, in Auckland he is got up in a tail coat and a Kilmarnock bonnet. In Aberdeen his expression is stern and dignified, in Central Park it is pained; he looks earnest in Ayr, vacant in Dumfries. Burns in the act of composition, Burns gazing at the evening star, Burns holding a bunch of daisies ... The range is truly eclectic, although inevitably some are more successful than others. 'Undoubtedly the most pretentious of all Burns monuments,' writes James Mackay of the structure unveiled in Kilmarnock in 1879 – 'a fusion of Scots Baronial, neo-Gothic and Italianate, with a dash of Baroque and a hint of Romanesque'.[1]

The centenary of Burns's death in 1896 was also widely marked. At the Mausoleum in Dumfries, wreaths arrived from around the world. The one sent by Burnsians in New South Wales was somewhat delayed. It had been placed inside a block of ice and conveyed to Scotland in the refrigerated hold of a ship normally used for transporting frozen meat. It finally reached Dumfries by goods train early in August, and was met by the town band and a large crowd, but although it had by this time begun to melt, the block of ice in which the wreath was entombed was still too big to be got through the gateway of the Mausoleum.

---

1. James A. Mackay, *Burnsiana*, Alloway Publishing Ltd., Ayr, 1988, p. 36.

There was an ambitious exhibition in Glasgow. It was held under the patronage of Queen Victoria and of a galaxy of the great and the good – dukes and marquesses, generals and archbishops, Lord Provosts and Members of Parliament, university principals and newspaper editors. Sir John Millais, then President of the Royal Academy, was an Honorary Vice-President, as was the historian W.E.H. Lecky; literature was represented by the oddly-assorted duo of Bret Harte and Algernon Swinburne. Lord Rosebery, whose premiership had ended so miserably the year before, accepted the honorary presidency; another patron was Andrew Carnegie – for many years it was *de rigueur* in the libraries he endowed in the United States (there were more than three thousand of them) to have a bust of Burns on display.

An unwieldy general committee was established. It included, as *ex-officio* members, not only the entire executive council of the Burns Federation, founded eleven years previously, but the presidents, vice-presidents and secretaries of all the clubs affiliated to it. These already numbered seventy – the Burns Haggis Club of Alloa and the Winnipeg St Andrew's Society, the St Rollox Jolly Beggars and the Scottish Thistle Club of San Francisco ... Happily there was also a much smaller executive committee with a strong leavening of Glasgow lawyers and businessmen, and they saw to it that the exhibition was ready by the appointed day in July.

In the six galleries of the Royal Glasgow Institute of the Fine Arts in Sauchiehall Street the committee assembled a remarkable collection. There were books and manuscripts, portraits and pictures. The Trustees of the National Gallery of Scotland in Edinburgh declined for some reason to lend the original portrait for which Burns gave sittings to Nasmyth, but the Skirving drawing in red chalk was there, and McKenzie's portrait 'Bonnie Jean and Grandchild' attracted much attention.

The book section of the exhibition was a bibliographical feast. The organisers had managed to lay their hands on 696 different editions, issued by 243 publishers in thirty-two cities and towns of the United Kingdom (which at that time included the whole of Ireland) – 303 editions in Scotland, 359 in England, thirty-four in Ireland. The editors of the catalogue expressed some disappointment at having been able to round up only some seventy editions from the United States:

> Only four of the greater cities are represented, while wealthy, populous, and progressive centres like Washington, Chicago, Cincinnati, San Francisco, St. Louis, and New Orleans do not appear at all. The presence in the list of relatively small places like Salem and Wilmington may be taken as evidence that Burns has been much more widely and frequently reprinted in the United States than would appear from this collection ...[1]

1. *Memorial Catalogue of the Burns Exhibition*, William Hodge & Company and T. R. Annan & Sons, Glasgow, 1898, p. 196.

There was also a section of translations and continental editions – Burns in Bohemian, Burns in Flemish, Burns in Hungarian, Burns in medieval Latin. Germany was strongly represented, and even the Old Enemy was catered for: *Burns in English*, translated from the Scottish Dialect by Alexander Corbett, Boston, 1892.

The most popular feature of the exhibition was the display of relics. A writer in the *Twentieth Century* in 1892 had poured scorn on the credulity of Church dignitaries in Rome who venerated such objects as a bottle of the Virgin's milk or a vial of the sweat of St Michael when he contended with Satan. Such excesses were clearly not to be expected in the land of Calvin and cakes, but the editors of the catalogue deemed it prudent to issue a mild disclaimer: 'Though no hall-mark of genuineness can be claimed on the ground of admission to the Exhibition, it is not to be supposed that any large proportion of the articles shown were of the nature of counterfeits.'[1]

The crowds who thronged the large gallery found much to excite their interest. Here was the poet's excise ink bottle and the Bible he had read when he was at Brow Well; here was a draught-board he and Gilbert had used at Lochlea, and here was his masonic apron and the jewel he had worn as Depute Master of the St James' Lodge at Tarbolton. There were two of his razors, his blunderbuss and several locks of his hair; there was Jean's rolling pin, and a pair of her black silk embroidered stockings. John B. Morgan had lent the bolt and two hasps from the outer door of Clarinda's house; the Kilmarnock Burns Club had lent a small egg-cup made from the old rafters of the steading at Mossgiel; J. R. S. Hunter Selkirk, LL.D., had made several items available from his collection, including 'a piece of wood which formed part of a joist on which the bed rested on which Burns died.' 'All are redolent of his humanity – scarce one of his spirituality,' wrote Duncan McNaught, the then editor of the *Burns Chronicle*:

Burns is no abstraction to his countrymen. His poetry is embalmed in their hearts, and his overshadowing personality pervades and is ever associated with it. Hence it is that everything connected, in the remotest degree, with his earthly pilgrimage is guarded by all sorts and conditions of men with a solicitude that is apt to evoke a smile from those outwith the pale of the national feeling.[2]

The 1890s saw important advances in Burns scholarship – much of it from outside that pale. In 1893 the Frenchman Auguste Angellier of the University of Lille brought out his magisterial two-part *Life and Works*. The first volume

1. *Ibid.*, p. 92. A substantial number of the Burns letters which passed through the auction rooms in the 1880s and 1890s turned out to be forgeries, many of them the work of an Edinburgh man called Alexander H. Smith. This enterprising citizen (he became known as 'Antique' Smith) managed to keep one step ahead of the law for quite some time.

2. *Ibid.*, pp. 91-2.

was a searching biographical study, the second considered Burns's poetry not only in its British context, but against a broader European background. To Angellier, Burns stands out in the literature of his native land as a somewhat isolated figure. In his view, he could find congenial literary asylum in the French tradition, and he draws interesting comparisons with poets of an earlier age like François Villon and Mathurin Régnier.[1]

In Britain the centenary was marked by two substantial works. William Wallace published his extensive revision of Dr Robert Chambers' four-volume study, first published in 1851-2, and Henley and Henderson produced a new text of the poems far superior to any that had previously appeared. The flamboyant Henley (Robert Louis Stevenson, a close friend, called him 'boisterous and piratic' – he was the model for Long John Silver), enlivened this Centenary edition with a brilliantly acerbic biographical essay, as readable today as it was in the closing years of Victoria's reign.

The German academic Hans Hecht, a godson of Brahms, published his excellent short biography in 1919.[2] After that, the centre of gravity of Burns scholarship shifted to North America, and the contributions made during the 1930s by such scholars as Franklin Bliss Snyder and J. De Lancey Ferguson have not been surpassed. Ferguson's edition of the *Letters* came out in 1931 and Snyder's *Life* the following year. Ferguson's original and penetrating study, *Pride and Passion*, which appeared on the eve of the Second World War, ended on a glum note: Burns's worshippers, he concluded, were ashamed of the best part of his nature and his work, and nobody else read him at all.

Ferguson was perhaps unduly despondent; academics sometimes are. His energetic fellow-countrymen did not see reading books and erecting statues as the only ways of paying homage to the bard. In St Louis, Missouri, there was a long-established Burns Cottage Association; in 1902 it had published a report of a project to build an exact replica of Burns's cottage at the Louisiana Purchase Exposition. During the First World War a young Scot called John Reith, later to become celebrated as the first director-general of the British Broadcasting Corporation, was despatched to the United States on a weapons procurement mission. Wounded in France, and with a vivid scar on his cheek to prove it, he found himself much fêted by the local business community in Philadelphia. On one occasion he stayed overnight with a wealthy family of Scottish descent. 'Next morning I was awakened by telephone at 5.30,' he noted in his

---

1. Villon, (c. 1431–1463), thief and murderer as well as poet, would easily find a place in *The Jolly Beggars*. He is remembered especially for his *Grand Testament* and for his *Ballade des dames du temps jadis*, with its celebrated refrain, '*Mais où sont les neiges d'antan?*' The life of Régnier (1573–1613) was less violent but equally dissipated. A disciple of Ronsard and a forerunner of Molière, he was a stylish and penetrating satirist. Burns would have approved of the licence he permitted himself in his language and of many of his sentiments: '*C'est honte de vivre et de n'être amoureux*' – 'it is shameful to live and not be in love.'

2. *Robert Burns, Leben und Wirken des schottischen Volksdichters*, Carl Winter, Heidelberg. There is an excellent English translation by Jane Lymburn, first published in 1936 by William Hodge and Co. Alloway Publishing Ltd. of Ayr brought out a new edition in 1981.

diary. 'They showed me with great pride that the grounds immediately in front of the dining room were laid out in boxwood hedges and little paths the same pattern as behind Burns' cottage at Ayr.'[1]

From 1924 onwards Burns became widely known in the Soviet Union through the translations of Samuil Marshak. A friend of Gorki's and celebrated in Russia as a children's poet, Marshak also translated Shakespeare, Blake, Edward Lear and A.A. Milne; by the time he died in 1964, his translations of Burns had sold more than a million copies.

The poems became available in Icelandic in 1924, Rumanian in 1925 and Esperanto in 1926. (The Faroese had to wait till 1945, and the Albanians until the 1960s.) Their appeal was not confined to the English-speaking world and to Europe. 'In order to understand China,' the philosopher Lin Yutang wrote in 1935, 'one needs a little detachment and a little simplicity of mind too; that simplicity of mind so well typified by Robert Burns, one of the most Scottish and yet most universal of all poets.'[2]

Interest in the life and work of Burns continued at a high level in the inter-war years, even if changed economic conditions meant that he was now less frequently immortalised in stone.[3] There was no check, however, to the commercial exploitation of the Bard. Memorabilia in porcelain and pottery had begun to appear early in the nineteenth century. Burns's friends in Dumfries commissioned a splendid three-gallon punch-bowl and four whisky jugs from Spode as early as 1819, and ceramics remained attractive to those whose enthusiasm for Burns was tempered with some aesthetic sensibility – the Globe Inn in Dumfries still possesses a delightful Staffordshire flatback figure of Tam o' Shanter and Souter Johnny, for instance, and in the middle of the nineteenth century items of salt-glazed stoneware were also produced at Portobello and other Scottish potteries. Later, the flood of souvenirs and mementoes was swollen by all manner of printed ephemera – labels for whisky bottles, calendars, match boxes and cigarette cards, beer mats, T-shirts and the lids of shortbread tins.

In the twentieth century, as in the nineteenth, Burns has been hi-jacked for a range of political purposes. The authors of the *Great Soviet Encyclopedia*

---

1. Entry for 16 May 1916, Reith Diaries, BBC Written Archives Centre, Caversham.

2. Lin Yutang, *My Country and My People*, New York, 1935. Another Chinese Burnsian, Dr. Wen Yuan-Ning, visiting Britain as a member of a Chinese goodwill parliamentary mission towards the end of the Second World War, was invited to propose the Immortal Memory in a BBC radio programme. Burns's treatment of common incidents and feelings, he said, reminded him very much of the poetry of his own country. ('Robert Burns: Songs and Poems to Celebrate the Anniversary of the Poet's Birth', BBC Home Service, 9.40 p.m., 25th January 1944.)

3. There were exceptions. James Mackay notes that Cheyenne, Wyoming, boasts an elegant bronze on a granite pedestal, erected in 1929; it was presented by Mary Gemmell Gilchrist, the widow of one of Wyoming's most colourful cattle-barons – and a native of Ayrshire. An enormous Burns Memorial was also put up in Canberra, Australia, in 1935. (Mackay, *Burnsiana*, *op. cit.*, p. 46.)

wrote about him as predictably as they did about Dickens. ('Burns, who had assimilated the progressive ideas of the Enlightenment, created an original form of poetry that was modern in spirit and content . . .') A pamphlet published in Vancouver in 1926 was entitled *Robert Burns, Patriot and Internationalist*. In Scotland, whenever there has been a revival of the fortunes of the Scottish National Party, some of its less sophisticated candidates have tended to evince a loud proprietary interest. In 1989, at the first Dumfries Burns Festival, an exhibition was mounted with the title 'For a' That'. It was advertised as having two aims – to shed new light on Burns, and to get more people thinking about contemporary art. One of the paintings on display depicted a newspaper billboard which proclaimed 'Robert Burns calls for Tougher Sanctions Against South Africa'.

Earlier, in the 1950s and 60s, he was the occasion of a controversy in which, improbably, philately became caught up in politics. A month after the 160th anniversary of Burns's death in 1956, the Soviet Union, rather mysteriously, issued a special 40-kopeck postage stamp. The British Post Office was notoriously conservative in the matter of commemorative issues, and when the Burns Federation and its many allies made a case for a stamp to mark the bicentenary of the birth, they came up against a brick wall.

Four years later, when it was announced that five stamps would be issued to mark the Shakespeare quatercentenary, Scottish tempers rose; in Ayrshire, the Stevenston Branch of the Scottish National Party produced a crudely-printed label decorated with the Lion rampant which read 'BOYCOTT THE SHAKESPEARE STAMPS! "NO PRECEDENT" FOR BURNS, WHY ONE FOR HIM?' The Labour government that came to power in 1964 adopted a more liberal policy, and two Burns stamps were eventually issued in 1966 – in time, somewhat raggedly, to mark the 207th anniversary.

In more recent times Burnsians have had to brace themselves against the impact of feminism. A charity event at the Kelvingrove Galleries in Glasgow in January 1992 was billed as Scotland's first women-only Burns Supper, although some of those present thought this a misnomer and argued that it should be called a Jean Armour Supper. 'We are going to make it more sophisticated,' announced one of the organisers. Champagne was served in place of whisky. A few men in kilts were allowed to be present to serve the haggis.

There had been a renewed flurry of interest in the 1920s in the question of what Burns died of. For most of the nineteenth century, to the extent that people thought about it at all, the demon drink theory had generally prevailed, with occasional suggestions that syphilis may have played a supporting role. Then, in 1925, a well-known Scottish medical man, Sir James Crichton-Browne, contributed a series of articles to the *Glasgow Herald*, and a new, sanitised Burns emerged – a lifelong invalid who had finally succumbed to medical ignorance and rheumatic endocarditis.[1] This was cheerful news for bardolaters, but there were those who remained sceptical. 'In order that the last lingering doubts about Burns's respectability should be dispelled,' George Malcolm Thomson wrote slyly in *Caledonia*, 'it only remains for an eminent obstetrician to discover that the ladies who saddled Burns with the paternity of their children were deluded by parthenogenesis, or hero-worship, or actuated by spite.'[2]

Although Crichton-Browne had taken his L.R.C.S. and M.D. at Edinburgh in the 1860s, his experience in clinical medicine was severely limited. For most of his life he occupied administrative posts in mental hospitals (he was Lord Chancellor's Visitor in Lunacy from 1875 until his retirement in 1922). He was also the son of a Dumfries doctor and a fervent admirer of his home town's most famous citizen. His views remained unchallenged for almost sixty years. Then, in 1982, two scholars at McMaster University in Ontario published a paper called 'Robert Burns's Illness Revisited'.[3] They reached the common-sense conclusion that unless Burns's remains were exhumed nothing could be proved and a great many things could not be excluded – they specified a rare disorder called polyarteritis nodosa, also known as Kussmaul's disease, in which inflammatory lesions occur in the arteries; systemic lupus erythematosus, another chronic inflammatory disorder of unknown aetiology; carcinomatosis, hepatitis, leukaemia and tuberculosis.

They also considered brucellosis, unrecognised in the late eighteenth century, always an occupational risk for those who worked on the land and, in the days before antibiotics, often a killer.[4] The brucellosis theory was further explored by Richard Hindle Fowler in the book he published about Burns in 1988. Fowler, a former Director of the Victoria Science Museum and a past Senior Vice-President of the Melbourne Burns Club, apologised for sullying the language with words like 'retrodiagnostics,' but devoted a whole chapter to Burns's medical history.

He made a convincing case. Brucellosis, or undulant fever, as it used to be called, would certainly account for a good many of the symptoms displayed by Burns during the last two years of his life. It is a feverish disease that can persist for years, sometimes in phases of remission. It can cause depression,

1. 'Burns from a New Point of View', *Glasgow Herald*, 4,5,7,8,9 December 1925.) At the beginning of the century Crichton-Browne had joined in the controversy over Froude's *Life* of Carlyle. In 1903 he contributed an introduction to Alexander Carlyle's *New Letters and Memorials of Jane Welsh Carlyle*. He diagnosed Jane as having suffered from 'masked insanity'. Froude's biography, he wrote, 'began with hero-worship and ended in a study of demoniacal possession'.

2. George Malcolm Thomson, *Caledonia*, or *The Future of the Scots*, Kegan Paul, Trench, Trubner & Co, London, 1928, p. 62.

3. W.W. Buchanan and W.F. Keen, *Scottish Medical Journal*, 1982

4. The causative organism of the disease, now known as *Brucella melitensis*, was identified by the bacteriologist David Bruce during the course of an Army Medical Service posting to Malta in the 1880s. Bruce, born in Australia of Scottish parents in 1855, later investigated the cause of tsetse fever in Africa and of trench fever during the first World War. He was knighted in 1908.

lassitude, loss of appetite, headache and enlargement of the liver. The manner of Burns's death, Fowler asserts, attracts a strong presumption of terminal pneumonia: 'Have medical Burnsians become an extinct subspecies of homo sapiens?' He goes on to suggest that Burns's condition may have been aggravated by lead poisoning, pointing to the practice of using metallic lead, or its oxide litharge, in the making or subsequent 'improvement' of wine (lead reduced acidity and helped to dispel cloudiness).[1]

This did not please orthodox Burnsians. 'We are now back to the tired old canard of drunkenness,' James Mackay wrote stiffly in 1992. 'Doubtless this perverse view will continue to be aired periodically till the very end of time.'[2] He was certainly correct in noting that the debate is cyclical. A year previously the Scottish writer and poet Alan Bold had published *A Burns Companion*. Bold, never a man to beat about the bush, called one of his chapters 'Burns and Booze'. The poet's letters, he declared, made it clear that he 'suffered from the guilt-edged insecurity of the bout-alcoholic'. Bout-alcoholism, he added, 'with its euphoric self-indulgence dissolving into remorse as the bout shakily ends, is often associated with manic depressive behaviour which, in turn, is often found in highly creative individuals'.[3]

Bold was not the first twentieth-century Scottish poet to court a *fatwa* from the Burnsian ayatollahs. The trail to that particular form of martyrdom had been blazed with characteristic recklessness seventy years previously by Hugh MacDiarmid in 'A Drunk Man Looks at the Thistle':

> You canna gang to a Burns supper even
> Wi'oot some wizened scrunt o' a knock-knee
> Chinee turn roon to say, 'Him Haggis – velly goot!'
> And ten to wan the piper is a Cockney.

That appeared in 1926, long before the days of legislation on race relations. Eight years later MacDiarmid compounded his offence with 'The Last Great Burns Discovery', the satirical tale of Burnsian-extraordinary Charlie Crichton. Charlie leads him through the tangled undergrowth of an old garden and then dramatically throws aside a last swathe of rank vegetation to reveal a little ruined dry old closet. The seat, though rotted away in parts, is wonderfully preserved:

> 'You don't mean . . . ?' I cried.
> He nodded solemnly.
> It was an august moment – the most impressive moment of my life – as we stood there in the gathering twilight, and he told me the slow but sure

---

1. *Robert Burns*, Routledge, London, 1988.
2. Mackay, *op. cit.*, p. 679.
3. Alan Bold, *A Burns Companion*, Macmillan, London, 1991, pp. 121–2.

steps, the ten years' unremitting study, that had led to his discovery and his final and absolute proof that (though, alas! there was no scrap of writing on the walls, no carved initials on the woodwork even) Burns himself had used that very place, that very seat; the only convenience he had used that was still extant – Burns himself, and Jean Armour . . .

In case that was too subtle, MacDiarmid rammed the point savagely home elsewhere in the same volume; it was not for nothing that he once described himself as 'the catfish that vitalises the other torpid denizens of the aquarium'. 'The Burns cult must be killed stone dead,' he pronounced:

Scotland will signalize that it has come to itself again and resumed its proper attitude to world affairs when it makes a bonfire of all the worthless, mouldy, pitiable relics that antiquarian Burnsians have accumulated at Mauchline, Dumfries, and elsewhere and reconcentrates on the living message of Burns's poetry the world-wide attention devoted today (at least once a year) to the mere man and his uninteresting love affairs and the ramifications of the genealogies of his acquaintances and the pocr bric-à-brac of his *lares* and *penates* and the witless lucubrations of the hordes of bourgeois 'orators' who annually befoul his memory by the expression of sentiments utterly anti-pathetic to that stupendous element in him which ensures his immortality . . .[1]

MacDiarmid's reputation as Scotland's greatest poet since the death of Burns offered no protection from the storm of fury which opinions like these drew down upon his head (he was also in the habit of mauling Sir Harry Lauder, whom he regarded as an equally deplorable manifestation of professional Scottishness). He came under attack not only in the Scottish press, but also in Canada, Australia and New Zealand. He was expelled from the Burns Club to which he belonged at the time and for years afterwards was treated in Burns circles as a pariah.[2] Twenty years after his death he is still seen by many as the wild man of Scottish literature. It is true that his political eccentricities and his virulent anglophobia can become tedious, but his views cannot be disregarded: 'He dynamites a building,' wrote his fellow-poet Norman McCaig, 'and when the dust has settled, what structures shine in the sun!'

MacDiarmid was not the only Scottish writer to fall foul of the guardians of Burnsian tradition in the inter-war years. Catherine Carswell was the daughter of a Glasgow shipping magnate. Working in London in the early years of

1. Essay entitled 'The Burns Cult' first published in *At the Sign of the Thistle: A Collection of Essays*, Stanley Nott, London, 1934.

2. MacDiarmid, whose politics were as fierce as they were incoherent, became something of a connoisseur of expulsion. A founding member of what was later the Scottish National Party, he was expelled for his communist sympathies; joining the Communist Party, he subsequently lost his party card for 'nationalist deviation'.

the century she and her journalist husband became close friends of D.H. Lawrence. Lawrence greatly admired Burns and at one stage had started work on a novel about him. In 1927, when Mrs Carswell was getting down to work on her book, Lawrence, in a letter to her husband, offered some characteristically vehement advice:

I always wanted to do one myself, but am not Scotchy enough. I read just now Lockhart's bit of a life of Burns. Made me spit. Those damned middle-class Lockharts grew lilies of the valley up their arses to hear them talk. If Cath is condescending to Burns, I disown her . . . You can't know Burns unless you hate the Lockharts and all the estimable bourgeois and upper classes as he really did – narrow gutted pigeons . . . Oh, why doesn't Burns come to life again and really salt them![1]

Cath was not condescending to Burns, and three years later many of her readers judged that he came brilliantly to life in her pages. Franklyn Bliss Snyder, at work on the other side of the Atlantic on his own judicious and scholarly biography, thought she wrote vividly and entertainingly, although he deplored the 'baffling manner' in which she had woven together fact and fiction. This did not bother John Buchan, who had employed his novelist's skills in some of his own biographies. 'It is really a wonderful performance,' he wrote to Donald Carswell. 'Beautifully architectured and brilliantly written. It seems to me also essentially a just book.'

The serialisation rights were bought by the *Daily Record*, then as now a popular newspaper with a large circulation, and all hell broke loose. To one Glasgow Member of Parliament (John S. Clarke, Labour, Maryhill), Mrs Carswell was a latter-day accomplice of the body-snatchers Burke and Hare, engaged in 'the resurrection of the ghoulish remains of great men'. Through the post, from an anonymous correspondent (he signed himself 'Holy Willie') there came a bullet; by using it in a quiet corner, he suggested amiably, Mrs Carswell would 'leave the world a better and cleaner place'.

Behind the scenes there were efforts to have the book suppressed; lawyers exchanged letters on the question of whether the publisher had infringed the copyright of the Burns Federation. It seemed that they hadn't. Orthodoxy had to be content with the sort of hellfire denunciation of the book contributed to the *Burns Chronicle* by the Reverend Lauchlan McLean Watt:

It is not far off from being the kind of record Satan might keep near the door of his dark abode, lest a repentant sinner might slip into higher places of peace after struggle, failure and victory – a book he might bring forward to prove a poor soul's previous convictions, in some final Court of Spiritual

1. Letter dated 5 December 1927. Quoted by Tom Crawford in his introduction to the new edition of Mrs Carswell's book published by Canongate in 1990.

Common Pleas ... It is, in much, an undocumented libel on the dead, compiled on a method of smelling out stories that have grown putrid long ago in the corners where even what had no love or pity in it was content to leave them to oblivion.

Burns would have enjoyed that. He would also have relished the contrast between the vacuous pieties of those who had appointed themselves to watch over his reputation and the earthier version of his legend which persisted in the folk memory – a version which found expression not only in the street lore of children in the slums of Glasgow but also in the work of Lewis Grassic Gibbon, the son, like Burns, of a small tenant farmer, and Scotland's most important novelist in the twentieth century:

> Well, the creature died, and he went to heaven and knocked like hell on the pearly gates. And St. Peter poked his head from a wicket, and asked *Who're you that's making a din?* And Burns said *I'm Robert Burns, my man, the National Poet of Scotland, that's who.* St. Peter took a look at the orders, pinned on the guard-room wall for the day; and he said, *I've got a note about you. You must wait outbye for a minute or so.* So Robbie sat there cooling his heels, on the top of the draughty stair to heaven, and waited and waited till he nearly was froze; syne the gates at last opened and he was let in. And Burns was fair in a rage by then, *Do you treat distinguished arrivals like this?* And St. Peter said *No, I wouldn't say that. But then I had special orders about you. I've been hiding the Virgin Mary away.*[1]

Some of the most perceptive writing about Burns in the middle years of this century came from the pen of the Orcadian writer Edwin Muir. A man of very different poetic sensibility from his one-time friend MacDiarmid (they fell out over the future of Scots as a literary language), Muir did not simply rail against the accretions which had overlaid the genius of Burns but placed a gentle finger on some of the reasons for them. Burns, he believed, had become so deeply embedded in Scottish life that it was almost impossible for Scots to see him simply as a poet, to regard him as they would Dunbar, or Hogg or even Walter Scott:

> He is more a personage to us than a poet, more a figurehead than a personage, and more a myth than a figurehead. To those who have heard of Dunbar he is a figure, of course, comparable to Dunbar; but he is also a figure comparable to Prince Charlie, about whom everybody has heard. He is a myth evolved by the popular imagination, a communal poetic creation, a Protean figure; we can all shape him to our own likeness, for the myth is endlessly adaptable; so that to the respectable this secondary Burns is a

1. Lewis Grassic Gibbon, *Cloud Howe*, Jarrolds, London, 1933, p. 173.

decent man; to the Rabelaisian bawdy; to the sentimentalist, sentimental; to the socialist, a revolutionary; to the Nationalist, a patriot; to the religious, pious; to the self-made man, self-made; to the drinker, a drinker. He has the power of making any Scotsman, whether generous or canny, sentimental or prosaic, religious or profane, more whole-heartedly himself than he could have been without assistance; and in that way perhaps more human. He greases our wheels; we could not roll on our way so comfortably but for him; and it is impossible to judge impartially a convenient appliance to which we have grown accustomed.[1]

It is not a reading that presents the Scottish psyche in a particularly flattering light, but it was a penetrating analysis and it remains so today. Certain aspects of the cult of Burns are without question the manifestation of a sense of nationhood which has survived the loss of sovereignty for close on three hundred years. For some Scots it expresses their feelings of political amputation, serves as an ointment to salve the wound of national hurt. Equally, the Protean quality to which Muir draws attention explains much of Burns's continuing appeal far beyond Scotland and the English-speaking world.

There is nothing disturbing or particularly demanding about Burns. He does not intimidate. He is not trying to convert us, or persuade us to vote for anything. He is a painter of morals but he is not a moralist; he invites us to look, but does not instruct us in what to think of what we see. He is agreeably lacking in intensity and fervour. He does not lead us prophetically to the heights or lower our spirits with disturbing insights into a future we have no special wish to see. He lacks the intellectual ferocity of a Carlyle and the philosophical cloudiness of a Wordsworth and we like him the better for it. He is not profound, or complicated or particularly subtle. He is ordinary, average, his poetry reassuringly concerned with the here and now and the everyday:

> 'Life's cares they are comforts' – a maxim laid down
> By the Bard, what d'ye call him, that wore the black gown;
> And faith I agree with th' old prig to a hair;
> For a big-belly'd bottle's a heav'n of care.[2]

In the half-century since the Second World War, the Burns 'Movement' has shown continuing signs of vigorous growth. In the early 1990s, for instance, the Canberra Highland Society and Burns Club spent A$3.5 million on a new clubhouse and saw an increase of 11,000 in its membership in the first twelve months of operation. The Club (it is number 882 on the roll of the Burns

1. 'The Burns Myth' in W. Montgomerie (ed.) *Burns: New Judgements*, William MacLellan, Glasgow, 1947, pp. 5–7.
2. Kinsley, 27. The bard that wore the black gown is Young. Burns is quoting his 'Night Thoughts' in the first line.

Federation) celebrates Burns Night and Hogmanay and St Andrew's Night in the traditional manner and offers bagpipe tuition and lessons in Scottish country dancing. It has diversified its activities considerably, however, since it was founded in 1924 by a group of expatriate ladies eager to prevent the withering of their Scottish cultural roots. Today, there are golf and fishing sections, facilities for darts, snooker and carpet bowls, a bistro and sixty-five gaming machines. Donations are made to local schools and charities, and the club is a major supporter of the Tuggeranong Little Athletics Association.

In Scotland, where it all began, development at club level proceeds at a more modest pace. The Ellisland Trust, however, together with two local authorities, recently commissioned a feasibility study on the restoration of the farmhouse to what it was in Burns's day, the conversion of the outbuildings to a museum and the remaking of Jean Armour's kitchen garden, and 1995 saw the opening of the Burns National Heritage Park at Alloway, where visitors may sample a three-screen and audiovisual presentation called 'The Tam o' Shanter Experience'. Such material changes had little influence on the pervasive Burnsian ethos, however. 'Be Inspired,' say the advertisements for the Cottage in the *Burns Chronicle*: 'Visit Us At This Hallowed Place'.

'This hallowed place.' Such phrases strike a note of cosy religiosity and remain as unappealing to many present-day scholars and critics as they did to De Lancey Ferguson in the 1930s. Fears that the critical intelligence on which Scots have traditionally prided themselves has been blunted are premature, however. A number of excellent studies appeared in the two decades after the Second World War, notably those by David Daiches and Thomas Crawford, and 1968 saw the appearance of James Kinsley's three outstanding volumes, based on a critical recension of nearly 800 manuscripts and including his invaluable literary and textual commentary.

Two hundred years after Burns's death, we are also much better equipped to appreciate his stature as a songwriter, although this has come about very slowly. J. C. Dick's pioneering work on the songs did not appear until some years after the centenary celebrations of 1896. In it he drew a comparison with Schubert, who had died at an even earlier age than Burns. A generous countryman had said of him that if he had lived, he would have put the whole German language into music: 'Of Burns it may be said that, if he had lived, he would have put the whole of Scottish music into verse.' Dick's advocacy did little to enlarge the painfully small and hackneyed repertoire of those called on to entertain the company at Burns Suppers; even today, most people would be hard put to it to come up with the words of more than a dozen of the three hundred and seventy or so songs which he wrote or revised or collected.

There are signs of change. The upsurge of interest in folk song in the years since the Second World War has no parallel since Burns's own day. This revival coincided almost exactly with the post-war rebirth of television, and the small screen has played a part in broadening the range of performance and making it less stereotyped. Donny O'Rourke, the Head of Arts at Scottish

Television, the commercial company which serves Central Scotland, has expressed himself pithily on the matter: 'My idea of an apt celebration of Burns Nights is not a room full of men making whoopee over the equivalent of a cultural kissogram.'[1]

He was rightly proud of his company's initiative in commissioning from Scottish Opera, as a Burns Night offering with a difference, a production of Cedric Thorpe Davie's *Life and Liberty*. O'Rourke did not, on the other hand, admire the long-running stage and television performances of the actor John Cairney: '*There Was a Man* established John Cairney as Rabbie's representative on earth, eradicating the Nasmyth and other portraits with a single toss of his pony-tailed head.' Feeling had been swamped by sentimentality. He also had his reservations about Burns songs delivered in what he termed 'besporraned *bel canto*'.

Jean Redpath's performances of Haydn's settings of Burns have been much admired in recent years, and she also collaborated with the American composer Serge Hovey, who in his pursuit of original tunes did not shrink from the occasional Bartókian dissonance. Another singer, Jo Miller, a member of the staff of the Royal Scottish Academy of Music and Drama in Glasgow, has testified to the technical challenge posed by the wide ranges and large intervals in some of the songs. She established, by a count of the songs in Donald Low's 1993 edition, that 88 per cent had a range of an octave to an octave and a fifth, and that intervals of sixths and octaves were common.

Jo Miller notes that some of Burns's bawdy songs are now increasingly heard in public performance, popular choices by women singers including 'Dainty Davie' and the unsanitised version of 'John Anderson my Jo'. She also cites the beautiful but seldom sung 'Jamie come try me'. James Dick, writing in 1903, declared that the compass of the tune was too great for ordinary voices, but Miller challenges this. She concedes that it is tricky to sing (the range is an octave plus a sixth), but points out that it can be adapted, retaining the character of the tune while reducing the high register hazards.[2]

In 1993 Donald Low published the first comprehensive and unexpurgated modern edition of all discoverable songs by Burns, and made it possible to listen with a fresh ear to the remarkable achievement of this man who never heard a symphony or a string quartet. He did not, as we have seen, compose lyrics that were subsequently set to music by others – as Schiller's, say, were set by Schubert or Herrick's by Roger Quilter. Burns reversed the process, sometimes devising words for a tune that caught his fancy, sometimes working like a sort of literary tinker, mending, expanding, strengthening, combining existing fragments.

The result is a corpus of work of great variety. Although he collected far

---

1. Donny O'Rourke, 'Supperman: Televising Burns', in *Burns Now*, ed. Kenneth Simpson, Canongate Academic, Edinburgh, 1994, p. 208.

2. Jo Miller, 'Burns's Songs: A Singer's View', in *Burns Now*, pp. 193–207.

fewer songs than Bartók was later to do in Romania and Hungary, they reflect a marvellously broad span of mood and emotion. Many of them were originally dance tunes – strathspeys and reels – but Burns, often through the confident liberties he took with *tempi*, achieved a range of expression and modulation which bears comparison with some of the *lieder* of Schubert or Wolf. They are strongly national in tone, and this has caused some critics to strain earnestly at a seeming paradox – the universal appeal of the poetry, the circumscribed life of the poet. It was, as Thomas Crawford has pointed out, another great national poet, W. B. Yeats, who helped them over the non-existent stile:

> The hailstone is a journeyman of God; the grass blade carries the universe upon its point. But to this universalism, this seeing of unity everywhere, you can only attain through what is near you, your nation, or, if you be no traveller, your village and the cobwebs on your walls. You can no more have the greater poetry without a nation than religion without symbols. One can only reach out to the universe with a gloved hand – that glove is one's nation, the only thing one knows even a little of.[1]

An international celebration seems in order, then, in 1996. But who or what exactly is to be commemorated? The man or the icon? The poet or the legend that has become entwined about him like a giant creeper? One particular strand in that legend might now repay closer scrutiny. As James Mackay has pointed out, advances in forensic science have made it possible to make genetic comparisons between persons long dead. If sufficient undegraded nucleic material could be recovered, it might be possible to compare a DNA profile of Burns with one constructed from the infant remains that lie buried in Greenock. That would, of course, require a second exhumation – a suggestion certain to be received in some Burnsian circles with as much enthusiasm as the cardinals of Turin used to show for scientific tests on their famous shroud. In the spring of 1994 the present author and his publisher nevertheless decided that it merited further exploration.

It seemed sensible to be in touch in the first instance with the Burns Federation. Stuart Proffitt, HarperCollins's Trade Publisher, accordingly wrote to the then President, Mr J.S. Morrison, acknowledging that the matter was delicate, but pointing out that this was one of the very few areas in which scientific advances had opened up the possibility of making a contribution to Burns scholarship.

Mr Morrison's reply was positive and cordial. Genetic comparisons, he wrote 'would certainly satisfy and finally answer the universal curiosity that exists, regarding Robert Burns, Highland Mary and an illegitimate infant.' He

---

1. Crawford uses the words as an epigraph to his 1960 study of Burns. They date from September 1888.

undertook to seek support for an exhumation from the President of the Greenock Burns Club, who were the owners of the lair, and also from the Federation's Convenor of Monuments. 'May I take this opportunity,' he concluded, 'of thanking you for courteously seeking our advice and assistance.'

It was a good start, and a letter from Peter Tait, the Director of Environmental Health of Inverclyde District Council, seemed equally promising. He confirmed that the Greenock Burns Club had bought the grave in 1920 on behalf of the Federation, and gave its precise location in Greenock Cemetery. He explained that the procedure for exhumation was to apply to the Sheriff, who would then require the District Council to issue a Statement of Feasibility – 'a description of the problems, or lack of them,' Mr Tait wrote, 'which would then be met in carrying out the exhumation'. It was then for the Sheriff to decide whether to issue a warrant granting the petition to exhume.

After this things went curiously quiet – no word from the Convenor of Monuments, no word from the Chairman of the Greenock Club. Then, early in July 1994, the diary column of the *Herald* in Glasgow printed an item headed 'Digging the dirt on Rabbie's love life'. It was a piece which could only have been written by someone who had seen the correspondence between Harper-Collins and the Federation. Greenock Burns Club, it reported – this was news to HarperCollins – had been consulted and was not happy at the prospect. And there was a hostile gloss: 'Mr McIntyre, the author, is no stranger to sensational revelations. His recent book on Lord Reith, revered founder of the BBC, revealed this dourest of Scotsmen to have been passionately in love with another chap.'

Before moving forward on the legal front it was plainly important to clarify the position of the Greenock Club. A letter to their President went unanswered; a gentle reminder elicited a brusquely negative reply from their Honorary Secretary; a further request for a more reasoned response was met with silence. Nor, in all this time, had there been any word from the Federation's Convenor of Monuments. In December 1994, however, the Federation's journal, the *Burnsian*, carried extracts from the minutes of his committee, and a reference to the 'sensationalising purpose' of the author made plain which way the wind blew in that quarter.

On other fronts, prospects were brighter. The construction of the necessary DNA profile of Burns himself could most easily be accomplished by subjecting a lock of his hair to the appropriate scientific tests. The Trustees of Burns Monument and Burns Cottage have such a lock of hair in their keeping at Alloway. The Secretary of the Trust made encouraging noises and asked for a request to be put in writing to his Chairman. An approach was also made to Professor Peter Vanezis, who holds the Regius Chair of Forensic Medicine and Science at the University of Glasgow. He expressed interest in the project, and confirmed that it would be possible for the necessary work to be carried out in his department.

Time now began to press, and it was decided to petition the Sheriff without more ado, emphasising that HarperCollins were proposing to publish a serious biographical enquiry, not a bodice-ripper. The reply from the Sheriff Clerk may simply have reflected a tradition of Scottish legal formality, but it sounded decidedly frosty: 'Dear Sir,' it began, 'I refer to your letter of 9 January 1995 which purports to be a Petition for Exhumation . . .' Such petitions, he advised, must be in a particular form, and must follow a particular legal style. It might be in our interest to consult a solicitor.

The Law Society for Scotland produced the names of a number of firms in Greenock, but now new obstacles loomed in the mist. A senior partner of the firm consulted announced that he felt unable to accept instructions – as a past chairman of a local Burns Club, he explained apologetically, he was unwilling to associate himself with a case that had already excited some controversy. He could not speak for colleagues in other practices in the town, but thought it unlikely that they would feel differently. Foolish of us to forget Burns's enthusiasm for freemasonry.

The Glasgow firm of Ross Harper were hampered by no such inhibitions, and one of their resident partners, Cameron Fyfe, was soon deep in the columns of the *Scots Law Times*. There he came across the cases of Cunningham, ET AL., 1871, and of Sister Jarlath, Petitioner, 1979. These led him to believe that neither a court order nor the consent of the Burns Federation was necessary; all that was required was the permission of the owners of the land, the Inverclyde District Council.

The officials of that body, however, now began to see complications where none had existed before. Although the Director of Environmental Health professed that he saw no difficulty with what was proposed, he felt the matter must be referred to his Chief Executive; he also felt that it might be prudent to take legal advice. The opposition of the Greenock Burns Club was well known locally, and any decision by the District Council would therefore be highly political; it might well therefore have to be referred to one of the Council's committees, and this, as we would appreciate, could well take several months . . . Old Fabius Cunctator, driving Hannibal crazy with his tactics of masterly inactivity in the Second Punic War, would have been full of admiration.

At this point (it was now mid-March 1995) came word that the Trustees at Alloway were unwilling to make their lock of hair available. Cameron Fyfe, the glint of battle in his eye, was all for going for broke – why not open up a new front in Dumfries and seek permission to exhume the body of the Bard himself from the Mausoleum?

'Nae man can tether time or tide.' The same, unhappily, applies to publishers' production schedules; reluctantly, we concluded that this time round at least our question must go unanswered, and that we must give best to those who did not want to know. It had to be conceded that the closing in slow-motion of the bardolatrous ranks had been an impressive spectacle.

The Burns industry began to make its arrangements for the bicentenary in good time. Advertisements for bicentenary car-stickers started to appear in the *Burns Chronicle* several years in advance. A bicentenary medal was also announced. Complete with ribbon and clasp, it would be struck in an edition limited to one thousand; Burnsians were advised to order early to avoid disappointment. An international festival director was appointed and it was agreed that he should work closely with the Secretary of the Burns Federation.

As the year of the bicentenary approached, presses around the world disgorged a flow of new material. From Beijing, the works translated into Chinese in an edition of 100,000. From Oconomowoc, Wisconsin, 'Mither Wit and Native Fire', a collection of articles by members of the Robert Burns Club of Milwaukee.[1] (These included 'A Preliminary Survey of Scandinavian Words in the Poetry of Robert Burns' by the Reverend Ernest O. Norquist. Mr Norquist is nothing if not thorough; his researches, he discloses, have thrown up no record of Burns ever having visitied Oslo, Copenhagen or Stockholm.)

From a Berlin publishing house, *Ich, Robert Burns*, by Dietrich Hohmann.[2] The *Burns Chronicle* found a German Burnsian to review it, but even he was struggling: 'This non-chronological structuring and frequently associative style of narration,' he wrote gamely, 'does not always make it easy for the reader to know exactly what is being narrated.' The editor of the *Chronicle* also appeared between hard covers. Peter Westwood's hobby is deltiology – he collects picture postcards. He has more than eight hundred specimens relating to Burns, and has used more than half of them as an intriguingly novel way of illustrating the life and works.[3]

In Japan, Burns's work has been enthusiastically received since the first translations appeared in 1906, but it has also, more recently, been put to practical use. At a Burns supper in Edinburgh in 1992, Seiichiro Otsuka, the Japanese consul-general, disclosed that Scotland's national poet was making a contribution to traffic management in Tokyo: when the lights turned green at pedestrian crossings, he explained, those waiting on the pavement were jollied over the road to the strains of 'Coming Through the Rye'.

The Bard has therapeutic uses, too. Reciting what he could remember of Burns was one of the ways in which the Scots-American hostage Tom Sutherland battled to remain sane during his captivity in Beirut.

The Immortal Memory – the Lassies – Oor Toon – Auld Scotia – The Land of Our Adoption – Here's Tae Us, Wha's like Us. The Scotch whisky industry is going to have an exceptionally good year in 1996. Crabby old Hugh MacDiarmid is not likely to figure on the toast list at many Burns Suppers during

---

1. Priscilla J. Kucik, ed., *The Robert Burns Club of Milwaukee*, Oconomowoc, Wisconsin, 1992.
2. Verlag Neues Leben, Berlin, 1991.
3. Peter J. Westwood, *The Deltiology of Robert Burns*, Creedon Publications, Dumfries, 1994.

the bicentennial celebrations, but one stanza from 'A Drunk Man Looks at the Thistle' cries out to be displayed at every top table:

> Rabbie, wad'st thou wert here – the warld hath need,
> And Scotland mair sae, o' the likes o' thee!
> The whisky that aince moved your lyre's become
> A laxative for a' loquacity.

For those who prefer not to make the commemoration a matter of quasi-religious observance, there are always the poems and the songs. He is not Dante, and he is not Pushkin. It was not given to him, as it was to Shakespeare, to illuminate our moral universe. He does not, all that often, make us think. But he makes us laugh, and he makes us cry, and in doing so, most precious of all poetic gifts, he heightens the sense we have of our common humanity. And that is why the lad who was born in Kyle belongs not just to the keepers of the flame but to the whole world.

> Lang hae we parted been,
>   Lassie my dearie;
> Now we are met again,
>   Lassie lie near me.

> A' that I hae endur'd,
>   Lassie my dearie,
> Here in thy arms is cur'd
>   Lassie lie near me.[1]

1. Kinsley, 290.

INDEX

READ MORE IN PENGUIN

In every corner of the world, on every subject under the sun, Penguin represents quality and variety – the very best in publishing today.

For complete information about books available from Penguin – including Puffins, Penguin Classics and Arkana – and how to order them, write to us at the appropriate address below. Please note that for copyright reasons the selection of books varies from country to country.

In the United Kingdom: Please write to *Dept. EP, Penguin Books Ltd, Bath Road, Harmondsworth, West Drayton, Middlesex UB7 ODA*

In the United States: Please write to *Consumer Sales, Penguin Putnam Inc., P.O. Box 12289 Dept. B, Newark, New Jersey 07101-5289*. VISA and MasterCard holders call 1-800-788-6262 to order Penguin titles

In Canada: Please write to *Penguin Books Canada Ltd, 10 Alcorn Avenue, Suite 300, Toronto, Ontario M4V 3B2*

In Australia: Please write to *Penguin Books Australia Ltd, P.O. Box 257, Ringwood, Victoria 3134*

In New Zealand: Please write to *Penguin Books (NZ) Ltd, Private Bag 102902, North Shore Mail Centre, Auckland 10*

In India: Please write to *Penguin Books India Pvt Ltd, 11 Community Centre, Panchsheel Park, New Delhi 110017*

In the Netherlands: Please write to *Penguin Books Netherlands bv, Postbus 3507, NL-1001 AH Amsterdam*

In Germany: Please write to *Penguin Books Deutschland GmbH, Metzlerstrasse 26, 60594 Frankfurt am Main*

In Spain: Please write to *Penguin Books S. A., Bravo Murillo 19, 1° B, 28015 Madrid*

In Italy: Please write to *Penguin Italia s.r.l., Via Benedetto Croce 2, 20094 Corsico, Milano*

In France: Please write to *Penguin France, Le Carré Wilson, 62 rue Benjamin Baillaud, 31500 Toulouse*

In Japan: Please write to *Penguin Books Japan Ltd, Kaneko Building, 2-3-25 Koraku, Bunkyo-Ku, Tokyo 112*

In South Africa: Please write to *Penguin Books South Africa (Pty) Ltd, Private Bag X14, Parkview, 2122 Johannesburg*

READ MORE IN PENGUIN

PENGUIN CLASSIC BIOGRAPHY

 Highly readable and enjoyable biographies and autobiographies from leading biographers and autobiographers. The series provides a vital background to the increasing interest in history, historical subjects and people who mattered. The periods and subjects covered include the Roman Empire, Tudor England, the English Civil Wars, the Victorian Era, and characters as diverse Joan of Arc, Jane Austen, Robert Burns and George Melly. Essential reading for everyone interested in the past.

Published or forthcoming:

Ernle Bradford	**Cleopatra**
David Cecil	**A Portrait of Jane Austen**
Roger Fulford	**Royal Dukes**
Christopher Hibbert	**The Making of Charles Dickens**
Christopher Hill	**God's Englishman: Oliver Cromwell**
Edward Lucie-Smith	**Joan of Arc**
George Melly	**Owning Up: The Trilogy**
Lytton Strachey	**Queen Victoria**
	Elizabeth and Essex
Gaius Suetonius	**Lives of the Twelve Caesars, translated by Robert Graves**